MW00800545

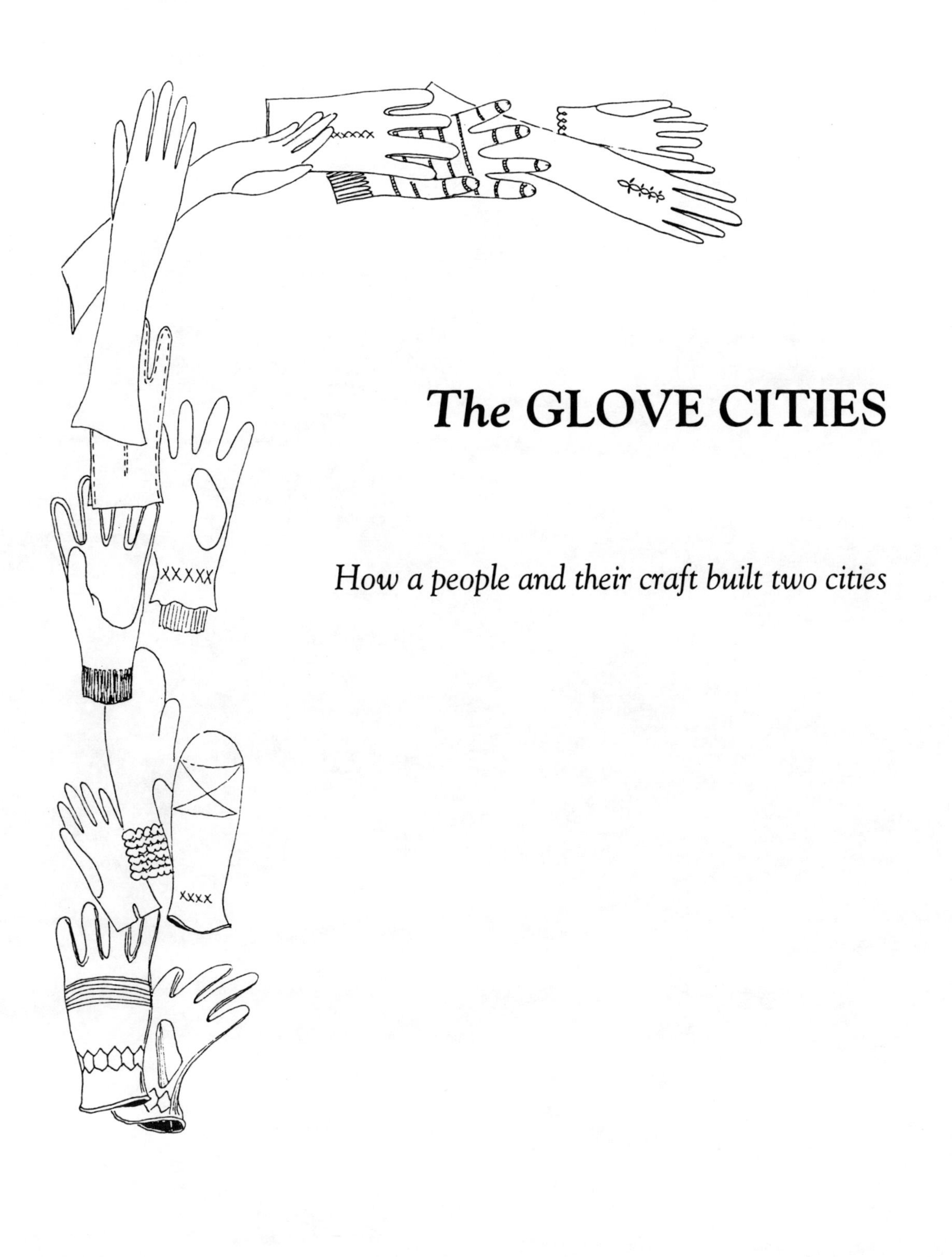

The GLOVE CITIES

How a people and their craft built two cities

The GLOVE CITIES

How a people and their craft built two cities

A sociological and economic history
Of the glove and glove leather industries
In Johnstown and Gloversville, Fulton County, New York

Barbara McMartin
with
W. Alec Reid

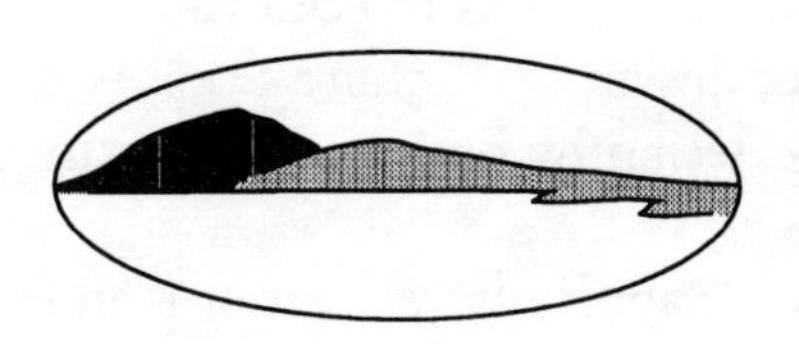

Lake View Press
1999

Lake View Press
339 Kasson Drive
Canada Lake
Caroga, NY 12032

Library of Congress Catalog Card Number:

99-094082

ISBN 1-888374-13-6

Printed in the United States
Cover design by Richard Loomis
Book design by Barbara McMartin

Cover Map: *Birdseye View of Johnstown, 1888*

Acknowledgments

My husband has been a full partner in this endeavor. He completed some of the research, made all the statistical analyses and summaries needed to understand the industry, and prepared all the graphs for the book. In addition he has read my work many times, discussed ideas with me, and helped assemble the final work. There is no question but that I could not have written this without him.

Betsy Folwell is a wonderful editor; after her first reading of this book, she made many recommendations, noted numerous areas that needed expansion, and recommended ways to improve the book's organization. Except for the fact that we never could find all the additional material to flesh out some of her suggestions, it was a pleasure to follow her advice. Especially helpful was the style sheet she suggested that reconciles archaic and modern terms and the various ways different companies have been named.

Thomas Walsh of Russo, Walsh and Walsh loaned us the *Birds Eye View of Johnstown* for cover art. My son-in-law Dick Loomis is a fine graphic designer. Using that map as the basis for his design, he created the cover. I am very pleased with it as I have been for all the covers he has designed for my other books.

Paul Brady spent many days at the Library of Congress researching the history of tariff legislation and even more days in the difficult search for census data, manufacturing statistics on domestic production, and import records. It was a truly noble labor and much appreciated. Two reference librarians at the U.S. Bureau of Census Library were very helpful to him: Trudy L. Williams and William L. Turner, Jr.

John and Lois Widdemer gave me tutorials on the glove industry so I could begin to understand its technicalities. John has discussed the industry with me, read several drafts, and made corrections and helpful suggestions. Bill Studenic was my resource on modern tanning and he introduced me to many other tanners. I really appreciated being able to learn about both industries from these three knowledgeable people.

Libraries are great places, made better by the help of fine librarians. Alyce Lanphere, who retired at the end of 1998 from the Gloversville Free Library, is one of the best. She not only gave us permission to copy much first source material, but let us do it at home so that as we wrote the book we had all the most important sources available. These included the Fulton County Glove Manufacturers Association scrap book; *The Glovers Review*; and numerous items from the library's vertical file. Alyce also found some of the more exciting bits of history we have used, such as the article by John S. Town. She has read the manuscript to help with the difficult job of reconciling all the various ways names are spelled in the different sources. Her replacement, Deborah Bucholtz, also helped us.

Special thanks are due the Manuscripts and Special Collections, New York State Library for the use of the Parmelee Diary, the many lovely letterheads, and invoices.

Barbara Germain and Debbie Calloway at the Johnstown Library were very helpful. We also used the resources of the New York State Library; the New York State Archives; the Schenectady Library; and the Baker Library at Harvard, for access to the R. G. Dun reports on Fulton County. Ted Comstock did research into union history using libraries at Cornell University.

Dr. Charles Noxon arranged for us to copy photographs and pamphlets from the Johnstown Historical Society's collection. He was most helpful.

The book owes much to the many people whom we interviewed. Our thanks to all of them:

George Agar
Eleanor Cirillo
Ann Lee Clough
Roderick Correll
Warren Dennie
Mark Dzierson
Herbert Engel
Morris Evans
Dr. Pasquale Fugazotto
Cyndie Gates
William B. Gates
William C. Gates
Sam Greco
James Hayes
Elbert Heacock
Dr. William Hesek
Ross Higier
Arnold Jaffe, Fownes
Earl G. Johnson
Anne Jung
Peter Kiernan
George Madnick
Lydon Maider
Joseph Morsheimer
Chester Nessle
Gerda Newbower
Fred Ohler
Joseph Pagano
Dominic Papa
Frank Perrella
Edward Perrone
Anita Potocar
Lester F. Pross
Stanford Pulrang
Dexter Risedorph
Humbert Saluzzo
Abe Seroussi
Anthony and Ann Pastore Sorrento
Lari Stanton, Aris
Mike Subik
Edward F. Vonderahe
Thomas Willard
Jack Woodcock
Richard Zuckerwar

Over the years, many people have given me historical material, maps, and photographs. I used them all in this book and thanks go to:

Richard Shell for his gift of the 1905 Atlas;

Daniel Halloran, for permission to use Georgianna Cole Halloran's reminiscence;

Ellen Percy Kraly, Department of Geography, Colgate, for census summaries of population and ethnicity in Fulton County;

Flora McMartin Wing, the McMartin trademark and patent;

Eleanor Reppenhagen, her research and articles on homework and glove-making courses at Gloversville High School;

Don Williams, for sample homework books and numerous clippings;

Fred Ohler, for historical materials;

Robert Valachovic, for copy of the Northrup engraving;

Alan Farber, for postcards;

Ann D. Gordon, Editor, *The Papers of Elizabeth Cady Stanton and Susan B. Anthony*, Department of History, Rutgers University;

Lester F. Pross, for permission to use essay on his mother;

J. D. Widdemer, for advertising photographs from the 1930s through the 1950s.

Years ago my husband made copies of many valuable photographs for the Fulton County Museum so that the copies could be displayed, thus preserving the originals. We used our prints of a few of these pictures for this book. The Gloversville Historical Association has the McMartin papers, some of which I had also copied years ago and the rest we were able to access with the assistance of Robert E. Murphy.

Gerold Zahavi, SUNY Albany, helped me with background on unions and the Communist Party. He has put the records of the 1914 Hearings of the NYS Board of Mediation on the internet for all to read.

William Towne, Asistant Manager, Amalgamated Northeast Regional Trade Board, Union of Needletrades, Industrial, and Textile Employees, AFL-CIO, has been an extremely valuable resource. We discussed important issues at length, and many times he supplied papers from the union files or books from his own collection to illustrate themes in union history. His careful reading of early drafts produced many comments that induced me to clarify or expand different points. His appreciation of the work in progress was extraordinarily encouraging.

Clyde Griffen, who has retired from the History Department at Vassar College, helped me find resources on other industries so I could compare them with glove-making.

Wanda Burch shared her knowledge of the Sir William Johnson papers. Years ago, Robert Bedford, former Johnstown historian who died in 1998, let us copy from his files many clippings that illustrated life in Johnstown. Judy Marcoux, archivist, City of Gloversville, helped us find some important photographs. Michael Shafer and Art Green, of the Gloversville Fire Department, also helped locate photographs.

Linda Madison, Fulton County Board of Elections and Sean Geraghty, Fulton County Planning Board supplied county records.

The Leader Herald is much appreciated for allowing access to microfilms of that paper and its predecessors, the *Morning Herald* and the *Leader Republican*. We also used the resources of the Evans Library of Fulmont Community College and were helped there by Peter Betz.

The Heacock family let us copy their treasures: licenses to manufacture leather, old bills and invoices, and family records. Thanks go to David C. Heacock, Elbert H. Heacock, and Mrs. Donald Peters.

William Hutchens shared material from his file on Hutchens & Potter Glove Co. and gave us permission to copy it. William Wormuth shared his knowledge of the Slovak community.

Richard Zuckerwar and Bob Hall helped us plan a visit to Grandoe's glove factory in China. Aniceto Delos Reyes and Cesar A. Co entertained us in Fuzhou and guided us through the factory and all its operations. It was a wonderful experience.

Joseph Conroy and one of his almost-retired cutters, Paul Pollak, gave us a tour of the Conroy factory and answered all our questions about glove making.

It was many years ago that I decided to write this book. I discussed aspects of the industry with several people who are no longer alive: Joe Perrella; Harwood Rowles; and my father Dr. Malcolm McMartin.

I only regret that I have not been able to talk to many others and that this book recounts only a few of the human stories that constitute the history of glove-making. I wish I could have used more because I have so enjoyed the personal accounts and interviews. My thanks to all who shared the life and times in these two cities to help me create the story of their industry.

Contents

Illustrations

Credits

Credits for postcards, sketches, invoices, and photographs accompany the art work in the text. Those not individually identified come from the author's collection.

Letterheads for Marshall & Co. , Daniel Hays, D. B. Judson, J. & W. S. Tooker, H. Jordan & Co., J. Wooster & Sons, John Ferguson, Northrup & Richards, Newton & Sloan, Moore & Peckham, Hutchinson, Decker & Co., Leonard & Decker, Peckham & Powell, Jas. A. McDougall, and Dempster & Place are reproduced courtesy of Manuscripts and Special Collections, New York State Library.

Glossary sketches come from an undated booklet published by Daniel Hays Co.

All advertisements unless otherwise credited come from *The Glovers Review*, courtesy the Gloversville Free Library.

All photographs of glovemen were taken in the late 1940s and early 1950s and put in a National Association of Glove Manufacturers scrapbook, which is now in the Gloversville Free Library.

Pictures

Pictures continued

Maps

Charts

GLOVERSVILLE, N. Y. BIRDSEYE VIEW

Foreword

Search for the Past

I grew up in Johnstown, New York, a small city, which was brought into existence by one of the oldest crafts in the world, glove-making. Johnstown and its larger, sister city, Gloversville, and several small surrounding communities in Fulton County shared a common industrial history.

Fulton County occupies a plateau a few miles north of and above the rich agricultural land of the Mohawk Valley. The county backs up against the Mayfield Hills, southern ramparts of the grander Adirondack Mountains to the north. The two cities both evolved from pre-Revolutionary War settlements.

Johnstown's story is not too different from communities all across America that grew with emerging industries, some based on old-world crafts, some on new inventions. The making of leather products flourished into a county-wide industry that before the turn of this century produced 90 percent of the men's fine dress gloves made in the United States. In this expansion, the industry impelled Fulton County into one of the richest counties per capita in the country. Then, like many nineteenth century craft industries, which depended more on manual labor than on machines, the glove industry waned. In the second half of the twentieth century, Fulton County became one of the poorest counties in New York State.

I have long been fascinated with this story of growth and demise, long wondered at the causes for both the success and the decline of the industry. No one, growing up in Fulton County in the last years of the Depression and World War II, could be oblivious to the forces at work here.

Although my father was a doctor and not connected with the glove and leather industry, most older members of the family and their friends were in some way related to the local glove businesses. My paternal great-grandfather founded a glove shop, the James I. McMartin Glove Company, in Johnstown in 1843. His three sons joined him in the business and continued it after his death in 1888. The James I. McMartin's Sons firm remained on Clinton Street until 1915. Well before that time, though, my grandfather had left to become a broker of skins and one of the first to import from the Horn of Africa the skins of hair sheep used for mocha leather. Very late in life he married a woman who had been his father's bookkeeper, and as I sit and study her records of gloves sewn, leather and thread bought, and sales to distant places, her elegant handwriting ties me to a long ago time. Like many other women in town, she worked in a glove factory, but she was also a cultured and gracious member of Johnstown's society.

The James I. McMartin Glove Company was larger than average and always comfortably successful, but it never expanded to become one of the county's larger shops. This has always puzzled me, so perhaps I began writing this book to find that answer as well.

My grandmother's father, William D. Foote, was typical of the glove manufacturers who struggled at first in farming or small businesses. His first venture was a grocery store, and during the expansion years of the 1870s, he began to make gloves. Like others of the time, his shop was partly in his house, and his family helped sew the gloves. Although he later established a separate glove shop, his business always remained small, little more than a family enterprise. However, some glove shops that started this way became very large and successful. The reasons they grew and others, like the Foote's, did not have always intrigued me.

Throughout its history, the glove and leather businesses in Fulton County were handed down from father to son. Brothers formed partnerships; glovers married the daughters of other glovers and as in the tradition of monarchies, cemented their efforts through these ties. Interrelationships in the communities were to me a wonderful part of growing up in a small town. Our family was connected by marriage to the Shults family, to the Evans, the MacIntyres, the Piersons, the Dawes, the Rowles, and others, all of whom figured in the glove business. Discovering this trait in my own background helped me see the role of family in the perspective of the whole industry. As I traced genealogical connections, I was able to identify the businesses with the greatest longevity and continuity. I began to understand the role of family in their tenure. The family nature of glove-making emerges as a dominant theme throughout most of the past two centuries.

However, discovering the financial structure of those family businesses proved to be almost impossible. Twentieth century financial figures, in general, are exceedingly difficult to acquire. Two incidents from my past illustrate the problems. I remember as a very little girl watching an elderly glove manufacturer park near our house. He drove a very old car. I asked my mother why he was so poor, why he did not have a newer car. She replied that the man was very rich, but in Johnstown it was not right to flaunt or even discuss your wealth. Not only did the manufacturers not show their wealth, they held knowledge of it very closely. Years later, when I was trying to raise funds for an exhibit on glove-making and tanning at the museum in Gloversville, I naively thought that wealthy glove and leather manufacturers might contribute. I quickly learned that most had moved away, many to spend their wealth elsewhere. Even the city's greatest philanthropist, Lucius Littauer, who gave money for the hospital and many other fine things, spent the bulk of his fortunes elsewhere. Littauer endowed the School of Public Administration at Harvard and established a foundation whose focus is now the country's environment.

Littauer's father, Nathan, was responsible for a part of Gloversville with an ethnic heritage that contributed significantly to its vitality. He encouraged Jewish immigrants to come to Gloversville and bring their skills to the glove industry. As waves of immigrants joined the Scots and English who were my ancestors, Fulton County became a polyglot community. Palatines from Germany had joined the Scots and English in the early days, working as farmers throughout the county. In the early nineteenth century, English, Scots, and later a few French-trained glovemakers made their way to the area along with New England Yankees. They were joined by a new wave of Germans, some trained as glovers and tanners and many of whom were Jewish. Later, near the turn of the century, a great wave of Jews from eastern Europe escaped the Russian pogroms and settled principally in Gloversville. The Slovaks, who came next, established a large community, mostly in Johnstown. The Italians were the last large group of immigrants who came to work in the glove business and they settled in both cities.

It was in this very mixed society that I grew up, living in a 1787 building near the center of town which also housed my father's medical office. That placed me downhill from the factory owners, whose substantial Victorian homes graced the upper slopes of William Street, but uphill from the homes of workers who lived nearer the railroad and Cayadutta Creek.

That mix contributed to the vibrancy of the schools. My high-school class typifies the way the glove and leather industry made it possible for immigrants to become independent and provide schooling for their children. Of my class of 110 students, perhaps half were sons and daughters of recent immigrants. And, almost a quarter of the class has gone beyond college to acquire advanced degrees in education, law, and medicine.

Many of them had mothers who worked—but they were able to stay at home and sew gloves. Federal and state regulations reflecting new social policies began to control homework in the 1930s, but many women retained individual licenses to continue working at home even after laws were enacted to control homework. The glove industry had spawned a type of homework that is very special: its second income lifted many families into the middle class, while allowing mothers to sew gloves at home and also cook and care for their children. The gradual elimination of homework is often cited as one cause of the region's decline. Whether or not this is true has always seemed a mystery.

These were strong families, often immigrants, who raised their children to succeed—and almost universally to leave their hometown and its dominant industry. Something inherent to the immigrant experience spurred families to push their children away from the county. Immigrant parents had a better life than in the troubled countries of Europe, but that was not good enough for their children. Few encouraged their children to become glove workers. Many parents struggled to provide higher education for their children and this inevitably led to them finding careers away from home.

No one who lived in the towns was very far away from the ubiquitous glove shops and large wooden tanneries and skin mills that produced leather for the glove shops. They were everywhere, some clustered near the center of town, others scattered in residential areas, never more than a few blocks from workers' homes. Interspersed were the small shops and factories that supported glove-making: tool makers, box makers, and so on. Looming above all were the three big industries that grew out of the wastes from glove- and leather-making: the glue factory, the hair mill, and the Knox Gelatin Company.

This rosy, if not quite accurate, picture of my hometown had a darker side. Among the things I remember was my father's concern when he had to treat a young tannery worker who contracted anthrax from working with imported skins. My father served as city health officer to supplement his income, and I remember the numerous phone calls of complaints about the horrible windblown smells emanating from the glue factory. I recall a man sitting in our front-hall waiting room who had huge sores from working in the tanneries. I heard a woman crying in pain from a sewing-machine needle that had pierced her finger and broken off beneath the nail.

I remember too the shouts and anger of men emerging from a union meeting at the Eagles Hall across the street from my home. From my safe front-porch vantage, I had only a hint of the strife that brought the men to strike in 1949.

So, it was almost foreordained that I should write this book. My research to write about the Adirondack hemlock-bark tanning industry and the months I spent investigating the glove- and leather-making artifacts for an exhibit I installed at the Fulton County Museum were just first steps in my preparation for this book.

Introduction

I naively thought that I could tell the story of the glove industry by documenting the industry's manufacturers and workers. I quickly realized that the story of these people, their dreams and failures, could only be told in terms of the underlying economic structure. My research had to find answers to such questions as how much was produced, how large was the industry, when did it peak, what caused it to decline. How did the industry shape the community and how did the community shape the industry? How did Fulton County's experience compare with that of other places in America?

These questions in turn made me ask how did national and international events affect the industry. What were the impacts of wars, the National Recovery Act of the 1930s, the Depression, tariff reductions, the loss of homework, unions, and free trade on the community? These questions sent me to a prolonged study of the national context.

To discover the financial history of the industry required that I produce a detailed statistical analysis of the industry throughout its history. These figures, compiled and charted by my husband, W. Alec Reid, are the basis for my understanding of the industry. However, we found that the raw data were scattered, given with different parameters, and generally difficult to compile over any period of time.

Obviously, glove and leather men were drawn to Fulton County with promises of wealth. And, just as obviously, understanding that wealth is essential to my quest to understand the county's history. Statistics from the second half of the nineteenth century, which come from the United States Census of Manufactures for 1850, 1860, 1870, and 1880, have information that can be interpreted to show individual wealth or size of production. In spite of all the gaps, errors, and inconsistent reporting, much can be gleaned to corroborate or enhance the skeleton of historical information from the period. More insights come from the early reports of the R. G. Dun Company, predecessor of Dun and Bradstreet. These are available for the period from the late 1850s to the mid-1880s.

After 1890, the country changed its methods of recording industrial production several times. It ceased documenting individual family-held companies. Gross production and import data are available, but often different categories of products are recorded. In the twentieth century only publicly held corporations had to make public reports and only one manufacturer with a plant in Gloversville falls into that category. As the twentieth century progressed, less and less information was given out about the number of employees or the production levels of individual firms. The Department of Labor provides a fair picture of the industry as a whole in the twentieth century but not of the individuals in it. Even within these constraints, we have been able to compile a fair picture of the size and value of the industry and some of its components. However, most statistical information comes from the entire county or from the two cities, so it has been difficult to write about glove-making in such outlying towns as Mayfield, Broadalbin, or Northville with the same level of detail.

I approached this book using methods similar to those I used in my 1992 history *Hides, Hemlocks and Adirondack History*.[1] That book and *The Glove Cities* are both based in the leather industry, but they tell very different stories. My earlier book describes the hemlock-bark tanning industry in the Adirondacks, which primarily produced shoe and boot leather from hides of horses and cattle. The cowhides were imported from California and Central and South America to huge tanneries in the wilds of upstate New York. Because tanneries consumed huge quantities of hemlock bark, they were located in dense forests, close to the source of the bark.

Though there were several early colonial tanneries making shoe and boot leather in Fulton County, only a handful of the bark-consuming giants were built between 1850 and 1890, and all of them were located on the fringes of the wilderness, not in the county's larger settlements. Very little heavy shoe and boot leather was initially produced in the Town of Johnstown, a political entity which included what is now both cities—Johnstown and Gloversville—and the surrounding area. (This, by the way, has changed in the 1960s and 1970s; while Fulton County had historically produced little shoe leather, it has produced much leather for clothing and shoes in those decades.)

From the beginning, Fulton County produced leather from tanned deerskins. Near the end of the nineteenth century, Fulton County gradually added the skins of sheep, goat, kid, pig, and other small animals to the deerskins dressed in the county. This book starts with the story of how the making of rough mittens from deerskins grew into the county's sophisticated glove industry. Skins of deer and other smaller animals when tanned are said to be "dressed," terminology used throughout the nineteenth century. "Hides" always referred to cows and horses, and just as "hides" and "skins" refer to two different kinds of animals, the processes of tanning and dressing animal skins to convert them to leather was very different from the tanning of hides. Today, with the use of chemicals, the processes have elements in common and the term for making leather from both hides and skins is now "tanning."

The resulting leathers have very different uses as well. Dressed deerskins were usually made into articles of clothing. Vegetable-tanned cowhides were used for sole leather and harnesses, heavy leather that did not stretch or have polish or added color. Tanned hides, when split, became the tops of boots and shoes. Even though these hides were also dressed with oils to make them pliable, the tanning process, initially based on a vegetable process that extracted tannin from hemlock bark, was totally different from the dressing of deerskins. Historically, that employed human urine and rotten eggs, as well as animal brains and other organic materials.

I agonized over the question of who would be the principal audience for the book. Should I write it for academicians or for the descendants of the thousands who worked in the glove and leather industries and the residents of the glove cities? The story cannot be told without details of the historical, sociological, and economic records, but I could not write a strictly academic book. Hence I have designed a compromise that places details of people, timelines, manufacturers, unions, and illustrative notes and quotes in narrow columns beside the historical narrative. I could have put these details, which will appeal to people who know the area, in appendices, but then the material would have been separated from descriptions of contemporaneous events.

The historical account is presented from the perspective of what residents of Fulton County saw and recorded of themselves, their industry, and their towns. Their sense of reality drives the narrative and occasionally mirrors the outside world. My goals in writing this book led me to weave the industry's technical details with the human story and the result is a complex narrative. Rather than introducing the work by foretelling the answers to my basic questions, I prefer to invite the reader to discover these answers as I did, bringing together the bits and pieces of the historical record. That way I trust there is some element of suspense in the unfolding story.

The map of Johnstown circa 1869 shows many of the early glove shops and skin mills.

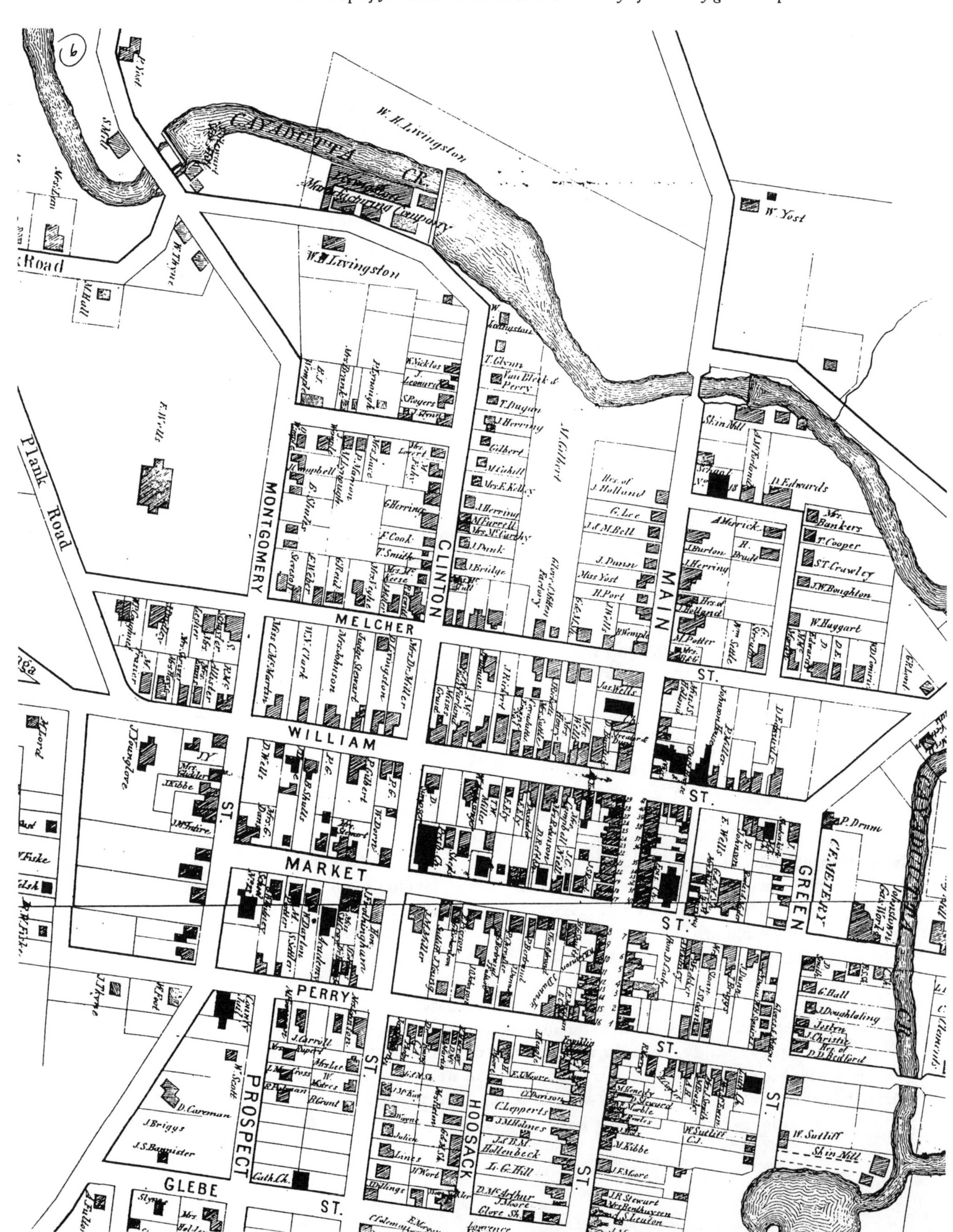

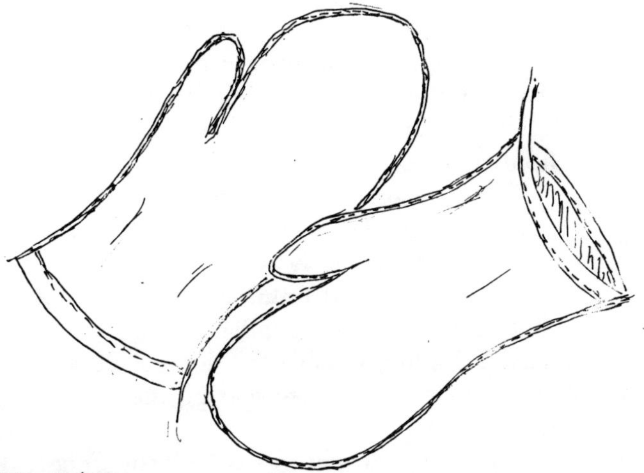

Beginnings

Just as the first streets of Johnstown were laid out as part of Sir William Johnson's planned town, it has long been assumed that the beginning of its glove industry was also planned and to a large extent predetermined. Johnson was born in Ireland and came to America to manage his uncle's estate, a large tract south of the Mohawk River. He entered public life under Governor George Clinton and moved to his own stone mansion north of the Mohawk River in 1742. Sir William served as representative of King George II, who gave Johnson his baronetcy and a royal grant of 69,000 acres that stretched north of the Mohawk Valley. Because of his service as major general in the French and Indian War, Johnson was appointed Colonial Agent and "Superintendent of All Affairs of the Six Nations and other Northern Indians." In 1761 and 1762 he built a baronial mansion with two guard houses six miles from his former home on the Mohawk at the edge of what is today Johnstown. The location placed him strategically between the settlements in the Mohawk Valley and the wild lands still dominated by the Indian Nations.

The extraordinary localization of the glove-making industry in Fulton County is an incident of much interest in the economic history of the United States. It seems to have had its origin among a colony of Perthshire families ... who were settled in the region by Sir William Johnson about 1760.

For many years the products were disposed of in the neighborhood, but about 1809 the goods began to find more distant markets, and by 1825 the industry was firmly established.

From the *Encyclopedia Britannica*, Eleventh Edition, 1911

Sir William also had a summer home at Fish House near the Sacandaga River, in what is now the Town of Broadalbin. Around 1760 he encouraged Scots settlers to immigrate to the Broadalbin area. The people of Breadalbeen and Perth named their new homes for the towns they had left. Among them were said to be several leatherworkers. Little record of glove-making comes down from these early times, but the many names from the second wave Scots people, who settled Mayfield and Broadalbin just before the Revolutionary War, later show up as the glovemakers in the Town of Johnstown—Burr, McDougal, Leffert, and McMartin to name a few.[2]

Sir William encouraged other Scots to settle in Johnstown, and he focused his town planning ideas on this area near his baronial mansion. The town was Sir William's dream and by 1770 he had attracted eight families to live there. The new settlement was close to both the farming areas to the east, Broadalbin, Mayfield, and Perth, and to the Indian trade routes emanating from Johnson Hall. Deerskins were plentiful and much sought for clothing. Learning Indian ways, eighteenth century colonial settlers began to dress deerskins, and a cottage industry in dressing deerskins for clothing developed along with all the other aspects of self-sufficiency common in upstate New York in the eighteenth century—burning trees to produce ash for lye and soaps, tanning cowhides for shoe and boot leather, spinning flax and woolens for clothing, collecting fat or wax for candles.

In establishing his town center near his baronial hall, Sir William gave the town's future industry an added start. The town attracted settlers from Scotland, England, and Ireland who had the special skills needed in a frontier outpost.

The transformation of deerskin-tanning from a frontier activity in many small communities in northern New York into the dominant industry in Fulton County probably owes its origin equally to Sir William's planning and the availability of deerskins. Deerskins were plentiful and easy to obtain through barter with the Indians. The could be turned into soft, pliable, and durable leather, suitable for clothing. It was an easy transition from using deerskins for clothing to making them into rough mittens for commercial trade.

Sir William sought to have Albany County divided, and in 1772, Tryon County was detached and Johnstown became the county seat. Shortly afterwards a courthouse and jail were erected. Sir William died before the start of the Revolutionary War.

After that war, Johnstown remained a legal and political center with life circling around its courthouse. New residents flocked to Johnstown and the surrounding area from Connecticut and other more crowded northeastern regions. They came also from other points in the county, which was renamed Montgomery County in 1784. The wave of immigrants now included many Scots, English, and Irish descendents of settlers of the New England states—the Yankees who fled westward. Descendents of the Palatines and Germans who had settled the Mohawk Valley also moved into Johnstown. Throughout the county, settlers clustered in crossroads that began to grow into small villages. Most people farmed, while the settlements grew around saw-, grist-, and woolen mills.

Accounts in local histories present the belief[3] that because of Sir William's death, Johnstown proper grew only very slowly during the next few decades. It is true that surrounding fields were not as suited to agriculture as land to the south along the Mohawk River. It is also true that Johnstown was removed from the main east-west routes along the Mohawk River. River towns were given an increased advantage in 1824 by the opening of the Erie Canal. Local historians later claimed that the canal temporarily stopped the town's growth—in fact they saw the period up through 1848 as the dark days.

In 1836, the Montgomery County seat was moved to Fonda. Perhaps the sense that it was a dark time arose from that brief period of Johnstown's political eclipse. Two years later Johnstown was restored as the seat of newly created Fulton County, which was severed from Montgomery County. Perhaps also it seemed a shadowy time because of the county's isolation and the many settlers who stopped briefly before heading farther west. To former historians it may have seemed a bleak time because so much about the early days of the glove industry are lost in history. In 1895, the local newspaper was exuberantly extolled the town's growth and industry in a historical review celebrating the centennial of the town's founding. What is certain is that the account was in error when it cast a pall over the growth of the first half of the century. As research reveals, the glove and mitten industry began to grow in the first decade of the nineteenth century and its growth proceeded gradually through the 1830s and 1840s, primarily based on the use of deerskins. The paper, following earlier historians, also erred in stating that Johnson brought in the first glovemakers. No trained glovemakers arrived until well after his death, so it appears that this myth was created to explain the seemingly miraculous beginning of the glove cities.

Mittens

At the beginning of the nineteenth century, only crude mittens were cut and sewn from the leather made from deerskins. Because relatively few deerskins could be converted into a very useful and rather valuable product, they were an good raw material for local industry. Further, deerskins were easily transported by traders coming from the north and west, so the industry was not initially dependent on water or rail transportation. And the finished mittens were light and easy to transport to markets, an ideal product to export from a remote town.

The primitive buckskin mittens and breeches made by the early settlers were due to the necessity occasioned by the rough, laborious work of the farmers and wood-choppers, leather being also cheaper than the products of the loom.
Washington Frothingham, *History of Fulton County*, 1892.[1]

The gathering of skins, the sale of gloves, and the use of a barter system depended on the seasons. Skins had to be gathered in cool weather—after the fall hunts—so that they could be delivered to Fulton County for tanning before they could rot or decay. Gloves were needed as fall approached, and late summer and fall were the time to sew gloves. This established the pattern of seasonality in the glove industry which persisted into the twentieth century. Traditionally, gloveworkers were employed for only a part of the year.

The area north of Johnstown was part of the Kingsborough Patent, which gave its name but not its spelling to a farming settlement called Kingsboro. Kingsboro was at the base of a mountain range that dipped down to the east and the broad fields and marshes along the Sacandaga River. Before the Revolutionary War, Kingsboro was a rough, frontier crossroads whose settlers traded with the farmers of Broadalbin and Mayfield and with their immigrants from Perthshire who had brought their leathermaking skills to America.

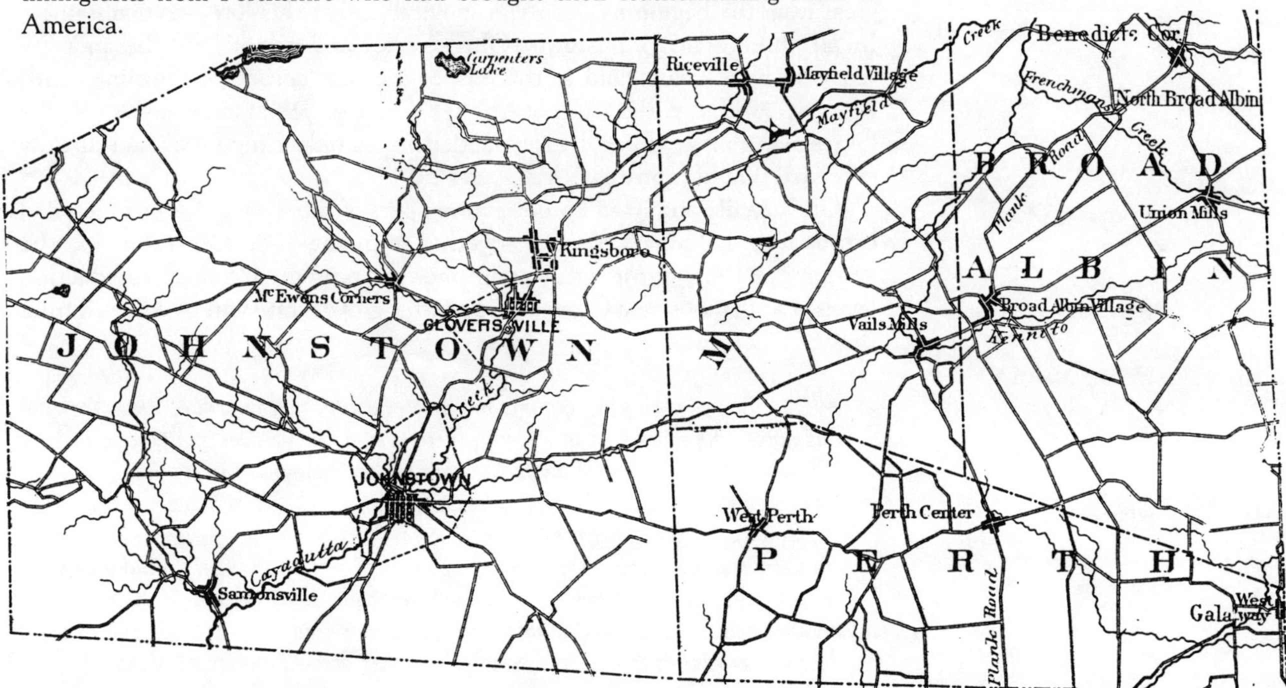

The 1868 J. Jay Stranahan and Beach Nichols Atlas of Montgomery and Fulton Counties *depicts the close proximity of Johnstown, Gloversville, and Kingsboro and their relationship to Perth, Mayfield, and Broadalbin.*

After the Revolutionary War, Kingsboro grew with immigrants from Connecticut and coastal states, descendents of Scots and English. A few settlers in the Kingsboro area in what is now northern Gloversville worked tin items, traveled to the western part of the state, exchanged their wares for deerskins, and converted these to jackets and breeches and later to mittens. They, too, must have learned tanning from those who had passed on Indian ways as well as from the immigrants from Scotland. Washington Frothingham, historian and author of a history of the county published in 1892,[4] retells this oft-repeated story of glove-making beginning with tin-making, so it has become gospel, but the beginnings of the glove industry in Kingsboro are well documented and logical. Quite simply, it was after the Revolutionary War that several of the pioneering makers of gloves and mittens had moved to Kingsboro and established mitten shops there.

The wide plain surrounding the Cayadutta Creek and its tributary Mill Creek south of Kingsboro was covered with a dense forest. The forest quickly gave way to farms and a settlement, whose beginning can be traced to the first decade of the century, about the time Kingsboro residents began making mittens from deerskins. Timber cutting to make room for the settlement that became Gloversville gave the city its first name, Stump City[5]. Within a decade Stump City's residents were also converting deerskins to mittens and gloves. Their homes and attached shops appeared along Fulton Street near the creeks and along the main road from Johnstown. By 1828, when the first post office was established, the settlement was renamed Gloversville.

As I was growing up, we believed that Johnstown had originated the glove and mitten industry and that it came much later to Gloversville. The commercial center of Gloversville began after 1820, but the glove and mitten industry had much earlier roots. The rivalry between the towns was great from the beginning, so it was inevitable that this lore was maintained. In all three areas, Johnstown, Gloversville, and Kingsboro, the industry seems to have taken hold at the end of the first decade of the nineteenth century. And, by the end of the 1840s, the production levels of the Gloversville area, which had expanded to include Kingsboro, had already exceeded that of Johnstown.

Gloversville and Kingsboro remained part of the Town of Johnstown and census records lumped the two together until the 1880 Census, giving the appearance that Johnstown was the more important. However, production levels that demonstrate Gloversville's faster growth rate can be inferred from the 1850 Census.

> *. . . Some years ago, and one hundred and fifty miles north of New York and about fifty miles west of Albany, there lived a few families in a place called "Stump City." It was wild and cold in the winter almost as Greenland. I have often seen the snow there six feet deep. O the long and dreary Winter! Most of the land was as poor as the snow was deep.*
>
> *Now this is the very spot where our city was "builded together." And it was done by the deer. . . One of those neighbors came home with a deerskin and another neighbor happened in at the time and they said, "What is the use of a deerskin unless it is tanned and dressed?" So they dressed it after a fashion.*
>
> *The next thing was to make mittens out of it. And they did that after a fashion too. But no sooner were the mittens made than everyone in the neighborhood wanted a pair.*
>
> *So other skins were bought and soon turned into mittens and gloves and moccasins, after a better fashion, and distant neighbors heard of the wonderful wares for the hands and feet in the winter, and they came miles to get them.*
>
> *Then poor cold "Stump City" with its three or four families began to "look up." Every man woman and child went into business. Even then they could not*

supply the demand. Distant towns sent word "We want some [mittens]." The peddlars started out with horse and sleigh in mid-winter, often with a great load of the precious wares tied with buckskin strings in dozens, and all packed nicely in a big box. Isabella Alden, 1888, from her book A City *Founded by a Deer.*

[*License to a manufacturer of* LEATHER.]

No. 38

WHEREAS Lemuel Heacock **of the county of** Montgomery **in the** State **of** New York **hath duly applied for a license to employ manufactory conducted in** the Tannery Containing Vats **situate in the county of** Montgomery **in the** State **of** New York **and owned by** Lemuel Heacock **of the county of** Montgomery **in the** State **of** New York **in the** Manufacture **of LEATHER during the term of** One Year **to commence on the** 19th **day of** April **1815, and to end on the** 18th **day of** April **1816**

NOW, KNOW YE, That the said Lemuel Heacock **is hereby licensed to employ the said manufactory in the** Manufacture **of LEATHER, for the said term of** One Year **as above defined, in conformity with the laws of the United States.**

Walter P. Beale

Countersigned at Johnstown **in the Collection District of** New York **this** 17 **day of** April **1815**

Charles Morris

Collector of the Revenue for the 11th ***Collection District of*** New York

For the Commissioner of the Revenue.

New York State granted Lemuel Heacock a license to manufacture leather in 1815.

Courtesy the Heacock Family

Pioneering Glovemen

Job Heacock and his sons were probably the first to make gloves in Kingsboro.[6] The Heacocks continued making mittens and later gloves from deerskins for almost two centuries. The ownership of the firm established by Job's son Lemuel is traced in the family tree, along with the shops belonging to other descendents of Job.

Job came to Kingsboro in 1791, and whether or not he began making gloves then, it is known that his son, Lemuel, born in 1786, had a growing business at the end of the first decade of the nineteenth century. Lemuel's brother Philander G. was also a glover and his sons had a separate establishment from that of Lemuel and his sons. Ezekial Case also tanned deerskins in Kingsboro as early as 1803.

Cod oil was used to dress deerskins and many barrels of cod oil were shipped to Fulton County from Boston and Rhode Island.

Mr Lemuel Heacock
Bot of [illegible] Humphrey
2 bar Oil @ $12 — $24.00
Albany 24 Mar 1825

Courtesy the Heacock Family

The first maker of mittens and gloves in Johnstown was Talmadge Edwards. He moved to Johnstown from Beacon, New York, and by 1808 had established a glove shop in his house at the corner of William and Montgomery Streets. He had a small mill to tan deerskins in a shed attached to his house. Edwards had been trained as a leather-dresser in England and in 1809 James Burr and William C. Mills hired Edwards to teach them the art of leather dressing. Mills and his son-in-law Burr established glove shops in what is now the center of Gloversville.

Burr began selling gloves in 1809 and introduced "the bucktail," for which he had a patent. Burr used a device literally covered with the tough hairs of a buck tail to smooth leather. (Burr's invention was replaced in 1874 by an emery wheel, first introduced by gloveman Daniel Hays. It was still called a buck tail.) Burr had a mill on Forest Street in Gloversville, just south of the corner of Fulton and Main streets that became the future city's center. Burr was succeeded nearby by his son James H. and grandson Harvey W.

William C. Mills began to buy deerskins from Holland Patent to the west of Fulton County in 1805,[7] acquiring about 400 to 500 skins a year. By 1809 he was manufacturing mittens. Two eponymous streets, Burr and Mills, are parallel to and immediately south of Forest Street. Today in Gloversville you can almost reconstruct the roster of pioneer glovemen and sometimes locate the site of their first shops from the names of the city's streets.

These common early start dates confirm that the making of deerskin mittens began within a decade in all three areas.[8]

The Heacock Family Tree

Descendents of Job Heacock maintained gloveshops to manufacture deerskin gloves for almost two centuries. The family's tenure in the business was longer than any other in Fulton County

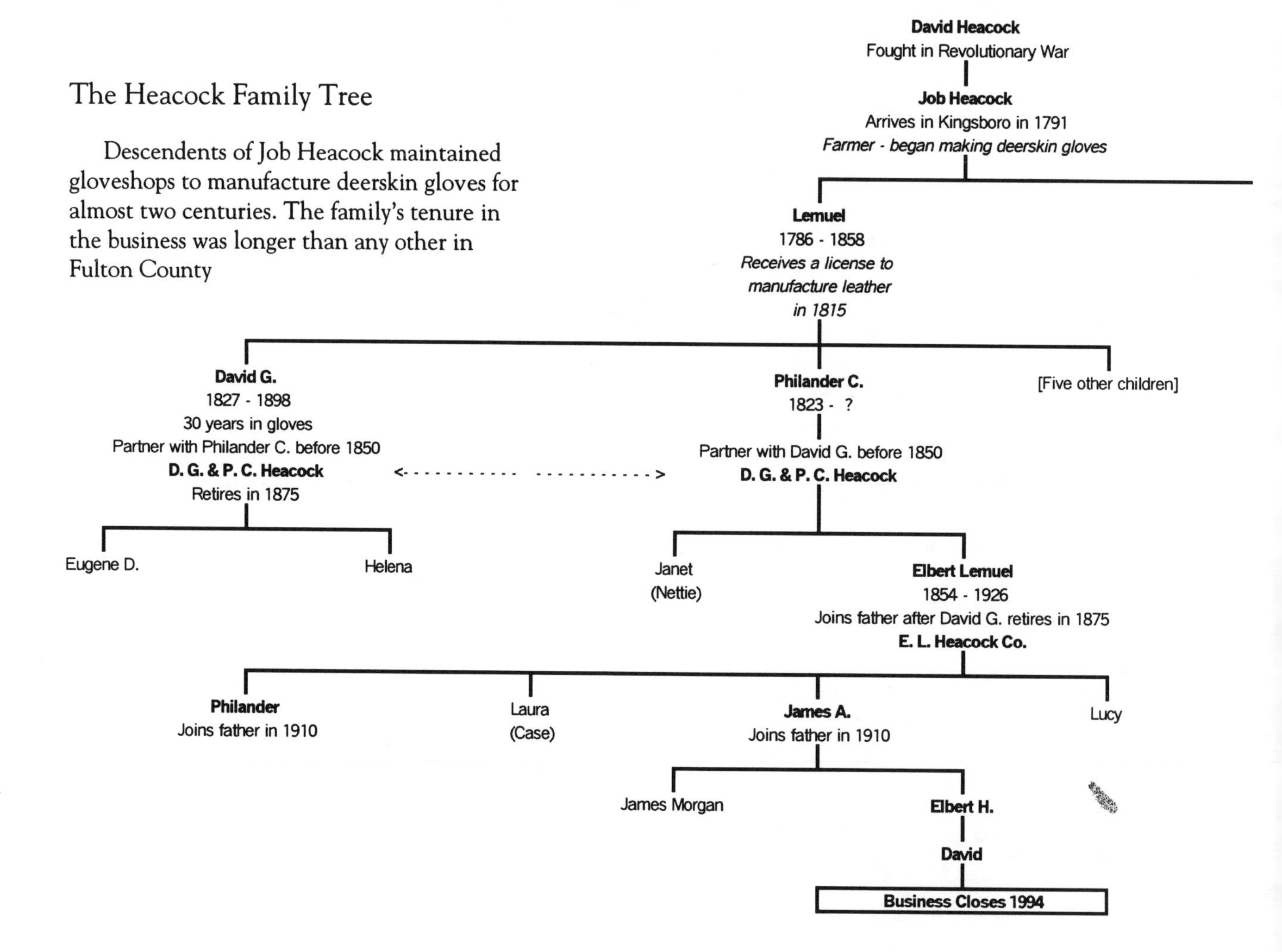

John Ward began making mittens in Kingsboro in 1810. The Leonard brothers, Josiah, Daniel, and Abner, started making mittens about 1820. Willard Rose began making mittens after 1830. It was probably about this time that the Town of Johnstown began to produce gloves as well as mittens. Although the gloves were crude, rough, and ill-fitting, they were well suited for outdoor work in the cold north woods.

The deerskin mittens produced locally could be sold by their makers who carried them to the west to trade in towns along the Mohawk River. In 1825 structured glove selling began when one of Philander Heacock's employees, Elisha Judson of Kingsboro, went to Boston with a cart loaded with gloves. In the course of a six-week trip, he returned with $600 in silver—equivalent to a year's wages for several men at that time, and worth about $8,000 today.

Elisha Judson's younger brother Alanson joined his brother in making gloves before 1830. Elisha's son Daniel B. became the county's largest producer of gloves in the 1870s and his firm continued until 1890.

Uriah M. Place (1832), John McNab (1836), and Humphrey Smith (1834) round out the roster of Gloversville's pioneers. Smith's brother, D. W., began making gloves about 1837 and he continued in the business for 50 years, working in later years for others.

In Johnstown, A. S. VanVoast began making mittens from deerskins in 1833. His factory later made gloves and continued in business until VanVoast retired just before 1890. Jonathan Ricketts, who came from England in 1839, was the first of at least four Fulton County immigrants who were trained in the glove and leather industry in Yeovil, which was then England's glove-manufacturing center.

Mitten manufacturing was a curious business, for at first the glover had to turn the deerskins into leather. Initially an Indian process was used, soaking the skins, scraping them to remove the hair, then tanning them by applying the brains of a deer. Later, brains of hogs were substituted, but were not as successful, because deer brains contain properties similar to 'soda ash' or fat liquors, while hog brains do not. This process was still used to some extent in the 1890s.

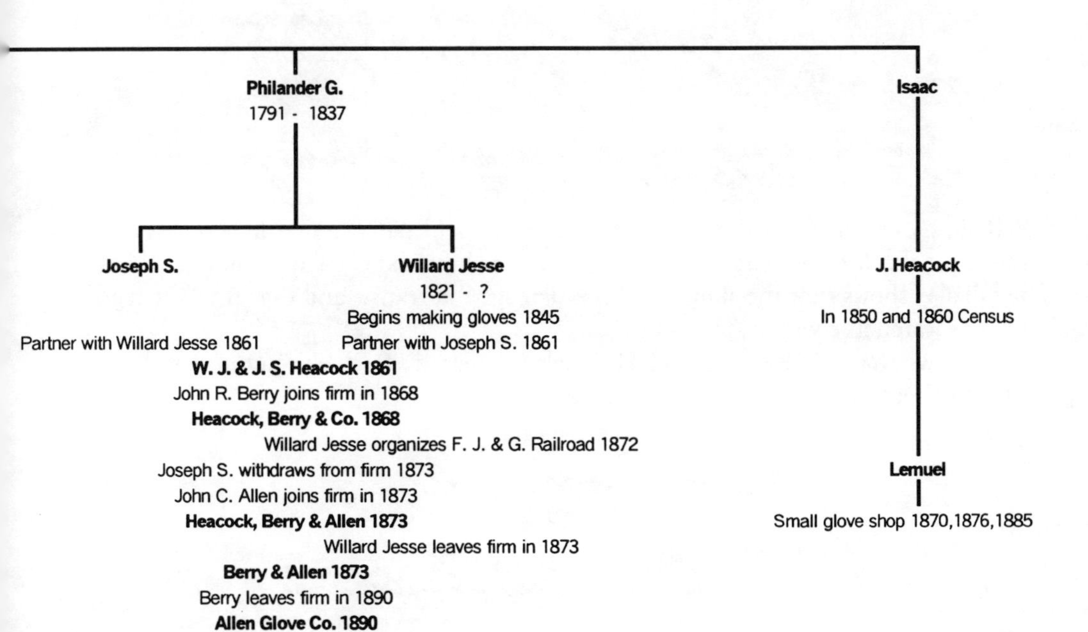

Courtesy the Heacock Family

Mr John McNab Junr — New York 5 August 1839
Bought of the American Fur Company

C #233	1 Bale 150 Shaved Deer	354	@ 43		152 22
234 a 236	3 " ca 200 Red & Blue " is 600 skins	1361	@ 40		544 40
237 a 243	7 " " 100 Grey " " 700 "	2056	@ 32		657 92
#1	1 " 27 Shaved Deer Imperfect 60 @ 43	2580			
	Damaged 20%	516			20 64
	30 " " " 61 @ 43	2623			
	Damaged 30%	787			18 36
	13 " " " 26 @ 43	1118			
	Damaged 50%	559			5 59
	22 Red " " 38 @ 40	1520			
	Damaged 20%	304			12 16
	33 " " " 57 @ 40	2280			
	Damaged 30%	684			15 96
	9 " " " 13 @ 40	520			
	Damaged 50%	260			2 60
	2 Grey " " 7 @ 32	224			
	Damaged 25%	56			1 68
	6 " Sound 29 @ 32				9 28
	3 Red Elk (24) at 3.00 per skin				9 —
2	1 " 25 Grey Deer Imperfect 42 @ 32	1344			
	Damaged 25%	336			10 08
	41 " " " 92 @ 32	2944			
	Damaged 40%	1178			17 66
	26 " " " 55 @ 32	1760			
	Damaged 50%	880			8 80
	1 " 7 Shaved Elk 71; 20 Red " 215; 13 Grey " 190 — 40 Skins @		3.00		120 .
					1606 35
	Cartage to TowBoat				1 56
	Cash				1607 91

Marked J McNab care of McKinley Fultonville N.Y. and shipped on board TowBoat Dry Dock

Manuscripts and Special Collections
New York State Library

As early as 1839, glovemen needed more deerskins than could be obtained locally. As the above bill of sale indicates, John McNab obtained red and grey deerskins and elkskins from a trader in New York City. The bill also shows that the skins had been damaged in transit and that the "Cartage to the TowBoat" from the warehouse was $1.56.

The invoice below shows that in 1846, Lemuel Heacock purchased "Red Musquito" deerskins, which probably came from Central America.

Johnstown Aug 31st 1846
Mr Lemuel Heacock Bot of C. B. Fosdick & Co.

5 Packs Red Musquito Deer skins
165. 158. 177. 173. 164 – 837
Tare – 5 = 832 @ 2/- $208.00

Recd Payt C. B. Fosdick & Co

Courtesy the Heacock Family

The 1840s—Early Industry

To me, the decade of the 1840s lives up to is appellation as a dark time only because of the mysteries surrounding the next stage in the growth of the glove and leather industry. This was unquestionably the decade in which the transition from home shops to factories began. This decade preceded the introduction of machinery either for sewing or for tanning, but it marked the beginning of specialization in the industry. Separate shops or parts of shops were established to accommodate the division of leather-making and glove-making operations. The transition is not described in local histories; it can only be inferred from the United States Census of Manufactures and other records. During the 1840s, as glovemen built separate structures for glove-making and tanning or dressing of skins, these buildings became known as glove shops and skin mills. Often one man or a partnership owned both a shop and a skin mill, but by the 1850s several men specialized in either tanning or glove-making. One of those was Eli Pierson, who built a separate tannery near the center of Johnstown in 1851.

Jonathan Ricketts was among the first of those who branched out from the dressing of deerskins. He began dressing sheepskins in 1841 "in the old McLaren mill" near the cemetery. According to Frothingham, around 1848, Ricketts began importing sheepskins from South America, shipping them by boat, canal, and wagon to his tannery. In 1855 he tanned about 40,000 sheepskins. Ricketts built a mill on West Main Street just east of the Cayadutta Creek in 1856 and continued in business there for about 25 years.

The first trained leatherworkers to come from France were the Bertrand brothers, Lucien and Theophilus, who arrived from Millau around 1840. They began tanning kidskins (the skins of young goats) in Johnstown in 1848, perhaps as early as 1844. This may have marked the beginning of the production of finer grades of men's gloves, but the industry did not begin the real shift to the manufacture of finer grades until after the Civil War.

The Old Ricketts Mill, Johnstown, New York

Kingsboro Aug 15, 184[illegible]
Burton Heacock & Co
Bot of Lemuel Heacock
3 Dz Mittens $7. — $21.00
7 — Do 5. — 35.00
7 Dz Gloves 6. — 42.00
1 Do Do 5. 5
$103.00

Courtesy the Heacock Family

The Bertrands' glove shop was the first of five manufacturing concerns established by trained French glovemen in Johnstown before the Civil War. The others were established by Louis Jeannisson, Ferdinand Vassier, Jean Joseph Riton from Strasburg (his sons Charles J. and Eugene later formed the Riton Brothers glove concern), and by the father of Emile Julien. The glove shop of William J. Larcombe, another Frenchman, was built later (1885).

James I. McMartin established his glove and mitten shop in 1843 on East Clinton Street. Also making gloves in Johnstown in the first half of the 1840s were D. H. Cuyler and Samuel and Howard Hill. About the same time, Marcellus Gilbert began to make gloves and mittens. He formed a partnership with David Wells and the firm of Gilbert & Wells built a separate tannery, becoming one of the decade's largest leather producers as well as one of the largest glove manufacturers.

A small leather pouch with folded receipts of the Heacock glove and leather shops tells all that is known about the finances and business practices of individual concerns in these formative years. In the 1830s and 1840s, Lemuel Heacock bought bales of deerskins from dealers as far away as New York City. These dealers also shipped skins of red deer from the south. The prices ranged from $.21 to $.24 a pound. Heacock paid freight charges from New York City to Fultonville that were about a third the cost of freighting between Fultonville and Kingsboro. The canal had proved its value! A barrel of cod oil for dressing skins cost $13 in 1824, $16 a decade later. In 1839 Heacock sold mittens at prices ranging from $5 to $8 a dozen pair, gloves at $7 to $8 a dozen. For many of his transactions, Heacock paid about half in cash with a promissory note given for the remainder. While it is impossible to draw any conclusions about costs and profits, it is interesting that a century later gloves were selling for little more—less than $9 a dozen for rough gloves.

What is amazing is the number of men who set up glove shops and skin mills. This great number of entrepreneurs distinguishes glove-making throughout its entire tenure in Fulton County. Large shops arose, and they, too, were numerous, but no single man or family ever dominated local industry.

From the inception of the glove and mitten industry, county glovemen counted gloves by the dozen. The practice survives.

The smallest shops continued to be attached to the owners' homes, as did most of those whose production was under $10,000 a year. By 1850, two small manufacturers produced leather and not gloves. However, the tradition of one manufacturer dressing deerskins and producing gloves continued through the next three decades and established the pattern of vertical operations that prevailed along with the trend toward specialization.

Women and glove shops

The female employees who sewed the gloves were usually the owner's wife or daughters or elderly relatives—mothers and aunts—who sewed in family circles in the women's homes. The sewing was at first as crude as the cutting. The women waxed threads to use with square needles. They drew the needles through the leather using backstitches or lockstitches. If a heavy work mitten was being made, an additional thin length of leather—a welt—was sewn into the seam to give it strength. These more serviceable mittens were designed for men who worked long hours out-of-doors in the cold. (At this time womens' gloves were handsewn from woven fabrics. Women who could afford the luxury of fine gloves bought imports from England and France.)

The gloves were mostly made by women. The Country people for miles in the vicinity came after packages of buckskin cut into the pieces to make a dozen pairs of gloves. Washington Frothingham, *History of Fulton County*, 1892.[2]

The smallest shops had only the owner and perhaps one other male to prepare skins and cut mittens or gloves with two to five women sewing gloves for them.

What did an early shop look like? For the smallest operations it was simply a room attached to the owner's house. The father occasionally purchased tanned deerskins, more often he dressed them himself. Then he cut out the mittens and gloves with shears, using simple patterns with only a front, back, and thumb piece. The front and back were often all one piece.

The patterns were made of pasteboard or wooden shingles, and the glover traced the outlines with sharp pointed pieces of lead called "plummets." Lore has it that the plummets were formed by pouring molten lead into the cracks between floor planks. The women and children sewed around a kitchen table and as they worked, they sat on the sewn mittens and gloves to smooth them. Children tied knots in threads just as they did in later years.

The first factories

Separate buildings for glove shops were erected during the 1840s for all the larger firms recorded in the 1850 Census of Manufacturers. These were mostly detached two-story, frame structures, often on the same site with the glovers' residence. Before long, back sheds, barns, carriage houses, and other outbuildings became shops adjacent to homes throughout the center of town. They were about the size of a modern two-car garage and you can still drive around town and spot some of these relics.

The compact square of streets designed by Sir William and the town's proximity to water sources (Cayadutta and Mathews creeks) made Johnstown an ideal location for the growth of the glove industry.

As the glove shops increased in size, the buildings adhered to a common design. On the lower floor there was a place to dress leather, upstairs a large table for cutting and a place to store leather and finished goods. Neighbors joined the owner's relatives to sew gloves. Bundles of cut mittens and by the 1850s rough gloves, with fourchettes and thumb pieces, scraps for welts, thread, and sometimes needles were tied together and distributed to the women who sewed. (Fourchettes, from the French for forks, are the pieces between fingers which give a good fit.) Almost all of the female employees worked in their own homes, a tradition that prevailed even as the transition to women factory workers began in the 1870s.

Finances and wages in the 1840s

According to the 1850 Census, which gives an overview of the financial picture of the industry at the end of the decade of the 1840s, most of the businesses remained quite small. In the Town of Johnstown, which included Johnstown, Gloversville, and Kingsboro, 52 firms or 80 percent of those reporting produced in one year less than $10,000 worth of gloves (the equivalent of about $180,000 today). Most also prepared their own skins. The shops whose production ranged from $5,000 to $10,000 usually had three males and upwards of 20 females, most of whom probably worked at home and part-time. Eleven firms produced between $10,000 and $20,000 worth of gloves and the two others had production valued at more than $20,000. These thirteen larger firms all had a substantial number of employees. The number of males employed in the larger firms ranged from four to six, while the number of females in those firms ranged from 15 to 36.

Alanson Judson was the largest manufacturer in Gloversville, while Gilbert & Wells was the largest in Johnstown, with annual productions in 1850 valued at $29,400 and $27,000 respectively. They employed 11 and 12 males respectively and 50 and 58 females.[9]

Only six firms in 1850 reported the value of their initial investments—and these were very small. The early Census of Manufactures is noted for incomplete information on overhead (costs of production) and historians believe that early manufacturers did not understand the concept of overhead. In this case, before any machines were used, overhead amounted to little more than the primitive factory buildings, which were crude and relatively inexpensive to build and maintain. Leather and gloves were much more valuable than wood and shingles.

Low overhead encouraged the proliferation of small shops, which seemed to be as productive as the larger ones. Wages, $25 per month for males, $8 a month for females, and raw materials constituted the bulk of basic costs. Profits appear to be substantial—averaging 28 percent of the cost of raw materials. The smallest shops made less profit, 25 percent, perhaps because they produced the poorer grades of gloves. The few larger shops averaged 38 percent profit, more than enough to account for the investment in buildings. (In the 1850s and for many decades after, manufacturers often failed to consider the cost of overhead—an easy thing to do given its small size in relation to the cost of raw materials. The smaller manufacturers often did not calculate their own wages as part of the cost of doing business—many glovemen failed to do this until forced to adopt decent accounting practices in the 1930s.)

For all the small amount of money required to set up a glove shop, there was always a substantial investment either in skins or later in tanned leather. The investment was a risk, but the amount earned from sales minus the costs of raw materials appears sufficient to insulate the early glove manufacturers from the vagaries of markets.

MARSHALL & CO.'S

PATENT LINEN THREAD

The 1850s—Decade of Change

By 1850, the products of the industry had begun to change. Finer grades of men's gloves were produced by the Bertrands with their imported kidskins. In the decade before 1860, others began to import kidskins for gloves, but sturdy work gloves remained the bulk of the production along with deerskin mittens. A local historian claimed that four-fifths of the residents of Gloversville were engaged in the manufacture of leather and gloves.[10]

Owners of the smaller shops joined together to sell their wares throughout the East Coast and in the cities in the Midwest. Gradually itinerant salesmen began hawking the gloves of several different home shops. The best evidence we have of how this worked is in a diary written between 1857 and 1864 by glove maker E. P. Parmelee of Broadalbin. He described moving his shop from place to place several different times. In 1859 he wrote that he loaded a wagon with gloves and mittens so that S. S. Capron, another glover, could then set out on a peddling trip.

The diary also shows how far glovers had to go to secure raw skins. Later in the same summer, Parmelee went to Albany to purchase sheepskins for his business. In August he had to ship a box of finished gloves to Capron in Steuben County. Apparently Capron could sell more goods than he had brought with him. In 1860, Parmelee went to New York City to purchase seven bales of deerskins. That year he prepared a huge shipment of gloves for one E. T. Newton to sell in Michigan.

His daily entries detail the tasks he accomplished each day from Monday to Saturday: "worked on patterns and tools, worked on the tools, staked cape leather, worked at egging leather, worked at cutting leather, making glove patterns, then cutting gloves."[11]

Although it was not initiallly installed in the glove shops, the gas industry in the county had a phenomenal growth between 1850 and 1860.[12] In 1856, Stewart Mills, a hotel owner, built a small gas plant for the Windsor Hotel, slowly extending gas service for illumination to a few churches and homes. In 1859 a new gas company, Fox & Demarest, was organized. That company built a coal-gas plant to serve the growing village of Gloversville with its 500 homes, an increasing number of the small glove shops, and population of 3,000 people. Johnstown also had a small gas plant, and later the two were merged into a larger plant, which served to light most factories until the early 1900s when electric power gradually supplanted gas.

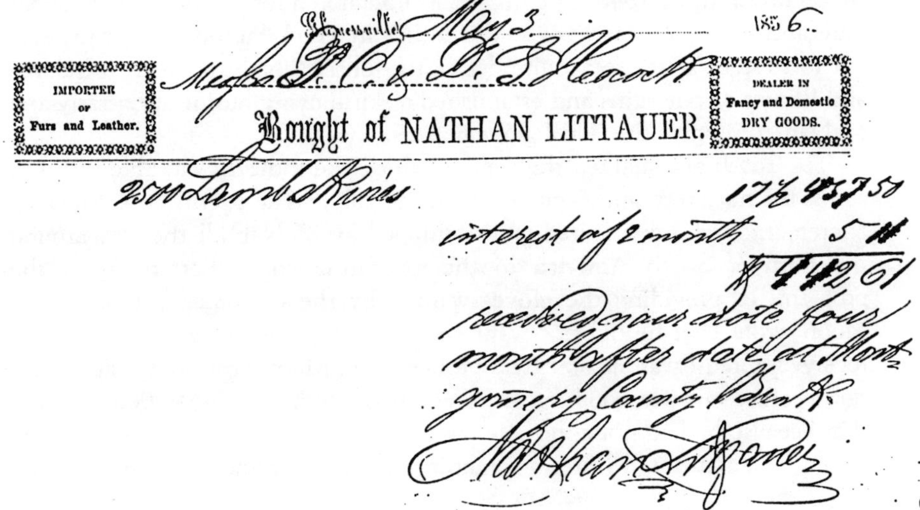

Gloversville May 3 1856

Messrs P. C. & D. S. Heacock

IMPORTER OF Furs and Leather.

Bought of NATHAN LITTAUER.

DEALER IN Fancy and Domestic DRY GOODS.

2500 Lamb Skins 17½ 437 50

interest of 2 month 5 11

$ 442 61

received your note four month after date at Montgomery County Bank

Nathan Littauer

In the 1850s glovemen sought different kinds of skins such as lambskins and kidskins. This bill of sale was signed by Nathan Littauer, Gloversville's most famous citizen. It indicates that he was giving Heacock two months with interest to pay for the skins.

Courtesy the Heacock Family

New factories and skin mills sprang up in both settlements. It is remarkable how many of the names from the 1840s appear as principals of glove firms in the next three decades. The decade from 1850 to 1860 was the time when all of the larger firms moved into factories separate from their homes. A few tanners located just two or three blocks from the center of Johnstown near the bottom of State Street hill and adjacent to the creeks. However, Jonathan Ricketts on Melcher Street, Eli Pierson on Market Street, James I. McMartin on Clinton Street, and Russell & Gilbert, whose factory was on Melcher Street, all had glove shops near their homes. In 1856, Jonathan Ricketts built a new skin mill on Main Street near the Cayadutta Creek, just a few blocks from his home.

In Gloversville, Alanson Judson's factory was on the corner of Fulton and Fremont, just east of the "four corners," the intersection of Fulton and Main streets. Numerous small glove shops lined the streets within a three-block radius of the corners. Two branches of the Heacock family had shops in Kingsboro that may date to this early time. McNab's skin mill was built on West Mill Creek (earlier named Bennett Corners Creek) and the D. C. & S. S. Mills huge skin yard was built at the confluence of that creek with the Cayadutta Creek.

Among the glovers with large separate buildings, some near or adjacent to their homes were D. C. Mills, H. Leonard, H. L. Burr, W. A. Kasson, and Uriel Case. S. Dodge had a huge kidskin factory behind his home, which was on North Main Street near Elm Street.

The area grew so rapidly that Gloversville was incorporated as a village in 1853. By 1857, so many skins were being dressed in Gloversville and surroundings that the first of the subsidiary industries was founded. Denton M. Smith established a hair- and wool-packing company that gathered and shipped hair and wool to carpet manufacturers, in particular serving the growing carpet industry in Amsterdam. Smith's company grew, passed from father to son to grandson Edward Smith Parkhurst, and by 1890 occupied a large (60 by 80 foot), three-story building on West Fulton Street.

In addition to those noted above there were Edward H. Allen, Peter Ballentine, Alonzo D. Brower (1848), H. C. Leavenworth, H. M. and J. C. Leonard, the McEwen Brothers, John McNab, James McSwiney, Hiram and John Parsons, the firm of Parsons & Sunderlin, Uriah Place, Isaac V. and John W. Place (1840), D. M. and D. H. Smith, J. W. and Elliot Thomas (1838), and the firm of Wooster and Steele (1844).

Thus while the 1850s saw the establishment of a few more new firms than were started in the 1840s, the decade is most noted for the building of larger mills and factories. This was also the decade in which Fulton County reached out to western states to acquire deerskins. John McNab traveled to Indiana and Illinois to buy skins and established a skin-buying business, Easterly and McNab, to supply other local glove makers.

The 1850s also marked the time in which the industry was able to reach across the nation to sell its gloves. John McNab had an agent, D. Z. Moon in Sacremento, who distributed gloves shipped by McNab all the way around the horn of South America to the California coast. Letters detail the problems of providing the gloves wanted by the customer. At one time, Moon wrote that he did not want the large shipment of gauntlets he had received. Credit was apparently a problem too. Moon protested that he was not wealthy but was good for any amount of credit up to $40,000. He said that because he had not contracted with any other glover in Gloversville he would be embarrassed (a term sometimes used for business failure and even

New York Feb 2/1855
McMartin Pierson & Co
Bot by Ston of Wm R Fosdick & Co
1 Bale 320 Mexican Deer Skins
Wht 552
Tare 2 = 550 lbs 40 220 00

bankruptcy) if the gloves were not promptly shipped. In 1861, Moon placed a huge order for gloves, mostly J. T. Plymouths (a type of rough work gloves). It is amazing that in just two decades, transporting gloves for sale had progressed from wheelbarrows and carts to ocean vessels.

Skins used in the James I. McMartin gloveshop, 1855
(From his inventory book)
Mexican deerskins
Florida deerskins
Shaved roans (sheepskin)
Musquitoe [sic] deerskins
Bolivar deerskin
Red deerskins
Fleshers (sheep)
Nutria hides
Lambskins

John S. Town and the first strike

A glove cutter who came to Johnstown in 1853 and worked for the James I. McMartin firm penned a reminiscence anonymously under the name "John S. Town." It was published in a local paper and survives only as an undated clipping. It is invaluable for its description of the way workers were paid:

The system in vogue in the early days did not allow the manufacturers to pay their employees their wages monthly. A man hired out on January 1st and worked all the year, and seldom saw any money. He got due bills which he traded out at the store and when the year came around if there was anything coming to him he got that in cash. When I first came to town to work, in 1853, living was very cheap, and the average wages were not much, if any lower than they are now. Men earned from forty to fifty dollars per month and considered it good pay. The first year I worked here I boarded at a tavern that stood on the site of the present City drug store. It was kept by Peter McIntyre, father of P. C. McIntyre, of Davies, McIntyre & Co. There I paid $2.00 a week. The next year I got a raise in wages and went to the old Cayadutta House kept by John Pool. That was considered the most desirable place in town to live and I paid $2.25 per week for my board.

I said we never had a strike in those days, but I forgot. We did, and I led the first one, so far as I know that was ever connected with the glove business. I was foreman at the time in James I. McMartin's beam shop, and as there was no union I was as much one of the men as any of the others. We worked from sun up to sun set. We got up at sunrise, beginning about April 1st and went to the shop and worked until 6 o'clock. Then we went home to breakfast and were back at 7. About 10 o'clock we all sat down for a rest and ate a lunch and had dinner at 12. We rested a few minutes at three and went to supper at five and then back to work again as long as we could see. The shop was never lighted up so the days were long in summer and short in winter. Well, one winter Mr. McMartin, who was a fine man to work for, was satisfied and so were we. Well, when the time came in the spring for us to go to work before breakfast, Mr. McMartin spoke to us about it and we objected. I said we were doing as much work as we did under the old plan and he said he knew it and was satisfied, but there

> *were other shops in town and he did not want to be the first to establish a new order of affairs. We told him we would just as soon be the first as the last. We could not come to an agreement for several days, but finally Mr. McMartin consented to try it and the other shops soon followed our example, and that was the beginning of the ten hour day in Johnstown.*
>
> *I remember once shortly after that the Fourth of July came and I wanted to use a little money. I had worked since New Years and had not had a cent, so I said one day, "Mr. McMartin, I should like to have three dollars for the Fourth of July." Turning to me with a look of amazement upon his face, he said to me in a tone of voice that expressed his utter inability to comprehend such a request, "John, what in the world do you want to do with three dollars?"*[13]

The financial picture at the end of the decade of the fifties was mixed. Even though Fulton County glove-making continued to expand in the 1850s, nationally that decade was marked by financial turmoil that culminated in the bank panic of 1857. This panic caused numerous bankruptcies across the country and a few in Fulton County, most notably the hemlock-bark, shoe-leather tannery at Newkirks.[14] Despite financial problems, the number of glove factories grew through the decade, though at a slower pace than in the 1840s: Only 72 glove shops reported in the Census of Manufactures of 1860, versus 59 from a decade earlier. Still, the transition from 1850 to 1860 was expansive, with 29 shops whose production values are over $10,000, although only 14 report more than 10 female employees.

Many of the new firms were in outlying parts of the county, where the new glove shops appeared to be more modern. Broadalbin reported use of the newly invented sewing machines, though many in Gloversville were experimenting with them. A few mills in outlying settlements had also begun to tan kidskins for glove leather.

Production values were up in general although the decade saw virtually no inflation. Fifty-one shops reported amounts of $10,000 or less for a year. Fifteen more reported productions amounts between $10,000 and $15,000, so the threshold of the 80 percent that constituted the smaller shops doubled. The 15 larger glove businesses were run by many of the same men who figured in the census a decade before. Hulett & Son, and firms belonging to

CITY HALL BUILDINGS, LONDON, C.W.

DEALER IN ALL KINDS OF LEATHER, HIDES, LASTS, BOOT TREES, Crimps, Linings, BINDINGS, &c., &c., &c.

LEATHER ESTABLISHMENT, RICHMOND STREET.

London, 17th March 1859

Mr John McNab

Bought of E. W. HYMAN,

THE HIGHEST PRICE IN CASH PAID FOR HIDES, SKINS &c., &c., &c.

To 1000 Lamb pelts in Pickel @ 10¢ $100,00

Recd payment by draft on Mess VH & Hull & co NY for 100,00

E W Hyman

Manuscripts and Special Collections
New York State Library

David H. Cuyler, the Leonards, the Thomases, and the Places joined the roster of larger shops. Employment levels grew, but not as fast as production values. Wages increased, with males earning up to $38 a month. Female salaries had generally doubled from a decade earlier and were as high as $18 a month—this in a period of little inflation.

The rise in the value of gloves produced may owe much to the quality of the gloves. Finer grades of leather produced finer gloves. Even though expansion of the industry seems to have slowed, profit margins did not suffer. In fact, according to the 1860 Census, that year was the peak of profitability in glove-making. The smallest shops, those producing under $5,000 a year, reported an average profit of 44 percent above the cost of raw materials and wages.

The slightly larger shops, producing between $5000 and $10,000 annually, were the least profitable, but still reported almost 41 percent. As production grew, profits soared, reaching an average of 81 percent for shops producing over $30,000 worth of gloves. These profits are so grand that in many instances one year's profit exceeded the total capital investment.

Alanson Judson, who emerged in 1860 with the largest glove-making operation in Gloversville, converted 22,000 deerskins into 4,200 dozen gloves with the help of 11 male employees and 50 women. The largest in Johnstown, Russell & Gilbert, employed 58 women and 12 men to produce 4,500 dozen gloves from 18,500 deerskins. Of the 69 firms in the census, 24 produced over 1,000 dozen gloves annually, 28 employed more than 10 females.[15]

Among other larger firms in the Town of Johnstown with significant production in 1850 that continued through the decade to 1860 were those of D. M. Burr, Samuel Hill, Austin Kasson, Eli Ward, and Frank Enos. In Johnstown village A. C. Churchill's glove shop (1844) became one of the larger firms, along with the shops of the Bertrands, James I. McMartin, and Anaius S. VanVoast.

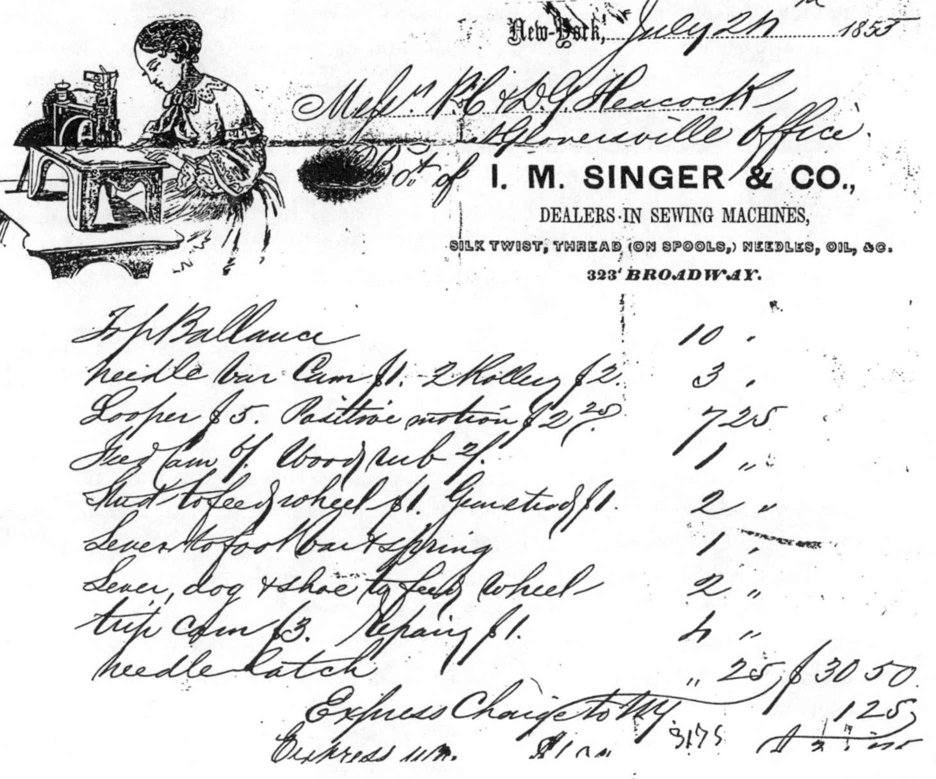
New-York, July 24th 1855

Messrs. P.C. & D.G. Heacock
Gloversville Office
Bot. of I. M. SINGER & CO.,
DEALERS IN SEWING MACHINES,
SILK TWIST, THREAD (ON SPOOLS,) NEEDLES, OIL, &C.
323 BROADWAY.

To Ballance — 10.
needle bar Cam $1. 2 Rollers $2. — 3.
Looper $5. Positive motion $2.25 — 7.25
Feed cam & Wood rub — 1
Stud to feed wheel $1. [illegible] $1. — 2
Lever to foot bar & spring — 1
Lever, dog & shoe to feed wheel — 2
[illegible] $3. Repairs $1. — 4
needle latch — .25 — $30.50
Express Charge to NY — 1.25
[illegible]

This bill for needles and parts for sewing macnines indicates that the firm of P. C. and D. G. Heacock was using Singer machines in 1855. This is proof that the firm was among the first to have sewing machines.

Courtesy the Heacock Family

The 1860s—Expansion

External forces shaped the way the industry grew in the decade of the 1860s. The newly invented sewing machines were improved enough to be adopted by glove-makers. The invention of dies revolutionized cutting. County manufacturers began making dies, adding one of the many industries spawned by glove-making. The Civil War had an impact in increased demand for gloves for the infantry and cavalry, but shortages of both leather and workers limited increased production. The burgeoning industry felt the aftermath of war much more strongly than the war years. Numerous new factories sprang up and the county began producing fine gloves. Marking post-war growth, a railroad finally reached the county in the last years of the decade.

The Civil War years themselves were static, with a sharp decline in new shops and a retrenchment in existing shops as owners left to serve in the Army. As 1870 approached and the country's population exploded, so did the glove industry in the county. The post-war years proved to be a time of exuberance and expansion.

The introduction of the sewing machine began to revolutionize glove-making and increase production. Many inventors had tried to perfect a sewing machine. A simple machine that sewed a chain stitch with a single thread was invented in France as early as 1830, and improved in the late 1840s. At the same time in New York, Walter Hunt devised a lock-stitch machine whose most important feature was the eye-pointed needle. He failed to patent this innovation, but others did in the 1840s, both in the United States and England. By the 1850s there were several companies producing sewing machines with these revolutionary needles.

Local history states that the first Singer machine appeared in the county at A. C. Churchill's factory in 1851 and the Singer company established an agency in Gloversville the next year.[16] These early machines needed constant repairs, they were very noisy, and at first were only used to stitch bindings, which reinforced seams. They could not be operated smoothly enough to sew gloves. David Spalding experimented with a chain-stitch machine made by Grover and Baker in 1854, but this too was inadequate for seaming gloves. Niles Fairbanks began using a Howe machine in 1856. This much lighter machine proved useful for the delicate work of sewing the curved seams of fingers and thumbs. The depression following the panic of 1857 caused a tight money situation that halted further experimentation with machines.

Sewing machines in Fulton County in 1860
According to the 1860 U. S. Census, there were 81 glove and mitten manufacturers:
76 had no sewing machines
1 had 2 sewing machines
1 had 6 sewing machines
1 had 7 sewing machines
1 had 11 sewing machines
1 had 14 sewing machines.

According to the 1860 Census, there were 35 sewing machines in glove shops in Broadalbin. Case & Roberts with 11, James I. Northrup also with 11, Parmelee & Capron with six, and Rosa & Burr with seven were the first glove shops in outlying areas of Fulton County to invest in the new machines. Interestingly, within a decade James I. Northrup took on a new partner and opened a large shop in Johnstown; others moved to larger quarters in Gloversville and acquired many machines.

The Civil War brought demands for gloves as well as boots and uniforms. This made the acquisition of machines a necessity, and they became so important to the industry that, by 1870, the factories in the two centers (Johnstown and Gloversville) had at least 1,303 machines, almost one for each of the 1,914 female employees tallied in that year's census. By 1878 one local distributor, Wheeler and Wilson, was selling about 375 machines a year.

Certainly the machines remained in the shops at first. They required too many repairs to warrant individual ownership, and they were quite expensive. Women in factories could use the machines for basic stitching, but handwork was needed for finishing, hemming, embroidery, and buttonholes.[17] While the manufacturers seemed to take the added capital investment in stride, few women could afford to spend $60 for a machine equipped with a "roll presser foot for leather," when the machine represented a third of a maker's yearly wage.

What a dramatic change this implies, though! By 1870 many women engaged in making gloves had begun working in the factories. However, it remains unclear how women's work was apportioned between factory and home. Certainly the new, larger glove shops were designed for significant numbers of factory workers, but homework for women remained an essential part of glove-making.

The 1869 *Nichols Beach Atlas for Fulton and Montgomery Counties*[18] identifies the location of the new glove shops that were built after the Civil War, presumably to accommodate sewing machines. Among the new factories in Johnstown were the large Rowles & Mister glove shop on Market Street near Green Street. In 1870, that factory accommodated 35 sewing machines, while Gilbert & Wells factory had more than 40.

In Gloversville Daniel Hays, A. Kasson, and A. Judson had shops in separate buildings on the same lots as their residences. A. C. Churchill's new factory in Gloversville had 50 sewing machines. Although D. B. Judson had just as many machines at his factory in Kingsboro, the company employed twice as many women, many presumably working by hand.

The tradition of women working at home was well established for the families of the men who built glove shops. It did not seem a major shift for women to enter the factories, which still appear as family enterprises. This was typical of nineteenth century paternalism in its "concentration on the family as the linchpin of the industrial order."[19]

1860 payments to sewers in the McMartin gloveshop

$5.00 - Mrs. Monroe
19.12 - Mrs. L. Pierson
5.12 - Mrs. Richard Demarest
3.50 - Mrs. Alvord
1.75 - Widow Mary White
12.00 - Mrs. Mary Ann McMartin,
9.00 - "
2.00 - "
30.00 - Mrs. C. McMartin
1.75 - Mrs. Jacob Shafer
1.75 - Mrs. H. Wethuber
.88 - Mrs. P. Carmichael
6.00 - Mrs. Mary Ann McMartin
10.00 - Mrs. Jacob Moltz
17.00 - Mrs. Katy O'Neil
2.00 - Mrs. Mary Ann McMartin
12.22 - "
30.00 - Christina McMartin
10.00 - Margaret Davis

Fine gloves

No longer were most of the gloves designed for rough work, now some were fine dress gloves for gentlemen and women. Harry S. Cole, a glover who had worked for two firms in London, Fownes and Dents, came to Gloversville in 1857. According to his son, Cole was the first to cut lightweight dress gloves in the county. (The story remembered by the son may be apocryphal because surely the two French glovers, the Bertrand brothers, were cutting fine gloves at an earlier date.) But, there is no question that fine glove-making started early, before the Civil War, and grew slowly but inexorably through the 1860s. By 1890 fine gloves accounted for the major part of the county's production.

At the end of the decade of the sixties, almost every glover was still making gloves from deerskins, however all but a few of the very smallest report using both kidskins and sheepskins. The shift to other leathers was accomplished in a few short years after the Civil War.

No longer were all gloves cut laboriously by hand. Frothingham credits Niles Fairbanks with designing a metal die for cutting gloves. E. P. Newton began manufacturing glove-cutting dies in Gloversville in 1859. Jacob Haag started manufacturing dies in 1869. Charles A. Brooks worked with him

Cutting with maul and die

Fulton County Museum

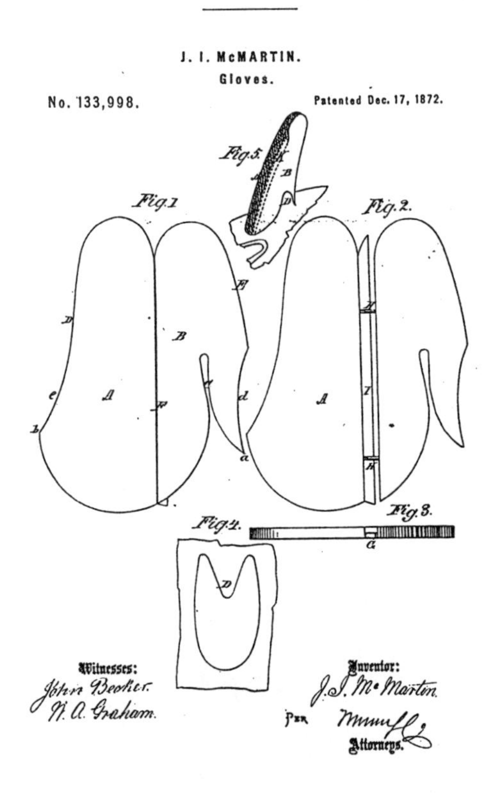

James I. McMartin filed this patent for a pattern for cutting his thumb design in 1872.

around 1878 and in 1880 formed a partnership, Titus & Brooks, to manufacture dies in Johnstown. That firm moved to Gloversville in 1885. This move is seminal: it not only marks the time when Gloversville had become the dominant manufacturer, it also highlights the clustering of support industries there instead of in Johnstown.

The dies were forced into the leather with heavy wooden mauls. The cutter had to have hardwood blocks on which to stamp the leather, and local businesses began to provide these blocks. Initially the ends of stumps sufficed, but finished blocks of many pieces assembled vertically so the cutting end was against the grain, not along it, provided better cutting surfaces.

Different glove manufacturers began to specialize: some continued to sew rough work gloves, others began to make fine men's gloves. This specialization makes it difficult to compare the profitability of different manufacturers.

Women doing hand-sewing at home began to specialize in such tasks as silking (stitching designs on the backs of gloves), hemming, and buttonhole making. At the same time, small shops began to concentrate on different aspects associated with making gloves: Some factory workers manufactured linings, others did black-edging (coloring the white edges of seams of dark leather gloves), and laying-off. Laying-off is the shaping and smoothing required to finish a glove, which became a separate craft with the advent of steam. power It evolved from simply sitting on sewn gloves to shaping them by smoothing dampened gloves on wooden forms. By 1890, steam from boilers was piped to tables fitted with hollow metal forms on which a dampened glove could be stretched and shaped. The steam softened the glove as it was being smoothed into its final shape. Layers-off joined the skilled ranks of makers, silkers, hemmers, and cutters.

Not only did agencies develop to sell sewing machines, but entrepreneurs started businesses to repair them. By 1876, Gloversville also had a producer of knives and machinery for leather manufacture, H. J. Anthony.

The year 1868 saw the establishment of the second of the industry's major subsidiary businesses. A. Brower & Son patented a process for turning the clippings from the flesh side of skins—the pates—into glue. They had a factory in each town. Robert Evans (father of Richard and Robert J. Evans, Johnstown glovemen) had a glue factory in Gloversville. The largest glue firm, Fulton County Glue Company, was built on Maple Avenue in 1869 and that factory continues today as Milligan and Higgins, still manufacturing glue from leather scraps and wastes.

All finer gloves were shipped in light paper boxes and local manufacturers had sprung up to serve the trade. John Drake started making boxes in 1859, E. H. Mills in 1861. The box company founded by J. W. Sisson in 1860 was still going strong in the 1960s. By 1876 there were two paperbox makers in Gloversville and three in Johnstown. All the boxes were made from straw—wood had been introduced for papermaking in the North Country in 1867, but it was another decade and more before wood pulp became dominant in the manufacture of paper products. If you count the farmers whose straw went into glove boxes as well as all the other support industries, it really seems that almost everyone in the county was a part of the glove industry.

Aftermath of war

The graph shows how the number of glove shops, skin mills, and leather manufacturers has waxed and waned over two centuries, reaching obvious peaks in the periods just after the three wars. The number of glove shops crested around 1875 in the aftermath of the Civil War and never reached that number again. Between 1865 and 1875 the county saw at least 200 new glove businesses. After 1875 the number of glove shops declined gradually with about 200 upstarts disappearing by 1895.

Undoubtedly, the small size of the shops accounts for their huge numbers in the 1865 to 1875 interval, but the Town of Johnstown's population explosion, 60 percent growth in those ten years, was also responsible for the increase.

From the 1860s to as late as the 1930s, a man cutting gloves at home, with a wife and one other female relative to sew, constituted a glove shop. Their products were made under contract for larger shops or combined with the gloves from several small shops with sales handled by a common agent. Few of these small shops advertised or are counted in the Census; almost none show up in the city directories. As a result, almost all of this book's counts of the number of shops at a given time are understated.

The post-Civil War phenomenon of the surge in the number of glove shops of both long and short duration is common to all postwar periods in Fulton County. The post-World War II era saw the second greatest upsurge in new shops while the years immediately after World War I brought a slightly smaller increase. Neither of these later periods had population increases similar to the post-Civil War period.

Population
Town of Johnstown
(includes Gloversville)

Year	Population
1855	7,912
1865	9,805
1870	12,273
1875	15,689
1880	16,626

Population
Fulton County

Year	Population
1855	23,284
1860	24,162
1865	24,512
1870	27,064
1875	30,155
1880	30,985
1890	37,650

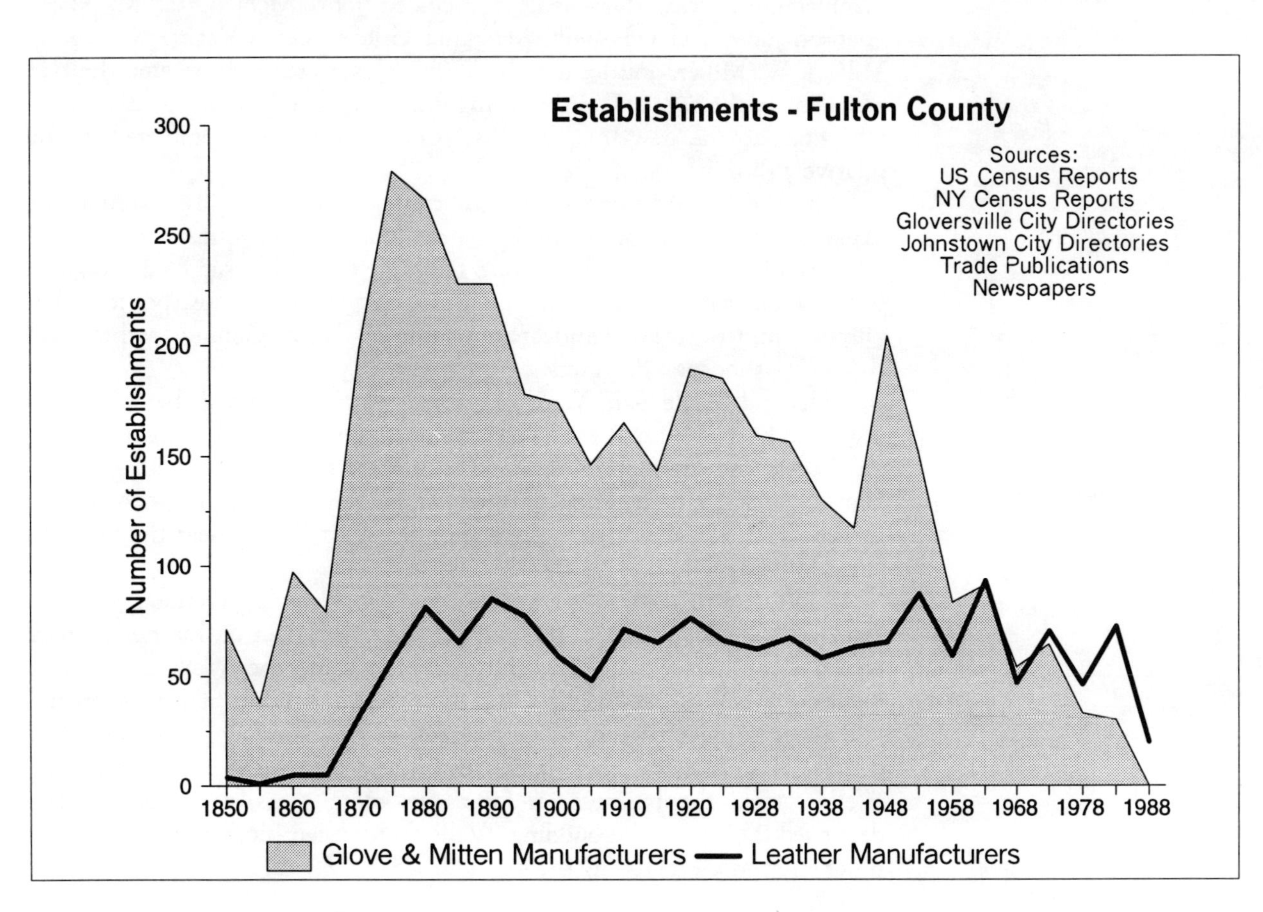

The F., J. & G. Railroad

In the late 1860s, new skin mills appeared along most waterways, the Cayadutta and Mathews creeks in Johnstown and the Cayadutta and West Mill creeks in Gloversville. Separate mills were needed to tan the growing variety of skins used in the county. Deerskins, sheepskins, and goatskins required different tanning methods; all involved a lot of water, which the creeks supplied. The creek also began to carry away the wastes created by the tanning processes, which were dirty and smelly and contained such wastes as flesh and hair. The pattern of establishing skin mills along the waterways was permanently fixed by the location of a railroad in the Cayadutta valley.

The completion of the Fonda, Johnstown, and Gloversville Railroad (F., J. & G.) in 1867 as far as Gloversville equalled the effect of the Civil War as a cause of the tremendous growth of the industry into the 1870s. An extension through Mayfield to Northville was completed in 1875, allowing outlying communities, particularly Mayfield, to share the county's growth.

Previously, several attempts to bring a railroad to Fulton County had failed, most notably a line proposed in 1836 that would have reached the county from Utica. The post-Civil War years proved a great time to channel interest in a railroad and this time men from the glove and leather industry led the way. The first attempt in 1865, spearheaded by W. J. Heacock and John Wells, was a proposal for a line from Fonda to Gloversville that would have extended to Wheelerville. This would have brought much needed firewood to the New York Central, but the plan quickly collapsed because that line's locomotives switched to coal.

The next year, 1866, a new board, made up mostly of leather manufacturers, was assembled. It included John McNab, U. M. Place, Alanson Judson, David Wells, Marcellus Gilbert, Lewis Veghte, George F. Mills, J. W. Miller, and John Peck. Willard Jesse Heacock became the first president of the railroad, withdrawing from his glove business to devote his attentions to the new line, the first part of which was completed in the relatively short period of a year.

With the railroad came a few significantly larger skin mills as well as the expansion of existing ones. Along the corridor north of Johnstown and into Gloversville, several new mills were built. At first these supplied the glove industry, but within a few years the area began to produce leather for other purposes and by 1890 significant amounts of Fulton County leather were shipped to shoe manufacturers.

Mills and Steele Skin Yards on Cayadutta Street joined the Mills Skin Yard and McNab's on West Fulton. Separate glove shops belonging to Day and Steele and the Place Kid Glove Shop were south along the Cayadutta. Leavenworth's and the shop of Wells and Plummer were north of Fulton Street. W. J. Heacock had a glove shop on West Fulton near the pond on West Mill Creek.

In Johnstown, Gilbert had two skin mills on Pleasant Avenue near State Street to take advantage of the pond created by a dam on Mathews Creek near its confluence with Cayadutta Creek. With the Wells glove shop nearby it is easy to see how the firm of Gilbert and Wells had the shop and mill space to become the village's largest glove manufacturer in the 1870 census. That title was short-lived, for Gilbert died in 1869, and although Wells carried the business on for a few more years, a devastating fire destroyed their principal building. Wells then busied himself with numerous other enterprises, including the new railroad.

In the years of postwar exhuberance, almost every one of the leaders in the glove business became a leader in the communities, using the wealth acquired from the industry to build up the towns. Many were involved in the street railroads or trolley-car lines that preceded the F., J. and G. as well as in the railroad itself. Glove manufacturers are listed as benefactors and trustees of libraries and churches; they were pillars of the community. Obviously they expected to gain from building up the communities, but there really was an air of altruism associated with their activities. Acts attributed to John McNab illustrate this: It was said that during one depression period he permitted the residents of his rental properties to remain even though they could not pay the rent.

Daniel Hays deserves a special note because of all the innovations he introduced in his business. From a modest start in 1854 when he carried leather in a wheelbarrow from house to house to be sewn, he bought out his father-in-law's interest in a small glove shop, Ward & McNab, and began to produce Plymouth pattern gloves. He hired a tanner from Plymouth, England, to begin to use English coloring techniques for his leather. In 1867 he became the first to use power from a steam engine for his sewing machines. He was also the first to use waxed thread for machine sewing. He saw the advantages of South American water hogs, capybara (known then as *carpincho*), in the early sixties and was the first to tan their hides in large quantities. He controlled the market on these "Para" deerskins by developing a special method of tanning for them. In addition to introducing the emery wheel to replace the bucktail, his factory used blowers to take the dust from finishing wheels. His factory was the first to have drying rooms for skins—before 1874, all the county's shops had dried skins in open yards. In 1864, Hays moved his shop to Main and Middle streets, where he remained for 25 years. In 1888 he began building a huge brick factory on Fulton Street near both water and a spur of the railroad.

In 1867, James H. Brown commenced the manufacture of gloves in one corner of his brother's wood-shed, on the side of the mountain, near Jackson Summit, on a capital of two hundred and fifty dollars and his first year's business amounted to $2,000. In 1871 he moved to the village [Mayfield], increasing his business quite extensively, until at the present time, 1877, he has the largest shop in the town, having 19 cutting blocks, and employing nearly 500 hands at different times during the process of turning raw material into neatly fitting gloves. His business now amounts to $125,000 per year, and is still increasing.
F. W. Beers & Co., 1878, History of Montgomery and Fulton Counties

Before the Civil War, the county produced only five styles of heavy buckskin work gloves: the Plymouth, the inseam mitten, the gauntlet, the ordinary button top, and the Montpelier. The writer who noted this had worked in a glove shop during the Civil War and his employer had told him "the time will come when so many styles will be made it will be almost impossible to enumerate them."[20]

The decade ended with a very bright financial picture for the county's glove manufacturers. It is noteworthy that almost all the larger glove manufacturers in 1870 were in Gloversville, not Johnstown. The profit levels recovered somewhat from the 1860 level, but the smaller shops in Gloversville were the least profitable, the mid-larger shops ($20,000 to $100,000 production) more profitable, and the largest shops were the most lucrative. In Johnstown there was relatively little difference in profitability in relation to the size of the shops.

Courtesy the Heacock Family

All Claims for Damages or Deficiencies to be ... in Five Days Receipt of Goods.

Kingsboro, Fu... n Co., N. Y., Aug 7 1871

Messr. P. C. & L. E. Heacock

Bought of D. B. JUDSON,

Manufacturer of and Wholesale Dealer in

Buck, Kid & Patent Cloth Gloves & Mittens.

Terms, ...

Branch Store 93 Pearl Street, Cincinnati, O.

The James I. McMartin inventory books are the only remaining information about the finances of a moderate-sized business.[21] McMartin noted the purchase of a double-entry ledger, but if he ever used it, it has not survived. His expense record is remarkably complete. However from the 1860s into the 1880s, he listed expenses for skins, payments to women who sewed, interest on loans, repairs to sewing machines, along with sausages, oysters, steak and roast beef, and other household expenses., which included piano, German, and dancing lessons and tuning the piano. His personal and business expenses were so mixed it is difficult to see how he understood whether or not he was making money.

Analyses of profitability are also suspect given that it is not clear whether the owners calculated the costs of new buildings or machinery and the real costs of overhead. Still, with 40 percent profit for the largest vertical producers, this was a very lucrative business. Wages were still low, though the 1870 Census makes determining this difficult: male and female wages are lumped together in one annual total for each shop, not the monthly reports as in earlier decades.

The increase in capital investment still seems modest, in fact low with respect to profit. The larger glove firms, known to have purchased many sewing machines, had a profit in just one year that ranged from 30 percent to 60 percent of capital investment. Greater productivity undoubtedly made the new machines seem like a relatively small investment.

In 1870, the largest and most successful glove businesses were those that had been in business before the war, in fact before 1860. They include A. C. Churchill & Co.; P. C. & L. E. Heacock; Heacock, Burr & Co.; and D. B. Judson. The latter two employed one hundred female workers and each had 50 sewing machines and produced more than $100,000 (about one million dollars in 1998) worth of gloves and mittens.

The 1870s—Retrenchment and Consolidation

The number of shops in operation in the interval 1870 to 1876 is staggering, with over 210 substantial enough to remain in operation for at least a decade. Even more telling is the number of shops of short duration, those that appeared in only one statistic, either the Census of Manufactures or one of the city directories. The postwar era brought promises of success and with it came the upstarts, 60 at least that were in business for only a year or two around 1876, at least 125 were in business for less than half a decade, sometime between 1870 and 1880.

Only 106 of the 210 firms identified appear in the Census statistics, perhaps because they were the most substantial, but sometimes because of anomalies in the reporting process. Information about the more than 100 shops identified but not described in the Census comes from many sources. One source of information about the numerous new businesses started by residents and newcomers comes from the R. G. Dun reports. That company looked at or answered queries on over 400 firms that had started business in the decade of greatest expansion (1870 to 1880) following the end of the Civil War. Of these firms, nearly 200 survived for at least half a decade and reported production levels to the census or were noted in the 1876 or 1880 directories. Another 64 lasted a half decade but do not show up on either the directories or the census. The rest are identified only in the R. G. Dun reports with notes indicating they existed for less than half a decade. These short-term firms—approximately 130 plus as many as 50 that appear only on the census or directory and not on the R. G. Dun reports—constitute two-fifths of all firms in existence during this period.

There were so many firms and the businesses had become so sophisticated that around 1870 the manufacturers formed the Fulton County Manufacturing Association. Little is know of its origins, but it was primarily concerned with helping glovemen price the expanding and complicated inventory of gloves. The association printed a pamphlet, "Estimated Cost of Goods and Recommended Prices." Accompany the total cost and recommended selling price to jobbers for each kind of glove or mitten is the caution, "This is for your own use, and strictly confidential" and "Goods sold to retailers should bring an advance of from ten to fifteen percent above the prices recommended for selling to jobbers." The gloves priced were made of buckskin (the most expensive); cloth, including woolens made of "chincilla" and "cassimere" [sic] (as expensive as buckskin); kidskins from young goats (half the cost of buck, except for the finest imported kidskins); and fleshers (a low-grade of sheep and goat used for the cheapest kind of work gloves).

The profits computed based on the Census of Manufactures did not include overhead and hence were larger than the pamphlet recommended. Most glovemen continued to ignore overhead, which made them think their profits were really greater than they were.

According to the pamphlet, 72 percent of the cost of making a glove was in obtaining and dressing skins. The buckskin for a pair of men's glove cost $1.00, roughly equivalent, considering inflation, to the cost of leather for a similar glove today—$10.00. The costs of production, at this early date, were broken down into piecework tasks such as cutting, laying-off, binding, sewing, and silking. In 1872 the total was less than $.20 a pair, which is about $2.00 in today's money. It costs at least $3.00 just to sew such a glove in the county today, and cutting and laying-off are additional. Labor costs

FULTON COUNTY MANUFACTURING ASSOCIATION.

ESTIMATE

OF THE

COST OF GOODS,

AND

RECOMMENDED PRICES

FOR

SELLING THE SAME,

ESTABLISHED BY THE BOARD OF DIRECTORS.

ALBANY:
VAN BENTHUYSEN PRINTING HOUSE.
1872.

BUCKSKIN GOODS.

	Buck Mitts, as they run.	Buck Mitts, No. 1.	Buck Mitts, No. 2.	Buck Mitts, No. 3.	Buck Mitts, No. 4.
Stock	$6 50	$8 05	$6 05	$4 33	$2 33
Dressing	1 30	1 30	1 30	1 30	1 30
Splitting, smoking and staking to cut	25	25	25	25	25
Pasters and paste	20	20	20	20	20
Welts and binding	30	30	30	30	30
Thread and silk	15	15	15	15	15
Binding on machine and silking	20	20	20	20	20
Making and trimming	63	63	63	63	63
Cutting	63	63	63	63	63
Box and case	16	16	16	16	16
Laying off	10	10	10	10	10
Sorting, mending and tying up	15	15	15	15	15
Rent, fuel, lights, ins., wear and tear of tools	15	15	15	15	15
Freight, carting and ex. in buying	10	10	10	10	10
Interest	63	63	63	35	35
Stitching of laps	......	......	......	......	......
Getting made	......	......	......	......	......
Facing	......	......	......	......	......
Silking	......	......	......	......	......
Buttons	......	......	......	......	......
Band	......	......	......	......	......
Coloring	......	......	......	......	......
Thread and silk	......	......	......	......	......
Pasting wrist	......	......	......	......	......
Total cost—(This is for your own use, and strictly confidential)	11 45	13 00	11 00	9 00	7 00
Recommended to sell at	......	14 50	13 00	10 50	8 00

Suggested price to jobbers of a pair of gloves, 1872

(Retail should bring from ten to fifteen percent more.)

No. 1 Buckskin mittens	$1.20
No. 1 Buck Plymouth gloves	1.35
Extra heavy Jack Frog Mouth mammoth sized gloves	1.65
Ladies fine buck unlined gauntlets, ornamented	1.25
Best heavy Cassimere imported kid palm gauntlets	1.40
All wool chinchilla imported kid palm, otter wrist	1.15
Domestic kid unlined	.75
Extra fine imported kid ladies gauntlets	1.25
Domestic kid ladies gauntlets	.90
Domestic kid felt lined otter wrist gloves	1.00
Common union wrist cotton lined flesher gauntlet	.45
Extra heavy union wrist felt lined flesher gauntlet	.65

were a much smaller precentage of the cost of a glove in 1872 than they were just a few years later. Furthermore, labor costs would not return to this low level until the industry moved to take advantage of cheap overseas labor in the second half of the twentieth century.

Much has been written about the failure of most small glove manufacturers to understand the true cost of their operations. That may be true, but as early as 1872 the association advised its members to consider freight, interest, and "rent, fuel, lights, insurance, and wear and tear of tools." The pamphlet advised selling prices that were on average ten percent above costs, a more realistic figure that considered overhead.

In Johnstown, the two principal new businesses of this period, the R. J. & R. Evans (1867) and the Ireland Brothers (1875) glove companies, appear to have been well financed. Both firms were able to build important brick shops within a short time of starting in the glove business.

Not everyone was so fortunate. My great-grandfather William D. Foote began making gloves in the early 1870s, financing his shop by selling his grocery business. His youngest daughter wrote of sitting at a table with her mother, father, and two sisters, watching them paste felt on the gauntlets produced in the father's shop, two blocks from their home.

> *Father's work in the little glove shop seemed congenial. Mr. Phelps [a glove manufacturer who had taught her father the ins and outs of the glove business] had an expert glovemaker who had been with him several years and she was now working for Father, too. . . . In the summer we had a buckboard wagon. It was very light with one seat but there was plenty of room at the back to carry the gloves which father took out to be made. . . . As children, we never seemed to have money to spend, but we never needed any. . . . It was in one of my early school days that I first felt the lack of money. I asked Father for five cents and he said, "No, I can't give it to you." Years later he asked if I remembered the incident. He said, "But you do not know how it hurt me to refuse you, I just did not have it, money was so scarce in those days."*
>
> *After Mr. Phelps had given up his business and retired, he used to come often and sit in the shop and talk with Father while he worked. One day there were two other men there and mother was called in. When she came back I was in the kitchen, and she told me they had put a mortgage on the house. I did not know what it meant, but I knew it was something bad. I do not think it was for a large amount, perhaps a thousand dollars. It must have been the business depression and panic of 1873.*[22]

Gloversville was becoming a compact little village. Many houses near the center of the village had glove shops adjacent to their homes. Three small shops nestled side by side on the southeast corner of Bleecker and Spring: A. Lowrey, Brownell & Helwig, and S. W. Jeffers. Their proximity hints at future partnerships.

LEONARD S. NORTHRUP, JOHN N. RICHARDS.

Office of

Northrup & Richards,

GLOVE MANUFACTURERS,

Broadalbin, Fulton Co., N. Y., Oct 5th 1876

OFFICE OF

J. WOOSTER & SONS,

Manufacturers of

Buck, Kid, Cloth, and Flesher Gloves and Mittens.

J. WOOSTER.
M. L. WOOSTER.
IRA WOOSTER.

Kingsboro, Fulton Co., N. Y., Feb. 20th 1874.

However, by 1876 all the larger glove shops in both towns were separate from the owner's homes. Despite the move to larger and larger factories, the pattern of smaller glove shops adjacent to or even part of the owner's residence continued all through this period and into the first half of the twentieth century.

In both communities, the late 1870s witnessed devastating fires that destroyed parts of the downtown centers. Fire protection was the impetus for establishing water districts and reservoirs. Within a decade both communities' water mains served major streets and businesses.

The Cayadutta, however, continued to receive the effluent from the skin mills strung along its course. That creek smelled and foamed and irritated, both literally and figuratively, for another century; and as more and more plants were built along and sometimes over it, flooding became a problem.

The 1870s witnessed the gradual completion of a number of larger new glove shops, for a time almost one a year: M. Beeber in 1870, Simon Hulett in 1871, and Charles Rose in 1872 moved their existing businesses into newly built larger accommodations. In Johnstown, two of the new glove companies, Ireland Brothers and Northrups (the latter relocating from Broadalbin), built substantial new factories in 1874 and 1875 respectively. Fidoe & Radford moved into a larger shop in 1878.

W. S. & M. S. Northrup & Co.
Market Street, Johnstown,
Built in 1875

Courtesy R. Valachovic

Original Ireland Brothers Factory, 1875-1879

Johnstown Historical Society

Throughout this period and into the 1890s both towns witnessed the building of numerous, very large brick glove factories. They were constructed on the same model as existing frame buildings, which were still being constructed. Both types were typically long and narrow to accommodate city lots, with rows of windows to provide light for the workers. The cutting rooms generally faced north for a more even light. Many of these brick buildings with three, sometimes four floors, survive today. At first a few were built with the sewing rooms on the top floor for better light, but these rooms were moved to lower floors as more efficient layouts were adopted.

The new brick buildings could accommodate steam to power ranks of sewing machines. After 1880, steam power, which had been introduced in 1875,[23] was turning most sewing machines in the newer factories. Steam engines turned long driveshafts. Individual machines were attached to the shafts by leather drive belts that could be engaged by the machine operator. Steam thus further concentrated the making of gloves in shops, although hand-finishing continued to be farmed out to workers at home. But there is little question that steam power enticed many women to leave homework in order to make more money in the factories. And it encouraged manufacturers to modernize their glove shops to accommodate the steam-driven machines.

Ireland Brothers Factory
West State Street, Johnstown
Rebuilt after fire, 1879
Johnstown Historical Society

The firm of R. J. & R. Evans had completed extensive improvements to its huge three-story, brick structure in 1879. This company, which produced heavy work gloves from deerskin for many years, added a twin brick structure to its State Street factory in 1891.

The first Ireland Brothers glove factory, built in 1875 of brick with a frame structure attached at the back, burned in 1879. The event is remembered because even though it was a big fire, no one panicked; the owners told the men to save themselves, but if they could to help save the business. A new and larger brick building was immediately erected, with three stories instead of two.

John Ferguson,
Manufacturer of Buck, Flesher, Kid & Cloth
Gloves & Mittens.
Gloversville, N.Y. June 7, 1876

Booth & Co., an English firm with offices in Boston and New York City, bought the Kent & Co. tannery in Gloversville in 1879 . By 1890 it was the largest tannery in the county, producing both glove and shoe leather. Charles Booth stayed at the Alvord House when he visited Gloversville in 1878. In a letter to his wife in England he described the town:

The houses are all, or ninety-nine out of a hundred, built of wood, . . . Every house has a verandah on one or more sides, or sometimes a great portico of classic pretension supported on huge wooden columns. The houses are all scattered about, the streets being wide and rather far apart and not built up, that nowhere are the houses packed together.
Almost all the people subsist one way or other on the glove trade, nine-tenths of all the gloves made in the United States being made here or in Johnstown, which is close by, half-way to Fonda, and all this industry is so new that men in it still remember the beginning of it. They make all sorts of gloves, except knitted ones; that is, they cut up all sorts of materials and sew them into gloves, and carry on the work in the family, men, women, and children all doing their share, and nothing needed but the pattern cutters (which they can lend each other) and a sewing machine.
Charles Booth, A *Memoir*, 1918

Pictures of the makers and silkers at Ireland Brothers, taken in subsequent years, show neatly coiffed women in dresses with mutton sleeves, all wearing aprons. The women are dressed so identically their outfits resemble uniforms. The men in the cutting room are all dressed in white shirts and ties—costumes identical to the owners or supervisors. Photographs depict an aura of propriety that must have been instilled by a paternalistic employer. The making rooms became an extension of home, all rooms appear clean and organized.

Company picnics are documented with photographs as well. The workers were looked after, for the Ireland Brothers company cared for its employees. But Ireland Brothers company was not unique. Not only did owners compare business conditions (while trying never to reveal any important details), but employees compared conditions. Business was so good workers felt free to pick up and find new employment, but most did not. They were dedicated to their shop, boasted that their employer was a fair man, and were prepared to spend their entire careers in one place. In 1915, James Ireland was proud of the length of time his cutters has stayed with his shop; some had been with the firm almost from the start.

Women factory workers were mostly single, young or spinsters, or older married women whose children had left home. Homeworkers were often mothers or the elderly, but there appears to be no exact separation between home and factory work with respect to age or status. Glove-making remained a craft—women were not just operating a machine, they were "making a glove." The ability to shift from home to factory gave women workers the ability to balance a sense of independence and a feeling of control with job security and continuity.[24]

The county's financial picture through the decade of the seventies is a mixture of growth, confidence, and turmoil, little different from the expansion of business all across America. Throughout the 1870s the county's production levels soared with the new buildings. Nearly a dozen skin mills

JAMES NEWTON. -OFFICE OF- C. A. SLOAN.

Newton & Sloan,

Glove Manufacturers,

Fulton Co. Broadalbin, N. Y. Mar 22 1877

-OFFICE OF-

Hutchinson, Decker & Co.,

GLOVE MANUFACTURERS.

Johnstown, N. Y., Sept 14 1876

produced each between $50,000 and $100,000 worth of leather. Fourteen glovers each produced gloves valued from $50,000 to $200,000. Almost all of these were what we would call today vertical enterprises. Carrying on the early nineteenth century tradition of a glover dressing deerskins as well as making gloves, these glove manufacturers also owned skin mills. Gilbert & Wells, again the largest, A. C. Churchill, D. B. Judson, Heacock, Berry & Co., and the newcomers R. J. & R. Evans and Daniel Hays all dressed skins for their own gloves.

There was a marked decline in glove manufacturers' profits during the decade of the 1870s as evidenced in the 1880 census, and the highest profits accrued to the established firms. Profits dropped on average from about 40 percent to 26 percent between 1870 and 1880, and apparently continued to decline through the 1880s, although this cannot be demonstrated as the Census ceased collecting the necessary data. It is not that glove shops made little money, it is just that the days of enormous profits were over. Competition, consolidation, and the country's generally poor economic climate following 1890 will be seen to limit the euphoria of Fulton County's industrial heyday.

There was, however, a dark side to the financial picture of the 1870s. Most of the successes accrued to men who had been in business before the Civil War. The huge number of firms that could not become established in this period, those that went out of business in a year or two, indicates how difficult it had become to gain a start in either the glove or leather business. Lack of capital for raw or dressed skins seems to be the root cause, and inability to borrow apparently stopped many individuals. The R. G. Dun Company's reports were used to evaluate the risk of lending to different businesses. The notes prepared by company agents located in the community illustrate the causes of failures, business dissolutions, and closures.

Death took a few (three) but drink stopped even more—R. G. Dun cited excessive drinking as the reason credit should be denied certain manufacturers. Presumably those who drank excessively were not good credit risks. Of the businesses with poor credit ratings, at least nine were bought out by other firms, while the owners of more than 20 other firms moved away, three of them under clouds of misdeeds or unpaid debts. The report called 15

Kingsboro dates from before the Independence, as does Johnstown. Gloversville, the new place, has far outstripped the others, but Johnstown is quite a place and is perhaps more solid-looking than Gloversville, and more solid too, at least there have not been so many failures there. Kingsboro is a very little place, and I daresay there have been no failures at all there.
Charles Booth, *A Memoir*, 1918

Office of LEONARD & DECKER,

MANUFACTURERS OF

Buck, Kid and Sheep Gloves and Mittens of all styles,

49 MAIN STREET.

Gloversville, N. Y., Dec. 21 1871

or more irresponsible, an additional few even dishonest. A dozen firms were just dissolved. The assets of businesses facing bankruptcy were assigned to other firms in ten or more cases, and presumably the assignee either loaned money or took over the business. Notes indicate that a few of those who failed just could not get credit. A handful returned to farming, some went to work on the railroad and at least one became a justice of the peace, while others became grocers, milk peddlers, or carpenters.

It was not uncommon for a wife to take over the business while the husband who failed "acted as an agent" for his wife's work. Not infrequently, a man threatened with failure put their assets, in particular real estate—home and glove shop—in his wife's name, protecting his family while he tried to work himself out of debt. Not a few of those who could not succeed in business became agents for others, the traveling salesmen who spread the county's gloves far and wide. Among the men who placed all their real estate in the wife's name was one of the county's larger glove manufacturers in the 1880s. Whether Mrs. J. M. Stockley started this way or was widowed is not known, but her glove shop was in business from 1876 to 1880.

Many women became the owners of glove or leather shops as a result of their husband's defaults, a few by widowhood. One woman owned a leather shop, another owned a leather shop in partnership with her brother. Six women were owners of record of glove shops, one was "hard working, but of little means," another "should have no credit." A rich wife was noted as a reason for credit, but an "expensive wife who keeps him back"[25] was a reason for no credit.

Not only was it hard for glovemen to obtain money to begin making gloves or dressing leather, but those with loans were at the mercy of business declines, changes in interest rates, and bank failures. The panic of 1857 was particularly hard and undoubtedly accounts for the slow growth of the industry between 1850 and 1860. Many of those who became successful had a period when R. G. Dun noted that they were "embarrassed"—temporarily unable to meet obligations—or were failing. Post-Civil War years were times of great population expansion, enormous growth in all industries, but still, the glove and leather industry experienced a significant number of failures.

Many of those who were able to continue in business acted as jobbers or worked under contract to larger manufacturers, letting the more successful assume the financial risk of buying the necessary skins or dressed leather. (The county's longest running family firm, the line established by Lemuel Heacock, survived as long as it did because it did work for others under contract.)

On the other hand, it is amazing how many of the instances where R. G. Dun called a glover a "man of limited means" and yet that man managed to become quite successful in later years. Reading between the lines in the financial reports hints at why some firms succeeded and why some grew larger and larger. Luck seems to play a part in the answer—starting business when small profits could accrue was fortuitous. But, not borrowing at all was

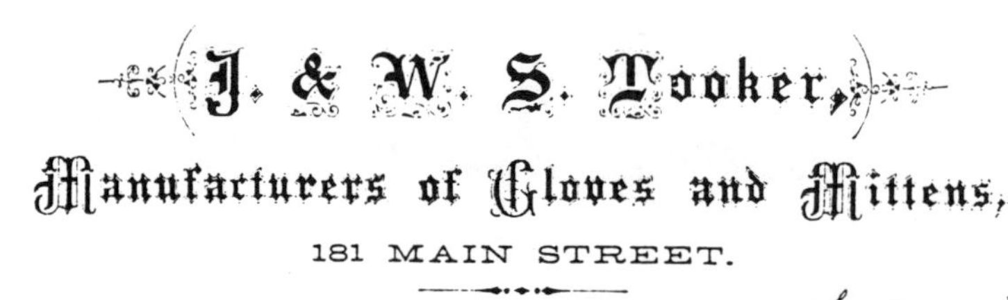
J. & W. S. Tooker,
Manufacturers of Gloves and Mittens,
181 MAIN STREET.
Gloversville N. Y., Feb 1 1875

Office of MOORE & PECKHAM,
Glove Manufacturers,
E. MOORE.
C. E. PECKHAM.
151 MAIN STREET,
Johnstown, N. Y., Dec 7th 1875

the surest way to success. It appears that a few established firms rarely borrowed. Some borrowed from family members. Over the years a few successful firms were able to grow because they could finance their own purchases of raw materials. The strong Scots heritage, the Protestant ethic, and caution mark the growing businesses of the 1870s into the 1880s.

For instance, it appears that my great-grandfather rarely borrowed large sums, never extending beyond that level at which he felt comfortable. His account books indicate that he frequently made partial payment for skins as he needed them, giving a promissory note for the remainder.

Throughout the 1880s, shifting partnerships were legion. Father to father and son or sons was most common in the nineteenth century, brothers or brothers-in-law often became partners. Sons-in-law took advantage of their wives' family connections. But unrelated partners were also common and more often than not shifted frequently—a few shops listed new partners almost annually. R. G. Dun notes several disputes among partners.

One troubled partnership resulted in the establishment of the industry's third subsidiary business. Charles Knox manufactured gloves briefly in partnership with L. Jeannison, who, according to rumor, refused to share the 1881 season's profits with Knox. The dissolution of that partnership was quickly followed by the establishment of Knox Gelatin Company, which opened a large factory near the railroad in Johnstown in 1890. Wastes from the leather mills—particularly the skins from the heads of calves—were washed, dried, and processed into gelatin, reputedly the only colorless and odorless source of gelatin in the United States.

In the glove industry, especially the smaller businesses, locations of shops shifted as frequently as partnerships. As smaller shops clustered near the main business areas in both towns, businesses moved with changing fortunes. Two men might share a building, then merge their operations, then split again within a year, sometimes remaining under the same roof.

Throughout the decade, glovemen continued to experience failure, bankruptcy, or embarrassment, the latter the euphemism most often used in the R. G. Dun reports. Business failures had varying results. In cases where assets were assigned to other glovemen or skin-dressers, a few owners were able to consolidate into larger businesses. In fact the companies that were able to buy up the assets of others indicates the birth of the larger and eventually most successful firms. These firms acquired the assets of failed businesses for 10 to 50 cents on the dollar. The assignees (33 identified in the R. G. Dun reports) included several of the largest and most rapidly expanding firms of the time—A. C. Churchill, L. Northrup & Co. D. B. Judson, J. O. Parsons, and the Heacocks.

Since working for others was always a possibility for sole entrepreneurs, an initial failure was not fatal. Among those who did not wish to work for others, some tried again and some went on unfazed by temporary embarrassments.

Peckham & Powell,

MANUFACTURERS OF AND JOBBERS IN

Gloves and Mittens,

NOS. 65 AND 67 MARKET STREET.

Johnstown, N. Y.

But even the more successful shops, those that did survive, had a period of loss—waves from the panic of 1873 swept over every business. Of the people whose credit was examined between 1864 and 1880, less than a quarter survived without any noted financial reversals.

Some firms grew quickly; owners, like Daniel Hays, the archetype of Fulton County successes, were noted as businessmen as well as manufacturers of gloves. Credit in general was hard to obtain, but foreign credit was denied all but the most stable businesses. Foreign credit allowed a skin dresser to bid for the sheep, goat, kid, and other special skins from abroad that were becoming dominant in the glove industry in the 1870s and 1880s.

Very few were able to get large credit—some had to pay cash for materials. Frothingham tells a story from a later era that illustrates how valuable credit was. Uriah M. Place had obtained a loan to set up a leather business. He and his wife were visiting her family in Utica when the blizzard of 1888 left them snowbound. Teams could not pull carriages over the roads for many days and the date his note came due was fast approaching. Place rode horseback for 60 miles through deep drifts to pay the banknote, thus assuring his reputation as a man who would never default on a loan.

No visible means of support. Careful, prudent, worthy of credit.
Two basic characteristics of county businessmen, according to the R. G. Dun reports.

Despite being occasionally slow to pay or temporarily embarrassed by turns in the market, most of the county's businessmen earned R. G. Dun's appraisal, "careful, prudent, unlikely to venture beyond ability to pay, worthy of credit." Few glovemen seriously overextended. It seems to be a phenomenon of the local industry that owners in this period only expanded when they could.

The owner of a glove shop had to be a multi-talented man, even more capable than the would-be glover of the early 1860s. Now, he had to know markets and style. He had to be able to judge the quality of many raw materials, he often shared the cutting of gloves with partners or hired cutters. He had to supervise the sewing and record-keeping, and arrange for salesmen. He had to be financially astute enough to know how and when to finance his production.

Many marvel at the intricate steps a maker had to perform to sew a glove, stitch decorations on the back of the glove, attach thumbs and fourchettes to the sides of fingers, all the while stretching and easing the leather so the seams were tight and smooth. More to be admired are the many facets of the work taken up by the owner of a small glove shop.

Women in Industry

From the beginning, there is no sense that workers were exploited; glove-making was never a sweatshop activity. The small shops were all family enterprises—an extension of farming and agriculture where a whole family was necessary for the many different activities and products. The first factories were simply extensions of family work. The origins of Fulton County glove-making as a family enterprise make it different from other craft industries. The differences probably account for the lack of union organization among those who sewed gloves until well into the twentieth century.

Just after the Civil War, the Noble Order of Knights of Labor was founded in Philadelphia. Throughout the 1880s the union attempted to organize leather workers in tanneries throughout the north, growing until it claimed 700,000 members by 1886. After1882, women were admitted to the Knights of Labor on an equal footing with men. Attempts to organize labor in the glove industry paralleled that in leather industry. The Knights of Labor had local assemblies in the county: one in Broadalbin, eight in Gloversville, and four in Johnstown. It is not known how many members were in the assemblies but they were organized around different skill groups: heavy-glove workers, glove-makers, block cutters, and stakers, with the majority being mixed glove and mitten workers.[26] The various groups met regularly and participated in negotiations over schedules with manufacturers, but staged no strikes before 1890.

A comparison of the growth of glove-making with the development of the textile industry explains the differences in union organization..[27] Textile production originated in Massachusetts after the Revolutionary War, a little earlier than Fulton County began to make deerskin mittens. Both industries expanded from a local enterprise to become an important part of the national economy at about the same time; both gained wide markets. The years between 1843 and 1846 saw the building of whole new textile towns in Massachusetts, just as the decade of the 1840s saw the establishement of many new glove firms in Fulton County. But here any parallels cease.

Towns like Lowell, Massachusetts, and Manchester, New Hampshire, were essentially run by one company; Fulton County's glove industry had numerous owners. The Amoskeag Mill in Manchester attracted many Irish workers in the 1850s and 1860s, French Canadians in the 1870s. Fulton County's settlers were initially native-born. Immigrants from foreign countries came later in more prolonged waves, but there was little overlap among the periods in which the different immigrant groups arrived. Hence the proportion of foreign-born workers in Fulton County never reached the 45 percent attained at Amoskeag in the 1890s.[28]

Looms for weaving textiles required large factory spaces, they were expensive and needed many factory workers to run them. By 1850, throughout the Northeast, women were employed in these textile factories and living in huge boarding homes away from their families. Only a few women remained in their homes hand-weaving patterns for which no powered looms had yet been developed. Steam powered the larger looms from the start, and continued improvements in the design of looms demanded that women had to work in the factories. In contrast, in Fulton County women were still sewing gloves in their homes and continued to do so even after the introduction of sewing machines in the 1860s. Gloversville had a few boardinghouses, Johnstown only four in the 1880s. There was one

Foreign born as a percentage of Fulton County's total population

Year	Percentage
1860	9.3%
1870	9.3%
1880	9.5%
1890	10.6%
1900	11.1%
1910	14.6%
1920	14.2%

large apartment house—on lower William Street—and a few attached homes, but single or two-family homes were standard, supporting independent family life.

The textile industry's prosperity rested on the exploitation of labor, and "labor became a tool, not a partner in enterprise."[29] In Fulton County, prosperity relied on the talents of entrepreneurs and their ability to entice family and neighbors into joining their ventures. Boardinghouses were a way of controlling labor in Massachusetts. Single men lived in the few boardinghouses in Fulton County, but few women did. Whole families moved to textile towns to work, and children as young as seven or eight were employed in the factories. Fulton County's children were rarely employed in factories, although many did help pull threads and tie knots for their mothers—at home and after school. In Massachusetts, women protested against the working conditions and participated in "turn-outs," a sort of strike, as early as the 1830s. There is no record of discontent among women in Fulton County, though this does not negate the possibility that it occurred.

Textile manufacture required huge capital investments, Fulton County's glovers could start with little except raw materials. Low overhead meant that expansion could be gradual and self-sustained.

The paper industry in the first half of the nineteenth century in Berkshire County, Massachusetts, offers another example where women workers played a significant role. As in the textile industry, women had to work in factories. Jobs ranged from picking and processing rags (wood pulp for paper was not introduced until after the Civil War) to finishing and sorting paper. Industrialization and mechanization meant that women were "mere cogs to the wheel," at wages well below that of men.[30] Men performed the tasks that required manipulating heavy machines, and although women's tasks could only be performed in factories, female workers did manual labor entirely without benefit of machines.

In contrast, in Fulton County the work of men remained unmechanized for most of the century. There was no great separation in the roles of men and women, even though their tasks were different. Despite the inequities of wages, women were essential to the industry and the equal of men in production and skill. Their roles were more a partnership.

Shirt-making and the sewing of collars became a vibrant industry in Troy, New York, just after the Civil War, employing women almost exclusively to sew and starch and iron.[31] Here women's labor was always performed in factories, but the female workers were able to experience a level of independence. This combined with an infusion of immigrant workers, mostly Irish, resulted in the creation of a union to further members' interests. The women struck in 1869 and the manufacturers (men) countered by forming an association to further their business interests, a move that ultimately destroyed the union.[32]

This organization of independent women is a far cry from the family-oriented society and work force in Fulton County. The closest parallel American industry may be the shoe and boot factories along the coast of Massachusetts, where a large percentage of female workers were married women living with wage-earning husbands.

The shoe industry in Lynn, Massachusetts, began earlier than the glove industry in Fulton County but its origin in small shops (called ten-footers because they were no more than ten-foot-wide square buildings fronting Lynn's streets) resembled the beginnings of early glove shops. As the industry grew and factories increased in size, the importance of women's outwork, the finishing or binding of uppers, grew equally. This growth was not unlike Fulton County's homework experience. Shoe-making combined both craft and factory techniques, but in Lynn factories increased in size much more rapidly as machines became more important. Lynn experienced a "Great Strike" in 1860, just as Fulton County's glove-making was emerging as an industry. In 1868, the Knights of St. Crispin championed workers' concerns for higher wages and Lynn experienced bitter strikes in 1878 and 1890 as well.

Differences between owners and workers became increasingly pronounced in the shoe industry. Paralleling this from the 1860s through the 1880s, the distinction between workers and employers in Fulton County continued to blur as workers emerged as entrepreneurs. Lynn's workers were becoming segregated by ethnic groups,[33] while there was little ethnic diversity in Fulton County before 1880. Further, all the personal anecdotes that this book quotes to describe the county's manufacturers before World War I illustrate their benevolence and concern for workers. This paternalism or humanism appears to have preempted moves toward unions and strikes.

Both the shoe and glove industries experienced difficulties in establishing standardization, but mechanization and division of labor became much more pronounced in the shoe industry. Lynn's factories were able to triple production between 1860 and 1870; Fulton County's production grew in that period but as a consequence of new businesses and workers, not because of increased productivity. As a result, Lynn emerges as a microcosm of the industrial revolution, which never really occurred in Fulton County because of the craft nature of the glove industry. Even with the advent of sewing machines, mechanization did not control gloveworkers and they were able to remain independent with a sense that they were in control of their work. Lynn and the shoe industry became a hotbed of radicalism, home to reformers and five generations of protesting shoe makers.[34] Fulton County's workers appeared comfortable with the work they were offered until the last decade of the nineteenth century.

Fulton County and Lynn were both one-industry areas, although the proportion of shoe workers in Lynn declined from 30 percent after 1880s as new industries arrived.[35] In contrast, the proportion of glove and leather workers in Fulton County remained well above 30 percent of the total population into the 1930s.

Workers in both areas were highly mobile, moving from job to job within the industry as they wished. But few of the conditions that gave rise to strife in Lynn—worker inequality, exploitation, and social conflict—were present in the early days of the glove industry.

A comparison with the glove industry in England yields similarities and significant differences. The glove industry in Yeovil, Somerset, England,[36] developed earlier than that in Fulton County, beginning in the last half of the eighteenth century. By 1830, a recession, attributed to laws which permitted the import of French gloves, decimated the work force. "Squalor and misery"[37] of Dickensian proportions gripped the town. The horrors brought by the industrial revolution to the larger manufacturing cities throughout England at this time did not spare this rural area. "Here were the ingredients of social discontent. Grinding poverty [contrasted with] the comparative affluence of parts of the town. Even in the hardest times there was money to be made in glove-making, with the rewards going to the successful entrepreneurs who sewed gloves in order to supplement their

Coat of Arms of The Worshipful Company of Glovers of London

meagre income. It is hardly surprising that a working-class consciousness expressed itself in the beginnings of political activity."[38]

As in Fulton County, almost every resident was engaged in glove-making, but in Yeovil the factories and homes bred tuberculosis. Given "the overcrowding and sedentary occupation of females. . . It is no uncommon thing to find in the winter season as many as eight or nine persons crowded in a space of eight feet square, sitting around a small table [sewing gloves] and with one or two lights, and seldom any fireplace for ventilation."[39]

Fulton County's workers suffered few such hardships. In the search for the reasons why this was so, differences in housing become apparent. Even in the first half of the nineteenth century, the housing stock for workers in Fulton County was superior to that of rural England. Squalor and disease were not totally absent, but almost everyone could find adequate work and housing. There were few tenements, some boardinghouses, but most workers lived in small frame houses. The compactness of the towns, their small size, and the integration of glove factories into the communities and their relative cleanliness permitted the growth of two handsome settlements more reflective of New England charm than industry.

Fulton County had no downtrodden worker class. Its workers were not exceptionally wealthy, but few were exceptionally poor. Workers supplemented their incomes with small farms, and farmers' wives sewed gloves. Families struggled together; extended families cared for single or widowed relatives. A middle class was beginning to emerge from the pattern of family enterprise.

The importance of women's homework sewing gloves increased as the factories grew. In part it reflected the owners' needs to keep overhead low. Homework grew along with the shift from family-labor systems to a wage-labor system as in shoemaking and other industries.[40]

Even as a few entrepreneurs became quite wealthy, the family nature of glove-making persisted with husbands and wives employed together. In addition, manufacturers emerged as leaders in the community, working to build the community itself as well as their own businesses. In the late 1880s and into the 1890s businesses became more stable and successful. Paralleling this, the owners' attitude toward their workers became more humanistic than paternalistic .

The 1880s—Success

Both Gloversville and Johnstown took on an aura of success in the decade of the 1880s as glove manufacturers began to produce increasing quantities of fine dress gloves. Skin mills were still concentrated along the creek and railroad corridors. The brick factories flaunted success and were still scattered throughout both towns. And, slowly, the gracious new homes of prosperous glovemen coalesced along a few handsome streets, proclaiming the growing affluence of these entrepreneurs.

In Gloversville, the most elegant residential streets stretched uphill from Main on Prospect, First, and Second avenues to Kingsboro Avenue, where elegant houses were set well back from the wide street. William and Melcher streets and the top of the hill above First Avenue outlined Johnstown's most prestigious area. But in both places mills were never far away. A knitting mill was built on upper Kingsboro Avenue; Hutchens & Potter built a glove shop on Third Avenue in Johnstown, not far from some of the most elegant homes. A large mill was built just west of Melcher Street only a little more than a block from some of William Street's finest homes.

The comparison with other industrial towns is telling. It is much more common to find factory enclaves separated from residential areas, clustered along riverfronts or railroads. Mohawk River towns such as Amsterdam, Little Falls, and Utica are like this, with residential areas perched on the bluffs above the river. In Johnstown and Gloversville, glove shops and even a few tanneries abut middle-class frame houses.

Throughout the county, ponds and crossroads spawned clusters of farms and each cluster soon had a few glove shops and small skin mills. Small settlements such as West Bush and Smiths Corners were typical. Larger settlements like Mayfield, Broadalbin, Northville, and Ephratah all had glove shops and skin mills. In both hamlets and the larger towns, the glove shops appeared, integrating industry in residential areas in a unique fashion.

1880, typical monthly payments to sewers in the McMartin gloveshop

25.00 - Lucy Fuller
14.00 - Magy Hare
20.00 - Sarah J. Hillsinger
17.62 - Clara Soule
3.00 - Annie McDonough
20.00 - Annie Cameron

Typical number of months worked in parentheses

Annie Cameron (9)
Maggie Hare (2)
Mary E. Gillespie (5)
Sarah J. Hillsinger (5)
Clare or Katie Soule (12)
Alida Irving (7)
Lucy Fuller (7)
Mrs. Peter Hio (3)
Annie McDonough (3)
Mrs. Anson Wentworth (3)
Mrs. Cymene Johnson (2)
Lib Gillespie (3)
Irene A. Scott (6)
Mrs. Jas. Van Duesen (3)
Margaret McMartin (2)
Mrs. Conymal (1)
Mrs. Carmichael (1)
Mrs. Kreins (3)
Mrs. Wm. Pierson (1)
Mary Wemple (1)
Annie McMartin (1)

Exerpts from James I. McMartin's cash book

1879
April - $1.00, Committee on Tariff
May - $2.00, fixing blocks
July - $2.25, Ferres and Dewey for new maul
July - $.50, shuttle
$.60, fix silking machine
$.77, presser foot for machine
Dec. - $1.25, dress block

1880
January - $12.25, Ferres and Dewey, for new mauls
January - $2.50, L. Daniels, preping blocks
March - $.75, circular needle for Maggie's machine
$1.00, preping blocks
$2.00 for preping blocks
April - $5.50, repair Lib's machine
July - $4.50, Annie McDonough, tying ends
$3.50, repairs machine
$2.00, dressing blocks
August - $.65, Kingsbury, repairs Lucy's machine

1881
January - $4.00, dressing (smoothing) and repairing blocks
$15.05, C. A. Phelps, for Block

Cutters at the James I. McMartin gloveshop, 1881

Henry Murray
Charles A. Phelps
Eli McMartin, son
James McMartin, son
Archibold McMartin, son
Daniel McMartin, son

Many members of a family working together was typical of Fulton County gloveshops.

In the 1880s there was a continuation of the building of new and larger glove shops: Rea & White in 1884, McDougall in 1885, Lebenheim in 1885, A. J. Zimmer in 1887, and Louis Meyers in 1888. Daniel Hays, who already had a large factory built in 1864, put up a much larger one in 1888. Construction of new shops continued into the 1890s: Berry Brothers (1890) and Kibbe & Parsons (1891) extended the building of glove shops into the decade of the 90s. Many of these, but not all, were substantial brick buildings that are still standing.

The smaller glove shops just sputtered along. Among them was the James I. McMartin & Sons shop whose production declined for a while in the decade before the death of James I. (1888), then picked up again as the sons took over. Even that small shop had contracts to produce gloves for retailers in LaFayette, Indiana; St. Paul, Minnesota; three stores in Chicago; and two in Boston.

The McMartin shop also made gloves for other companies in Fulton County. This is in a tradition that continued through this century. If a company could land an order too large to fill or one that required more leather than could be obtained, the owner farmed out a part of his order to other companies with slack. The only drawback is that he had to pay more to the subcontractor than if he made the gloves in his own shop.

Because of their huge size skin mills and tanneries were traditionally wooden frame structures. The last half of the 1880s saw many skin mills expand into new and larger mills: Levor in 1885, J. Q. Adams in 1888, Topp in 1888, Roucoules & Larcombe in 1889. Four new mills were built in 1891: Robinson, Wood, Thompson & Lord, and Lebenheim. New buildings for manufacturing leather were roughly equally distributed between Johnstown and Gloversville, with the number of substantial mills in the two areas being comparable (Johnstown, 24; Gloversville, 27).

The expansion of new glove shops in the 1880s occurred principally in Gloversville so that by 1890, there were roughly twice as many shops in Gloversville as in Johnstown. And as at the beginning of the decade, there were more of the larger glove shops in Gloversville and their production values where higher. However, Gloversville's largest in 1880 had disappeared. D. B. Judson's production reached $375,000 in 1880. With 500 employees, his vertical operation was the county's largest. It is interesting to speculate on its demise, for the entire operation disappeared before 1890. Judson's illness was the direct cause, but it is a puzzle that no family members (he had mostly daughters) or employees kept the business running.

Built in 1885

Built in 1889

Miller, Argersinger & Co. Established in 1870 on Mill and Water Streets, Johnstown

Built in 1885

A Glossary

Fine gloves—new techniques and materials

The production of fine gloves involved new materials and techniques. In later years manufacturers' association, industry periodicals, and some of the large glove companies produced articles and elaborate booklets on the making and wearing of gloves. The following descriptions are taken from various pamphlets, particularly an undated one prepared by Daniel Hays Co. The types of skins, methods of tanning, procedures developed for making fine gloves, and terms used to describe all of this remained in use in the county even as that industry disappeared. Hence this section should serve not only as an introduction to fine glovework, but as a glossary for reference throughout the book.

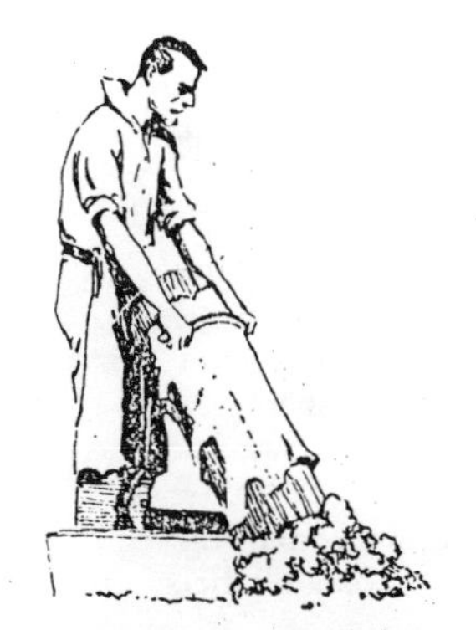

The "Beam" on which fine skins are dehaired and defleshed.

The greatest change in the industry in the 1880s came from the increasing importation of different skins from many foreign sources, and this dictated new operations in skin mills. Domestic and foreign lamb and sheep skins, calf and elk, horse and foreign hogs, dog, capybara, kangaroo, and many types of deer and antelope from Central and South America and northern Africa were all used. Mocha skins from a northern African hair sheep made an especially soft glove leather.

These skins were dried or salted or both dried and salted and shipped from all over the world to Fulton County, bringing with them dirt, insects, and diseases. Tanning these skins was a much dirtier and more dangerous business than simply dressing locally killed deerskins.

Knee-staking

Tanning is simply a means of preventing leather from putrefying when wet. Each type of skin required a different tanning method. The processes were not understood at the time; in fact, they were not fully understood at the end of the twentieth century. Processes depended on the different kinds of skins, their condition, and the skill of the tanner. Raw skins, dried and stiff, will putrefy quickly if wet.

Dried or salted skins were first **soaked** to clean and soften them and remove the salt. Often skins were painted with a depilatory to loosen the hair and make it easier to scrape off. The next step was **beaming**, or scraping away the hair and wool using a curved knife (beaming knife) on the skin, which was stretched across a rounded board (beaming board) in a beam room. These beam rooms were messy, dirty, smelly, foul places.

Next, the skins were **limed**, or soaked in slaked lime, to loosen any flesh or hair that remained. **Fleshing** followed; this is when all flesh is removed. (For both **unhairing** and fleshing mechanical drums fitted with sharp blades gradually replaced the laborious task of scraping skins by hand with long knives.)

Some skins were then **pickled**, soaked in a weak solution of sulfuric acid and salt to remove the lime, soften the fibers, and separate the fibers of the skin so that the tanning liquor would penetrate. Leather in this state is said to be "in the pickle," and in more recent times, skins have been shipped to the U. S. in the pickle, that is partially tanned, rather than salted and/or dried.

Fulton County Museum

Arm-staking

Next, the skins were **staked** to soften them before a variety of chemicals or oils could be applied. Staking required physical strength. In **knee-staking**, the worker used his knee to move a skin back and forth across a dull blade

Skins used in the James I. McMartin gloveshop, 1880
(from his inventory book)

Jacks (deer)
Little Greys
Blesbock deer
Venezuela deer
Antelope
Elk
San Juan deer
Blacktails (deer)
Matamoras (Mexican deer)
Fleshers (sheep)
Mohawk from sheep
Black Kid (sheep)
German Kid
Bark Fleshers
Indian Tan (deer)
Para (deer from Paraguay)
Florida Indian (deer)
Western deerskins
White sheepskins
Russett lamb
Imported kidskins

held in a vertical stand—the knee-staker. Alternatively, the worker used a dull blade attached to a short handle—an **arm-staker**—and work it across the skin. These forms of staking held nothing like the danger that a worker faced after the twentieth-century invention of the Slocum Staker—a mechanical device that thrust a moving wheel at the worker as he moved the skin beneath the thrusting arm. No wonder **Slocum Stakers** were called the "no-finger" machines.

In **chrome tanning**, which came into use in the 1890s, these processes were followed by a salt bath, more washing, then the skins were placed in a drum filled with chrome salts. The skins were now leather, that is they will not putrefy, but they would still dry hard and stiff, so they had to be given one more treatment, usually soaking in an emulsion of soap and oil. Dyed and softened by knee-staking, then polished, the skins were ready to be made into gloves.

In **oil tanning**, buckskin and chamois were dressed with an oil, initially cod oil. This oiling process originally took four months and required up to 200 different operations. After soaking, kneading to soften, liming, unhairing, and fleshing, the **grain** or hair (skin) side was **friezed** (removed) with a sharp knife. Then the skins were soaked in cod oil, kneaded, and hung to dry very slowly, then heated to produce leather. Oily skins were then soaked in a solution of soda ash and the emulsion of oil and soda (**fat-liquor**) was saved for a later step. After several rinsing steps interspersed with more kneading, the skins were hung to dry. Dampened skins were treated with the fat-liquor and hung outdoors to bleach, four days in summer, two weeks in winter. After staking with a fine emery wheel, the skins were dyed and ready to be cut into gloves.

Alum tanning was devised for soft-finished leather such as suedes and later used for mochas (see below). A paste of egg yolks, flour, salt, and alum was used to tan suede kidskins and lambskins. It was a laborious and time-consuming process in which the paste had to be worked into the skins in a series of operations that involved as many as 30 steps. Throughout the end of the nineteenth century, huge shipments of eggs brought by rail from distant farms still constituted the basic tanning agents, with one Johnstown firm alone using 12,000 dozen eggs in a year.[41] Buckskins and chamois were dressed with cod oil—a process that required up to six weeks preparation.

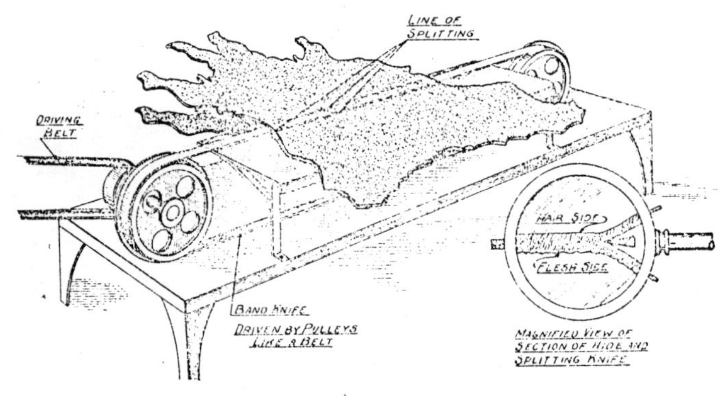

Diagrammatic illustration of skin splitting machine.

After tanning, some skins were **shaved** to make them even enough for the finest dress gloves. The use of heavier skins meant that some had to be split to create thin enough leather. The shoe industry had developed splitting machines in the 1870s and 1880s for splitting cowhides into sufficiently thin for use as the tops of shoes and boots. Similar devices were adapted for **splitting skins** to produce smooth leather from the grain side along with a soft-finished leather for suede or soft finishes from the flesh side.

Glove Leathers

The county became the focus of a global market as it began to produce fine gloves. In branching out from domestic and foreign deerskins, skins from many different kinds of animals were brought to the county from all around the world to be tanned. However, even as the county's glovemen sought different skins, competition from European manufacturers limited supplies. Europe had a long tradition of glove-making that enabled glovers there to establish control over African skin markets. Some county shops were able to obtain fine glove leather tanned in Europe, but here, too, competition from European glovemen made this increasingly difficult.

Sources of **glace** (smooth) or grain surface leather:

Kidskins from young goats produced the finest quality grain leather, very thin and flexible. (Alum tanned).

Lambskins from young sheep produced a slightly lower quality leather than kidskins. (Alum tanned).

Schmaschens from still-born lambs was less durable, but very thin.

Cape, tanned from haired or coarse-wooled sheepskins, was used in the late 1800s for fine men's gloves. It was strong and pliable, but not thin enough for fine women's gloves. During and after World War I, advances in chrome tanning allowed cape skins, originally from South Africa, later from the Orient or even Spain, to be shaved to produce a leather as thin as kidskin or lambskin but still strong.

Goatskins from Spain, South America, South Africa, and India were made into a style of gloves, called chevrette, worn primarily by men.

Horsehides from young horses came from around the world and were made into motoring gloves.

Pigskin or **Peccary** gloves were made from Mexican and South American wild hogs. They had a coarse grain and were very durable. (Chrome tanned).

Calfskin was not introduced for fine glove leather until 1926. It was made from the skins of young calves from the United States, Russia, and Poland. (Chrome tanned).

Grain deer or **buckskins** from South and Central America, Mexico, and China could be finished with a pebbled grain. (Chrome tanned)

Dogskins, imported from all around the world, were occasionally used for glove leather.

Sources of **suedes** or soft finished leather:

Buckskins from deer from Mexico, Central and South America, and China produced durable men's gloves with a soft finish when oil tanned. The grain surface was cut off and the hair side given a velvet finish.

Chamois skins from the small antelope from the Caucasus had all but disappeared as a glove leather by the 1930s. Splits of lamb or sheepskins, oil tanned so they resembled chamois were given the animal's name.

Doeskin referred to the skin of sheep or lamb with the grain side split off.

Reindeer from Russia and Siberia produced the finest, most durable, velvet-finished gloves.

Suede was made from South African kidskins or lambskins that were finished on the flesh side. (Alum tanned) Imported suede was suitable for the finest women's gloves.

Fleshers, splits of lambskins or sheepskins where the grain surface split was used for low-grade suede gloves. Fleshers were also used for book bindings.

Mocha was produced from hair sheep from northern Africa; the grain was friezed (removed) to give a velvet finish.

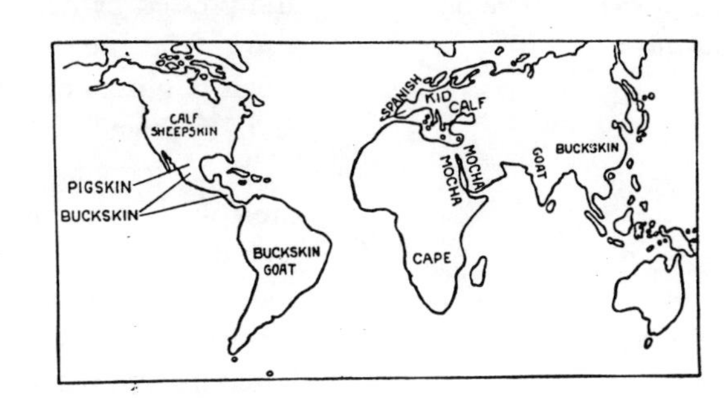

Tanners and skin dressers were skilled men, almost artists, because each type of skin required a different process. Manuals such as August C. Orthmann's *Tanning Processes* contain more recipes for dressing, coloring, and finishing leather than a cookbook.

As the tanning industry grew, more employees were needed. The gap was filled by unskilled or less skilled workers. This growing pool of laborers included immigrant families that came from the low end of the social stratum, impoverished regions of eastern Europe.

Until the 1890s, county manufacturers had little access to the best skins; the European monopoly over kidskins made them especially scarce. In addition, the county had few workers capable of making women's gloves that could compete with the French and English gloves.

Cutting

Upon the cutter depends the manufacturer's profit.
Striking cutter, 1914 hearing

The production of fine gloves required new techniques of cutting and sewing. The county adopted methods of European glove cutters or table cutters. **Table cutting** brought a new level of art to the craft of cutting gloves. Block cutting and cutting with heavy dies and mauls, which had typically been used for the rougher grades of gloves, were phased out with the decline in making work gloves. By 1890s an elite class of table cutters had appeared, men who could cut skins for the finest gloves. These men were masters at figuring out what a skin could produce. Their craft was highly skilled, for no two skins were alike.

A **table cutter** had to carefully select skins from which matching gloves could be cut. Then he dampened and stretched and pulled the skin to reveal any imperfections. Next the table cutter figured how to cut out the **tranks**, rectangular pieces whose size corresponded exactly to the length, style, and size of the glove to be cut. To do this he had to measure the amount of stretch in the leather so that a glove would fit the hand whether the hand was open or closed. (Make a fist, and note that the circumference of your hand is greater than when it is relaxed.) In table cutting, the skin is stretched horizontally as well as vertically so the finished glove would fit snugly.

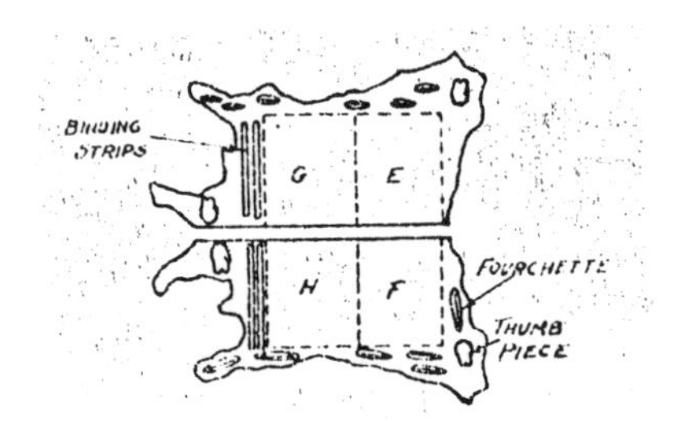

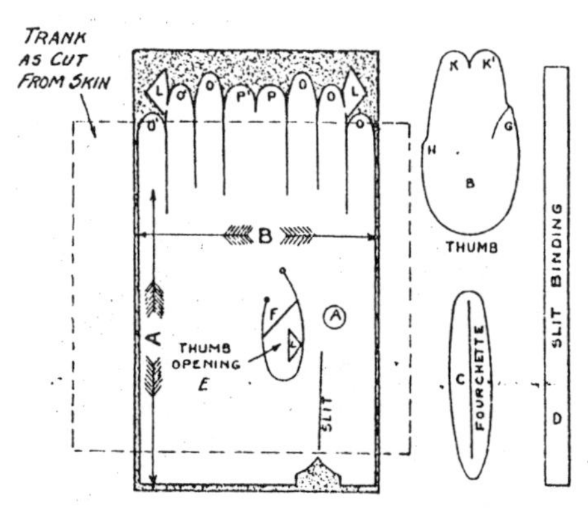

Diagram shows how leather was stretched before cutting the trank.

The cutter had to cut the rest of the parts of the glove to match the tranks: thumbs, **fourchettes** (either long thin rectangular strips or strips with a triangular end that form the sides of fingers), **bindings** (reinforcements for hems and seams), and **quirks** (small triangular pieces inset between the fourchette and the back of the finger to make the glove fit more smoothly). Then he stamped each piece with an identifying number and the size. (**Sizes** corresponded to the circumference in inches of the palm, measured just below the fingers. There were many sizes—7, 7 ¼, 7 ½—and so on, reflecting how perfectly gloves were supposed to fit.)

Initially, the parts of a fine glove were cut from the trank by hand with shears, but early in the twentieth century, machine-driven cutting dies came into use to cut the glove from the trank and also make **slits** to separate the fingers. Several pairs of tranks of a given size were placed under movable dies and pressed by hand or power to cut out the glove. These **slitting machine** also cut out the thumb holes and separated the fingers. Then all the pieces of a pair of gloves or several pairs all of the same size were tied together to go on to be sewn.

Many manufacturers hired skilled cutters from England or France to train their workers. Some immigrants were already expert table cutters, having served apprenticeships. The European tradition of apprenticeships was adopted with modifications in Fulton County. Here apprentices were not indentured to the master craftsman. In England, typically an apprenticeship lasted for five years, although one cutter remarked that the first two years the apprentice served to fetch things for his master. In Fulton County three years of **apprenticeship** were considered adequate to produce a trained table cutter, and one manufacturer remarked that given an intelligent youth, six months training would suffice. Apprentices received their board and their clothes, and perhaps $.50 a week spending money. Cutters were so protective of their profession that for many years only the son of a cutter was permitted to become an apprentice.

Various types of cutting were devised to reflect more efficient or economical ways of cutting gloves. In **pull-down cutting**, or **American table**

cutting as it was sometimes called, leather was stretched in one direction only with the cutter estimating the amount of stretch in the skin. Then, the glove was stamped out without first making a trank. Pull-down cutting did not require as high a level of skill as table cutting and offered lower pay for the cutter. It was practiced on the lower grades of gloves, with inferior quality leather.

As slitting machines became more powerful, they evolved into **clicker-cutting machines**. By 1935, these had become such an important part of glovemaking that an editor of a glove magazine described them in enthusiastic terms. He wrote that these "homely" machines combined the block and maul of old-time block cutting with electric power. "The clicking machines dies are lighter than the ordinary die. They are open at the top so that when the glove is to be cut directly from the skin as in block cutting, any defect in the leather can be seen. The operator places his die where he wants it, swings the arm over the die, touches the release, the arm clicks, [the die is pressed onto the leather] and the glove is cut. The arm is easily swung back into place and the man and machine are ready for the next move. No heavy old-fashioned die and ten-pound maul to be picked up and set down."[42] The cutter still had to stretch the leather, but in one direction only as in pull-down cutting. After the glove was cut out, thumbs and fourchettes were punched out in the same way. This kind of mechanical cutting, which omitted the step of cutting tranks, gradually supplanted table cutting.

Slitting machine
H. H. Steele Glove Co.
Fulton County Museum

Styles

As the county began to focus on making fine gloves, local shops branched out into many different styles. The trend continued through the late 1930s, when the county produced almost as many women's fine gloves as men's. Fashion dictated new designs through the thirties, then changing lifestyles called for different kinds of gloves.

Among the different styles were **gauntlets**, gloves with large cuffs, often used as men's heavy work gloves, but sometimes with elegantly embroidered cuffs in fine leathers for women.

Among the women's gloves were **mousquetaires** in 8- to 20- button lengths or styles such as **slip-ons, strap wrists, novelty cuffs, lined gloves**, or those with clasps. For both men and women, there were special gloves for **driving** or **sport** such as golf or skating.

Sitting on a high stool alongside a table was a man of over seventy whose hands had by no means lost their cunning. He was laying off black Glaces [gloves of smoothed and polished leather] *by a method he learned in his youth before the Civil War. One or two primitive wooden tools were the only mechanical appliances in evidence. . . He picked up a delicate glove, straightened out and stretched the fingers, shaped the top, and as the process continued tucked the fourchettes into place as deftly as a woman tucks the finest hem on a dress.* Historical article in a 1918 issue of *The Glovers Review*.[3]

A FULL LINE FROM GLOVERSVILLE

Producing a glove

In **making** or putting the glove together, first, the thumbs are sewn in, then the fourchettes and quirks are sewn in place, and finally the **fingers are closed**, that is the finger seams are finished.

Silking is the stitching of designs on the back of a glove, usually three rows of stitches that are mostly decorative but do improve the fit of the glove. There are many different styles of silking, some of which include stitching a cord onto the leather using a two-needle machine. Each different type of embroidery or silking has a special name. The threads in silking have to be "pulled" and tied.

In **laying-off** a dampened, sewn glove is placed on a steam-heated form to work out wrinkles and give the glove its finished shape and appearance.

Polishing refers to finishing a glove of smooth leather with a finishing or velvet wheel, a suede glove with a brush wheel.

Sewing gloves—stitches

As with embroidery, a wide range of stitches gradually evolved for hand-sewing gloves. With improvements in sewing machines, it was possible to develop machines that could perform the special stitches.

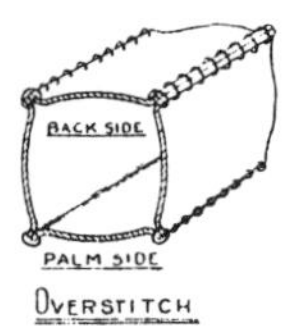

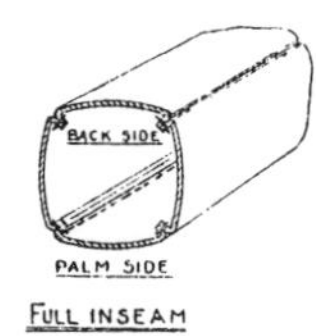

Outseam - The glove is stitched with the right sides out, thus the seam is visible.

Welted - A narrow strip of leather is sewn into the seams for strength.

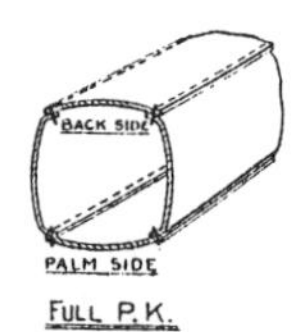

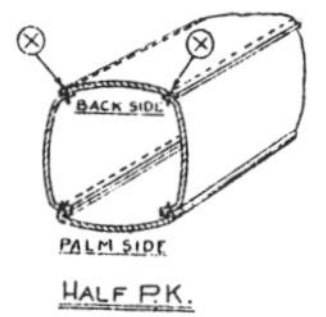

Half Pique - The back of the fingers are sewn pique and the palm is closed inseam.

Prixseam and Gauge - The English prixseam machine and the gauge machine are used produce an outseam glove.

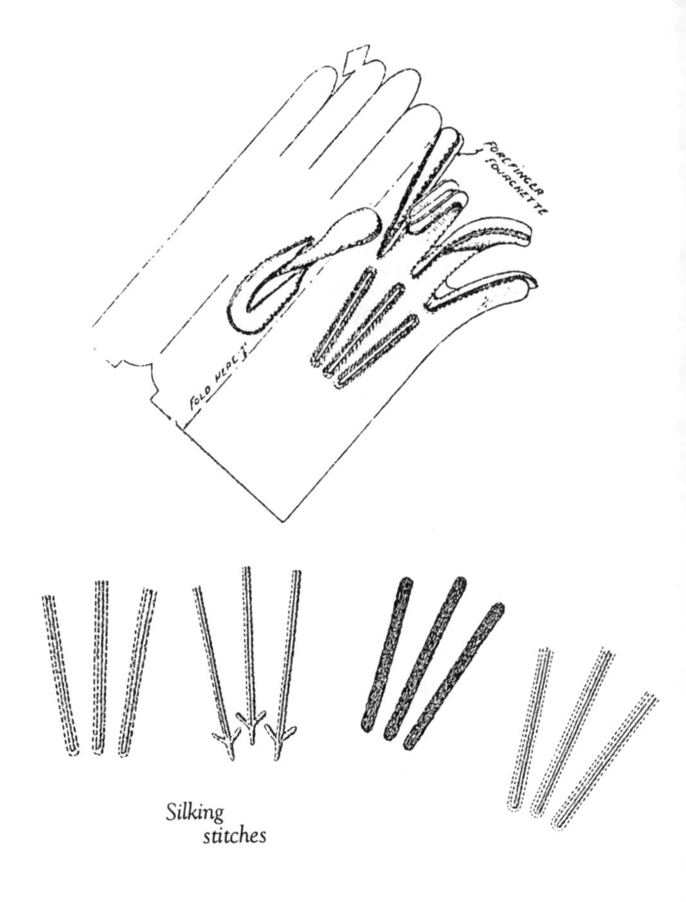

Silking stitches

Overseam - With the wrong sides of the gloves together and the edges exactly even, the seams are stitched and at every stitch the thread also loops over the edge.

Inseam - The right sides of the glove are placed together and stitched, usually with a lock stitch. The seams are trimmed and the glove turned rightside out so no seam is visible.

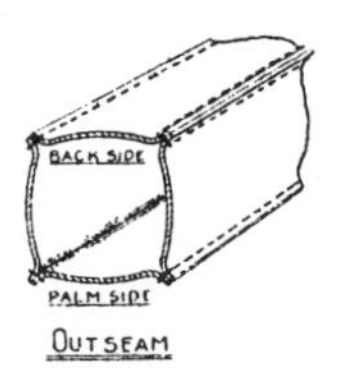

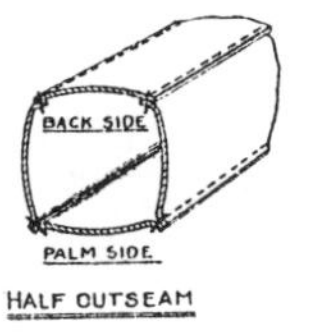

Full Pique - P K - The seams are sewn flat with one edge overlapping the other. The stitching shows on the finished glove. This is a very difficult seam to make, especially when closing fingers. The seam is placed over a small steel post through which the needle works and the leather is pushed very gradually over the post so that only a few stitches are made at a time.

Triple stitch - This is outseam stitching with a special machine that produces two stitches forward and one back so that each stitch is tied and the thread cannot ravel.

Homework in the 1880s

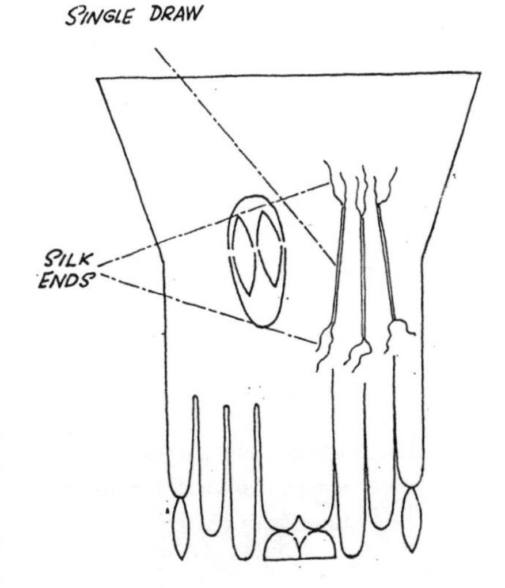

Even as factories were growing and more and more women were working in them, women continued to work at home. A charming vignette about the work of women and the shortage of places to board comes from letters written by Susan B. Anthony to a friend. She stayed in Johnstown from April to August of 1884 to be close to Elizabeth Cady Stanton, who was a Johnstown native. Stanton had returned to care for her father who was ill. Anthony joined Stanton so they could plan a women's suffrage conference in Johnstown and work on their memoirs of the women's movement. In all the two women's talks and writings, there is no reference, other than this letter, to women working in glove shops.[43] Securing the vote for women was obviously more important to these ladies than protecting women from local factory work. Incidentally, the wife of one of Gloversville's principal glove manufacturers, Mrs. Churchill, was chosen as vice-president of the new suffrage organization.

Parenthetically, Susan B. Anthony boarded at the home of Widow Henry on William Street, the same house in which I grew up. As she described her stay,

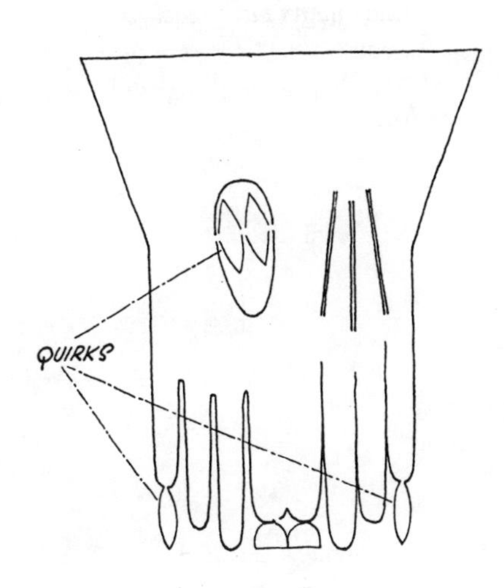

> *Here I am—settled in Mrs. Stanton's old home town—a block & a half away from her place—in a lovely sunny parlor chamber—of a widow lady—with one daughter & a niece—"we four & no more"—are to be the family—My room fronts East with two good old fashioned windows—& extends back the full width of the house—with one west window—into which—now—the sun is streaming in most lovely through a lovely white lilac bush or tree—So you can think of me, all this blessed summer & mayhap away into autumn—basking in both the morning & evening sunlight!! It is the nicest bit of good luck for me—the Hotel man & everybody said it was no us[e] to look—that every house was ful[l] that would take a boarder! This is the glove making world so every woman & girl that must eke out her income or make one stitches on gloves—the two girls here make button-holes—& nothing else.*

Not a word of condemnation about women having to work!

About the same time Isabella MacDonald Alden, who wrote many books and articles and edited her own magazine, often using the pen name "Pansy," wrote of the glove business in Gloversville, where she grew up. Her works were mostly directed at young people and often had a religious theme (her husband C. R. Alden was a Presbyterian minister).

Her story, *A City Founded by a Deer*, simplified the city's history.

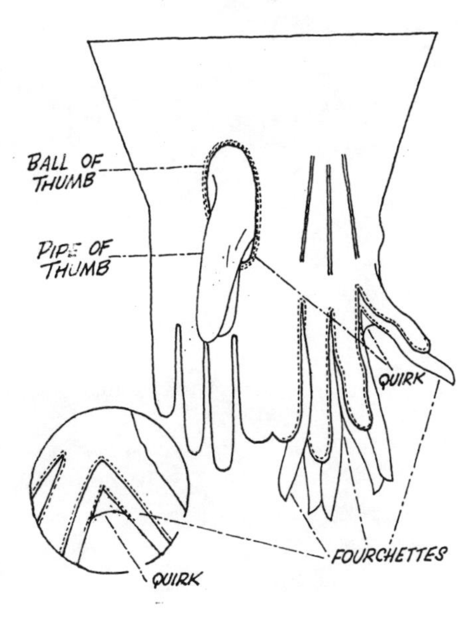

> *A real city now [1888] occupies the place of "Stump City" and its name is Gloversville. . . Go through the streets and you'll be surprised to see how busy every man, woman and child still is. It's one of the last places to go if you want to rest.*
>
> *There are machines and machines often many in the same house and from early morn till long after sunset they hum and buzz til you'd think everybody and the very air would go crazy. No one goes crazy, however. The hum has become the sweetest music in Gloversville. It annually makes money for them to the tune of millions, and I am glad to say they pour thousands of it into the Lord's treasury.*

Here are children and women working and not a note of disapproval from a champion of families! Homework in the cigar industry in New York City was being condemned in the late 1870s. Samuel Gompers called homework a new form of slavery.[44] This form of homework was seen as being so horrible that measures to regulate cigar-making in the home were adopted. Throughout the 1880s—when battles were waged over the condition of homeworkers in other industries—no such protests appear in Fulton County. This difference continued into the following decades, and the next chapter shows that the family nature of the glove industry and the independence of women workers accounted for the apparent sense of contentment of the county's homeworkers.

Manufacturers

The art of making gloves has long been a prominent feature in the prosperity of Fulton County, yielding a comfortable support to all thus engaged, while many have reached wealth.
Washington Frothingham, 1892[4]

Who were the glove and leather manufacturers who had brought the industry to the 1890 level that foretold such great future expansion? Washington Frothingham published a *History of Fulton County* in 1890 that attributes the growth and prosperity of Fulton County to the strength and character of its preeminent inhabitants. The men whom Frothingham chronicled as the backbones of the communities were the leading glove and leather manufacturers.

Of the 33 members of the old guard prominent enough to warrant biographical sketches by Frothingham, only one was foreign-born and more than half had grown up in Fulton County. Of the nearly 500 families considered important enough to rate mention, Frothingham identifies 61 as being foreign-born. All but 11 of the 61 worked in either the glove or leather industry. Their origins were English (22), German (16), Prussian (three), Austrian (one), Hungarian (one), Irish (three), French (nine), and Scots (six). Approximately 80 others, all native-born, were profiled as important in one of the two industries. Of these 60 percent were born in Fulton County, 40 percent were born elsewhere in the state or the country, with a significant number of the latter coming from nearby communities such as those in Saratoga or Montgomery counties. Among those born in this country, German ancestry was more than double English; Scots ancestry was almost as common as English, with French and Dutch far behind. Of the foreign-born, six were Jewish.

These numbers are offered as indications only, because Frothingham was not consistent in giving the origin of all the people he noted as being in the industry. Nevertheless, they do underscore the Anglo-Saxon origins of those in Fulton County's glove and leather industry in 1890.

At the end of the nineteenth century, as in earlier years sons followed fathers into the industry, creating a strong family tradition among owners. Some gloves shops were owned and managed by the same family for two, three, even four generations.

Growth of the Jewish community

An event, hardly mentioned by contemporaries, was the gradual shifting in the county's ethnic makeup, a shift that began in the 1860s and reached a peak in the two decades that bracket the turn of the century. The origin of the shift can be traced to one man—Nathan Littauer. Littauer emmigrated from Breslau, Germany, in 1848, to Albany, where he became a peddler.

Among the wares he took to surrounding communities were the needles and threads used by women who sewed gloves. By 1856 he had established a store on the corner of Fulton and Main streets in Gloversville, the hub of the growing community. Receipts for thread and needles and ledger accounts of purchases from Littauer are among the papers of the McMartin and the Heacock glove companies.

Acting as an agent for the wares of smaller firms, he expanded his sales of gloves by opening a store in New York City in 1866. This pioneering sales operation was copied in later years by many Fulton County firms. In 1866 he also began to manufacture gloves in a middle-sized shop capitalized at $40,000 and employing 15 men and 30 women, with 20 sewing machines. That year he produced $55,000 worth of gloves.

Two of his sons, Lucius and Eugene, took over the glove business in 1883. In 1890, just a year before Nathan died. The sons moved the business into a new, larger glove shop that employed 140 cutters and 450 other workers. They added a leather mill in Johnstown to their operation and a store and warehouse on Broadway in New York City. The expansion of the Littauer Brothers factory will be discussed in the next chapter, but the father was responsible for something much more important to the glove industry than his factory.

Nathan Littauer and his sons encouraged the growth of a Jewish community, which reached its cultural peak in Gloversville after 1890 with the height of the glove business. Nathan Littauer was able to provide a welcome community for Jewish immigrants and encouraged many Jews to settle in Gloversville. where a neighborhood of homes and shops owned by Jewish families arose around their synagogoue. Lucius later contributed to the library, the hospital, and most importantly the Jewish Community Center, which became the focus of Jewish family life.

The Littauers employed many Jewish immigrants, a number of whom went on to establish businesses of their own. Among those who were able to leave Littauer and start independent enterprises was Gustav Levor who began producing leather in 1875. By 1884 he had built a new skin mill that employed 140 men. Like Littauer, he, too, employed many fellow Jewish immigrants. Louis Meyers started as a cutter with Littauer and was able to open his own glove factory in 1877, moving to a new larger building in 1890. The legendary Sam Goldwyn started work in a tannery before moving on to the lights of Hollywood.

Others, like S. and H. Lebenheim (1877), were able to start factories shortly after arriving in Gloversville. A. Klein began making gloves in 1868 and continued in partnership with his son after 1891. H. Knoff began dressing leather in 1861. Max Beeber took as partner Jacob Lehman in 1867 and by 1870 was able to build a new three-story glove factory. His success rivaled the Littauers' and he soon had a warehouse and glove store on Broadway in New York City.

All of these Jewish entrepreneurs provided ready work for the wave of eastern European immigrants who came directly to Gloversville to find work in the city's glove shops. The wave began as a trickle in the 1880s, accelerated through the 1890s, and peaked in the early 1900s. Some were untrained laborers, others were trained glove-cutters. They were a new kind of worker, used to dealing with labor strife and social unrest. They changed the nature of Gloversville's labor force, and their legacy is the hallmark of the decades that bracket the turn of the century.

The wave of eastern European immigration in the 1880s can be traced to one event in 1881: The death of Czar Alexander II of Russia marked the end of a period of liberalism. The new government began a wave of persecution and pogroms of the Jewish population that stretched across the Pale, the east European area that stretched from the Baltic to the Black Sea. This in turn sparked an exodus that brought a million Jews to New York City in the following three decades and an even greater proportional increase in Gloversville's Jewish population. The social unrest that followed the pogroms in Europe accompanied the immigrants to America and inexorably changed Gloversville's work force.

There were a few Jewish families in Johnstown in the nineteenth century; most migrated to Gloversville, where they were decidedly more welcome. There is no question but that prejudice was fundamental to the way the communities grew. It was not just that Jewish people felt more comfortable in Gloversville, they must have felt less so in Johnstown. Discrimination in nearby resort communities was a dirty little secret that kept Jewish people out. At the time of World War II, there were but three Jewish families in Johnstown. The success of Jewish glove and leather manufacturers—and they were very successful—contributed to the separation between the communities. One manufacturer whose business continues into the late twentieth century commented that these men were shrewder and smarter than the old-line family businessmen. They were poised to lead the industry in the next two decades.

The decade of the eighties was the prelude to the crest of production in the county's glove industry. In the 1880s the larger glove shops continued to dress their own leather stock. The county's operations remained primarily vertical, although there were now separate leather manufacturers. Most had only small businesses, and only one, Booth & Co., produced a substantial amount of leather ($300,000 worth in 1880) for others to turn into gloves. Booth & Co. continued to be the dominant county tanner into the next century, and in 1892 the company employed 350 men and tanned 1.25 million skins and 140,000 hides.

Frothingham wrote a very complete history of Fulton County through the year 1890, giving many more details of people, families, and professions than included here. His book complements this first section, but does not provide answers to questions such as how did things happen and why. It has been difficult to pull these answers from the evidence of this long-ago time. The county's relative isolation, its heritage, its valued and trained immigrants, and the vision of a few entrepreneurs all contributed. But, of all the reasons why glove-making developed as it did in Fulton County, one thing stands out: the industry was the effort of an entire community, its residents working together, building their towns, and finding a unique niche in the economy of our growing country.

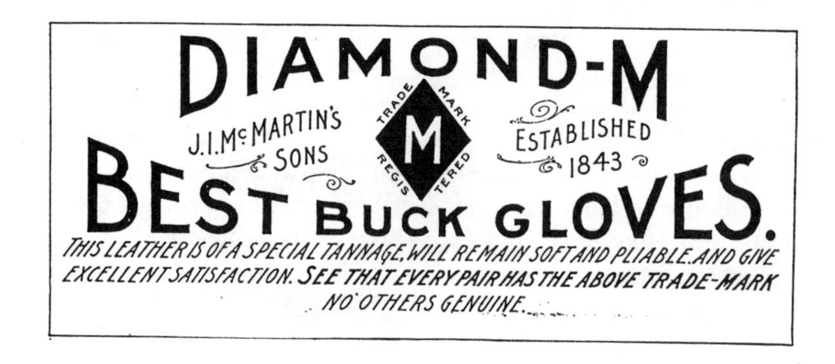

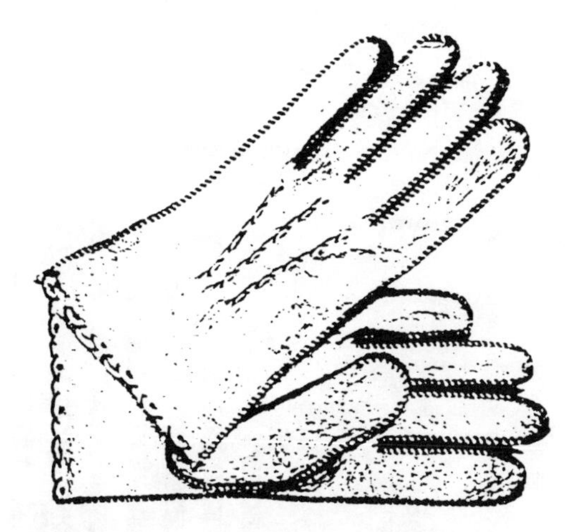

Maturing Industry

1890 to 1915

When business is bad throughout the United States, [the Fulton County] glove business is dull.[1]
Albert Aaron, superintendent of Louis Meyers & Son

The year 1890 saw the acceleration of the fine glove industry that became Fulton County's claim to fame. The quarter century following is remembered as the brightest times even though there were bleak stretches. And, while the industry was enjoying some of its greatest successes, the seeds of its eventual demise were already germinating.

Fulton County's economy paralleled the country's ups and downs throughout this period. In the United States, the 1890s and the first decades of the 1900s were a time of wonderful expansion, conglomeration, and turmoil. Workers and their unions began to promote social causes, strikes were rampant, and unions struggled to make economic gains for their members and to become accepted in America.

The depression of 1893 led to the formation of the United States Leather Company, a corporation formed by merger of almost all the hide tanners in this country. Its assets were the tanneries and hemlock forests that provided the bark that still supplied tannin to make shoe leather from cowhides.

The 1893 depression continued until 1897. The good times that followed brought a strike by Fulton County's cutters, one that gained them the only substantial raise they had prior World War I. The good times lasted until about 1903. Sometime after 1904, the local industry peaked. There was a deeper depression nationally in 1908 and it caused glove workers to leave for other industries. In 1912 when Johnstown and Gloversville were both "employed to capacity" and some companies were behind in their orders, the industry was already beginning to shrink. The general decline that followed was exacerbated by the threat of war.

Despite these ups and downs, the county's economic picture was very bright. Statistics show just how much the county gained. Between 1890 and 1900, there was a 47 percent increase in value in the county's glove production. In the same decade immigrants increased the local population by 33 percent,[1] while the number of workers rose by 59 percent, implying an huge increase in two-income families and in the number of part-time homeworkers. Johnstown produced 40 percent as much as Gloversville.

Population

	Fulton County	Gloversville	Johnstown
1890	37,650	13,864	7,768
1900	42,842	18,349	10,130
1910	44,534	20,642	10,447
1920	44,924	22,075	10,908
1930	46,560	23,099	10,801
1940	48,597	23,329	10,666
1950	51,021	23,634	10,923
1960	51,304	21,714	10,390
1970	52,637	19,677	10,045

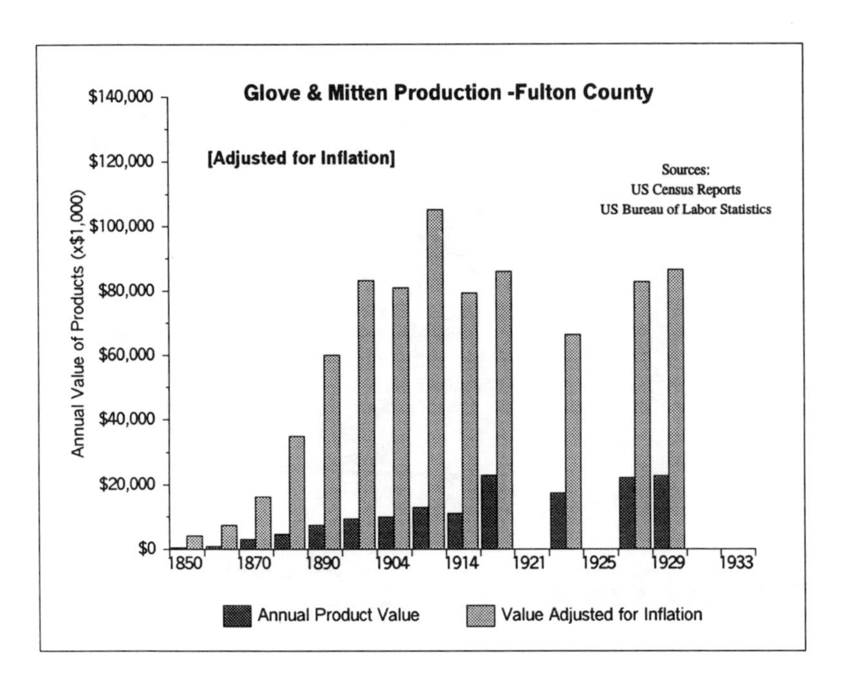

In 1900, the county produced 57 percent of all gloves produced in the United States.[2] By 1905, Fulton County's 145 establishments produced 48.3 percent of the value of all gloves produced in the United States.

In 1905, 82.4 percent of all workers in Fulton County's 13,340 wage earners were employed in the glove and leather industry. In Gloversville alone the proportion was even higher, 87.6 percent. One-third of all county residents were on glove or leather company payrolls.

In 1909, 41.4 percent of all Unites States glove businesses were located in the county and they produced 54.7 percent of the value of all gloves produced in the United States, down slightly from 56.4 percent in 1899. The rise in the manufacture of dress gloves accounted for a disproportionate rise in the product value.

In 1909, 12,950 people worked on gloves in Fulton County, more than one-third of the county's population. There were slightly more females than males employed in the local glove industry.

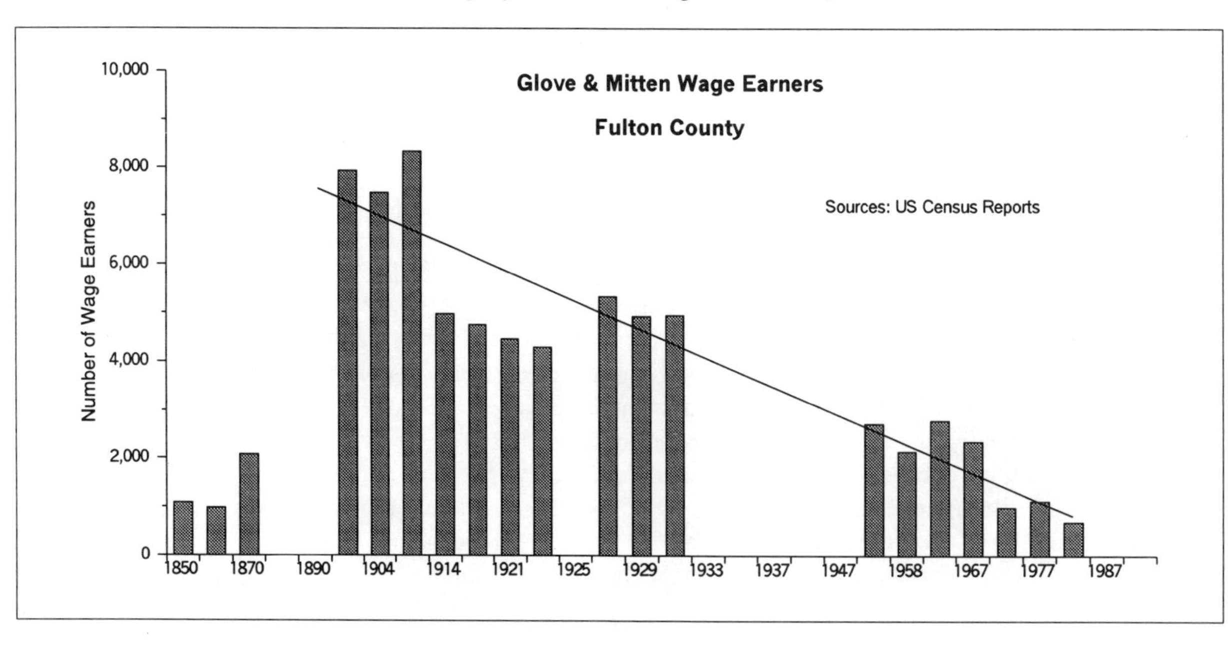

Representatives of sixteen glove manufacturers, seven of whom were still in business in 1934, joined together in 1897 to form the American Glove Association. They created the organization primarily to obtain higher tariffs on imported gloves, but also to exchange ideas and socialize. At about this time, the local industry began publishing the *Glove and Leather Review*. The Fulton County Glove Manufacturers Association succeeded the earlier association in 1902. It continued under different titles—The Glove Manufactures Association and The Glove Manufacturers Association of the State of New York—until it merged with the National Association of Glove Manufacturers in 1923. Starting in 1902, a private company began publishing *The Glovers Review*, which related association news and reflected association policies. This review is a vital source of information on the industry through the period until 1940, when its publication ceased.

The interval between 1890 and 1915 was a time of great growth in the county's glove business, and, although it was not evident at the time, that business peaked shortly after 1900. In the same period, glove workers experienced a time of strife and struggle which culminated in 1914 in a prolonged strike and lockout. The inevitability of the approaching strike parallels the ominous approach of war. Hearings conducted in 1914 by the New York State Labor Department's Board of Mediation not only describe the strike, but their record also provides insight into workers' lives and conditions throughout the previous 25 years. This chapter makes extensive use of the hearing record.

The year 1890 was a watershed year for Fulton County's glove and leather industry because it marked the culminantion of several events—changes in the tariff laws, movement of work-glove manufacturing to the western United States, increases in imports, attempts to make fine ladies' gloves as well as fine mens' gloves, electricity for power, increased immigration from eastern Europe and Russia, social unrest, and the rise of unions locally. All these events are interrelated; most can be dealt with sequentially to describe the county's economic expansion. However, two events occurred simultaneously and so interconnectedly that making the choice of which to deal with first becomes very difficult. There is no justification for dealing with changes in tariff laws before describing the move west of the manufacture of heavy work gloves or the reverse. I chose to describe changes in tariff laws first.

American Glove Association, 1897

Northrup Glove Mfg. Co.
Jacob Adler & Co.
Julius Kraus
Mason Campbell & Co.
Rea, White & Carter
Littauer Bros.
E. K. Scheftel & Co.
Ireland Bros.
Louis Meyers & Son
Schwartz, Schiffer & Co.
P. P. Argersinger & Co.
John C. Allen
Dempster & Place
Bachner-Moses Co.
Hutchens & Potter
Daniel Hays Co.

Tariffs

The result of that tariff [1890] was that the industry of manufacturing men's gloves began in this country, an industry that to-day gives employment to 20,000 working men and women at the American rate of wages.
Lucius Littauer, 1914

Tariff Rates for leather gloves

1789	7½%
1792	10%
1812	110%
1816	30%
1835	29%
1837	28%
1841	23½%
1842	20%
1846	30%
1857	24%
1861	30%
1862	45%
1864	50%
1872	50%

Tariffs are credited with the birth of the fine glove industry in Fulton County, even though it is now known that the start occurred more than two decades earlier. Until 1890, tariffs played a minor role in that development. Historically, the United States used tariffs on such items as woolen and cotton cloth and steel for three different reasons: to protect and nurture young industries, to provide revenue, and finally to allow American industry to compete with low foreign wages. The spike in tariffs in 1812 was directly related to the need to raise revenues for the War of 1812. From 1816 until just before the Civil War, tariffs on imported gloves began to reflect the need to help the domestic industry. In general, the period from 1832 to 1860 was one of great vacillation in tariff policy, created by periods of inflation and deflation, prosperity and depression.

Tariffs were raised in 1860, 1862, and 1864. Three sources were tapped to fund the Civil War: a tax on all goods produced in the country, the introduction of an internal revenue tax, and great increases in tariffs. Foreign-made gloves were taxed at 50 percent. Between the end of the Civil War and 1872 many bills were introduced in Congress to reduce tariffs, but none passed, until 1872 when an across-the-board ten percent reduction was considered. The conservative and generally Republican glove manufacturers in Fulton County were well represented at that time by John M. Carroll, who became a Congressman in 1871. He succeeded in having gloves exempted from this reduction, thus protecting his constituents.

The year 1883 marked the first general revision of tariff laws since the Civil War. A tariff commission, appointed in 1882 and made up largely of protectionist members, studied the matter and made recommendations for changes in legislation. The tariff on gloves, both men's and women's, was raised to 50 percent, while most tanned skins had a tariff of 20 percent. It is interesting that manufacturers described the 1890 tariff law, whose added protection for gloves is described below, as being primarily responsible for the county's fine glove industry; but in truth, the 1883 tariff had to have been just as important.

In 1887 Democratic President Grover Cleveland urged the removal of all duties on raw materials and a reduction in duties in general. The Republicans, with the election of President Benjamin Harrison in 1888, were successful in reversing the Democratic stand. The McKinley Tariff Bill of 1890 broke from the tradition of *ad valorem* duties, where assigned duties were a percentage of the glove's value. The new law differentiated gloves by length. The minimum tariff was 50 percent, and additional duties were imposed for ladies' gloves over 14 inches in length and on men's gloves.

Cleveland's reelection in 1892 resulted in the tariff act of 1894, in which the duties on many goods were reduced, but not on gloves. That act created an additional category of ladies' gloves with increased duties on those over 17 inches. Tranks—partially cut gloves—had the stiff duty of 75 percent, thus protecting the growing number of cutters in the local industry.

The tariffs on men's gloves remained constant until 1897, while women's and children's gloves were increased slightly. With the election of McKinley in 1896, Republicans were returned to office, and in 1897 Congress passed the Dingley Tariff Act, which raised duties to 57 percent.

In 1914, William J. Stitt, a foreman for the Jacob Adler Glove Co. said he believed it was the 1897 Dingley Bill—with its great increase on the duty on foreign gloves—that "was the beginning of the fine goods industry in the county." He thought it permitted the glovemen to experiment and see how successful they "would be in making the finer grades of gloves in competition with Europe."[3] No matter which year was credited, there is little doubt that tariffs played a major role in creating the county's fine glove industry.

At this point, the tariff story, which is so essential to understanding what happened between 1890 and 1915, is best described in the words of Lucius Littauer, the county's premier glove manufacturer, who was also a member of Congress between 1898 and 1907 and one of the county's staunchest Republicans. (The glove industry was represented in the New York State Assembly by another local gloveman, Daniel Hays, also a Republican, who was elected to the Assembly in 1898.)

In testimony before the Ways and Means Committee in 1908, Littauer traced tariff history from the manufacturer's perspective. He noted that the industry had begun by producing buckskin gloves for working men: "this happens to be the only country in the world where the workingman earns sufficient wages to afford him the luxury of protecting his hands with a pair of gloves." Glove production in the United States in 1908 was still more than 65 percent work gloves. Littauer testified that even with the 50 percent *ad valorem* tariff rate in force between 1883 and 1890, American manufacturers could not compete with foreign manufacturers. He claimed that until 1890, all fine gloves were imported, and that the McKinley Bill added a dollar a dozen tariff to the 50 percent *ad valorem* rate. "The result of that tariff was that the industry of manufacturing [fine] men's gloves began in this country, an industry that to-day gives employment to 20,000 working men and women at the American rate of wages."[4] Littauer continued,

> *The McKinley Bill lasted only a few years and we came before this committee, then presided over by Mr. Wilson. Despite the fact that on that portion of the gloves schedule which concerned ladies' gloves the McKinley rates were cut in two, we yet were able to demonstrate the justice and necessity and propriety of fostering this business of manufacturing men's gloves that had been started under the McKinley Bill, and the Wilson Bill gave us higher duties than the McKinley Bill. . . Then in 1896, when the Dingley Bill was under consideration, the importation of men's gloves had been reduced to 62,000 pairs and our glove making communities began to grow."*

Littauer went on to describe the inequities of the 1897 bill with respect to different types of skins. Still, all of the locally produced men's gloves were made with imported skins, which commanded a duty of 20 percent. Littauer compared the wage scales for different types of sewing, demonstrating that European rates were much lower. His testimony continued with some exaggerations with respect to home ownership and wages in the county. But he summed up the needs for a high protective tariff:

> *During the fifteen or eighteen years that we have had a protective tariff on men's gloves, our savings bank deposits, . . . have increased 212 percent. There is no trust, no combination, no selling organization, no millionaires in the glove business. Domestic competition has extended through 329 factories. There is close and active competition, and large production, at only a fair profit.*

Despite the fact American women appeared to prefer imported gloves, Littauer felt domestic manufacturers could make "the best in the world. . . . If

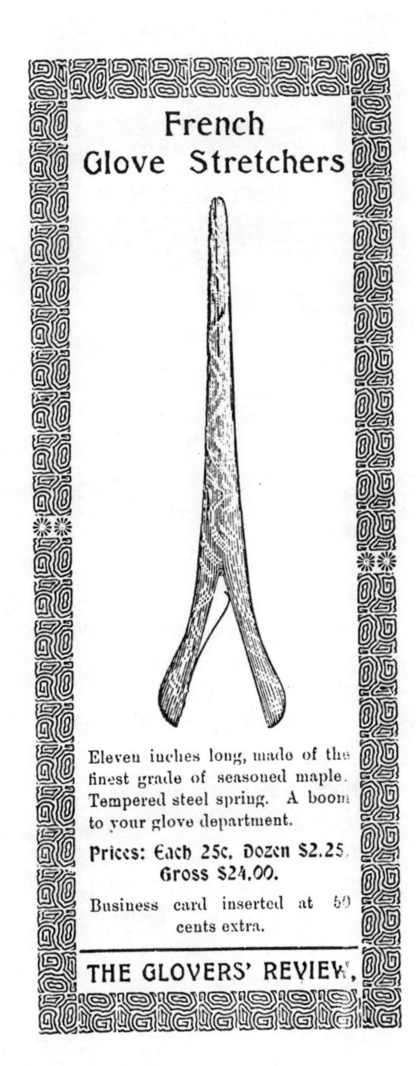

There are eight times more women's gloves than men's gloves consumed in this country. At present only about five percent of the women's gloves used in this country are made here, the other 95 percent being imported. When the Americans are put in a position where they can make women's gloves with the prospect of profit, then there will be real competition and the result will be that the consumer will get a better glove for the same or less money.
George C. Potter, quoted in *The New York Times*

you give us a proper opportunity, we will demonstrate on ladies' gloves, and we will give 50,000 working men and women in the United States employment at American rates of wages." He attempted to prove that at the same time a sufficient number of stylish gloves would continue to be imported to equal the current revenue produced by the tariff.

"There is no question tariffs raised the industry after 1890, but protectionism has developed a trained labor force, so fortunately situated in living and working conditions and with such prospects of immediate growth as to entitle the industry to at least temporary continuation of protectionism." When Daniel W. Redmond wrote this analysis of tariffs and the glove industry in 1913, he also added that "the present method of fixing the rate of protection . . . is responsible for the excessive rate and the improper distribution of benefit of the rate between manufacturer and laborer."[5]

In 1909, the Fulton County Glove Manufacturers Association presented the Ways and Means Committee with a proposal for a tariff schedule that left the tariffs on men's gloves as they were and charged women's gloves solely on length, not on skins used. These proposals were encompassed in the Payne Bill, which would greatly simplify the tariff law and eliminate some of the arcane arguments that had tied up collection under the previous law.[6]

The Payne (Payne-Aldrich) Bill was passed in the spring of 1909 and drew immediate charges that it would "work untold hardship upon women all over the country"[7] from the manager of the Boston department store in Milwaukee. Other retailers also opposed the bill, claiming that gloves would become too expensive for working girls. The Democratic party's platform of reducing tariffs to reduce prices for workers was beginning to take hold, even as the bill was passed. The New England Drygoods Association protested that "to tax every man and woman in this country who wears leather gloves for the benefit of the already too highly protected domestic manufacturers is an outrage that should not be tolerated."[8] Despite all the fuss, when the Payne Bill went to conference between the Senate and the House, tariffs on gloves remained essentially unchanged from the Dingley Bill of 1897.

Not only did the manufacturers work strenuously for higher tariffs, they were so strong in pursuing the support of county workers that the workers felt compelled to vote for higher tariffs and for a Republican Senator, not without misgivings. A cutter for Bachner-Moses-Louis recalled how the manufacturers "organized a parade in this city and one of the most shameful things you ever saw, when all the girls and women and old men were fighting for a reduction in the tariff and we were said to be demanding a high tariff to save our homes and our jobs."[9] The cutters believed that if they supported a higher tariff and if it was adopted, they would receive a wage increase. A cutter for George Mandrill Co. was angry that this did not happen: "We were told from shop to shop that if the McKinley Tariff was passed they could afford to give us a ten cents raise. When the McKinley Tariff became a fact, we were not organized. . . . We made no concerted effort and we did not get it. Later on came the Wilson bill. . . . Again when the Dingley bill was passed we thought then that it was time that we ought to have it a little different from what we had and when we appealed to the manufacturers we were told that the increase in the tariff did not mean anything."[10]

Woodrow Wilson's election to the presidency finally gave the Democrats the opportunity to lower taxes. In a special session of the sixty-third Congress in April of 1913, House Ways and Means Committee chairman Oscar W. Underwood introduced a bill to reduce tariffs and supplement government revenues through increased income tax. *The Glovers Review* informed manufacturers that the tariff had to be changed as it was a Democratic pre-election pledge, but "with the accompanying promise that it would be done in a way so as not to injure or destroy legitimate industry." While it was intended to cheapen the price of commodities for the people, the *Review* saw that this would be accomplished "without regard to the conservation of their employment or maintenance of their purchasing power. And this is not alarming monopoly and 'Big Business' nearly so much as it is the smaller, highly competitive industries."

George C. Potter, co-owner of Hutchens & Potter, sent a letter to R. G. Dun & Co. with figures correlating business failures and tariff cuts. He also wrote to *The New York Times* analyzing costs and duties in an attempt to show that higher tariffs would result in lower cost and higher quality domestically produced gloves. *The New York Times* reworked the same figures to show that Potter's ideas were a "near absurdity."[11]

On April 14, 1913 Gloversville merchants with a lot of support from the *Morning Herald*, organized a mass demonstration to protest the Underwood Bill. A series of editorials in the paper entitled, "Standing at Armegeddon" inspired workers to join the parade. Not only were all factories and leather mills shut down, but stores and offices closed so all could march in the parade or attend the mass meetings. Numerous speakers addressed the meetings and if the local paper's report is verbatim, the talks were rather dull and uninspiring.[12]

Parades were a part of every celebration and protest. The Four Corners of Gloversville was the scene of many parades, as in this photograph from the the late 1890s. This was probably a July Fourth celebration, but the tariff-protest parade in 1897 or even the one in 1913 would have looked like this. Notice the trolley lines that carried workers to the mills and glove shops

Gloversville City Archives

So dense was the throng that the police were kept busy keeping the thoroughfares open to allow marchers to pass through. The multitude followed the pageant the entire length of the march to Bleecker Street Square where the paraders broke lines and proceeded to various theaters where the mass meetings were to be held.
Morning Herald

The Glovers Review claimed that the manufacturers had no part in organizing the protest, though they did march in the parade. Who did they think would believe they had no role in the event? Here, at a time when the working people of America were staunchly behind the Democratic platform, Fulton County's workers—Democrats, progressives, and socialists—were allied with the generally Republican manufacturers.[13] The manufacturers were strong enough to demand the workers' allegiance.

The industry's protest ranged far beyond Fulton County. William Reiss, a Chicago glove manufacturer, importer, and retailer, argued that "a better measure for the fostering of the European glove industry at the expense of home factories could not possible be framed."[14]

The Underwood tariff bill reduced the duty on men's gloves from a maximum of $4.00 to $2.75 a dozen on unlined gloves. With many amendments and different rates on various kinds of gloves, the bill was adopted on October 3, 1913. As a result, the county's glovemen felt they had to reduce prices on their principal product line "to give us at least half a chance of competing with Europe."[15]

Other manufacturers, such as Abraham Lehr, president of Dempster & Place, believed that 1913 marked the point at which the county's glove business became acutely affected by competition from foreign gloves. Chicago retailers said they would buy from Europe if the prices of foreign gloves were lower. One retailer warned that "the American glove manufacturer must find a way to meet foreign competition or quit."[16]

Between 1913 and 1922, the Underwood Tariff served as a step toward free trade. Its influence on free trade would have been greater if it had not been for the intervening war, which limited imports.

The county's glove manufacturers believed that imports from England increased 48 percent after the 1913 tariff reduction. Whether this was true or not, the reductions in tariffs reduced local production, forced some manufacturers to become importers, and generally left all of them fearful for the future. This fear was compounded by the spreading war in Europe, but before we discuss the way the war temporarily put the glove industry back on course, we have to examine other aspects of glove-making in the county in these crucial two and a half decades.

Loss of Heavy Glove Business

The United States is the only country in the world in which the manufacture of work gloves is of any importance.
United States Tariff Commission, Second Annual Report, 1917-1918.

Beginning in the 1870s, glove shops began to emerge in the central and western parts of the United States. They were closer to the sources of heavy leathers, cowhides and horsehides that went into rough and serviceable work gloves. Fulton County continued to produce work gloves, some from heavy leathers, although many, like the R. J. & R. Evans Glove Co. made them from deerskins as well.

Large factories appeared in Chicago, then Wisconsin and Minnesota, and finally all the way west in San Francisco. In addition to proximity to raw materials, these factories had many advantages over the Fulton County shops: All work was done in the factories, which were better organized. Workers had to keep regular hours; they did not have the independence of the cutters and makers in Fulton County. And wages were lower.

Fulton County glovemen could not compete with western glove manufacturers. They gradually relinquished the heavy glove trade, taking up instead the making of fine men's gloves. This turnover to fine gloves coincided with the peak of the heavy glove industry's move west. (This was the same period in which county manufacturers benefited from changes in the tariff laws.) Except for buckskin gloves, three-fourths of heavy gloves were made in the west by 1897. Glove factories in the Midwest continued to expand through the first decade of the twentieth century. Just behind New York State in value of production were Wisconsin, Illinois, and California; Wisconsin had quadrupled its production in the decade between 1899 and 1909 and Michigan's production was increasing at an even greater rate.

Carloads of machines from Fulton County were shipped to the new factories. It was reported that Omaha, Nebraska, tried to get William Topp to move his entire factory to that city. Conditions in western shops were as severe as in Fulton County, occasionally even worse. In addition to fixed work rules and set hours, western employers gave no vacations and no pay when a worker was ill.

In 1902, a thousand glove workers in Buffalo formed a union to ask for parity with Fulton County's wages. In 1903, western cutters asked for parity with cutters from Fulton County; western operators wanted one-third more pay to bring their wages up to Fulton County's rates. Union organization was strong, and Chicago became such a hotbed of union activity that some manufacturers there—the larger companies at least—began to move even farther west. The strike at Eisendrath Glove Co., one of Chicago's largest firms, was settled by arbitration granting the workers a union shop. Competition was becoming so severe that manufacturers in Chicago denied workers a raise in the 1903 strike that eventually fizzled.

Because wages of western glove workers were lower than those in Fulton County, local manufacturers claimed that they could not compete with western firms. Even the R. J. & R. Evans Co., which had always specialized in work gloves, stopped making some kinds of heavy gloves, particularly cheap sheepskin gloves, by mid-1903. By 1910, 95 percent of new glove businesses were being established outside Fulton County. Milwaukee became a center for manufacturing heavy gloves; the Twin Cities of Minnesota produced heavy leather work gloves for farmers.

Two facts from this are important: The wages of Fulton County workers set industry standards. The movement of glove manufacturing away from Fulton County was accomplished even at the approach of the county's most productive period.

Fine gloves—new challenges

The making of fine gloves was not taken up until after 1880, but since then rapid progress has been made so that now men's fine gloves are here made which are equal, if not superior, to any foreign make. Ladies' fine gloves are mostly imported, and the domestic manufacturers have as yet been unable to equal the European makers in this class of goods, chiefly owing to the difficulty of obtaining the finest grades of skins which are but little exported to this country.
The Glovers Review, *June, 1906.*

After the loss of the manufacturing of rough gloves to the west, Fulton County's glove-making survived primarily because the tariff on men's gloves allowed the county to focus on making better quality gloves. By 1905, Fulton County produced 86.5 percent of all men's dress gloves. There was no comparable increase in the tariffs on most women's gloves and production levels on women's gloves would remain low until the mid-1930s.

However, in 1903, *The Glovers Review* still conceded that "the very best gloves, as all know, are made in France, and neither Canada nor the United States has ever pretended to compete with her in fineness of quality, but in the medium grade and rougher goods the United States is peer of the world." A few manufacturers like James Ireland produced quality women's gloves, but tariffs, lack of fine skins, low European wages, and the superior skills of European workers generally inhibited the county's entrance into the market for women's gloves. Except for the war years, America never produced more than 20 percent of women's gloves sold in this country. Certainly the different tariff rates on men's and women's gloves accounted in part for the disparate levels of production, but fashion preferences and quality were major factors.

In the early part of the nineteenth century, local manufacturers opened salesrooms in New York City or placed their gloves in the new department stores. The industry took pride in advising wearers which styles were appropriate for different occasions and even which kind of stitching was most appropriate. But, domestic production of fine gloves was limited by the fact that few of the county's workers had the skills and techniques of European workers.

There was a third reason the production of fine gloves remained at low levels: the Europeans had a corner on the fine leathers imported from around the world, especially the markets of lamb, sheep, and goatskins. Fulton County glove manufacturers had sought a replacement for the scarce foreign skins and leather. They had found that domestic lambskins were an unacceptable substitute for foreign skins.

The making of Mocha gloves was in its inception distinctively an American industry, and at the present time [1909] they are manufactured almost exclusively in the United States.
The Glovers Review

A first break in Europe's hold on leather had occurred around 1885. The skin of a hair sheep, found in the Arabian peninsula and northern Africa, had been impossible to tan into a fine leather. Because of its low cost it was used only for cheap grades of gloves and shoes. This sheep has no wool at all, but a coarse hair similar to goats. American ingenuity turned the skins into mocha. Without this development, the county would not have been able to continue to expand the production of either men's or women's fine gloves.

A Fulton County tanner, M. S. Northrup, developed a method of friezing or scraping the skin side of hair sheep to remove the grain. When pumiced and treated this yielded a "beautiful, velvety nap, which can be colored to any shade desired, despite its delicate texture. The hair sheep were called mochas from the anglicized spelling of a port on the southwestern coast of the Arabian peninsula. According to local lore, the first shipment of these skins arrived with a shipment of mocha coffee from that port. A mocha glove is durable and retains its appearance as long as the best, and has better wearing qualities than most any other kind of glove."[17] Europeans tried to copy these techniques, but in general preferred American mochas. The Northrup Glove Company in Johnstown specialized in tanning mochas, though other companies also took up the manufacture of mocha.

Not only were mochas harder to tan, but cutters considered them much harder to cut because "they are so faulty and not so easy to handle."[18] But they became the staple of the county's fine gloves and sustained the industry in the years between 1890 and 1915.

As the use of mochas expanded, a trading network developed along the east coast of Africa and the Red Sea. A series of dealers and agents collected skins for shipment in bales "of six to eight score" and brought them along the coast to Aden. Lumped with other skins and sold by the score, only an expert could tell what part of the world they came from and analyze the color, weight, manner of skinning, condition of the cured skin—its thickness, clearness, and smoothness of grain, and the absence of insect blight and decay.[19]

By 1908, nearly eight million mocha skins were shipped from the port of Aden, most brought by caravan or native dhows from Yemen, Eritrea, Somaliland, and the African coast as far south as Mombasa. The black-headed mocha sheep from Somalia was considered to be more desirable than the white-headed or red-headed varieties from other areas. Every native herder participated by removing skins from the sheeps' carcasses and hanging them to dry in the sun. They sprinkled them with naphthalene to inhibit insects.

Johnstown Historical Society

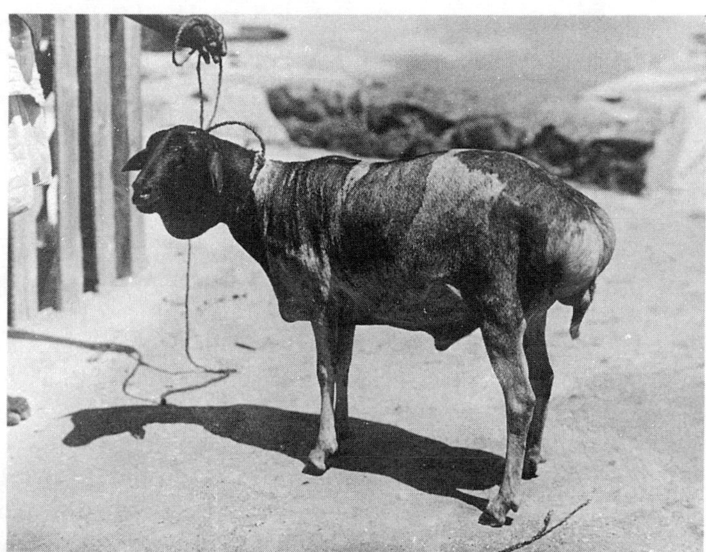

Johnstown Historical Society

Shipped in bales, the skins were tanned in Fulton County by a process that required more steps than any other leather. They were soaked in large, water-filled vats to remove dirt and poisons, then placed in lime solutions until the hair became loose. Machines had been perfected to do the work of removing hair formerly done by beaming knives. Next the skins were returned to a lime solution until it was possible to remove the grain. This was accomplished by knives in a traditional beaming process. Then the skins were again soaked to remove the lime. Mocha skins were tanned by repeated applications of egg yolks, alum, and flour in rotary drums. This replaced the chemicals removed in the liming process.

Next the skins were hot-air dried in a drying room, then moistened again in bins filled with damp sawdust to prepare them for knee-staking that would make the skins soft and pliable. Then the skins were put on revolving wheels faced with emery. These wheels, which replaced bucktails, were still called "bucktails" and they gave the skins the beautiful, velvety surface characteristic of mocha. The egging process was repeated, as well as more drying and knee-staking and applications of the bucktails. Finally the skins, which were then pure white, were ready to be dyed and sent to the glove manufacturers.[20]

It is interesting to note that around 1910, sales of mocha skins to Europe expanded because the Americans insisted on having the skins in their hands before they authorized payment, while the Europeans immediately paid the native dealers. The financial squeeze on Fulton County glovers was thus pushed on to the Arab merchants who had had to pay for the skins they accumulated in Aden. This elliptical evidence is just one of many signs of how difficult were the finances of the county's glovers.

As late as August of 1914, the manufacture of women's leather gloves in the United States was very limited and confined to mocha, suede, chamois, doeskin, and some cape and glace gloves. At that time, Europeans produced 90 percent of women's gloves sold in America, while 70 percent of fine men's gloves were made here. Of all the fine gloves made in the United States, however, 85 percent were produced in Fulton County.[21]

Louis Meyers & Son was becoming a major producer of women's gloves around 1910, and by 1914 half that company's production was in women's gloves. Irelands produced some ladies' gloves from the time the company was formed and it continued to be a leader in the production of fine women's gloves as the company began to focus on fashion and style. But Littauer's always made a less expensive dress glove without benefit of the finest leathers.

Changing Ethnicity

A change in the enthnicity of manufacturers and workers accompanied and in part accounted for the growth in the fine glove industry. This occurred in the first decade and a half of this century at the same time as the deaths of almost all the old guard of glove and leather manufacturers, most of whom had started businesses in the county in the years before or just after the Civil War.

As an example of how death and illness affected business, consider what happened to the firm of D. B. Judson. Not only had his glove business, which produced mostly heavy work gloves, closed before his death in 1894, but the tannery he built, one of the area's largest, changed hands. Judson had built a large factory in 1870 in northwest Gloversville for Thomas Foster, who dressed kid leather for Judson's glove company for two decades. When Judson withdrew from the glove business, Foster sold the skin mill to Julius C. Bleyl, and Bleyl continued to dress kid leather under contract to Winslow Bros. & Smith, a Boston shoe-manufacturing company. Bleyl ran the business until 1920 when it was sold to the Boston firm, which continued to produce leather under the Bleyl name through the 1940s.

Replacing the old guard was an emerging group of new entrepreneurs, many of whom were German and Austrian Jews who led the way in building new and larger factories. These were men trained in the glove or leather business, who had come from European cities, occasionally bringing enough money to establish new businesses. They became the owners of the largest glove shops. Most of the German Jews had found their way to the county in the years before 1890, but their impact was greatest just after that date.

The largest of their factories can be ranked in terms of the number of their cutters. These listed below give start dates and the number of cutters employed in 1914 where such information is available.

In Gloversville:

- Littauer Bros, 1866, 150 cutters
- Jacob Adler & Co., 1885, 120 to 125 cutters
- Louis Meyers & Son, 1885, 140 to 150 cutters
- Elite Glove Co.—(Ralph and Isaac Moses), 1905, 55 cutters
- Dempster & Place—with the death of George Place, the new president was Abraham Lehr, 1887, 100 cutters
- Lefi, Bachner, Hall Co. with Abraham Bachner a partner, 1908, 25 cutters
- Bachner-Moses-Louis, 1900, originally Bachner-Moses, which had been established by Joseph Bachner, a glove cutter from Warsaw in 1880, 120 cutters

Among the tanneries led by German Jews was one owned by Gustav Levor, which specialized in tanning sheepskins from Brazil and Argentina. Levor perfected a method of tanning white leather that was used extensively for shoes, so unlike most Fulton County firms, this factory's leather was destined for East Coast shoe manufacturers.[22]

Several of the middle-sized shops in Gloversville were owned by gentiles: Daniel Hays; Fownes (owned by the English firm) with 60 to 75 cutters; and V. Perrins & Cie, (a division of a French company) with 40 cutters.

They come practically straight to Gloversville. Gloversville is the head of the glove trade of the United States and every Glover throughout the world knows that.
Gloversville cutter George Taylor, testifying at the 1914 Hearing.[3]

Deaths among the old guard, 1890-1915

- Frank P. Zimmer, partner in A. J. Zimmer & Co.
- Hon. James H. Burr, active for 50 years, Member of the State Assembly, began manufacturing buckskin gloves in 1844
- D. B. Judson, dead at 75 with 50 years in the business
- John Veeder, age 72
- Louis Meyers, 40 years a gloveman, first with Joseph Adler, then with his son
- M. Sexton Northrup, the inventor of tanning processes for mocha, age 64
- George H. Hilts, in business for 39 years
- Julius Quackenbush, age 72, started in business in 1859
- Delevan Hewitt, age 66
- David S. Dempster of Dempster & Place, had built large plant in 1887
- Richard Evans, age 56
- Ferdinand Jeannison, age 50, first in business with his father, later at Littauers
- Edward H. Drumm, age 68, started making gloves in 1863
- S. C. Burton, Wm. L. C. Rubsamen, W. W. Hubbard, Wm. T. Lintner, Lucien B. Young all died in 1909
- J. D. Lefler, age 57, leather dresser and glove manufacturer
- P. P. Argersinger, age 66, started glove business in 1862, firm continued by his son John and son-in-law, A. Judson Baker

Deaths among the old guard, 1890-1915

David Ireland, age 56, born in Scotland, served as salesman for his brothers' firm
John C. Allen, age 71, originally of Heacock, Berry & Allen, Allen alone after 1890
Julius Kraus, age 66, from Vienna, Austria, started own business in New York in 1869, moved to Gloversville in 1880, the first to import cape and suede
Uriel Case, age 99
Daniel McEwen, Sr., age 91
Charles W. Rose, age 78, started factory in 1862
George M. Place, age 53, vice-president of Glove Manufacturers Association
L. S. Brown, in business for 45 years
Joachim Lebenheim, age 71, born in Germany, started leather dressing firm in Johnstown in 1869, moved to Gloversville with sons until 1908 fire destroyed their building
Daniel Hays, died in 1913, age about 80
Alvin V. Quackenbush, age 64
Marcellus Burr, age 67
Wm. H. Brower, age 75
Max Beeber, age 90 years, lived in New York city, retired from Swartz, Schiffer & Co. in 1895
Ottis E. Potter, age 68
Frank Pauley, age 82, came from Prussia in 1853, started buckskin business in 1859
Charles A. McEwen, age 71, started glove business in 1874
John M Shaw, age 63, of Gloversville Auto Glove Co.
Mark M. Hall, age 81

Johnstown firms were almost all middle-sized with Anglo-Saxon, Protestant owners: Ireland Bros, 35 cutters; R. J. & R. Evans, 50 cutters; Hallock & Stewart, 50 cutters; Northrup Glove Co., 30 cutters; George Mandrill, 30 cutters; Hutchens & Potter, 50 cutters; and Lucas & Kennedy, 35 cutters.

Immigration from eastern Europe produced a dramatic change in the working population. The pogrom launched by the Russians against the Jews of the Pale in 1881 started an outflow from Poland, which was then part of Russia. The result was that in the 1890s, Russian-born Jews (Hebrews as they were known locally) gradually replaced the English, Scots, French, and Germans as the largest ethnic group in the table-cutting fraternity of skilled workers. Immigration from Russia continued until World War I.

In the shtetls, the small towns of the Pale, Jewish workers had been oppressed, exploited, and ill-treated.[23] Fleeing poverty, these immigrants were for the most part young workers who brought their families, seeking permanent settlement in the United States. Among them were a number of skilled workers, especially those skilled in needle trades. Great numbers of them settled in New York City and slowly entered the garment industry, which was largely in the hands of German Jews. It was logical that those who were trained in the glove business would make their way to Gloversville, where so many German Jews were establishing glove businesses.

As persecutions and labor strife continued in eastern Europe, those who remained began a class struggle, marked with the growth of unions and numerous bitter strikes throughout the 1880s and 1890s. Immigration rose steadily with peaks in 1892, 1904 and 1905, and 1914. Those who came to America in the 1890s brought no sense of unionism, but they were imbued with a sense of struggle, social reform, and radicalism. This led immigrants toward the socialist ideals, which were developing in this country primarily in New York City, and ultimately into the unions.

By 1900, over 90 percent of the garment industry in New York City was in Jewish hands and "eastern European Jews were taking long strides toward driving their German cousins from the industry."[24] The influx of eastern European Jews into Fulton County's glove industry had many parallels with their rise in the garment industry. There were, however, major differences in living and working conditions. Garment workers were crowded into tenements and forced to work in sweatshop conditions. Housing was better and working conditions, though not ideal, were noticeably better in Fulton County than in the garment industry.

Herbert M. Engel, born in 1918, son of an immigrant from Warsaw, grew up in the Jewish community of Gloversville. In *Shtetl in the Adirondacks*, he wrote about the strong family and religious ties that united the Jewish community, and also about the gulf that separated the German Jews from the Russian Jews. As the new factory owners increased the number of jobs available in Fulton County, the new eastern European Jewish immigrants sent letters to relatives back home, encouraging more and more to settle in the county.

As in New York City, the Russian Jews in Fulton County were poorer and noticeably different from the German Jews in their religious and social life. The German Jews, who had become manufacturers, were richer, more cultured, and more sophisticated. The Russian and eastern European Jews were either cutters or became apprentice cutters in the shops established by the German Jews. At Meyers, 80 percent of the cutters were "Hebrews" from Russia. At Littauers and Adlers the proportions were even higher, and in all these shops the majority of the women who sewed gloves were also new Jewish immigrants.[25] However, Littauer's factory superintendent for many years was Alfred C. Saunders, born and trained as a cutter in Worcester, England. He was employed at Littauer's between 1880 and 1917.

It was not long, however, before a few of the eastern European Jews became owners themselves. The process was certainly slower than in the garment industry in New York City, but it was inevitable. S. Schrecker, who came from Austria, worked at various factories in Gloversville, his last job as superintendent at Meyers. In 1913 he was fired, and with $3,000 in compensation or severance pay, he started his own business, S. Schrecker Glove Co. Abraham Zuckerwar, a rabbi and trained glove cutter, came from Warsaw in 1891 with his two-year old son, Jacob, to cut gloves in Gloversville. Although Jacob also became a cutter, working for Bachner-Moses-Louis Gloves and other firms, he was not interested in the glove business and was selling shoelaces at the time he married Schrecker's daughter Marguerite. Because of the marriage he joined his father-in-law in his new venture, which grew until today as Grandoe Corp, it is one of the county's largest importers and distributors of gloves. The company expanded from the start, for within a year of its formation, S. Schrecker Gloves reported assets of $17,588 and liabilities of $8,750—a net worth of over $8,800.[26]

No group changed the social structure of the communities and the character of the glove industry as greatly as the Jewish immigrants from eastern Europe. The county's immigration paralleled that of New York City with peaks in the early 1890s, the middle of the first decade of the 1900s, and the years just before World War I. The political activism that grew out of the persecutions in Russia and the resulting social unrest developed simultaneously in New York City and other cities where Jewish immigrants clustered.

Gloversville, with its established Jewish community, offered a welcome place to settle. Jobs were plentiful. Many of the eastern European men were skilled glove cutters, willing at first to train unskilled fellow immigrants. Life in the shtetls of the Pale was easily transferred to Gloversville's growing

Lucius Littauer not only expanded his father's glove business but he also continued his father's example of caring for the community. In 1891, Lucius Littauer gave money to build Gloversville's hospital, naming it after his father, Nathan. Over the years Lucius contributed additional funds to enlarge the hospital.

Jewish community. Oppressed, exploited, and ill-treated workers found a haven in this country's freedom. Gloversville's workers, like those in New York City, must have retained ties with events in Europe and followed the growing class struggle and the increasing number of strikes. Jews here and abroad simultaneously developed a sense of social justice and protest against exploitation of labor. As labor unrest grew in America, strikes were called.

At the same time, the county's factories were greatly expanded. A large part of the growth came in Jewish-owned factories and discrimination against Russian Jews by the German Jews was only one aspect of changing ethnicity. Discrimination existed at many levels. For example, the wealthier glovemen from Johnstown had summer homes at Canada Lake, an attractive nearby resort where Jews were not welcome. The wealthiest Jewish glovemen vacationed in Europe, taking long tours to glove centers as well as to spas and cities like Berlin and Paris. Harry J. Louis of Bachner-Moses-Louis Glove Co. made a three-month automobile tour that took him from Scotland to Marienbad, the Black Forest, and the Austrian Tyrol.

Fulton County's Foreign Population in 1910

England and Wales—1144
Germany—1074
Ireland—693
Scotland—86
France—175
Canada—289
French Canada—96
Italy—971
Hungary—257
Austria—616
Russia—859
Small contingents from Switzerland, Spain, and Greece

There were several other waves of immigration that affected the glove industry. Early on, most of the county's German population were descendents of Palatines who had settled in the Mohawk Valley and moved into Gloversville and Johnstown to find work in the glove industry. A second wave of Germans, mostly Catholics, settled in the county, many of them in Gloversville near their church, St. Francis de Sales, which was established in 1891. This church was known as the "German Parish," because it served immigrants from the "central empires of Europe." Many of these Germans were trained cutters and makers.

A few Italians came as greengrocers, but gradually leather workers from the Naples region found work here in the early years of this century. Their greatest impact on the county's work force was felt after World War I.

The arrival of Slovaks is attributed to a fluke, and the story is probably apocryphal. It is said that a stoneworker from a tiny town, Kuty (population 1,200) in a poor area in the Little Carpathian Mountains in western Slovakia arrived in America looking for work in the mines of Johnstown, Pennsylvania. He was directed to a train to Johnstown, New York, found work in a tannery, and started an influx of Slovaks that lasted for several decades. (A history of the town of Kuty notes that the population there dropped precipitously as residents moved to "Johnstown, North America.")

These immigrants had had nothing under the Austria-Hungary regime that ruled their homes. The *grof*, the monarchy's Jewish tax collectors, took 40 percent of the farm produce, the monarchy took another 50 percent, and the poor farmers were left with only 10 percent. All Slovaks were required to learn Hungarian and they could also speak German, but they were forbidden to speak their native Slovak on the street. This sparked an exodus from many small settlements around Kuty, a region of rolling hills, forested but not wild. In the wave of emigration many extended families left the region. They hoped to return, and over the years a few did go back and forth between Johnstown and and the region around Kuty.

Some immigrants from Kuty came to Fonda by train and were met by a farmer named Grannis who helped them find a house and work. Others walked all the way from New York City. Charlie Rauster's Hotel, which became the American Hotel, was the center of Slovak immigrant life. Some immigrants stayed there at first; others boarded in houses run by families who had preceded them.

Slovak immigration into Fulton County reached a peak around 1905, at which time there were already a hundred Slovak families in Johnstown. In the 1930s when immigration dwindled, more than a thousand had found homes in Fulton County. The men in the first generation in America were unskilled and found work in the local tanneries, often doing the most difficult and physically demanding tasks. At first the women—wives and unmarried sisters and daughters—found work as domestics. Bill Wormuth, whose grandfather came to Johnstown shortly after the turn of the century, remembers that this first generation was an accepted part of the community. Gradually, the second generation of women found work as makers in the glove shops, and he remembers that task stigmatized them as "dumb foreigners."

A two-story brick schoolhouse on West Main Street, built in 1860, became the James I. McMartin's Sons glove shop in 1909. After a fire in 1914, the building was purchased by the Slovak Gymnastic Union Sokol, Assembly 99. Until 1930, the building was the hub of social activities for the Slovak community as well as a theater for plays, a gym for gymnastic events, tables for pool and cards. The Slovak community built St. Anthony's Catholic Church in 1915.

Like many others whose earnings in the tanneries were limited, Slovak families were still able to accumulate money. They bought and sold land, built houses, and lived not just on the north end of town but on the streets approaching the Knox Gelatin Plant and on farmland on the very southern edge of town. All wanted their children to be educated.

Wormuth, unofficial chronicler of the Slovak community, supplied these notes as well as the information that his grandfather had brought his father and mother and eleven brothers and sisters to Johnstown. His grandmother was the first Slovak woman to drive a car. Dr. William Hesek, whose grandmother was related to Wormuth's grandfather, became the physician for the Slovak community.

The change in ethnic background between 1880 and 1910 demonstrates the change in family structure and glove workers, although a majority of the county's foreign born in 1910 were still Anglo-Saxon. The biggest difference in the county's foreign-born population came from the immigration of Italians and eastern Europeans in the first decade of the twentieth century.

For Nineteen-Thirteen

Try Fear & White gloves. There is a trade in your town or city that will appreciate F & W. Hand-wear.

Our new creations for 1913, in Cape, Kid and Suede are now ready and, as a whole, value and quality are more pronounced than ever.

Quality for quality your money can not buy better.

You can have samples

TO
FINISH

FEAR & WHITE

Makers of the Leather and the Gloves

GLOVERSVILLE, - - NEW YORK

F. SHULTS. S. DUNN. W. PERKINS.

THE RELIABLE GLOVE CO.

Successors To ROBERT REA & SON

MANUFACTURERS OF

FINE KID, CAPE and SUEDE

GLOVES

ESTABLISHED 1880

Cor. Yale Street and 4th Avenue - - - - GLOVERSVILLE, N. Y.

Expanding and Modernizing Factories

Business activity

1902

Elite Glove Company relocated from Boston and took over the Pauley factory. Elite produced primarily women's gloves of lamb and kid.

G. Spaulding Co., manufacturer of gloves, was formed with a capitalization of $50,000.

H. H. Steele with A. J. Lebenheim expanded Steele's company into the Excelsior Glove Works.

Pings and Pinner of New York City moved to Gloversville with work for 40 cutters.

1904

The Johnstown Mocha Mill, a new corporation, took over the business of Otto Geisler.

Littauer Bros. and Louis Meyer & Son added to their factories.

Jacob Adler Glove Co. added new machinery and a boiler.

1905

Bachner, Moses Co. enlarged its factory in 1905 by adding a second cutting room.

Lehr & Nelson added a floor to employ more cutters.

Hutchens & Potter doubled their space with a three-story addition.

Richard Evans & Sons (successor to R. J. & R. Evans) began building a new factory and in 1907 bought the George A. Stewart leather-dressing plant to expand its operations.

Lucas & Kennedy began building a three-story factory.

James Ireland announced plans to build more space.

Several glovemen banded together to form the Johnstown Glove Co. with eleven mills; included were David and James Ireland, George C. Potter, and Hillabrandt and Hallock.

Despite the daunting problems of heavy glove manufacturing heading west, labor unrest, and tariffs, glove manufacturers maintained a remarkable confidence in the future. Much of the expansion occurred in Gloversville. Three new firms were established in 1902 alone. Because the R. G. Dun reports after 1890 are not available to the public and almost no individual financial records have been discovered, it has been difficult to learn how these expansions were financed, however. The year-end account book of the W. N. Zimmer & Son glove firm[27] indicates large bank loans in the early twentieth century, about the time that firm expanded its glove shop. Glovemen also had to finance their purchases of raw material as well, but such details are not known. The most that can be said is that the glovemen claimed, and still do claim, that they felt that they were in partnership with their banks.

Modern technology was also incorporated into many newly built or expanded glove shops. For example, the Carmen Glove Co. was remodeled to include both electric power and lights. Electric power for lighting came to Johnstown in the form of a generator temporarily installed in the tannery owned by John Q. Adams, with the generator driven by that mill's engines. Shortly afterwards, a waterpowered electric plant was built at Cayadutta Falls, south of Johnstown. Gas continued to be used for lighting in most homes and factories. Gloversville's power company was incorporated in 1890 using steam generators and quickly began to power street lights and some industries, in particular the glove factories: within a year Gloversville factories had acquired 500 electric-powered sewing machines.

Glove factories took on a more efficient structure with most of the new buildings having sales rooms, shipping departments, and offices on the first floor, making room on the second, a cutting room on the third floor, and stock rooms on the fourth floor. In design, all the buildings remained long, thin rectangles with the smaller side facing the street and rows of windows lining the longer sides. Natural light was still essential for cutting and for making, despite the use of gaslights.

Louis Meyers and Sons modernized with a rest room for women and a smoking room for men! Obviously the wonder accompanying these improvements hints at just how primitive were the nineteenth century factories.

Expansion was not limited to Fulton County factories. Companies like James S. Ireland enlarged or relocated their New York City sales offices.

To finance the expansions, many companies, beginning in 1903, reorganized as stock companies: Among them were Northrup Glove Co. with $200,000 capital and A. S. Rosenthal as one of the principals. Daniel Hays also incorporated at this time.

Leather and skin mills expanded as well. The county was still dressing large amounts of deerskins and a new factory for that production was opened in Gloversville. The trend away from verticality in the industry is evidenced by the increasing number of leather manufacturers that were independent of glove operations. Construction of tanneries reached a peak in this period, although more new tanneries than glove shops were built in the three decades after World War I. A newspaper editor described the tanneries as "mammoth wooden structures built around the turn of the century. They hover over the small clapboard houses that are crowded together in the surrounding neighborhoods, and sometimes cast dark shadows over the lives of the working people that live in these houses."[28]

An amazing aspect of these new mills was their "modern" features. For instance, Stockamore's mill had a "slow burning" slate roof with an efficient layout capable of producing 200 dozen skins a day—tanning on the first floor, staking and finishing on the second, stock rooms on the third, and drying rooms on the fourth and attic floors. And, the men were provided with toilets and washrooms!

In 1908 expansions in the glove business reached new heights and the following year there was a veritable game of musical chairs as going concerns sought larger factories. There were too many moves to enumerate, so only the activities of the largest glove shops are listed.

From the time the Glove Manufacturers Association started publishing *The Glovers Review* in 1902, the magazine was full of elegant ads, enlivened with engravings of the proud owners' factories. Among the fanciest artwork was the advertisement of Richard Evans and Sons (successor to R. J. and R. Evans) for Revanson Gloves. It depicted their four tanneries and factories

Karg, Tomlison and Butler began building a new brick structure, and within two years, the company, now called Karg Brothers stopped producing gloves and only dressed skins.

J. H. Stockamore's new leather mill was a four-story, 50-by 100-foot structure.

Robinson Bros. large mill and Booth and Co.'s addition were started in 1902.

S. H. Shotwell took over the Filmer mill and expanded its operation to dress mocha.

Maylander Bros. built a five-story addition to their leather mill, which included a sprinkler system.

Bellis & Klein was a new partnership. The company's new building was equipped with a sprinkler system.

Lucas & Kennedy boasted that their new three-story addition had radiators.

Radford & Langford moved into a four-story building and added an elevator and "good ventilation."

A younger generation of glovemen entered new partnerships: J. A. Batty joined with Harold B. Northrup and George A. Veeder joined with L. B. Jerome.

1907

Tannert & Co expanded.

Wood & Hyde was incorporated at $200,000.

Gloversville Auto Glove incorporated at $25,000.

Not everyone fared equally well. Raymond & Hillock became Raymond and Stewart, then Stewart and Briggs, then Wm. T. Briggs alone before closing in 1907.

1908

Guaranteed Glove Co. incorporated.

Klopot Glove Co. moved a plant from Boston to Gloversville.

Fownes, the English glove firm, began building a four-story plant on South Main Street in Gloversville to accommodate its 500 workers.

Northrup Glove Co. added steam power and 70 more machines for makers.

1909

Wertheimer Glove Co. and Hayes and Gates expanded.

New incorporations: Loucks Bros. at $60,000; Empire Glove Co at $4,000; Dunham, Peck at $50,000.

C. A. McMartin & Co. joined with Lichenstein and Windsor.

Ideal Glove Co., which started in 1909, folded within a year and sold off its equipment.

1910

Expansions continued at an accelerated pace in 1910. J. H. Danforth expanded by creating space for 75 cutters; its old building was just large enough to hold the shipping department for the enlarged operation.

McDougall, Dewey, Co. was incorporated with the two principals and their wives as officers.

George A. Veeder acquired a new three-story building.

1911

V. Perrin & Cie., the French firm, announced plans to build a factory in Gloversville.

H. G. Hilts and Co. evolved from H. G. Hilts and Son and in 1914 purchased the much larger factory formerly owned by Rea and White.

Karg Bros. added a 200 HP steam boiler for a new heating system to dry leather.

1912

Laurence Mills purchased the interest of John Hayes in Hayes and Gates, forming Gates Mills, which continues to this day.

Dempster and Place acquired a three-story building next to their factory and constructed a bridge between the factory and the new annex. The addition allowed them to include a women's rest room.

Moves, additions, and consolidations affected S. Schrecker, Sutton & Hibbard, H. Higier, Wm. M. Gant, F. A. Rupert, Lebenheim & Lansing, and Imperial Glove Co.

Charles Tannert Co. was swallowed up by Lefi, Bachner, which shortly became Lefi, Bachner, Hall.

New buildings were also erected in the county's outlying villages. Among the larger was the Mayfield Glove Co., incorporated with $100,000 capital.

Cape Glace Mocha

Men's Women's Children's

Meet satisfactorily a growing demand for a better-made and better-value glove than producers have previously provided.

LITTLE'S GOOD GLOVES

are desirable and distinctive. They're made of specially selected stock and stand for quality, style, fit and superior finish.

THEY'RE OUT OF THE RANKS OF THE COMMONPLACE.

ELMER LITTLE, Manufacturer, - Johnstown, N. Y.

capable of producing buckskin, horse, and sheepskin automobile gloves and gauntlets.

Such confidence in a time when the country's population was expanding relatively slowly is amazing. Even more extraordinary is the fact that the glove shops and factories built between the late 1870s and 1915 were virtually the last new glove buildings erected until recent times, when huge warehouse-type structures were erected to accommodate the importing and distribution of foreign-made gloves. Over the years buildings have been remodeled to make them more efficient and there were a few additions, but for almost a century, no one invested in new factories. More than any other facet of the glove industry, this failure to continue building shows the way the industry had stopped expanding.

Even as a few really large firms emerged, the field of glove shops became increasingly crowded, because the expansion between 1900 and 1914 included many small- to moderate-size shops. Competition escalated so that all the manufacturers had to have felt coerced by powers outside their control. The loss of tariff protection and worker discontent in the form of strikes only made matters worse. Manufacturers survived by keeping wages down and by fighting union organization. The larger factories retaliated by trying to tighten procedures and operations, but that, as we will see, only fueled worker's discontent.

And, for all the improvements in factory construction, some of the older buildings showed their age. "Not fit for cattle or pigs" was how some cutters described their factories. "There is a lot of dust, a lot of unsanitary conditions, and right above your head, you have got rafters and lots of dust coming into your nose and lungs and the windows and shades aren't washed, I don't know when, but I do know they are dirty as rags."[29] In some factories the men worked in spring and autumn without light beyond what filtered through the side windows.[30] Gaslight, still used in many factories, was never considered adequate for cutting gloves.

Gloversville, N. Y.

"They wear out, but they take their time about it.

There's Refinement of Style, Strength of Character and Long Life in every pair of

Labor Unrest, Unions, and Early Strikes

The American Federation of Labor, formed in 1881 in Pittsburgh as the Federation of Organized Trades and organized in 1886 in Columbus, Ohio, began the fight for an eight-hour day. Starting in 1896, locals chartered by the AFL began to organize tannery workers in various parts of the leather industry. The formation of the Amalgamated Leather Workers Union of America, AFL, in 1901 grew rapidly from charters in 65 cities, two of which were Johnstown and Gloversville. In the West, the leather union staged a strike at one shoe-leather tannery with 3,000 workers, which was settled without a strike on terms that provided a nine-hour work-day with no reduction in wages and no discrimination against union men. It did not, however, grant a union shop.

AFL leadership, under Samuel Gompers, had courted big business, and after several disastrous strikes in 1903 and 1904, entered into the "Chicago agreement," which called for compulsory arbitration and peaceful settlement instead of militant actions. The union gave up the right to strike for five years. This sense of cooperation with employers and abandonment by union leaders had parallels in Fulton County. Nationally, it led to a decline in union membership. Finally, in 1913 the AFL union disbanded. Locally as well as across the country, union members in both the glove and leather industries felt they had been abandoned by the national leaders.

Labor organization had begun in the county in the 1880s under the Knights of Labor. Local unions functioned primarily to negotiate schedules with the manufacturers. The AFL began organizing county workers in the 1890s. Cutters were at the center of the county's labor unrest and union organization. The International Table Cutters Union (an independent group) began holding meetings in Fulton County in 1895. In 1897, the cutters struck for ten weeks and received a ten percent increase in the wage schedule established by the manufacturers.[31] Not only did the cutters have to "fight" for ten weeks to get the raise, they had to promise to support the tariff. "Mr. Littauer instructed us to vote for the [protective tariff], and we got the protective tariff, and we had to turn around and strike ten weeks to get a ten percent increase."[32] The men felt they had been betrayed because the manufacturers had linked their request for wages to the passage of the protective tariff and then failed to increase wages.

The International Table Cutters Union held its eighth annual meeting in Gloversville in 1902 with 200 members attending. G. H. Taylor was elected president. The reinvigorated organization reported that Fulton County workers wanted to establish a new union, the International Glove Workers of America, which would be an amalgamation of glove unions within the AFL. In January 1903, 18 delegates from Gloversville, one each from Boston and New York, and 14 from western states established the new union and Taylor became its first president.[33]

Skirmishes on the county's labor front occurred again in 1902 and early 1903. Table cutters at W. L. Sporberg Co. in Gloversville struck in early 1902, claiming their wages at that shop were 25 percent below the schedule established by the National Glove Manufacturers Association. Cutters struck Hutchens & Potter in October 1902 because they refused to work with the one nonunion man employed at the firm. Newspaper accounts supported the manufacturers: "Should the Table Cutters' union be allowed to dictate to the owner of a glove factory whom he should or should not employ? . . . The strike was recently called off by the union leaders, the one nonunion man over whom the dispute arose becoming a member afterward. . . . We understand that there are only six or seven nonunion table cutters in Fulton County, and that sixteen days' wages should be lost by union members simply because one of these nonunion men was employed, would almost be farcial were it not such a serious matter for the employees who have lost much in wages . . . No agreement was made by the fir to hire only union men or to discharge nonunion men.."[34]

There was unrest in the skins mills as well. One of the Johnstown dressing mills was struck with the claim that the current wages of $1.75 a day were below average—and they were. John Stockmore's mill was paying even less, $1.50 for a ten-hour day.

Union activity and unrest increased through 1903 in the two cities around 1903, but few of the numerous county glove unions were actually incorporated into the new International Glove Workers Union. In Gloversville the unions remained separate and included Pique Makers, Block Cutters, Silkers and End Pullers, Glover Finishers and Layers-off, Prix-seam Workers, Gauge Makers, American Table Cutters, Lockstitch Operators, Overstitch Makers, and International Glove Table Cutters. Johnstown had an office of the latter union and the Waxthread Glove Makers Union. Leather workers were represented in both cities by their respective Leather Workers Unions, and Johnstown had a separate Beam Hands Union. Each of the Gloversville unions had regular meetings, once, sometimes twice a month, and most gathered at union offices in the Littauer Building on Main Street.

The extraordinary number of unions undoubtedly represents the fact that each group identified its craft and its needs as being unique. The profusion of different unions, each negotiating a separate schedule with the manufacturers, must have seemed chaotic to the owners. The number of unions must also have rendered them individually weak, especially as only two had national affiliations. The proliferation of unions certainly strengthened manufacturers' control over wages and work policies. It was not until after World War I that the glove-worker unions consolidated into three main unions, and even these three often failed to work together until they consolidated in the late 1960s.

Fulton County unions were not only concerned with wages, but with the way wages were calculated. The industry had gradually shifted from paying a worker's grocery bills to monthly paychecks, and by 1910, almost all shops were paying workers biweekly, but never an hourly wage. Throughout the entire period and all the way through the twentieth century one practice stands out as a problem to introducing modern factory organization—piece-work pay for individual tasks. Granted, there was probably no other way to pay for work that accounted for the difference in skills among workers. And, piecework reduced manufacturers' overhead. If the piecework rate was adequate, the worker could decide how much he or she would do, hence the manufacturer's needs were not paramount. A worker who found the rates too low had to work as fast and as long as possible, provided there was work.

A loose confederation of manufacturers had joined together in the early 1890s to establish a schedule for piecework for cutters and makers throughout the industry. Schedules for different tasks were established and published in the early 1890s. A schedule for 1893 lists rates per dozen for table cutting, without differentiating between the types of leather. The schedule also gives various rates for silking and sewing or making gloves using different techniques—overstitch, pique, etc. Fine handwork was listed on the schedule, with rates given for different types of hemming and hand sewing. The copy of the schedule we have has many amounts crossed out; the new penciled rates are all higher for women's work, and cutters' rates are unchanged.

According to one manufacturer, schedules were established because "as the business developed and increased in size and importance and people became more generally employed the factories that were running regularly all the year around felt that it would be a better thing for the manufacturer and a better thing for the employee to have regular weekly rates of wages and out of that was developed the schedule."[35] However, even among association members there were minor variations in parts of the scale. Non-association members adhered loosely to the schedule, but were much more likely to offer smaller wages. From the time the first schedules were published, manufacturers, even those who were members of the associations, granted different rates to workers. This was done to reward better workers, compensate for slow times, and many other reasons; but if the workers who did not benefit discovered the variations, the practice often created bad feelings

The industry used such complicated schedules because there was no other way to account for the different elements of the craft and the skills they required. This is a further indication of how glove-making differed from the requisites of industrial factory practices "where the making of a product has been broken into myriad tasks, where each worker knows but one task and needs little or no training to master it."[36]

There were small adjustments to the wage schedule—some up, some down—between 1897 and early 1903. For example, block cutters at the Johnstown Glove Co. returned to work in January 1903 after a month-long strike; they gained minor changes in the schedule that included a 15-minute "coffee and bun break."[37]

Five hundred block cutters struck firms in both cities in March of 1903. Manufacturers offered a wage of $2.00 a day, although a few factories were

Partial 1893 Schedule
Fulton County Museum

DECEMBER 11, 1893.

TABLE CUTTING.

Item	Rate
All Men's, Ladies', Misses', Youth's, or Cadets', not over four-inch top of Imported or Domestic Lamb or Sheep, Colored or Cr[illegible]an, Suedes or Mocha Castor, rags out (that is, skins cutting less than a pair), whether for inseam, overseam, pique or any other kind of sewing, with bindings or gores, thumb quirk or English thumb, including bell or flare tops, whether with ridele or blue mark including numbering and sizing, but without punching of thumbs, fourchettes and hands	.70

EXTRAS.

Item	Rate
Punching and trimming thumbs and fourchettes	.10
Punching and trimming thumbs, fourchettes and gloves	.20
Finger quirks	.05
Laps	.03
Coltskin, Calfskin and Buckskin	.15
For each extra two inches of length	.15
Cutting mochas, rags included	.05
Mitts, thumbs not punched	.55
Mitts, thumbs punched	.60
Mitts, thumbs and hands punched	.65
All Boys' gloves and mitts 10c. less than above.	
Lamb linings	.50
Ladies' gauntlets with small cuff, thumbs and fourchettes punched	.90
" " " large " thumbs and fourchettes punched	1.00
(If Ladies' gauntlets are bound, 5 cents extra.)	

DOWLING.

Item	Rate
Per dozen gloves, four inch top	.25
" " " four to eight inch top	.37 1-2
" " " eight to twelve inch top	.50
" " " Colt skin	.35

MAKING OUTSEAM, TRIMMED.

Item	Rate
Gloves not hemmed, with or without quirk	.80
" all outseam, extra	.20
" combination backs, extra	.20
" Tilbury extra	.20
Mitts, men's or ladies', with or without slits	.30
" Boys', with or without slits	.25

MAKING PIQUE GLOVES.

Item	Rate
Fitting up without quirks	.50
" " with quirks	.60
Closing	.75
Mitts, half price of gloves.	

MACHINES AND POWER.

All machines owned by manufacturer to be rented at 40c. per week and kept in good order at operator's expense. Power to be charged at 40c. per week.

Fine Table Cut Work. Making Inseam.

THUMBS AND FOURCHETTES TRIMMED IN UNLINED.

Item	Rate
Unlined, hemmed once or twice in shop	.75
" if hemmed on overstitch, less	.05
Quirks, stitched twice extra	.10
Ladies' gauntlets, for hands only	.55
" " " cuffs, hemmed	.35
" " bound	.40
Lined gloves, made with linings complete	.80

already paying $2.40 a day (wages, however, ranged as low as $1.62 a day.) In May, the block cutters were still out on strike and the table and pull-down[38] cutters were locked out. A stalemate had developed.[39] In March, shortly after the strike began, a group of cutters organized the Co-operative Glove Company in an attempt to compete with existing manufacturers and thus put added pressures on the owners.[40]

The manufacturers were sufficiently pressed by the union wage demands that it is no coincidence that the beginning of the strike marks the virtual end of all manufacturing of cheaper grades of gloves in Fulton County. The wages demanded by the cutters were greater than the manufacturers' profits.[41] Since work gloves could be produced more cheaply out West, the county's manufacturers had no choice but to focus on the more expensive dress gloves.

Labor problems engulfed the glove industry across the entire country. Manufacturers in Chicago retaliated by instituting a policy of no vacations, fines for being late for work, and an absolute guarantee of an open shop. These events were duly noted in Fulton County.[42]

In Fulton County, the strike of pull-down cutters and the lockout of block and table cutters was ended on June 3, 1903, when the International Table Cutters and American Table Cutters rescinded a no-cut order for buckskin gloves and agreed to arbitrate the other matters. The shops reopened.[43]

The agreement for arbitration was similar to that agreed to by AFL leather workers nationally. In the uniform settlement, Johnstown cutters benefited the most. Workers on many types of gloves were accorded raises in fixed daily rates and the block cutters' day was fixed at ten hours during the week and nine hours on Saturday. The New York State Department of Labor estimated that $300,000 in wages had been lost in the eleven weeks of the summer 1903 strike. After fourteen weeks, the strikers each received only $16 from their union.[44]

Labor strife continued nationally in other industries as well, most notably in coal mining. Unrest was spreading again in western glove manufacturers

Partial 1904 Schedule
Fulton County Museum

..SCHEDULE OF..

Prices for Table Cutting

Adopted by The Fulton County Glove Manufacturers' Association.

This Schedule to be in Effect From December 21, 1903, to December 21, 1904.

Imported or Domestic Kid or Suedes,	$ .88
Mocha Castor or Mocha Reindeer, or Friezed Lamb or Sheep, but not more than two rags cutting less than a pair of gloves may be included in each dozen skins,	.93½
Mocha Castor. Reindeer, or Friezed Lamb, if for Lamb or Fur Lined Gloves, or where two inches or more of extra leather is required,	1.03½
Craven Tan, Napa, or Dipped Lamb or Sheep,	.95
Craven Tan, Napa, or Dipped Lamb or Sheep, if for Lamb or Fur Lined Gloves,	1.05
Real Kid, or Goat and Deerskins,	1.00
Indian Tanned Deerskins,	.95
Little Jacks,	1.20
Cabretta and Mocha Kid,	.99
Coltskin,	1.10
Calfskin,	1.05
Chamois or Fleshers, White, Smoked, Light Fawn, or Dipped Mode colors,	.84
All other colors including Pearl,	.88
Ladies' Wide Cuff Gauntlets, flare included, but not bound,	1.20
Ladies' Wide Cuff Gauntlets, flare included, including binding,	1.25
Ladies' Gaunts, with cuff up to 2½ inches wide, including flare,	1.05
Automobile Gaunts, not combination,	1.50
For Dowling the Cuffs of Ladies' Gaunts, extra,	.10
All Mittens 18 cents per dozen less than corresponding gloves.	
Boys' Gloves not to exceed 8½ inches of leather for lined or 8 inches for unlined and 2¾ inches in top length, nor cut on cadet patterns,	.80
Gloves and Mittens of German Deer, 16½ cents per dozen above price paid for cutting Mocha.	
Cutting Lamb Linings,	.70
Cutting Fur Linings,	1.00

and manufacturers anticipated trouble would erupt in the fall.[45] Chicago was called a "hotbed of union labor."[46] Workers there wanted a schedule patterned after the scale adopted in Fulton County. When a strike was called it quickly fizzled out—two Chicago manufacturers decided to move to Wisconsin.

In November Fulton County's glove manufacturers decided to put off adopting the schedule that had been proposed in the arbitration settlement until the men agreed to an open shop. As in the rest of the country, the true reason for the unrest emerged: Manufacturers wanted a non-discrimination clause and the unions did not and this forced a strike. When the cutters began the strike for a union shop, the union claimed that only two table cutters were not members of their organization. The manufacturers replied that they would not deal with the union until there was an agreement "whereby there shall be no discrimination between union and nonunion workers."[47] The cutters refused to work with men who were not members of the union. The shops closed again—the lockout that lasted from December 21, 1903 until June of 1904.

The employers saw the union demands as workers wanting "to operate their own factories and hire their own workmen."[48] *The Glovers Review* reported that employers had "advanced wages," creating the best-paid skilled workmen in the United States, with clean sanitary workrooms, and pay twice a month in full. Whether or not this was true, the manufacturers believed in their own benevolence. The manufacturers claimed that the International Table Cutters Union (ITCU) had increased the initiation fee for membership to $100, a rate so high it would deter any more table cutters from coming to Fulton County.[49] In February of that year, factories were advertising for nonunion cutters.

Employers began to place orders with foreign firms as there was no sign of a settlement. The strike/lockout dragged on for months until April, when a few (no more than 50) cutters returned to work. In May foreign orders for the fall season were so large that it was estimated that no more than 50 percent of the cutters could find work if they wanted. The strike had actually stimulated imports of foreign-made gloves and manufacturers were worried that "foreign houses would obtain almost entire control" of the country's glove market.[50]

In May, the Glove Manufacturers Association announced that there would be no further dealings with the International Table Cutters Union, that current schedules would be maintained, that there would be no shop committees and no collection of dues in the factories. A resolution by association members, announced in May 1904, left no susbsequent room for negotiation: "No further conferences will be held with the representatives of the Table Cutters' union on matters connected with the present strike, no matter how long it may last."

On June 28, the strike/lockout was finally called off. The manufacturers were pleased that they were able to "maintain the open shop, the only real issue of this unpleasant controversy."[51]

Before 1904, the union had a relatively strong organization with, they claimed, 98 percent of the table cutters. The cutters felt they could take any grievances to a factory and "most invariably it was always settled agreeably."

As a result of the strike of 1904, the union was left powerless. *The Glovers Review*, in noting that the ITCU voted to reinstate all union members who had returned to work before the strike was called off, had made a "pitiful confession of weakness. In fact, it seems almost like an informal dissolution of the union. . . . There is obviously an end of all discipline and consequent power of the union."[52] *The Glovers Review* quoted at length a *New York Times* editorial that assured the glove manufacturers that they were not alone in the struggle to maintain an open shop policy. Noting that there were 7,000 members of the Boiler Maker's Union on strike in the New York City shipyards, the editorial came out against closed shops, stating "the demand is one impossible of recognition by either labor or employers of labor."[53]

In 1914, one cutter recalled the results of the earlier strike, "It was a curse on the people. It seems to me that the manufacturers are taking advantage of us, we being weaker . . . because we are divided now. I say it is worse than civilized warfare. The defeated country cannot be oppressed. Because we have been defeated ten years ago, we are oppressed."[54]

James S. Ireland, a member of the association, conceded that the breaking up of the union in 1904 "broke up all direct conference between the employers and the employees." On the other hand, the cutters believed that the association was not formed to take united action on tariff matters, but "primarily to crush the union. . . . [In 1904], the manufacturers starved the workers into submitting to nonunion conditions."[55]

Between June and December almost all cutters were laid off. This layoff occurred at the time the Wilson tariff bill was before Congress. When the men were called back to the shops, they were told they "could resume work, but at a reduction." In 1905 four or five shops struck again and recovered some of the reductions in wages. Sporadic strikes affected tanners and skin dressers—the knee stakers at Johnstown Mocha Mill struck in August 1905, opposing the replacement of pay based on piecework with a wage of $2.00 a day.

When the union lost its fight for a closed shop, union strength declined. In the 1903-04 strike for a union shop, the parent AFL craft union abandoned the local. By September of 1905, the International Glove Workers of America held its annual meeting in Chicago, not Fulton County. The next year it was held in Milwaukee, and Gloversville had lost the national headquarters of the union to Chicago. "Westerners agreed that the industry is rapidly spreading to the middle west."[56] The cutters felt the union had deserted and betrayed them, and as a result the struggle for greater wages and a resurgence of union organization was pushed into the background until 1913.

Unions were losing battles for union shops all across the country, and workers were struggling to share the wealth created by their efforts. The country as a whole was undergoing a movement toward socialism. The glove industry was still in its infancy after the Civil War when union formation and strikes became prevalent in other, more mature industries. This lag in the glove industry's development in comparison with the growth of the shoe or textile industries undoubtedly delayed any union movement in Fulton County. Union activity in the county might have increased after 1900 even without the influx of immigrants and their concepts of social justice. But it is probably no coincidence that glove workers began to protest their conditions about the same time there was a major shift in the ethnicity of both manufacturers and cutters. Certainly some of labor unrest in Fulton County can be attributed to the new immigrants among the cutters and to union struggles elsewhere.

The Fulton County Glove Manufacturers Association

In December of 1902, the Glove Manufacturers Association was reconstituted with the primary goal of securing high tariffs on gloves manufactured in Europe. They claimed their members included three-fourths of the glove and mitten manufacturers in the county representing 80 percent of the county's glove production. (This figure may be questionable in light of a statement in 1914 that the association members produced fewer gloves than non-association manufacturers. In reality, the industry was so secretive that no one knew.) In actuality, there were about 30 active member firms, and although many of the county's larger shops were included, the claim they represented 80 percent of the county's production is certainly an exaggeration.

One member, Abraham Lehr, president of Dempster & Place, later (circa 1914) estimated that firms in the Association produced 40 percent of the county's gloves, though others claimed the percentage was much higher. The county's larger firms accounted for 50 percent of the total production, and a number of the larger firms were not in the Association. Among them were Louis Meyers & Son, Fownes, Hallock & Stewart, Lehr & Nelson, and Lefi, Bachner, Hall.

In 1905 a permanent secretary was hired. Meetings appeared to have been social events with no records of issues discussed. Tributes to departed members, like recognition in 1908 of M. S. Northrup and George Hilts, were duly noted in *The Glovers Review*, which, although independent of the Association, always reflected the organization's views.

The Glovers Review was a strange journal, full of elaborate advertisements, notes on salesmen's trips, news of promotions and bankruptcies in the industry, glowing descriptions of new buildings, history and lore on gloves and their manufacture, fashion tips on wearing gloves, import data on gloves and leather, details on tariffs, and talk of shortages of workers and leather. By 1902 so much of the industry was moving west that the vast majority of notes on new factories dealt with events outside Fulton County. There was scant mention of any labor unrest.

Glovers, especially in Johnstown, were a close-knit group socially. Marriages solidified that structure; for instance in just a year or so after the turn of the century, Carrie McMartin married Richard Evans, James M. Evans married Nellie Ireland, E. C. Shotwell married Katherine Argersinger, and a grandson of Alanson Judson married a daughter of P. P. Argersinger. All these marriages were duly noted in *The Glovers Review*.

Expressing the glovers' confidence, the *Review* enlarged its format in 1910, but the content on its glossy sheets was little changed.

The newly strengthened association also continued to fix rates for piecework in meetings with committees of the various unions, a process which grew more cumbersome with each schedule revision. For instance, the schedules for table cutting established in 1900 and 1904 gave different rates for various types of skins as well as for different styles. Every step in making a glove was negotiated individually. This complex system of determining wages outlived the association.

The roster of 32 firms in the Association in 1904:

Jacob Adler & Co.
J. C. Allen & Son
P. P. Argersinger & Co.
Bachner-Moses
G. C. Berry
Clark, Easterly & Co.
J. H. Decker, Son & Co.
Dempster & Place
Elite Glove
R. Evans & Sons
Fear & White
Hutchens & Potter
G. H. Hilts & Son
Ireland Brothers
Kibbe & Radford
Lucas & Kennedy
Lehr & Nelson
Littauer Brothers
Mason, Campbell & Co.
G. W. Mandrill
Wm. McDougall
J. P. Miller & Co.
Northrup Glove Mfg.
J. A. & A. V. Quackenbush
Rea, White & Carter
T. E. Ricketts & Son
The Spaulding Co.
Streeter, Hackney & Co.
Schwartz, Schiffer & Co.
Charles Tannert
The Daniel Hays Co.
Louis Meyers & Son

Changes in the Industry

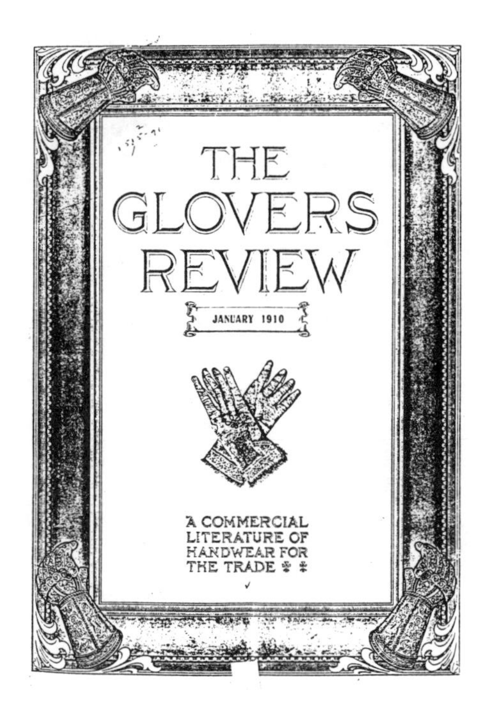

"Changes in the industry" is almost a euphemism for how the glove business matured. Changes occurred at a turtle-like pace. Glovemen were constrained by traditions from their fathers and their fathers' fathers. Fulton County developed connections with the rest of the country, but in many ways remained a provincial backwater. The elegant New York City showrooms contrasted sharply with the dusty factories wallowing in both custom and leather scraps. The long period (1890-1915) with little change in the economy and very slow growth in the cost of living only exaggerated the glove manufacturers' fear of adopting new ways in selling or manufacturing. It was only the few aggressive entrepreneurs, mostly in Gloversville, who were able to bring initiative to the industry. The county displayed a conservatism, perhaps born on the Anglo-Saxon origins of its leaders, that proved a drawback both to the worker and to the manufacturer.

Glovemen had been selling gloves by the dozen in standard monetary units (viz. $9.50 a dozen or $10.00 a dozen, but never $9.73 a dozen) for so long that they would not cut prices even by a few cents. This practice permeated the retail market. A glove should cost $1.00 or $1.50 or even $2.00, but not until much later could it cost $1.69. No one believed these strange practices could or should be changed. Despite efforts to standardize sizes, retailers still complained about the lack of standard measurements for gloves.[57]

Even stranger, and more difficult to deal with, was the tradition of revolving sales and accepting returns of unsold merchandise. A manufacturer would guarantee the retailer that unsold gloves could be returned at the end of the winter season. The gloves could be shipped out again, if styles did not change too radically and if the gloves were not dirty or shopworn, but the manufacturer, not the retailer, bore the expense of poor sales. Oddly enough, this method of sales persists today among the few remaining Fulton County glove firms. Book publishers in this country accept returns, but the practice does not occur in any other branch of the clothing industry.

Traditionally glove manufacturers had taken orders far in advance with the distribution of goods made chiefly through wholesalers. There was a long evolution from this practice to that of selling direct from the factory to the retailers. This advance required a more expeditious production of goods than the manufacturers could accommodate.[58] The retailers were notorious for placing orders late. Glovemen either had to gamble on the rate of future sales and buy expensive leather on speculation or risk not being able to fill orders in the Christmas rush. Either way, workers were often unemployed or not fully employed in late winter into spring and compelled to work longer hours in the fall.

The Glovers Review noted in 1902 that most factories used systems and methods "in vogue dozens of years ago." It was not until the summer of 1902 that shops began to close on Saturday afternoons in June, July, and August. Shops did not even offer time for a coffee break until after a strike of block cutters at the Johnstown Glove Co. in 1903. One of the goals of the 1903 strike was a ten-hour day. (The state's "54-hour law" limited work hours and in 1912 was amended to include hours for women and children.)

Throughout this period, many smaller firms went out of business in the few years before 1903 as the whole industry was consolidated into fewer and fewer companies.

A few glove firms tried to expand the tradition of close relations between owners and employees into a more modern organizational structure. For instance, when Northrup Glove Co. incorporated in 1903, it tried to enlist the heads of departments and other employees as stockholders, to "secure the earnest cooperation" of its workers.

Making had always been women's work and required great manual dexterity, but the heavier parts of the process were done in the factories, and the term "operators" came into vogue to replace "makers." A few men were even employed as operators.[59] Still, the bulk of the manufacturers continued to save capital by not providing machine space and thus continuing homework over which manufacturers had little control. Furthermore, unlike shoe manufacturing, in the glove business machines never replaced handwork totally.

In an effort to improve their business operations, manufacturers struggled to overcome the seasonality of the business so they could offer steady employment. This proved to be an almost impossible task. Because retailers never ordered gloves for the following winter until late spring or summer, salesmen were not even sent out during the winter months. Factories were more than busy in summer when workers wished for time off, and work continued heavily into fall, when many men wanted to go hunting. Many factories closed for a week in summer, and all closed in December when the push was over, partly for the holidays, partly for inventory, and partly because there was little work.

The seasonality of work had suited the factories—in winter they were dark. Cutters and makers could not see well, and those companies with buildings that depended on natural light went to much shorter days. In the mid 1890s, many shops operated for only seven months, some for eight, and a few of the biggest shops for nine months.

In being able to offer work for the whole year, as some tried to do around 1910, the manufacturers believed they had raised workers' wages without increasing the rate at which they were paid. "The systematic employment in all the factories here, due to steady work, running 50 weeks per year, has made a very large increase in the income of all the operators, not only cutters and sewers."[60] George Potter of Hutchens & Potter believed that the cutters' earning capacity had actually doubled between 1897 and 1914 because his shop was able to offer steady employment. He noted that his profits as a manufacturer had shown no such gain.

Irelands, which kept a record of its cutters and had a stable workforce so comparisons could be made, had documentation to show the wages of its cutters "were practically doubled" between 1896 and 1913. The cost of living nationally rose 18 percent between 1900 and 1913 and at the same time the wages for union manufacturing jobs rose about the same percentage. For nonunion jobs the percentage rise almost doubled as well, but the average weekly pay was half that for union jobs. A cutter's weekly pay was halfway between that of union and nonunion manufacturing workers nationally.

At best, only a few manufacturers were able to offer employment for 48 weeks. Running a business that operated 48 or at most 50 weeks out of 52 was difficult for the manufacturer. It was very hard on the workers; only a few of them—the best workers—enjoyed full, year-round employment.

Even as the manufacturers struggled to offer steady work, many cutters had no work from January to July in the last years before World War I. Others cutters had to accept lower wages to continue working when business was slow. In the smaller shops this seasonality was much more pronounced than in the larger shops.

An owner of a silk mill was critical of practices in the glove industry. He summarized his observations in an address to the Glove Manufacturers Association. He deplored the way the locals clung to

> *their old ways of making leather gloves, until that branch of the trade has been lost to the west. Glovemakers who emigrated west took along a knowledge of the business, but they also took along a disposition to welcome innovation. The Gloversville pieceworkers are independent. They consider that as long as their employer is not paying them for their time, they are at liberty to come and go as they see fit. Not so in the west. The western manufacturer figures his shop space worth so much, and demands that pieceworkers and all others work steadily at their benches the entire day. As a result, they have gotten greater production. Then they are near to the leather tanneries. Now they even ship and sell coarse gloves in the east.*[61]

Fulton County's tradition of piecework rates and independent contractors, which marked the industry in its early years, gave way to a form of independence that did not lead to modern factory organization. This lack of organization limited both owners and workers.

One small step toward organization came as shops began to specialize on different operations. This separation of work into different types of shops became even more pronounced in future years. Gloves were sent to special shops, some of them quite small, for different tasks like making and laying-off, or those like hemming, silking, and sewing buttonholes that remained handwork operations. The nature of the industry limited real organization of factory work beyond the 1880s factory design which placed different operations on descending floors to create a smooth flow from leather to glove. The workers, especially the cutters, faced too many variables, so it was not possible to quantify standards. Cutting—and sewing—remained an art and a craft. It never became manufacturing in the sense that machines operated by a handful of workers were dominant.

The larger manufacturers expanded their sales forces, often maintaining salesmen who traveled for many months during the year and sold gloves on a commission basis. A few firms had as many as four salesmen covering different regions of the country.

Many firms also maintained sales rooms in New York City. Sam Goldwyn (formerly Goldfish) moved from the position of foreman at Bachner-Moses to New York City, where in 1911 he was in charge of the Elite Glove Company's office.

BACMO WASH
LEATHER GLOVES

Bachner-Moses-Louis Co.
Manufacturers of BACMO Gloves
Gloversville, -:- New York

Even with all the new factories, fires continued to plague the county's glove and leather manufacturers. Coal-fired boilers and heating systems were prone to fires. The tanneries were most apt to burn and their stored chemicals and inventories made the fires more devastating: the Lebenheim, Karg & Fennel, and Maylander mills burned, with destruction of all skins, most of which were not owned by the mills, but were being tanned under contract for different glove firms. One of the largest fires was at the G. Levor tannery (pictured) in 1913, in which the mill was totally destroyed. A short time later, in December 1913, the G. F. Troutwine mill caught fire. This could have been as disastrous a fire as the Levor tannery, but the blazes were limited by an automatic sprinkler system.

Over three dozen fires occurred in glove and leather shops between 1900 and 1914, nine alone in glove shops in 1911. Even the Fulton County Glue Factory burned with a loss of upwards of $100,000. The Adams tannery in Johnstown burned in 1917 in one of the worst fires that had ever occurred in that city. The mill, considered one of the best equipped in the county, was leveled and the loss exceeded $300,000.[i]

Few fires were of suspicious origins, and most owners just started over, either at other sites or in new mills. Almost all fires were partially, if not totally, covered by insurance. This was an expense all the owners had finally accepted, but as *The Glovers Review* observed, "despite being covered by insurance, the interruption, as in all such cases, must be borne by the firm."[ii]

That fires were of great concern is shown by a magnificent folio of maps, printed in 1905, which identifies each building in Gloversville, its source of power, presence of night watchmen, and location of outbuildings. This was all the information needed by fire companies to quickly address an alarm.

Gloversville City Archives

Between 1890 and 1915, the glove industry spawned two new and related industries. Knitting mills, one of which remains a part of the county's economy today, began as the industry needed knitted silk both for ladies' gloves and for linings for leather gloves. This important component of the county's manufacturing began in 1893, when John P. Shanahan and Thomas Kyne started the first silk mill in the D. B. Judson shop in Kingsboro. A series of retirements, new partners, expansions, and reorganizations culminated in 1906 with the formation of the Gloversville Silk Mill, which continued until it was sold to the Van Raalte Co. and moved to New Jersey.

Silk for linings became so important in the 1890s that other mills were started. George and William Holmes and Alec Crounse formed the Fulton County Silk Mill, also in Kingsboro, in 1901. After Ernest Jones joined the company, he and William Holmes built the brick structure on Kingsboro Avenue that today houses several small leather and fabric businesses.

The Gloversville Textile Company was in operation for a decade before it moved to Tonawanda, New York, to become the Niagara Silk Mill. The Normandie Silk Mill, run by James and George Batty, also operated for just over a decade. The Cayadutta Knitting Company in nearby Fonda was rescued from bankruptcy with new money from the Littauer brothers, who became principal owners.

The Johnstown Knitting Mill was established in 1893 by William Wooster and John G. Ferres and later William T. Briggs joined the firm. The 40 by 200-foot brick building continues to serve as the company's headquarters, in which members of the Briggs family are still principals.[64]

Growth of the knitting industry was limited by the way the glove industry permeated every facet of local business. A representative of the Gloversville Knitting Company, E. M. Slayton, told a group in Milwaukee that Fulton County's glove industry so totally dominated the local economy that he had had to move part of his knitting business to Oneonta, New York.

Also in this period, a second major business arose to support the glove industry's growing need for machines and dies. H. J. Anthony Glove Tool Manufacturing Co. dates back to 1893, Curtin & Hebert to before 1903.

The companies merged in 1913 into Curtin-Hebert-Anthony, then became Curtin-Hebert, the largest concern of its kind in the county. The company started out manufacturing cutting dies for gloves. It pioneered in designing and manufacturing steam laying-off tables. In 1903 it also produced buffing machines, finishing forms, sueding machines, stretchers, trimmers, and sewing machines. One of the company's innovations was a mechanism that could turn sewn gloves right side out with a blast of forced air. The company later developed clickercutting machines, and repaired all kinds of machines required for glovemaking. (Curtin-Hebert was still in business in 1998, making dies. In later years, as the industry required fewer dies, the firm branched out into the manufacturing of tools and machines for other industries.)

Other related businesses

Box-making waxed and waned with the glove industry. At least eight box makers were in business in the two cities in the early 1900s, two in Johnstown (G. Johnson and S. E. Trumbull) and six in Gloversville (J. W. Sisson, Charles F. Allen, J. E. Brown, J. H. Drake, H. VanAntwerp, and F. Wurtzburder).[3]

A half dozen businesses provided the glove industry with thread, several others sold lining materials and woven labels, fasteners, and buttons.

GLOVE CITY CUTTING DIE AND MACHINE WORKS.

Illustrated & Descriptive Gloversville & Johnstown, 1907

Living and Working in the County

The housing pattern in Fulton County strongly favored single or two-family homes. In 1890, the county had 7,627 dwellings housing 9,181 families, with an average of nearly five people per dwelling and just over four people per family. This equates to 1.2 families per dwelling, well below the state average of 1.5 families per dwelling.[65] Even the two-family houses were separated by small yards bordered by tree-lined streets. Compare this with the families of garment or glove workers in New York City who lived in multi-storied tenements or tight rows of brownstones.

Johnstown had one multiple-family frame dwelling on William Street. Known as the "Wayne Arms," this ten-apartment structure was built in the 1870s. (It had so deteriorated by the 1930s that all signs of its original elegance had disappeared.) It stood next to a two-family brick structure that resembled a New York City brownstone. Five double-family structures were built side by side on Washington Street to form worker housing that later became known as "the ten commandments." (This too became a slum before World War II.) Both were substantial dwellings when they were built. Except for two-family dwellings with one floor for each family, there were very few other multiple-family structures in either town.

In Fulton County housing costs remained relatively steady in the interval between 1890 and 1915. A worker's home was typically in a two-family frame structure, with two, occasionally three, bedrooms on each floor. The buildings were substantial enough that many of them survive. The rent for one floor was about $12 a month. Of the nearly 10,000 homes in the two cities in 1910, 59 percent were rented.

Two thousand dollars would buy a decent single-family home. Many sold for between $1,700 and $1,800, but that represented three times a cutter's annual wage. One elderly cutter (73 years) was still working in 1914 because even though he owned "a little cottage," he had no other savings. A worker could become a homeowner with a payment of $50 and the assumption of a large mortgage. Still, 24 percent of the homes were owned free and clear by the occupant, and only 17 percent of the homeowners had mortgages.

Factory workers waiting for the trolley on a cold, wet day circa 1900.
Gloversville City Archives

I have no money in the house. I owe the butcher and the grocer. I wish Saturday would never come. I never have any money.
Cutter at the 1914 Hearing

The owners with mortgages did not consider they owned their homes. They paid about $10 a month interest on their mortgages, a total of $30 a year for taxes, so that with upkeep, the cost of owning was about the same as renting. However, the prospects of owning a home outright were dim.

Housing problems were especially severe for large families—those with three or more children could not find places to rent. Heads of large families felt they had to buy a home although they knew they could never pay for it. Many cutters thought that "the houses own the cutters," not the other way around; they thought the houses would prove "a millstone around their necks for the rest of their lives."[66]

Workers' homes in Gloversville seemed to cluster near the center of town, in an area north of Burr Hill (which later became Meyers Park), near the Cayadutta Creek and the mills, west of Broad Street, and along Spring Street and its intersecting streets. By 1905 a small Jewish enclave was developing east of the armory. It was the next decade before eastern European immigrants made inroads in the community. Originally, they clustered on Market Street close to their house of worship, which was led by Abraham Zuckerwar. Zuckerwar helped form the Knesseth Israel congregation and raise funds for the building of the synagogue. According to Herbert Engel, who grew up near the synagogue, there was never a ghetto; Jewish residents lived throughout Gloversville, except on the west side, choosing sites as close to their places of employment as possible.

Tannery owner Gustav Levor built this fine home on Prospect Avenue in 1892.
Gloversville City Archives

In contrast, before 1905, some of the old-guard glovemen had joined other Gloversville businessmen in creating a few streets of beautifully well-built larger homes. These lined Kingsboro Avenue from Fulton Street to Second Avenue and graced the adjoining sections of First and Second Avenues. The houses along Kingsboro were set back from the street, emphasizing the elegance of these stately buildings. Among the glovemen who built in this area were two members of the Judson family and A. J. Zimmer and G. M. Place. Other fine homes belonging to glovemen were spread through the town, such as the Heacock homes and the estate of D. B. Judson in Kingsboro, the Dempster and Stewart homes on Bleecker Street, and the McNab home on Fulton Street.

Lucius Littauer lived on South Main not far from the homes of the Churchills and Zimmers. The wealthier Jewish residents built along North and South Park streets, but with no great concentration of showier homes. In fact, the wealthiest of the German Jews, like Nathan Littauer's son Lucius, kept apartments in New York City. For them, even the best locations in Gloversville were still a provincial backwater.

Large amount of the industry is in the hands of home workers, both in the town and country districts.
Encyclopedia Britanica, 1911, *under* Gloversville

As a footnote to the growth of Gloversville, it is interesting to observe that through the 1880 and 1890s very few streets were paved and most of these were lined with cedar blocks. Bricks were only used to pave the major thoroughfares. It wasn't until 1912 that 1.5 of the city's 51 miles of streets received a concrete pavement, though by then cement sidewalks were common along most streets, even the remaining dirt tracks.

In Johnstown, workers' homes were everywhere except along the heights of South William Street and some of its cross streets. By 1905, South William Street, a broad thoroughfare lined with majestic elms, had a magnificient row of elegant homes built by glovemen such as Robert and Richard Evans, J. P and P. P. Argersinger, J. Ricketts, J. Northrup, and the Irelands, Kennedys, and Woosters. Uphill and just around the corner from William Street stood the Knox Mansion, Rose Hill. To this day, the fine woodwork, stained-glass windows, elegant main staircases, tall windows, and broad porches of these graceful homes express the wealth and good taste of the city's conservative glovemen.

Homework in the county expanded even as the number of factories increased. There are figures to show the number of women in factories, but only rough estimates of the number of homeworkers. Single women often started in factories, married, and after the birth of children began sewing at home. Older women preferred to sew at home. Spinsters and widows chose either factory or homework at will. As children left home, women returned to the factories. But, both classes of workers shared a basic commonality: they remained very independent employees.

Women were appointed to supervise factory making rooms. Two women owned glove shops in the years around 1900: Mrs. F. Beach and Mrs. I. A. Leonard of Gloversville.

All machines owned by manufacturers to be rented at 40 cents per week and kept in good order at operators expense. Power to be charged at 40 cents per week.
December 11, 1893 Schedule printed by the Glove Manufacturers Association of Fulton County.

Women who worked at home used treadle machines or did the handwork that was essential to fine gloves: silking, hemming, making buttonholes, pulling ends, and so on. With the the advent of electric power around 1890, women in factories used electric-powered machines, but it was another decade or more before women working at home had them. After the turn of the century, electricity became available to private homes and women began to use and, on rare occasions, acquire power-driven machines, buying them outright. A few manufacturers sold women machines, making deductions from the womens' earnings to pay for them over time. Most factories loaned machines to home workers.[67] A few factories made women financially responsible for repairs to their machines. Through 1900 and into the next two decades much homework was still handwork, but women were acquiring machines at such a rate that by 1911 there were 1,300 electric motors powering machines in private homes.[68]

Manufacturers still delivered packets of cut gloves and later picked up the sewn gloves. Many people who grew up in Johnstown or Gloversville and who were interviewed for this book remember pulling coaster wagons of cut gloves home to their mothers. Among those who did this was Charles Noxon, who became a professor of geography at the University of Maine.

Johnstown Historical Society

In the years between 1890 and 1915, more than three times as many women as men worked in the glove industry, but the number of women factory workers was roughly equal to the number of male employees.

Notice how many of the women's surnames appear to be Irish.

Johnstown Historical Society

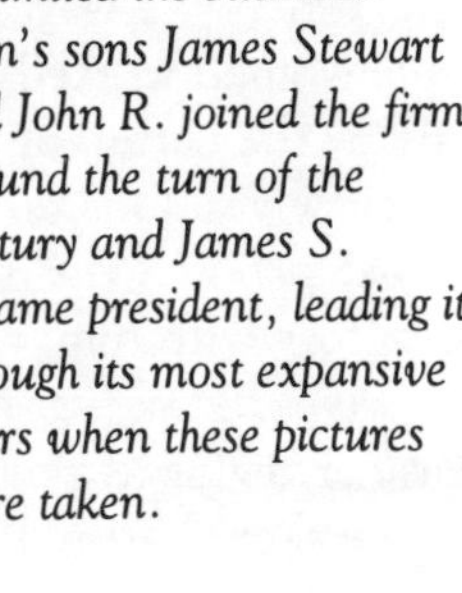

James, John Stuart, and David Ireland founded Ireland Brothers in 1875. John died in 1891 and the remaining brothers continued the business. John's sons James Stewart and John R. joined the firm around the turn of the century and James S. became president, leading it through its most expansive years when these pictures were taken.

Johnstown Historical Society

Johnstown Historical Society

Some women were more adept at sewing and were able to earn reasonable wages working at home. Some women with large families had to work long hours to do both housework and homework. Others only worked until they earned what they needed, and manufacturers had to hustle to find workers when there were large orders. Almost none of the women found employment year-round. They faced uncertainty, times of unemployment, and occasional long hours. Some felt pressed to work such long hours as to conjure images of garment-industry sweatshops, but these were the exception, not the rule.

The result of the variability of women's work was that manufacturers had little control over their work force. Manufacturers had to work hard to keep the best makers and find new ones. The uncertainty of the work force was taxing for all the glovemen.

As factories grew, so did the role of working wives. When the wages of working men, especially cutters, declined, more and more women worked out of necessity and not just for extra money. The testimony by the cutters at the strike hearing in 1914 is a mine of information about their wives. One cutter claimed that for every worker in a glove shop who had a home the wife would either "be working on a machine or in the same factory with him, with his children being looked after by the neighbors."[69] The wives did not earn as much in the home as in a factory, but the difference was narrowing as women acquired powered machines. One cutter was proud of the fact that in 1914 many "have motors installed in them," running on electricity the same as in the factories.

If a canvass could be taken of every glove cutter or anyone who works in a glove factory and has a home, you could either find his wife working on a machine or his wife working in the same factory with him, and his children being looked after by the neighbors.

A. J. Lewis, cutter at A. Perrin & Co.

Having a wife who worked was not always desirable. The cutters in particular resented the fact their wives had to work. One wished to make a good living "and not compel my wife to help, and I do not think that a wife ought to be a partner with me in the factory." One man said that when he was single he had money and thought that his wife would never have to work. "I laughed at everybody. But when it comes to the second month's rent after I was married, I had to force my wife to work. . . . In order to enable my wife to earn that little money I have to help wash the dishes and help the children and I don't think a man who has worked three years to learn a trade should have to resort to dishwashing so his wife can use a machine."[70]

The wages ranged from a woman with two children who might average $5.00 a week, another with electricity who made $6.00 a week, one who could earn $10.00 a week, another with two children apparently able to make that much, while a sporadic worker made only $2.00 a week. Even a woman with seven children had to earn $2.00 a week. But all this depended on whether a woman could "get good work," which was not always available. One maker, whose wages were particularly high, worked in one factory and sewed at home for another factory. It was even possible for makers' wages to exceed that of their husbands who were cutters.

Sometimes factory workers took work home so they could take care of their homes and sew enough to earn the money they needed. "She never can go at seven o'clock in the shop. She must do housework. She goes at half-past eight in the shop, then works overtime at night."[71]

Workers felt reasonably comfortable in the 1890s because expanding business meant jobs were plentiful, but the cost of living rose about 20 percent nationally between the end of the 1890s and 1914. With wages failing to keep up with inflation, workers began to feel financially pressed on all sides. Workers who had been employed in New York City believed that meat and fruit were cheaper there than in Fulton County. One cutter said he paid $.25 a pound for meat in 1914; it had only cost $.16 a pound in 1900.

For many money was always tight. The cold climate meant that the average home needed seven tons of coal a winter, and often there was no extra money for it. With luck the coal dealer might defer payment until spring. Almost everyone owed back bills to the butcher. Many wanted to see their children better dressed and better fed. One worker with four children had his "boys on the corners selling papers. I want my boys in school, and one of them is a painter, and I wish I could give him a good education. . . . I have two good Christian girls, one of them works for five dollars a week in a store, and another girl is over 17 and she makes a little money in the shop when there is work."

That is the rule here in Fulton County, a good many of the women have to work and if it weren't for the women it would be hard to make a living.
Jacob Pitonberg, a Gloversville cutter.[4]

With a wife who had been sick for ten months, one worker ended up $150 in debt. In another family struck by illness, the mother could not work and two of the four children died, perhaps from tuberculosis.[72] One family with four children managed only because they lived with in-laws.

Living and working conditions differed markedly between Johnstown and Gloversville. As the union spokesman Julius Ehrlich observed in 1914, some shops were better than others, and it was generally conceded that the better shops were in Johnstown. The union believed there were good shops as well as poor ones. There were manufacturers who had earned excellent reputations among the cutters: "If all the manufacturers in the two cities would treat their employees as the employees in J. H. Danforth Co. are [treated], they would not have any strike."[73] During the 1914 strike, one member of the committee representing the cutters' union testified that they had the greatest respect for all the Johnstown manufacturers in general.[74] It was generally conceded that Johnstown cutters were more fortunate than Gloversville cutters with respect to shop practices.[75]

How much did this difference come from the changing ethnic mix in the two places? Johnstown's manufacturers were almost all Anglo-Saxons; many were descendents of glovemen who viewed the workplace with paternalistic concern. Gloversville was the locus of vastly larger shops with much bigger and more ethnically diverse workforces. Numerous Jewish manufacturers were among the new entrepreneurs, but the greatest change was in the work force.

Ireland Brothers Picnic 1903
Company picnics were very popular and almost every glove shop had a picnic in July.

Johnstown Historical Society

Bells and whistles rang at seven to wake workers, at eight to summon them to start work, at noon and one to mark the noon hour, and again at five to end the day. In 1997, Dr. Charles Noxon, whose mother sewed gloves at home, remembers the "symphony of bells" as happy moments in the day.

Even the larger factories in Gloversville tried to maintain the sense of family of the past. Picnics were provided for workers—the trip to Sacandaga Park was most popular. Booth Company's picnic there in 1902 drew 5,000 people! The employees of Louis Meyers & Son had a Mutual Aid Association, which held a reception and ball annually to raise funds. A thousand attended the reception at the factory in 1912, and by 1914, the reception had to be held at the state armory in order to accommodate the 2,500 who attended. *The Glovers Review*'s observation was ironic in light of the escalating labor unrest: The event was "a striking demonstration of the good feeling which exists among the employees of the Gloversville factory."

One story in particular illustrates the differences between the Johnstown manufacturers and those of Gloversville, or more properly the old-time manufacturers and the newcomers. George Cole was a Johnstown glove manufacturer in the first decades of the twentieth century. His niece Georgiana Cole Halloran grew up in Cohoes but spent part of every summer vacation with her aunt and uncle in Johnstown. Her aunt, an exuberant entrepreneur, did not sew gloves; she had an antique business and a hair-dressing business, and she dabbled in making hair dyes for women.

The niece's reminiscence shows the paternalistic or humanistic side of the industry. Some of the pitfalls encountered by this caring gloveman can be gleaned from other sources. Cole acquired a new cutting machine in 1903 that enabled him to increase his cutter's output tenfold. His two-story frame shop was destroyed in 1907 by a fire that started in the laying-off room. Even with insurance, starting over was difficult, and he went into bankruptcy the next year. The appointment of a receiver allowed the business to continue, and within a year Cole settled with his creditors for 10 cents on the dollar—26 creditors were paid in full, but 40 others who were owed $7,600 received only $760. Cole was back in business, only to fail again. He went into bankruptcy in 1912, owing $4,000. Like almost all the glovemen who struggled, he survived, and his business continued.

Georgiana Cole's reminiscence

At the time he [my uncle, George Cole] first started in this business, Johnstown and Gloversville were largely engaged in the manufacture of gloves and mittens. Manufacturing was by means of small scale operations; the cities were filled with small factories, and practically everyone over twelve years of age was engaged in the glove business in some way or another. Uncle George's factory was in back of his house, and as I think of it now, the smell of leather comes back to me. As soon as we arrived in Johnstown, we couldn't wait to get out to the "glove shop," to be greeted by all the employees and welcomed back to Johnstown. It was a friendly business, conducted in a small-town, paternal manner.

Most of the neighbors worked in the glove shop and many of them lived in houses owned by Uncle George. Sometimes they paid rent, more often they didn't. But he had a way of balancing it out in terms of service on one side and rental and loans on the other that made him a profit and kept the people happy and prosperous. He was a good businessman; he got orders, the work was turned out, everyone involved lived well and was happy.

Each of the employees seemed to feel that the business belonged to him or her. This often produced differences of opinion and led to heated arguments as to administrative procedure. There were no employee representatives—each employee represented himself. There were no labor troubles; each employee felt a personal interest in the business and considered production of more importance than his grievances. When grievances existed they were brought up immediately and "thrashed out" on the floor of the shop in open forum and settlement arrived at before any further work was done. Then, the problem settled, attention was again turned to the business of production. Gloves were manufactured; invoices sent out; checks came in and the "help" was "paid off."

Many of Uncle George's employees were women and this seemed strange to us Cohosiers, for during my childhood in our city the housewife was simply a housewife; she did not engage in outside employment. Once when my father was visiting in Johnstown he was asked what my mother did. He replied that she took care of her home and children. "But what does she work at?" he was queried. And I think industrious housewives in Johnstown were rather astounded to learn that she had no other job than of housewife and mother. All the women in Johnstown worked on gloves; if not in a glove shop, then at home. The small glove factories were scattered throughout the city, and it was not necessary for any woman to go far from her domicile for employment in the glove trade. Imagine having an employee open her kitchen window to call to her boss that she wouldn't be in to work that day because of some personal business which she explained freely at the top of her lungs?

The system of production control was completely different in those days. A manufacturer didn't wait for an order before producing; he produced the merchandise and then went out and sold it. When he got the opportunity to make an advantageous buy in material for the production of a certain type of glove or mitten, he bought and produced. When the order was nearing completion, he went out and found a customer, getting the best price obtainable. This meant that a manufacturer often found himself pretty well crowded for space and when this happened he took a sales trip to dispose of the stock on hand. On one of these sales trips to New York City, Uncle George called on a customer named Goldstein and dickered with him on the price of an order. Neither would budge and Uncle George left for more fertile fields. Goldstein called up the factory, told John Cridland (who ran the business during Uncle George's absence) that he had bought the order in question at a stated price (Goldstein's, not Uncle George's), that he was putting a check in the mail and the goods should be shipped immediately. This sounds rather unbelievable today; but business was conducted in a more haphazard fashion then, and Goldstein got away with it and got the gloves at his price. When Uncle George returned home and found that he had been outsmarted, he planned a retaliatory move. On his next trip to New York, he called on Goldstein and told him that he appreciated business cunning and had great respect for him as a customer. He was, therefor making him an offer of a special lot of gloves which had been manufactured with a slight defect, at an excellent price. He showed a righthand glove, with some small imperfection. Goldstein made the purchase of the gloves on the sample, "as is." When the shipment arrived, Goldstein had a large shipment of righthand gloves. In order to get a shipment of lefthand gloves to match those he had bought in the "as is" deal, he had to pay Uncle George's price.

The men and women—the Forkers, Dueslers, and Cridlands—who worked in Uncle George's factory were such an intimate part of it and of Uncle George's family that they all seemed to be one individual unit. In those days, illness in the family of a worker had an effect on production comparable to the effect of the illness of the President today on the stock market.

Much of the glove work was done by workers at their homes. This work was delivered and picked up by my older cousins. They used horses during my early childhood, and in the bad winter weather a sleigh was required instead of the usual delivery wagon. Some of the work was delivered to workers in the country and going along on one of these trips was a thrill for us.

Owners Squeezed

The first decade of the twentieth century may have been the high point for the county's glove industry, but it was scarcely that for the county's workers and manufacturers. Workers were squeezed between low wages and rising costs, but the way the manufacturers were squeezed by competition both at home and abroad, by rising overhead in new factories, by shortages of raw materials, and by difficulties in borrowing money was just as great. Even as a few succeeded and were able to expand and a few were able to build large homes, times remained shaky for most of the county's glove manufacturers.

The number of bankruptcies is indicative of the pressures on the county's glovemen. It seems surprising that the strike of 1903 and 1904 did not produce more bankruptcies, but then perhaps it isn't. It is possible that the industry had overproduced, and the strike allowed manufacturers to reduce stocks and preserve capital. This was certainly the case a decade later, at the time of the 1914 strike. The years after the depression of 1893 to 1897, the period from 1897 to 1903, saw a minor upswing in the economy, with low unemployment nationally. Therefore everyone was caught by surprise when the huge New York City firm of Schwartz, Schiffer and Co. failed, owing a half-million dollars. The firm had a factory in Gloversville and had succeeded M. Beeber and Co. in 1893. When the parent company failed almost every manufacturer in Gloversville and Johnstown was on the list of creditors. Among them was the Gloversville firm of James McSwiney. It too failed, owing $12,000, as a direct result of Schwartz, Schiffer and Co.'s failure.

There were few bankruptcies in the next few years, but the pace of failures picked up in 1912. George B. Cole, George A. Veeder, and Frank Ardizzone failed in 1912 as did the New York City firm Wilson Glove Co., which had a factory in Gloversville. In 1913 Robert J. Williams of Gloversville was able to transfer his property to creditors to avoid bankruptcy. McDougall & Dewey failed in 1914 as did Henry Lebenheim.

An ever-present cloud over the members of the association were the antitrust laws. Manufacturers were seriously worried about possible charges of collusion. It is difficult to imagine how individuals who were so competitive and secretive could be viewed as acting in concert, although they did work together, albeit in ways that did not invoke antitrust laws.

Federal antitrust laws had resulted from the economic forces that created large conglomerates and trusts at the end of the nineteenth century. The Sherman Act was adopted primarily in response to John D. Rockefeller, Sr.'s virtual control of the country's oil production and refining through his Standard Oil Co. Section 1 of the Sherman Act of 1890 focused on group behavior by banning every "contract, combination, . . . or conspiracy" in restraint of interstate or foreign trade. It prohibited price discrimination. This did not apply to the industry's setting a more or less uniform wage schedule. Section 2 of that act did not apply to Fulton County's industry because it was directed at monopolistic practices of individual firms.

Between 1898 and 1902 almost 200 new trusts and huge new corporations were formed in the United States, some in such industries as steel, coal, and sugar. The Sherman Act proved vague and ineffective and in 1914 Congress passed the Clayton Act. That act was concerned with practices of pricing and affected mergers that served to restrain trade. Outwardly, little of either act applied directly to Fulton County, but the manufacturers, especially those in the Glove Manufacturers Association, were afraid that it might. Competitors might set prices, but competition kept prices low since not all glovemen were members of that organization. Members were cautious in talking about the wage schedules, noting that the association's schedule was not in force throughout the county's industry. They worried that the association might be considered a means of controlling competition. They maintained that their organization was primarily concerned with keeping tariffs high. And even to this day, some glovemen claim that there were subjects they did not dare talk about—or admit to talking about.[76]

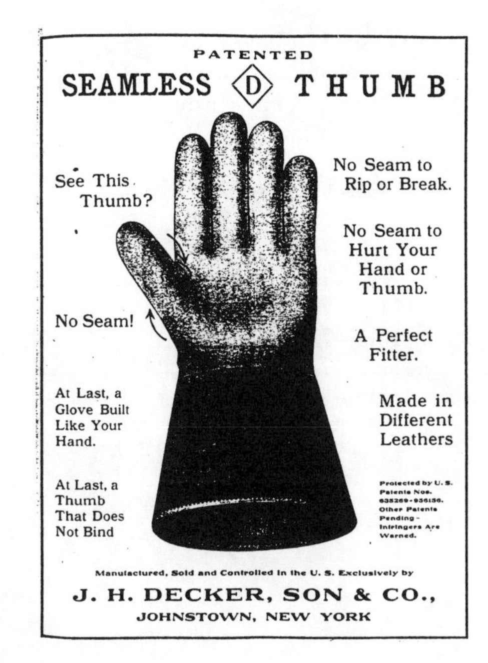

Even though a few large glove companies had emerged in this period, it is almost comical to compare the giants of an industry like Rockefeller with the huge number of small businessmen who constantly competed for a share of the glove market. Even the largest firm, Littauer Brothers, could not be considered a monopoly, capable of controlling trade and prices. The manufacturers' association tried to control wages, but not prices. The few large glove companies that emerged did not grow by swallowing up competitors. Competitors' assets, comparable to the cost of starting a business, were small in relation to the constant expenses of acquiring raw materials. Smaller firms simply dropped out when faced with problems, the more successful ones just grew. This growth pattern may be inherent in craft industries; certainly such growth has similarities with what occurred in the shoe industry. A few large shoe firms emerged as the industry abandoned the manufacturing centers along the East Coast. The Endicott Johnson company, organized in the early 1900s, began making shoes near the source of shoe leather about the same time the heavy glove business left Fulton County for the Midwest.

The greatest source of pressure on glove manufacturers was competition within the industry. At the 1914 hearing, George C. Potter agreed with other manufacturers that local competition had always kept wages and costs in the county down.[77] With 150 competitors, manufacturers had to keep profits to a minimum. During the times of high tariff they were able to undersell the tariff protection, but in general local competition offset the effects of any tariff reduction.[78] Abraham Lehr, president of Dempster & Place, felt that competition between local manufacturers precluded their ability to increase wages.[79]

In the strike in 1903, some strikers, primarily cutters, started manufacturing gloves and underselling other manufacturers. In a curious twist, they began competing with the same manufacturers they were striking. The factories could be undersold because, as Albert Aaron of Louis Meyers & Son later testified, "a man does not have to have any tools of any kind to speak of in order to start glove manufacturing and he can undersell us because it does not cost him anything to sell the gloves. He makes them in one or two rooms, possibly in the back of his house and gives them outside to make and he has no expense."[80] Aaron believed that sales by small manufacturers to larger firms proved the small firms could make gloves for less money.

This emphasizes the difference between the trusts of the day that controlled whole industries in order to raise prices and drive out competitors at will and the many firms in the county which were all prevented from raising prices because of competitive forces. According to George C. Potter, "local competition has always been rather severe in the glove business, and the Washington authorities object strenuously to any combination for the

Value of imported gloves
In million dollars (today's dollars in millions, in parentheses)

1904—4.6	(63.8)
1905—5.4	(74.5)
1906—9.2	(127)
1907—10.2	(133.9)
1908—7.8	(102)
1909—7.5	(102)
1910—7.5	(98)
1911—7.2	(94.3)
1912—7.8	(98.9)
1913—7.6	(96.4)

For seventeen years the manufacturers of Fulton County never knew a time when there could be an increase [in wages]. ... Something would always come along to prevent it.
Dialogue at the Hearing.[5]

raising of prices, and that is a question that they always ask us in our tariff discussions. They seem to believe that we have a glove trust here ... [but] it is plain that we have not."[81]

There was another side to the fierce competition in the industry—the one feature of the glove industry that had no parallel in any other industry of equal magnitude, and it stemmed from the absolute individual independence of the manufacturers. There were almost no combinations; the Littauers' interests in several firms was the one large exception. None of the influences of trust monopoly which stifled competition in other industries were evident in Fulton County. A man with small capital could always enter the field and challenge larger concerns.

Growing competition from imported gloves increased pressures on manufacturers. At the turn of the century there were many more glove manufacturing establishments in Europe than in America. As in Fulton County, most were undoubtedly small. *The Glovers Review* quoted statistics showing 1,100 shops in Germany, 350 in Austria-Hungary, 225 in France, 190 in England, 100 in Italy, 50 or so more in both Norway and Spain, and about 30 in Russia. Nearly 1,000 of the glove shops in Germany produced only kid gloves—a fact that helps explain the problems American glovemen had obtaining kid leather.

America imported 5.5 million pairs of kid gloves in 1899, 6.4 million in 1900, and 5 million the next year. Fulton County's efforts to produce more women's gloves was beginning to affect German production. In 1902 German manufacturers were hurting, the following year their industry was said to be waning. In 1905 an industry-wide strike hit Germany, with 400 to 500 cutters and all the women workers off the job. Germany's leather industries became so depressed that the country imported no cowhides from America for its shoe industry in 1905.

The French began to feel the competition for skins in 1907 as the price of some grades rose by 50 percent. The industry in France began to decline the following year and this was reflected in a slump in American gloves imports.

Many Fulton County manufacturers began to import gloves and sell them along with their own production. In 1912, James S. Ireland started importing fine gloves from the Vallier factory, one of the largest in Grenoble. Ireland said, "They do business all over the world, in fact the American end of the business is a small end of it and I suppose that is because we handle it." This wry Scots humor shows just how conservative and perhaps timid were the Johnstown manufacturers.

When a company like Perrin & Cie received cancellations of two or three dozen gloves to be made in its Gloversville factory, it had the advantage of switching the business to its French and English factories. The company recognized that the county lost much more than just the wages: future business would shift to Europe as well. Because retailers who had ordered their domestic gloves from the company for many years were ordering from abroad, Perrin & Cie speculated that their factory in the county would continue to decline. This forced them to cancel plans for a new factory in Gloversville.[82]

The only recourse available to manufacturers was to keep wages down. The strike for a wage increase in 1897 brought a 10 percent increase and established table cutters' wages at $.95 a dozen for cape gloves, $.90 a dozen for kid gloves, and $1.00 a dozen for mocha. When established this was intended to provide the cutter with wages of $2.00 a day. Although wages were adjusted somewhat in 1903, they remained essentially the same through

1914. A 1909 increase in the rate for some forms of cutting was offset by reductions in other forms. Actually, because the 1897 strike had sought to win back some of the money taken from the cutters in 1892, wages varied little from well before 1890 until 1914. The only significant changes were in the larger shops that could provide more weeks of employment.

A new schedule was published at the beginning of 1903, but it contained no general increase. What purported to be the first revision in the uniform schedule since 1897 was published in 1905, establishing new rates for cutters, makers, and silkers. In 1907 J. H. Decker Inc. "voluntarily" raised the wages of the firm's block cutters from $.12 1/2 to $.18 a dozen. It was charged that certain manufacturers began to offer cutters work at "pull-down" rates, which were substantially lower than table cutter rates.

Toward 1914, manufacturers began to offer $.30 an hour for some kinds of cutting.[83] In the standard 9-hour day plus a half day on Saturday and 50 weeks of work, a cutter could average $27 a week. Few good cutters wanted the hourly rate, implying that their potential wages were greater than they admitted in 1914.

But there is no question that glove workers' wages stayed about the same throughout the first decade of the century. They failed to keep up with the wages of most skilled workers. Prices were relatively stable as well—white bread remained at 5 cents a loaf until 1912. The value of a dollar fluctuated only slightly between 1890 and 1910, then declined gradually as war approached. Average wages of all industries rose by 20 percent between 1900 and 1909, and almost as much again between 1910 and 1915. In the first decade of the century, union workers in other industries across the country were earning substantially more than Fulton County's cutters, approaching 40 cents an hour by the end of the decade. Inflation and the local decline in earning power was real.[84]

The wages of garment workers in New York City were comparable, with little real growth in the first part of the century. In fact, depending on how the cost of living is calculated, garment workers' wages actually declined.[85]

According to one cutter, "a pull-down cutter is simply a table cutter who is not required to put as much time and skill into his work."[6]

Although pull-down cutters were paid lower rates for their work, in some cases such as at Littauers, Class A pull-down cutters were doing the same work as table cutters, producing gloves sold for the same prices as table-cut gloves, with pay that ranged from $.60 to $.80 a dozen versus $.95 to $1.05.

Not only did pull-down cutters receive lower rates for their work, they found it difficult to get promoted to table-cutting jobs because the manufacturers could pay them less.[7]
Cutter at the 1914 Hearing

Cutting Department
Ireland Brothers, 1915
Johnstown Historical Society

Slitting and Trimming Department, Ireland Brothers, 1914

Johnstown Historical Society

In the 1914 hearings one cutter said he would offer to work six days a week if his employer would just pay his grocery and meat bills.[86] But, many manufacturers testified that the cutters' wages were not as low as they claimed.

At Littauer's a cutter could make from $2.80 to $3.00 a day if he was fast. In this shop the superintendent estimated that 60 percent of the workers were efficient and could make this wage, 25 percent were moderate workers who could earn $2.60 a day, and the rest were slow and earned much less. At Littauer's the average of all cutters was $14.85 a week, which was below the current wage of a skilled worker in other industries. Low as these wages were, they were two and a half times the wages in Europe.[87]

At the Northrup Glove Co., cutters averaged $18 a week when they worked, or an average of $15.60 a week for the entire 52 weeks in a year. This was nearly $200 a year more than the $600 average yearly wage the cutters claimed they were making in 1914.[88]

Manufacturers had other means of limiting wages. When business dropped off, some, like the Jacob Adler Co., just opened later and closed earlier, thus limiting the amount of time cutters could work. Of course, in down times, the slower workers were the first to be let go. By 1914, George Mandrill's firm was working on short time all year and capped cutters' wages at $15 a week.

But the independence of the cutter was such that he could rebel when his wages were cut, and as one said, "That struck me as being such unfair treatment that I rebelled and the cutters stuck by me. . . . The intent to reduce our prices per dozen was too clearly shown and I soon left Meyers shop and I will never go there again."[89] Mobility among craftsmen, so lacking in most industrialized businesses, was Fulton County's hallmark.

Further, every cutter had the potential to be an entrepreneur. This gave him hope that he could move up in life. It may account for the fact that much of the time there was little outward resentment between workers and owners. After all, even the most successful glovemen had their bad times.

Decreasing supplies of leather created one more problem for manufacturers in this supposedly best of times. At the turn of the century, a great many of the fine skins used in Fulton County for gloves were imported already tanned from Europe, and the finest skins were French. The county's tanners, who had great difficulties obtaining the higher grades of untanned skins, were running at a loss or making a very small profit. In addition, they suffered from a shortage of skilled workers. As a result, the price of leather began to rise along with everything else. A sharp ten percent rise in the cost of all grades of fine domestic leather in April of 1905 was followed by a 25 percent rise within a month. This exacerbated the forces squeezing the glovemen.

This rise in the cost of leather made it seem certain that the price of gloves would advance. This became even more inevitable as a shortage of skins resulted in many cutters being laid off, just as orders were peaking. Glovers were competing with automobiles for leather. Sheepskins were needed for popular lined coats in 1906, at the time there was a worldwide decline in sheep.

Prices of skins rose. Quality declined, and manufacturers could get fewer gloves from a dozen skins. The rise in leather prices between 1903 and 1906 was unprecedented. Prices on deerskins and heavy leather rose similarly. By 1912, the increase in the cost of leather over the past decade approached 50 percent and there was a significant scarcity of all grades. The demand for leather jumped in 1914 as European countries declarated war. Fulton County had only a three-month's supply on hand (125,000 skins at a full cutting rate).

Cost Dozen skins	**1903**	**1906**
Cape	$14.50	$18.00
Kid	$11.00	$14.00
Domestic cape	$7.00	$10.50
Mocha	$9.60	$12.00
Suede	$7.00	$11.00

In addition to all their other problems, manufacturers were faced with a growing shortage of workers, especially makers. Almost from its first issue, *The Glovers Review* published editorials worrying about the shortage of workers, especially women "operators." The August 1902 issue estimated that the county could use 1,000 more operators. This may not have been an actual shortage, but a reflection of the way the industry was planning to expand. In February 1903, there was a note about men working as makers,[90] and although a few men did operate machines doing heavy work, their numbers as makers remained infinitesimal compared with women.

In the aftermath of the 1903-4 strike, as manufacturers rushed to fill orders, the shortage of makers became more pronounced, and there were many advertisements for new workers. *The Glovers Review* commented that it was "strange that more young women do not take up this work" in light of the fact that the average wage was higher than that of salesgirls.[91]

The scarcity of makers became so pronounced in early 1905 that by August the Glove Manufacturers Association considered establishing an independent school to train them. The association's school actually started in the fall of 1905, and by early 1906 turned out 40 makers who found employment. Another 23 were in the program and more were expected, with May bringing "an abundance of applicants."

Even in mild depression of 1908 there was still a shortage of workers because the slows time caused many to leave for other industries.

In mid-1909 the Gloversville Board of Education decided to establish a vocational school connected with the public schools to address the problem of the inadequate supply of trained labor. That training was necessary was evident from the origin of the upper level of workers. "By far the greatest number of superintendents, foremen, and managers are of foreign birth. They obtained and hold these positions because of superior training."[92] By June 1911, the Public Vocational School was able to hold an exhibit showing the

Our most pronounced trouble, however, has been in getting operators to turn out to work.
D. Quaile of Daniel Hays & Co., 1907[8]

work of its students on its 16 sewing machines. The class could now make finished gloves.

There was a growing shortage of trained cutters as well. A cutter who taught an apprentice was able to increase his production and hence his earnings since the production of the apprentice was considered part of the teacher's output. The apprentices were not even put on the payroll. One cutter received an enormous wage, but "he had a healthy young apprentice with him and it was a double wage. [Since] most of the boys we are learning the trade [sic] have to sell Sunday papers on the streets here to get spending money,"[93] it was little wonder that few wanted to study cutting.

By 1914, fewer and fewer single men were training to be cutters. The vast majority of cutters were married—and married men often felt trapped in their jobs. Family responsibilities compelled them to stay in the industry and stopped them from taking a chance at anything else. "Single men won't go into the glove business any more. It is very hard to get an apprentice today, and the man who has a son, it is the last thing he will do today, put him on as a glove cutter."[94] The number of apprentices in 1914 was as little as a quarter of the number at the turn of the century. "Only as a last result—when other channels were not open to his son—would a father be compelled to teach his son to cut gloves for a living."[95]

The shortage of workers began to affect production. Attempts to increase production of fine gloves made the shortage of trained workers even more critical. In addition, the continued seasonality of the industry exaggerated the scarcity of trained cutters and makers. "Even during the lull between seasons, there is not an over-supply, and there seems to be no certain way of equalizing production to give employment to an average number of operatives, the year round."[96]

Homework offered no real solution: "As long as the manufacturer must depend upon having a large part of the sewing done outside the factory, he is obliged to keep a sufficient number of homeworkers on his list to protect [his ability] to fill orders in the busy seasons. The fact that for one reason or another the persons who work in their homes may stop taking work at any time necessitates the constant addition of new names to the list of outside workers. In Fulton County, the limited population from which workers may be drawn adds to the difficulty of obtaining the required number." The shortage became so acute that women from distant counties were recruited, and one firm even reached all the way east to Vermont to obtain makers.[97]

Both homework and piecework pay for factory work were seen as impediments to the manufacturer in his attempts to organize his production.

There has never been a time of long profits in the glove business.
George C. Potter, 1914[9]

Glove manufacturers' profits during this decade of peak production may never be known. In 1902, *The Glovers Review* observed that a profit of 10 percent of gross sales satisfied most manufacturers, but noted that profits were rarely adequate. That was almost the last mention of profits ever made in the magazine. Manufacturers became increasingly secretive about their businesses. The magazine hinted at the manufacturers' jealousies: "It is not uncommon that a good citizen will surprise himself by discovering a subconscious resentment at his neighbor's success; and a sneaking pleasure at his business loss." The industry was too competitive: "There will always be some who think they can produce gloves cheaper than anyone else, and until they discover their mistake and are wrecked financially, they cause a very fierce competition." *The Glovers Review* concluded that there was "no likelihood of better profits" in general.

Only the hearing of the 1914 strike gave a further glimpse of their finances. The capital investment and profits of ten companies was surveyed and the results show that manufacturers did not have a very large return on investment. For instance, the 1913 profit of all ten concerns amounted to $2.4 million calculated in 1990 dollars.

Profits based on capital investment

Year	Capital	Profit	Percent
1910	$1,308,000	77,000	5.8%
1911	1,325,000	76,000	5.7%
1912	1,419,000	137,000	9.6%
1913	1,672,000	192,800	11.5%

Manufacturers claimed their profits were less than 5 percent of gross revenues. The ever-conservative and self-effacing Johnstown gloveman James S. Ireland said it might be possible to raise cutters' wages if it would not hurt sales and profits. "I think it would be up to me to see that I got a small profit out of it; if I could, of course, naturally."

It is not entirely clear what manufacturers meant by "profits." From the industry's beginnings through most of the 1800s, a gloveman continued to figure the costs of his raw materials and the wages he paid his workers, subtract that from the amount he received for his gloves, and consider the difference as his profit. He never figured his earnings as wages. When manufacturers began building large factories, they began to revise their view of overhead. But for most of the smaller manufacturers, the inability to understand the true cost of their product was carried over into the twentieth century. By the early 1900s, most manufacturers included rent and insurance when they computed costs, but they were only beginning to consider the expenses of selling as part of the cost.[98]

By early 1914, shadows of approaching war in Europe began to add to the worries of the county's glove manufacturers. Imports of leather for fine gloves were threatened by disruptions in shipping. The need to use heavy leather for shoes, boots, and harnesses appeared certain to deplete the stocks needed for manufacturing heavy work gloves for civilians.

Hides, skins, and leather are so thoroughly world commodities, and used for so many different purposes, that even the supply of stock for the manufacture of heavy leather working gloves, which is almost an American industry, will be seriously affected by this crisis.[10]
Editorial in *The Glovers Review, 1914*

By the summer of 1914, prices on all grades of leather had risen again, and production of heavy leather had so closely matched the needs of all industries that prices would have risen even without the advent of hostilities.[99] Manufacturers were at a loss to understand the disruption war might bring. It was possible that tanneries would receive additional hides from Central and South America that would normally have been shipped to Europe, but then, European bankers' control of those markets might limit United States' imports. While scarcities of all imports threatened Fulton County's production, the domestic hides used in heavy gloves and sewn almost exclusively in the western United States kept production levels near normal in the western glove factories.[100]

All this led to a decline in business and an increasingly uncertain future. Given the ups and downs created by the glove industry's seasonality, it was difficult for glovemen to understand the extent to which their businesses were shrinking. Much of the uncertainty facing the manufacturers was of their own making. They were inexorably hemmed in by tradition. They were afraid to raise prices for fear the public would not buy. They were afraid to veer from the practice of selling a dozen gloves in standard monetary units.

Manufacturers were aware that business had begun to decline in 1913. They had received many letters cancelling orders, asking for additional time to settle accounts, or returning gloves for credit.[101] The prospect of war cast a pall over future orders.

Workers, Unions, and the 1914 Strike

The cutters, who numbered 1,765 in 1914,[11] included
Russian Jews—500
Native-born Americans—400
Italians—300
English—300
Germans—110
French—80
Scandinavians—50
Czechs and Slovaks—25

Most evident in the early years of the twentieth century was the changing class of workers. Russian-born Jews gradually became the largest ethnic group in the table-cutting fraternity, replacing the English, Scots, and French. As they became dominant, these eastern Europeans, who brought the art of table cutting to the county or learned it here, became a force for change within the industry and a source of labor unrest.

Union organizers conceded that there had been a very harmonious feeling between employers and employees between 1897 and 1904, "a bridge upon which they both walked," but the gap between them widened from 1904 to 1914. Union workers recalled with nostalgia the time before 1897 when "we were having picnics, and the manufacturers were with us. He was more democratic in those days than he is today."[102]

In the words of Julius K. Ehrlich, member of the conference committee of the strikers in the 1914 strike, the period from 1897 to 1914 was one of struggle with little reward. Another cutter claimed that he and his fellow cutters had waited for a wage increase for all of the decade leading up to August 1914, in spite of the fact that they had requested a wage increase three or four times.

Sometime after 1904, the manufacturers cut the rate paid on silk-lined gloves and reduced the rates paid for cutting bindings. Julius Ehrlich admitted that in 1910 the manufacturers had granted an increase of 2 cents per dozen on kid and suede gloves and 6 ½ cents on mochas, but because the union men felt this hardly compensated them for the earlier reductions, all the cutters believed there had been no real wage increase in the decade. The raise in 1897 "is all the increase we have had in seventeen years."[103]

According to the union, these concerns about wages were the principal reason that approximately 1,500 glove cutters struck almost all of the glove firms in Fulton County on August 21, 1914. This gradually idled 15,000 other workers. With few exceptions, the manufacturers were united in their "conviction that neither the present nor future trade outlook holds any promise upon which to logically base an increase" in wages or other production costs.

The strike was so devastating to the region's economy that the New York State Board of Mediation and Arbitration convened a series of hearings in the county. Although the board issued its findings and recommendations in late December of 1914 and although the cutters gradually returned to work, the issues that brought about the strike were not settled at that time. The union did not win the wage increases recommended by the board until well after the start of World War I and the union lost virtually every other issue. On the other hand, the manufacturers achieved only a Pyrrhic victory for the industry had begun its ultimate decline.

Workers in Gloversville were the first to decide to strike, but within hours Johnstown workers agreed to join them. Johnstown workers felt their conditions were comparatively good with respect to those in Gloversville. "The stories we heard from our fellow glove workers, . . . for instance in Meyers shop, were bloodcurdling." The men dropped their tools because of wages, not because of conditions. In Johnstown, in summer there was "lots of air, lots of light, lots of rooms, everything is frequently cleaned." The owners of Hutchens & Potter wrote the *Johnstown Republican* that a committee of

Opposite page:
Map from 1905 Century Atlas of Fulton and Montgomery Counties, *showing density of glove shops and skin mills near the center of Gloversville.*

4
2
WEST
CLINTON ST.
COTTAGE
CHURCH ST.
N. SCHOOL ST.
BLEECKER
ELM
MIDDLE ST.
FREMONT
N. MAIN
W. FULTON
E. FULTON
ST.
WASHINGTON
CARPENTER
FOREST
GAS
ST.
ALLEY
VINE ST.
CAYADUTTA ST.
SCHOOL ST.
S. MAIN
BURR ST.
PARK
F. J. & G. R. R.
F.J. & G. R.R. Co.
(ELECTRIC DIV.)
Creek
Cayadutta
Station
Coal House
Coal Co. of Fulton Co.
Glove City Feed Mill
Opera House
First M.E. Church
Presb. Church
Masonic Bldg.
Elk Club
Hotel Lincoln
City Hall
Gloversville Free Library
Congreg. Church
Cong. Ch. Pars.
Littauer Bldg.
Hotel Kingsborough
Keystone Hotel
I.O.O.F. Hall
Fire Sta. No 2
Star Creamery
Bapt. Church
Post Office
Iron Foundry H.J. Anthony
1st Bapt. Ch.
Littauer Bros. Glove Mfy.
Central Ho.
Glen Teleph. Co.
Wadsworth Livery
C.J. Holden
W.H. Demarest
Eugene Littauer
W. Filmer
Louis Meyers & Son

the company's cutters "had assured the owners that they had absolutely no grievance against us." The workers claimed they only went out because one of their number would not join the union. In a letter to the owners, the cutters wrote that "some if not nearly all of your men now out, are out through fear."[104]

However, there were actually many other causes for the strike. Gloversville cutters, and some from Johnstown, protested discrimination in wages against pull-down cutters. They fought for wages, improved conditions, and relief from the dreaded practices in taxing. Underlying all these concerns was the fact that the future of the union was also at stake in the 1914 strike. Ehrlich, the most articulate of the union spokesmen, testified that cutters "have been rebuked for preaching unionism in the workshops, and since the strike began this conference committee has been told by local mediators that it is not so much a question of an increase in wages with the manufacturers as it is their opposition to anything that looks like unionism on the part of glove workers. Unionism in this glove center has to receive a black eye, said a local mediator to the conference committee. . . . The manufacturers can rest assured that they will never crush the spirit of unionism."[105]

There was more than a hint of socialist goals among the leaders of the strike. Herman (Bert) Abbott, another cutter, appealed to the mediators in the 1914 strike: "In a city flooded with food, fuel, clothing, shelter, and luxury, we have half-starved children, overworked mothers, [fathers worried about their property and their] crowded, cold, and cheerless homes. If that is the action of certain individuals that cause these miserable conditions, then we say, they are accessories to the crime of starving little children and the renewal of chattel slavery. If these appalling conditions are due to competition and private ownership of industries, then the business system today stands condemned and the quicker the state owns and controls the glove industry, the better for the community, for no industry has a right to exist that can not pay its employees a living wage."[106] Both Ehrlich and Abbott appeared to be well-read, especially versed in the writings and ideology of the country's socialist leaders.

Fulton County's workers may have learned of socialist ideals through their union, but socialist philosophy was not unknown to residents in general. The Johnstown Grand Opera House had a series of talks in a Socialist Lyceum course. Among the speakers who visited the county, was a prominent socialist, Mrs. Ella Reeve Bloor. Her research was the basis for Upton Sinclair's book, *The Jungle*.[107]

In describing the beautiful homes the manufacturers had built around the turn of the century, one cutter protested that the money to build them did not come from "those fellows who ride in automobiles." It came from the workers like himself. He had seen Littauers go from one cutter to a hundred, Adlers the same. He believed that workers like him were responsible for the city's growth. "Those beautiful places are most all built up out of dishonesty or cheating honest toil."[108] Many of the workers who went out on strike must have shared such thoughts.

While the 1,500 workers who went out on strike represented a huge majority of the county's cutters, a few firms were not struck: Pannaci, Malone, Loucks, and Faultless. About 190 cutters chose not to strike at these firms and about 200 others went back at various times during the strike with the promise of greater wages: 90 cutters scattered among several small shops were enticed by the full advance of $.25, 70 cutters at Fownes returned after being given a $.15 per dozen raise, and 35 or so at Hallock & Stewart returned with the same increase. When Fownes offered a raise of $.15 per dozen, the union advised cutters to accept that across-the-board increase.[109] Some union leaders believed that all the cutters would be willing to return to work with the same increase. Even among other firms there were a handful of non-strikers. (three out of 40 cutters at Davis & Fleischer, four or five out of 55 at Elite, eight at Bachner-Moses, eight out of 30 at Mandrill's, and five out of 25 at Hutchens & Potter.) The men at Fernandez were enticed back to work with a promise of a raise, but as soon as work caught up, Fernandez reneged and cancelled the arrangement.

In September, an unsigned article in *The Glovers Review* analyzed the problems facing the manufacturers but raised "the point of a 'living' wage upon which the cutters' demand is specifically based. There is a human factor as well as a wage factor involved in the question. The blame which may attach to the manufacturers for this strike is found chiefly in their long-continued failure to properly deal with the human equation."[110]

At the end of the first decade of this century, the owners of the newer, larger glove factories were forced to devise methods that would make their operations more efficient. Gone were days when an owner, with his son or brother and perhaps one other, could sort and cut gloves for a whole shop. This type of operation persisted only in the small shops which served primarily as jobbers[111] for the larger manufacturers. These smaller shops could undersell the larger ones because they could pay less and because the owner had lower overhead.

Realistically, what could the larger factories do to increase efficiency? There were no new machines, no new methods, no new science. Glovemaking was a labor-intensive craft. A worker's efficiency was limited by his mental and physical capacity. Some were fast, some were moderate, a few were just plain slow workers. Paying for piecework appeared to recognize these differences, but barely rewarded the slow worker. Slower or less-skilled cutters were a problem, and one owner claimed that the cutters themselves "acknowledge that there are many of them who do not cut gloves properly and should not be allowed to cut." Cutters resisted hourly pay. They worked when they wanted. William J. Stitt, a partner as well as foreman in Jacob Adler & Co., described their work habits:

> *The men come at ten in the morning and stop at twelve and if they don't come back in the afternoon we don't know it. They have had the freedom of coming any time in the morning that they like and leaving at any time in the afternoon. It might be it is not a good thing for the cutter. It is certainly not a good thing for the general oversight of your business. The business started here in a very moderate way, in small shops, and as the small shops have developed into larger shops the same easy way of going along continues, and where we have a number of small shops, where the men are allowed to do about as they please, that feeling is carried into the larger shops.*[112]

Owners of the larger shops could enforce more regular hours but not much else. Further, there were thousands of skins to sort, a hundred or more cutters to supervise, operators to oversee, homeworkers to keep supplied with gloves to sew, plus the sales and shipping of gloves, the ordering of leather and other supplies, and the necessary record keeping.

Shops with two or more partners often divided the work so one did selling, one looked after finances and buying of leather, and one oversaw the factory itself. An owner often had to hire a manager to supervise his factory. Still that job was too big for one manager. He had to hire men to sort the leather and distribute it to the cutters. He to make sure the cutters did not waste any leather, that they got the maximum amount of tranks, thumbs, and fourchettes from it.

The owners began to devise a staff hierarchy. The assistant superintendent at Meyers had the optimistic, additional title of Accountant and Efficiency Man. In other large shops, the most-experienced cutters took on the new role of sorting and distributing skins to other cutters. In the process, they decided how many pairs of gloves a batch should yield and passed the batches out to individual cutters as they saw fit. Here was a place the owner or shop manager could exact greater efficiencies. He could demand, through the sorter, a fixed number of pairs of gloves from a given batch of skins. No longer was the cutter king, making all the decisions concerning what the leather could produce. The increase in the cost of leather made it imperative that the owner "get the best results from the cutter."[113] In addition, problems could develop at every step in the process, not just from the cutters.

This method of fixed distribution took on an ominous name. It was called "taxing," and the man who assigned bundles of leather and calculated how many gloves each bundle should yield became known as the "taxer." In the 1914 strike taxing became the focus of complaints about working conditions.

Getting the best from a skin was no simple matter—a seamstress can devise the best way to put a pattern on a yard of material, but no two skins are the same. Deciding how to cut a skin introduced countless variables. Taxing could be fair, but it could and did lead to abuses. Efforts to increase production through taxation only angered the cutters and exacerbated their belief that they were underpaid.

Alfred Saunders, Littauer's superintendent, had come to America from England as an experienced gloveman. In his job at Littauers, he said, "I never heard the word taxation until the last two years [1912]. We used to call it sorting and estimation."[114] Every firm, even the more modest ones, had someone who sorted and estimated the skins. Taxing, by its very name, appeared ominous to Gloversville's cutters.

Not unexpectedly, the transition went rather smoothly in the more humanistic, moderate-size shops in Johnstown. Factory owner J. K. Northrup considered his shop "more or less a family operation."[115] He had two men who had worked for the company for over 30 years, five for over 20 years, and ten for between 10 and 15 years. "Every man who is working there is trusted." There were no problems with the distribution of work. James S. Ireland continued to call the process "sorting," and he believed his Johnstown firm had no complaints. If a man needed more skins to fulfill his quota, he was given them. "Of course, I suppose if we had a lot of new men and didn't know with whom we were dealing we would not be that way." [116]

The greatest number of complaints seemed to come from just a few shops in Gloversville, most notably from the Louis Meyers & Son factory. The complaints came from the shops with the largest number of new, immigrant workers. The owners may have directed the taxers to be fair, but everyone felt pressured to produce more. Some of the poorer cutters could not produce the taxed amounts with any consistency. Disputes arose. "Now, if a man persistently cuts less gloves than the foreman taxes them to get, and another

Taxing

The leather has not been good, they are more inferior every year, and in order to meet the tax, the men who put up the skins are, of course, crowded by the boss or employers. I don't say the man who owns the factories, but the man who gives out the skins is between the glove cutter and the boss, and on the one hand the man that gives out the skins is constantly driven by the boss and crowded, to crowd the skins more and more, then he in turn has to crowd, gradually crowd the cutter more and more to get the gloves out of the skins, and the skins are constantly getting poorer and poorer, and that would necessitate the wages, my wages gradually decreasing every year.

Edward N. Etman, cutter at the 1914 Hearing.[13]

man having the same class of work produces the correct quantity, isn't it natural to suppose that the man is very slack or careless in his work, so we must have some sort of record in running a large business and preventing waste wherever possible. . . . We cut in the course of a year several hundred thousand dollars worth of skins and unless we keep some sort of record our business would not be stable, we could not run it at all."[117] It was Adler's policy that if a cutter consistently failed to get the number of gloves which the skins would produce, he would be the first to be dropped. At Littauers, such a man would be given warning and time to improve, but ultimately discharged if he did not measure up.

The greatest problems did not come from the regular cutters, but from times of extra rush, when a few extra cutters were hired, and "they may not be as expert as the more regular cutters and they possibly have a little difficulty once in a while which the man has to show them how the skins can be produced into the gloves required."[118]

In some factories, when a cutter did not produce what was expected, he was subject to fines or damages. The cutters claimed that threat of fines made them nervous. Manufacturers offered a different story: One factory reported it had fined some $30 in a 20-month period in which all the wages totaled over $125,000. All manufacturers, who fined men when they did not meet their tax, claimed that the amounts exacted were small. One superintendent explained another source of the cutters' anxiety: "The noise that is made up on the top floor through the singing and shouting and carrying on like boys is enough to drive me, to prevent me from being able to add up a column of figures. And I have to send out to ask the men to please stop. That makes the men more nervous than the taxation."[119]

One cutter thought the way taxing was done made "it impossible for the cutter to get the proper tranks." If a cutter had to keep looking around for needed scraps, he was constantly worried "whether he was going to be fined or fired. . . . [But the manufacturer] has bought a number of skins at a certain price to cut out a certain number of gloves and he has got stuck and he is going to try to get it out of the help."[120] Another cutter was quite eloquent in his description of the problems: "If you are to read the bible, how the Jewish race were told to go around and pick up straw for making brick, and that they would allow them to make the brick, and then they told them to go around and look for hay, that is just the way the taxation goes here; you get the skins and then you have to go around and look for fittings, you got to waste your time around the shop looking for fittings."[121] Even though the cutters complained that they had difficulty finding scraps from which to cut matching fourchettes or thumbs or wasted time chasing extra scraps through a huge floor of cutters and piles of scraps, there were always enormous amounts of scraps, which the owners could sell periodically.

Taxing was not an American innovation. In fact it had been used in Europe for some time, undoubtedly because those countries had a longer history of producing fine, table-cut gloves. And Europeans taxed more heavily than Americans, or at least that is what Fulton County's manufacturers thought.[122] One manufacturer marveled at the quantity cut from skins in Europe and considered that that was part of the reason Europeans were able to make gloves so much more cheaply than Americans. Albert Aaron, superintendent at Meyers, justified the practice of taxing by saying, "I don't doubt that the men would prefer to have the skins not taxed, but we have to go back to the question of competition, in particular our competition with Europe."[123]

There were other insidious aspects to taxing in some factories: If a glove at whatever stage in its production was found to have defects, the blame was pushed back through makers and inspectors all the way to the cutter. Cutters believed that even in the shops which claimed cutters were never fined, fines where extracted from pay envelopes after the worker had signed for his wages.

Jacob Adler Glove Co. had its share of complaints about taxing, but foreman William J. Stitt claimed that the taxers "are all former cutters themselves. The relations between them and the cutters working for them are quite friendly. . . . Of course, there may be a mistake made on either side once in a while, but as far as our shop is concerned there has always been a pretty good feeling between the cutters and the men over them. . . . The whole manufacturing business here, the glove business, has been run on a friendly line."[124] His statement might seem hypocritical in light of the way the manufacturers suppressed wages.

However, Stitt was fully aware of his company's inability to regulate the factory. To eliminate the potential for abuses between taxers and cutters, Adler's employed a sort of ombudsman, a floorwalker, whose job it was "to walk through the cutting room and act as go-between between the cutter and what troubles he might have and the foreman as it has now got beyond our personal attention. This man serves to review the 'estimating' and rearrange the cutting scale if necessary." Stitt claimed his firm never fined a cutter "for shortage on his tax."

Favoritism by taxers did exist; some cutters paid their taxers to obtain better skins and easier estimates. A principal in Lefi, Bachner, Hall said he watched "the skins to see that there is absolutely no favoritism shown. If we can divide our lots and are in condition to watch them, every cutter gets the same work."[125] One manufacturer admitted that in his shop "one man had entire charge of estimating and it was within his power to do whatever he pleased as regards favoritism to the cutters in general. [He received] either presents or money." The owner claimed the firm put an immediate stop to this, but one modern manufacturer recalled that even in the 1950s and 60s, favoritism went on in his factory and he was essentially powerless to stop it. After all, the business depended on the work of the estimator.[126]

While abuses on the part of heavy taxers left some cutters feeling threatened, a few cutters were also guilty of abuses. One stole skins, another sold scraps that were large enough for tranks.

Cutters' and manufacturers' views on taxation were far apart. Manufacturers believed that the foremen taxed on the number of gloves an average cutter could produce. The cutter believed that "If there shows up a lot of cutters the [foreman] shall tax a little tight and squeeze more because there are more cutters and a few weeks later it is getting busy and many cutters don't show up and we can't get the gloves cut and they tax a little less so it goes like a regular stock market."[127]

But at the bottom of the problem was the fact that some cutters were scared: "Whenever there is anything wrong, when you see four or five foremen in there around you, you look like a little lamb among lions and they will put questions to you and keep you in terror all of the time. Now, I don't feel that is right in a free country, a democratic country like this. It may be all right in Russia, but they would not stand for it here."[128]

In 1914, striking cutters were as concerned about addressing problems of taxing as they were anxious to increase their wages. Taxing was a threat to their wages but an even greater threat to their independence. What started as a way of improving efficiency was held against the manufacturers. The protests were fueled by rumors started by a few bad situations. It is ironic that both the cutters' desires and the manufacturers' attempts at modernization were doomed.

The cutters chose a very unfortunate time for a strike and I told the committee so.
William J. Stitt of
Jacob Adler & Co.[12]

This was the setting in which the cutters decided to call the 1914 strike, but it is ironic that they could not have picked a worse time.

Comparison of glove production between 1909 and 1914
(Figures in parentheses are in 1990 dollars)

	1909	1914
Gloversville	$8,869,000	$7,309,000
	($120,662,745)	($90,324,622)
Johnstown	$3,258,000	$2,914,000
	($44,569,440)	($36,017,104)
US total	$22,525,000	$20,296,000
	($308,142,007)	($250,858,567)

As the chart indicates, the county's total production slipped from nearly 50 percent of the Unites States' total in 1909 to 40 percent in 1914, but the United States' production dropped overall as well. When the 1914 strike was called manufacturers had a much larger stock of gloves on hand than they had ever had before.[129] This overstocked situation combined with the shortage of leather for future work meant that the strike indirectly benefited the manufacturers—they actually had only enough leather for four weeks.

The workers appear to have called the 1914 strike as a last resort. They were totally frustrated and lashed out at any and all slights in the shops because they could not budge manufacturers on wages. They felt impotent and threatened. They anticipated that war would mean increased production levels but in truth they knew nothing about the effects of war.

The State Board of Mediation and Arbitration held six days of hearings in the first half of October 1914. On the 21st of that month, the board summed up the hearings and reported that "the low average cutters' wage, $13.50, was not adequate and would be entirely insufficient to afford a bare living wage if it were not for the earnings of the wives of the cutters, who are forced to work at home or in the factory in order to eke out a living for their families."[130]

The mediation board concluded that the cutters' wages were too low and that the manufacturers' returns (profit on capital) though "not large" did not preclude their granting an increase in wages. The mediators recommended that the manufacturers correct abuses in taxing and that the cutters conform to regular hours, but most importantly that the manufacturers should grant an immediate increase of $.15 a dozen.[131] The union accepted the compromise. This was less than the $.25 the union sought, but just what several manufacturers had been willing to give.

Despite the mediation board's recommendations, members of the Glove Manufacturers Association refused to grant the raise. The cutters and their union had no power; they could no longer fight. The manufacturers were so pressed they believed they had given all they could. The economics of the time was killing what was left of the manufacturers' paternalism. Only the coming war and its inflation would finally bring higher wages.

Because the manufacturers absolutely refused to grant the recommended $.15 raise, the strike or lockout continued. (The workers had struck, but it is obvious that the manufacturers had cut back manufacturing opportunities. This had become a classic lockout.) In December, *The Glovers Review* summed up the situation: "With the present depression in business and demand for gloves curtailed to a point where it is making no serious tax upon the present supply, there would be a great lack of steady employment for the cutters if they were willing to work. So, call it a strike, a lay-off, a lockout or what you will, the fact remains that it is largely a condition."[132]

November came with no change, but an event on the 12th of that month caused the union to lose community support. On that evening, two brothers, Ralph and Isaac Moses, who owned the Elite Glove Company,[133] were walking home. An assailant (who was never identified) emerged from shadows to slash Isaac's neck. He survived—a doctor's office was nearby—but the act of violence helped bring an end to the strike.[134] The cutters could no longer justify their families' suffering and the strike ended officially on January 19, 1915. The glove manufacturers' victory was total. They had won again, but this proved to be a hollow victory.

As 1915 began, the war in Europe expanded, and the glove shops had more work—although the problems of obtaining skins became even more acute. The union had totally misjudged the effect of war and the strength of the association. The union collapse was total.

The old Glove Manufacturers Association folded as well, but only to reorganize as an even larger and more powerful group. In October of 1915, the Glove Manufacturers Association of the State of New York was formed, with president Frank L. Easterly, vice-president George C. Potter, treasurer U. G. Patterson of the C. W. Rose Glove Company, and James S. Ireland returning as secretary. Almost all the members of the old association joined the new one, along with enough new members so that the new organization could claim that its membership employed 80 percent of the table and pull-down cutters in the area. The association's first act was to "fulfill a promise made about a year ago, during the strike, when it was publicly announced by a large number of the employers, that when conditions throughout the industry were such as to permit of the making of an advance in wages, such advance should be voluntarily granted."[135] Consequently, cutters wages were raised ten cents a dozen, not even the $.15 that had been recommended. Both inseam and overseam sewers were also granted a raise of ten cents a dozen.

The defeat of the local union stands out in comparison with the results of a series of strikes that occurred a few years earlier in the garment industry in New York City. A settlement in 1910 had created a sort of closed shop or "preferential union shop," where union rules prevailed and union members were given preference. What differences between the glove and garment industries accounted for the disparate strike results? Were the manufacturers really that powerful or was the union's timing to blame? Both are probably true, but it is also possible that there were too many workers for the level of business and too many manufacturers.

Some insiders alllude to an ethnic difference. A few eastern Europeans were becoming entrepreneurs in the glove industry, but nowhere near the proportion of those who were beginning to dominate the garment industry in New York City. German Jews owned some of the largest shops and held positions of financial importance in others, but the sons and grandsons of the Fulton County's English and Scots owners continued to run a large percentage of the glove shops. While Jews consitituted the largest ethnic group in the cutters' union, they were never a majority.

At the same time, workers throughout the country were beginning to win benefits. Ford Motor Company even instituted profit-sharing. Given the fragmented nature of the glove industry, it is no wonder that owners did not provide workers any real benefits. None would be provided until unions gained strength long after World War II.

Buried in the production statistics and records is the fact that Fulton County's glove industry had peaked. It would be a long time before the extent of the decline would be obvious to glovemen because in the decline, ups and downs masked the trend. What is most amazing is that the county was hardly aware of this high point. The years that produced it were fraught with problems—poor working conditions for the cutters and sewers, difficulties for the manufacturers, threats of increasing imports. Ominous clouds were gathering on the horizon.

Several skin mills shifted from producing glove leather to tanning leather for the shoe industry. Besides Bleyl's, Booth and Co. stopped making leather for gloves by 1902; Northrup & Miller tanned shoe leather after 1912.

In this period of national stagflation, from 1890 to 1914, the glove industry reached its maturity in Fulton County, but the consolidation and growth of large factories during this period was made possible primarily by a freeze on real wages.

A middle layer of management emerged from the ranks of workers. These new foremen did not always have the same humanistic attitudes toward workers. Piecework provided no benefits to workers, and this was especially hard for women. Nor did it provide unemployment insurance or paid vacations. Workman's compensation was just beginning under a New York State law that made such insurance compulsory as of July 1914.

Despite the strength of the Glove Manufacturers Association in dealing with workers and the unions, the organization could not act with a single directed policy in raising prices or wages. Few manufacturers were able to overcome the provincialism that characterized the county's glove manufacturers. Local competition strangled many firms. The owners' independence was beginning to limit their ability to conduct business. It presaged the unfair competition that would burden the industry in the 1930s. And, the independence of the cutters, despite their defeat, led them to demand wages that no craft industry in America could ultimately support.

Among the workers in the county, there was a pervasive belief that the manufacturers kept other businesses away. "They don't want any other industry here because the manufacturers realize that we would have other places to work." This theme is evident in many conversations and interviews with county residents today—they believe it happened, but there is no hard evidence. But, something intangible did help the turn-of-the-century manufacturers keep wages down and that something did reinforce the one-industry dominance of gloves and leather. It could have been the general flight of industry from the Northeast. It could have been the area's aging infrastructure. It could even have been the harsh climate. Whatever the cause, Fulton County's plight resembled the one-industry problems of Schenectady and General Electric or the Berkshires and the paper industry. The failure to attract new industry was one more factor that would ultimately limit the economic viability of the Fulton County.

Even as the county approached the decades in which it basked in its reputation as the premier manufacturer of fine gloves, the handwriting was on the wall—the industry as it was developing could not survive.

In this period a large proportion of the industry had not only moved west, it had begun an inexorable flight from the county. "After the last tariff bill went into effect," one manufacturer "seriously considered the opening up of a foreign factory."[136] Despite paying wages below those of skilled workers in other industries, the gap between the cost of glove production in Fulton County and that of foreign countries continued to grow. For the manufacturers the strike's end was a hollow victory because there were already signs that the industry was moving away. Mounting problems—shortages of workers and raw materials—would increase pressures on glove manufacturers more and more.

I had thought I would have to look to the post World War II era to find the causes of the industry's demise, when in fact the seeds of its decline were already present before the turn of the century: shortages of workers and materials, competition, lack of organization, unions, cheaper places to manufacturer gloves than in the county, and lack of new investment on the part of manufacturers. All these were evident even before gloves became less important as fashion, before fabrics began to replace leather for gloves, before the last wave of immigrants sent their sons and daughters off to college and brighter futures. At the time the county's industry was reaching its highest levels, all the aspects that led to its ultimate virtual demise were present. As in a Greek tragedy, those elements were obvious, but not to the participants. The globalization of the industry, competition, both at home and abroad, pressure for wage increases, shortage of workers desiring to do low-paying handwork, and the flight of the industry from the area all foretold a future decline. At the outbreak of World War I, local manufacturers were beginning to import more and more fine gloves. The war would stop this and temporarily halt the flight of business from the county, but not for long.

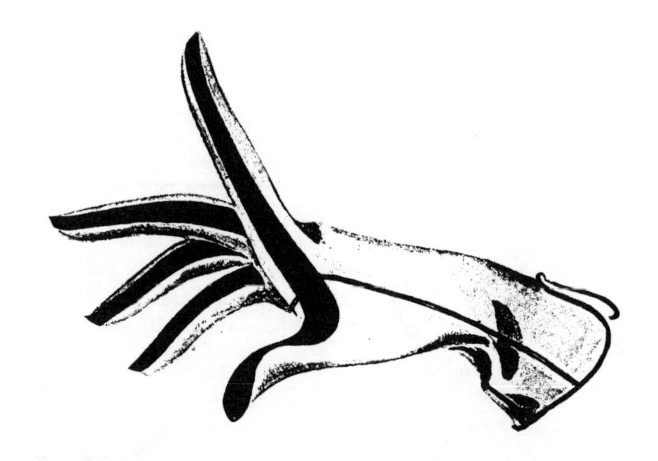

Between the Wars

World War I and World War II serve as bookends of an era in which many changes in the glove industry did little to slow the inevitable decline of glove-making in Fulton County. In the period between the wars, the ethnic makeup of the county's two main centers changed dramatically and in different ways.

The foreign-born population of Johnstown, only 14 percent in 1900, jumped to 30 percent in 1930. Into an immigrant mix dominated by Germans and Irish in 1900 came Eastern Europeans, mostly Slovaks, who accounted for almost 20 percent of the foreign-born population in 1910, and 30 percent in the twenties and thirties.

The percentage of foreign born in Gloversville was comparable to that in Johnstown, but the mix was quite different. Eastern Europeans migrated to Gloversville in the first decade of the century, along with a large number of Jews, but in 1910 they did not constitute as large a proportion of the population as Germans. In the next decade Italians became the dominant foreign-born group.

By 1915 Johnstown's Slovak community was strong and well organized with its *Sokol* and church. Many in this ethnic group went into the leather business. From the men who first worked as unskilled laborers in the tanneries emerged a second generation who owned or managed tanneries—Mike Subik, Fred Simek, George Valachovic, and T. Kralovich.

Bill Wormuth recalled how his grandfather worked in Maylander's tannery until he was 75, when Mrs. Maylander gave him a 200-acre farm in North Bush as a reward for his long service. Some Slovak men went to work in glove shops; Wormuth's father worked for Ireland Brothers for 40 years, first as a layer-off, then a shipping clerk, then as a clicker cutter.

His mother worked there as a gauge maker. His grandmother sewed at home, and like every family in town, the children pulled the ends of threads so they could be tied. A large number of Slovaks went into the knitting mills, such as Swears and Scotsmoor. As Wormuth remembers, "everybody's mother worked, women always worked, and they were proud of their work." Families were large, but quickly assimilated into the community. Intermarriage, opportunities for higher education, and chances to advance

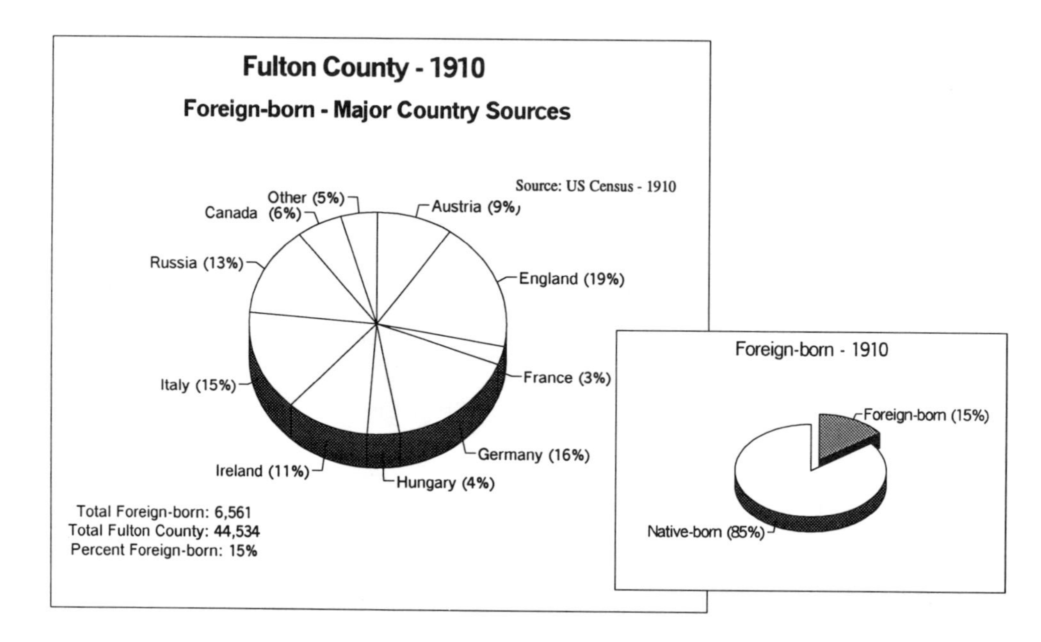

soon undermined the clannishness of the Slovak community. Its members, like those in other ethnic groups, profited from work in the glove and leather industries and worked for the future of their children, whom they encouraged to branch out into other endeavors.

Slovaks settled at first near Karg's mill and the northern part of Johnstown. Their Catholic church, St. Anthony's, experienced a period of conflict and many members left to form the Sts Cyril and Methodius First Presbyterian Church. When that failed the splinter group joined Johnstown's very staid and proper First Presbyterian Church.

Italian immigration started a little later than Slovak, but surged in the decade before 1920. In Johnstown the percentage of Italian-born reached 15.6 percent in 1920; it was 16.7 percent a decade later. Everyone worked, and from their large families, many children grew up to work in the glove

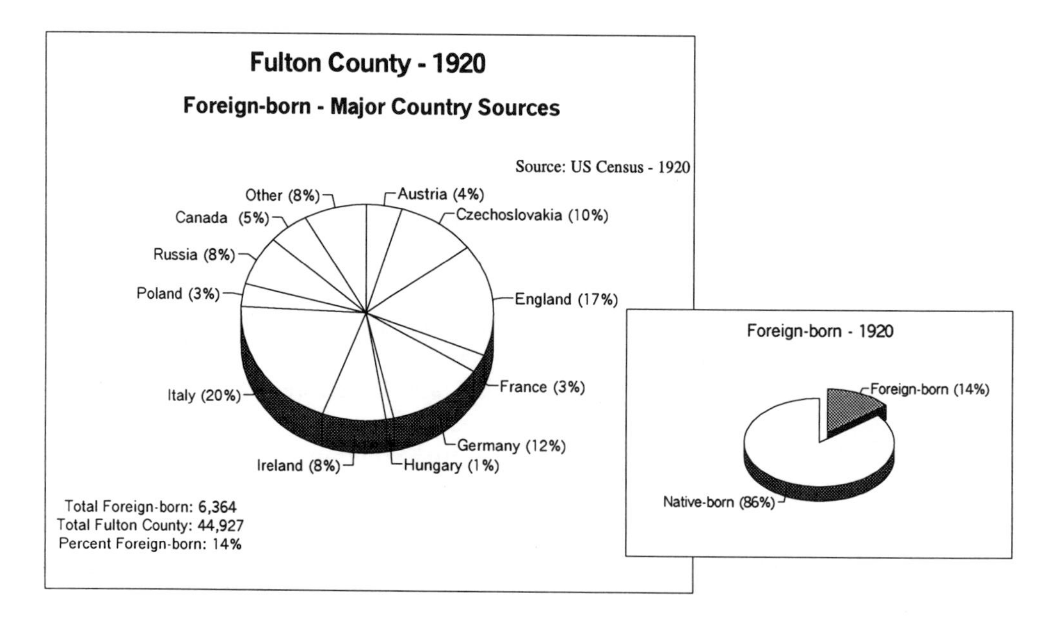

factories. In Gloversville the proportion of foreign-born who were Italian was well over 20 percent in 1920 and remained about 20 percent in 1930, when Italians constituted the largest single ethnic group. (However, for all the immigrants who made their way to the county, the proportion of foreign born never exceeded that of America's big cities.[1])

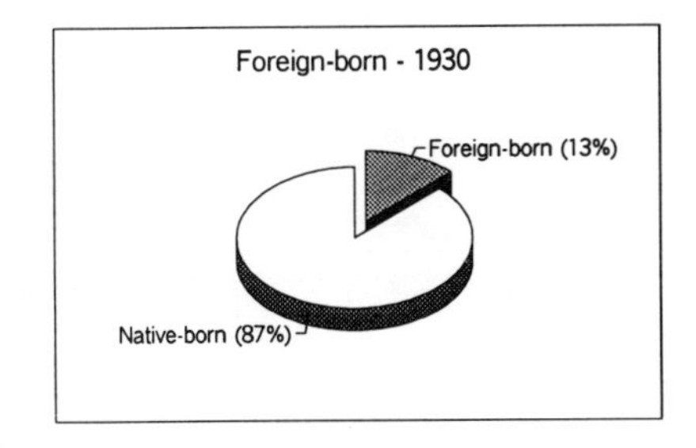

Italian men often worked as cutters. Whether they had been trained in Italy or apprenticed in America, they were an independent lot. Many established small glove shops in their homes or in factories others had outgrown. This brought a new group of entrepreneurs into the glove industry, some of them among the more successful in the decade between the wars, and still more who established businesses after World War II.

Many Italian families were very poor. They settled on Park and Pine streets and Bloomingdale Avenue, the area they dubbed "Hungry Hill." Almost every Italian woman sewed gloves at one time or other. Many did throughout their whole lives. For Italian families it was not exceptional for wives to work; throughout America Italian wives were regularly employed in many industries.[2]

Ed Perrone's family is not quite typical—it was considerably larger than average. His father came from Italy in 1893 and worked as a cutter at Meyers; Ed, who related the family's history to me, learned cutting there as well. His father's first wife died at the birth of her eighteenth child. He remarried and had six more children, of whom Ed, 79 in 1997, was the oldest, and Rene, at one time head of Liberty Tanning, was the youngest. Joe, the oldest in the first family, had a glove shop, Perrone Gloves, on Cayadutta Street in Gloversville. All of the 24 children worked in either the glove or leather industry. Ed does not remember feeling the Depression; Meyers was a good place to work in those years. But, the family was poor. They owned their own home, but slept four to a bed and most left school early to go to work. When Ed left trade school at fifteen, he was a better cutter than his instructor.

Humbert Salluzzo has a slightly different story. His father was not a cutter, so Humberto could not become an apprentice. His father had had a

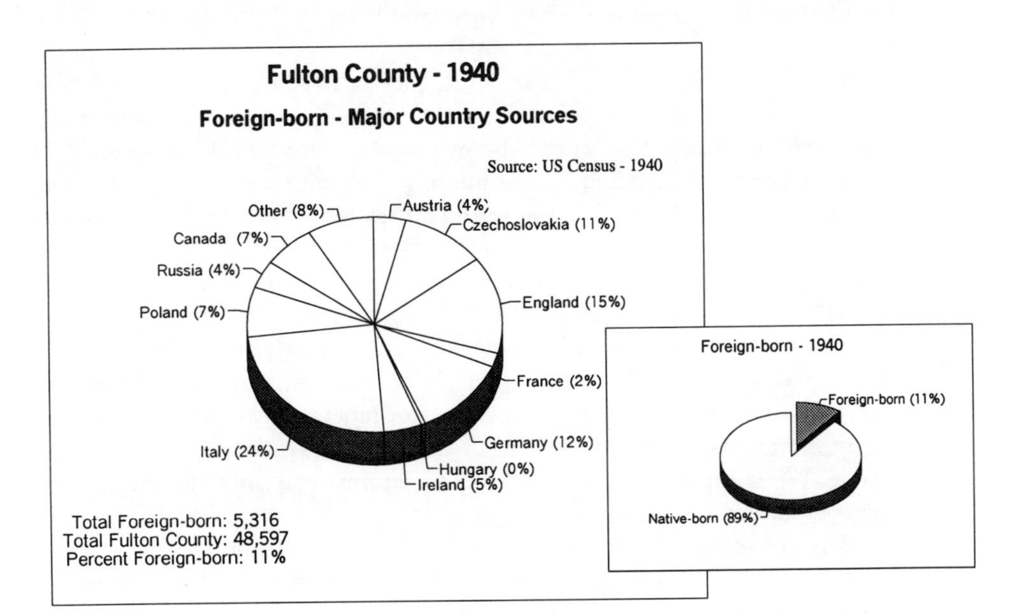

stationery store in Naples and did not like living in the States; his mother learned to sew gloves and used a treadle machine all her life, turning out a dozen perfect gloves a day. The family moved back and forth between Naples and Gloversville, but the mother was always the breadwinner here.

Saluzzo remembers that discrimination was very real: a house he rented was sold out from under him because the son of the owner did not want to live next to an Italian. Both Perrone and Saluzzo are certain that Italians were the best cutters, and they remember the noise of the cutting rooms and the way the cutters told jokes all day long and the older generation of cutters who owned big cars and dressed in white shirts and ties.

Pasquale Fugazzotto—now a pediatrician in Pennsylvania—remembers growing up in Johnstown's close-knit Italian community in the late Depression and war years. His father served in the Italian army in World War I and came to America when he was 21. He worked at various jobs around the country before settling down in Johnstown and marrying in 1930. He worked in the glove business for 64 years, retiring three times, and died at the age of 93. Fugazzotto's mother sewed at home until the children were grown, then she worked at Gates-Mills. Fugazzotto remembers that the whole street worked, and that most of the sons and daughters left for college as he did. His parents were very frugal, but saved enough to buy a home. His father was never a member of a union, although his mother was. This angered his mother, and she made his father go to his employer to arrange retirement income.

The Irish constituted Johnstown's third large ethnic group. Many had arrived in the nineteenth century. Irish immigration continued into the 1930s. Even though many Irish women sewed at home or in the shops, few Irish men established shops of their own, and those that did started later. The Cleary Tannery was in operation after the World War II and into the fifties. Joseph Conroy, in 1997 the patriarch of the county's glove industry, did not establish his glove shop until World War II.

Immigration slowed in the twenties due to restrictive legislation and remained low in the thirties. The total population of both Johnstown and Gloversville was stagnant in these years and actually decreased after World War II.

In the years before World War II, the picture that emerges is of two very vibrant communities with the work force continually enriched by new immigrants who were eager for work. The newcomers were quickly established in the communities. They found good housing, they found good places to raise families, and, after the turn of the century, they sent their children away—to college and to work. For most of the immigrants, the glove industry was a stepping stone to economic freedom and success. And of all the reasons uncovered in a deeper look at the industry between the wars and in the search for the reasons why the industry slipped so greatly after World War II, one explanation stands out: The number of immigrants slowed and almost stopped; the immigrant working class was not renewed. It is possible that immigrant workers extended the life of the industry long after it was truly viable. When immigration stopped, manufacturers had only one choice—to take production overseas.

A major source of information on the shops, the ethnic groups, and the areas they settled is the city directories. A comparison of directories over the years throws light on the changes in the ways the communities saw themselves. Initially the directories, which were first published in 1867, did not record women workers, or identify women glove workers by their occupations in the same way as they did for men. This had more to say about the subservient role of women in the late nineteenth and early twentieth century than it did about the amount of work women did. They were the backbone of the glove industry from the start, and yet it was not until the early 1930s that women glove workers were identified by their occupation. However, female teachers, bookkeepers, clerks, and so on were listed by their profession long before women sewers were noted. This is, perhaps, an indication of the fact that the communities were beginning to assign female factory workers a lower status, that the directories reflected not only gender discrimination, but growing class discrimination.

The 1920 *Gloversville Johnstown Directory* rarely identified cutters by their place of employment. This may be a subtle confirmation of their independence, the fact that they contracted out their work at will. Pocketbook workers appeared in the 1920 directory. Retired people were also listed. Whereas people who sewed gloves were previously referred to as glovers, now there was a category of "makers." In later years as more and more women had to give up homework, the directories adopted "operators" for that category.

The directories listed a few women glove manufacturers over the years: Mrs. J. M. Stockley, circa 1880; Mrs. F. Beach and Mrs. I. A. Leonard of Gloversville, circa 1900; Grace Filmore, 1924; Mrs. Mary Principe and Mrs. Anna Gillmen, circa 1932.

In 1920, only nine boarding places were indexed, including Gloversville's YMCA. Related businesses had proliferated: merchants of chemicals and dyes; manufacturers of metal dies and blocks for cutting; suppliers of fasteners; importers of leather; splitters; dealers in raw skins, glove remnants, silk thread, and sewing machines; and sewing-machine repairmen.

Also listed are several silk manufacturers. In the 1920s, a number of Johnstown residents listed knitting mills as places of employment. (Fulton County was a cradle of the knit-fabric industry, which gradually expanded to surrounding communities like Ballston Spa and Palatine Bridge, but that story is beyond the scope of this book.)

By 1930, the directory listed die cutters separately from cutters. Glovers became glove makers. Also listed for the first time were a number of phone operators, bookkeepers of both sexes, and night watchmen.

Tannery workers there were divided into splitters and kneestakers. By 1930, glove makers were divided into specialized occupations like brushers, layers-off, and hemmers. The number of company presidents, vice-presidents, foremen and forewomen, bookkeepers, and stenographers in the 1930 directory points up the growth of a large and separate level of management within the glove shops.

Few women became managers of glove companies, even though sewers remained the backbone of production. Nationally, in 1920, only one in fifteen married women was employed. By contrast, in Fulton County almost every woman married to a cutter or layer-off also worked, usually sewing gloves. The directories give evidence of the fact that an increasing number of foreladies and union officers rose from the ranks of the sewers.

The distinction between male workers and entrepreneurs remained blurred as a man might be listed as a cutter one year, as a manufacturer the next. In the smaller shops, owners' wives occasionally served as bookkeepers and sewers, but very few wives of the owners of larger glove factories were employed. Among women there was a real class distinction in the county. From this time date a number of women's clubs and a coterie of women of leisure.

World War I - 1915 - 1918

The county began producing gloves for the Army during the Civil War when the M. S. Northrup Glove Co. made 2,500 dozen pairs of gloves dyed green and brown for use by the northern armies. Daniel Hays, Littauer, and Richard Evans manufactured gloves for the army during the first decade of the twentieth century and were in a good position to produce gloves during wartime.

As logical as it would seem that war would bring good times to manufacturers of gloves and uniforms, two things kept this prosperity from the county's glove makers. One was the long period that war gripped Europe before the United States became involved and the country's slow efforts toward mobilization. The other was that, by World War I, most work gloves came from the West and Midwest, and Fulton County was so totally focused on fine men's dress gloves that its manufacturers benefitted only slightly from wartime production.

The early war years were a contradictory time. During 1915, the year after the devastating, five-month strike, business recovered very slowly. A majority of the workers found work, though many only part-time, and all factories resumed operations, though at less than full capacity.[3]

Shortages in leather forced the work-glove industry to begin to substitute canvas and other fabrics for leather for heavy-duty gloves. In 1916, the changeover in Fulton County to fine gloves was virtually complete, with 95 percent of the country's production in fine gloves concentrated in Fulton County. That production, however, depended on foreign sources of leather, primarily kidskins from Europe. At this point, prices of skins rose sharply, speculation hit the leather industry, and manufacturers were afraid to accept orders. This happened at the same time the country and the county were experiencing a sense of prosperity. The decline in exports from Europe prompted *The Glovers Review* to encourage manufacturers to build on the industry's successes, specifically, the use of chrome-tanning methods that allowed domestic production to rival that of Europe in quality and the development of washable leather for gloves.

Despite the shortages, by mid-1916, the county's business had improved so much that every available cutter and maker was busy.[4] At the same time, however, orders for foreign-made gloves also began to increase.

Just as factories were expanding, raw materials suddenly became harder to obtain, while prices continued to escalate. In 1915, the British Navy blockaded Germany and Austria. France put an embargo on the shipment of kidskins to the United States. A shipment of Arabian blackhead sheep for mocha was lost when a ship was sunk in the Mediterranean. Louis Meyers & Son managed to circumvent the British blockade of the shipment of gloves from Europe but it is not clear how the company did this. As the war curtailed Europe's glove industry, prices there rose.

Europe, primarily Germany, had shipped 80 percent of the coal-tar dyestuffs or aniline dyes used in the United States. The war stopped shipment of dyes and caused a crisis in the leather industry. By 1917, even needles had become scarce, and far more expensive. That year, the government released German patents on dyes so American companies could produce them, and E. I. Du Pont Powder Company began their manufacture.

By 1918, the shortages were becoming so acute that the industry started using cotton and wool materials. Gloves were made of a newly perfected fabric, sueded cotton, developed and produced in mills in the southern United States. An editorial in *The Glovers Review* recalled the disdain local manufacturers had for coarse cotton gloves produced elsewhere, but in a very short time manufacturers in the eastern United States began to offer fine cotton sueded gloves, at remarkably high prices. A footnote to the expansion into fabric gloves is the observation that Japan had already stepped into the void by creating new factories to produce fabric gloves. The county reconciled itself to fabric gloves by pointing out that the "distinctly American" cotton and wool die-cut gloves, "made on the outseam on the lines of leather gloves . . . are very attractive in appearance."[5] But even here shortages threatened to limit production. Manufacturers were so desperate they experimented with ways of making "artificial leather" from cotton and wool.

Parenthetically, the wartime introduction of new kinds of fabric gloves would plague the county's manufacturers after the war. Cheaper fabric gloves would begin to supplant women's fine leather gloves, just as the county was making inroads in that market.

During the three years (1914-1917) that the United States did not participate in Europe's war, the county's manufacturers seemed oblivious to the war, or as if they were trying to ignore its consequences. On April 6, 1917, the United States formally entered the European conflict and the first American troops were sent abroad on June 26, 1917. *The Glovers Review* for 1917 says little about the county's role in the war; it seems as if manufacturers were having difficulty coming to grips with worldwide events. Only as 1917 drew to a close did the review mention the United States' expanded preparations for war and the prospect of needing most sheep-glove leather for soldiers' coats. The supply of heavy leather skins decreased as animal production, both at home and in South America, declined.

Just as the country entered the war, the ever-optimistic glovemen were speculating on what the effect of peace might be on the prices of raw skins.[6] *The Glovers Review* concluded that scarcity of transportation and competition would keep prices high. That newsletter observed ruefully that war is better for manufacturers of heavy gloves than the producers of dress gloves like those in Fulton County. The county's glove manufacturers were probably no more isolationist than the country as a whole, but they went to great lengths to keep production normal. The manufacturers conformed only reluctantly to government-imposed, wartime limits and controls.

In March 1918 the Hide and Leather Control Board (a federal wartime agency) informed the Tanners Council that the government would need the entire production of sheep and lamb leather for clothing for the army. Shortly afterwards the federal government began to limit local production. The conservation committee of the War Industries Board restricted the number of styles that could be produced in the county, the colors that could be used, and the length of the gloves.

The year 1918 revealed just how severe were the problems of producing fine gloves in wartime and the extent to which the county had lost momentum by abdicating to the West and Midwest the production of heavy gloves. Fine leather was needed for everything but gloves—watch straps, field-glass cases, bindings for manuals. Horsehides were made into glove leather. Long gloves were no longer in style; Paramount Glove Co. of New York City took out a large ad in *The Glovers Review* offering to make two pairs of short gloves from returned long silk and fabric gloves.

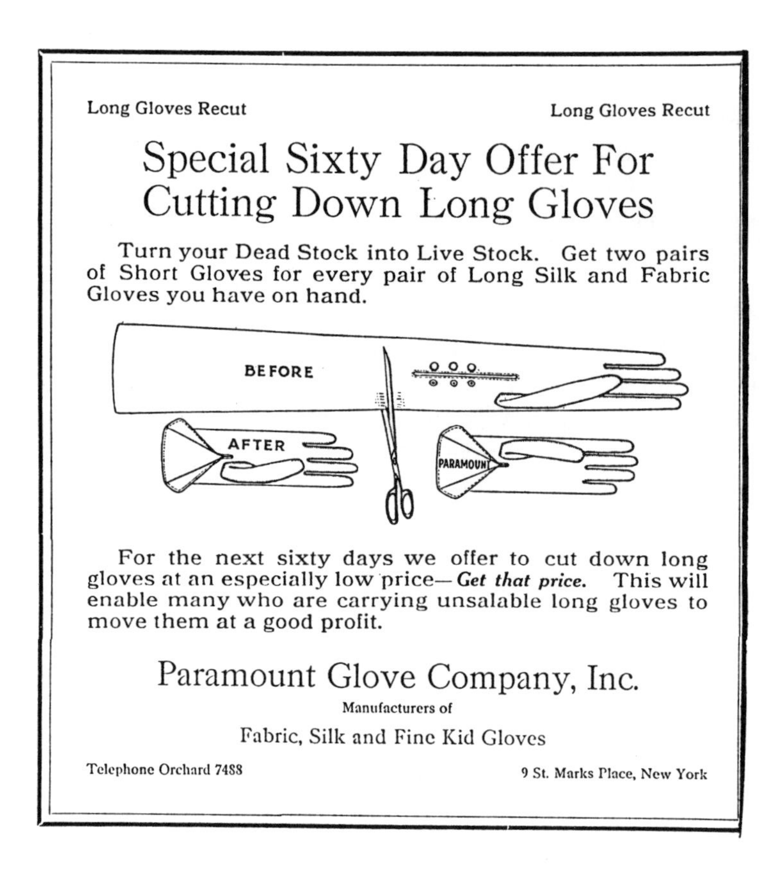

Only toward the end of the war did the government begin buying gloves in large quantities. It was early 1918 before the county's manufacturers began to realize what war could do to their business; they estimated that they would have to devote from between 25 to 30 percent of their production to government orders. Still, their concerns focused on fine gloves. Their efforts to maintain stability in their part of the industry make it seem as if they were wearing blinders.

In March 1918 the government placed a ban on imports of foreign skins, and a member of the Congressional Military Affairs Committee exhorted local manufacturers to accept that prohibition as their way of supporting the war effort. By April 1918 the price of leather gloves had almost doubled, and the county's manufacturers could obtain almost no glove leather. In May the War Industries Board fixed the price of all raw skins, but there was little domestic production to make up for the shortages of foreign skins because sheep farming in America was declining.

By mid-1918 fine glove manufacturers were unable to fill orders for fall because all raw materials had been "commandeered by the Government." But, Ireland Brothers advertised that regulation military dress gloves, which it was supplying to the government, would make great Christmas presents. That company remodeled a brick house near its main plant to increase production of government gloves.

By July even stocks that could be used for second-quality gloves were in short supply. Almost belatedly, in mid-1918 the government geared up to send three million more troops to France by the spring of 1919. The county was already working at full capacity, and dedicating 50 percent of its labor force to supplying gloves for the 1.5 million men who had already been sent overseas. In September 1918 the government created a War Service Board to place the glove industry on a wartime basis. James S. Ireland was nominated chairman of the board, which had five subcommittees, only one of which represented the light leather industry of Fulton County. That subcommittee was also chaired by Ireland and its only other member was Albert Aaron of Louis Meyers & Son. Midwesterners represented the heavy leather or work glove industry, the wool fabric work glove industry, and the cotton fabric work glove industry; New York City manufacturers represented the fabric glove industry. Colors, styles, lengths of gloves, packaging, and boxes were all severely regulated by these committees.

In September the county's glovemen noted that the influenza epidemic had curtailed sales of gloves. With the signing of the Armistice on November 11, the war was over. The county's boom in glove production lasted less than a year. Any prosperity gained from the war was concentrated locally into a few months in 1918. Labor shortages caused wages to rise, but only briefly. Supplies of skins limited production. Manufacturers could enjoy greater profits, if any, for only a short period.

At the end of the war, restrictions on imports and production were removed, contracts were cancelled selectively so as not to create unemployment, and plans were made to remove price limits on skins. But the prospects of normality did not relieve the worries of the county's manufacturers. *The Glovers Review* reminded them that so many animals had been slaughtered for the war effort with little replacement of herds and flocks that for "years to come, the leather from [sheep, lamb, and kid] skins is going to be one of the scarcest materials in the world."[7] Even at the end of the war, the *Review* could note that "so few fine American leather gloves are made from skins of domestic origin" that their production is identical to that of foreign manufacturers. Despite the higher quality of locally made gloves, leather shortages induced increased production of fabric gloves and this in turn led to the creation of the Fabric Glove Manufacturers Association of the United States. This new association, formed by manufacturers of silk, cotton, and wool gloves, would function separately from the National Association of Glove Manufacturers in future years. It included among its members several county businesses as well as fabric glove manufacturers from upstate cities like Glens Falls and Balston Spa.

A shortage of workers and the industry's dependence on hand labor inspired other worries for one writer in *The Glovers Review*. He noted that at war's end that fine glove production had decreased by 60 percent and he predicted it would remain at that low level "until we can get a sufficient number of men back to the cutting tables and educate others to fill the places of the men who will never return."[8]

Between 1909 and 1919, glove production in the county dropped by 25 percent. This decline in production happened at the time European production dropped to about a quarter of its pre-war level. Four million dozen pairs had been imported annually before the war, now competition from abroad amounted to no more than a million dozen pairs.

Wage increases accompany conflicts and World War I was no exception. Cutters had received an increase at the end of 1915, but it was below what they had fought for in 1914 and early 1915. Cutters received that pay hike and then some at the end of 1916 when they gained a 25 percent wage increase. At the same time sewers gained 17 percent, and bonuses of two to six percent were given to those who work more than a 48-hour week. As a result of increased war work, wages were raised again at the end of 1917. Then, in May 1918, Fulton County's manufacturers granted cutters a raise of ten cents a dozen in order to keep up with rises in the cost of living.[9] This was the fourth raise in three years, resulting in a total of between 40 and 50

1915

The firm of Bachner-Hall was established by C. J. Bachner, who had started in business with his father, Joseph Bachner.

1916

H. G. Hilts added to its sewing and cutting capacity.

Jones & Naudin, dealers in imported leather, erected a large new building in Gloversville.

Fownes began an addition to their factory.

The Buckskin Glove Company added a new three story addition.

Thomas E. Ricketts, who began making gloves in Johnstown in 1867, retired. His firm continued as Boyce-Lazarus, with its former salesman and bookkeeper as principals.

1918

Hallock & Stewart incorporated with a capital of $300,000.

The Lefler Tannery of Johnstown was fitted up to manufacture fine cotton cloth for sueded gloves.

Adams & Co., buckskin tanners, replaced their tannery, which had been destroyed by fire.

Herbert Topp's factory was totally destroyed by fire.

Bachner-Moses-Louis hired Leonard W. Grant, a well-known manager.

R. Antevil & Co. leased the Schermerhorn building.

Bachner Brothers moved the manufacturing of its Atlas Fabric and die-cut wool gloves from Oswego to a new building attached to the rear of Bachner-Hall's Bleecker Street factory.

percent increase in wages over the rates prevailing at the end of the strike in 1914.

The Glovers Review observed that there recently had been no strikes and no lockouts in the leather glove industry although several had occurred in silk glove operations and in the tanneries. The lack of strikes was attributed to the "stable character" of the leather glove workers and the wage increases granted by the manufacturers.

A record wave of strikes swept through many industries during the war years and the early twenties.[10] The cutters' strike in 1914 had devastated local unions. The weakness of the unions combined with an upsurge in work toward the end of the war kept strikes and unrest to a minimum locally, in contrast to the national scene.

"Forget the past"

It is not easy to forget former prices and qualities, but it is absolutely essential to do it. . . [A manufacturer can operate much more profitably if he does not] constantly make comparisons with conditions that prevailed in 1913.
Editorial in *The Glovers Review*, June 1918 [1]

The Glovers Review began 1918 with an article castigating the industry for its backward (the review called it Chinese) accounting practices. In it was a note from a Kansas City manufacturer who bragged about his strong grasp on "our manufacturing by knowing daily what we have available, will make, ship, and the promises we can safely give [reduce prices] on orders received."[11] Fulton County's smaller manufacturers employed bookkeepers to record hours worked or pieces sewn, wages, and materials used, but none computed or projected profit and loss with any accuracy. Glovemen still struggled from the purchase of leather to sales with no clear idea of the total costs.

The wartime imperative for greater productivity did encourage factory owners to reconsider theories of building design. *The Glovers Review* advised owners of both multi-story structures and smaller one-story factories to adopt a progression of operations that offered easy and efficient handling of both incoming and outgoing materials, good light, ventilation, and room for workers and machines.

Elite Glove Co. built in 1915
Fulton County Museum

In the war years, a few new factories opened while others expanded. Many new corporations were formed in efforts to raise cash for these expansions, but mostly for restructuring existing buildings. Even though the list of expansions and incorporations in the county is impressive, the comparable list describing similar development in the West and Midwest is at least 20 times longer.

In 1915 Elite Glove Co. completed a new factory in Gloversville with fireproof stairwells; a restaurant; 3,500 panes of glass; separate rest rooms for men and women; and enough space in the four-story structure for 500 workers. Its principals were Ralph and Isaac Moses and J. H. Lautterstein.

Daniel Hays increased its common stock, added to its building and rearranged operations to promote efficiency and increase production by 50 percent. The new factory layout followed the pattern that had been developing and that all new firms would follow: leather stored on the top—fourth—floor, cutting below, sewing next, laying-off below, and shipping on the ground or basement floor.

Several tanneries were built, in fact many more new tanneries than new glove shops. A few mills were producing shoe uppers and leather for products other than gloves. The firm of Gustav Levor, which had started making white leather for shoes before 1890, built a new tannery building in 1915 to increase its production of shoe leather and washable suede glove leather. That expansion allowed his company to maintain its control of the market for white kid used for uppers.

Also in 1915, Richard Evans & Sons erected a two-story building to produce washable cape leather as that company had shifted production from work gloves to fine gloves. With a new structure, Wood & Hyde increased its output of washable cape for gloves. Liberty Dressing Company, Gloversville, incorporated with Arthur K. Hamm, John N. Ruff, and Frank A. Patten as principals. Patten's father had learned the glove business in Yeovil, England, and brought his family to Gloversville in 1884 where he ran a glove shop until his death in 1905. Frank Patten had started in his father's glove business.

Wartime also brought prosperity to the silk mills. Adirondack Silk Mills, a new corporation, began producing silk gloves in Gloversville. Superior Silk Mills, with Samuel Rothschild, W. Donald Hyde, Jasper J. Stanyon, and Robert N. Russell, incorporated in Gloversville in 1919. Russell sold out in 1930 and established Acme Glove Corp. in Fulton County; the Fenimore Fabric Co. in Cobleskill; and Superior Silk in Prescott, Ontario.

Also in 1919, Kingsboro Silk Mills was formed and took over Normandie Silk Mills' building. Three of the mills survived into the late 1930s, all in Kingsboro: The Fulton County Silk Mills (founded in 1901), Kingsboro Silk Mills, and Superior Silk Mills. (Note "mills" all are plural in original.)[12]

Near the end of the war, Gloversville and Johnstown manufacturers must have sensed a future shortage of workers. This explains why they began to set up businesses in the county's outlying centers and in nearby communities, even though factories in the two cities had not returned to full production. Fear & White opened a branch factory for sewing gloves in Wells, Hamilton County, in May 1918. Christie & Wilkins of Mayfield had factories in Northville and Herkimer. Kingsley & Mansfield of Northville purchased the two-story factory of Ressigue & Partridge in order to expand their operation. Borst Glove Co. purchased a large Broadalbin factory formerly owned by Littauer Brothers.

Closings

Remarkably few firms closed in the war years. Among the oldest to close was Mason, Campbell & Co, which had been established in Johnstown in 1869.

C. S. and G. W. Schermerhorn, one of the few manufacturers of heavy gloves in Gloversville, closed in 1918 after 32 years.

Deaths and retirements in the war years

Edgar W. Starr, leading tanner, age 79. He had worked for several firms before taking over Starr and Geisler.

Sherwood Haggart, age 72. His father had been one of Gloversville's pioneering glovemen.

James Stewart, of Raymond & Stewart, then Stewart & Briggs until Stewart retired in 1904.

Frank L. Easterly, age 56, of Clark-Easterly Glove Co. Gloversville.

George B. Hallock, age 42, of Hallock & Stewart, Johnstown.

William C. Potter, retired co-founder in 1889 of Hutchens & Potter.

The Decade of Optimism - 1920-1929

Slow Recovery

Up to May 1, 1922, business was so stagnant it almost required a stethoscope to hear its heart beat, but since then there has been a steady recovery in orders.
The Glovers Review, July 1922

The beginning of the decade was marked by very slow recovery in the glove industry. The end of the war brought the immediate confirmation of fears regarding the supply of skins, which continued to sell at prices well above the government rates fixed during the war. "Manufacturers will have to work on quarter or half time for many months, because they have not the leather."[13] The government's cancellation of orders had little effect on the reduced production; instead shortage of leather was the main deterrent to recovery.

Suddenly sueded cotton gloves became such an important part of the industry that Congress began considering tariffs on them in order to preserve and develop the business in the United States. The Tariff Commission commented that it was "an open question whether American manufacturers can continue to make cotton gloves in competition with Germany and Japan"[14] after normal conditions were restored.

France and England were experiencing problems similar to those of the county's producers of leather gloves: short supplies; rising wages; and escalating prices, whose effect on the market could not be gauged. Germany's leather trade had been ruined. Europeans were attempting to import leather from America. During the war, some leather had been shipped directly to the United States from Africa and Saudi Arabia, but quickly that shipment was redirected to England and Europe. Competition resumed at an alarming rate.

By May of 1919 prices for raw skins of all kinds the world over were soaring. Domestic leather for automobile gloves and men's cheaper gloves was also in short supply. Still, orders for leather dress gloves soared, but a new problem emerged: it was impossible to find all the workers needed. An editorial in *The Glovers Review* reflected that for years glovers had claimed that cutting gloves was highly specialized process, passed from father to son and that sewing requires skill equal to cutting. "Yet, for years the wages of glove cutters—artisans though they may be—have been far below those of carpenters, plumbers and automobile mechanics."[15] No new cutters were learning the trade, and the county, the editorial estimated, had 20 percent fewer cutters than before the war.

The depression of 1922 diminished sales of fine leather gloves, and unemployment meant a downturn in sales of work gloves, alhough the ever-optimistic *Glovers Review* saw "signs of life in the leather work glove industry" in mid-1922.[16] Both the coal and railroad strikes were settled in late 1922, meaning those workers could again buy gloves, but that helped midwestern glovemen, not the county's.

In 1922 factories in the United States and in France had cut prices "to the bone" and were "marking time for want of orders."[17] That year the enormous devaluation of German currency brought rapid rises in the cost of living there. This compelled a high increase in wages. German exports dwindled all through 1923, partly because of American tariffs, partly because of British anti-dumping efforts, and partly because of these monetary problems.

Czechoslovakia, with 36,000 glove workers, was emerging as a source of gloves, as 90 percent of that country's production was destined for export. The protective tariff law of 1922 extended duties to agricultural products and raised the general tariff level by approximately 36 percent.

Expansions
1920

Milton E. Trumbull remodeled his factory to produce velour gloves.
Stockamore Leather Co. purchased a Gloversville tannery.
Liberty Dressing purchased a tannery on Burr Street.
C. L. VanDoren & Sons and White-Smith Glove Co. consolidated into one firm.
Dempster & Place Co. expanded on Bleecker Street.
Imperial Glove Company moved to a new factory on Eighth Ave.
Gates-Mills & Co. doubled the size of its plant on North Market Street, Johnstown. With remodeling this created room for 80 machines and a modern arrangement. Sprinklers were also installed.
Chapman, Finch & Smith, a new glove concern, Johnstown. In 1922, George H. Chapman sold his interest to the other two partners and established George H. Chapman & Sons in Johnstown in a three story brick building on North Perry Street.
Boyce-Lazarus Co., Johnstown, and G. W. Mandrill, Gloversville, each became corporations.

Countries other than the traditional European manufacturers were attempting to build up indigenous glove businesses. In 1923 representatives from Mexico visited Gloversville looking for instructors to help establish a glove industry there.

In the 1920s, without a strong labor movement, the gains of productivity [went] into plant, profits, and speculation. [2]

In the twenties, in contrast with what was happening in the rest of the country, Fulton County saw few new and more modern factories, even though there were many additions and remodelings. One of the more compelling characteristics of the county's industry is the fact that so few completely new factories were built after World War I. In fact, the stock of brick factories built between the 1870s and the early 1900s housed most of the county's glove shops right up until the closing years of the industry in the 1960s and 1970s.

A number of companies incorporated as ways of protecting its officers, but many raised capital in this way to increase business capacity. They bought a few new sewing machines, but many of the clicker-cutting machines, which were not only becoming standard for slitting glove tranks but were being used for cutting gloves directly from a stretched skin. One wonders if these machines ultimately replaced the table cutters or if the later shortage of table cutters accelerated their installation.

Association activities

The Glove Manufacturers Association of the State of New York continued active in Fulton County through the war and the early 1920s with some of the same officers: James Ireland, Albert Aaron of Meyers, and U. G. Patterson of C. W. Rose.

"The National Association of Leather Glove Manufacturers was organized in June 1918 in Chicago for the purpose of cooperating with the government in furnishing gloves needed for various branches of the army with the least disturbance to civil business."[18] Its 30 members were mostly western manufacturers of heavy gloves, whose aggregate production totalled two million pairs. It started in 1917 and 1918 in informal meetings on glove contracts and was initially associated with garment manufacturers. Its real beginning, however, stemmed from the end of the war, and after 1920 it began to hold semiannual meetings.

The national group was invited to hold its convention in Gloversville in 1922, a prelude to the joining with the county-based Glove Manufacturers Association. In June 1922 the fifth annual convention was held in Gloversville, a joining of eastern, western, and Canadian glove manufacturers. The formal application of the New York group to join the National Association of Glove Manufacturers (NAGM) was accepted, along with a statement of the new group's objectives: the furtherance of national legislation for the glove industry, national cooperation to secure trade benefits, the stimulation of public interest in wearing of gloves, and the elimination of trade abuses. The group decided to hold two meetings each year, one in the East and one in the West. The Glove Manufacturers Association of the State of New York[19] became the Fulton County Group within the NAGM. The NAGM claimed it represented 90 percent of the glove manufacturing industry in the county, a higher proportion than any other trade organization according to Department of Commerce figures.

The secretary of the NAGM exuded an air of optimism at every meeting. The meetings were generally very social affairs, however, the newly strength-

Expansions

1920 Continued

VanVleet Co., manufacturer of automobile gloves bought a building owned by Bachner Bros. Glove Co. on Spring Street.

Bachner Bros Co. and Bachner-Hall Co. leased building on South Main, owned by Louis Meyers & Son, and formerly occupied by Littauer Glove Corp.

Julius Bleyl Co. incorporated, taking in Frank G. Allen of Winslow Bros & Smith, one of New England's largest tanneries.

Andrew S. Ardizzone & Son enlarged its shop in 1920

1921

V. Perrin & Cie, occupied a new factory at East Fulton and Fremont streets—brick, new vertical arrangement, "as in all newer factories."

The American branch of Fownes Brothers & Co. incorporated with a factory in Gloversville for leather gloves and one in Amsterdam for silk and other fabric gloves. This company started as an English firm in 1777, and opened its first office in America in 1887.

We have striven after volume and forgotten that profit, not volume, is our main reason for entering and staying in business.
Secretary Roy Cheney of the National Association of Leather Glove Manufacturers.

ened joint organization did introduce several important benefits for members: a credit information service; an exchange of information on buying, selling, and merchandising; a collection service; as well as advice on fashion, style, and advertising. In subsequent years, members were given the latest information on tariffs.

The spring 1925 convention was held at the Hamilton County Inn and Country Club at Lake Pleasant in Speculator. The accommodations and golf course proved to be so pleasing that for years after it was the scene of the spring meeting.

Albert Rosenthal was elected president of the NAGM at its tenth annual convention (1927) at the Hamilton County Inn. Secretary Roy Cheney was as usual optimistic, noting that the past two years had been very good and that there was reason to expect the next year to be even better.[20]

In 1929, the spring convention was held in Gloversville instead of in Hamilton County, and there were hints that all was not well in the industry. The organization's secretary preached that manufacturers had made "an idol of volume. We have striven after volume and have forgotten that profit, not volume, is our main reason for entering and staying in business."[21] Was he becoming acutely aware of the industry's bleak future? Under his leadership, the association had petitioned the Department of Commerce to conduct a survey of the glove industry. "We are going to find out first what is actually wrong with our industry before attempting remedies," reported secretary Cheney.[22]

Between 1919 and 1927 there was only a slight increase in the number of workers in the glove industry, 5,279 to 5,690, but just over a million dollar increase in the glove workers' wages, $5.3 million to $6.3 million. The value of gloves produced increased from $22.8 million to $31.7 million.[23] This was well beyond the rate of inflation, which was less than four percent.

Fulton County Tanners Association continued to function from 1920 into the 1930s and requested affiliation with the Tanners' Council of America in 1933. The Fulton County Chapter of the Tanners' Council had officers from Alma Leather Co., Twin City Leather Co., John V. King Co., and Martin-Deichsel Co., which was represented by Walker McMartin.

The Glovers Review

In 1924, a third periodical devoted to the glove industry was established: the British *The Glover* joined the French *Ganterie*, founded in 1918 and of course the *Review*.

The Glovers Review continued publishing independently of the National Association of Glove Manufacturers, although it functioned as that group's principal means of informing members about happenings in the industry and association policies. James Warbasse, who took over *The Glovers Review* within a few years of its establishment in 1902, served as editor and publisher until his death in mid-1920. He was knowledgeable in business and law. His legacy was the peculiar style he imprinted on the magazine, which survived long after his death—a mix of statistics, glove history, advice, personal notes, jokes, and fancy, with the text supporting ever more ornate advertising. He established the formulaic approach to the newsletter and its air of optimism that persisted until the review ceased publishing in 1942. Beginning in 1912, Malcolm G. Hughes became associate editor under Warbasse.

It is no crime to make a profit on a glove transaction.
James Warbasse, editor, *The Glovers Review.*

At the association's national convention in 1923, a speaker urged manufacturers not to forget Warbasse's maxim, "It is no crime to make a profit on a glove transaction."[24] Warbasse's knowledge of the manufacturer's conservatism and timidity was at the base of his many editorial comments urging them to act in a more businesslike fashion.

In 1922, under editor Bethune Grant, Jr., the review featured even more clever asides. A column called "Short Lengths of News," the name inspired by short-length gloves, featured personal notes describing buyers, retailers, and vacationing glovemen. The review added a page of new factories and reorganizations called "Mousquetaires and Strap-Wrists" after two other glove styles.

A 1925 article entitled "Theory of Glove Prices" discussed reasonable profits, but not in a manner that could really help glovemen. The manufacturers were not given a clear picture of the relation of costs and overhead to pricing. Articles detailed inventory procedures for the 1925 income tax law. In 1926 the journal had fewer articles and more ads. That year it also began publishing complete monthly records of both domestic production and imports. A gloveman could no longer ignore what was happening in the industry.

As trade names became the norm, the review dutifully recorded all those for gloves in a 1927 issue. Novel names like Bobbie Ritz, Arabuk, Hika, and Excelsior, join such traditional ones as Vallier, Meyers Make and Revanson, which were based on the manufacturers' names.[25]

Throughout the 1920s and 1930s, the amount of news and personal items concerning western manufacturers overwhelmed items from Fulton County. Advertising expanded and personal notes included information on buyers and department stores. When there was insufficient news to justify the growing number of pages of advertising, the editor added such features as a glossary to glove making, a guide to wearing gloves, notes on fashion, sources of leather for gloves, and historical essays on the industry.

In the 1920s, the county began to challenge France's dominance in the production of women's gloves. They did this by emphasizing style and new products as well as fine manufacturing techniques. County glove firms hired glove designers, most of whom were locals with experience in the industry. Many manufacturers (including Alexette, Ireland Brothers, Louis Meyers) established lines of ladies' gloves and fashion became increasingly important as a way of determining the kinds of gloves produced. Among the leaders in fashion was Isabel S. Ireland, daughter of James S. Ireland.

In 1923, *The Glovers Review* dwelt on the fashion acumen of Parisian women, but the next year the periodical began to talk about style from an American perspective. "Style to the Rescue" was a headline that encouraged glovemen to pay attention to fashion.

At its fall meeting in 1924, the NAGM began to focus on ways of merchandising gloves, and it hired Byron G. Moon to manage the industry's advertising campaign. That year *The Glovers Review* offered five dollars for the best story containing clever selling ideas. It also published a style chart identifying the proper gloves for different occasions and directions for putting gloves on and taking them off. Changing styles brought new opportunities—Martorelli Brothers advertised in 1926 that the company would convert gloves to new "cuffed novelty" styles.

The first fruits of the association's attempts to advertise gloves and encourage more people to wear them resulted in a slogan, "*In Any Event - Gloves*," that seems quaint today. The manufacturers expected the slogan to raise glove consciousness. In 1925 the association adopted the campaign "Display with a purpose" to encourage retailers to feature gloves, and to do this the group reached out to the National Association of Retail Clothiers and Furnishers. Men's fine gloves were to be promoted with the line, "Dress Well and Succeed."

Expansions

1922

Boyce-Lazarus Co. purchased a large, three-story brick building on North Melcher Street and remodeled it to double its floor space.

Vogue Glove Co., Gloversville, increased its factory space and issued new stock to pay for it.

William J. Stitt, who had been connected with Jacob Adler & Co. for 47 years, became sole owner of that glove firm.

Silvernail-Mosher Co. of Gloversville, glove manufacturers, closed. It had taken over Clark-Easterly Co. in 1919 and operated for a short time as a jobbing company.

1923

Edward J. Lucas purchased the interest of Martin Kennedy in Lucas & Kennedy of Johnstown. Lucas was born in England of a family of glovers and started a glove business in 1890. The company had its own tannery and one of Johnstown's larger glove factories.

1924

H & P Glove Co. incorporated under the leadership of George C. Potter.

V. Perrin & Cie, with factories in Grenoble and Gloversville, incorporated as Perrin Glove Co.

Crocetta Brothers purchased a large factory in Gloversville. By 1929 the company had offices in both Boston and New York City.

Scotsmoor Co. incorporated and set up a new facatory building to produce wool gloves and linings.

1925

Daniel Hays Co. of Gloversville took over Dempster & Place Co.

Joseph M. Rubin & Sons leased the former C. W. Rose Co. factory, discontinuing its production in New York City to concentrate its activities in Gloversville.

Wood & Hyde erected a two-story brick addition to its tannery.

Production of fine gloves peaked in 1927. That year and the next were certainly the epitome of an era of luxury. But Fulton County had to share that high point with Europeans, whose exports to America crested simultaneously with the county's output.

Increasingly, the county began to produce gloves designed for specific activities. Automobile gloves were a staple of production throughout the twenties. One of the most unusual automobile gloves was produced by Daniel Hays Co.; on the back of the left hand was attached a piece of cut red glass with a reflective base so that a driver could signal turns at night.

"Stop" Signal glove for Autoists

The Daniel Hays Company has originated a clever signal device for automobile drivers for use at night. It consists of a piece of red glass, cut with facets, or diamond shaped and silvered on the under side like a mirror, which is affixed to the back of the glove for the left hand. When desirous of signalling a car behind him, a driver has only to extend his hand outward so that the rays of the headlights of the car following strike the glass and he immediately gets the "slow down" message.

Utilitarian gloves, sport gloves, and special gloves became increasingly more important. As a portent of things to come, the industry recognized that people who attended football games needed gloves. In 1928 several glove concerns banded together to design and make gloves for Commander Richard Byrd's expedition to the South Pole. During the trek, the team sent a radiogram asking for more gloves, which were shipped by transcontinental air mail to San Francisco to be put on board a steamship bound for New Zealand in time for transfer to a second ship headed for Antarctica.[26]

Fabric gloves, cheaper than leather gloves, became more acceptable for dress wear throughout the 1920s, especially for women. American manufacturers appear to have reduced their production of fabric gloves as imports of them increased. There was a notable drop in domestic production of fabric gloves toward the end of the decade of the twenties.

As designs and styles proliferated and business improved, manufacaturers felt confident enough to increase glove workers' wages through the 1920s, although only after the first few years of the decade. World War I had brought real increases in wages as well as more full-time employment; but following the war there was a decrease in the total amount of wages paid. This was partly as a result of a downward adjustment of the wage schedule, which in turn reflected the reduction in work available around 1920. That year, a committee of six employers and six workers met to outline an increase in wages in the work schedule, "not to avert a strike, for one has not been threatened" . . .

Our No. 999
Selected by
The Antarctic Expedition
Led by
Commander Byrd

Streeter, Hackney & Co.
JOHNSTOWN, NEW YORK

> *There is an element in increasing wages in an industry working on a piece price schedule which must always be considered and that is it often operates to curtail production. An employee turning out a number of dozens per day, for instance, to yield, at the existing rate per dozen, $35.00 per week, may be satisfied with the earning which he or she can make by the production of a lesser number of dozens at the increased wage rate. This is overcome [in some] industries by the insistence on a certain fixed number of hours work per day. But in this industry that rule has not been applied to factory workers and cannot be applied to the large number of workers on gloves in their homes.*[27]

A wage increase of 10 percent was granted in March of 1920. But *The Glovers Review* in April noted that young men in construction trades could earn as much as $25 a week and no longer wished to apprentice to learn to cut gloves.

A conference of workers and employers agreed on a general increase in the schedule of wages of between 13 and 14 percent effective January 1, 1923. The schedule was adjusted again at the beginning of 1926 and later that same year a joint committee agreed to another raise, which would become effective on Labor Day of 1926 and continue through the end of 1927. This raise brought the highest rate paid in the glove trade, exceeding even the high point reached in wartime. Cutters received yet another increase in their wage schedule in November 1929.

In the twenties, wages were rising at comparable rates in most industries across the country. Good times and a growing shortage of workers forced wages up in Fulton County as well. However, the reasons wages rose in the county and in the country were significantly different: Increases in productivity accounted for increased pay throughout the country.[28] There was no parallel growth in productivity in Fulton County. Cutters became more productive as a result of the new machines, but there was no way to increase the productivity of sewers in this basically craft industry.

Over all of the local increases in wages loomed the prospect of lower and decreasing wages in Europe. Local glovemen could not compete with the lower prices of imports and tariffs were not helping.

Throughout the post-World War I years, benefits for workers were slow in coming, but some employers were more advanced than others. Daniel Hays touted a "Square Deal" policy, in which a happy worker—happiness derived from health, progress, opportunity, and prosperity—would be able to achieve self-respect. Both management and employees had responsibilities toward that end: cooperation, loyalty, and good work habits from employees, to be complemented by safe work places, opportunities for workers, and just return for efforts from the employer. This outreach to workers may appear to have been an attempt to lay to rest the socialist movement, and perhaps it was a way of pre-empting union organization.

It is likely that Hays' Square Deal was inspired by a similar program established in the early 1920s at Endicott Johnson Corporation, makers of shoes in Endicott, New York. That company's booklet on its version of the square deal explained its labor policies and expressed "an ideology whose primary goal was the establishment of an industrial community in which the interests of workers and managers would be perceived as inextricably bound."[29]

Hays must have done a good job convincing his employees of the worth of his approach, for a statement of the Square Deal was signed by all of Hays' employees in an ad in *The Glovers Review*. Hays' employees even started a publication called the "Hays Square Dealer."

In 1923 the company celebrated several long-term employees—six who had worked continuously for Hays for over 40 years, nine for 30 years or more, 13 for 20 years, and 16 for ten years or more. Building and maintaining worker loyalty was an important facet of employee relations and Hays did it very well. A dinner for all employees and their families, with about 300 attending, certainly enhanced worker satisfaction. In 1925, Louis Meyers & Son also presented gold watches to employees who reached the 25-year milestone. This practice expanded to all the larger glove companies. (Later—in 1935—the Hays company would recognize the value of its cutters by having them autograph each table-cut glove, the signature on the left glove, the mark identifying it as table-cut on the right glove.)

Expansions

1926

Peerless Tanning Co. of Johnstown incorporated.

Superb Glove Co. moved from Gloversville to a large brick factory on Market Street in Johnstown.

Two companies enlarged their buckskin tanneries: John Johns added a concrete structure and Floyd VanAllen took over a tannery building to establish the Buckskin-Mocha Mill to use his original process for coloring buckskin.

C. W. Rowles & Son and Leon F. Swears bought the Hewitt & Hillock factory on North Perry Street with plans to share the building.

Hewitt & Hillock purchased the three-story brick building at the corner of West State and North Melcher that had been the Weare & Chant building.

Louis Meyers & Son moved their New York headquarters into a larger location on Park Ave.

1927

The Johnstown Tanning Co, relocated to the "Red Mill" in 1927 in order to tan lamb, rabbit, and other fur leathers into washable leather suitable for gloves.

The Napatan Co., formerly under sole ownership of F. W. Lebenheim, became a corporation, with Lebenheim as president and William G. Loveday as vice-president.

Rowles-Newnham Glove Corp incorporated with Harwood S. and William C. Rowles and John Newnham. Rowles & Mister had started in 1859 and on the death of founder William Rowles, his son Charles W. continued the business, taking in his son, Harwood S. The concern became C. W. Rowles & Son. The William C. Rowles in the new corporation was the grandson of the founder William Rowles.

Expansions
1927 Continued

Two corporations merged: Bachner-Moses-Louis (Bacmo) of Gloversville and Postman Co. Inc. of New York City became Bacmo-Postman with a million dollar capitalization, producing fine gloves. The merger united "the strongest and best known concerns in the American end of the glove industry," according to *TGR*. Bacmo was started by Joseph Bachner and Joseph Moses in 1892.

S. Schrecker Glove Co. bought the former Dempster & Place glove factory on Bleecker Street, which consisted of three large brick buildings. The main building, which had been enlarged in 1920, housed the cutting room on the fourth floor, making on the third, laying-off and examining on the second, and executive offices and shipping on the first floor.

1928

Albert Rosenthal, who had joined the Northrup Glove Co. (founded in 1869) in 1923, became sole owner of the company in 1928.

Acme Glove Co. of Gloversville became a corporation.

1929

George F. Conrey, manufacturer of children's gloves, moved into larger quarters.

Smith & Travers purchased the H. H. Steele factory in Gloversville.

Richard Evans & Sons incorporated.

G. Levor purchased the George F. Troutwine & Sons tannery to add to "their already large plant."

Daniel Hays Co. merged with George Updegraff & Sons, Hagerstown, Md. Cross Glove Co. purchased Updegraff's Gloversville factory.

Manufacturers shut their plants for the week surrounding July 4th for the first time in 1920, and this closing practice has continued locally to this day. But there were still no paid vacations.

In 1920 a writer in *The Glovers Review* suggested that many benefits would come from profit-sharing plans, a radical idea at the time. Such plans would be especially valuable in keeping employees.[30] There were no proposals for retirement plans, but pensions did not become an issue for most American workers until after World War II.

In 1919 the supply of imported skins was barely beginning to recover from the war years when a drought hit South Africa, reducing both the quality and quantity of skins available. A severe drought in 1919 and 1920 also reduced flocks of hair sheep in northern Africa. If droughts were not bad enough, consider the effects of the tribal wars that followed in countries around the Horn of Africa. They resulted in the butchering of vast numbers of the sheep in 1920 and 1921, animals whose skins never reached America[31].

W. Donald Hyde of Wood & Hyde was stationed in South Africa for four years to buy skins for his company. He reported that farmers were breeding South African sheep for greater wool production, and this lessened the quality of the skins for tanning.[32] It is little wonder that prices of leather for fine gloves remained high into 1922.

Prices of domestically produced heavy leather for work gloves also rose, as much as 50 percent in just three months at the end of 1922. The shortage of horsehides for work gloves limited production in 1923, even as the volume of orders finally began to increase. Optimism in the work-glove industry was predicated on the weather; predictions for a hard winter stirred all the manufacturers to find ways of increasing production. Prosperous agricultural conditions gave the work-glove industry reason to expect higher sales, because farm workers were important buyers of work gloves.

The cost of leather for fine gloves continued high in 1924. This contributed to the squeeze felt by glovemen; prices should have been raised to reflect costs but buyers were rebelling against higher prices. In the next few years, prices of most other commodities declined but the cost of hides and leather continued to rise rapidly through 1927. This put additional pressure on glovemen, who were also confronted by a changing marketplace: The mid-twenties also marked the beginning of the gradual shift away from the fashion dictates that compelled women to wear gloves.

The importation of various exotic skins like alligator, snake, or ostrich for glove leather sparked the growth of tanning those skins for uppers for shoes and eventually for leather clothing. In the 1920s and 1930s, leather for gloves began to consume a smaller part of the region's production. This trend continued until now, at the end of the twentieth century, when the principal leather dressed locally for gloves is once again deerskin. But the story of how tanning has come full circle back to deerskins is for later.

Imports of fine gloves began to pick up in 1921, but *The Glovers Review* saw an improvement in the leather glove industry in general at the end of that year. However, for all the talk among Fulton County glovemen about producing fine gloves, that still meant men's gloves because imports of men's fine gloves remained limited. Even though county production of women's gloves was gradually increasing, a large proportion of women's fine gloves were imported. Americans wanted the cachet of French designs, especially in gloves.

Although Fulton County's production of women's gloves rose during the decade, from less than 15 percent to almost 30 percent of the county's total, it did not approach the level of domestically produced men's fine gloves until the 1930s. Even then the narrowing of the gap between men's and women's production levels was only accomplished by declines in the men's sector, not an absolute increase in women's glove production.

The U. S. Commerce Department began recording import levels after 1909 and producing statistics on domestic production starting in 1924. The domestic reports represented "a little more than 95 percent of the production capacity of the industry."[33] Imports of leather gloves rose sharply in 1920, dropped in the mid-20s to pre-war levels, and rose to a peak in 1928. These statistics, published in *The Glovers Review*, should have frightened glovemen.

The rise in domestic production in the mid-1920s came almost entirely from men's part-fabric work gloves. The production of men's fine gloves and leather work gloves was static through the 1920s. None of the information available supported the optimism expressed by the *Review*. Nor is there any indication that glovemen used the reports to change their practices. In fact, their irrational exuberance encouraged them to increase capitalization and production capacity; but the extent to which they increased production capacities challenged reality.

In 1924 glove buyers from all the large department stores flocked to Europe, fueling the surge of imports. That year, the national association sent its secretary to France to enlist French manufacturers to participate in a joint publicity campaign to encourage the wearing of gloves.

The volume of imports rose in 1926 and 1927, spurted upwards in 1928, then started to fall dramatically. Much of the rise was due to the increase in foreign-made work gloves, the cheaper heavy leather or combination leather and fabric gloves. These imports should have set off an alarm throughout the industry.

Expansion into other Fulton county towns

1920

Borst Glove Co. of Broadalbin increased its capitalization.

Stewart & Jerome in Mayfield, incorporated.

1924

Children's Glove Factory established in Mayfield in a new three-story building.

1928

W. N. Wilkins Son & Co. of Mayfield and Northville.

1929

LaRowe Glove Co. of Northville purchased the factory and equipment of the Northville Branch of the W. N. Wilkins Co.

Northville Glove Manufacturing Co. incorporated.

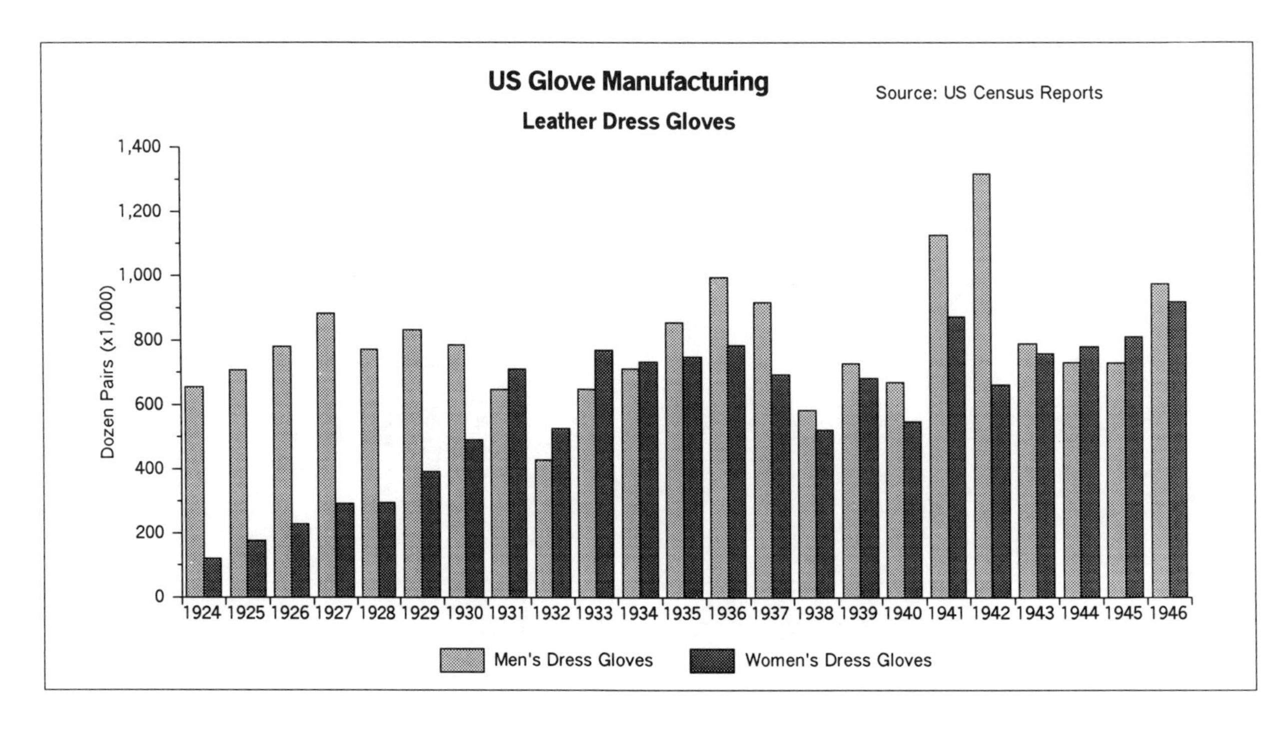

No American ever considered that European glove operators were adequately paid, and American manufacturers have for years realized that even at the higher wages prevailing here they were having a hard time to compete with other industries in holding a class of intelligent and skillful operatives necessary in the industry. Yet at the prices which prevailed for gloves they felt themselves powerless to pay more.
The Glovers Review[3]

In the 1920s there were no significant changes in tariffs to benefit glovemen. In 1921 Congress proposed tariff legislation for leather gloves that would return to the provisions of the Payne-Aldrich bill or its successor, the Underwood bill, with the exception that for certain types of stitching, the new rate would be less. The duty on men's gloves, not over 12 inches in length, would be $4.00 a dozen; the duty on women's and children's gloves, not over 12 inches in length, would be $3.00 a dozen and $.50 a dozen for each inch in excess of twelve. Additional cumulative duties were specified for different linings and embroideries. Further, the duty on all gloves was to be not less than 37½ percent *ad valorem.*[34]

In 1926, England considered imposing a tariff in order to protect British glove manufacturers. It is a sign of the times that competition from the continent, in particular from Czechoslovakia, was becoming very severe. England was forced to give protection to its emerging fabric glove market. The next year, the "London Correspondent" of *The Glovers Review* reported that continental manufacturers were shipping fancy gloves to England at prices that barely covered the cost of production.

Obituaries in *The Glovers Review* are an important resource and they served to punctuate the changing times. Deaths in the 1920s of Jewish manufacturers, most of whom had come from Germany or Austria, marked the closing of the era in which an elite class of entrepreneurs had fueled the greatest expansions in the industry. Some of the Jewish entrepreneurs who died in this period had already moved to New York City. Others, like Eugene Nessel (who survived the decade), chose to live there at least part of the time.

Others who died were sons and grandsons of glovemen who had started working during the Civil War. Their deaths often brought about the demise of the families' businesses.

In the decade of the twenties, one event stands out—the closing of Littauer Brothers Glove Co. The company modernized and expanded its firm on Gloversville's Main Street in 1921, and reorganized as Littauer Glove

The
BELLIS & KLEIN
BULLETIN

Leather	Linings
Pickled Skins	Cotton Fleece Lining
Raw Sudans (A H A BRAND)	Astrakhan
Raw Mochas	Jersey Cloth
Turkish Pickled Skins	Elastic Webbing
China Crosses	Wrist Webbing

Corp., with a capitalization of $787,500 and Lucius Littauer, E. Harry Mierson, and Paul Gottschalk as principals. The corporation added another factory in 1922 and in 1923 began to produce gloves at an auxiliary plant at Cranberry Creek, Broadalbin.

Littauer's general manager Mierson died in 1927 and he was succeeded as vice-president by his widow, who died a year later. After these deaths and the decision by Lucius Littauer to retire, the corporation tried to sell its stock. The attempt failed and the corporation reorganized its stock structure in 1928 to make a sale more desirable. This too failed and in 1928 the corporation closed its factories.

Did the Littauer factory close because of Lucius' age, because he was getting tired? Or because of the illness of his brother, who was active in the management of the Gloversville factories? Or was Lucius prescient, fearing that the glove industry as he knew it might not survive? Whatever the reason, Lucius Littauer began a new career as a philanthropist, and the extent of his philanthropies attest to his success as a gloveman.

His gifts to Gloversville included an enlarged Nathan Littauer Hospital (the original building became the Littauer home for nurses), as well as a public swimming pool. He contributed to the Jewish Community Center. His gifts nationally far exceeded his contributions to Gloversville. He created a scientific endowment at a New York hospital to develop a cure for pneumonia and he endowed a chair at Harvard, his alma mater. At the very beginning of 1929, on his seventieth birthday, Lucius N. Littauer announced the formation of the Littauer Foundation and endowed it with one million dollars. The foundation would serve the "cause of better understanding among all mankind." In 1929 he gave Harvard University 12,000 rare Hebrew books and added 2,238 more volumes to this collection in 1937. In 1935, in the depth of the Depression, he endowed the Graduate School of Public Administration at Harvard. In 1937 he contributed a hundred thousand dollars to the New School for Social Research in New York City and gave an endowment to the National Hospital for Speech Disorders.

In later years he lived in New York City. On his death in 1944 he was hailed as Gloversville's leading benefactor and a man who had "inherited a small business and built it into a fortune through many industrial moves."[35] What his obituary did not note is that the foundation for the seven- to ten-million-dollar fortune, which he gave away during his lifetime, was amassed primarily from his Gloversville factory, from the labors of that city's workers.

In 1927, as domestic glove production of all kinds reached a peak for this supposedly "big decade," the Department of Commerce identified 232 leather-glove factories in the United States. New York State had the largest number, 154. Cloth and part-cloth gloves were produced by 131 manufacturers, and Ohio had the most, 22, with New York next at 21.

The commerce department's summary for 1929 shows just how vibrant was Fulton County's glove industry, and also clearly hints at the way it was beginning to shrink. The county had 138 of the 257 glove manufacturing establishments tallied, and it continued to hold a majority of the industry's wage earners, 4,928 out of 9,203. The county produced 58 percent of the value of the country's glove output, over $22.6 million out of the total of $39.1 million. Gloversville's statistics for number of workers, amount of wages, and value of production were roughly three times the comparable figures for Johnstown, although Gloversville had just a little over twice as

Deaths in the 1920s in the Jewish community

1921

Aaron J. Lebenheim, principal of H. H. Steele & Co., which owned Excelsior Glove Co.

Gustav Levor, immigrant from Prussia, age 73, built tannery in Gloversville in 1884, rebuilt it after a fire in 1912 with a concrete and brick building. He tanned mostly shoe leather and some glove leather.

S. Schrecker, 63 years old, came from Austria in 1887.

Moses Schwartz, worked for M. Beeber & Co., then formed a partnership with Joseph Schiffer, taking over that company, which became Schwartz, Schiffer & Co.

1924

August Klein, age 59, born in Austria, manufacturer of buckskin gloves as A. Klein & Son, later as Bellis & Klein. That company's factory had an impressive reception room which doubled as a meeting place for Gloversville's glovemen.

Asa B. Bellis, age 70, had been a superintendent at Booth & Kent before forming Bellis & Klein.

Frederick W. Ittman, age 86, born in Germany, was for many years a leather dealer.

Gustave C. Straus, age 72, had been with the Lefi-Straus Co. after 1896 and Gloversville Welt Co. after 1903.

1927

Wolf Horowitz, of Horowitz & Arbib, died at age 65. He was born in Russia and tanned glove leather through his entire career.

1929

Eugene Littauer died at age 69, partner with his brothers in Littauer Brothers from 1883 to 1921.

many manufacturers (88 versus 37), implying its shops on average were bigger than those in Johnstown.

During the twenties, a few concerns closed, mostly because of the deaths or illnesses of their principals. The numerous incorporations suggest that owners were looking for capital to expand or make their enterprises more secure. The decade emerges as one of expanding investments, and Fulton County's manufacturers participated in that growth all the way.

In 1929 the county had 12,000 registered automobiles, almost one for every four residents. Eighty percent of industrial workers owned their own homes, most of which were supplied with gas and electricity. But, as *Business Week* observed a few years later, "in 90 percent of the homes, women sew gloves all day long to fatten family incomes."[36] The county ended the decade with production levels remarkably similar to those of 1915, and not far below the 1927 peak. The county prospered in the decade, but not at the levels of the rest of the country.

A few glovemen felt the crash of 1929, men who had invested in the stock market or who were dependent on banks for operating cash. But the crash did not bother the majority as much as might be expected. Their capital investments were relatively low: little new capital had been required for new buildings or expansions in the 1920s. The manufacturers remained very conservative, buying only as many skins to cut into gloves as they thought they could sell. Some overproduced—the competition was fierce—but the problems were nothing new, and initially only marginally related to the crisis in the stock market.

Deaths among leading glovemen changed the industry more than outside events. Deaths closed many shops by ending familly dynasties. Deaths in the 1920s and 1930s and into the 1940s took many of the German Jews and a few of the eastern European Jews who had built large and important glove shops. A sign of the transformation of the industry is the fact that relatively few of these leaders were replaced by Jewish businesssmen.

Other deaths from this period:

1920

James Radford, age 77, a cutter who came from Worcester, England, to Fulton County in 1864, and was principal successively in Fidoe & Radford, Kibbe & Radford, and in 1909 Radford & Langford. Burt Brown became a partner in 1914, then Harry S. Hall joined in 1917. Langford retired in 1930, Brown died in 1938, and Hall continued the firm into the forties, when it employed about 25 workers.

Henry B. TenEyck, owner of Bias Fabric Binding Co.

1921

Julius C. Bleyl, born in Bleecker 1854, founder of tannery bearing his name.

George C. Berry, age 56, owner of George C. Berry & Son, successor to Berry and Allen.

1922

Samuel B. Brown of L. S. Brown & Sons, Gloversville, age 47.

1923

Leonard Argersinger, age 74, had been a Johnstown tanner, in later years taking his sons into the business.

William C. Hutchens, age 62, co-founder of Hutchens & Potter Glove Co.

Ralph R. Chant of Weare & Chant, age 65, born in Milbourne Port, England.

Bethune M. Grant, age 90. He was born in Glasgow and began cutting gloves before blocks and dies were invented.

Edward W. Fiske, general manager of Kingsborough Glove Co. age 61 [suicide].

A laying-off room
Courtesy Fulton County Museum

1924

Henry Knoff, born in Germany, died at age 86. He began working in the glove business in Gloversville in 1850 and established his own enterprise in 1870.

M. Bradford Northrup, age 85, of Northrup Glove Manufacturing Co.

Eugene Riton, age 60, had worked with his father, Joseph, who was one of the first to manufacture table-cut gloves in the United States. His father and uncle Eugene had come to Johnstown from Millau, France and the uncle worked with the Bertrand brothers. At his death, Eugene was one of the few remaining cutters who could cut gloves without using any dies, hand-slitting fingers and thumbs in the French method.

William N. Zimmer, age 79, veteran of the Civil War and gloveman for more than 50 years, started in 1870 with his brother J. S. Zimmer. Continuing alone after 1897, W. N. took his son Bert S. Zimmer, born 1883, into the business in 1905, renaming it W. N. Zimmer & Son.

John C. Hillock, a founder of Hewitt & Hillock, age 66.

1925

Thomas E. Ricketts, age 84 years, born in the glove center of Yeovil, England, started manufacturing gloves in 1869 and sold out to Boyce-Lazarus in 1917.

Nelson Dutcher, age 61, a leading leather merchant.

1926

Mark H. Dewsnap, age 82, for 40 years a salesman for Louis Meyers

William C. Hackney, age 62, 1926, glove manufacturer, with Hackney & MacIntyre and later Streeter, Hackney & Co. in partnership also with Frank Prindle. At Hackney's death the firm consisted of his son George S. Hackney and son-in-law, Robert M. Milford.

John Q. Adams, age 83, of the Adams Buckskin Co., started making gloves in 1862, had several partners including his son and grandson, and in 1920 added a new concrete structure to his factory, which became the largest and oldest firm in the world for oil-dressed buckskin leather.

E. L. Heacock, born 1854, became head of the Heacock firm in 1871, and took his sons into the business in 1910. The firm was already the oldest in Fulton County.

E. Harry Mierson, vice-president and general manager of Littauer Glove Corp., age 62.

James Heagle, age 84, still making gloves in his own small shop.

1927

James Ireland, age 77. He was born in Forfar, Scotland, and established the Ireland Brothers firm in 1876 with his brothers John and David. In 1927, Ireland Brothers was administered by James S. and John R., sons of John.

1928

William M. Grant worked for Northrup Glove Co. for 27 years, then in 1913 started his own company and later took A. E. Pearson as partner.

George J. Chant, age 67. He was born in England and became a partner in Weare and Chant and in Chant Brothers.

Seymour D. Tomlinson, organizer of Karg, Butler & Tomlinson, age 80.

Leonard W. Grant, age 50. manager of A. C. Lawrence Leather Co.'s business 1906-1918.

Samuel Lehr of Lehr & Nelson. On his retirement in 1917, he had moved to New York City.

Lewis C. Fox of Superior Glove Co.

Fred M. Ward of W. N. Wilkins Glove Co. of Northville

1929

James M. Evans, age 52, son of Richard Evans, original partner of R. J & R. Evans glove firm, brother of Richard M. and partner with him in the firm after 1908.

James K. Bradt, glove manufacturer since 1883.

Cutting tranks, courtesy Fulton County Museum

The Depression and Big Government - 1930-1941

Deaths in the 1930s

1930

Ralph A. Moses, born in 1872, organizer with his brother Isaac of Elite Glove Co., which began making gloves in Gloversville in 1901.

Joseph Moses, partner with Joseph Bachner in Bachner & Moses, later Bachner-Moses-Louis, noted as a able businessman and financier as well as a designer of new glove styles.

1931

Joseph Bachner, age 75, born in Warsaw, one of the originators of the Jewish Community Center, partner in the Bachner-Moses-Louis firm. Before the end of the decade, that firm would be bought out by Jacob Zuckerwar of S. Schrecker Co.

1932

James McMartin, age 70. He was the sole proprietor of the James I. McMartin Sons' firm from 1910 to 1917.

Henry P. Gates, age 74, commercial traveler for Northrup and other companies until 1900 when he organized Hayes & Gates with John Hayes. This became Gates & Mills, then Gates-Mills-Driscoll, then Gates-Mills, Inc., which survives in the late 1990s.

Emil Alexander, age 78, born in Berlin, where he learned glove making. In business for 50 years after 1874 as Alexander Glove Co.

The decade began with a new round of tariff increases that benefitted county glovemen, but changes in the country's politics soon ended this reprieve. In June of 1930 a new higher, and more protectionist tariff was imposed on imported gloves. It called for a duty of $6 per dozen on men's leather gloves, not over twelve inches in length. Women's and children's were assessed at $5.50 a dozen pairs, plus $.50 for each inch over 12 inches.[37] Other duties were assigned for different fabrics, trims, and stitching. Further, the duty on all gloves was to be not less than 50 percent ad valorem. These rates were considerably higher than those of 1921, the duty on men's gloves was increased by 50 percent, on women's and children's gloves by 83 percent. For the first time, women's gloves enjoyed a tariff nearly comparable to men's.

The graph on page 138 comparing production levels of men's and women's dress gloves shows the strengths of tariffs in determining domestic production. The production of women's gloves had gradually increased through the twenties—a mirror image of the decline in production of men's dress gloves. The equalization of tariff rates for men's and women's gloves enacted in 1930 is immediately evident. The county continued to produce more men's than women's gloves, but except during the early years of American's participation in World War II, 1941-1942, the differences were slight.

In 1931, under President Herbert Hoover, Congress passed the Smoot-Hawley Act which raised tariffs by an average of nearly 53 percent, the highest in the country's history. Enacted as the country was engulfed by Depression, this tariff was opposed at home as well as abroad. European countries also raised tariffs and even Great Britain, long an advocate of free trade, adopted protective legislation.

Smoot-Hawley was a major issue during Franklin Roosevelt's first campaign for the presidency. In 1934, the United States stopped levying fixed duties and began negotiating trade agreements with different rates applied to individual countries. In general, this "Reciprocal Trade Treaties" act had the potential to lower the duties on all types of gloves. From this time on, questions of duties center on specific types of gloves or problems in individual countries.

Japanese manufacturers began copying styles of American knit wool gloves before 1935 and selling the gloves in America at a fraction of the domestic manufacturing cost.[38] American industry hoped to obtain a partial embargo on imports from Japan. Hearings held in late 1935 at the urging of the association were instrumental in obtaining a ruling that required that the duty on certain types of gloves be paid on the standard wholesale price of the comparable American-made glove instead of the declared foreign value. The Japanese discovered ways of circumventing this ruling and the association again petitioned the Tariff Commission to investigate the situation.[39]

Congressman Frank Crowther, who represented Fulton County, appealed for a trade adjustment in early 1936, stating that glove imports had reached a level equal to domestic production.[40] In 1936, additional tariffs were levied on German gloves, under the claim that Germany had subsidized its industry.

Czechoslovakia was granted a huge reduction in the tariff rate in early 1938. Isaac Moses of Elite Glove Co., chairman of the association's tariff and prosperity of the glove industry of this country."[41] Czechoslovakia had exported about 1.5 million dozen pairs to the United States in 1935 and 1936, and 2.2 million dozen pairs in 1937. The executive secretary of the manufacturers association presented evidence to support a call for increased tariffs. The testimony included facts to show that the American glove industry was operating at only half capacity, that there was resistance by buyers to American-made gloves in favor of those from Czechoslovakia, and that, according to records of the Bureau of Labor Statistics, when glove workers have full-time work their earnings, compared with the earnings of workers in the principal industries of the country, were among the best-paid wages in the country.[42] Also revealed was a complex arrangement in which a Czechoslovakian munitions manufacturer with large sales to Turkey had its funds in Turkey frozen. To overcome this, the Czech firm procured Turkish skins at above cost and sold them to Czech firms at below cost. This, combined with low labor costs, permitted the Czech glove manufacturers to undersell American manufacturers.

Hints of the coming Depression appeared in the glove industry as early as 1928 with declines in the demand for both fine and work gloves made of leather. Thus, once again, signs pointing to a retrenchment in the leather glove industry appeared even as many manufacturers were achieving some success.

The financial records of only one firm in this period survive. Every year from the early 1900s on, W. N. Zimmer had recorded his assets and liabilities. His son Bert S. Zimmer left public school after the eighth grade and attended Gloversville Business School. Bert joined his father's glove business in 1905 and took over the task of keeping the company's records. This one notebook offers so much insight into the workings of a glove company that it is doubly unfortunate that no comparable records are available. The family counted as assets their horses, buggy, harnesses, and blankets as well as the value of gloves produced for other companies such as Ricketts, Northrup, and Louis Meyers & Son. Business profits grew substantially between 1916 and 1918 and the company borrowed heavily from local banks. The company sold gloves at a great loss in 1921, did no business for the first six months of 1922, although the business showed a profit in the mid-twenties. The owner's net worth peaked in 1928 and declined as the business failed to show a profit in every year of the decade of the thirties except 1939.[43]

There are those who remember the Depression of the 1930s as having less effect on the county than other places. That may be true. There still were jobs, but partly because the work force was shrinking. There was work, but not full-time employment; employers tried to spread the work around, so all would have some income. In the rest of the country, there were attempts to limit women's work because of the Depression, but this was not possible in Fulton County, where women who sewed were essential to the production of gloves. The ratio of sewers to cutters remained constant in good times and bad.

Even in the best of times, competition made it difficult for most manufacturers to survive. Although the county enjoyed relatively good times in the twenties, workers and owners alike still had to struggle. The Depression, though more severe, was nothing new. It was not a bad decade: years at the beginning and end were poor, but 1935-37 were actually quite good years. In Fulton County, no one starved, no one prospered, and most

1933

James Windsor, age 72, a founder of Windsor-Northrup Co., born in England where he began to learn the trade.

1934

Edwin L. Meyers for 30 years head of Louis Meyers & Son, Inc., born 1866. Although he supervised the firm's Gloversville factory, he lived in New York City.

Albert G. Rosenthal was the period's most shocking death. He had been head of Northrup Glove Manufacturing Co. and former president of the NAGM. He committed suicide, jumping from the 21st floor of the Commodore Hotel in New York City. He was born in 1873 in Hamburg, Germany, and learned the glove business in New York City.

1935

Thomas A. Sutton, age 62, founder of Sutton's, a glove manufacturer in Johnstown; joined by his sons, Milton and Francis in 1926.

Josiah G. Danforth, age 61, founder and sole owner of the eponymous glove company, located in Mayfield, the largest manufacturer of children's gloves in Fulton County, some sources say the world.

Melvin E. Bradt, age 60, glove manufacturer with his father.

Frank Brower, age 64, of Brower Brothers.

Frank Martorelli, age 74, born in Naples where he learned gloving. Later he worked in Grenoble, then for Louis Meyers & Son, before becoming associated with Martorelli Brothers.

Harry Speare of Speare Glove Co., age 52. He was born in Vilna, Russia, where he learned glovemaking. In 1927, Samuel Starr became his partner; later Samuel Madora joined the firm. Starr's father was born also in Russia.

1936

Ed Karg, founder of Karg Brothers, age 68.

Frederick Rulison, tanner.

1937

Eugene D. Heacock, age 75.

Adolph Nessel, a retired Gloversville manufacturer, died at his home in New York City.

Darius Filmer, age 82, Gloversville tanner since 1890.

Nathaniel T. Weber, age 86, Johnstown tanner since 1875.

Emile Julien, age 80, former glove manufacturer. His father was one of five French manufacturers who made table-cut gloves in Johnstown before the Civil War.

Robert A. Rea, age 85. He had been a member of the firm of Rea, White & Carter, then president of Dempster & Place.

Andrew Studenic, age 49. He was with Independent Leather Co. of Gloversville.

Frank Adams, age 66, surviving member of the A. M. Adams & Son firm that produced alum-tanned glace sheep and lamb skins.

Daniel W. Mason, age 70. His father was a founder of Mason, Campbell & Co., where Daniel was employed.

1938

Rudolf Seykota, age 53, with Jacob Adler & Co. then when that company liquidated, he set up his own company. He was known for patterns and designs that improved the fit of gloves.

George B. Groff, age 44, proprietor of Groff & Co.

Burt L. Brown, age 54, of Langford, Brown, & Co.

Karl Gerstl, Secretary of the National Glove Manufacturers Association.

William T. Dovey, age 71, firm of C. H. Dovey & Son.

Julius Morbach, age 64, of Wolf & Morbach .

James Curtin, age 79, of Curtin & Hebert, manufacturer of cutting dies.

continued to find some work. The romantic aura attached to the industry in modern times comes partly from this decade, which is as far back as most people's family memories or experiences can reach. It is touchable history, very real, easily translated into glowing terms—a Depression that hurt but did not destroy glove-making.

The Depression did not stop the formation of new concerns—in fact the times seemed to accelerate it. While a few firms closed, several firms incorporated. Others consolidated. A few moved to larger quarters, but there were almost no new buildings. Most of the mergers reflect stronger firms taking advantage of weaker ones. From those who capitalized on the hard times and expanded emerged some of the largest firms of the 1990s.

S. Schrecker Glove Co.'s expansion began in 1926 when it purchased the former Dempster & Place building, a four-story factory on Bleecker Street. In 1933, the company took over as annex to their factory the building occupied by John Snell & Son on Bleecker Street. The next year it built a large three-story steel and brick addition to the Bleecker Street shop in order to make room for more sewers. The addition almost doubled the company's factory and with three stories on top of a one-and-a-half-story basement. Table cutting was on the top floor, making on the second floor, leather sorting on the first floor. The company employed 500 workers, who had been crowded in the older former Dempster & Place building.

In 1936 Jacob Zuckerwar, who had married Schrecker's daughter, became president of the company and continued the company's policy of catering to the jobbing trade, producing gloves on commission for others. That year the Schrecker company purchased the interest of Harry J. Louis in Louis-Bacmo-Postman for a reported $120,000.[44] This increased the number of employees under Zuckerwar to 600. In 1938, S. Schrecker Glove Co. took over the wholesale glove business of Marshall Field & Co. of Chicago. S. Schrecker also acquired Marshall Field's trade name, Alexette, and began to handle imports of leather and wool gloves under the name Alexette Gloves, Inc.[45]

Schrecker's was not the only company to function primarily as a jobber for other manufacturers, but it seems to have been the most successful. That freed the company from having to tie up huge sums in leather and raw materials and enabled it to grow, right through the Depression.

Compare this with the fate of the Richard Evans & Sons glove company, which folded in 1937. This company descended from a firm established in 1868 by Robert J. Evans, which became a partnership of Richard and Robert J. two years later. In 1898 Robert J. Evans retired and Richard took as partners his sons Richard M. and James. The father died in 1908 and the sons continued the business until James died in 1929. Richard M. was head of the business from 1929 to 1937.

The firm had made work gloves long after most manufacturing of that kind had moved west, but it did try to establish itself in the fine glove trade. For unstated reasons, the company's "attempts to handle varied lines of gloves were responsible for the decision to discontinue the business."[46] What was there about the Depression that forced this company to close? At its peak it employed 300 in the glove factory, one of the largest brick glove shops in the county, and 200 men in the tannery, which was capable of turning out a million feet of leather in a month.

The way the company closed speaks volumes about the old-time Johnstown glovers, for it illustrates their stature and uprightness. The Evans family recalls how Richard M. had built a large, three-story, frame house on William Street, replete with two-story-tall Doric columns. When he decided to close his business he was on the verge of bankruptcy; the end of 1936 was a very difficult time, with the glove business beginning to drop again. When he closed the business in early 1937, he paid all his bills and settled with all his creditors and retired to his William Street home, only to rent out the top floor in order to make ends meet.[47]

The unanswered question is, How could Zuckerwar expand at the same time Richard Evans was forced to go out of business? Was the fact that Schreckers had produced gloves under contract for others who sold to department stores solely responsible for the disparate results?

RESIDENCE OF RICHARD EVANS.

From *Illustrative & Descriptive Gloversville and Johnstown*, 1907

NGMA, *The Glovers Review*, and *Gloves Magazine*

In 1930 the National Association responded to signs that the industry was suffering by postponing its fall 1930 convention and glove fair. But few in the organization seemed to realize the extent of the country's problems. In mid-1931, association secretary Roy Cheney, in his annual report, expressed the opinion that the Depression the country had been experiencing was definitely approaching its end. The report contained not one shred of evidence except his "feeling" that this might be the case.

Throughout the 1930s, Fulton County glovemen maintained their focus on fine leather gloves. There is little indication that they experimented with other types that might be more useful. At a time when such things were cast aside, fine gloves were a luxury. In order to call attention to their finest products, the association established a committee on "branding" to select a design to distinguish table-cut gloves.

From the early 1930s on *The Glovers Review* was laden with statistics of exports, imports, and domestic production, but skimpy on news of the glove industry, except personal notes. In the depths of the Depression, it added a column of jokes—called quirks—that are marginally humorous, perhaps as a way of cheering up its readers.

Ireland Brothers typifies the reliance on fine gloves and fashion. Isabel Ireland, daughter of one of the founding brothers, managed the company's New York office from the 1920s until the company closed in 1958. She made yearly trips to Europe. In 1932 she spent nine weeks surveying manufacturers in France, Germany, Belgium, and Czechoslovakia. Ireland Brothers represented Vallier, a French glove manufacturer, in the United States.

1938 Continued

Frank J. Argersinger of Argersinger Brothers, leather splitters, age 57.

Delos Brower, age 82, glove manufacturer.

Isaac Moses, age 63, head of Elite Glove Co., active in National Glove Manufacturers Association.

Samuel B. Morrell, age 72, head of the Gloversville Auto Glove Co. He had been connected with the glove industry in Gloversville for over 40 years.

Sidney Argersinger, age 91, the oldest retired glove manufacturer. He was a member of the firm of John H. Decker & Son, founded by his father-in-law, John H. Decker.

Daniel McMartin, age 82, born in 1856, dealer in mocha.

William J. Adams, age 66, president of Adams Buckskin Co. founded by his father.

1939

George B. Cole, age 72.

Isabel

Ireland Brothers led the way in trying to gain business by focusing on quality, table-cut gloves. Isabel helped Ireland's emphasize contemporary style all through the 1930s. In 1934, she was profiled by the *Review*'s new female writer in an article that extolled Miss Ireland's fashion acumen and design skill. "Gloves by Isabel" became the hallmark of Ireland's production. For years she traveled to Europe to size up the fashion scene, create designs, and keep Ireland Brothers at the lead in producing glamorous women's gloves.

Deparment stores played a big role in selling ladies' gloves.

In 1932 *The Glovers Review* encouraged the industry to promote novelty styles and fabrics as a way of enticing buyers. The association held fashion accessory shows in New York City in 1935, 1936, and 1937. The *Review* hired Mary Craig Usina as a representative in New York City to keep tabs on the retail trade in gloves and fashion items. Her first column in 1936 mentioned styles created by Ireland Brothers and the Northrup Glove Co.

The *Review* was redesigned in mid-1934, with different and more modern headline type, and renamed *Gloves Magazine*. That year, a female assistant editor, Bessie C. McClain, began to write columns for the magazine, emphasizing glove news as well as fashion. Her columns did something none of the previous editorial writers, all male, had ever done: She produced a few very acerbic columns about labor practices, one of which described the iniquities of competition in terms no male writer for the *Review* ever expressed. In most ways, however, *Gloves Magazine* remained the same old journal.

In the spring of 1934, fabric glove manufacturers formed a separate association as part of the National Association, which had changed its name to the National Association of Leather Glove Manufacturers (NALGM). Fabric gloves had come a long way since their introduction in World War I, in part because their lower prices had made them affordable in the Depression years.

Other business activity in the Depression

1931

Supreme Glove Corp. was organized with Herman J. and Charles Serfis, owners of Serfis Glove Co. which was to continue as a separate business.

Martorelli Brothers incorporated.

Merger and incorporation of H & P Glove Co. (Hutchens & Potter) of Johnstown and The Unique Glove Co. of Gloversville, capitalized at $400,000.

1932

Newman Glove Co. of Johnstown, opened in January.

R. Antevil & Co., Gloversville, new factory.

John Naudin took over Jones & Naudin as Jones continued with Fulton County Silk Mill. Jones & Naudin continued handling leather and raw skins for gloves.

LaRow Glove Co. in Northville was dissolved and the assets sold at auction.

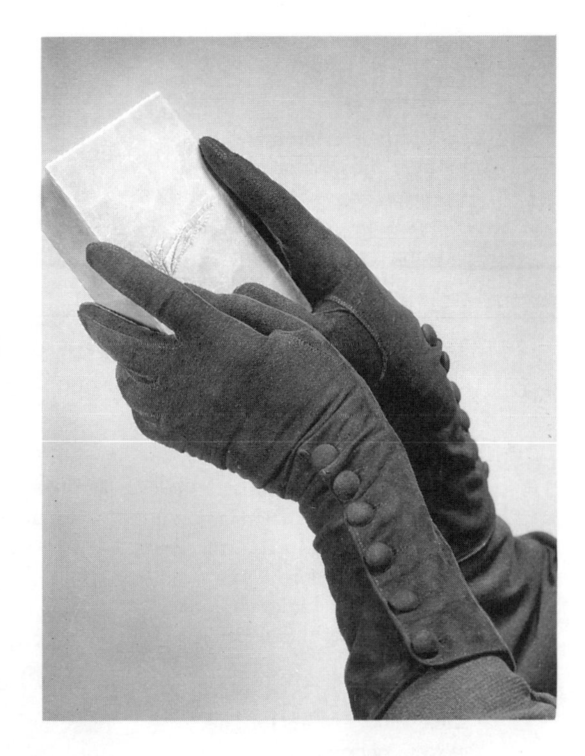

Elegant glove by Bacmo
Courtesy J. D. Widdemer

Throughout the thirties local members of the association engaged in collective bargaining with the unions, a continuation of a custom that had begun in World War I. Association leadership was very concerned about the fact that some manufacturers did not adhere to the agreed schedules and were breaking ranks by reducing quality standards.

At one point in the depth of the Depression, June 1937, editor Grant must either have felt an unusual need to fill the pages or a sense of foreboding for the industry and a desire to document its past. He began publishing a historical sketch of glove manufacturing in Fulton County, largely based on the work of glove manufacturer and historian M. Sexton Northrup (which also served as a resource for this book). Grant's notes for his history sum up shared problems. "I have endeavored to verify things that have been told me as facts, I have found an amazing amount of seeming contradictions, largely because there is so little corroborative, documentary evidence."[48]

The NALGM's secretary Karl Gerstl died in 1938 and was succeeded by James J. Casey, Jr. A student in economics at Boston College who already had a law degree, Casey brought a new perspective to the local industry,[49] most of whose manufacturers did not have a business education.

Casey's impact on the glove industry figures largely in the story of the industry after World War II. His goal was to "develop a very active trade association."[50] The association had taken steps in that direction just before Casey was hired. Under the direction of Louis Rubin of Rubin Gloves, who was elected association president at the spring meeting in 1938, Louis Postman presented a plan to assess members an aggregate of $100,000 to create a fund to "promote the superior quality of American-made gloves." Members would be assessed an amount proportional to the quantity of gloves their firms cut.[51] The fund, the advertising campaign based on style, and the work of a national advertising agency finally got off the ground in the spring of 1940.[52]

The widow of James Warbasse sold *Gloves Magazine* at the end of 1939 to Philip Banker and Don Willard. Both men were county glovemen; Willard had an artistic flare and a desire to work in a more creative field than the glove business. They were defeated by the economics of the times and the magazine was bankrupt within a few months, its equipment auctioned in September 1940. Banker committed suicide shortly afterwards.

Ben Kaplan and Milt Kristt, who purchased the rights to the magazine, sold *Gloves Magazine* in early 1942 to the Haire Publishing Co., of New York City. Haire combined it with that company's *Fashion Accessories* publication, circulation 6,000. At the time of the sale, there was speculation that *Gloves* might one day become a separate journal again, but that was not to happen.

Business activity during the Depression
1933
Steinberger Brothers Glove Co. purchased the business and factory of Adam W. Klopot, who continued to manage the company.
John Snell & Son moved to larger quarters.
Sutton Glove Co. moved into a new three-story building on South Melcher Street in Johnstown.
Allen A. Bornstein, head of Aborn Glove Co, purchased a building in Johnstown five times larger than the one he had occupied previously.

The National Recovery Act

Between 1929 and 1932, manufacturing in the United States declined by almost 50 percent and the value of production declined even more. Nationally unemployment reached 25 percent in 1932-33, rising from 4.5 million in 1930 to eight million in 1931, to 13 million in 1933.

The number of men's dress gloves, the staple of Fulton County's production, declined from 800,000 dozen pairs to half that many in the same interval. Unemployment in the county increased, but employers began to spread work among the cutters and sewers, giving everyone some employment some of the time. Violent protests, huge marches by unemployed workers, and demonstrations against both government and employers marked the national scene. The level of despair in Fulton County's glove industry was not sufficient to bring about similar unrest, but a widespread strike did occur in the tanneries in 1933.

Franklin Delano Roosevelt was elected president in 1932 with the expectation that he could bring about national recovery. In 1932 and in 1936 when Democrats again prevailed, Fulton County remained a Republican stronghold.

In short order, Roosevelt's administration advanced many programs to deal with the growing Depression. General Hugh Johnson, who would manage the National Recovery Act (NRA), pushed forward the idea of "self-government in industry under government supervision." He felt that unrestrained competition was responsible for the business decline. Workers were at the mercy of greedy manufacturers and needed the protection of wage and hour laws.[53]

Out of these beliefs came the the National Recovery Act, the centerpiece of New Deal legislation, adopted in June of 1933. It was designed to end the country's widespread depression and deal with unemployment. Every industry was to appoint a governing board and establish a code of fair competition within that industry. The federal government would license businesses operating within the code and exempt them from existing anti-trust laws. Association members were acutely aware of restrictions in the Sherman Antitrust Law. Lest they forget, *The Glovers Review* reminded them that the aim of the law was to secure "free competition," that there could be no attempt to fix prices and no restraint of free trade.[54] Thus, glovemen welcomed the NRA's suspension of the Sherman Antitrust Laws and the promise that it would eliminate questions of price fixing. On the other hand, it is hard to imagine an industry more beset by competition and the promise of "fair competition" must have been very appealing to the county's glove manufacturers.

Section 7A of the NRA guaranteed collective bargaining and prohibited employers from stifling unions or interfering with union organization. It also established maximum work hours and minimum wages. Businessmen in general were unhappy with the guarantee of collective bargaining and questioned whether the act compelled employers to recognize unions.

Concerns about competition overshadowed county manufacturers' worries about any benefits unions might gain from the NRA. An article from *The Glovers Review* demonstrates why members of the National Association of Leather Glove Manufacturers were so enthusiastic in their support of NRA's promise to control the extremes of competition:

> *They tell me in New York that table cutters have found a new way of cutting—their own throats. You remember the higher wage scale that went into effect after the strike a year ago [1934]—the one which they say put two pattern-cutters working where one table cutter worked for before? Well, that was just the beginning. After NRA gave up the ghost, an effort was made to get table cutters to agree to a lower wage scale in New York City. As a union, the table cutters turned the suggestion down cold. . . . Then as individuals, some of these same table cutters put up a table in the kitchen at home, or maybe two or three if they have a couple of relatives who are not having much work. Each one can cut maybe 25 dozen a week. Perhaps they have a friend who can slit then, and*

1934

J. Castiglione & Co. leased a new factory.

Karg Brothers incorporated their tannery and took on a new manager, David S. Van Santen.

Sanges Glove Co. purchased an existing three-story factory.

Harry R. Bradt leased the Lucas & Kennedy tannery in Johnstown.

The Goodheim-Crossley Glove Corp. was organized to manufacture gloves in Mayfield.

1935

Liberty Tanning, variously Dressing, Co. was defendant in a lawsuit charging its construction over Cayadutta Creek was responsible for damage to four other tanneries that were flooded out.

Dawes and Hann, in existence since 1900, making fur-lined gloves, incorporated.

H & P Glove Co. purchased the tools, machinery, and stock of Josiah H. Danforth Co. and employed some of the latter's salesmen. The Danforth factory was purchased by Acme Glove Co.

Elmer Little & Son built a three-story addition to increase space by 50 percent.

Jacob Adler & Co., organized in 1862, closed at the end of 1935.

1937

H. G. Hilts incorporated in 1936 and in 1937 merged with Willard Glove Co. The consolidated firm, Hilts-Willard, was located in the Hilts building in Gloversville. Hilts had been in business since 1878; Ellery G. Willard established his business in 1936 after having represented Louis Meyers & Son on the road for 20 years.

other relatives to sew them. In other words they become manufacturers. . . . They cut down their own table-cutting wages and figure everything at rock-bottom, offering their production at ridiculously low prices. The old-time manufacture tells me he finds it cheaper to shut down his cutting and sewing rooms and buy from these cutters. [55]

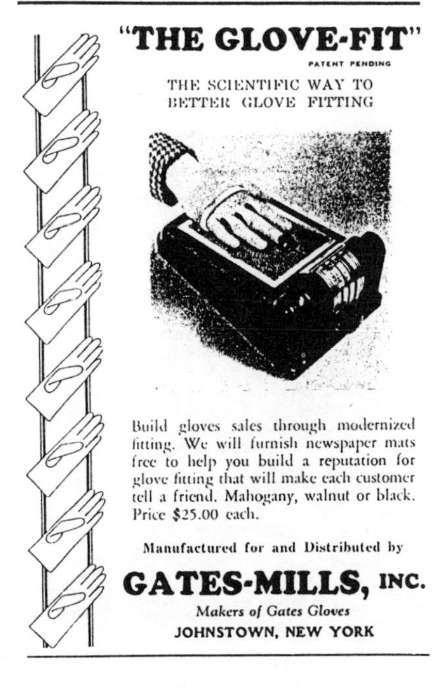

Fulton County's glovemen were inspired to act to limit competition. They were well aware of declining business: boxes in each month's issue of *The Glovers Review* in 1931 and 1932 tallied retail sales in key cities across the country and showed sharp declines in sales over previous years. At its 1933 annual meeting, the association quickly appointed a committee to draft their code of fair business ethics. Quite expeditiously, the group established a number of committees designed to improve business practices, which were to be a part of each industry's code. It is amazing how the association jumped at the opportunities required by the new laws, when it had seemed as if the industry would never adopt modern ways. One might conclude that the manufacturers were dragged kicking and screaming into a new world of business simply because the new codes required the industry to establish new methods of accounting. They might never have done so on their own.

William C. Gates, descendent of one of the founders of Gates-Mills, remarked to the author in 1998 that modern management wondered how their company managed to survive in the Depression. On learning of the NRA accounting requirements, he recalled that in 1934 the company hired an accountant, Bob Eckstein. Gates said that members of the firm had always believed that Eckstein's accounting ability had saved the firm. One wonders if his hiring was solely in response to the NRA.

Perhaps glove makers were enthusiastic supporters of the NRA because business conditions were so desperate, or more likely because they saw the other benefits. As perceived by the NAGM, the NRA would help the manufacturers fight the Depression by controlling the "10 to 15 percent who exploit labor to the point where the rest of the industry can not compete fairly and profitably."[56] Association president Albert Aaron summed up the industry's response to the NRA by noting that the intent of the act was "to help the industry prosper and save itself from bankruptcy, . . . to control its production that we shall not again have these proverbial 'fat' and 'lean' years, and finally, as well as probably most important, is the idea of compelling the industry to pay its workers a wage in keeping with the accepted standards of living in America, regulate hours, prevent sweat-shop conditions, and forever do away with either direct or indirect slashing of wages to below our agreed schedule of rates."[57] In other words the manufacturers saw the act as controlling "unfair" competition and were eager to embrace it.

(The manufacturers' reluctance to act unless pressed has a parallel in later years when union shops prevailed. In the seventies and eighties, glovemen would say the unions were a necessary thing—they needed someone with whom to negotiate. But by the time they realized this, the struggle for union organization had gone on for a decades.)

A representative of the Ernst & Ernst, a national accounting firm, summarized the government's actions for association members. He noted that in the past cooperation in the industry met with indifferent success and that it was possible that government action did present a great opportunity for the glove industry to do things it had failed to accomplish in the past—or even things the industry failed to recognize as necessary.[58] He summarized the

Business activity during the Depression
1938

A farmer took down the old Daniel B. Judson factory on Glove Street, Kingsboro, to use the lumber for his barn. Sixty years before it had been one of the area's most imposing plants.

Crocetta Bros. purchased the former high school building in Fonda for its fabric glove division, Artcraft Glove Co.

Aris Gloves built a three-story addition to its Gloversville factory, doubling its capacity and adding about 150 more workers. The company was previously Steinberger Brothers Glove Co. with Arthur and Robert Steinberger and Adam and Winslow Klopot. The next year, Aris was licensed to produce the Merry Hull glove which had been made by the Daniel Hays Co.

J. M. Rubin Glove Co. purchased the very modern Perrin factory as an annex.

THE GLOVERS REVIEW

Retail Glove Sales

October 1932

For the month of October 1932 retail glove sales showed a decrease as compared with October 1931 according to six Federal Reserve districts reporting. The average decrease was 23.1%. The average stocks on hand for four of these districts was 34.6% under October 1931.

District	Per Cent of Gain or Loss Sales	Stocks
Boston	—26.0	*
Chicago	—21.0	—39.7
Cleveland	—26.1	—31.3
New York	—16.1	—37.9
Richmond	—24.6	—29.7
San Francisco	—24.9	*

(* Not Reported)

Gloves and Costume Jewelry

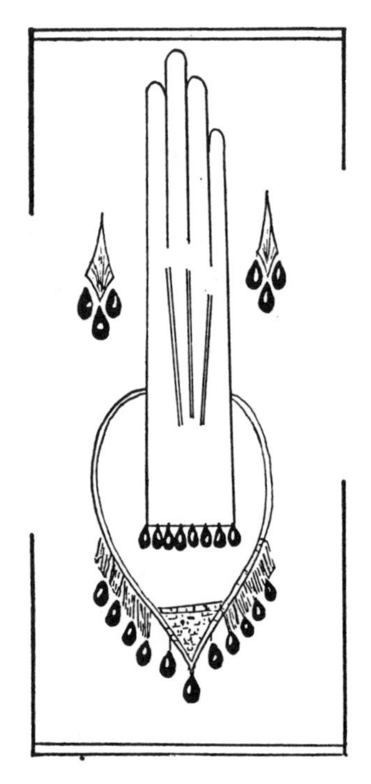

An ensemble of gloves with necklace and ear drops designed by Chanel for Steinberger Bros. Glove Corp.

provisions of the act as 1) providing supervision or control of the industry by the government, 2) suspension of antitrust laws with respect to those who meet the other requirements of the act, 3) establishment of a code of business principles, 4) permission for agreements between competitors to regulate conditions, 5) price stabilization, 6) a guarantee of collective bargaining for employees, and 7) the appointment of the trade association as the agency for carrying out the law and dealing with the government. He envisioned membership in the association as not merely essential, but an asset for the manufacturers. For association members these were great inducements to act.

The NRA had another salutary affect on the association: the number of new and associate members jumped. Of the 56 active members attending the 1933 meeting, six were from New York City and four from the Midwest, and the rest were from Fulton County. Almost the same ratio applied to the 27 new members in July and the 39 added in August, 34 in September. By its spring 1934 meeting, national membership in the association had grown to 232 manufacturers, leaving only 104 firms that had not joined the group.

On the adoption of the glove code of fair competition, a local code authority was established to implement the National Recovery Act and to determine a uniform minimum wage scale for the industry. In November 1933, James S. Ireland was appointed to the code authority along with Francis Sutton, also of Johnstown, two representatives from the Midwest and Louis Postman of New York City. Ireland resigned as chairman at the association's spring meeting in 1934, and talked of his support for the NRA.

An immediate result of the adoption of the code was the cutting of employment to 44 hours a week, then to 40—this in an industry where factories had been open for 55 hours a week. A minimum wage for both piecework and time-work was established at $.32½ per hour, beginners $.22½. Homework was to be eliminated as quickly as possible, "within six months of the date of the approval of the code, employers had to reduce their outside work by at least 25 percent, and another 25 percent reduction had to be made within a year of the date." The code authority would study the timetable for the final 50 percent reduction. There could be no selling below cost and each employer had to keep and provide records of employment, hours, wages, wage rates, production, orders, billings, stocks, and raw materials. Table-cut gloves were to be identified and fines were established for unauthorized use of that label.

Bethune M. Grant, Jr., editor of *Gloves Magazine*, showed his deep understanding of the industry's intrinsic problems in his observation that the NRA plan would greatly benefit business because it would force manufacturers to confront methods of cost accounting. He noted that "until after the war, much of the cost accounting in the glove industry was by rule of thumb and guess work. Some manufacturers never paid themselves a salary. One man, perhaps 30 years ago, figured that cutting linings did not cost him anything. He said it was no one's business if he went to his factory each morning before breakfast and cut enough linings to last during the day."[59] The editor believed that with such practices there could be no market stability, hence no wage uniformity. "When trade falls off in any line of business the tendency has been to lower wages, which depresses purchasing power. This sets up a vicious cycle and reacts to the disadvantage of the retailer. Buyers frequently say that they are not concerned about getting gloves at low prices. What they have to watch out for is to buy their goods as favorably as neighboring stores."

Association secretary Karl Gerstl opined in 1934 that "for years glove manufacturers, subject to the sometimes over-keen competitive methods of other manufacturers, have wished that there was a way to place competition upon a fair and equal basis, to compel observance of wage schedules, uniform cost accounting and fair methods in selling merchandise. These things are now possible through the code."[60] This silver lining in the code accounts for the way it was so heartily endorsed by glove manufacturers in spite of the fact that one primary purpose of the law was benefits for workers.

Manufacturers seemed to have expressed no objections to the wage and hour parts of the law, but they were concerned with proposals to limit homework. Glove manufacturers were concerned about the small glove shop owners who depended on homeworkers for most—even 100 percent—of their sewing. They claimed that its elimination would "take from many families in Fulton County one of the main sources of income." They feared the "adjustment to these new conditions would be a serious problem."[61]

In mid-1934 several amendments were proposed for the glove code. One would extend the code to include manufacturers of fabric gloves. Also, a conflict arose concerning the code's wage scale. The eastern scale based on piecework was contrary to the western scale based on hourly wages. The National Recovery Administration, through the code authority, decided the issue by extending piecework rates to the entire industry, but western manufacturers continued to protest that this would not fit their methods.

In 1935 both manufacturers and the code authority argued in Washington that the different wages for 2,000 separate tasks created a wage scale too "bulky" to manage.[62] Louis Postman said that the wage scale "destroyed the principles of collective bargaining [because] it is possible to bargain only upward."[63] It was proposed that all reference to piecework be removed from the wage scales of glove workers, thus bringing the glove code closer to codes in other industries. A basic minimum would be substituted. This pleased western manufacturers but proved locally to be just as contentious, because of the difficulty of applying an hourly minimum to the widely different operations found in the county.

The code authority began to inspect factories for compliance and the enforcement committee began to hear and settle labor complaints. Inspections of 124 of the 332 known plants found individual cases of underpayment to workers. At a meeting of the Fulton County group, the manufacturers agreed that the code authority's work was to be commended. At the same time, in the fall of 1934, the workweek was temporarily extended from 40 to 44 hours to permit greater production. In early 1935, the director of the compliance division found 27 "bootleg" factories producing more than 1,500 dozen table-cut gloves that were not manufactured according to the code.[64] One glove shop, R. Antevil & Co., was found in violation for underpayment, and for coercing workers to give back the funds when the company did correct the pay.[65]

The fair trade practices committee of the association proposed that manufacturers could save $200,000 if they refused to allow retailers to cancel orders without penalty or return gloves not sold. A new and stronger set of fair trade practices was adopted by the association in early 1935.

The National Recovery Act was scheduled to expire in June of 1935. Congress was considering the Wagner Bill, which would have strengthened the protection given labor. The courts were considering challenges to the NRA, and finally on "Black Monday" of 1935, the Supreme Court declared the act unconstitutional because under it the legislature had delegated powers via the codes and because the Chief Justice perceived distinctions between direct and indirect interstate commerce.[66]

The National Labor Relations Act (NLRA or the Wagner Bill) became law in July of 1935. Robert Wagner, a U. S. Senator from New York State, believed that higher wages would increase workers' buying power and that in turn would stimulate the country's economic growth. His bill, the NLRA, created a public policy to encourage collective bargaining through independent unions and guaranteed a fair procedure for determining bargaining rights and for the disposition of charges of unfair practices.[67] (The Social Security Act, which was passed later that year, capped Roosevelt's reform legislation.)

The wool-glove branch of the association had voted to recommend continuation of the NRA and the code authority. Bethune M. Grant, Jr. wrote an editorial in *Gloves Magazine* in support of the code, which turned out to be an obituary for the NRA. "Perhaps," he wrote, "the Glove Code went too far. Perhaps too many reforms were attempted at once." He mourned the loss of the provision that goods not be sold below cost. He did not describe the controversies that brought about the failure to renew the code.

Just before the association's annual convention in 1935, the chairman of the code authority reviewed the code's accomplishments: uniform operation of factories, limited work hours, rules for fair-trade practices, and more detailed production reports. It was anticipated that termination of the NRA would not affect glove prices and the wage and hour conditions of the code would go on even without the act being in place. The association voted to continue these standards until the end of the year. It is wonderfully amazing that when the act was eliminated, the association even embraced the continuance of detailed recordkeeping.

But, as the editor of the *Gloves* noted, manufacturers did not put the improved statistical information provided by the government and the magazine to use: "If glove people would only learn to use the statistics given month after month to estimate the capacity of the wholesale market against the purchasing power of our 120,000,000 people and then 'allot' themselves something like their own proportionate share of production, there would be less dumping and more money made."[68]

A footnote to the social legislation of the thirties: New York State adopted a law in 1935 creating unemployment insurance for workers and a payroll tax to pay for it, although it was not the first state to do so.[69]

Domestic glove production, which had dipped precipitously at the end of 1934, began to rise, reaching a peak in the early fall of 1935, just before it dropped even more steeply toward the end of that year. Much of that increase was in work gloves, and orders for leather mittens for Civilian Conservation Corps workers accounted for a good part of that increase. The county received none of the government orders for the CCC; they were all filled by Midwestern firms.[70]

An increase in production peaked again in the fall of 1936, following the seasonality of the industry, but the decline that followed, with a slight rebound, reached at the end of 1937 the lowest level that the industry recorded in the first half of the twentieth century.

A slow and not quite consistent upturn through 1938 left the editor of *Gloves* confident again. There was reason for his optimism; all of the county's 900 cutters were employed. However, even this rosy view had a dark side. At the time of the 1914 strike, the union had 1,400 to 1,500 cutters. Death and attrition had claimed 36 to 40 percent of the cutters in two and a half

School for gloveworkers

A cutting school, established in Gloversville in 1927 continued into the 30s, in cooperation with the State Education Department and instructors from the local industry. The course was eighteen months long. The students were paid $57 a week, monies advanced by the association.

In 1909 Gloversville High School established sewing classes and continued these into the 1930s. Night school sewing classes there started in1929.

decades! Further, it was obvious that mortality among cutters would continue to rise. Of the 1,023 table cutters employed in the county in the early 1930s, the average age of those under 65 was 45 years. Many cutters continued work past 65, and death and illness were decreasing their numbers at a great rate, perhaps as high as 64 a year, with few replacements. In 1933, the cutting school had only six students and only 20 apprentices were scattered in the shops. This small number could never correct the imbalance.

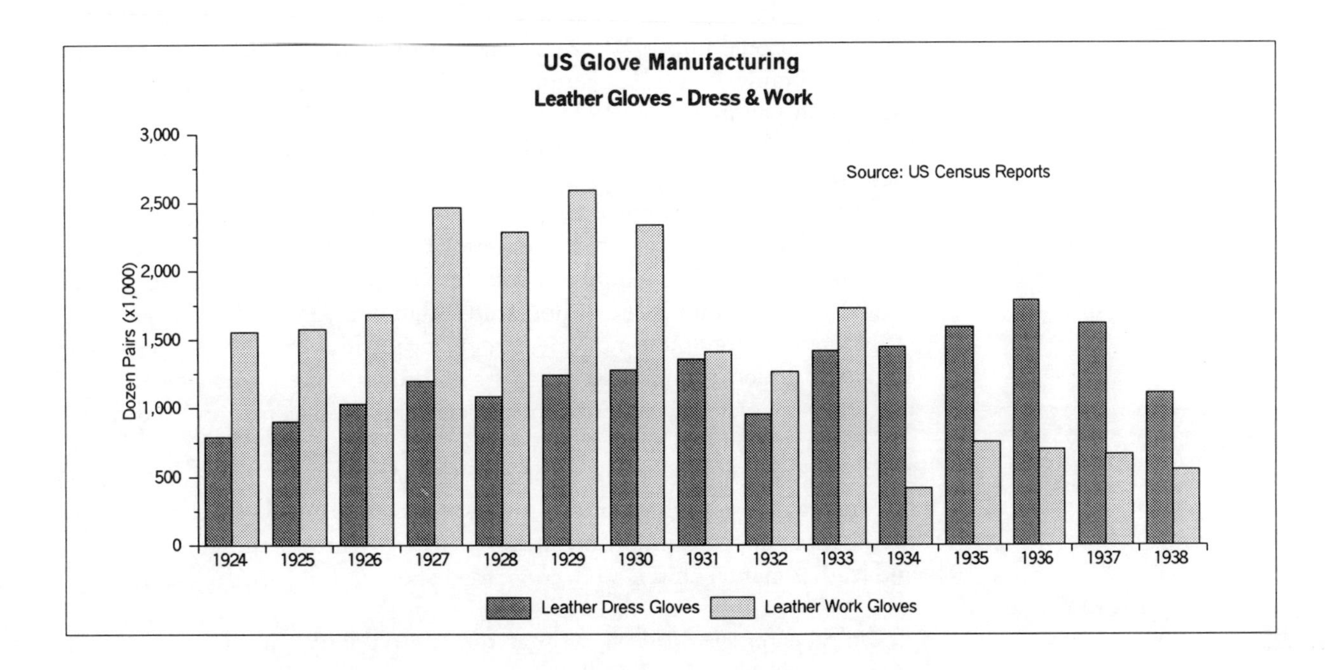

Unfortunately the census statistics for production levels circa 1910 and 1938 are not precisely comparable and it is difficult to establish the figures just for Fulton County. However, the number of pairs of fine leather gloves (presumably almost all made in the county) is known for several years that offer telling comparisons: 1.3 million dozen pairs in 1910, 1.1 million dozen pairs in 1938. The decline in the number of table cutters should have made the decrease greater, so these figures probably reflect the widespread use of clicker cutters. The decline is real, but given that 1938 reflected the depth of the depression, it could have been greater.

Already the clouds of coming wars began to affect the shipment of skins. The fighting between Ethiopia and Italy threatened to limit the shipment of blackhead mochas.

As different kinds of skins became rarer and more expensive, the industry tried many new sources for gloves. Pigskins from Mexican peccaries were tanned for many things, but not for gloves due to their extreme thickness and imperfect surfaces. In the early 1920s, Karg Brothers tanned between 20,000 to 25,000 peccary skins a year. Ed Karg experimented with splitting the skins and had two pairs of gloves made from them. A Canadian saw their possibilities, and gradually the retail industry began to offer pigskin gloves. As pigskins became acceptable a new source was found in Brazil. However, this did not prove very stable because in 1935 the Brazilian government decreed a closed season on killing peccaries, and it considered an embargo on their shipment.

Unions and Strikes

The Depression led to an increase in union membership both nationally and locally. Union membership in the American Federation of Labor had declined after World War I all across the country,[71] and union activity was relatively dormant in Fulton County's glove businesses as well. As a first step toward national affiliation, Fulton County's glove cutters reorganized in 1933, with almost all cutters joining a new union, which became Local 69 of the International Glove Workers Union of America, an AFL affiliate. The union, claiming it was bargaining for over a thousand men, obtained an increase in pay in August 1933, pending adoption of the code called for in the NRA. The sewers, emboldened by the cutters, began to press for an increase as well.

The local glove-workers' unions did break with one established policy that gave preference to senior workers when work was short. During the Depression, the unions permitted work to be spread around—some worked alternate weeks, some worked short shifts—but everyone had some work.

Nationally, the labor movement revived in the years between 1932 and 1939 with union membership rising from three to nine million members in that interval, aided by government policies and the Depression.[72] Although the AFL grew by 500 thousand members in 1933, another 400 thousand in 1934, its leadership was weak.[73] Fulton County's union activity paralleled the national rate of growth of unions in this interval. Just as businessmen across the country opposed union organization in the thirties, the county's glove and leather manufacturers were concerned about union growth.

Utilization of labor without restrictions was central to the innovative heart of the American economy. . . . Earlier in the century, aggressive employers under the banner of the open shop had broken the power of many established craft unions precisely so that engineers and managers could impose their version of efficient, unrestricted production. Union work rules, contractual grievances and seniority rights, and other union-imposed regulations and customs, [businessmen] believed, stifled the creative genius of the American system.[74]

Clarence Carr and the tannery workers' union

After 1932, Communist and Socialist philosophies gained influence in several national unions, but there is scant evidence that these philosophies penetrated the glove unions—even the cutters' union, whose leaders had represented Socialist ideals in the 1914 strike. However, Communist philosophy played an enormous role in the activities of the tannery workers' unions, primarily because of the influence of their charismatic leader, Clarence Carr.

In 1933 organizers led by Louis Solomon from the left-wing Needle Trades Workers Industrial Union (NTWIU), came to Gloversville to organize Fulton County's fur workers in a dozen or so small shops. The union was the creation of Communist leaders in the International Ladies Garment Workers Union and the International Fur Workers Union.[75] Secretary of the NTWIU Benjamin Gold was an admitted Communist. After staging a four-week strike, the union won recognition, and moved on to organize mocha tannery workers. Carr, who grew up in Fulton County and worked for different tanneries, joined Solomon in organizing other tanneries. The

Independent Leather Workers Union of Fulton County was established in the summer of 1933 with all the mocha workers joining the new union, which was headed up by Carr.

Carr started work as a Slocum staker at the Martin-Deischel tannery, but most of Carr's early life is an enigma. According to labor historian Gerald Zahavi,[76] Carr ran for local office as a Socialist, was a member of the Industrial Workers of the World (IWW, the "Wobblies"), and the Communist Party of the United States of America. He ran for Congress on the CPUSA ticket in 1934 and 1936.

As Carr described in "The Early Years," his treatise on *Organizing the Fulton County Leather Workers*, the struggle to unionize Fulton County's tannery workers began when he spearheaded an organizational drive. Besides asking for a wage increase, the union was seeking recognition and a closed shop. Carr claimed that at the start of the strike in October 1933, 2,300 men—only a third of whom were union members—walked out of 33 tanneries; the local newspaper reported that many were still at work. The union said the Tanners Association was at the root of the strike because its members would not recognize the union. The Tanners Association refused to bargain with the Independent Leather Workers Union as called for under the NRA Leather Industry Code. Carr charged that a worker affiliated with the union had been fired. The Tanners Association countered with a broadside charging that the call for a closed shop was in direct violation of the leather code.

The union threatened to picket every tannery and the threat of violence impelled Gloversville's mayor to put every policeman on duty the next morning. Carr charged that police were escorting strike-breakers to the tanneries. The union appealed to the NRA in Washington but the appeal was returned to the local code committee. The union staged mass meetings and cavalcades of cars through the city's streets. Within days, members of the Tanners Association decided to close the tanneries, and according to the *Morning Herald* it did so "as challenge to strikers who defy the NRA Board which is attempting to effect conciliation."[77]

A small note in that paper read "COMMUNIST ORDERED FROM STRIKE MEET, An unidentified woman was ejected by the Sergeant-at-Arms of the strikers' meeting last night in the Eagles Hall for distributing copies of 'The Daily Worker,' the official Communist newspaper in America."

The union protested the presence of a tannery employer on the code committee. Within a day, two representatives of management resigned from the committee in an effort to move the conciliation process.

The newspaper carried the text of a speech by NRA administrator Hugh S. Johnson before the national convention of the AFL, in which Johnson said that under the NRA strikes were unnecessary. The newspaper editorialized that his words might have been delivered for the benefit of the Glove Cities and noted that the union risked losing public support.

Because of protests by the strikers that all members of the code committee were associated with the tanneries, the NRA appointed an outside mediator. A report from the Department of Labor was leaked to the local newspaper, which was then able to reveal that "one man taking part in the present labor difficulties in the Glove Cities [Louis Solomon] is an officer of the Communist Party and was an important figure in another strike of a similar nature in a Pennsylvania city."[78]

The Tanners Association

In 1936 attorney Lydon Maider arranged for the incorporation of the Tanners Association, which was formed to deal with the emerging union. From then on, with the exception of the time he spent in the service, he served as counsel to the Tanners Association.

At the time the organization was founded there were four merchandise tanneries, outfits that bought raw skins, tanned them, and sold them as finished leather. They were J. C. Bleyl, a division of Winslow Brothers & Smith of Boston; Wood & Hyde; Gloversville Leather, headed up by Joseph Mendel; and G. Levor & Co. In the late thirties, G. Levor, which tanned primarily shoe leather, created Framglo Tanning Co. and expanded into glove leather.

There were nine contract tanners: Cane Tanning Co.; Independent Leather Mfgr. Corp.; Liberty Dressing Co.; Peerless Tanning Co.; Reliable Tanning Co.; Risedorph Tanning Co.; J. G. Robinson; Geisler & Lehr; and Twin City Leather Co.

Leather dealers and merchants engaged in buying raw skins and contracted with tanners to turn them into leather. The leading dealers were Hess & Drucker, Horowitz & Arbib, Jones & Naudin, Ernest Pryor Leather Co., Kurt Schaeffer, Harold J. Smith Leather Co., and Spanish-American Skin Co. Henry Tauber came from Switzerland to Gloversville in 1936 and established Spanish-American Skin Co. with his wife, who was the daughter of an owner of a tannery in Tarrassa, near Barcelona.

In an interview with the author in 1996, Maider described the range of skins tanned in the county during the thirties and the level of competition—"very fierce"—among the different companies. None of the tanneries employed more than 100 workers, except G. Levor, which had over two hundred employees. Maider believes the union was successful in organizing tannery workers because the tanneries were so small and that the person in charge of the workers, the foreman, had enormous control over them. According to Maider there was "no question the situation, the labor relations, was bad." A committee of the tanners was designated to deal with the union; its members included Benjamin Dennie of Wood & Hyde; George Meyer of Liberty Dressing; Arthur Cane of Cane Tanning; and Fred Rulison, who was a merchandiser of horsehides and supplied Johnstown's baseball manufacturers.[79]

In meetings through the second week of the strike, the arbitrator S. Park Harmon failed to bring the two sides together. Harmon's proposal for a settlement included a clause that coincided with the tannery owners demands—the removal from the ranks of the Independent Leather Workers Union of "certain elements," that is the Communists.[80] The Association of Tanners claimed that a split was developing in the union and that there would be a revolt if Louis Solomon and Jack Golden, the labor advisors from New York, did not return to New York City. Tannery worker David Canfield began leading an insurrection against the outside Communists and according to Carr, the men were asked to leave the Glove Cities. Also, according to Carr, Canfield was using the red scare to confuse workers, was acting as a strike breaker, and was trying to establish a company union.[81]

MONDAY, OCTOBER 23, 1933. THE MORNING HERALD

STRIKE SEEMS NEAR END AS SOLOMON AND GOLDEN CEASE ACTIVITIES HERE

Except for a decision on wages, the strike appeared to be ending after three weeks. The proposed settlement included union recognition and collective bargaining, mutual protection of each side against strikes and lockouts, a sharing of work when times were slack, and the establishment of grievance committees to handle disputes within the tanneries. The union's strike committee approved the proposed settlement, which included a temporary raise in wages. Meanwhile, there were several clashes at two tanneries where workers tried to return and windows were broken.

The Tanners Association rejected Harmon's proposed settlement and countered with one containing three fundamental differences. The union took out a large ad the next day stating that the newspaper's account of the differences erred and showing that the two proposals had only minor differences. Both proposals contained the condition that the union not merge with any national union during the term of the agreement, but it could affiliate with another Fulton County union.

The union held two mass meetings and met with Assemblyman Harry F. Dunkel, who was serving as the union spokesman, and tabled, then rejected, the tanners' proposal. As the strike entered its fifth week, "night raiders" broke windows in several tanneries and union strikers set up guards to protect the tanneries.[82] The union charged that the Tanners Association was holding up the settlement in order to destroy the union.

On November 1, Adams Buckskin Co. withdrew from the association and signed with the union. The union strike committee voted to allow settlements with individual companies. Adams reopened and its hundred workers went back to work amidst rumors that other tanneries would soon break ranks. Two Johnstown tanneries, H. W. Topp Co. and Edwin Vosburgh, Inc., also nonmembers of the association, were about to sign with the union.

TUESDAY, NOVEMBER 7, 1933. THE MORNING HERALD

TANNERY OPERATORS 'SEEK TO CRUSH UNION BY STARVATION ROUTE,' CLARENCE CARR SAYS

A hearing in Washington before the NLRB was scheduled and welcomed by the strikers but not the tanners. G. Levor Co. obtained a court order restraining union picketing. Levor remained open until numerous skirmishes between strikers and "loyal workers" finally convinced the company to close. The union replied by bringing 500 picketers to Levor's instead of 200.

A group of citizens attempted to bring the tanners and the union together, but were rebuffed by the chairman of the local leather industry code. The strike was definitely hurting the county. Two thousand men were on strike, of whom Carr claimed 1,500 were union men. Carr charged that the association was trying to "crush the union by the starvation route."[83] The secretary of the Tanners Association charged that union members had not been permitted to vote on the association's proposal; the union countered that the vote had been unanimous. Then the tanners voted to withdraw their proposal for settlement and the union sent a telegram to President Roosevelt asking for help.

Rumors abounded that four tanneries were considering ways of settling the strike: Martin-Littell, Levor, Wood & Hyde, and Karg Mills. Levor said it would not sign with the union, but would make an agreement with its employees. Wood & Hyde and Liberty Dressing signed with their employees, and the tanners asked that local police forces be augmented given the possibility for violence.

Benjamin Gold, representing the Needle Trades Workers Industrial Union, was indicted for restraint of trade and conspiracy, hiring gangsters, and using violence to pursue union goals. In reporting his indictment, the local paper noted that he had earlier addressed the local union. Louis Solomon returned to the area and spoke at a mass union meeting, stating that the Communist Party was a political party like the Democrats and Republicans. The union had asked him back as advisor because the strike had not been settled within 48 hours of his leaving two weeks earlier.

The NRA sent a new mediator, the tanneries announced they would reopen, and the union prepared to strengthen picket lines. The Glove Cities were a pot about to boil over. The mayors of both cities said any threats or intimidation would bring arrests. On November 14 David Canfield was beaten up and Charles Cole was arrested for the assault, which allegedly involved a group of strikers abducting Canfield and driving him to an isolated location. Other arrests followed. The tanners decided not to reopen the mills, and several members sought injunctions against picketing.

After two days of hearings, the mediator, New York State industrial commissioner Elmer F. Andrews, recommended that the workers should return without discrimination against them for union activities. His other recommendations were similar to earlier union proposals. The union accepted the November 17 mediator's recommendations "as a basis for negotiations," but not in their present form. The "fiery" meeting at which the proposal had been considered was enlivened by a harangue by Miss Rina Evans, a Communist, who railed against the government, the NRA, and the tanners. Two union leaders had her thrown out.

The sheriff had a hundred men deputized to protect workers should the tanneries reopen, but the reopening was postponed for several days while the tanners considered and reconsidered the mediator's recommendations. The tanners, accused of carrying on a lockout, restated that the tanneries had closed after the union began the strike on October 6, more than six weeks earlier.

The mediator, angered by reports of Solomon's speech in favor of Communism, refused to meet with union leaders when Solomon was present.

After a day of "restlessness and disturbances bordering on near-riots," where a thousand strikers congregated at G. Levor and Martin-Littell tanneries, the union called a truce—but not before a car, carrying workers attempting to elude strikers, hit a young child. Windows were broken at one Johnstown tannery; fights broke out between strikers and non-strikers.

Despite three more days of conferences, both sides continued to disagree with the mediator's proposals and presented their own conditions, which seemed to be drawing them further apart. The NLRB ordered both sides to accept the mediator's proposals. Senator Wagner issued a mandate for both sides to end the strike, to no avail.

After seven weeks, the mediator was able to get the two sides to agree and the strike was over. Workers could choose their own union, they were guaranteed collective bargaining, and a grievance procedure was established. Although the union won recognition and a significant wage increase for tannery workers, it did not gain a closed shop.

The two cities had suffered greatly and supply stocks, though varied, were short enough to hamper glove production. Mochas were in the shortest supply because workers at the mocha tannery had staged a three-week strike earlier in the summer in addition to participating in the October strike. The settlement in Fulton County was still not complete, however. Mocha tannery workers had asked for a ten percent increase, the manufacturers asked for a ten percent decrease. The outcome was that 250 workers finally went back to work with the guarantee that wages would remain as they were at the time of the walkout.

From the 1933 conflict emerged a small Communist cell in Fulton County that continued until 1949.[84] Carr later wrote that "the leather workers in Fulton County conducted a constant struggle against the tannery bosses" for the next seventeen years. Despite organized labor's gains—and some feel that it was the most successful strike in the county ever[85]—the union struggle continued.

Despite the fact that the strike seriously disrupted the local economy and threw the cities into turmoil, it was just one of many similar strikes. As the local paper noted, "Since the NRA codes went into effect, the number of workers on strike has increased sharply. Through 1932 there were few strikes, but after the summer of 1933 the number of strikers nationally rose dramatically."[86]

Carr never concealed his Communist party affiliation. It never seemed to affect his leadership of the union. "Carr's popularity rested on a genuine affection for him and an unyielding faith in his honesty and integrity—characteristics attested to even by his enemies."[87]

The county's glove unions

How much did the Independent Leather Workers Union's struggle influence glove unions in the county, which were also mostly independent and not affiliated with national unions? Their nonaffiliation may reflect the independent nature of local workers or it may be that the small number of workers in the county meant that larger industries—like the garment, construction, coal, steel, and auto industries—were more fertile fields for labor organization. Whatever the reason, for many subsequent years local glove workers felt they could handle union matters without the help of a national organization.

During March 1934, Local 69, International Glove Workers Union of America began to press for higher wages, and committees representing the different kinds of work held discussions with manufacturers. A denial of a wage increase for cutters brought a strike vote on April 5, and other county glove workers joined the walkout on April 13. Even though an agreement was reached within two weeks, workers did not return because manufacturers declined to adopt the new schedule before it was approved by NRA officials. The strike had spread to glove workers across the country, and although it ended on May 14 in Fulton County, Milwaukee's 750 glove workers stayed out in an attempt to win union recognition. They did not return until July when they were granted wages equal to those in Fulton County—it is significant that Fulton County's wages were still leading the industry. Even New York City manufacturers had lowered the schedule for fine leather gloves below that of the county, and this issue was taken up by the code authority.

Primarily as a result of the NRA, committees of glove workers and manufacturers began to wrestle with the question of wages on an annual basis. In 1935 the NAGM drafted a plan for arbitration which "should prevent strikes and other disastrous interruptions of business." It called for arbitration panels and appeals panels, and means of enforcing the plan if and when it was adopted.[88] The *Leader Republican* printed the entire text of the agreement. The association stated that it was acting on the union's suggestion when it created the agreement, but the pact went nowhere at the time.

The International Glove Workers Union—representing table and pull-down cutters—voted to continue the wage and hour provisions of the NRA when that act was declared unconstitutional (as did the manufacturers association). Workers struck Tryon Co. because that company had made an agreement recognizing the union under NRA, but later repudiated the agreement.[89]

The same union called a walkout at Louis Meyers & Son over the issue of pattern cutters using "a 'spud' knife and rule," methods that were restricted to table cutters. The manufacturers suggested appplying the arbitration plan, but the union settled when Meyers agreed to enforce the existing schedule and address all kinds of complaints from sewers, binders, and layers-off.[90]

An agreement in the summer of 1936 extended the wages schedule in the table-cut industry for 18 months to the end of 1937, and called for longer work weeks just before Easter and Christmas, provided workers were employed to the fullest. In 1937 labor problems shut two county knitting companies. That year there were strikes by table cutters in New York City, dissatisfaction among pattern cutters, and strikes among Czechoslovakian glove workers. Notes in the local papers informed Fulton County workers of strikes and problems in the glove industry in the rest of the country and in Europe.

The county's labor unions banded together in December, 1937 to form the United Labor Committee (later the United Labor Unions or ULU), which grew to include a dozen Fulton County unions, most of which were not glove or leather unions but representatives of other groups such as telephone workers. Frank McMaster of the Joint Council of Glove Workers quickly replaced Carr as head of the new group, because of concern for the Independent's Communist leanings.[91]

As the Depression deepened in 1938 and conditions grew worse in the county, something else was beginning to happen; the whole climate in Fulton County changed, probably in a short few years around 1938. Gone was the feeling of cooperation between employer and worker, lost was the conviction that people could work together to solve problems, missing was the sense of paternalism that made workers believe that employers cared for their welfare. It is hard to determine just what started the shifts, probably it was the result of many things. Perhaps it was the deepening of the Depression. Possibly it was a repercussion from the tannery workers' strike of 1933. Whatever the cause or causes, each side began to blame the other for the industry's decline.

In 1938 the NAGM began studying the various operations in glove manufacturing in order to establish a minimum wage basis for the industry. Special certificates were supposed to be issued to apprentices and learners of sewing, but these certificates were held up by delays in implementation of the Wage and Hour Law.

In October 1939 a $.30 minimum wage was to take effect, but the Apparel Industry Committee in Washington, which included glove manufacturing, recommended a $.35-an-hour minimum. This the glove manufacturers opposed, but concluded that if it were to be adopted, it should take effect at the beginning of a season, not after orders had been received. The federal Fair Labor Standards Act had established the minimum at $.25 an hour for a 44-hour week in 1938, raising it to $.30 an hour for a 42-hour week in 1939.

Because wages were really computed on piecework rates there was general confusion about what the minimums meant. Mrs. Elizabeth Bunn, president of the operators branch of the union, testified that a $.40 hourly minimum would have little effect on the county, yet a report done in conjunction with the study of homework stated that a fifth of all factory workers received less than $.30 an hour. The NAGM's director Casey pointed out the inconsistencies in Mrs. Bunn's statements.

The government tried to halt the handsewing of gloves in Puerto Rico because the workers there did not receive the basic minimum hourly rate. The Daniel Hays Company had been contracting such work and the government brought an injunction against the company.[92] Attempts to increase handsewing in Fulton County increased costs so greatly that English handsewn gloves became competitive.

Manufacturers claimed that tariff concessions by the United States were the reason they had to ask for a 17 to 20 percent reduction in the wage scale in 1938. The workers actually granted a ten percent reduction that went into effect in the spring of 1938.[93] In answer to union charges that glovemen were not doing enough to stimulate sales, manufacturers tried to show how effective their 1938 sales campaign had been. For a short two months things looked better,[94] but, as a writer to the local paper stated, there was no reason to expect glove sales to pick up when so much of the country was unemployed.[95]

New union leaders emerged. Calls went out to strengthen the unions, and the unions began to dispute among themselves. The layers-off called meetings to organize all the day-hands in the industry.

Frank McMaster, chairman of the Joint Council of Fulton County Glove Workers; Gordon Blake of the Table Cutters Union; and Joseph A. Nelkin of the Layers-off Union issued broadside after broadside to the paper, attacking the manufacturers and stating that they had not done enough to increase business. Nelkin and McMaster led the fight against the wage reduction.[96]

Mrs. Bunn joined the fray and claimed that the manufacturers had tried to mislead the public in blaming the union for the manufacturers' inability to bring more work to the county.[97] Union attorney Harry Pozefsky claimed that manufacturers were sending gloves to makers outside the county. The layers-off led the fight against the reduction and voted to strike in August.

They categorically rejected the manufacturers' offer to submit their grievance to a board of arbitration. Listed among the union's demands were conditions describing an arbitration process, which the union now desired, and provisions for a union shop.

The level of rhetoric rose with the heat of summer and as fall approached machine operators at Imperial and Crocetta glove companies briefly joined the striking layers-off. With the repeal of the ten percent reduction in mid-September, the layers-off strike was over, but not before a spate of inflamatory paid notices had been placed in the local papers. The restoration included the sewers as well but the cutters had to wait until their contract was negotiated in 1939.

Under Mrs. Bunn, the operators union was becoming a force to be reckoned with. She prepared a complaint to the National Labor Relations Board claiming that the glove manufacturers were not bargaining fairly with block cutters on the wage schedule.[98] She urged members to rally against companies diverting work to Puerto Rico and to towns outside Fulton County.

Nelkin's proposal to unite all glove workers in the county in a joint union appears to be an attempt to increase his personal influence and power. Hints of struggles between union leaders emerge from reading between the lines of the newspaper articles but there is no hard evidence. Frank McMaster resigned as head of the joint council after the unions failed to unite.

Because there was little reason to hope that the Depression would soon end, the relationship between the unions and the manufacturers deteriorated rapidly. Both groups had claimed authorship of the proposal for table cutters to stamp their own work as a hallmark of quality, but the manufacturers retained the right to affix the stamp. Nelkin charged this was a power grab by the manufacturers, and the issue became tied to the manufacturers' distribution of work to the different kinds of cutters—at the expense of the table cutters. Nelkin claimed the stamp had become "a toy of the manufacturers rather than a protection of quality and workmanship."[99] The issue was quickly settled, but it is typical of the petty problems that were blown out of proportion by both sides.

In the spring of 1938, Clarence Carr urged the members of the Independent Leather Workers Union of Fulton County to affiliate with the Congress of Industrial Organizations (CIO). That organization held its first convention in 1938, but it had its origins in John L. Lewis' Mine Workers Union in 1935. Lewis believed that the American Federation of Labor was incapable of organizing the vast majority of American workers. He challenged the AFL leadership and eventually withdrew the United Mine Workers from the AFL, taking with it several other unions to form the CIO. In recruiting both skilled and unskilled workers and the mass-production workers of modern industry, the CIO focused on workers' social welfare. To expand the ranks, it welcomed anti-capitalist radicals, Socialists, and even Communists in its organizing campaigns. Within two years it attracted four million members.[100]

Benjamin Gold spearheaded the attempts to organize leather workers into the International Fur and Leather Workers Union of the CIO, in which Gold served as president. That union had been formed from two unions (Fur and Leather) in 1938, both of which were militant organizations. Labor historian and chronicler of the Fur and Leather Workers Union Philip S. Foner describes that union's struggles to counter the corrupt practices of the

AFL, which, according to Foner, had "betrayed [leather workers] again and again."[101]

Preferring their independence, Fulton County's leather workers under Carr rejected proposals to join the IFLWU in 1938 and again in 1939. One union worker said that Carr ably represented the interests of the workers of Fulton County. Even though Carr was a Communist, union members felt that they could control the policies of the union as long as it remained independent. They hesitated, however, "to join forces with a larger organization whose policies they would be unable to formulate."[102]

During 1938 Carr's Leather Workers Union tried to organize the Surpass Leather Co., which retaliated by firing two union workers. The union called a strike and set up picket lines; confrontations between workers and the police and deputy sheriffs ensued. It was 1933 all over again, only this time the NLRB authorized a "consent" election so Surpass's workers could vote on having Carr's union represent them, and the workers returned pending the election. According to Carr, "Surpass launched a vicious anti-union campaign. . . . Workers known to be sympathetic to the union were sent home. . . . Pro-union workers were taken off their regular jobs and given lower-paying ones. . . . Under those conditions, the Union lost the election."[103] Carr's union filed unfair labor practices complaints against Surpass, and the NLRB ruled in favor of the group, ordering the company to recognize the union. "This was the first time that the Labor Board had ever ordered a company to recognize a union that had been defeated in an election."[104] Surpass, which had another plant in Philadelphia, announced that it was closing its Gloversville tannery—something the union later learned the company had planned all along. Lydon Maider, representing Surpass, filed an exception to the NLRB ruling.[105] (Two years later, the NLRB settled the dispute by declaring the company was not guilty of unfair labor practices when it did not bargain with the union, but that the worker whose discharge precipitated the strike had to be reinstated.)

In 1939, after several months of negotiations, the tanners reached an agreement under which the union was recognized as sole bargaining agent. Tanneries would be "preferential" shops, i.e. preference would be given to union men. Choremen (laborers) would receive wage increases. And all disputes would be negotiated. This agreement was to hold until January 1, 1941.

Partly because of the labor turmoil that gripped Gloversville and partly because of the closing of Surpass Leather Co., mayor Chauncey C. Thayer appointed a fact-finding committee whose report, after five months of study, was issued in March of 1939. The unions protested the organization of the mayor's committee and its exclusion of union leaders. The committee interviewed workers and manufacturers and concluded in their report that the "great mass of workers in the community favor unions." It found that most strikes and walkouts could have been avoided and that with few exceptions they were for "organization purposes solely and mainly."[106] It also found that there had been "wholesale abuse of the right to strike and walk-out and that walk-out and stoppage of work and strike have been used as a weapon by the union leaders first to strengthen their role on organizing purposes and, secondarily, to threaten and intimidate the manufacturer, resulting in chaos." Further, strikes had a detrimental effect upon business, businessmen, the rank and file of the workers, and the community. The report called for an elaborately defined board of conciliation, which could not arbitrate but, with management and labor cooperating, would mediate disputes. The committee also recommended that the city enact laws to regulate peaceful picketing. Given the weight of the findings, the recommendations were relatively mild. Nonetheless they were immediately opposed by union leaders, who claimed the committee must have had a "sinister purpose." The committee interviewed 40 workers, but no leaders of the unions representing the county's 7,000 workers.

While these disputes were going on, an industry subcommittee in Washington was trying to establish a minimum wage for glove work. Jim Casey, representing the association, protested that $.40-an-hour minimum wage was too high but the unions supported that level. Data collected by the union to support that minimum showed that 98 percent of table cutters earned $.40 or more, 97 percent of layers-off earned that much. Among the sewers earning more than the minimum were 96 percent of the silkers, 96 percent of the pique operators, 78 percent of the outseam operators, 57 percent of the pique fitters, 60 percent of the gauge makers, and 83 percent of the over-seam makers.[107] The union claimed the minimum wage would affect between 10 and 12 percent of all workers.

The minimum wage established in May 1940, after much dispute, was set at $.35 an hour for the dress-glove industry, $.32½ for the work-glove industry. Pay for piecework was to be adjusted so that such workers could earn the minimum. The newspaper quoted Mrs. Bunn as saying that as many as a thousand workers in the county would receive pay raises, but that fabric glove workers would benefit the most.[108] In May a committee of the leather industry recommended to the Wage and Hour Administration that tannery workers receive $.40 an hour.

Across the country unions grew ever stronger in 1939 and early 1940 as the country began rearming in the face of Hitler's expansion in Europe. Union leaders saw this as a time to improve the condition of workers who had fared so poorly in the Depression. Labor unrest gripped the country and filtered into the county. Through 1940 and into 1941, "it became the duty of militant laborites—and Communists prided themselves on their record of militancy—to defend workers' rights regardless of the cost to the defense effort."[109] Nationally, in the two-year interval that preceded Nazi Germany's 1941 invasion of Soviet Russia, there were many strikes in defense industries, a number of them fomented by Communists.[110]

The Independent Leather Workers Union of Fulton County finally, in August of 1940, voted to join the International Fur and Leather Workers Union of the CIO as Local 202.[111] Whether from dissatisfaction with the new union or company efforts, a group tried to organize a new union at G. Levor. Carr claimed it was to be a company union, and Local 202 passed a resolution calling for all organized labor "to combat the anti-union forces" working in the county.[112] The CIO sponsored a mass meeting and the NLRB was called in to conduct the election. Newspaper accounts of the election and the vote count read like a mystery thriller, with suspense, confrontation, and tension. The independent Adirondack Leather Workers Union won, 136 to 79. The new union signed a two-year contract with Levor in June of 1941, making that company's tannery workers the highest paid in any shoe-leather industry in the country, giving them a rate higher than that paid to any beam shop worker in Fulton County's glove leather tanneries.[113] Overtime, seniority, and arbitration were all part of the agreement. The independent's victory did not stop another county union from joining a national organization. In the spring of 1941, the Layers-off followed the example of the tanners' union and became Local 292 of the Amalgamated Clothing Workers, CIO.

The Glove Workers' Union had won a "sweeping victory" in January of 1940 when the federal court in New York City held that 25 manufacturers, representing 90 percent of the industry, had agreed to pay back wages and overtime due their employees under the Fair Labor Standards Act of 1938. Defendents among the county firm's were Acme, Aris, Bacmo-Postman, Balzano, Crocetta, Imperial, Louis Meyers & Son, J. M. Rubin, S. Schrecker, Van Vleet, and J. Bachner. The Operators Union took credit for bringing the case, which involved mostly homeworkers and workers in Puerto Rico, to the courts.[114] Casey was quick to point out that the county's manufacturers had not been proven guilty nor had they admitted guilt.

Throughout this, despite union efforts to raise wages of workers in Puerto Rico, pay there remained low. As late as 1944, sewers in Puerto Rico doing handwork on gloves received $.18 an hour, while cutters earned $.24 an hour. The wage differential encouraged Fulton County manufacturers to send work to the island in increasing amounts.[115]

Union leaders representing Table and Miscellaneous Cutters, with 1,000 and 400 members respectively, agreed to merge in early 1940, but the members of the latter union soundly defeated the proposal. Disputes between the unions flared in negotiations with manufacturers in the next few months.

As a result of negotiations within the glove industry in 1940, the joint council agreed to the formation of a joint conciliation board (two union members, two manufacturers, and an impartial chairman), a sort of clearinghouse to investigate any violations to the schedule. The board hired an independent investigator, John Yanno.[116] The cutters at the Henry G. Lesser Glove Co. struck in the summer of 1940 because their schedule was less than the one agreed to by the association. Lesser, who was not an association member, had to conform.

An alleged violation of a part of the settlement agreement precipitated a strike at Superb Glove Co. in September 1940. The event is recalled to this day[117] as an example of union excesses; the union sees it differently. The union had won the right for authorized members to enter the shop to adjust complaints. Owner Jules Higier denied access except at specified times. When a union leader arrived to check on a report that one worker was not paying union dues, the official was denied entrance, so the union struck. The union claimed the three-day strike was the result of Higier's failure to live up to the settlement and that the strikers should be reimbursed for the wages workers lost while striking. This was considered "a test case to determine whether an employer should be made to pay damages for the loss of time suffered by striking employees."[118] The arbitration board set up by the state (one representative of the union, one from the company, and a member of the state board of mediation) decided that the company did violate the labor agreement, but that no damages should be assessed. "The arbitrators venture to suggest that the convenience of the employers might well be considered by the Joint Council." The union had to pay the strikers' lost wages, estimated at $4,000. Higier summed up the event: "Because of the failure of one employee to pay monthly union dues of $.50, it is a shame to call out the entire working force with a weekly payroll loss of approximately $10,000."[119]

A Look Back

WHAT'S THE MATTER WITH OUR GLOVE BUSINESS?

(This is the first of a series of 12 articles presenting the findings of a survey of conditions in Fulton county's glove and leather industry.)

THEN and NOW

Headline in a series in *The Morning Herald*, 1940.

The decade of the thirties ended with the industry in as great a state of confusion as it had been at the end of each of the previous two decades. The community and visiting buyers were both aware that something was radically wrong. Even as the Depression was ending, the glove business continued to shrink. The smaller, more conservative manufacturers were just muddling along with little change to their habits. A few big firms had closed, particularly Littauer Glove Co., Richard Evans & Sons, and Jacob Adler & Co. In a letter to the local paper in March of 1940, one leather buyer wrote that concern for the loss of tanneries locally was only part of the problem. "To see such a feeling of helplessness in [this] city was the greatest shock."[120]

By 1940, improvement in the economic picture appeared to be so fragile that one local paper—*The Morning Herald*—ran a series of articles entitled "WHAT IS THE MATTER WITH OUR GLOVE BUSINESS?" The series started with a look back, noting that in 1932 more than 90 percent of the families in Johnstown, with a population of under 10,800, owned their own homes or were paying for them with low mortgages. At that time there were 3,100 telephones in the community and 3,500 pleasure automobiles, more than one for each family. "Why," a disgruntled resident asked, "did we come through one Depression so well only to get into this," referring to the sad state of the glove business.

Worker discontent was as great a concern to the community as declining business. Wage negotiations that started in 1940 collapsed into a nine-week "war of nerves," in which there were no settlements between manufacturers and the various unions, led by the county's United Labor Union. The lack of progress toward settlement sparked both the letter and the articles. (Quotes in the following pages are from those articles.)

When asked where did the industry's troubles lie, Casey, recently appointed secretary of the association, replied, "union leadership. . . . They

WHAT'S THE MATTER WITH OUR GLOVE BUSINESS?

(This is the fourth of a series of 12 articles presenting the findings of a survey of conditions in Fulton county's glove and leather industry)

Praise for Unions

won't listen to reason. . . . They want a closed shop, what practically amounts to a check-off. They want domination over everybody that works in our shops. If they haven't got their union dues paid up—O.K. they can't work. They want to drive out homework." The leather buyer quoted above thought that unionleaders ought to be more responsive to "the limits of worker's earning power," and he suggested a comparison with four years previous to show how worker's lives and earnings had improved.

Women in the best homes did homework because they wanted to, Casey said. "There's one woman [union] leader[121] who is death against homework. But she raised her three children with the help of homework. Now they are grown up, she has a private, weekly income from an award growing out of the death of her husband, and a nice union job and is working besides—and she wants to abolish homework. That's fine for her, but what about other women who have children to bring up?" A manufacturer claimed that "the unions want us to abolish homework but they don't want much said about it outside. They don't dare start an open campaign for the end of homework. They know the people . . . would rise up against them. I'd like to see homework put to a vote in Fulton County."

Casey claimed that union demands for increases in the schedule for hand-sewn gloves would drive that business from the county. Western firms were doing handwork at well below the county's rate, and workers in Puerto Rico were about to become exempt from minimum wage laws. Without union concessions, manufacturers predicted "business will go, no question about it."

A few union cutters expressed disagreement with union policies. They were unhappy about wages paid union negotiators and the lack of accountability for union funds. Union leaders "know all about unions," one said. "If we open our mouths they look at us as if we were ignoramuses."

One manufacturer thought unions were a good thing because they did protect the workers, and he cited an example of a foreman who took money from workers by selling them things they did not want or accepting gifts. The manufacturer also thought that owners could and should get along with the unions. He cited an instance in which one manufacturer had cheated workers and claimed that in keeping such "chiselers" in line, the union actually helped the "decent" manufacturers. He feared "the competition of the newly arrived cheaters as much as the unions."

One article in the series gave an example to show that the unions did not always practice democratic ways. When Gloversville's mayor had called a fact-finding committee to discover what was wrong with local business, five women from the Operators Branch of the Fulton County Glove Workers testified about harmful working conditions in their factories. They were "disciplined" by union leaders, who threatened to take their union cards away and did fine the women.

Average pay rates for union leather workers were from 20 to 30 percent higher than comparable wages in the rest of the country. That was a factor in keeping costs high for county glove manufacturers. One article in the series was devoted to the way cheaper, mass-produced fabric gloves were cutting into the sales of leather gloves.

A leather manufacturer complained that the strike of 1933 had spoiled the "spirit of fellowship" between owners and workers. "Once the employer had an intimate interest in the welfare of his men." When workers faced problems, those "who were so hot for the union are finding out the union isn't there to help them." The tannery owners noted that realistically their biggest problems stemmed from the loss of markets in Europe, especially

WHAT'S THE MATTER WITH OUR GLOVE BUSINESS?

(This is the fifth of a series of 12 articles presenting the findings of a survey of conditions in Fulton county's glove and leather industry.)

Domination or Democracy

Czechoslovakia. Canada was also taking much business away from the county. Another manufacturer faulted the unions for not organizing his competitors in other states.

The attorney for the Operators Union, Harry Pozefsky, talked about the problems of unbridled competition among manufacturers. "What kind of competition?" he said. Manufacturers "couldn't hope to meet the kind that had scattered homeworkers all over New York and Vermont, making gloves on a shoestring, selling them for what they would bring." He hoped the union could help end "the competition no one could hope to meet without grinding the worker down to serfdom."

Jim Casey believed that labor in general had been fair, but that some union leaders had shown disrespect for the industry by demanding unreasonable pay schedules. He noted that piecework rates had increased but annual earnings of the county's workers had seriously decreased because the county had lost so much business in the past 20 years, and especially in the past four years. While he assigned much of the industry's problems to the loss of full-time work, it does not appear that he had a real solution. He believed the unions were in a better position to address this, but instead of saying how they might do it, he attacked the "man-eaters" in the unions. Organized labor had to clean its own house, and if not he saw only one other solution: "an association of employers strong enough to meet the unions on an equal footing and intelligent enough to deal fairly with fair dealing unions." Casey believed that a proper balance of power between employers and employees was essential.

Not all the tempests over the report of the mayor's fact-finding committee were created by the unions. The head of the local Kiwanis Club attacked the series as "news at any price" without respect to whose feelings might be hurt and the good they might accomplish.[122] An editorial in the paper defended the articles, claiming "there is one thing the union leaders can't stand—criticism. . . . They are sacred cows. . . . always right . . . above and beyond blame of any kind."[123]

No one in the industry seems to have realized the depths of the industry's problems. Glove-making, which had begun to flee the county in 1890, was moving away at an alarming rate, impelled by a tidal wave of high costs, high wages, labor unrest, low profits, poor management, and changing styles and times. Even today, with the benefit of hindsight, there seems to be no obvious way the county could have stemmed the flight of this industry. The second World War would temporarily stop that flight and bring a very transient sense of hope as the country recovered, but in many ways local glove-making was already becoming a thing of the past.

The county was confronted with insurmountable problems: increasing wages nationally; a work force no longer willing to work for wages that could support the industry; the loss of a new immigrant population with workers willing to accept lower wages as a means of climbing up the economic ladder. In addition to problems of workers and wages, there were problems within management. Men who had spent endless hours sorting leather, cutting some of the skins, and worrying about people to sew were ill-equipped to face the unions and bureaucracy. There were still those who risked much to start new glove ventures, but there was a difference between the entrepreneurs of the late thirties and earlier decades. All glovemen of the late thirties needed much better business skills.

Homework

Although she gains her livelihood by work with her own hands, the glove homeworker's labors are creatively varied. Besides finding time to be an efficient housekeeper and a devoted homemaker, she spends the greater part of the day expertly fashioning fine gloves. After successfully packing her children and husband off to school and work, removing all traces of the hurried breakfast, and tidying her few simple rooms, the lady and her machine become one for the rest of the working day. However, she finds a few minutes now and then for a lettuce sandwich and a glass of milk, a twenty-wink nap, or the forcible eviction of crabgrass from her chrysanthemum garden. While she is busy closing pieces of leather into semblances of gloves, hemming them with tiny strips from huge balls of binding, or carefully trimming away the small bits of excess leather, dozens of pairs are piled around her, waiting for her especial skilled touch to make them fit for the windows of Saks Fifth Avenue or Powers and Dawley. Fine Arabian mochas and soft powdery doeskin, coarse, brittle pig and tough, heavy horsehide all receive the same patient stitch from her experienced fingers. Her work is not boresome, but always changing. Gloves in eggshell and black, in deerskin and in suede pass under her needle each day. She sews by her sunniest window and trims in the shadiest corner of her garden. She is the creator of handcovering for the finer ladies of New York and for cavalry officers in Virginia, for the students of Father Oberlin's school and those at Miss Jones Pre-kindergarten playroom. She who keeps others well-dressed and warm is not a laborer, but an artisan who loves and lives with her work.[124]

Lester Pross, 1941

Lester Pross wrote this tribute to his mother for a freshman English class at Oberlin College. As the essay indicates, homework was a respected profession. In his mother's case, it was also a necessity—her husband spent many years in a veteran's hospital as a result of injuries suffered in World War I.[125]

One more discordant theme joined the litany of strikes and unrest that rose to a crescendo of anger and distrust toward the end of the thirties—the issue of homework. Questions about the propriety of this vital component of the county's industry had been raised in discussions leading up to the wage and hour provisions of the NRA. There were some provisions regulating homework in the Glove Code adopted under NRA. The homework law of New York State was amended in 1935 to permit inspection of homes at any time. This, in addition to provisions that extended the law to all homeworkers in the state, gave the commissioner of labor power to determine which industries in the state could have homeworkers, and issued permits to employers who could dispense homework, to homeworkers themselves, and to the owners of properties where homework could be done. Residents could only work in their homes, no children could be so employed, and employers had to keep records detailing homework. With the provisions for inspection, unclean homes could be ordered clean and would be reported to the Board of Health.[126] In 1938 the federal government passed the Fair Labor Standards Act which required employers to keep additional records covering homeworkers.

Just how much the unions were able to achieve in the struggle to control homework is an open question. As early as June of 1938, the Operators Branch under Mrs. Bunn tried to make plans to unionize homeworkers, "in order to protect the homeworker."[127] The right of a sewer to work at home did not receive serious government challenges until November 1938, when the Division of Women in Industry and Mimimum Wage of the New York State Department of Labor began investigating county glove shops. Minimum wage and homework laws had already been applied to laundries, beauty shops, and the men's and boy's clothing industry, and were being considered for the artificial flower industry.[128]

STATE OF NEW YORK
Department of Labor
Bureau of Homework Inspection
80 CENTRE STREET, NEW YORK CITY

CERTIFICATE

TO DO INDUSTRIAL HOMEWORK

This CERTIFICATE is granted under the provisions of Article 13 of the Labor Laws of 1935. It is issued subject to revocation upon the exercising of the Commissioner's power under Section 351.1 to prohibit homework in any industry after proper study and consideration.

to Mrs. Viola Handy — Mayfield, N.Y.
Name of homeworker — Address — Fl. — Apt.

and to ....
Names of other members of family, 17 years of age or over, to help with industrial homework

These premises are dwelling.
Specify whether tenement or dwelling

leather gloves and mittens — Sewing.
Article manufactured — Process

Jerome & Co. — Mayfield, N.Y.
Name of employer — Address

NO PERSON OTHER THAN THE ABOVE NAMED MAY DO INDUSTRIAL HOMEWORK

Form 2—ORIGINAL
8-2-35-5000 (6-1024)
Inspector Clerk, E.F.Horgan. Date 9-28-35 (M)

At the same time, the Administrator of the Fair Labor Standards law scheduled hearings in Washington to address a complaint by Mrs. Bunn that manufacturers had compelled workers to sign untrue wage reports indicating they had received the $.25 hourly wage. Her letter of complaint contained the observation that even manufacturers were anxious to regulate homework because they considered it "one of the greatest forces of unfair competition."[129]

James Casey testified for the manufacturers, stating there were 2,000 homeworkers in the county; that because of the seasonal nature of glovemaking, not all sewers could be accommodated in the factories during peak production periods; that the elimination of homework would result in serious unemployment in the county. Harry Pozefsky, lawyer for the Machine Operators Union, estimated that there were 5,000 homeworkers in the county and that county manufacturers were recruiting homeworkers outside the county, perhaps 1,500 new workers within a radius of 75 miles. He concluded that the only way to regulate homework was to eliminate it altogether.[130]

Casey and Mrs. Bunn sparred over the number of homeworkers who had applied to be able to work at less than the minimum wage. The hearings quickly concluded as Casey wanted them to, resulting only in added requirements on manufacturers' record keeping. There were to be no restrictions on the rights of manufacturers or homeworkers. Each worker was to have a handbook in which the employer and employee were to record piece rates paid, wages earned, hours worked, overtime, and Social Security deductions.

In the spring of 1939, Congressman Lord read a letter into the *Congressional Record* from a homeworker and farmer's wife, protesting application of the minimum wage to those who earned under $200 a year. Mrs. Bunn attacked the writer as an exploiter who helped distribute homework. Frank McMaster of the Joint Council urged union control over homework and insisted that there be no "runaway factories" sending homework outside the county.

In order to understand what was happening to the industry, it is necessary to profile both the factory workers in Mrs. Bunn's union and the homeworkers she was trying to protect. By 1940, the majority of homeworkers were born in America; already a second generation was maturing—the typical homeworker was an older worker. Half of a sample of 535 county homeworkers were at least 48 years old, and only 12 percent were under 30.[131] Half of all leather-glove homeworkers had been in the industry for at least 24 years, 35 percent for more than 30 years.[132] Factory workers were slightly younger, but 30 percent were over 50.[133]

For every ten factory workers there were nine homeworkers sewing gloves.[134] Homeworkers were not earning the minimum wage due to many factors, including the commission fee of work-contractors. Factory workers received 10 percent more than homeworkers for similar piecework. While the median earnings of factory workers were $14.02 per week in 1938, for homeworkers the median was only $6.31 that year although it rose to $7.01 in 1939.[135] Seasonality differed slightly between the two groups: 21 percent of factory workers were employed less than 30 weeks during the year, and only 22 percent had employment during 50 weeks or more.[136] For homeworkers in 1937-38 the median number of weeks worked was 28, but that number jumped to 44 in 1939-40, making home employment almost consistent with factory work.[137]

The report's most striking comparison, however, revealed that in 1941 an average week's earnings for a glove-factory worker had slipped below that of women in many other manufacturing areas such as the garment and shoe industries. Glove makers were also less well paid than candy makers, who were generally lower-skilled women. Further, the glove industry's seasonality meant that glove workers' yearly wages were significantly below wages in most other industries.[138]

The average annual earnings of all glove workers decreased 33 percent between 1929 and 1939, while the average decline for the country was 26 percent. In 1929, New York State's glove workers had higher annual earnings than workers in any other state. The fact that this was reversed in 1939 led the report to conclude that homework was a root cause.

The massive report broke down wages among different pieceworkers, average lengths of time worked, and variations with respect to locality in the leather, fabric, knit, and fur glove industries. It attempted to show that hourly rates among homeworkers were well below minimum wages and that both workers and manufacturers had conspired to show that minimums had actually been paid. It itemized expenses faced by homeworkers and savings accruing to manufacturers because they did not have to provide space and machines.

Most employers distributed homework directly to the homeworker, and although some was distributed through contractors, it has been difficult to discover just how much of a problem this created. One indication of the problem comes from a case involving a contractor in Oneonta who had not

School days are here again!

And with them opens a big market for children's gloves, worthy of special promotion during the fall months of volume purchasing.

DANFORTH GLOVES

contributed to the State Unemployment Insurance Fund. After a prolonged investigation, it was determined that the glove manufacturers (Daniel Hays and Fownes) were not responsible, that the contractor was.

A camouflage to abolish homework.

Union leader Mrs. Bunn continued to increase pressure against homework. Miss Kate Papert, acting director of the Women's Division of the New York State Department of Labor, was in charge of investigating the homework question. Just as Miss Papert was starting inquiries in the county, the association called a mass meeting of manufacturers to fight imposition of restrictions that Casey claimed were a "camouflage to abolish homework."[139] The proposed restrictions would limit homework to those who could prove to a division doctor that they could not adjust to factory work, who were physically or mentally disabled, or who were caring at home for an invalid. Further, a homeworker could only work for one employer. When Casey claimed the division was about to abolish homework, Miss Papert said that was not so, and hinted that older women might be allowed to continue working at home.

The county's response to threats against homework were varied. Every day a new article appeared in local papers with charges and countercharges. The County Board of Supervisors adopted a resolution against abolishing homework, one more example of local government siding with manufacturers rather than unions. A civic committee that included the Chamber of Commerce and union leaders sought data on the effect the proposed restrictions would have on the county. Miss Papert's letters included the clause "because of age" as well as physical or mental handicap. The manufacturers requested that imposition of any order of restrictions be delayed at least a year, but the union wanted no delay beyond that necessitated by a public hearing. Miss Frieda Miller, commissioner of the NYS Department of Labor, said decisions would await the publication of the department's survey of conditions in the county.

A barrage of letters to the editor joined the daily news articles. One writer claimed that "The main aim behind it all has been to put every operator under union control . . . [with] greater union membership and consequent dues for the right to work in the county."[140] The same writer queried manufacturers about their plans. The manufacturers replied that they were holding on in hopes of better times. They felt they were doing a civic duty in continuing to provide work. The writer concluded with the question, "Should a manufacturer be compelled to provide further manufacturing space and add further equipment with a business that cannot show a reasonable profit as it is?"[141]

The newspaper launched an opinion poll on proposed homework restrictions. The paper's question, "Do you want homework eliminated in the glove industry, or so restricted that it will be practically eliminated?" called for a yes or no answer. Even though its wording calls for a no answer, the actual tally—1,890 to 34—was overwhelmingly against restrictions. One homeworker, a mother of three, wrote the paper that she could not do her housework and work in a factory and enjoyed the convenience of working at home.[142]

The manufacturers did a survey using Department of Labor statistics to determine the proportion of work done inside and outside the factories, available space in factories for more workers, and preferences of workers for factory or homework. Bert Bower of Acme Glove Co., Adam Klopot of Aris

Northrup Gloves

SINCE 1869

MOCHAS will star

in the Fall Fashion Picture

Glove Co., and Maurice Postman of Bacmo-Postman all disputed the labor department's statistics on wages for factory and homeworkers.[143]

Another editorial equated Nazi bombs dropped on Great Britain with Miss Papert's assertion that "neither the factory nor homeworkers in the glove industry can make a decent living."[144] The paper took issue with the fact that the labor department's study was based on earnings reports from 1937 and 1938. In those years, a half of all leather glove homeworkers earned less than $169 a year, and half of knit glove homeworkers earned $277. A quarter earned less than $100, and only one percent received over $800. Even during the next year's improved conditions, two percent of factory workers and half of homeworkers earned less than six dollars a week. The report used statistics like these to back up the need for welfare and other public aid.

The median wage for homeworkers actually doubled between 1938 and 1940.[145] The newspaper claimed, as did Jim Casey, that in 1941 cutters were earning from $40 to $60 a week, makers from $30 to $40.

The New York State Labor Department's findings were a foregone conclusion, the result of manipulating statistics to justify the outcome. When the Labor Department's bomb was actually dropped, in May 1941, the county was given a year in which to adjust to the new restrictions on homework. Further hearings were scheduled to clarify the restrictions. The Order Prohibiting Homework in the Glove Industry was modified to create a number of exceptions that would help preserve the county's traditional homework. In addition to physical or mental disability and care for an invalid, the new restrictions included an exception that permitted women to receive the new certificates if they could not adjust to factory work because of age. Only workers who had certificates prior to April 1, 1941 could receive new certificates, and all workers had to be covered by Workmen's Compensation. A company could have no more homeworkers than it had factory workers. Glove firms had to distribute the work free of charge and could distribute no more than a specified weekly maximum amount of homework for each type of work or combinations of different types of work. The handbooks would record all this for the Department of Labor.

DEPARTMENT OF LABOR
UNITED STATES OF AMERICA

Home Worker's Pay Roll No. ....

Social Security No. 096-10-0619

HOME WORKER'S HANDBOOK

Home worker: Name Mrs Harry L Pross

Address ....
(Number) (Street)

....
(City) (State)

Employer: Name [illegible] GLOVE CO.,
[illegible]VILLE, N. Y.

Details from the labor department survey:

In New York State there were 321 glove factories employing 15,183 workers, of whom 10,621 were women. Two-thirds lived in Fulton County and nearly half of the rest in surrounding upstate counties, Montgomery, Saratoga, and Otsego. Homeworkers in New York City constituted thirteen percent of the total.

Fulton County women had 84 percent of the certificates for homework, but only 68 percent of the homeworkers, because homework was distributed so widely upstate, many of them in the Cherry Valley.[4]

The study had based the need for exceptions in part on public pressure, in part on analyses of homeworkers, and this data gives a vivid picture of those who sewed gloves at home. Not only had most been sewing for many years, but 69 percent of homeworkers had worked in a factory at one time. Most had left factory work because of marriage or to have children, and only a small percentage had felt they were too old for factory work. The majority were married (78 percent in Fulton County); only six percent had never married; and 15.6 percent were widowed, divorced, or separated.[146] Families were small, and a third of the women surveyed said caring for children was the principal reson they preferred to work at home. Some women just did not like factory work. A considerable number said their earnings were not essential, just "pin money" for extras, something to do to keep busy or pass the time, or help put a relative through college. "May of these workers indicated that if homework were abolished, they would stop working."[147]

Manufacturers were apprehensive about restrictions on homework. Not only were workers getting older, but it was very true that many did not want to work in factories. Manufacturers were finding it difficult to obtain workers as shown by the great distances over which they were sending work to be done. "The reason for the use of homeworkers most frequently given by employers interviewed in 1940 was the inability or unwillingness of homeworkers to come into the factory and the consequent necessity for sending work out to the homes in order to obtain the services of highly skilled operators."[148]

But, a shortage of factory space was also an important reason. Seasonality, the lack of machines, and an undersupply of factory workers were also given as arguments against restricting homework.

The manufacturers were not unanimous in wanting to preserve or restrict homework; some felt that controls might adversely affect workers and thus the community. When restrictions were put in place, someone—a manufacturer, perhaps—established a neighborhood "job" shop near Eighth Avenue in Gloversville where local residents could come and sew, yet be near their homes. Several different manufacturers supplied the gloves to be sewn. Women set their own work schedules; they could quit in time to meet their children after school and they were close enough to their homes to return for lunch. Possibly this ingenious means of circumventing homework restrictions was unique.[149]

A hearing was held in New York City in early June before Frieda Miller; a second hearing was held a day later in Gloversville. Fueling the controversy were several statements made in New York City: A representative of the Consumer's League said that "homeworkers were the 'parasites of industry' and worked in 'dirt and filth'." A union representative called for a boycot of gloves made by homeworkers.[150] This prompted a homeworker to communicate to the newspaper her outrage at being described as unclean. Her comments were fairly typical of the feelings of county homeworkers: "My grandmother and my mother made gloves all their life in their homes." She wrote that she raised a family of four by sewing on gloves in her home, all the while bringing her children up to be clean. She believed children would be robbed of their education if the work is taken out of the homes.

That set the stage for high drama at the Gloversville hearing, which attracted people from the chambers of commerce of nearby towns, who joined many others in opposition to the proposed bans. An editorial described it as "charged with emotion, freighted as it was with so much importance for so many of our county residents. . . . [with] feet stomping, booing, and cheering."[151] The Jewish Community Center was packed when the Johnstown city attorney made the first of nineteen statements opposing the restrictions. Eleven people testifed for the restrictions, with union leaders calling for full implementation by January, not May. Four and a half hours later with tempers "frayed" the hearings were adjourned for ten days, but not before Johnstown's health officer (the author's father) testified that he believed limits on homework would increase the number of people on welfare.[152]

The report did not address the seasonality of work or the fact that many homeworkers did not work full time. This fact was pointed out by Victor Harrison, an attorney representing a group of homeworkers. The rest of the testimony from public officials, civic leaders, union leaders, clergymen, local officials, and female home and factory workers was followed by arguments already expressed. *The Morning Herald* editorialized "it is difficult to see how State Industrial Commissioner Frieda S. Miller can fail to recognize that she was misled, either deliberately or otherwise."[153]

Factory workers were encouraged to attend the second hearing, but again the applause seemed to favor those opposed to the new restrictions. An editorial commenting on the second hearing emphasized the testimony of one homeworker, who "owned an automobile, had a good and attractive home, was active in church affairs, and was able to finance her church activity by homework. She had been doing it for years. . . . It helped her to a better home and to a more active place in the community. Far from being a disgrace or a means of exploitation, to her it was a blessing."[154]

Factory workers applauded Miss Miller; homeworkers applauded James Casey. Casey insisted that homeworkers were essential for the kind of fine gloves made in the county. Representatives of several smaller manufacturers testified to the hardships their companies would have; they employ only cutters (no makers) in the factories. Homeworkers' attorney H. Andrew Schlusberg spoke of homework as a "cottage industry" and union attorney Pozefsky jumped on "this new phrase—sounds like a prospectus of a real estate development."[155] Pozefsky challenged Schlusberg for not championing equal pay for home and factory workers. Pozefsky assailed the fact gloves could be produced more cheaply outside factories, in homes where manufacturers did not have to pay for power or equipment.[156] Only ten percent of all machines were owned by the factories and loaned to homeworkers.[157]

Glove manufacture dominates the industry of Fulton County and glove homework has become an established and time-honored occupation for the working women of the region.
NYS Department of Labor Report

Page from the NYS Homeworkers Handbook adopted in 1941. The book belonged to Mrs. Viola Handy
Courtesy Don Williams

WITH RESPECT TO EACH LOT OF WORK RETURNED

Day, month, and hour work given out ¹	Day, month, and hour work returned	Lot number or kind of work	Piece rates paid	Amount returned	Hours worked on amount returned	Wages for work returned: Gross amount earned	Legal deductions ²: Social Security tax	Legal deductions ²: Other	Net amount paid	Day and month paid
(a)	(b)	(c)	(d)	(e)	(f)	(g)	(h)	(i)	(j)	(k)
7 3 41 1 30	7 3 41 1 30	[illegible]	35	172	23	860	9		851	7 3 41
7 11 41 2 30	7 11 41 5 3[illegible]	"	35	107	12	533	5		53[illegible]	7 11 41
7 18 41 11	7 18 41 4	"	35	61	7 1/2	305	3		302	7 18 41

The headline on July 2, accompanied by a particularly grim photo of Miss Miller, announced that the "State Orders Homework Ban to Start May 1—Homework Hearings Failed to Change Terms of First Order." In clarifying her decision, she said that the order would not abolish homework, but through restrictions and rules eliminate its evils. In giving her reasons for not changing the order to permit women with young children to do homework, Miss Miller said 50 percent of homeworkers have no children at home under eighteen years of age. She observed most women could adjust to factory work and that there was much misinformation circulating in the county—the order would not abolish homework, only regulate it.

The one hundred homeworkers who had attempted to revive the Fulton County Homeworkers' Federation before the second meeting claimed they represented 500 homeworkers. It quickly drew the ire of the joint council, which protested that the federation had no standing as a union, that it was disseminating false ideas about the new homework order, and that homeworkers would be accepted by the operators union. Within a month the new federation claimed "tremendous" membership growth.

In the end, homework was regulated more stringently, but not abolished. On the one hand there is the very thorough statistical report of the Department of Labor; on the other hand it would seem that there were other motives for imposing the regulations and that the welfare of the workers was not paramount in anyone's mind. In the long run, it did not matter. This last gasp of worker reform, which had started with Roosevelt's New Deal, ultimately hurt county workers more than it helped them. Homeworkers were an aging group. Sewers in general were already in such short supply, and wages so uncompetitive that work was being sent to Puerto Rico. By 1939 some 34,435 dozen pairs of leather gloves and 36,422 pairs of fabric gloves were being sewn there, which represented less than 1.5 percent of production on the mainland, but proved an inevitable wedge in future production. Daniel Hays Co., Louis Meyers & Son, Superb Glove Corp., J. M. Rubin & Sons, and Crocetta Bros & Co. were leading the way.[158]

It is ironic that today thousands of people in New York State are working at home for the same reasons glove workers wanted to do homework: to raise a family, be a homemaker, avoid commuting, be independent. The only difference is that today the homeworker is more apt to use a personal computer and a fax machine instead of a sewing machine. And, the few remaining homeworkers in Fulton County still require a certificate from the state while the computer-bound homeworker needs no such authorization.

RICHARD EVANS & SONS, INC.
JOHNSTOWN, NEW YORK

Within months these local problems in the glove industry would be overshadowed by events in Europe. In 1938 Germany invaded Czechoslovakia and took over the leading glove producing centers there. Neither France nor Belgium were able to produce the quantity of leather gloves that had been coming from Czechoslovakia. *Gloves* estimated that American women were consuming the production of 700 foreign table cutters. If this supply were to be curtailed, the review deemed the decreases in exports sufficient to spur American business and even create a shortage. Nevertheless, glovemen were still protesting new trade agreements, especially those established with England and Canada in November 1938.[159] Casey's solution to this was to urge local glovemen to focus on fashion, color, and prompt delivery and to convince retailers that "buying American-made gloves . . . will provide good insurance in the years to come" when European gloves are no longer available.

As conditions abroad worsened, and Germany took over some of the Czechoslovakian production, the United States placed a 25 percent duty on German goods. The English market was also reducing its imports; over 700 glove workers in Yeovil were unemployed.

In 1938 shipments of gloves from France had reached a near-record level for the decade and might have gone higher had not all imports been curtailed by German advances. However, it was not until 1941 that the war totally eliminated imports from Europe. This combined with increasing government contracts at last brought a sizeable increase in the county's glove production. Prosperity, in turn, temporarily lowered the conflicts between manufacturers and workers.

The county still faced many domestic problems. In 1939 nonunionized shops in New York City produced 20 percent of fine gloves and seriously undercut local manufacturers. The government was placing more and more contracts for gloves and taking steps to prevent overbidding by manufacturers with limited production capacity. To do this, the government placed limits on the ability of small manufacturers to subcontract work they could not produce. This would spread government contracts around and give more businesses a share of the work. But almost all of the government orders in late 1940 and into 1941 went to western manufacturers—county bids were consistently too high.

Negotiations on the 1941 schedule started and ended peacefully, with the cutters "accepting" 11 to 17 percent wage increases.[160] The cutters' union claimed more than 1,500 workers (an inflated number) and another labor shortage loomed. The Board of Education started classes again for cutters in the spring with 16 students.

Approaching war did not completely calm the local labor scene. All the cutters at Crocetta's, except those working on government contracts, struck in February 1941, and all the striking men quickly found work in other shops.[161] By midsummer 1941, two other plants were having labor troubles. Cutters at Sutton's went on strike because the company refused to recognize the union. A jurisdictional dispute between the Adirondack Leather Workers and Local 202 IFLWU of the CIO precipitated the strike at Milligan & Higgins Corp. glue factory. Adirondack won the right to represent glue-factory workers by a 48 to 3 vote. In a subsequent ad touting its accomplishments, Adirondack claimed Milligan & Higgins employees had been ambushed and beaten, shots were fired, and property damaged.[162]

James Casey, looking ahead, warned those attending the association's spring 1941 meeting that "there was no permanent prosperity in a war economy."[163] Indeed wartime economy brought less prosperity to the county than might be anticipated. The editor of the *Morning Herald* understood why the county was receiving such a small amount of government contracts; 80 percent of government orders were going west. "In the first place it must be admitted that our factories are no longer equipped to produce in large quantities the most wanted Army gloves."[164] Throughout the thirties, only a few factories had been enlarged, none truly modernized. No manufacturers in the county were capable of mass-producing the well-made work glove western manufacturers could make. But, the editorial continued, the county was not even getting a fair share of government orders for finer gloves. Local costs were so much higher that manufacturers asked the government to give Fulton County "a differential concession of 15 percent on account of labor costs." The county had priced itself out of the glove business.

Expansions and moves

1940

Acme Glove Corp. took over the manufacture of "Kislav" gloves, a $1.5 million annual business, from the New York City manufacturer.

Leon F. Swears, manufacturer of seamless knit gloves, took over the four-story building formerly owned by the George H. Chapman Glove Co. The building was adjacent to Swears' existing plant.

Fabrics Associated of New York City took over the Grewen Factory and enlarged its knitting capacity.

Baggs-Texier Corp. moved into new and larger quarters.

Scotsmoor purchased a building as an annex to accommodate 60 additional workers.

D. H. P. Co. and Garfall Brothers moved into larger quarters.

1941

G. Albano & Co. of New York City opened a branch factory in Gloversville.

Daytona Glove Corp. was incorporated by a Pennsylvania couple who bought the former Tipaldi shop.

Aris Gloves, Inc. built a large two-story addition to its Gloversville factory.

A Glove Buyers' Guide to the Gloversville Market

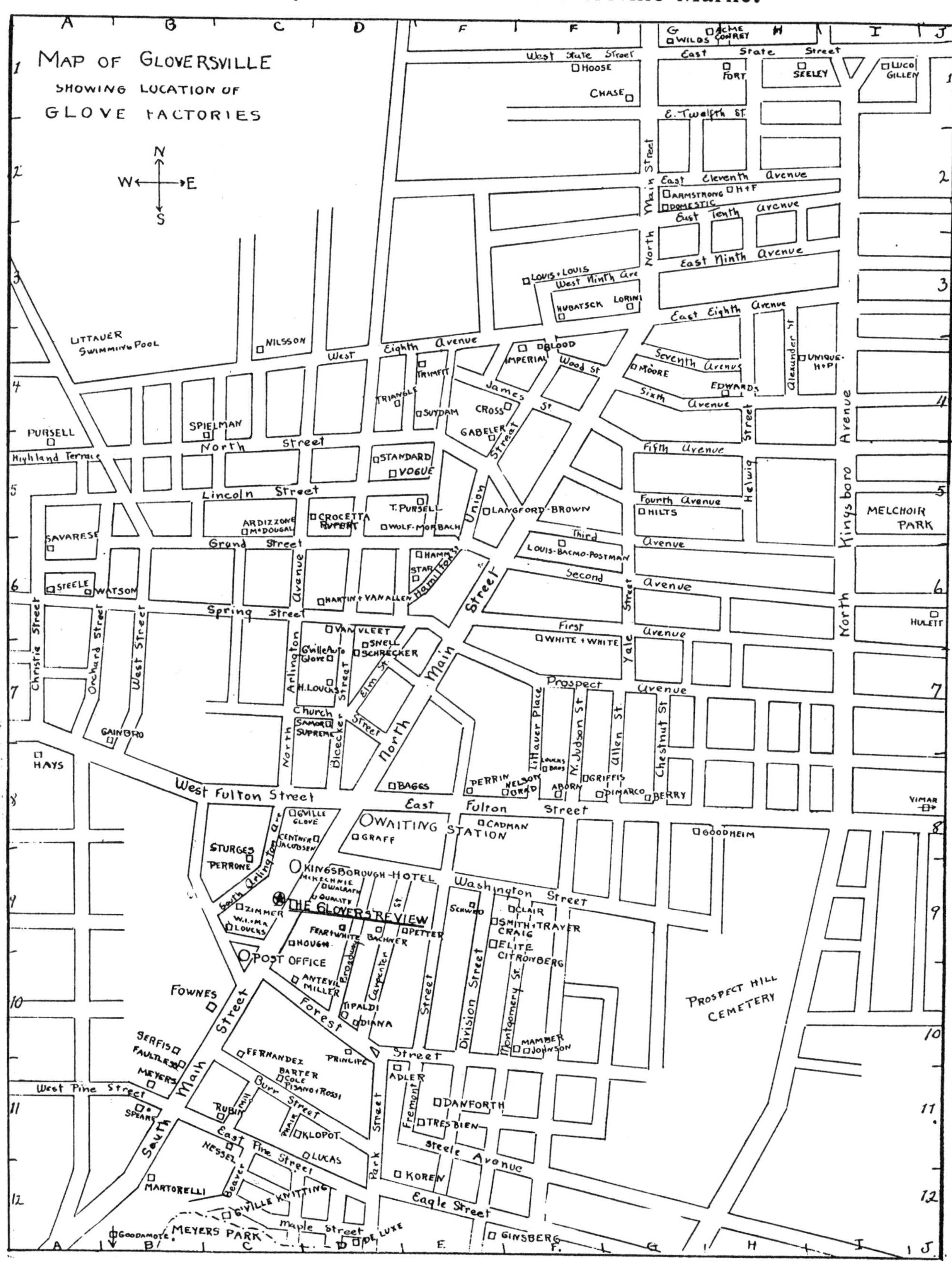

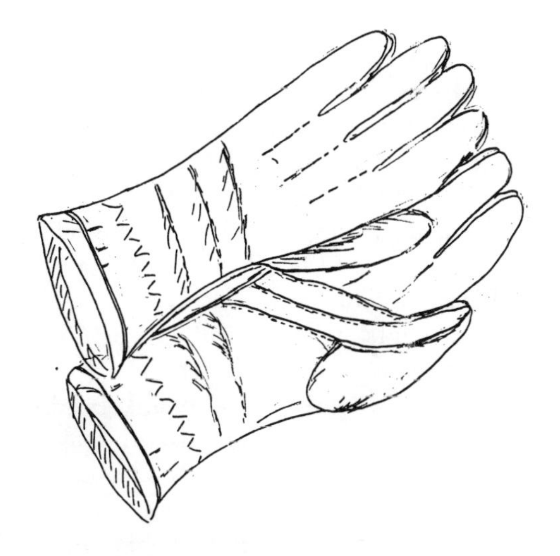

World War II and the Decade of the Forties

No one seems to worry about getting rich in this frontier atmosphere—perhaps because so few ever did. But no one in this citadel of glovedom starves.
John Lear, *Saturday Evening Post,* May 1947

The world was consumed by war in the first half of the 1940s. After a brief period of quiet in early 1941, Fulton County was consumed through the rest of the decade by a different kind of battle—among labor groups and between labor and management—whose denouement left the county as defeated as if it had been at war. Unions made many gains through the decade. A few manufacturers realized large profits. The county's glove industry experienced a very brief resurgence during the war and again around 1948, when there was a sharp increase in the number of glove shops. Despite these positive indications, by the end of the decade, the county's inexorable decline had regained momentum, becoming a downward spiral that was to drag on for nearly 50 years.

The recital of skirmishes is long and dense and ultimately a very depressing litany. It is remarkable in that between 1939 and 1955 none of the disputes involved all of the glove industry at one time. Fulton County's labor problems were not unique. Similar conflicts were occurring in almost all other industries, even those that were essential to the war effort and to the nation's postwar recovery. What was exceptional about events in Fulton County in the forties was the constant struggle between management and labor and the way wages increased to a level that ultimately contributed to the industry's decline.

On June 22, 1941, when Hitler attacked Russia, the United States stepped up its preparations for war. Communists and other pro-Soviets and left-leaning unions abandoned their efforts against preparations for war and "became ardent supporters of beefed-up military production."[1]

Just after Pearl Harbor (December 7, 1941), the AFL and CIO agreed to a no-strike pledge that called on the unions to forego strikes for the duration of hostilities.[2] This pact limited strikes for a time, but after 1942 disputes nationally became "more and more open and contentious,"[3] and strikes all across the country began to impede the war effort. The most egregious was the 1943 coal miners' strike called by John L. Lewis.

In 1943, when Congress passed the Smith-Connally bill, which would prohibit strikes, the United Labor Unions of Fulton County urged President Roosevelt to veto the bill on the grounds that it would split the labor movement from the war effort.[4] The unions castigated local Congressman Bernard Kearney for voting for this bill.

In January 1942 President Roosevelt established the National War Labor Board (NWLB) to resolve labor disputes. Throughout the war, all settlements, including those granted in response to rises in the cost of living, were subject to NWLB aproval. This served to put a lid on wage increases. The NWLB and the National Labor Relations Board (NLRB) played a role in almost every wage or strike settlement in the decade.

Nationally, one of the NWLB settlements was the "Little Steel Formula" which, in July of 1942, gave a wage increase to steelworkers that was much lower than they sought. Despite protests, the NWLB followed this settlement as a precedent and continued to mete out lower wage increases than workers desired. The NWLB actually strengthened the hand of unions by establishing a "maintenance of membership" policy, which meant that if a union had a contract with an employer, all newly hired workers would automatically become dues-paying members after their first fifteen days on the job.[5]

Despite the no-strike pledge, the number of strikes across the country in 1943 rose to over 3,700, involving nearly two million workers who were on strike for triple the number of days compared to the year before. Union activity and localized strikes in Fulton County mirrored the national scene. However, the independent nature of local unions and their nonaffiliation with national unions meant that most Fulton County workers were narrowly interested in wages, and not national labor issues. There is no evidence that increased union strength reduced the fragmentation and independence of local glove unions or involved union members in real discussions on the value of unionism. The tannery workers' union, however, was already strong and continued to engage its members in labor activity.

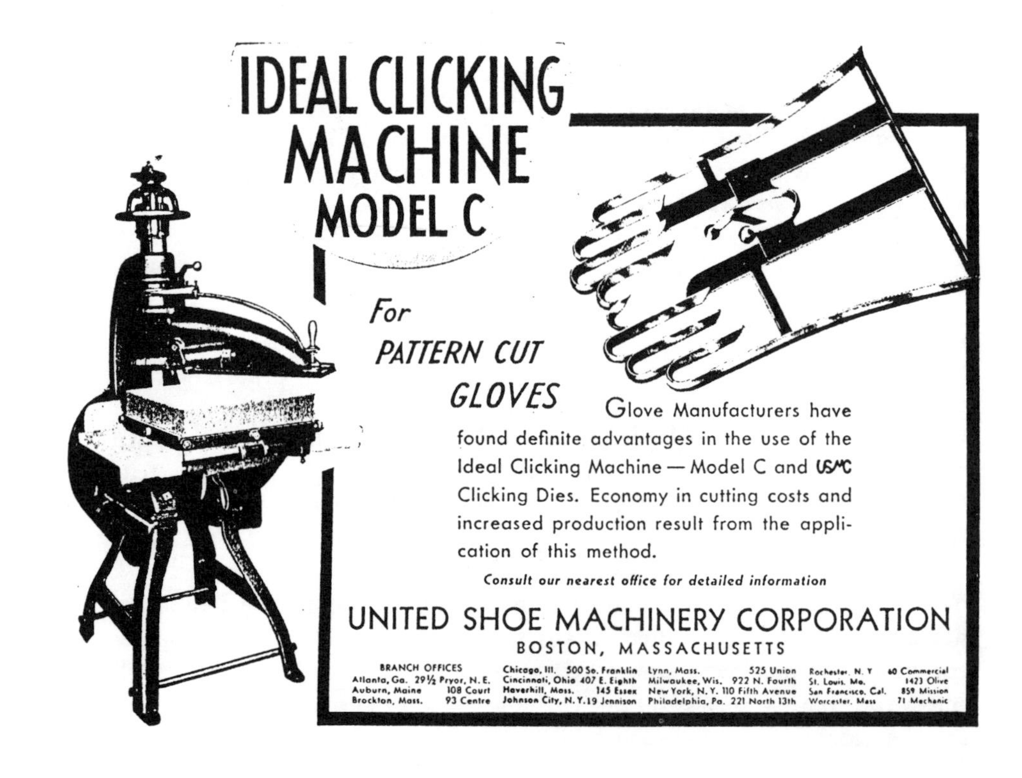

Every decade in the history of glove-making reflects the character and background of the glovemen who led the industry at the time. By the 1940s, the cross section of glovemen presented the wide spectrum of the county's people. At the end of the 1880s Frothingham was able to portray the glove industry through biographies and sketches of its principals. Obituaries and biographies of the manufacturers of the 1940s likewise help paint a picture of the great decade of Fulton County's glove industry.

Some of these leaders were well established before 1940 and relevant notes about them can be found in earlier chapters. Beside the heads of the glove association, they include W. N. Zimmer, Josiah Danforth, Harry S. Hall, William G. Loveday and the Napatan Company, Frank Patten and Liberty Dressing Co., and Samuel Starr of Speare Glove Co. Some of these firms continued into the postwar years as well.

Because many manufacturers of the forties played important roles in later years, short notes them are given in the postwar chapter. Glove manufacturers so described are Nathan M. Chase, Robert J. Evans of Lewis & Evans Glove Co., John DeGrand of Acme Glove Corp., Daniel C. Miller, Fred C. Miller, Bela Albert Loose and Herman Wille of Triangle Glove Co., Joseph Leibl, Adam Klopot, and Mario Papa. Tanners active in the forties who figure in the later chapter are L. James Risedorph of Risedorph Tannery, Corp., J. Edward Lotze of Peerless Tanning Corp., Abraham S. Fink of Reliable Tanners, Inc., and Arthur H. Cane of Cane Tanning Co., Inc.

The side-notes in this chapter include short notes on some of the lesser-known manufacturers, often those not members of the associations, as a way of demonstrating the rich diversity of the leaders of the forties. Many of the men who emerge as entrepreneurs in the glove and tanning industries in the forties were sons of immigrants from eastern Europe and the Pale. Joseph Bachner came from Warsaw and two of his sons, C. J. and A. J., were active in the forties. Abraham S. Fink's parents came from East Prussia and Lithuania in the 1880s. Bela Albert Loose was a glove cutter in Hungary. The parents of Joseph Leibl emigrated from Prague to Milwaukee. Samuel Starr, born in 1870 in Russia, arrived in Gloversville in 1906. Louis H. Albert was the son of an immigrant from Poland. Daniel Clair's father had come from Warsaw. Max Bernstein was the son of Russian immigrants.

Many of the glovemen had good educations, though not necessarily educations that would suit them for the local industry. A. J. Bachner had a law degree from Yale. In addition to Lucius Littauer, at least three other Gloversville glovemen went to Harvard.

MARTORELLI BROS.
Fine Table-Cut Gloves
GLOVERSVILLE, NEW YORK

1940s
Firms and Glovemen

Clair Glove Co. was established in 1918 by Joseph Clair who came to Gloversville in 1906 from Warsaw. He retired in 1945. His son Daniel entered the business in 1929 and became president in 1940.

Hubert J. Clifford was the son of Caleb Clifford, a cutter who emigrated from England to Gloversville in 1880. Hubert worked for Berry & Allen for 17 years, then in 1907 with his brother Arthur became associated in Clifford Brothers glove company. Arthur died in 1943 and Hubert continued the firm through the forties.

James L. Cahn was the son of Sigmund Cahn, an immigrant from Mannheim, Germany, who worked as a skin and hide merchant in New York City. James, a graduate of Harvard, established Alma Knitting Mills in 1941.

John Bonacker, son of a German immigrant, started working for Gloversville Leather Manufacturing Co. in 1915. In the mid-1940s, he became general manager of the firm.

R. W. Brauns was born in Prague in 1897, the son of a leather manufacturer who settled in Gloversville in 1905. In 1919 Brauns, with Fred W. Shire, organized Twin City Leather Co., custom dresser of glove and garment leather. He served as an officer of that company through the forties. Shire, who was born in England and learned glove cutting there, started work in Gloversville as a cutter in 1895.

Max Bernstein was the son of an immigrant from Russia who settled in Utica. Max graduated from Harvard and had a degree from New York Law School. He gave up his practice in 1917 and in 1921 became associated with Horwitz & Arbib, dealers in leather and importers of raw skins. Bernstein became president of the firm in 1927 on the death of Wolf Horwitz, and the firm, known as Horwitz and Bernstein, Inc. continued through the forties.

The County at the Beginning of World War II

The war saved us. Without the business created by war, we would have folded.
Ellery Willard, owner of Hilts-Willard[1]

As war in Europe escalated, the county's glovemen felt buoyed by prospects of increased business, but the county was ill-prepared to take advantage of those prospects. At the beginning of the decade, the county faced an unusual dichotomy: unemployment remained high, while concurrently there was a shortage of trained workers. At the start of 1942 some 2,000 Fulton County workers were drawing unemployment insurance. Even with the country gearing up for war, unemployment remained a problem all through 1942. Unemployment insurance was extended to those who found work for no more than three days a week, providing weekly wages were below $24. The Labor Department reported that Gloversville had the dubious distinction of being the only area in the state with "a surplus of manpower and a deficiency of women available for employment."[6] Though female workers were in short supply elsewhere, the problem was especially acute here. There were not enough women working as sewing-machine operators to allow for full employment of cutters. (Workers were needed at the ratio of one table cutter to three sewing-machine operators, one pattern cutter to five-sewing machine operators, or one block cutter to ten sewing-machine operators.)

The war effort quickly drew women into the labor force across the country. Nationally the ratio of women to men in the work force increased through the war years, although it was not until 1975 that it reached 50 percent. That ratio for glove workers in Fulton County had exceeded 50 percent for many years.

However, in Fulton County, where women were already the backbone of the labor force, women did not hesitate to leave their glove-sewing jobs for more glamorous and lucrative work. This exacerbated the already short work force of skilled makers and operators. The cost of living was rising and workers were leaving the glove shops for better paying jobs, even for beginners, in arms plants in Schenectady, Ilion, and Watervliet.

County glove manufacturers were desperately seeking defense contracts, but could not make bids low enough to win them. The Consolidated Cutters Union would not consider wage reductions that might make such bids successful.[7]

The local Committee on Civilian Supply proposed that glove manufacturers pool their resources, with ten leading manufacturers dealing directly with Washington and distributing work to all glove shops. As of early 1942, the government had contracted for five million pairs of gloves, but the county had received as little as six to eight percent of those contracts. Local tanners fared no better for they were not equipped to handle the horsehides favored in government contracts.

Local sentiment, expressed in a *Morning Herald* "Eye Opener" editorial, questioned the government's moving the glove procurement office to Chicago, even though that city was now deemed to be the center of the glove industry. The editorial noted that "Without a doubt there has been a strong swing in glove manufacturing to western cities. Yet it seems incredible that this swing could have been so swift or so extensive as to take from our county its leadership as a glove city."[8] What really is incredible is that the local newspaper did not recognize that the swing had been going on for so long. For the heavy glove industry—the volume industry—the shift had been complete for a long time. The Midwest had even expanded its production of leather gloves for the military. The trend away from the county had been in progress for such a long time, yet no one had perceived its consequences.

Firms and Glovemen, continued

Paul J. Baker, whose father had a leather manufacturing business in Boston, graduated from Harvard in 1910 and took a course in chemical manufacturing at Pratt Institute. He worked as a chemist in New York City until 1928, when he took a job with Gloversville Leather Manufacturing Co. He became its president in 1946. The company, founded in 1912 by Joseph W. Mendel, employed 60 to 90 workers.

Louis H. Alpert, son of a Polish immigrant, graduated from New York University in 1930, and founded Bell Glove Co., manufacturer of ladies gloves in 1938. The firm employed about 100 workers in the forties.

James T. Dowdall, son of an Irish immigrant, worked as a machine repairman under Frank Curtin until 1934 when he established the Fulton Embroidery Works, glove art embroiderers. He originated and adapted many stitch designs used by county manufacturers.

Stanley R. Ketchum started work in a glove factory in 1932 and with his brother Elwood L. began manufacturing gloves under the name Ketchum Brothers Glove Co. In the forties the firm employed about 30 people.

Frank Kiernan, grandson of Irish immigrants, began working as a stenographer for Louis Meyers & Son, Inc. in 1919. In 1939 he became general manager of that firm, all of whose officers were living in New York City in the forties. The company adopted the trade name Meyers Make for its gloves in 1944.

Twelve leaders in the glove industry agreed that better production methods were essential. Initially the union opposed manufacturing operations in which one worker specialized in a particular operation, but trials that showed that workers could increase output and earnings cleared the way for such "streamlining."[9] One manufacturer even hired an industrial engineering firm to redesign his operations, and after convincing the unions that the streamlining did not mean a "speed-up," he was able to institute new methods.

Labor leaders met with glove manufacturers to discuss ways of cutting costs. The Committee on Civilian Supply reported slow progress: some operations would have to be cut to make local manufacturers competitive, the union was balking, and manufacturers stated they would not pay for "work that is eliminated."[10]

Because of opposition only one manufacturer tried to upgrade his shop to modern designs and work methods. It is difficult to comprehend the industry's continued reluctance to change. The whole county was still operating as if glove-making was a colonial craft. Not since the old factories had been "modernized"—with bathrooms and operations reorganized so materials moved in one direction—had any manufacturer invested large sums in plant or equipment.

Machines that would do special stitches, such as the pique machines, were manufactured until the mid-forties. These Singer machines had a thin post so the operator could sew pique stitching in such small areas as fingers. In general, however, machines from the nineteenth and early twentieth centuries, many times repaired and still serviceable, remained in use. As recently as 1950, sewing machines in some shops were still driven by belts from an overhead shaft, and one current manufacturer remembers working as a "belt-boy," fixing the drive belts that wore out or broke with great regularity.[11] A local manufacturer said that when the industry moved off-shore, especially to the Philippines, these ancient machines were shipped to the new factories. In fact, until recently, most foreign manufacturers only purchased new tables and motors to run the old machines.[12] The basic class of machines used in making have not been manufactured since the end of World War II. Around 1945 "sewing machine manufacturers abandoned the glove industry," which became dependent on the skills of a few machinists to keep the old ones running.[13]

It was not so much the need for new equipment that impeded modernization, it was the difficulties in separating operations and attempting mass production through specialization. But as one manufacturer observed, "we are not General Motors." Nor would they ever be. Still, manufacturers proposed setting up a model factory in which modern methods could be tested. This proposal went nowhere because in June of 1942 the Operators Union voted to oppose the construction of such a factory on the grounds that any change would have an adverse impact on the current wage schedule.[14]

In the summer of 1942, the Office of Price Administration (OPA) put a price ceiling on gloves sold to retail outlets. Now both manufacturers and workers were being squeezed again. In addition, all the efforts to reduce prices of gloves to win government contracts were to little avail. A September 1942 government contract for two million pairs of gloves awarded only 150,000 pairs to the area (Crocetta and Elite of Gloversville, Northrup of Amsterdam). In November the county received a contract for 580,000 pairs of leather-palmed knit gloves. A panel of the National Labor Relations

Harry G. Hoose worked as a painter and decorator for 23 years before establishing a glove manufacturing business at the rear of his home in 1919. His firm continued producing gloves through the forties.

Ernest A. Hamm was the son of a Johnstown glove cutter who immigrated from England in 1873. He worked for Elmer Little & Son for thirteen years before establishing the glove firm under his name, which continued into the forties.

Frederick W. Geehr ran a liquor store in Gloversville in the 1930s and in 1940 became Secretary-Treasurer of Reliable Tanners, Inc.

Frank R. Morrell attended Union College and worked as a glove cutter until 1939, when he established the F. R. Morrell Glove Co., which employed 32 people in the forties.

F. J. Marshall was the son of a Canadian lumberman who moved to Hamilton County. He started as a bookkeeper and in 1936 established the F. J. Marshall Co., which specialized in splitting and shaving leather.

Adelard Normandin was one of the few French-Canadians to work in the county's glove industry. Born in 1879, he learned glove cutting in Canada. He moved to Gloversville in 1924 where he worked as a cutter until 1945, when with his sons he established the A. Normandin & Sons Glove Co.

Alvah H. Rogers ran a retail business in Gloversville from 1892 until 1925. In 1917 he was one of the organizers of Kingsboro Silk Mills, Inc. and became president of that company, which also had a plant in Daisy, Tennessee. In the forties, the company's annual business exceeded a million dollars.

Howard E. Schermerhorn was co-owner of Schermerhorn Perforating Co., makers of glove decorations, which he established in 1940. The company employed about 16 workers.

Lauren Sart started work as a meatcutter after World War I, and then in 1920, went to work for Geisler & Lehr, leather manufacturer. In 1936 he started a leather glove laying-off business, Sarts Laying Off Shop, which employed six people in the forties.

Bernard J. Shields, son of an Irish immigrant who worked in a tannery, began work as a bookkeeper for E. S. Parkhurst & Co. in 1902. He became vice-president of the wool and hair firm in 1938.

Samuel Siman was born in Warsaw where his father worked as a glove cutter. The family moved to Gloversville in 1912, then to New York City, where his father had a glove manufacturing business until 1940, when the son brought the family's Metropolitan Glove Co. to Gloversville.

Norman Winig was born in 1906 in Vienna, Austria where his father was a glove manufacturer. Norman was educated in Vienna and worked for a year in England and then with his father's firm until 1938. In 1940 he moved to Gloversville and established Winig Glove Co., which employed 100 people in the forties.

Robert J. Traver was the son of a glove manufacturer in Gloversville. He went to work for his father in 1932 and after the death of his father in 1945, he was sole owner of the glove firm under his name, which employed 25 people.

Frank E. Sweeney's father came from Ireland to Gloversville to work in a tannery. The son learned the tannery business, then became a commercial traveler for the J. E. Danforth Glove Co., and in 1920 established a brokerage business to buy and sell hides and skins.

William H. St. Thomas was president and treasurer of E. J. Wilkins Co. in the forties. This later became the St. Thomas Company, which closed in 1995. St. Thomas was brought up in Wisconsin and worked there as a factory manager for a shoe company before coming to Gloversville in 1936 to serve as manager of the Wilkins company, which made all sorts of leather products.

Board denied a union request for a 25 percent wage increase in October 1942 because, the panel claimed, so little war work was being done in the county and the cost of living in the county had not risen unduly.

At the end of 1943, county glove manufacturers obtained a contract worth $3 million for Army gloves, but only because nineteen local companies agreed to share the contract. In the spring of 1944, the Army met with 55 local manufacturers to discuss a joint award of "millions" for secret glove work for the Army Air Force. At first all anyone learned was that the gloves were for the extreme cold temperatures of high-altitude flight. Tanners quickly agreed to "cooperate" in turning out the cabretta leather specified for the contracts. Twenty-four firms bid on the contracts and ten firms began work on the 300,000 pairs of gloves ordered. An Army expediter was sent to oversee production. A shortage of women workers, particularly pique and triple stitchers, was so acute a patriotic appeal call for workers went out, noting that the project was already behind schedule.[15]

The government's encouragement of wartime cooperation between the glove companies was needed and it permitted the manufacturers to circumvent the cutthroat competition that had for so long curtailed the local industry. (One wonders if this precedent underlays the dark episode that occurred 45 years later, when some of the county's leading glove manufacturers were charged with collusion.)

In 1944 the War Production Board put a freeze on tanning several kinds of leather unless they were needed for government work. In Fulton County the shutdown was necessary so that the county could manufacture the special Army Air Force gloves, and this essentially stopped all civilian glove production. A year later, just as the war was ending, 50 triple-stitchers struck four shops,[16] tying up a special Navy contract. The women were unhappy with the average eight percent raise given all workers.

Still local business kept getting contracts. Even though there were few as large as those two mentioned, the county received war contracts totaling over 23 million pairs of leather gloves as of the beginning of 1945.[17] This averaged out to about five million pairs of gloves a year.

A report for the entire industry gives the United States wartime production for the Army alone at over 127 million dollars worth of gloves between July 1, 1940 and August 1, 1945, representing about 127 million pairs of gloves. The largest production was in 1943, with just short of 40 million pairs, followed by 33.5 million pairs in 1944, 26.6 million pairs in 1942.

Even though the average five million pairs of leather gloves a year produced in the East is well above the three million pairs produced in 1941, these figures indicate that the county received not much more than 20 percent of government contracts during the war. Nor was the county's production substantially greater than previous capacity, given that the 1941 levels were still depressed.

A few manufacturers did quite well, however. Even with open bidding, the contracts for developing special gloves proved particularly lucrative. Collective memory holds that the war years were great, but it is possible that just a few good contracts were enough to brighten the glove manufacturers' impressions.

Glovemen might have benefited even more from war work if an acute shortage of leather and skins had not developed. In 1943, Congressman Kearney arranged for an import ban to be lifted so that British doeskins could be imported and the county could continue making fine gloves.[18] Leather had become so scarce and valuable that in 1944 there were several incidences of thefts of skins.[19] Tanners anticipated even tighter supplies in 1945.

In 1945 hunters across the country donated 8,000 deerskins to be tanned. Carr's Local 202 collected an additional 2,500 deerskins. The union auctioned the tanned skins to glove manufacturers, but the winning bid was an out-of-county manufacturer, the Consolidated Slipper Corp. of Malone, which would make trigger gloves for the Army. Richard Parkhurst, chairman of the Gloversville Chapter of the Red Cross, suggested that the union use the proceeds from the sale to purchase a mobile blood unit for the American Red Cross.[20] Instead, the union supported the purchase of two ambulances and a canteen, but as a reflection of the union's sympathies, one of the ambulances was sent to the Russian Army through the Soviet Red Cross.[21]

Leather shortages were reflected in pressure on costs. In response to this, the OPA raised the price ceilings on leather in March of 1945 by nearly 25 percent and again by 6 percent (10 percent on imported skins) in mid-1946.

Overseas production

Surreptitiously, in the late thirties, a few county manufacturers started contracting work overseas, a move that would ultimately bring an end to local manufacturing. The Goldsmith Co. of New York City employed 3,800 workers in Puerto Rico to sew gloves by hand for two cents an hour, which meant $.80 for a 40-hour week. Gloversville's Daniel Hays Co., which also had factories in Fultonville, New York, and Rutland, Vermont, shipped materials to the Goldsmith Company, which sent them to Puerto Rico. The finished products were sent back to Hays's Gloversville plant. Goldsmith also produced gloves for Louis Meyers & Son, Superb Glove Corp., J. M. Rubin & Sons, and Crocetta Brothers, presumably in Puerto Rico. The Glove Workers Union brought charges against these companies, which resulted in the Wage and Hour Division of the U. S. Department of Labor issuing an injunction against all of them. The complaint against the Hays Company charged that "Among the competitive advantages so obtained have been the ability to undersell many of its competitors in and out of New York and the ability to divert business from competitors to the depression and demoralization of the glove manufacturing industry and to the creation and spreading of labor conditions detrimental to the maintenance of the minimum standard of living necessary for health, efficiency, and general well-being of workers in the glove industry."[22]

Wage hearings went on for years. In 1941 a Puerto Rican spokesman said that the island industry sought only handwork and did not want machine work as was done in Fulton County. In 1944 the question of a minimum wage for Puerto Rican workers surfaced again. A labor board panel recommended it a two-cent-an-hour raise (from $.18 to $.20 an hour), but representatives of the county's unions argued for a $.40 minimum, to make island wages more nearly equivalent to those in the county. In 1947 the unions were still fighting for increased minimums in Puerto Rico to the United States' standard $.40, this at a time when the Fulton County minimum was already $.50 an hour.

Before the end of the decade, most of Fulton County's larger glove shops were sending gloves to the island to be sewn. Everything that happened in the industry from 1939 on must be evaluated from the perspective of this initial move away from the mainland.

Plants moving out

1942

Kingsboro Silk Mill had established a plant in Tennessee in the late 1930s. Much of the company's government work was done at this plant. By mid-1942 all its operations had moved out of Gloversville.

Heagle Glove Co., maker of the first golf glove (circa 1897), closed.

Aircraft Glove Co, with Patrick Crocetta president, opened a factory in Johnson City, Tennessee.

1943

Elite Glove Company closed and its workers were absorbed by Bacmo-Postman. Elite moved all its operations to its factory in Middletown, New York.

1945

Van der Essen opened a new shop in Olean, New York.

1946

Bacmo-Postman opened a branch in Scotia, New York.

Expansions

1942

Bacmo-Postman, Jacob Zuckerwar president, purchased the former Kingsboro Silk Mill plant on East Twelfth Avenue.

Independent Leather, organized several years earlier by Anthony and Andrew Studenic, purchased the defunct Richard Young tannery.

Aris Glove Co. bought the factory of Artcraft Glove Co. of Fonda and moved its Brooklyn operation to the area to take advantage of the excess of workers available.

1943

Gloversville Knitting Co. took over Royalknit. Edward Vonderahe became manager of the Johnstown branch, formerly Royalknit, of the Gloversville Knitting Co. Ralph O. Collins, treasurer, and Lucius N. Littauer, president of Gloversville Knitting.

Gates-Mills enlarged its factory.

Louis P. Van der Essen, a returning disabled veteran, reestablished a shop for embroidering gloves.

Organized Labor in the Forties

Themes in the conflicts

Glove workers had won a ten percent increase in 1941, even before the glove business began to pick up. That year a ten-member Labor-Management Committee was established. The next year, the committee, functioning under the Fair Labor Standards Act, recommended an increase to $.40 an hour minimum wage for all 38,000 glove workers in the United States. The minimum established in July 1940 had been $.35, and the proposed increase would affect about 16,000 workers, principally heavy-glove workers in the west and relatively few of those in Fulton County. Of the 7,000 workers locally, only about 350 factory workers and 1,200 homeworkers were affected by the increase to $.40 an hour, indicating the extent to which wages of Fulton County's leather-glove workers exceeded wages of glove workers in the rest of the country.

At the same time, the committee considered banning all homework as a means of preventing "circumvention of the minimum [wage] throughout the nation."[23] In the end, the government agency backed off and said it would honor state certificates. But the threat of new wage rates and federal restrictions covering homeworkers prompted Casey to protest that the move to push sewers into factories was another step in the abolition of homework.[24]

—R. ANTEVIL & Co.
glorifying
the
American
glove
Won't you join us?

Homework continued to be a contentious issue into 1943, when the U.S. Department of Labor dispatched a group to make a complete checkup of local industry. Four agents issued summons demanding that homeworkers appear with all their employment records. The newspapers editorialized on the way this New Deal effort terrorized older workers.[25] Employers' problems with homework continued through the end of the decade. Numerous incidences of women working without permits—required since 1938—brought fines to employers, mostly small shops, in 1945.[26] In 1946, two larger firms, Bacmo-Postman and R. Antevil, were fined for homework violations.[27]

The Federal Wage and Hour Division of the Labor Department did permit manufacturers to employ "learners or handicapped or superannuated" workers, numbering no more than ten percent of the factory's work force, at $.25 an hour.

The calculation of overtime presented problems. The NALGM wanted to pay overtime on the basis of hourly rates computed on the average of an individual's hourly earnings.[28] It took a government mediator a week of hearings to settle this issue[29] and the question of whether overtime meant more than eight hours a day if a worker did not work more than 40 hours in a week.

NLRB hearings in Washington on the wage issues stretched into the summer of 1944. Andrew Schlusberg, lawyer for the association, claimed that cutters were earning upwards of $110 a week, over $1.50 an hour.

Operators won an eight percent increase in 1944, cutters a 10.6 percent increase. In 1945 the Block Cutters Union won increases that ranged between 18 and 26 percent. And that year the Leather Workers Union received a retroactive five percent raise with a ten cent bonus for shift workers.

Near the end of the war, when the National War Labor Board recommended an increase in the minimum wage to $.50 an hour, the

Operators and Day Hands Union requested that the Management-Labor Committee put that raise in effect immediately.[30] Day hands who had worked at least six months were granted the $.50 minimum.

In March 1946 the Layers-off Union won an eight percent wage increase retroactive to October 1945. This settlement was based on the claim that the "Little Steel Formula" was no longer valid. The same year Block Cutters won an 18 to 26 percent wage hike.

Despite these gains, the unions were preparing increased demands for the 1946 contracts. The Operators and Day Hands Union wanted 33 percent, and the Consolidated Cutters and Shavers Union wanted 30 percent. Both unions wanted the new contracts to include hospitalization and life insurance clauses, closed shops and check-off systems, a minimum $.65 an hour, and the right to reopen the contract if economic conditions warranted. The cutters under Blake settled for a ten percent wage boost.

Among the most significant union gains in this period were those dealing with workers' benefits. In April 1946 a contract negotiated by Carr's union won an agreement for a fund for workers' health insurance. The fund, financed by a contribution by the manufacturers of two percent of the annual payroll was precedent setting. That same year, the glove unions and manufacturers worked out an agreement with an insurance company for a policy covering all 6,000 workers. Paid for by the manufacturers, the policy included life insurance, hospital and surgical care, and disability benefits. The amounts were small, even for the time, but it was a beginning.

Conflicts among and within the unions

The decade of the forties was marked by numerous conflicts within and among the county's unions. In the leather industry, the controversy between Carr's Local 202 and the independent Adirondack Union centered at Bleyl's tannery, where both unions competed to organize its workers.

In 1941 an audit revealed that the Operators Union needed to improve its record keeping. The union's financial problems, though minor, were enough to spark a dispute between the leadership under Mrs. Bunn and a rump group said to favor affiliation with the Adirondack Union. Leonard J. Hannig beat Mrs. Bunn in the race for president of the Operators and Day Hands Branch in April 1942. In December he attempted to have the union vote to affiliate with the AFL, but that failed. The union was also courted by the Amalgamated Clothing Workers of America, CIO.

In July 1944 the Consolidated Cutters and Shavers Union called a mass meeting to consider affiliation with either the AFL or the CIO. Arguments imbued a sense of drama in all such meetings, and the speeches were rarely more impassioned than at this meeting. Some championed affiliation on the grounds that local manufacturers would have to contend with the many small shops being established outside the county and only a national union could organize workers there. Union member Joseph Nelkin noted that factories were opening all over the country and things were changing so that even women were doing cutting. Julius Ehrlich, a longtime member of the Cutters' executive committee and a compelling spokesman for the union during the 1914 hearings, opposed affiliation and asked that the union find out what an international union would do with their dues. The strongest argument for affiliation was the example of New York City workers whose international union had won wages far in excess of those in the county. The workers finally voted to ask representatives of national unions to speak to

1943 continued

Karg Bros. purchased the Maylander factory in order to increase production. Maylander Co. had tanned leather since 1856.

Joseph Simek and Marshall McKay acquired the old Johnstown Mocha Mill and its equipment at public auction. The mill was one of the county's largest tanneries. The men moved the equipment to the Teetz-McKay mill.

Ernest Kabat purchased the Gloversville glove shop owned by Everett Karg in order to open a new glove concern.

Bell Glove Co. bought a factory on East Fulton Street.

The Cross Glove Co., subsidiary of Mark Cross, leased the former Updegraff factory to increase production.

1944

Swears leased a building adjacent to its North Perry Street factory to further increase production of knit gloves.

Three new firms occupied the former Elite Glove Co. Factory: Geraldine Novelty Co., Metropolitan Glove Co., and Winig Glove Co.

Modern Tanning Co., owned by Howard Stern, purchased the Howden plant in Gloversville.

1945

Sanges Glove Co. purchased a three-story building on South Main Street in Gloversville.

Bell Glove Co. added new space in order to expand.

Stewart Filmer took over the empty Charles H. King tannery in the north end of Gloversville.

The Main Glove Co., reorganized under George W. Denton, purchased the old Littauer factory

The Adelman Leather Co. took over a three-story building to expand its operations.

them, but by vote in November, they decided against any affiliation, 696 to 397. The question they voted on did not specify a particular international union.

In 1944, when the War Labor Board finally approved the offered eight percent wage increase, the board of the union representing the cutters quickly accepted it without calling for a membership vote. This provoked an opportunity for a splinter group under Joseph Nelkin to challenge union president Gordon Blake.[31] It seemed like petty squabbling, but Blake said that the rumors of wrongdoing by union leaders that were circulating could split the union "wide open."[32] Blake defeated the charges and his slate won reelection by a margin of three to one with 818 of the 1,259 paid-up members of the Cutters Union voting. Another battle in 1944 took place between the Layers-off Union, then a part of the CIO Amalgamated Clothing Workers union, and both the Cutters and Operators unions.

In 1946 CIO sympathizers tried to unseat Gordon Blake, head of the Consolidated Cutters Union. The local paper sided with Blake, editorializing that "unfortunately not all unions have been as well managed as well as our own independent cutters and shavers organizations."

Within the cutter's group there were three unions competing among themselves and disputing the rights to perform different tasks. Within the Operators Unions, the schedule calling for different rates for different tasks had always been a source of contention. One group would win a slight rise in the rates and that would become a source of dispute in the next round of schedule negotiations. A job survey in 1944 addressed the question of unequal pay for different tasks. Walter C. Taylor of the U. S. Department of Labor and a group of engineers performed the study. The report, issued in 1945, attributed the disparity of pay for different kinds of piecework to the fact that the prevailing rates had "grown like 'Topsy' and bear out the statement that has been made that both parties have used pressure bargaining, and have had no real foundation or basis on which they could determine the rates."[33]

Union strength was increasing and several unions joined in the United Labor Unions Council, with president Charles Hildreth. The ULUC reached out to county unions outside the glove and leather industry, and in August 1946, the ULUC began a campaign to fight rises in the cost of living. Clarence Carr, whose union was also a part of the ULUC, tried to convince that group that wage increases did not necessitate price increases.[34]

A rise of 5.8 percent in the cost of living in 1947 allowed the unions to seek an increase, and although there seems to have been little opposition, the manufacturers proffered a contract that called for improvements in benefits but no increase in wages. With relatively quiet negotiations both sides reached an agreement for a five percent rise in wages. In secret ballots the Operators and Day Hands and the Consolidated Cutters and Shavers approved the contract. Perhaps the workers were taking into account declines in available work. Cutters' Union President Blake noted the number of men who were unemployed or working staggered weeks to spread the work around. The Layers-off voted a similar contract under protest.[35]

The decade's last negotiations between the glove unions and manufacturers were relatively quiet. The Operators and Day Hands Union rejected the manufacturers' version of a proposed 1949 contract because it could lower as well as raise wages in relation to whether the cost of living went up or down. Because of the poor economic conditions and unemployment in the county, all glove-union negotiations quickly bogged down. Both the Cutters and Shavers and the Layers-off unions reached a settlement based on the same wage scale as in 1948. However, the Operators and Day Hands were still holdouts in June, though their objections shifted to a clause that would have eliminated higher pay for workers at factories which traditionally gave higher wages. The Operators and Day Hands wanted equal pay for all classes of glove work.

Both the unions and the manufacturers debated at different times whether to submit disputes to arbitration. In 1941 during discussions for the 1942 wage schedule, the manufacturers joined the union in rejecting arbitration in favor of mediation. As part of the recommended settlement, the NWLB obtained an agreement that arbitration would be a part of future schedules discussions. In a 1945 walkout, involving all the unions, operators held out for arbitration. When the layers-off finally agreed to arbitration, they could not agree on the arbitrators. However, arbitration had definitely become a part of labor negotiations in the glove industry.

Strikes in the glove unions

Reports of strikes in later years mention the industry-wide strikes of 1939 and 1955, ignoring the fact that the forties saw a series of small strikes and labor skirmishes. Local 292, CIO, which was trying to organize the knitting plants, called a strike at Gloversville Knitting Co., which lasted for thirteen weeks before ending in January, 1942.

The Joint Council opened negotiations on the 1942 schedule with demands for a 25 percent increase. At a series of meetings with as many as 2,600 workers present, the council voted to strike in early March 1942, after rejecting a ten percent general increase over the 1941 schedule. While the manufacturers were delaying a decision whether to submit the wage issue to arbitration, cutters at Gates-Mills walked out. The manufacturers finally joined the union in rejecting arbitration and asked the War Labor Board to step in. The mediator made no progress until November when he ordered that no wage increase be given.

The unions in the Joint Council established strike committees. All the workers at Alexette, which later became a part of Grandoe Corp., walked out briefly in a dispute over one man's non-payment of union dues.

In October 60 workers at Alexette struck again, this time over wages. This is another of the stories that are still recounted to show the foibles of local unions. It seems that the company wanted to reward three workers with a five cent an hour increase. The union said all had to have the increase, and the company had to agree, provided it was acceptable to the War Labor Board.

In negotiations on the 1944 contract, the Layers-off rejected the association's five percent increase as did the Cutters and Shavers and the Operators. The increase was less than that won by workers in New York City. With a strike vote pending, a Labor Department conciliator helped bring the unions to an agreement for a ten percent increase, which the cutters and operators accepted. The manufacturers rejected this increase, stating that the ten percent represented their overhead on the ceiling on gloves, which was already as high as their costs. The manufacturers also refused to grant a week's vacation, which had been part of the package. The unions deferred making a strike threat so that the War Labor Board could become involved again.

Deaths

1940

Everett M. Kennedy, head of Scotsmoor, which he had helped found in 1916 by taking over the Wessell Knitting Co.

1942

Bert Bower, age 55, head of NALGM for two years, superintendent of Elite, partner with Benjamin Postman in Vogue Glove Co., and treasurer of Acme Glove Co.

James Stewart Ireland, age 68, president of Ireland Brothers.

1944

Lucius N. Littauer, age 85, at his summer home in New Rochelle.

1945

Otis Alva Chase began manufacturing gloves in 1912 in a partnership with Ward Van Wie. After Van Wie's death in 1930, Chase organized Domestic Glove Co.

In the spring of 1944, the panel established by the War Labor Board granted cutters a 10.6 percent increase, retroactive to January 1 and all workers a week's paid vacation. The wages of shavers and the other two groups were held up pending a Labor Department survey of the industry. In June, the War Labor Board's panel denied the raise to the other workers, and workers again began talking strike. The issue was complicated by the fact that manufacturers had a tentative agreement for a 10.6 percent increase in the government contract if the workers were given that pay raise.

The union objected to the fact the manufacturers were going to get the 10.6 percent increase anyway. Union leaders impressed the rank and file with the fact that no appeal would be heard if the workers were on strike. So the rebellious cutters went on "vacation"—despite the union debate in which one worker asked "What if 10,000 soldiers went on vacation?" The vacations started at Bacmo-Postman and spread to Superb, Alexette, Meyers, Rubin, and Martorelli glove shops, and then to Buscarlet, Daniel Hays, Barter Brothers, and Bell glove companies. Work stopped on the special Navy government contract. The vacations lasted about a week, until a government official convinced the cutters that the only way they could appeal was if they were working. At the mass meeting where workers voted to end their "vacations," senior union leader Julius Ehrlich urged them to return, but as he spoke he was heckled by younger union members.

The issues in this dispute were clouded by a battle between the unions. The Layers-off, Amalgamated Clothing Workers, CIO faced off against the Cutters and Operators unions over who was to represent the workers at Bert Kennedy's Capital Glove Co. and whether agreements reached in Gloversville would be the same in that company's Albany plant. Again the War Labor Board was dragged into a dispute, this time to address the layers-off claims of interference from the local unions.[36]

The NLRB regional board replied to this request for a wage increase by calling for a "re-study" of the matter, another job evaluation survey. That survey did not get started until the end of 1944. A group of engineers accompanied Walter C. Taylor of the U. S. Department of Labor to the area. In the meantime, manufacturers made plans to issue "vacation checks."

In the last days of the war, opposition to the settlement granting an eight percent wage increase and the readjustments in the schedule started as soon as it became final. A group of women sewers, special triple-stitchers working on the Navy contract, struck over the eight percent increase. In 1945 workers also struck Glovecraft (formerly Albany Glove) over pay differences between factories in Gloversville and Albany. Cutters struck Gates-Mills over piecework rates. Layers-off struck to force the manufacturers to reopen the settlement, but the manufacturers refused to discuss the issue unless the men went back to work.[37] This walkout stopped the shipment of finished gloves and a mediator was called in. Both sides took out large ads in the local papers, the manufacturers claiming the union did not follow the terms of the contract, the union holding out for collective bargaining.

The end of World War II did not bring an end to local union disputes. In August 1946 cutters at Meyers walked out over the wages for cutting smaller skins. That year, operators at five glove shops struck without the approval of union leadership in an apparent misunderstanding of the settlement terms accepted by the other unions.[38] Gloversville Knitting Company employees joined the strife when Frank McMaster of the ACW Local 292 (CIO) called a strike that lasted four weeks. In addition to granting increased wages, the company, desperate to increase productivity, obtained an agreement that the union would try new piecework rates and incentives for a 90-day trial.

Unionism and the tanneries

Through the forties, just as many disputes, strikes, or skirmishes occurred in the tanning industry as in the glove industry. In August of 1942, a dispute at Liberty Dressing idled 100 workers, but the WLB ordered the plant reopened.

Wage negotiations between Local 202 and the tanners reached a virtual impasse in early 1942 because the government had placed a ceiling on the price of leather, but none on wages. Wages of the county's tannery workers were already higher than those in Philadelphia, Wilmington, and out west. The deadlock was submitted to the National War Labor Board for arbitration, but that board had so many other more important disputes involving war production that this dispute was not addressed for some time. The NWLB took until September to settle the dispute between the manufacturers and Local 202 by recommending an average increase of $.44 a day, but this was less than the ten percent increase the 1,000-man union had rejected earlier.

Clarence Carr was elected to a ninth term as president of Local 202 in February 1942. In 1943, when the Adirondack Union's contract with G. Levor was expiring, Carr's union again petitioned the NLRB for certification as the union at that company. In the meantime, the Adirondack Union had won a wage increase for G. Levor workers. The dispute escalated during the two months it took the NLRB to decide to call a hearing as requested by Local 202. Adirondack president, Jack Burns signed a large ad placed in the local papers reminding Levor workers that in 1941 the union had won many things lost in the previous seven years under the Carr union. The ad also reminded the workers that Adirondack had won a 17 percent raise that had made tanners at Levor "the highest paid shoe tanning workers in the world." It called Local 202's leaders "Reds," identifying both Benjamin Gold, of the International Fur and Leather Workers Union and a founder of the country's Communist Party, and Clarence Carr. Referring to Local 202's leadership, the ad described "their doctrine of class hatred, industrial unrest and 'down with the bosses.'"[39] When the consent election was held, the Adirondack Union retained the right to represent Levor's workers, winning 152 to 99 over Local 202.[40]

Local 202 did win recognition at Martin-Deischel and in 1943 asked for a wage increase for tanners there. Carr protested the inclusion of Benjamin Dennie as chairman of the tanner's negotiating committee on the panel established by the War Labor Board and managed to have Dennie removed. The NLRB rejected the union's request for preferential hiring, a clause that had been left out of the 1942 contract with the Tanners Association, though it did continue the union membership requirement.[41]

Apparently Local 202 was able to continue fomenting discontent at Levor's because in October of 1943, Charles Stefic, who was associated with Local 202, and three others refused to pay Adirondack dues. Adirondack workers—350 at Levor's—struck to force the company to fire the men unless they paid their dues or quit. Fourteen workers paid their back dues and all the employees returned. However, Stefic was fired, and Local 202 then charged Adirondack with three unfair practices: intimidation of voters at G. Levor elections, that Adirondack was a company union, and that the company had discriminated against Stefic when it discharged him. Adirondack countered that they should not have lost a half day's pay and that the workers should have been discharged immediately.

Wages at other tanneries remained a contentious issue. Local 202 sought a wage adjustment in 1943 for mocha tannery workers at Geisler & Lehr and Martin Deischel Corp., but this was denied. In 1944 Karg Brothers gave their tannery workers a raise, without its being authorized by the NWLB, so that board gave the company a "stiff penalty."[42]

Finally, in early 1945, Carr announced that the union had obtained a directive from the War Labor Board granting union members retroactive pay, five cents an hour and ten cents bonus for off-shift workers. This settlement meant the area's 17 tanneries had to pay $100,000 to about 800 workers. Also in this agreement the union was granted, for the first time, check-off privileges, which required employers to collect union dues.

The year the war ended was a terrible one for industry strife. Not only did the various unions dispute the 1945 settlement, but Carr called all members of the Leather Workers Union out for a day in late November in order to "impress upon tannery owners" that the tannery workers were going to demand a 30 percent increase in their coming contract negotiations.[43] The overflow at Eagles Hall on the day of that walkout was so great some were turned away because of lack of standing room. Those who attended the meeting also passed resolutions supporting a $.65-an-hour minimum wage, better unemployment benefits, and enactment of the Fair Employment Practices Act prohibiting discrimination in employment. Then in December, 40 Local 202 workers struck Bleyl's tannery in a dispute over a conveyor that brought more work to some men than to others.

In 1946 the union settled with individual firms with wage increases ranging from $.15 to $.22 an hour. Carr claimed the union would only strike those tanneries that did not comply with the union's wage requests. The union was driving a wedge in the newly incorporated Tanners' Association. As the contract was running out, the union called a strike for April 1 against the tanneries which refused higher wages. An all-night negotiating session brought a settlement based on an increase of $.15 an hour, which was between $250 and $420 per man per year as well as the precedent-setting health insurance fund. This was the first such benefit obtained by any union for any of the county's glove or leather workers. The increase proved inadequate because by the fall of 1946 Carr's union was demanding a second wage increase in its current contract, which was to run until the end of 1947.

At the start of negotiations for the 1947 contract, Adirondack Leather Workers at Levor's agreed to a raise of $.10 an hour, bringing them to a minimum $1 an hour. Carr seemed ready to accept an offer $.15 an hour for Local 202 workers, but even that was rejected by union members as being below the increases in the cost of living. Negotiations with Local 202 dragged on for six months, and Carr was finally able to get a $.10 an hour raise for his leather workers, despite the fact the county's three glove unions had settled without a raise.

As talks got underway for the 1948 contracts, the NLRB issued a decision that was a severe blow to Local 202. Based on the Taft-Hartley Act, the NLRB ordered a consent election at the Loewenstein Tannery, but ruled that Local 202 could not be on the ballot because that union had not filed an "affidavit of non-communist leadership." The issue of Communist leadership is central to the decade's last strike.

Aftermath of War

In the postwar years, the county took on a perverse rhythm—slowdowns after the first of the year, union threats and unrest boiling up until the year's contracts were settled, manufacturers' optimism and a short respite with golf and camaraderie at their spring association meeting, a year-end speed up of work and a flurry of late orders, and then the layoffs. In January the cycle started all over again.

The nation's return to domestic production was far from smooth, but Fulton County experience was far worse because a plague from the past—seasonality—once again controlled production. Sales normally slumped after Christmas, but the county was shocked when nearly 2,500 block and table cutters were furloughed at the end of 1946. Price ceilings on most kinds of gloves were removed in August 1946. This permitted glovemen to ask that the cost controls on leather be removed. Skins were in very short supply and glove manufacturers needed to be able to compete for them worldwide. The glovemen simply planned to pass the leather costs along to purchasers.[44] The shortage of skins grew worse through early 1948 when stocks of leather in local tanneries reached a 25-year low, primarily as a result of competition for skins from reviving European tanneries and glove shops.

Nationally, the labor movement gained in strength following the end of the war, but growth was stopped by a number of issues and events: Communism, the election of Harry S. Truman, spiraling inflation, and finally the 1946 passage of the Case bill and the 1947 passage of the Labor-Management Relations Act of 1947, commonly known as the Taft-Hartley Act. The latter act superseded the NLRA. It banned closed shops and provided an 80-day injunction against strikes that endangered public health and safety.

Truman's call to enact the Case bill in May of 1946 brought a vituperative letter from the heads of all the local unions. The leaders objected to the terms of the bill as they interpreted them: granting government control of the right to strike; repealing the Norris-LaGuardia Act, which banned anti-labor injunctions; scrapping much of the New Deal's Wagner Act, abolishing seniority; and permitting the firing of strikers. Union leaders called the legislation "brutal, repressive, fascist-like [that would] in effect destroy the American Labor Movement." The letter castigated Truman for siding with big business.[45] The Taft-Hartley Act imposed even greater restrictions on unions and strengthened management, but its most controversial features were "its limits on the right to strike and the requirement that union officers had to sign anti-communist affidavits."[46]

In early 1947 everything in Fulton County started to go wrong. Already, less than two years after the end of the war, there were 4,000 unemployed workers in the county, drawing $72,000 weekly unemployment. Most were from the leather glove factories, but some were from the tanneries as well. This was far from a record, though: 5,500 workers had drawn unemployment insurance in 1939, before the war brought an upturn in business.[47]

In 1946 nine firms enrolled in a program for on-the-job training for veterans, with government allowances supplementing apprentice-level pay. Later that year, the Gloversville School System established classes for table cutters in its Vocational and Adult Educational program. Seventy students joined the first class, from which 36 graduated in February 1948.

Firms and Glovemen
1946

Passaro Glove Co. bought a factory in Mayfield owned by Crocetta.

Ace Glove firm was established by Robert Cerrone and Edward Cammarota.

Elmer Little & Son incorporated with capitalization set at $350,000.

Groff & Co, jobbers, moved into a larger plant.

Topps purchased the old Grewen fabric factory in order to make fur-lined gloves.

Maurice Sandfield and Frank Antevil purchased the Streeter & Hackney (founded 1897) factory and equipment and renamed it Sanville Gloves. (George Hackney, grandson of the founder, had become a partner in 1920 and in 1925 Robert Milford, Seth Fosmire, William Van DerWerken, and J. Eddy Smith joined him as partners.)

Henry J. Lesser established a leather-trading company.

Gould Glove Co. of Philadelphia bought Lewis & Evans, Inc.

French Glove Manufacturers, Inc. established in Johnstown.

Joseph Conroy purchased the former Lucas & Kennedy glove factory and V. G. Brooke, owner of a new firm established in 1943, purchased the old Conroy factory as both companies were expanding.

H. F. B. Tanning; Gloveskins, Inc.; Simon Glove Co.; and Paramount Glove Corp. all formed new corporations. Modern Tanning Corp. was formed from two corporations: Modern Tanning Co. and Leather Products, Inc.

Superb Glove Co. purchased the old Meco Hotel which it had been using for four years as a glove shop housing a hundred sewers.

Ma Kay Glove Firm and Vogue Novelty Manufacturing Co. incorporated.

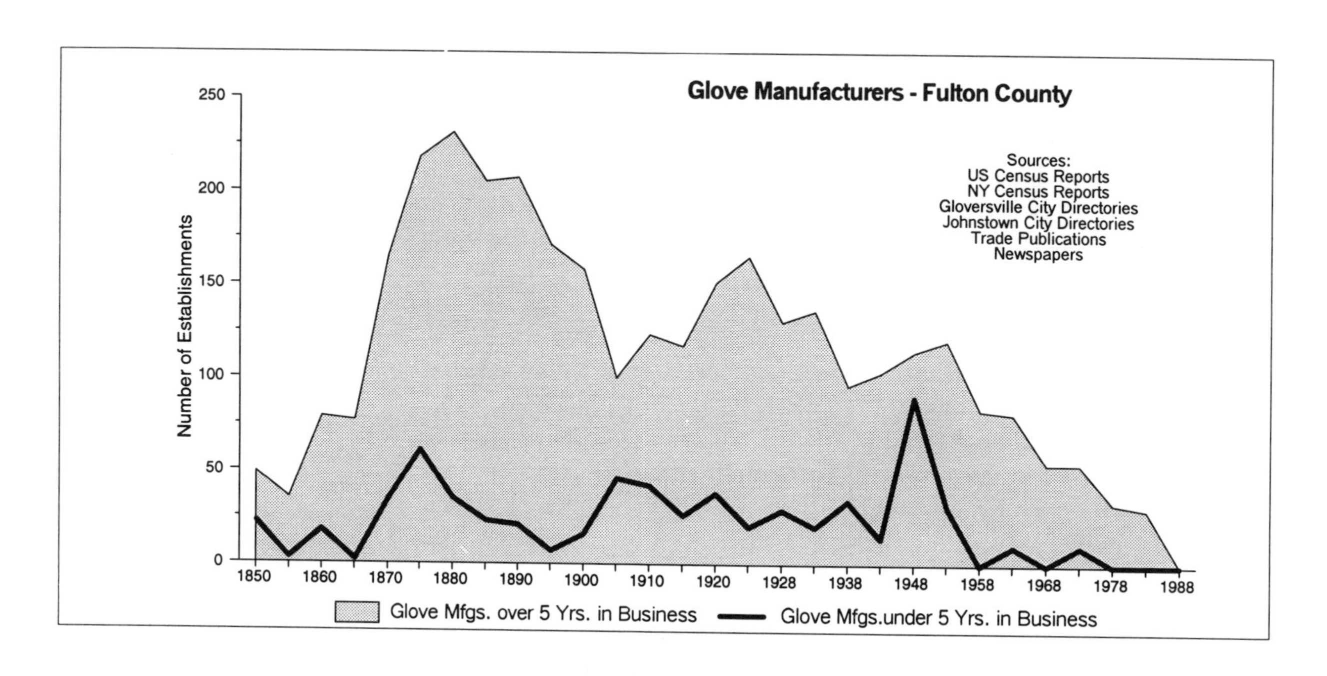

Notice the 1948 spike in the number of glove manufacturers in the county and how most of the new firms lasted for less than five years.

The number of glove shops surged in 1947 and into 1948; it was every man for himself. However, the number of workers and the level of production did not keep pace with the number of entrepreneurs. Just as quickly as shops opened, they were closed; 1948 was the crest. One of the shops to open and close within a year or so was Ketchum Brothers Glove Co., which started in 1946 but filed for bankruptcy in February 1947. Earnings for many companies fell that year; Fownes reported a 20 percent decrease from the previous year.[48]

The problems of obtaining capital hurt many upstarts. For years, glovemen had borrowed heavily to obtain skins and gambled that their gloves would bring large profits. It was said that manufacturers' credit kept the county running. One story demonstrates the power of that credit: Joseph P. Conroy was expanding his business in the late forties. He was thinly capitalized yet borrowing heavily, "stretched to the hilt." In 1949 his bank imposed a limit on other borrowings and discovered that Conroy had greatly exceeded that limit, so it cancelled his line of credit. Conroy paid the bank immediately but could not renew his line of credit because he had "broken faith," a euphemism for lying about his worth. Conroy made an assignment of all his assets to a credit committee, which brought an action against the State Bank of Albany for having been paid as preferred creditor. The bank lost the case three years later and had to restore $60,000 to the credit committee. Thus Conroy reestablished his ability to borrow and was able to continue in business.[49]

Joseph Conroy

Unemployment and the increasing instability of the glove shops did not deter the unions from asking for further increases. The layers-off wanted another 10 percent in their 1947 contract. In spite of the fact that Local 202's contract ran until the end of 1947, Carr and that union filed a 30-day strike notice in March 1947, asking for a cost of living increase. A worker wrote the paper asking for a secret vote on the strike question, claiming that at the mass meetings, "it is all staged by loud cries, led by a few well-placed stooges."[50]

In 1947 the county's United Labor Unions Council (ULUC) adopted a platform calling for many federal reforms concerning housing, income tax, unions, a $.75-an-hour minimum wage. The ULUC was roused to action by the passage of the Taft-Hartley Act. That group of unions had rallied 4,000-plus members for a one-day strike to protest its passage.

Glovemen were becoming desperate. Slumps in sales and increased competition prompted them to slash prices of leather gloves by 20 percent in the spring of 1947, a gamble they hoped would increase volume.[51]

At the time the county's future was actually quite bleak, a story in a national magazine painted a bright picture of the the glove cities. In May 1947 the *Saturday Evening Post* published an article by John Lear extolling the local glove industry. Called "The Temperamental Wizards of Fulton County," the piece seems to have forever frozen the way the county sees its past. It elevated a few myths to the stature of gospel, romanticized the industry, and hid its darkest secrets. Lear's hyperbole makes entertaining reading and gives the impression that the worker attributes he exaggerates were the norm.

However, Lear was right about one thing: the absolute independence of county glove workers, especially the cutters, whom he correctly called a "vanishing breed." The description of cutters working in white shirts and ties, a dress code that had prevailed since the previous century, enhanced their feeling of self-importance, their stature in the middle class. I remember how the article impressed me with the wonder of the town we lived in—more cars, telephones, and privately owned homes than anywhere else. No one I talked with in the county mentioned the fantasy the article concealed. No one pointed out the high levels of unemployment, the way the decline in the industry had only been temporarily interrupted by the war.

Perhaps it was Lear's splendid image of the cutters that inspired their union's extravagant demands in negotiations for the 1948 contract. In March the Cutters and Shavers had rejected a five percent increase with eight percent for block cutters by a vote of 640 to 43. The union wanted 22 percent. A strike was imminent.[52] The union reduced its demands to a 15 percent increase. This time the Operators and Day Hands joined the Cutters in rejecting the offer. The manufacturers had added a clause that stated that the offer to the unions was automatically withdrawn if one of the unions rejected it. The manufacturers held firm at eight percent, but finally all sides agreed to ten percent. Meanwhile the country was considering an increase in the minimum hourly wage from $.40 to $.75 an hour. In opposing it, Casey said that this meant there were some workers whose piecework pay dragged the average down, who would have to be discharged if they could not meet the minimum.

The manufacturers' annual meetings had followed traditional themes throughout the war: support for the war effort and worry about what might happen after the war. A member of the National Association of Manufacturers told the group that it would be the responsibility of industry to provide jobs for returning veterans.[53]

At the end of the war, an independent group spurred on by Andrew Haire, who had purchased the old *Gloves* magazine, proposed a "Glove Institute" to deal with problems in the leather and knit glove industries. Haire claimed it would not compete with existing groups, like the association, but there is the sense he considered the old association obsolete.

In June 1948 the manufacturers talked again of ways to overcome the seasonality of the business. The outgoing president of the Glove

1947

Richardson & Schism, Wessendorf Brothers, Mario Papa & Sons, and Castiglione Glove Co., Ossan Novelty, Salka Leather, and Nash Leather companies were all incorporated. Superb Glove Co. was incorporated with $400,000 capital.

Bermyn Gloves increased its capitalization to $100,000.

Loewenstein, Inc. of New York City, purchased the Cane Tanning Co.

Mark Cross Co. made plans to enlarge its Gloversville factory.

Buscarlet Glove Co., makers of Kislav gloves, purchased the Van Vleet three-story factory, built in the 1930s and one of the most modern factories in the county.

1948

Commodore Glove and Greentree Leather Company were incorporated.

Leavitt-Bogardus Corp, a new corporation, took over the Warren Miller & Sons mill, which was the last of the old-time buckskin leather-dressing plants.

Aris Manufacturing Co. was incorporated with capital of $100,000. Vincent Mario and Alfonso Sanges were named managers of the Gloversville plant by Arthur Stanton, head of Aris Gloves.

Geraldine Novelty Corp. purchased the Bacmo-Postman factory. Geraldine Novelty closed its Poughkeepsie plant and planned to hire 200 workers as well as consolidate its operations in Gloversville.

1949

Alexette Glove Co., bought the three-story factory on Bleecker Street owned by the Dix Fur Company. At one time it had been modernized to house the Gloversville Auto Glove Company.

Joseph Perrella Glove Shop purchased the four-story wooden Mark Cross factory.

Deaths

1947

Elmer Little, age 77, founder and senior member of the firm bearing his name.

Albert Aaron, age 76, retired manager of Louis Meyer & Son.

Peter MacIntyre, age 92, died shortly after the death of his son, James. They had been in partnership in the firm of Davies-MacIntyre & Co., founded in 1900.

1949

Daniel Higier of Glovecraft and Crescendoe, age 55

Manufacturers Association, Milton Gluckman, of Fownes, saw the industry from the perspective of a New York City manufacturer. He told the group that "there is something wrong with the current glove business, but that it was only a question of time before a solution would be found." Gluckman cited retailers' high prices, lack of styling and colors, poor merchandising, antiquated production methods, and inadequate promotion as causes for the industry's ills.[54]

One wonders instead why the manufacturers were not looking at such causes as their antiquated factories, seasonality, high costs, high wages, cutthroat competition, and overseas competition. These are the problems that we now see and that they had observed in the past. Perhaps manufacturers found it was easier to look at answers they could address, a promotional campaign for instance. Perhaps they had no real solutions for the hard problems so it was better not to dwell on them. Their optimistic facade was all that kept most of them in the business.

Casey told of one store returning a large amount of unsold gloves to a manufacturer, some of which did not even come from the manufacturer. He wondered why the industry still accepted unsold goods, why the manufacturer had to deal with such problems. "I suspect that top management in the glove industry is giving too much of its valuable time to more menial jobs, and not sufficient time to the big, broad problems that lie ahead." Most of the small-shop manufacturers I can picture from those days were still content to cut a few gloves and sort piles of skins, to lose their worries in physical labor. They tried to ignore troubled business conditions, and most did not have a clue about how to address the larger issues. The association should have been able to help them, but in the end it too was powerless.

Business was slowing all across the country, exacerbating local conditions. In the fall of 1948 retailers delayed their orders so county unemployment remained high. Costs were so high manufacturers were unwilling to produce gloves without firm orders.[55] Those who were working were doing so on staggered schedules so real wages were down, and workers were leaving the area for Amsterdam or Schenectady. Casey predicted that when Christmas orders came in, the glovemen would be unable to fill them. His prediction was right. By the end of October, manufacturers had turned away orders for 7,000 dozen pairs of gloves because they could not make them in time.[56] As a result, the leather glove business in the county decreased by 20 percent over the previous year.

Nor was the outlook for 1949 any better. Leather prices were rising, and Europe was buying most of the fine skins, even those from South America, which had previously gone to the United States. The postwar years were still seen as a period of adjustment.[57] As more shops closed, some, like Passaro Gloves, which had purchased a factory in Mayfield in 1946, filed for bankruptcy.

Although association members undoubtedly discussed the worsening economic situation, one issue continued to overshadow all their public debates: the perennial issue of free trade and tariffs. Daniel Higier replaced Elmer Little as president of the association at the June 1944 meeting. Jim Casey, who had issued his share of platitudes over the years, made a prescient speech at that meeting that is remarkable for two reasons—its divergence from the county's longtime attitude toward tariffs and the strengths of its warnings. Parts of it deserve quoting, for what the speech portends for the county's future.

"Lower production costs on one side and more satisfactory markets on the other side [are needed]. . . . How do we stand on foreign trade? . . . Each of us likes to speak of foreign trade as such, but don't ever make the mistake of thinking that foreign trade can be divorced from lower tariffs and removal of trade barriers. . . . Only two weeks ago our Secretary of State advised us that no industry would be permitted to survive if it had to depend on high tariffs and subsidies." Casey went on to cite a speech before the American Tariff League in which Burton E. Wheeler talked about the selfishness of the Republicans present and their lack of understanding of world problems, and he warned them they would receive little help from the current administration. Casey continued, "It sounds reasonable to me to say that, unless we trade with other countries, we can not hope to sell to them." He said that in order to employ returning servicemen and keep labor costs low, industry had to increase sales, foreign sales in particular. Despite the glove industry's dependence on tariffs, the country would actually need lower tariffs.

In spite of Casey's strong words the association continued to agonize over tariffs, in particular the Trade Agreements Act of 1934 and the succession of laws that reduced tariffs. These discussions would continue until the organization's last days. The inevitability of free trade as discussed by Casey had little impact on association policies. At war's end, county manufacturers were once more concerned about the impact of European imports on their business.

As tariffs resurfaced as the focus of the association's activities, Jules Higier, a vibrant leader and excellent choice, was named chairman of a committee to fight tariff reductions. In 1942 Higier, co-owner of Superb Glove Co., had been given a civilian-military position as glove technologist with the Quartermaster Corps. He was sent to Europe at the end of the war, and on his return in December 1945, he reported that glove factories and tanneries in France, Germany, and Czechoslovakia were relatively undamaged and that exports, though slow to resume, would soon pick up. The threat of lower tariffs had not yet materialized.

John Naudin, who was a native of France and head of Jones & Naudin, a local leather-trading company, joined the government in 1944 for an assignment in France to aid in the rehabilitation of leather factories in Belgium, France, and Luxembourg. On his return a year later, he stated that it would be a long time before the county's tanneries would feel any competition from Europe.[58] Alan Rothschild, of G. Levor, was also sent to Europe at the end of the war to survey the situation there. The somewhat contradictory analyses of conditions in Europe could do little to allay the fears of county manufacturers.

By the spring of 1945, the association's struggles, the weight of his work, and possibly the limited financial future offered by the manufacturers' group prompted James Casey to offer his resignation. Those attending the spring conference voted to put Casey's resignation aside until a replacement could be found, but the manufacturers did hire Harry A. Moss as an assistant to Casey. Moss graduated from Notre Dame and had a law degree from St. Johns University. He had worked for the American Tariff League and his appointment was a sign that tariffs would remain as the association's main concern.

Even though the war was not yet over, that 1945 spring conference gave the impression of business as usual. Higier talked about the tariff committee's work to protest the continuation of the Reciprocal Trade Agreement, which was to extend for another three years with an added 50 percent reduction in

DHAYSTEX

Daniel Hays' designing has conspired with Lastex, the miracle yarn, to produce the smartest of all velvet gloves. Black, brown, wine and white.

The DANIEL HAYS COMPANY, Inc.

Gloversville, N. Y.

tariff rates. Adam W. Gimbel of Saks Fifth Avenue predicted that manufacturers would have to compete with goods from foreign markets and work to provide a product the American market would want.

By the spring meeting in 1946, the manufacturers were once again considering advertising and promotion as a means of stabilizing the industry even as they heard concerns about inflation and rising costs of raw materials. (The war's destruction of herds worldwide echoed events following World War I.)

Jules Higier

Jules Higier, whose experience made him the obvious choice to continue heading up the association's tariff committee, felt the world trade picture was so unsettled that new tariff measures might be postponed. However, this proved not to be the case: before the end of 1946, the manufacturers' group was engaged in trying to thwart the government's move to cut glove tariffs by another 50 percent. Even the well-traveled Higier did not seem to comprehend the government's desire for free trade. One wonders how much his optimism in the face of lower and lower tariffs can be attributed to the fact that Fulton County was a quiet backwater, out of the mainstream of developments in Washington. Or was it because he was already contemplating moving some of his operations to Puerto Rico?

The threats from abroad took on a new twist when Stern's department store in New York City ran an ad touting the quality of French kidskin gloves and in the process disparaged American gloves. Jim Casey, the association, and even local newspapers rushed to defend the county's honor.

Labor joined the association in fighting the proposed tariff reductions as before. Congressman Kearney, representing the area, opposed further reductions in the tariff rates. Casey, several union leaders, Jules Higier, and Edward Vonderahe, representing the knit-glove industry, traveled to Washington to make the case for glove tariffs, claiming that industry could not survive without them.

Casey supported the knit-glove manufacturers' attempts to keep tariffs at their current levels, claiming that any further reductions under the 1931 Smoot-Hawley Act would gain foreign workers only pennies while causing irreparable harm on the domestic industry. Casey pointed out that from 1927 to 1941, imports accounted for nearly half of all gloves sold in the the United States.[59] In 1947 he traveled to Switzerland to attend an international trade conference and continue his fight to retain tariffs. In an interview in the *New York Tribune*, Casey stated that glove workers in America earned $60 a week, compared with $14.42 in England and $12 in France. He claimed the livelihood of 40,000 Americans depended on the tariff.[60]

The year 1947 saw another blow on the tariff front. The General Agreement on Tariffs and Trade (GATT) was approved by President Harry S. Truman under the provisions of the 1934 Trade Agreements Act, which meant that Congressional approval for GATT was not required. This measure attempted to simplify the mass of confusing concessions and agreements that grew out of the 1934 act. In addition to systematizing U. S. and world trade policies, GATT contained an "escape" clause which was intended to protect domestic industries against foreign competition. The escape clause would do little to help the county.

The county seems to have spent the summer and most of the fall of 1948 sweating out the announcement of the new tariff rates. It turned out that the glove industry's tariff cuts were remarkably small, well below the reductions in other industries. The tariff on men's gloves was reduced from 50 to 40 percent, on women's from 30 to 25 percent. However, the tariffs and duties on knit gloves were reduced significantly, something Edward Vonderahe, chairman of the tariff committee of the National Association of Wool Glove Manufacturers, called a "serious blow" to that industry.[61] Even the leather glove industry's victory was hollow because France devalued the franc in the beginning of 1948, making that country's gloves cheaper by half.

At the end of the war, several government contracts for gloves were cancelled. While government business slowed down, it never completely stopped. In 1948 one-third of the knit gloves made in American were produced for the government. County glove manufacturers received substantial orders for leather gloves from the Navy in 1949, and Elmer Little was low bidder on a 180,000-pair contract. Such contracts had saved local industry during the war, but in the late forties they were too small to keep it going.

The euphoria of postwar expansion was very short-lived. The threat of unemployment rose as the county, like the nation, faced the difficulties in returning to a peacetime economy. By 1948 the fragile state of all the new glove factories was becoming obvious. These clouds on the horizon inspired the county to once again look at its industrial base. A labor and management forum on the future of the glove industry, held in early January 1948, proved to be a dialogue between opposites. Three optimists—George H. Meyer of Liberty Dressing, Leonard Hannig of the Operators Union, and, of course, James Casey of the association—debated Gordon Blake of the Cutters, Clarence Carr of Local 202, and Donald Willard of Hilts-Willard. Willard, more a realist than a pessimist, said that because of the nature of the industry, "it does not appear that mass production will ever be possible in the glove industry." Despite the fact that American workers were the most productive in the world, he believed that the glove industry, as one of the few handicraft industries left, would always remain outside any technological revolution.[62] Even Casey was cautious, stating that he felt manufacturers could not absorb rising costs and risked pricing themselves out of business.

In the 1940s fabric and knit gloves were replacing leather gloves. High styles and affordability made them desirable.

Courtesy J. D. Widdemer

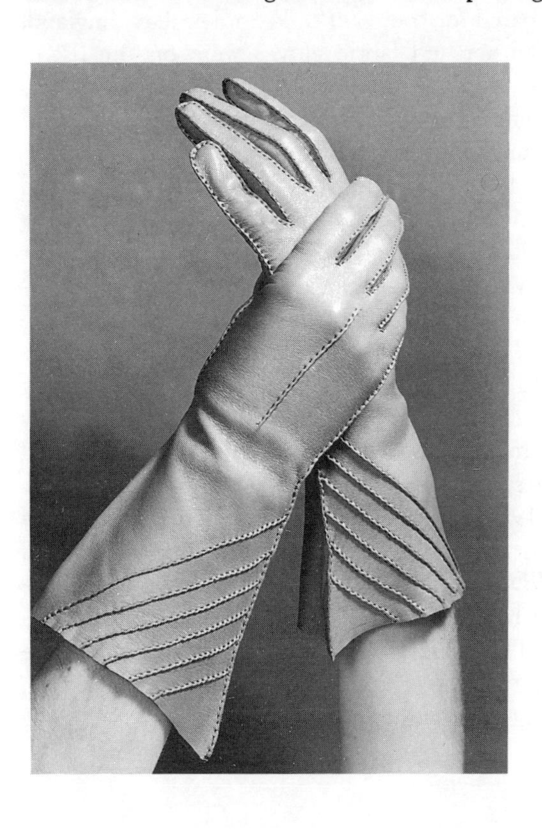

In January of 1949, Casey made yet another trip to Washington—only one of many he would make in the next few years. This time he told the House Ways and Means Committee that the NALGM and the Association of Knitted Glove and Mitten Manufacturers (AKGMM) were opposed to a three-year extension of the Trade Agreements Act because of the low wages of foreign glove workers.[63] He followed up with complaints before a Congressional committee on the difficulty and red tape involved when a manufacturer did protest hardships to the U. S. Tariff Commission. Congressman Kearney supported local efforts. Casey asked that the extension be for one year only.

Harry A. Moss, Jr. moved from assisting Casey to focusing on the Association of Knit Glove Manufacturers (AKGM), whose members were facing increasing competition from Japan. The wage difference, $9 a week for American workers versus $.11 a day in Japan, made Japanese knit gloves so inexpensive that it appeared the Japanese were dumping them on American markets. Leon Swears, Johnstown knit-glove manufacturer, traveled to Japan, ostensibly to find out what could be done. Imports, supported by United States' attempts to revive the Japanese economy, were hurting many industries like toys and silk, but the 385,000 dozen pairs of knit gloves imported from Japan were almost as many as could be sold in the country. Casey pointed out at a hearing chaired by Senator Joe McCarthy that the Army was training Japanese workers and actually selling these competing and subsidized gloves back home. The Supreme Command of the Allied Powers in Japan had approved an export price for gloves without discussing the matter with American manufacturers. In August 1949 the command did reduce the quantity of exports somewhat. The campaign against Japanese knit gloves picked up momentum through 1949, and in November the Tariff Commission postponed a decision on knit-glove tariffs. The AKGM was gratified that it was not an outright denial and kept fighting for higher tariffs.[64]

In 1950, as Harry Moss prepared for the tariff talks in Torquay, England, it was understood that both leather and fabric gloves were on the list of commodities subject to tariff cuts. Among the facts county leaders marshalled to prove their arguments against the cuts was the observation that American glove products had almost never been exported. The industry went so far as to say they must have protection or "face extinction."[65] The whole county rallied to the fight. The county supervisors appointed a committee to help. The way local business and political leaders brought Congressmen, individual letter writers, unions, and even the State Commissioner of Labor together to influence Washington is one of the glove industry's brighter stories. Even *The New York Times* described how the county's 50,000 residents were uniting to save their industry.[66] A large contingent of county leaders, led by Jim Casey, took the message to Washington to testify before the Congressional Committee for Reciprocity. The local paper said that "the unity and cooperative spirit were worthy of the highest praise."[67]

Nearly a year later, in May 1951, seventeen countries meeting at Torquay decided to lower tariffs on all but two of the 1,300 items under consideration. The tariff on men's leather gloves would remain the same as in 1947, the tariff on women's gloves would be raised by ten percent to 35 percent. The county had won a victory.[68] The Council of Importers protested to the Committee on Reciprocity, but could not change the decision.[69] Once again, the county had rallied to prolong the viability of its industry.

The Strike that Shook the County

During the war seven tanning operations started up, increased capacity, or moved to new, larger plants. The Tanners Association incorporated in December of 1945, choosing Maider and Maider as the law firm to represent the group. John N. Forster, who had been with the New York State Board of Mediation, was named the Tanners Association's Director of Labor Relations. The county's tanneries were entering a new era, and while tanning for glove leather was declining, tanning of other skins and hides for shoes and garments was increasing.

Despite changes in the industry, the tanneries suffered in the postwar depression as much as the glove factories had. The 1949 slump was becoming so bad that Carr announced that the leather workers would meet with public officials and manufacturers to see what could be done. He also noted that the other local unions (those in the glove industry) were in their fourth round of negotiations for wage increases. His union, Local 202, was only about to enter its third round since the war.[70]

The Adirondack union signed contracts with the two tannery companies whose workers it represented for increased hospitalization benefits and more paid holidays (five). The contract was to last until April 1950.

In March Carr announced that Local 202 would seek a $.25 hourly increase and other benefits from the tanners. In pushing for this seemingly modest raise, Carr, who was starting his eighteenth year as head of the tannery worker's union, had started down a path that would prove extremely devastating to the county. As July and the summer furlough approached, workers struck Independent Leather.[71] When employees at nine of the vacationing tanneries returned, workers at Geisler & Lehr joined the strike. The Tanners Association decided to cease production at all its members' plants. According to the local paper, "Association members claimed that present conditions in the industry are worse than at any other time in 30 years."[72] Carr called their action a "lockout." If the shutdown turned into a lockout, union members would have to wait seven weeks for unemployment insurance. Carr immediately declared it was "just a shutdown" so that members would be eligible to receive unemployment insurance after a one-week wait. Advertisements placed in the local papers by the Tanners Association claimed that the union's wage request the previous October had been rejected because the owners could not meet it and that the union had brought forth the same wage request in June. Association members offered a contract based on no wage cuts.

Talks went nowhere, but union leaders instructed their workers to return to work on Tuesday, July 19. They came back and found no work. Given the union threat that no raise meant no contract and no contract meant no work, Tanners Association members acquired no new skins for themselves or their customers, because, if there were a strike, the skins would spoil. As a result of the stalemate, 1,000 workers at 19 tanneries were out of work. The tanners said there would be no more talks until the union withdrew its financial demands.

There followed a barrage of advertisements in the local paper and both sides distributed flyers. Tanners Association members wrote of the money they had lost in delayed contract negotiations brought about by the "unbusinesslike union." In one ad they asked, "Who ever heard of starting a strike to involve an industry when business is so bad?" Never had the tannery

From October, 1948 to June, 1949—month after month—we met with the same reply, "We [the tanners] will sign a new contract, but no 15 percent increase." Our local began to mobilize its members and resources to force the tanners to grant a decent wage increase. On June 15, the tanners locked our members out after a dispute in one of the shops ended in the workers striking the plant.

This set the stage for one of the most heroic struggles in the history of the leather workers of our country—the Gloversville strike of 1949-50. It is also a story of betrayal of the Fulton County leather workers by their so-called "friends" in the labor movement—both AFL and CIO.

Clarence Carr writing in *The Leather Workers of Fulton County*

Tanners Association Members, 1948

Alma Leather
J. C. Bleyl
F. Rulison & Sons
Fear and White
Geisler & Lehr
Gloversville Leather Mfg. Co.
Independent Leather Mfg. Co.
Karg Brothers
Liberty Dressing
Martin-Deichsel Leather
The Napatan Company
Peerless Tanning
Risedorph Tanning
Reliable Tanners
J. G. & T. Robinson
Teetz-McKay Leather
Twin City Leather
Wood & Hyde

owners shown such solidarity. They tried to convince union members that their own union leaders had made decisions without consulting membership. They pledged to continue all health, accident, sickness, and death benefits for a month, then they extended the coverage for another month.

"Why," the employers asked rhetorically, had there been a "deadlock, since October 1948?, since January 1949?, since June 1949?" The ad answered because the union did not believe the Tanners Association when it claimed it was in the worst business depression in their history, demand for glove leather was worse than the poorest years of the 1930 depression, glove leather production had fallen from 8 million skins during the war to 5.3 million skins in 1948. Bold type proclaimed that by August 2, workers had lost $100,000.

As the Tanners Association saw the union's past actions, Local 202 had asked for a ten percent increase in 1941. In 1942 the War Labor Board gave them 6.5 percent. In December of 1946, the tanners offered increases equal to ten cents an hour. Six months later the offer still had not been accepted, but settlement was rushed through at that rate just before the Taft-Hartley Act was to take effect. The association claimed that the delay meant each worker had lost $100 in those six months.

These arguments did not move union members, so the association started on a new approach—union busting. An ad blatantly stated that no members of the association would ever again deal with the Communist-led Local 202. They assured the workers that they would not operate without a union contract, and would deal with any *other* union they chose. The union countered with an ad revealing a "conspiracy" in which some association members met with AFL leaders in an effort to force tannery workers "into a company union." The tanners did not deny the meeting, stating they were only seeking a non-Communist union. According to the Taft-Hartley Act, no union could be certified unless its officers signed pledges denying Communist Party membership. From the start of the strike, Carr refused to sign such a pledge. In August 80 members of Local 202 who had served in World War II took out an ad supporting the union.

By August the tanners were using the Communist threat to justify their decision not to deal with Local 202. The tanners took their stand to a group of citizens and their labor representative Forster told them the issue was not wages, but Communist leadership of the union. He claimed that the union was preventing him from increasing the wages of the lower paid workers, the 150 who receive on average $.97 an hour. The average pay for all workers was $1.67, and 400 workers earned over $2 an hour. The union claimed the average was $1.37. (The manufacturers later corrected the figure to $1.62, quoting U. S. Department of Labor statistics to show that the average for all industrial workers in America was $1.33, and of all tannery workers, $1.34 an hour.) The tanners offered to open their books so the public could confirm their claims. Even with these apparently correct accounts of the wage scales, the Tanners Association was unable to sway public sentiment to their cause.

By September leather stocks were so low that it appeared that some glove shops would close. Retail sales in Gloversville and Johnstown were off as much as 30 percent. The union held firm and challenged the head of the Tanners Association to debate. The county's United Labor Council considered whether to support Local 202 and in September the Operators and Day Hands voted to offer "moral support." In a secret ballot, the Consolidated Cutters and Shavers not only refused to lend financial support to Local 202, the cutters' union even denied the Local 202 moral support.[73]

Challenges to Carr's leadership arose within the union. A few members of Local 202 took out an ad offering to put the question of union affiliation to a secret vote—this in answer to management's claim that the union was afraid of a secret ballot. By September AFL organizers were at work in the county, touting their democratic ways and soliciting support for a NLRB vote to certify a new union for the tannery workers. Not only did ads attack Carr and Ben Gold, the avowedly Communist head of the International Fur and Leather Workers Union (IFLWU), they attacked Bernie Woolis, who entered the local struggle. (Woolis had tried to organize the Virginia Oak Tannery in Virginia for the IFLWU.) One notice from the Foremen and Supervisory Group of the Leather Industry called Woolis the "field Generalissimo of the Commies of the IFLWU." As the struggle escalated, the Gloversville radio aired a report that the tanners had imported goons. Local 202's policy committee again called for a secret ballot on that union's right to represent the county's tannery workers.

A notice placed in the local paper by the American Legion condemned Communism and stated that the organization believed there was communistic leadership in the county. The tannery workers held mass meetings and a parade in early September as they were finally able to apply for unemployment insurance. The clergy got into the fray. A Presbyterian minister preached about the selfishness or self-interest that had been placed ahead of common welfare, all the while carefully avoiding condemnation of either side. Gloversville's Protestant and Jewish clergymen took out an ad asking for a fact-finding group because both factions needed to realize "that their responsibility to the community overshadows any special interest."[74]

The newspapers were full of letters to the editor. One predicted that buyers would go elsewhere, that the county no longer had a monopoly on leather gloves. Another resident wrote that wages were "decent" and commented on the way workers shortened their work day to please themselves. Another equated local Communism with events in Czechoslovakia. The editor wrote that it was "Time for a Change," that by September workers had lost a half million dollars in wages, that the whole area was suffering. He reminded readers that Clarence Carr had run for Congress on the Communist ticket in 1936.

In mid-September Local 202 offered to leave the CIO and submit to certification by the NLRB if the tanners would agree to negotiate. The union's proposal "to remove itself from Ben Gold's IFLWU does not ring true," according to an editorial.[75] Neither the local paper nor the Tanners Association believed this would solve the dispute, which was growing more savage daily. A group of foremen from the tanneries placed ads in the local paper that contained a list of violent acts—a woman hit over the head after dark, a leather worker beaten by three assailants, another worker's tires slashed, workers and foremen alike receiving anonymous threats. The Tanners Association countered by reminding readers how Clarence Carr had fought to bring the Independent Leather Workers Union into the IFLWU, that Carr was an admitted Communist.

The county's struggles were not occurring in a vacuum. At the national level, the CIO was fighting its Communist image. Eleven board members were on trial in New York because of their party membership. The state CIO board condemned the leftist leaders of its member unions and declared at the state convention that they would be challenged at the national CIO convention.[76]

October brought another round of broadsides. The AFL organizing committee talked nobly of their labor heritage while blaming Local 202 for all the delays. The AFL had enough signatures (30 percent of the workers) to petition the NLRB for an election to determine who should represent the union. The NLRB scheduled a hearing to determine if there was a consent agreement to hold an election.[77]

Local 202 did manage to win a settlement with Knowles and Frank, Inc., a small tannery that was not a member of the Tanners Association. The contract represented about a ten percent raise and improved benefits. At the same time, pickets prevented a shipper from removing skins from Liberty Dressing for shipment to Canada. Liberty Dressing claimed the skins had become infested with worms as a result. Gordon C. Blake of the Cutters union used the disarray to suggest that all workers in Fulton County should be unified in one big independent union.

In mid-October Local 202 disaffiliated itself from the IFLWU and changed its name to the Independent Leather Workers Union (ILWU) in order to get a place on the NLRB election. The new union elected the same officers who had led Local 202. In an open letter, Ben Gold recommended that the membership instruct their officers to comply with the "Fascist" Taft-Hartley law and withdraw from the international union. He pledged "full moral and financial support" for the local union from the international.[78] This move necessitated another round of hearings and a further delay in an election to determine tannery worker representation. The United Leather Workers Union, AFL, objected to placing the new Independent Leather Workers Union on the ballot. The Tanners Association called the new union a "phony." The newspaper editorialized that the "so-called 'disaffiliation' comes too late to ring true."[79]

At the NLRB's informal hearing the issues appeared so involved that there was no "consent agreement" for an election, although the examiner said the NLRB would tentatively recognize the new Independent Union, over the objection of the Tannery Association's counsel, Lydon Maider. There was no agreement on who should be able to vote if the NLRB were to call an election. A formal hearing had to be scheduled, and the record (Case No. 3-RC-50) would go to a five-man NLRB board in Washington for a decision on whether to order an election.

The formal hearing did not get under way until the end of October. At the hearing, Maider protested that one of his witnesses had been "threatened with personal violence last night." Union attorney Harry Pozefsky replied that both sides had been threatened and that Carr "has received threats of everything from murder to mayhem." Maider tried to establish if there was a relationship between the local and the international and whether the local fronted for the international. He was able to show that officers from the international—including Woolis—had been in the local offices almost daily since the "disaffiliation." Maider revealed that the union was in debt to the international and Carr finally admitted that the debt totalled nearly $5,000.

It was becoming obvious that no workers would return to their jobs before the end of the year. The strike had gone on so long that Carr arranged for carloads of coal be delivered to the strikers, fuel donated by the Furriers Union. The International Fur and Leather Workers Union contributed $8,000 to the ILWU that had replaced Local 202.

A letter to the editor (signed "Hard Times") claimed that 41 tanners outside the county were preparing bids to tan glove leather. It claimed that English doeskin was being shipped to the county and that because of currency devaluation its price had dropped 30 percent. Furthermore, fabrics were fast replacing leather for gloves so fewer skins would have to be tanned locally. By this time, fabric gloves represented 70 percent of all retail glove sales.[80]

In spite of all that had happened in the last few months, Carr asserted that the mills would operate "only when we have a wage increase and have a signed contract with our union, not one dictated to us by the NLRB." The union was as resolute as ever, condemning the strike-busting efforts of company unions and the "vicious, greedy, and ruthless efforts" of the Tanners Association.[81]

On November 24 the NLRB ruled that an election would be held for the approximately 900 tannery workers within 30 days and that the ILWU would *not* be on the ballot.[82] The Independent's disaffiliation was called a "matter of form rather than of substance."[83] George Meyer, president of the Tanners Association, said they had known all along that the union was "a wolf in sheep's clothing." Workers would have a choice between "no union" and the AFL, but the International Textile Workers Union of America—a "right-wing" CIO union with a local in Amsterdam—began circulating petitions that it be placed on the ballot. That union had to scramble to get on the ballot because the NLRB designated December 9 for the election, and just days before the election it was certified for the ballot.[84]

The newspaper looked forward to "a day when ballots will supplant baloney." Its editorial was vicious in its descriptions of Carr, Charles Hildreth, and James Martin (Carr's son-in-law), describing their "demonic and snarling manner, [their role as] higher paid stooges of Ben Gold's union who hang around the Glove Cities because they love to prey on distressed communities." It accused union leaders of using such phrases as "Hitler-like" and "fascist" when they described the tannery owners. The local paper had stirred sentiments enough that it appears that public opinion did not favor the union. Certainly local businesses did not, nor did the local governments.

The ballot day finally arrived, but the cities' hoped-for resolution did not. In a move that stunned everyone, the members voted *no*. Because the independent tannery workers did not vote for affiliation with either a right-wing CIO union or the AFL union, the stalemate continued. At the membership meeting, the vote had been 493 for "no union," 180 for CIO affiliation, 144 for AFL. That left the industry without an NLRB certified bargaining agent for a period of one year, after which another election could be held.

Carr asked the tanners to resume negotiations with his union and also for the intervention of the United States Conciliation Service and the withdrawal of the New York Mediation Bureau. The tanners voted "not to deal with any Communist union, no matter what it is called."[85] According to Lydon Maider, some of the tanners were weak financially, so the members "created a pool of money to keep the weak ones afloat."[86]

Gordon Blake, president of the Cutters and Shavers Union, revealed that before the election Carr had offered to combine his Independent Leataher Workers Union with the Cutters and Shavers, but the latter turned the offer down.[87] The NALGM said that half the glove shops in the county were running short of leather or had exhausted their supplies.

Representatives of the International Textile Workers Union, CIO, decided to "completely withdraw" from the local labor scene after being repudiated by the leather workers. They left town after closing the union's Gloversville office.[88]

Nationally the split within the CIO grew wider. Six unions accused of being Communist-influenced were dropped from the parent union for non-payment of dues. These "left-wing" groups included the longshoremen, public workers, and food, tobacco, and agriculture workers.

By the end of December, newspapers announced the formation of a new union—Upstate Leather Workers Union—led by Elwood Baker, a nephew of tanner Fred C. Rulison. Carr's group lost no time in taking out an ad that charged that the union was the creation of the Tanners Association and an effort at strikebreaking, their "last desperate trick." Upstate signed a contract with one tannery and Baker's Meco (a neighborhood of Gloversville) home was stoned and windows broken. The list of violent incidences was growing: the tires of the secretary-treasurer of Peerless Tanning had been slashed and the wife of a city patrolman, possibly mistaken for the wife of a striker, was slugged.

The *Morning Herald*, which held to the tradition of almost never putting local news on the front page, placed an editorial on that page alongside national news. The piece championed the efforts of the new Upstate union to sign with the Tanners Association and suggested that Carr, Hildreth, and Martin should bow out of the picture.[89] Upstate was able to sign with two small tanneries, Cleary Tanning and Knowles & Frank, giving their workers a $.20 an hour raise.

Two days later, someone smashed a large plate-glass window in the West Eighth Avenue lunchroom used by the Independent Leather Workers Union to distribute food to members. Carr tried to get the mayors to defer collection of strikers' taxes or to agree not to have them evicted if their taxes were unpaid, pending the end of the strike/lockout.

In a vain attempt to find a way to end the dispute, the ILWU appointed a new negotiating committee and asked the tanners to meet with the committee, led by Arch Hine. A citizens' committee "organized itself" to try to settle the six-month-old labor dispute.

During the strike, the county's situation had become desperate. Unemployment escalated: out of a population of 9,000 working people, 7,000 were jobless, and of those 1,328 had exhausted their unemployment benefits.

Tanners also suffered. Two owners of the Teetz-McKay Tannery sold their interest to the third partner, Marshall D. McKay. McKay broke with the Tanners Association, signed with the ILWU, and announced plans to reopen the tannery. The settlement called for "the largest hourly increase in 16 years of collective bargaining in Fulton County"[90] and was slightly higher than the settlements won by Upstate. The greatest pay raises were for the lower paid workers.

George Meyer, head of the Tanners Association and of Liberty Dressing, called that tannery's workers to a meeting to discuss returning to work. A majority of the workers voted not to enter the mill, although fourteen did meet with Meyer. The other members of the Tanners Association decided to deal directly with their employees in an attempt to reopen the mills. While the county was speculating on the date the 17 still-striking tanneries might reopen, Carr declared that his union men would not act as strikebreakers. The union men voted to reject any proposal that would eliminate or destroy the ILWU.

The tanners announced January 25 as "O-day" when the tanneries would reopen. The ILWU countered with a $500,000 suit for breach of contract, charging that the association "agreed in writing at the time the dispute began that they would not attempt to reopen their mills until a settlement of differences had been reached provided the union would agree to remove from the perishable state skins then being processed."[91] On the 25th, many pickets—but only 51 workers—showed up at the tanneries. The news story on Janurary 26 was big enough to make the front page again. The tanners were confident that workers would gradually return to their jobs, but Fred Rulison signed with Upstate. Rulison's workers attempted to return on January 27 and Johnstown's police chief was slightly injured trying to prevent picketers at Rulison's from rolling over a car full of returning workers. A front page picture showed how picketers at Geisler & Lehr had overturned a car. Several men were arrested for this incident and one was quickly sentenced to a 30-day jail term. Two men tied up the night watchman at the Loewenstein leather factory but failed in their attempt to steal the company's payroll.

The records of the Common Council of the City of Gloversville imply an anti-union bent. The mayor declared "A man has a right to enter into business and to conduct that business without undue dictation from pressure groups in the community." While protesting that law enforcement was the council's only concern, his statement continued, "Violence has been used in an attempt to intimidate free men and to overthrow the peace and security of the community."[92]

At this time, labor strife was rampant across the country. The escalating strike of John L. Lewis's coal workers and President Truman's possible intervention managed to push the tannery strike from the front page for a few days.

With few workers showing up, the tanneries were virtually shut again. The owners contacted all their employees telling them that if they did not return their jobs would be considered vacant and given to someone else. Only three dozen more men showed up before the tanners' deadline.

Carr was fighting furiously to prevent other tanners from signing with any but his union. Pickets appeared at F. Rulison & Son and Wood & Hyde. Owners of ten of the thirteen tanneries still on strike informed the mayor of Gloversville that they would hold the city liable for any damage to their tanneries when they reopened. They were trying to force the city to police the strikers and protect strikebreakers. The county sheriff responded by hiring extra deputies.

By February 2 Fred Rulison announced that his tannery was back at full production. Napatan and Independent Leather Co. were approaching that level as workers slowly came back. The Tanners Association extended their deadline for the men to return to work. This only made matters worse: a confrontation developed between 200 picketers, augmented by 25 women sympathizers, and 70 policemen at Independent Leather Co., but that company's workers were able to enter the plant without injury.[93] However, two men were arrested for creating a disturbance at Karg tannery as workers began to return there.

Three out-of-town members of the Fur and Leather Workers Union and five members of the Independent Union met with Johnstown's mayor to ask that deputies be withdrawn. They claimed that these temporary law enforcers were causing the violence. The mayor replied that the deputies would be withdrawn only when the picket lines were reduced.

"Bomb Exploded on Fred Rulison Porch" was the headline on the front page of the February 4 *Morning Herald*. Rulison's lovely First Avenue home had been built by glove manufacturer George Place in 1904. No one was hurt and the porch was only slightly damaged by the homemade bomb, which police believed was "meant merely to frighten."[94]

The independent union, its numbers dwindling, met and voted to offer a reward for the arrest of the bomber. Of the 250 men present at the meeting, half were from outside the county, representing many different union councils. ILFWU president Ben Gold was not present, but his assistant promised enough financial support to prevent "starving of any."[95]

At Independent Leather Co. another three dozen men reported for work, and police had to use "tear gas to quell a melee" there. Police lines, formed to repel pickets and let workers through, were jostled and "a flurry of fisticuffs and club-swinging" ensued.[96] At Karg Brothers the next day three deputies and a returning worker were struck by lead pipes allegedly wielded by two pickets. A scuffle ensued; police again used tear gas. One of the women sympathizers claimed she was attacked by police. Cold, snow, then rain quieted the picket line for the next few days, but the work force climbed to over 400 in mid-February.

The Independent Leather Workers Union placed an ad in the local papers charging that the tanners were driving the cities into bankruptcy, that the tanners were employing scabs and strikebreakers in an attempt to smash the union. The union mounted large contingents of picketers to march on different tanneries, starting with Karg Brothers on February 17. A pipe was hurled through a window of the homes of two of the men who had returned to work. With the encouragement of management, 92 workers at Karg's attached their names to a February 21 advertisement proclaiming they had returned to work, "contrary to the statements of Clarence Carr that there are only a few of us."[97]

Bradt Tanning was not a member of the Tanners Association. Its workers formed a new union, Local 1712 United Tannery Workers, of the right-wing CIO. As tannery workers returned to work, they petitioned the international union for representation. Gradually, in the early days of March, they were joined by workers at Independent Leather Co., Filmer's, and Karg's. Karg Brothers became the first to formally recognize the new union as a bargaining agent. By March 20 eight tanners from the association and one non-association firm also recognized the new union.[98]

On March 8, 90 workers at Independent Leather Co. left their jobs to challenge union picketers. The number of men returned to work was more than 550. By March 9, when workers from Reliable and Geisler & Lehr voted to join Local 1712, its membership had swollen to over 450. With the March 10 addition of Twin City Leather's workers, the new union now had members in ten of the county's tanneries.

By law—Taft-Hartley—no new election to choose a representative union could be held for a year, but the tanners decided to recognize Local 1712 in each shop where a majority of workers had signed up with that new union. Although Taft-Hartley prohibited a closed shop, Local 1712 was to be a union shop with check-off privileges.

Carr appealed to CIO president Philip Murray to remove the right-wing leaders from the Fulton County tannery scene. The CIO, which was gradually replacing its left-led unions with right-wing organizations, denied Carr's appeal. The wage increases the new local was asking—an average of $.20 an hour—were more than Carr was able to gain. In April workers from two more tanneries joined local 1712, bringing the total to thirteen.

The tanners balked at Local 1712's wage requests, however. In May the head of the new union, John J. Maurillo, charged the tanners were not bargaining in good faith. In April, five weeks after the talks between the tanners and the new union broke down, Maurillo said, "It seems that while Communism may have been the alibi during the past nine months, they had other reasons besides. . . . The employers were taking advantage of what they believe to be the defeat and demoralization of the workers."[99]

This account, prepared almost entirely from newspaper accounts, differs significantly from a description of the nine-month struggle written by Martin Fishbein in *The Leather Workers of Fulton County.*[100] Carr, writing in 1972 summed up the denouement of the strike: "All the hard-won gains of years of struggle were wiped out. Wage cuts, speed-up, and job discrimination became the order of the day. Any worker daring to protest was promptly fired with the approval of the union."[101] Philip S. Foner in his history *The Fur and Leather Workers Union* wrote the strike's epitaph: "Whatever the final outcome, the struggle of the heroic tannery workers of Gloversville and their leaders will forever remain an epic in the history of American labor."[102]

It is difficult to imagine an industry and a locale in which two major strikes could have been called at such inopportune times—the cutters in 1914 bucking competition and then war and the tannery workers in 1949 facing another depression, a real decline in the glove industry, and the crest of the national wave of red-baiting. The tanners not only had the Taft-Hartley provisions to help them, but they benefited from the anti-Communist climate that gripped the country. The tanners had tolerated Carr's leadership of the union for eighteen years. This makes plausible the charge that they were only using the red scare as an excuse to break the union.

From the perspective of 50 years, it is easy to see how the tannery owners could succeed in ousting the union. What is difficult to understand is the incredible difficulty they had in doing that. It may be easy also to understand men like Carr and Woolis who really believed in socialist solutions to labor problems. It is hard to fathom the depth of support from the rank and file of the county's union members. It is also difficult to reconcile the strengths of such a charismatic leader with the shortsightedness that made Carr so completely misjudge the national scene and anti-Communist sentiments.[103]

In 1954 Benjamin Gold was convicted of perjury for saying that in 1950 he was not a Communist. The NLRB moved to disqualify the International Fur and Leather Workers Union, of which Gold was president.

Carr died in 1974, and Bernard J. Woolis gave the eulogy at his funeral in Gloversville. "For years, Clarence was elected President of the Union over and over again by the leather workers, who admired the rugged honesty and devotion of their rank-and-file leader."[104]

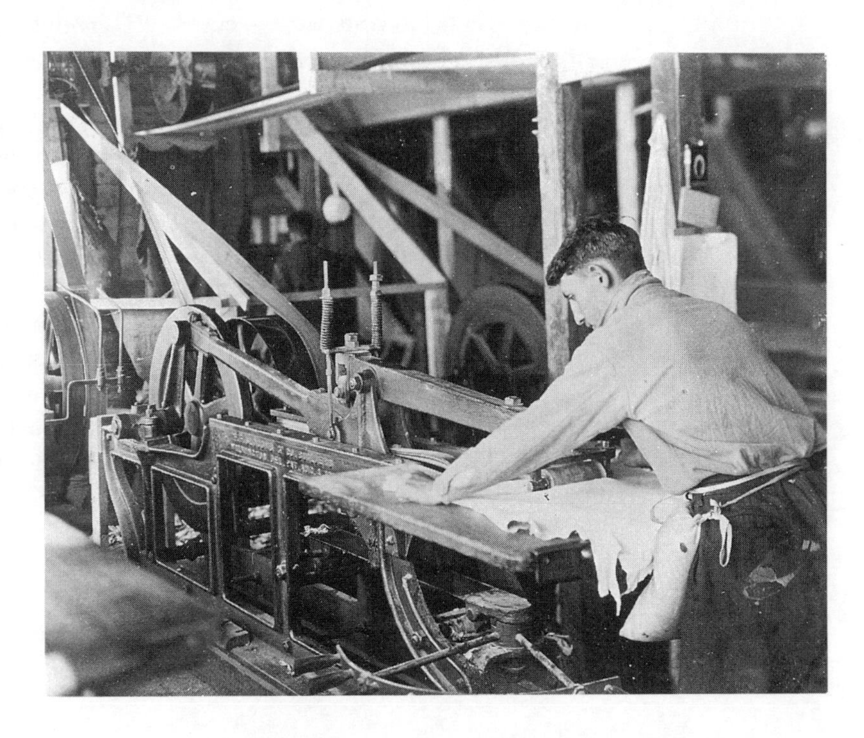

Using the infamous Slocum Staker
Johnstown Historical Society

The End of the Forties

The leather-glove industry was suffering; its decline and near-demise now seemed inevitable. In 1949, depression, the tannery workers' strike, and tariff concerns meant there was scarcely one positive headline concerning the industry in the local papers all year. To make matters worse for the glovemen, a federal grand jury in Utica began to look into all phases of the glove business, presumably to learn if any antitrust laws had been violated. After six months, the grand jury, which heard testimony from 65 county industrial leaders concluded its study without issuing a single indictment.[105]

Just as the tanneries were getting back to work, the glove unions opened negotiations for the 1950 contracts. The manufacturers asked the unions to consider eliminating the 15 percent cost-of-living adjustment in the current contract and placing a freeze on fringe-benefit increases.[106] The manufacturers' case was strong: business conditions were poor; there was widespread unemployment—78 percent of the work force of 9,000; and 76 glove businesses had folded between 1946 and 1950.[107]

After the strike, 5,615 remained unemployed in the county, as many out of work as in 1939. Unemployment remained high in the next few years, which led many to believe that the strike had done permanent damage to the local economy.

Then, like a bolt out of the blue, in the summer of 1950, the U. S. Attorney General filed a complaint against 28 local glove manufacturers charging violations in the antitrust laws. Casey was named as well. The government sought to enjoin the manufacturers and the two glove associations (NALGM and AKNGMM) from "combining and conspiring to stabilize the selling prices of gloves."[108] These charges hung over the manufacturers for three years, until November 1953 when seventeen firms associated with the NALGM agreed "to halt alleged restraints of trade."[109] Nine knit-glove manufacturers did the same, with both groups stating that to defend the charges would be too costly and time-consuming. Neither group had to admit wrongdoing.[110]

The defendants were accused of "agreeing on prices, terms, and conditions of glove sales; exchanging information on production; and circulating a blacklist of jobbers and retailers refusing to accept uniform terms and conditions of sales." The Justice Department stated that it had started the action in order to "restore competitive conditions" in the glove industry.

Association members had never discussed prices and production in formal meetings, but the social hours offered many opportunities for informal agreements. Most of the manufacturers belonged to one of each cities' premier clubs: the Eccentric Club in Gloversville and the Colonial Club in Johnstown. Both were male bastions dating to the turn of the century. Women came for dances and special events, never for the businessmen's lunches at which there must have been talk of the local industry. Because lunches at the Eccentric Club were communal, it was no place to discuss business with out-of-town customers. Almost every Johnstown gloveman had lunch at the Colonial Club at least once a week and some every day.

At the time of the settlement, newspaper reports stated that NALGM members accounted for 90 percent of the country's annual production of nineteen million pairs of leather gloves, valued at $47 million or $309.6 million in today's dollars. Ninety percent of the knitted gloves (15 million pairs, worth $17 million or $112 million in today's dollars) were produced by members of the Association of Knit Glove Manufacturers. County manufacturers named were Acme, Gates-Mills, Glovecraft, Daniel Hays, Hilts-Willard, Imperial, and Speare glove corporations and Ireland Brothers, Boyce-Lazarus, and Superb glove companies. Louis Meyers and Fownes with corporate headquarters in New York and J. Rubin, a New York City partnership, were also named along with two companies from Chicago and three from Wisconsin. Local knit-glove manufacturers included Gloversville Knitting, Scotsmoor, Sternwild Knitting Mills, and Leon F. Swears.

It is instructive to see how from all this turmoil one firm could rise and expand. The company's success appears to be due to the owner's willingness to move away from the county and exploit opportunities elsewhere. The firm may well have been the first of the county's shops to make the necessary moves—moves that in the next 40 years all but two or three others would either follow or perish. It was prophetic that the company was owned by the man whose voice in calling for higher tariffs for gloves had been the loudest and clearest. The man was Jules Higier.

Superb Glove Co. had started as a partnership owned by brothers Jules and Daniel Higier. The company moved to Johnstown in 1926 and was incorporated in 1940. Both men were active with the NALGM, Daniel heading up that group's tariff committee for years and serving a term as its president.

The two men founded and incorporated Crescendoe Gloves in 1945 to make fabric gloves. In a short time that company developed a superior cloth fabric for gloves and an advertising program that continually expanded sales. In 1948 the Higiers built a factory in St. Johnsbury, Vermont, where 300 women sewed Crescendoe gloves.

They also employed some 4,000 women to hand-sew gloves in Puerto Rico sending leather from Fulton County to the island to be sewn into gloves for Superb. Because of the Higiers' part ownership of Karg Brothers tannery, theirs was one of the last strong vertical operations in Fulton County.

Daniel Higier died in 1949, but Jules kept expanding the business. Crescendoe's success in fabric gloves allowed the factory to operate year-round in Fulton County, and by 1950 forced the concern to look for larger quarters. From producing grey fabric gloves, Crescendoe quickly swept the fashion market with unbelievably bright colors, and all the company's styles had musical names such as Overture, Allegro, Symphony. Jules' son Ross remembers how a musical dictionary was consulted every time the company planned to introduce a new line of gloves.

Jules Higier ran a very tight glove shop. He was the first gloveman in the county to use computers. In the late fifties, he installed a Sperry-Rand Univac computer in his factory to process his business accounts.

In its search for larger quarters, Crescendoe-Superb was wooed by southern states, but decided to remain in Fulton County, purchasing the 75,000-square-foot former Adams Mill. However, the renovated plant, which would produce a small quantity of gloves, would serve primarily as the home office and distribution center for gloves made in Vermont and Puerto Rico. This prototype of a home office and distribution center in the county with work done elsewhere is now typical of the majority of the county's surviving firms. Jules Higier, who championed higher tariffs until his death, was one of the first to expand manufacturing beyond the county.

As part of the ongoing tariff hearings a Department of Labor study analyzed Fulton County's underlying problems. The report emphasized the long-range decline in the wearing of leather gloves and consumer preference for fabric gloves. It minimized the effects of tariffs on the decline. The report summarized the past decade, which included the so-called boom years of the war, with appalling statistics. The Glove Cities, as one-industry towns, experienced a one-third decline in the number of employees covered by unemployment insurance in the years between 1941 and 1949. In the same period, manufacturing decreased by an even greater percentage, with the greatest decline in leather products.

Between December 1949 and May 1950, 1,800 people exhausted their unemployment entitlements. Between 25 and 30 percent of workers in the leather-glove industry were not employed full-time in the spring of 1950. Labor contracts called for work to be shared. Workers were employed for one, two, or three days a week, or for short hours, or for alternate weeks.

In 1940 Gloversville had 23,300 residents and Johnstown, 10,700. Fifty-four percent of the workers in these two cities were employed in the glove industry. The cities had not grown in 20 years.

Elections to choose a union for the tannery workers were scheduled for September 1950. Filmer Leather Co. and Johnstown Leather signed with Local 1712, the latter with the first contract in the entire leather industry in which the company paid the costs of insurance while the union held the policy and chose the insurance company. In a NLRB-supervised election, 600 workers in ten tanneries voted for the union, a final resolution to more than a year's turmoil. The left-wing union was dead. A last attempt to bring unfair labor practices charges against the Tanners Association and 18 tanneries was dismissed in April 1951.[111] Carr seemed to have disappeared from the scene.[112]

Fulton County Museum

Hindsight is wonderful, but it does not offer answers to the mysteries of this seminal decade. Did the militancy of the leather union inspire the glove unions to ask for ever greater wages? Was it true that keeping some tariffs on gloves only deferred the inevitable? If there was so much new industry, why were all the glove shops housed in the tired old factories built decades before? Was the fact that glove manufacturers were resigned to being importers a sign that they knew local industry was doomed? Were the only optimists returning servicemen who had worked in the mills and whose war experience inspired them to become entrepreneurs?

Would it have made any difference if the glovemen had combined into a handful of larger firms, big enough to modernize and improve productivity? Could this have leveled the playing field, or restrained competition without going against the antitrust laws? If a few had been individually stronger would this have strengthened the industry in general? Would an industry concentrated in a few large manufacturers have obviated the need for the NALGM? The fundamental question arises: Could larger firms deal effectively with such a handcraft industry, especially in an area whose residents were as independent as those in Fulton County?

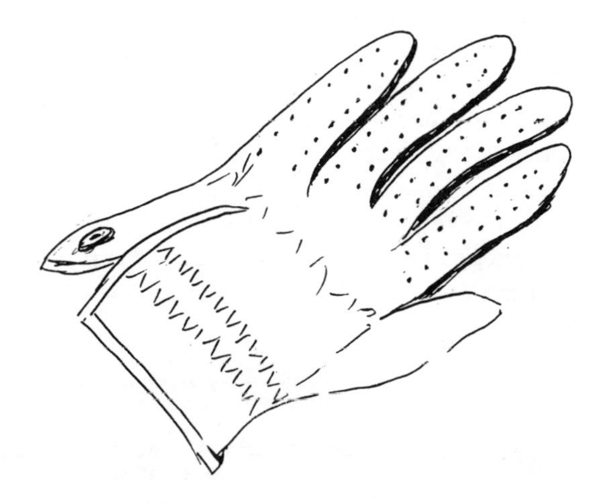

The Decline Accelerates

As a former manufacturer in a labor-intensive industry (knitted gloves) now virtually defunct here, I point out that the greater "efficiency" of foreign makers consists mainly of much cheaper labor rates—as low as one-fifth of American rates. When only a few small industries were hurt, who cared? Now that the pinch becomes apparent in the bigger ones, Congress is listening.

What is a fair share of the American market? All?
Edward F. Vonderahe[1]

Postwar exuberance, confidence, and savings had induced a number of new entrepreneurs to establish glove shops immediately after the war. These were not modern, up-to-date shops; most were small, almost cottage industries in the tradition of the past century. The post-World War II spike in the number of glove shops in Fulton County was all over by the beginning of the second half of the twentieth century. It was so short-lived that few of the startups survived long enough to participate in mergers. They simply disappeared.[1]

All the reasons for the decline that occurred in the glove industry in the second half of the twentieth century had been established before the end of World War II; no impetus was needed to further shrink the industry. After the first sharp decline about 1950, the number of glove shops remained fairly stable for the decade. In the sixties, the decline became precipitous before levelling off at the end of the decade. Through the end of the 1990s, the drop in the number of shops, big and small, was constant but more gradual, until manufacturing in the county all but disappeared. However, all through the decline a few new shops continued to appear, though these too, with one or two exceptions, soon closed.

The decline in manufacturing paralleled that of all the Mohawk Valley towns and was no worse than what happened in Schenectady, Amsterdam, Little Falls, or Utica. In 1952 the valley was the most heavily industrialized area in the state, with 47 percent of its workers engaged in manufacturing.[2] The decline was so great that today many cities have actually lost population: Utica's loss, for instance, has been far worse than that of Fulton County.

Nationally, the decades of the fifties and sixties saw "the rise of a new phenomenon: an affluent working class. Real gross national product expanded by $350 billion; real weekly earnings for production workers leapt 70 percent."[3] The basic wage rates of production workers in major industries "rose by 45 percent in the later forties, another 56 percent in the fifties, an additional 44 percent in the sixties. Even with substantial inflation, the growth of real earnings was a remarkable 41 percent."[4]

Sixty percent of all American families were now members of the middle class. There was little chance that workers in a craft industry that could not be industrialized and that faced stiff competition from abroad could join that leap into the postwar middle class. Furthermore, Fulton County's workers historically had received high wages compared with other glove and leather workers throughout the country. And, given the relatively low cost of living, the substantial housing stock, and the fact that two-family incomes had given the county's glove and leather workers cars, telephones, and the wherewithal to send their children to college, the county's workers felt they had already joined the middle class. Now it was a question of keeping up with the rest of the country, which was passing them by. The craft jobs offered by the glove and leather industry would soon relegate the county's workers to a lower economic status.

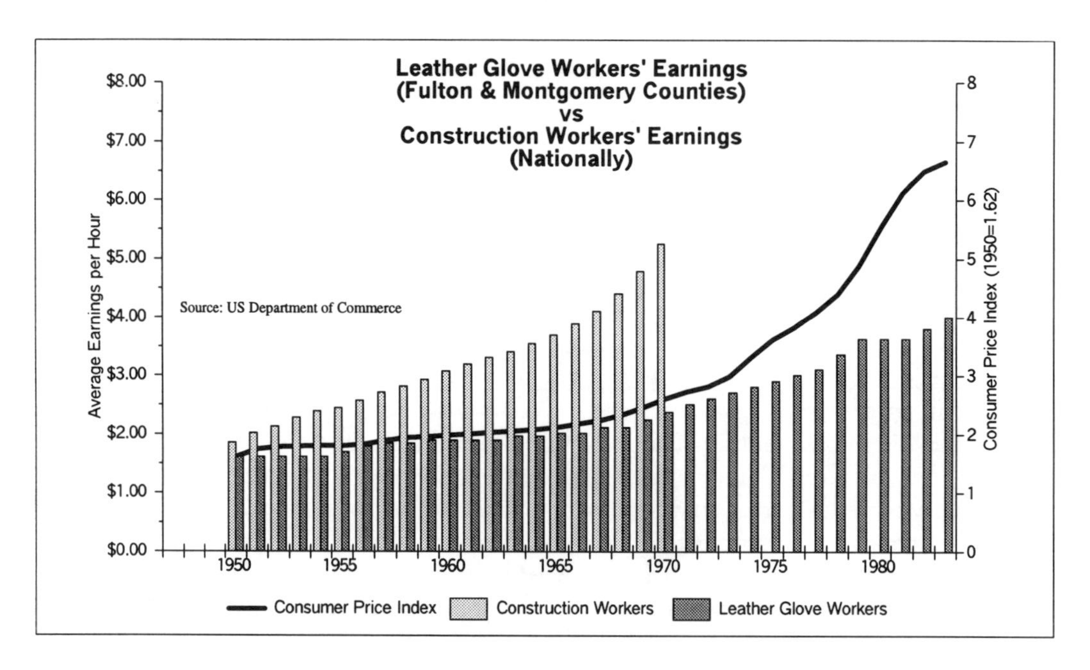

The chart indicates the growing disparity between the wages in the glove industry and in the building trades. By the late 1990s the difference accounted for the county's economic decline. One of the most competent clicker cutters left in the industry enjoys full employment because his employer gambles on future sales just to provide work for him for the entire year. The cutter is considered a valuable asset because his work is so good. But, he does not earn much over $13.00 an hour, although his wages are still calculated on piece-work rates.[5] Is there another industry in the country in which such a highly skilled worker is paid so little?

Glove manufacturers, on the other hand, could not hope to compete globally using the county work force. Sustaining themselves in the 1930s by increasing their imports of gloves and beginning to send jobs offshore, manufacturers sought out new sources of skilled, low-cost workers. Events of the next few decades disclose a parade of manufacturers establishing partnerships or building factories, first in Puerto Rico, then in the Philippines, Japan, India, Indonesia, and finally China. Only a few diehards continued to make gloves in Fulton County. Their attempts are analyzed at the end of this chapter. However, even Joseph Conroy, who, of the survivors, held out the longest against moving overseas and who is the only large-scale manufacturer still making gloves in the county, now contracts 85 percent of his gloves overseas. Conroy began importing gloves and ski gloves from Japan in the 1960s.

In 1950 Fulton County still produced 90 percent of all men's leather dress gloves made in the United States.[6] This figure had not varied much over the years.[7] What changed and increased inexorably was the amount of fine leather dress gloves sold in America that were produced overseas.

By the end of the 1950s, it was obvious that tariffs would never again protect county workers. The United States had become a part of a global economy and one of the most important supporters of free trade. This would not change. Duties and tariffs became so low that local manufacturers were able to generate profits in the gloves they imported. However, as importing became more complex and required larger amounts of capital, there has been a gradual attrition among county glovers who imported gloves. The big firms, Gates-Mills and Grandoe for instance, got bigger and one of the biggest, Aris, attracted a corporate takeover by a conglomerate.

After World War II, local unions kept up the barrage of strikes and negotiations to raise wages and benefits. Nationally, securing workers' benefits became a major part of all contract negotiations. Before the fifties, union-derived benefits played a minor role in the lives of the vast majority of industrial workers. In Fulton County, the unions finally began to join together and ultimately form one union which was able to secure benefits that included pensions and hospitalization, but the rates won were low, the conditions onerous, and the results not generally appreciated by those who continued to work under union contracts. Although union workers won benefits such as health insurance, a retirement plan and pensions for Fulton County's glove workers did not become effective until 1971.

Nationally, labor relations relied more and more on arbitration and collective bargaining. This dependence stemmed from the no-strike laws imposed during World War II and efforts of the National War Labor Board and the National Labor Relations Board. With improved grievance procedures and arbitration, many unions in the fifties and sixties were reluctant to go on strike. In contrast, glove workers in Fulton County staged numerous strikes against individual companies in those decades and general strikes in 1955, 1963, and 1965. The unions engaged in protracted negotiations for almost every contract.

The resurgence of the Republican party, heralded by the election of General Dwight Eisenhower, and the deaths of the leaders of both the AFL and CIO (William Green and Philip Murray respectively) made 1952 a pivotal year in the evolution of the country's unions. The old order of the thirties and that decade's labor militancy gave way to a new social concern within unions. This in turn led to a merger of the AFL and CIO in 1955. Perhaps it was the example of this merger that finally inspired the county's unions to join together and ultimately to affiliate with a national union.

Organized labor's successes in Fulton County only came about as the glove unions were inevitably shrinking as employment in the industry declined. Residents who have lived through the local downswing are content to blame the unions and their demands, but the unions were not the root cause of the county's decline—they may not have even hastened it. They were doing no more than defending the rights of workers in the same way as unions in every other industry in the country.

Nationally, unions were involved in the civil-rights movement and the protection of the rights of minority workers, especially women. With no growth in its immigrant class and an existing viable female working class, these struggles bypassed the county.

Job analysis as a basis for wage structures became important nationally in the 1950s. Attempts at job analysis had crept into the glove industry's schedule negotiations in the forties, but made little headway in the county. Arcane arguments over piece rates consumed an enormous amount of time and left many workers feeling they were cheated. For instance, layers-off thought cutters' rates exceeded theirs. The incredible variety of tasks performed by makers made it difficult to assess the schedules as a whole. Even within the unions, workers argued over increases in the ever-more complex piece work schedules, which even the unions felt were becoming unfair.

Gloversville and Johnstown were never large producers of leather in the context of our national output, they were only large in the realm of glove-leather manufacturing. Now that has changed. The biggest tanneries, like Karg Brothers and G. Levor, have closed. No longer was it possible to import significant quantities of capeskins or the skins of goats and hair sheep from Africa. The countries that produce these animals have stopped exporting raw skins in order to provide jobs in their own initial tanning operations. It is not unusual for a gloveman in Johnstown to contract for the sale of a large quantity of gloves, to order skins from Nigeria, ship them to a factory in India, then bring the finished gloves to America.

Mills here dye and finish splits of cowhides that have been tanned in South America. And, since the early 1980s, many of the remaining tanners have returned to dressing deerskins. The leather industry here has come full circle, while the glove industry has spiraled off to third-world countries, looking for ever-cheaper labor.

The ethnic makeup of both communities stabilized in the years following World War II. Not only were there no more waves of immigrants, but the populations of both cities began to decline. The Italians had made up the largest group of immigrants in Gloversville before the war, but soon the second generation was assimilated and educated, and many left. The number of Italians who became manufacturers is significant: the Papa, Crocetta, Perrone, Martorelli, and Perrella families all had more than one entrepreneur; Humbert Salluzzo, Vincent Sanges, J. Pagano, and James Castiglione also had glove shops. Some of the other Italian glove shops were smaller and a few lasted but a short time: the Balzano, Ambrosino, Licardo, Mosconi, Persico, Pisano & Rossi, Principe, Scarella, Tibaldi, and Vecera & Sweet shops fall into this category. Sam Greco's new (1996) glove shop is one of the county's few survivors.

Churches reflect ethnicity

In Johnstown, people of Italian heritage began to outnumber the Slovaks. And, a curious thing continues given the small size of the city: For years three Roman Catholic churches have served the twentieth century's three principal immigrant communities: St. Patrick's was built in 1869 primarily for the Irish community. The Slovak community erected St. Anthony's in 1915. The growing Italian community built the Church of the Immaculate Conception in 1925. Their start dates reflect the periods of immigration. Only St. Patrick's maintained a school.

In Gloversville, St. Mary's was built on Pine Street in 1871 and had many immigrant members, especially the Irish. In 1891 the congregation of that church moved to a new church on Fremont Street. The older church became St. Francis de Sales and served the German community. Our Lady of Mt. Carmel was built by the Italian community in 1922. All three churches had parochial schools.

A fourth Roman Catholic Church, Sacred Heart, was built in 1921 on northern Kingsboro Avenue to serve the expanding city; it survives. St. Mary's merged with Our Lady of Mt. Carmel to form the only other surviving Catholic church in Gloversville.

The Fifties—Expansion Overseas

Fulton County's glove industry in the fifties is characterized by unemployment, decline, the move to produce gloves offshore, and the futile attempts by the community, workers, and manufacturers to deal with events they barely understood. In 1950 the county produced 1,139,000 dozen pairs of leather dress gloves and 5,332,000 dozen pairs of fabric gloves. (Census records do not indicate how many of these gloves were sewn off-shore and how many were produced wholly in Fulton County.) The local work force was declining as 1,550 people from the county found work at General Electric in Schenectady. Aris Gloves discontinued making gloves at its Gloversville plant, although work continued at its fabric-glove plant in Fonda. The firm, headquartered in New York City, continued to import gloves.

In January 1950 5,125 Fulton County workers were unemployed. The decline in work for table cutters alone was so marked that they sought a contract to permit them to work as block cutters for the first time. This needed the agreement of 75 percent of the block cutters and twice block cutters failed to vote that majority. Finally, in February 1951, block cutters granted table cutters the right to do the work. The acceptance of this measure illustrates much more than the depth of unemployment: it indicates that the waning art of table cutting was doomed.

By midsummer 1950, employment levels rose slightly, but only because the country was again at war. The Korean conflict began at the end of June 1950, and for the fourth time, a war came to the rescue of the local economy. Eight Gloversville and five Johnstown firms shared a $2 million government contract in early 1951.[8]

As government contracts for the Korean War brought increased work for leather glove manufacturers, Gates-Mills, Pitman Glove Co., and Mario Papa received the biggest contracts. Most contracts specified deerskins, and the tanners did not have enough for all the orders pouring in. In December they asked the state to reopen the deer season to harvest more deer, but sportsmen shot that idea down. Tanners experimented with cowhides, which had formerly been used for work gloves. The National Production Authority claimed all deerskins and horsehides for the armed services.

With 60 percent of the industry's leather glove production dedicated to the military by March 1951, NALGM executive director Jim Casey worried about the county's ability to meet domestic production needs. Since the beginning of the Korean War, the military had purchased $34 million worth of leather gloves (not all in Fulton County). Suddenly the manufacturers were "begging for employees."[9] But at the same time, the unemployment picture in the county continued to be so high in early 1952 that Senators Herbert H. Lehman and Irving M. Ives and Representative Bernard W. Kearney petitioned the Department of Labor to have Fulton County listed as a federal critical area. This resulted in a federal labor department hearing, an investigation by the New York State Department of Labor, and a contingent of local leaders, mayors, and members of the chambers of commerce traveling to Washington.

Before the end of March, the county was certified as "a surplus labor area" eligible for federal glove-contract aid.[10] This permitted local manufacturers to enter into negotiated bidding on more than a million pairs of gloves.[11]

Milestones in the glove industry

1950

Joseph P. Conroy incorporated at $100,000.

1951

Daytona Glove Corp. bought the building formerly occupied by Aris, Inc.

1952

Alexette Bacmo Glove Corp. was formed by consolidation of Alexette and Bacmo-Postman Glove Corp.[2]

1953

Bankruptcy of Broadalbin Mills, Inc. for $420,000. Through Reconstruction Finance Corporation, the government attempted to continue a knitting business at the company's factory in the village.[3]

Buscarlet Glove Co., founded in 1940, suspended operations at the end of 1953 because of a scarcity of top-grade glove leather.

1954

The Van Buren & Co. glove firm of Mayfield closed after 59 years in business.

Daniel Hays Co. reelected James W. Green, Jr. president and made plans to celebrate that firm's centennial.

Acme Glove Company, in business for a quarter century, merged with Daniel Hays Co. Acme was established in 1930 by John DeGrand. He previously had been bookkeeper for Gloversville Auto Glove Co. His father had immigrated from Belgium and worked as a tanner in Gloversville.

George C. Potter died at age 89. He had headed the firm he established with William C. Hutchens in 1889 through 1948.

1955

Elmer Little & Son, Inc. bought the former H. & P. Glove factory in Johnstown. Jules Garfall, deerskin sportswear manufacturer, took over the Elmer Little building.

1956

Edward and Robert Perrone announced the construction of a new glove factory for their company, Westbrook Glove Co., at Berkshire, the area on the extension of East Fulton Street, Gloversville, near the proposed arterial highway.[4]

1957

Jacob Lazarus, co-founder of Boyce-Lazarus in 1916, died at age 73. He was born in Russia and came to America around 1897.

Chase Glove Co. was dissolved. Founded by Nathan M. Chase in 1919, it became N. M. Chase & Son when Raymond J. Chase entered the business. N. M. Chase was active in the business until his death in 1941.

Caleb Walrath, president of the Fulton County Paper Box Co., died at age 64. He co-founded the company in 1923.

1958

Lawrence P. Mills, co-founder with Henry C. Gates of Gates-Mills in 1912, died at age 68.

Ireland Bros. closed after 84 years.

Harry E. Hilts of Hilts-Willard died at age 83.

Clemans J. Bachner died, age 66. He had been in the glove business for 45 years and in 1923 had founded C. J. Bachner & Sons, which employed upwards of 60 people in the forties.

Daniel Hays Glove Co. ceased its fabric-glove line, selling its trademark "Finger Free" to Van Raalte Glove Co. That line had been developed twenty years before by Merry Hull under a patent that expired in 1958.

W. Nelson Wilkins, president of Wilkins Glove Co., Inc. of Mayfield and former head of NALGM, died at age 54.

The state labor department reported that the "glove industry was in the doldrums."[12]

Unemployment continued to rise through 1953. By the end of that year, Gloversville's Common Council was debating what could be done to stem the slowdown in the glove industry.[13]

Although the national economy, and even that in the Mohawk Valley, improved during 1955, the county still had over 1,500 drawing unemployment insurance at the end of that year. The county was in the incongruous situation of having a surplus of jobs, but a shortage of trained and competent workers.[14] And even though business was strong, many of the larger glove manufacturers continued to operate on a stagger system.[15] The unions broke with their tradition of seniority just as they had during the Depression, allowing all to share in the available work.

Until the 1950s, waves of immigrants had provided more glove workers than there was available work, except during the fall rush. The contradictory condition of too few trained workers and high levels of unemployment began in the 1950s and continued for the next two decades. The aging work force, decline in immigration, high wages demanded by trained workers, and efforts by manufacturers to keep labor costs down all contributed to produce this anomalous situation.

Orders in early 1956 fell off considerably; Jim Casey thought the drop was caused by higher prices. That year, when the National Census Bureau reported a sharp decline in employment and value of shipments in the leather-glove industry between 1947 and 1954, Casey challenged the data on the grounds that the census data was skewed—that 1947 was a peak year and 1954 was not a good year. It is amazing that Casey's rose-colored glasses even tried to tint statistics. Employment dropped between those years from 6,482 to 3,251 and the value of shipments after deduction of costs declined from $17,958,000 to $9,759,000. No matter which years were used, the trends were obvious, and Casey seems to have abandoned any sense of realism in an effort to preserve his optimistic views on the future of glove-making in the county.

At the end of 1957 one-third of the county's cutters had been laid off and the rest were working parttime, while imports climbed. Local glove manufacturing in 1957 was 25 percent below that of the previous year. The tannery business for 1957 was also below the year before. Jim Casey's year-end prediction for 1958 was, for the first time, pessimistic.

In 1957 the local paper ran a series of articles on the need to diversify industry in Fulton County. One segment summarized the loss of glove factories, tanneries, and jobs in these industries. It quoted the 1954 New York Department of Commerce study that concluded that "the economic welfare of the county exists primarily because of 'welfare aid, unemployment benefits, and out-of-town employment.' "[16] The county's welfare payments ranked ninth in the state. General Electric, which employed over 2,000 workers from the county and Amsterdam, was starting to cut back its presence in Schenectady and this too increased local unemployment.

A second article in the series quoted a study made by the State Teachers College at Albany that added a new twist to the county's poor employment record. In addition to observing that homeworkers worked when and if they wanted and table cutters earned what they wanted in a few hours and then went home, the study concluded that glove workers were now abusing the unemployment system by "taking jobs just to be laid off and get unemployment insurance."[17] The article reiterated the extent of aging among glove workers. Unions were castigated for barring assembly-line production.

The county received over $2.7 million in unemployment insurance in the first nine months of 1958. The unemployment level in Gloversville in 1958 reached 22 percent, while the state level was only 8.5 percent and nearby Utica's rate was 12 percent. As bad as the figures are for 1958, at the beginning of the following year 5,137 were unemployed in the county. This caused union leader Mrs. Florence Roberts to state that "the glove industry in Fulton County has come to the very last phase of its erosion.

Even though unemployment reached such high levels, the number of graduating high school students going on to institutions of higher education (this included technical and vocational schools) had climbed from around 20 percent in 1935 to 45 percent 20 years later.

The tariff victory at Torquay in 1951 was a brief success and had relatively little effect on local manufacturing. Two and a half times more women's gloves were imported from France in 1951 than in 1950.[18] Local manufacturers claimed that the French government's established exchange rate amounted to subsidizing the industry.

Local glove manufacturers voted to petition the U. S. Tariff Commission to restore the tariff on gloves to the level of 1930, taking advantage of the escape clause written in the General Agreement of Trade and Tariffs (GATT) because of "injury to the domestic industry.[19]

The Republican shift away from protectionism had little effect on the county's political bent. Throughout the decade of the fifties until the present time, the county has remained Republican. Democrats made inroads in city elections, but allegiance to the GOP, born in the tariff struggles of the late nineteenth century, continued even as Republicans espoused free trade. Registered Republicans had always outnumbered Democrats: 4.4 to one in 1929, 5.2 to one in 1932, 4.3 to one in 1952, the ratio dropped in 1957, but only to 3.5 to one.[20]

In 1955, the Organization for Trade Cooperation (OTC) became the permanent secretariat for GATT. Protectionists were afraid that the country could lose sovereignty through the OTC. Others charged that the country was handing over to foreign governments the power to set U. S. tariffs.[21] Hence the county was not alone in its struggle against lower tariffs.

At the beginning of 1955, 25 textile groups joined the fight against reciprocal trade legislation. With "unprecedented unity," country-wide press coverage, and Congressional help, the battle moved to Washington where some of those pleading for tariff relief claimed that government offices were treating them poorly.[22] Casey and Harry Moss, representing the knit-glove industry, added to the testimony. Moss claimed that in two years eight of 30 knit-glove manufacturers had gone out of business and employment had dropped from 4,000 to 1,500. Speaking for the American Knit Glove Association, he lobbied against lower tariffs through 1955. The threat of higher tariffs was so great that Japan considered imposing export quotas on its manufacturers of knit gloves. As United States domestic production continued to decline, Hong Kong, with its even lower wages, began to challenge Japan's export business.

The county responded with alarm to President Eisenhower's call for powers to further lower tariffs. Abandoned even by Republicans, the county's position became increasingly precarious. The county estimated that the 1954 imports of about 95,000 dozen pairs of foreign-made gloves represented a loss

1959

The Darby Glove Co. factory in Northville, formerly owned by Walker LaRowe Glove Co., burned.

Alexette-Bacmo Corp., the largest glove manufacturer in the county, became the Grandoe Corp.

Ellery G. Willard, owner of Hilts-Willard Corp. died in a car accident, age 76.

Joseph Schwed died at age 81. He came from Poland in 1891 and was one of the Jewish immigrants from the Pale who became a glove manufacturer, establishing Schwed Glove Co. around 1924.

Superb Glove Co. consolidated with Crescendoe Glove Co.

Harry A. Moss resigned as executive secretary of the American Knit Glove Association.

to table cutters alone of about $400,000 in wages. Gloversville remained one of New York State's two critical areas with respect to unemployment. Despite many protests, the government announced plans to lower tariffs by 15 percent over a three-year period. Partly as a result of local protests, both leather and fabric gloves were omitted from the 1955 list of goods on which tariffs would be reduced.

In May 1958 the National Planning Association, a private-sector organization that studies economic policies in order to influence public policies, compiled statistics to show "that the fine table-cut division employs only 325 table cutters, many above the retirement age and all on part-time employment; that the fine dress glove is practically all imported from foreign countries, and that the elimination of such a small industry from the national manufacturing picture would have no serious economic consequences when placed upon the block of international trade agreements."[23] William F. Wessendorf, Jr. wrote a letter to the editor of the local paper, protesting those findings; he nevertheless concluded that "the future of the Fulton County glove industry was doomed."[24]

It is also true that many countries were circumventing tariff agreements. Japan used the exception for horsehide work gloves, which had a very low tariff, to produce "pony-hide" dress gloves with the same low tariff. The tariff situation, "not good" according to Jules Higier, cast a pall over the 1958 NALGM's spring convention.

In 1952, because so many workers were unemployed or employed in other industries, a panel was assembled to discuss what was wrong with the county's leather glove industry. In a forum at the Jewish Community Center, speakers offered five solutions for the county's ills: newer ideas, better production methods, unionization of workers outside the county area, production of gloves that are in demand, and higher tariffs. Although in hindsight these recommendations would not have solved the county's ills, they were logical responses.

The county did make one significant response to the loss of business. In 1952 it formed the Fulton County Development Corporation to bring new industry to the area and assist existing industries. By 1954 the group had attracted three new industries employing 500 workers by 1954.

In 1953 a representative of the Tanners Council of America castigated the glovemen for not "pitching merchandise toward women's way of thinking, for not producing and promoting products of quality." Leonard Rossi, editor of *Leather and Shoes*, noted that the production of leather gloves was half that of 25 years earlier, despite a population increase of 35 million in that time.[25] Cotton and other fabric gloves were replacing leather, and glovemen were urged to improve merchandising to stem the trend.

A publicity campaign mounted by the NALGM in 1954 generated little euphoria; within a month a panel of citizens, which included a local minister and the guidance director of the Gloversville Schools, charged that glove manufacturers were not doing enough to promote glove sales. One speaker noted that while the cost of cars and homes had doubled, wages in the glove industry had only increased by 20 percent. Casey defended the manufacturers and noted that "too much stress is placed on the present condition of the industry and its results, rather than on the causes." But instead of talking about the causes and possible solutions, he justified the manufacturers' actions by listing all the positive things they had done.[26]

Grandoe Emerges

Jacob Zuckerwar

The fifties saw the emergence of the Grandoe Corporation as the single entity that dominated production in the county. In 1952 Alexette Bacmo Glove Corp. was formed by consolidation of Alexette (maker of women's gloves) and Bacmo-Postman Glove Corp. (men's gloves).[27] Jacob Zuckerwar, president of Alexette since 1921 and of Bacmo-Postman since 1935, became chairman of the board and his son Richard C. became president of the new corporation. Grandoe Gloves Inc., named for a soft sueded-cotton fabric, was the family's fabric glove division. In 1959 the name Grandoe was given to the entire corporation.

Leo Louis, Bud Ross, and George Madnick rounded out the list of the company's top management. Then as now, relatives were prominent in the company: Ross was a son-in-law. Only George Madnick, plant superintendent, was not; his parents had come from a very poor town in Poland to run a meat market in Gloversville.

Grandoe stands out because it continued to expand in the county into the sixties, as other companies declined. For all the shrewdness the company displayed in these expansions, it was not among the first to begin the exodus of companies sending work out of the country, primarily to Puerto Rico.

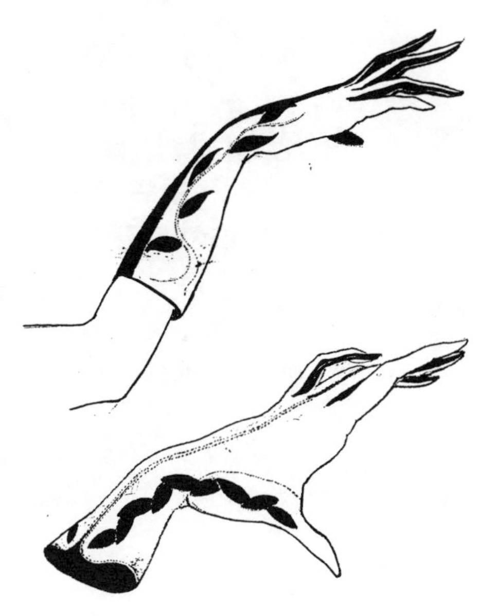

Designs by Anthony Sorrento

The larger companies all hired designers, though one designer said that many glove firms copied styles from competitors. Anthony Pastore, Sr. came to Gloversville from Naples when he was seventeen. He had trained as a cutter, but he was a natural artist and learned to design gloves. He became a principal designer for Grandoe and was the mentor for his son-in-law, Anthony Sorrento, who also designed gloves for Grandoe. Sorrento started work at Grandoe in 1944. His wife, Ann, learned to sew gloves at the Tibaldi factory, whose owner was her father's cousin. Ann's mother's family, the Procitas, immigrants from Italy, also had a small glove factory. Their experience is typical of the interconnected families from Italy who worked together.

Sorrento remembers never being out of work, even in bad times: "Richard Zuckerwar was good to his help." Sorrento had fond memories of being asked to drive him to the races during the Saratoga season. He received a modest pension, but "all in all they treated us right," well enough to afford a small condominium in Boca Raton.

Right: Two designs by Leo Newbower, who with his wife, Gerda, fled Austria after the Nazi takeover. He designed gloves for Grandoe for a decade and later worked for Jules Higier.

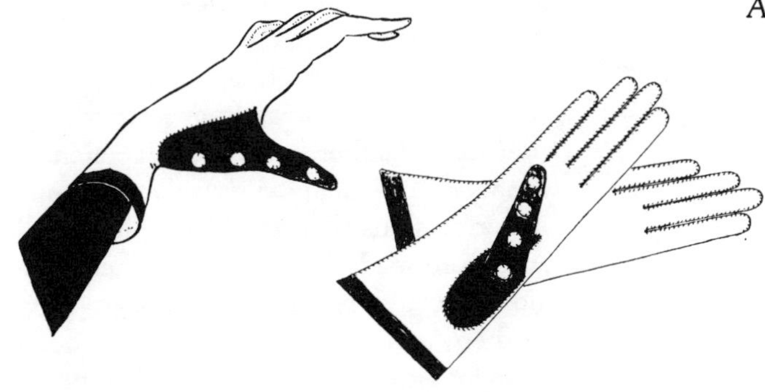

An article in *The New York Times* in February 1955 created an uproar by describing the way the county was divided over solutions to its slump. Author Murray Schumach stated that "progressive businessmen strongly favor any reasonable measure that will attract new industry.Their opponents are wary of experiments and distrustful of newcomers."[28] He pointed out that the population of the state had risen from 2.5 to 15 million in the previous two decades while Gloversville had grown only slightly and Johnstown not at all. "Business leaders both here and in Johnstown attribute conservatism to one factor. They say dominant members of some old and wealthy families are content to live on sizable inheritances and small returns on business investments here."[29] This observation undoubtedly had merit, however, its author failed to remember that those same businessmen provided whatever work there was. There is still no hard evidence that new business was kept out as many residents believe. The head of the Johnstown chamber of commerce in a letter to the editor was able to list the community's numerous economic improvements.

Fulton County glove manufacturers had for a long time sought new markets and tried to develop new products. Special gloves for various activities are such an important part of modern life that it is surprising to note that the first golf glove appeared around 1897. It was manufactured by the Heagle Glove Co., begun in 1866. After the death of founder George Heagle in 1927, the company was run by his daughter, Florence Heagle. Golf gloves, washable gloves, waterproof gloves, ski gloves, and baseball gloves supplemented traditional work gloves or long, embroidered ladies' gloves. Don Willard, of Hilts-Willard, developed the first short-fingered golf glove.[30]

The move to find new markets was especially strong after World War II and the subsequent decline of government contracts, but none of the innovations was enough to sustain the local industry. Glovemen sought new niches and innovative products that would outcompete other manufacturers. However, they had to share recognition for their one significant achievement in this period with local tanners. In early 1953 tanners joined glove manufacturers in establishing a research fund through the University of Cincinnati to develop washable leather for gloves. Research on many fronts followed: General Electric developed a silicone finish for garment leather, and in 1955 a new leather-cleaning solution was developed.[31] That year, the Cincinnati project announced a new washable leather, LaunderLeather. It required three years and $100,000 to accomplish this technical success. In 1955 a group representing eleven of the county's tanners set up the Washable Leather Research Corporation and moved the research facilities from Cincinnati to Gloversville in order to maintain quality standards for the new process.[32] Tanners withdrew their support from the Washable Leather Research Corp. in 1962, closing the operation primarily because its ten-year mission was complete.

Logo from the 1955 NAGM advertising campaign to market washable leather.

In 1953 Karg Brothers announced something that had the potential to reverse the trend away from leather gloves: it developed a tanning process that made leather both water-repellant and washable.[33] In fact, because of advances in chemistry, American tanners were producing leather from imported skins that was comparable to European tanned kidskins, allowing American-made ladies' gloves to compete with the French. But American glovers could not expand enough to take advantage of the new glace leathers, and 90 percent of local production was used for garments, leaving little for gloves. Wood & Hyde Leather Co. of Gloversville had become one of the largest garment-leather tanning companies in the world. The company produced a color film entitled "The Magic Touch of Leather," which won a first place at the International Film Festival in New York.

In 1966 association president Joseph Perrella used the example of golf gloves to show how manufacturers could find new sales niches. In the next few years, finding markets and seeking innovations helped sustain glove-making. In the mid-sixties, Joe Bachner, president of Bacson, purchased machinery to make a thermal lining fabric for gloves. "Thermoliners" would be used in ski, dress, work, hunting, and driving gloves.[34]

Joseph Perrella

Outwardly, the NALGM responded with unfounded optimism to every new sign of the industry's decline. It offered few solutions and by the end of the decade was actually becoming duplicitous in its actions and pronouncements.

At the beginning of the decade, with new government contracts and the tariff victory at Torquay, the manufacturers had something to celebrate at their 34th annual convention in 1951 and decided to reissue the trade manual *Glove Life*. Speakers noted that long gloves were currently more stylish than short.[35]

A firm, hired by the association, conducted a survey of women across the country. It showed women preferred leather gloves, but liked the wider color variety and washability of fabric gloves.

Seasonality still plagued the industry: by summer 1952 labor shortages were making it difficult to fill fall orders.[36] A shortage of all types of lined gloves developed that fall and optimism about the following year resurfaced. The fact that 1952 imports dropped 30 percent below the level of 1951 helped fuel that optimism. The 1953 NALGM spring meeting brought a caution from executive secretary Casey that "only the fit will survive."

In the perennial belief that promotion would solve the industry's ills, the leather glove manufacturers announced a bicentennial celebration for 1954. How the industry ever decided that 1754 was the beginning of the glove industry is a mystery, but a press release in the *Boston Globe* mentioned a "small wood tannery in the forest-wrapped hills of New York's Mohawk country."[37] It claimed Gloversville was built on the site of the original tannery and went on to confuse oak tanning with the dressing of skins. It falsely stated that the county's pioneering Scotch highlanders were all members of the famed Glovers' Guild of Scotland. The article completely garbled history in an attempt to create a myth worthy of an advertising campaign, which speaks to the county's desperation. Jim Casey began the celebrations by claiming that 1952 was the county's peak year for glove production. Irving R. Glass, of the Tanners Council of America, joined in the celebration that included movies, television, and a banquet.

That year the glove manufacturers' 37th annual spring meeting featured style and fashion, tariffs, and optimism. Nothing seemed to change, except the new president of the group was a Wisconsin manufacturer. Despite the reduction in tariffs, Casey's 1954 year-end outlook was upbeat with respect to leather gloves in the coming year.

The 1955 NALGM convention drew representatives of 175 firms[38] and Casey tried to stimulate confidence in the future (the recapturing of lost markets) with ideas on how to promote the new washable leather. A press and advertising campaign extolling the new leather appeared in numerous publications.

As the fall surge in glove-making began in 1955, Casey observed that the only things keeping the county from record-breaking production levels were a lack of experienced workers and the shortage of leather. The minimum wage of $1.00 an hour was to go into effect in March 1956, and manufacturers worried that the increase in the cost of a pair of gloves would range from $.20 to $.60 a pair.

The 39th convention in 1956 elected Douglas Hays of Ireland Bros. as the NALGM's new president. The programs featured a talk on the importance of handgear to the military and a call by Casey for the industry to meet the price challenge of exports from countries with lower wage structures through competitive prices and fashions.

The association's 40th convention, Casey's twentieth, brought remarks about vital challenges and another dose of Casey's optimism, this time for the industry's ability to retain markets.[39] A month later, the group announced "the most gigantic undertaking in its history"—the inauguration of a glove-shipping service with overnight delivery to New York City.[40] Actually, economical glove distribution was becoming a problem, as Dominic Papa testified at a small business conference in Washington. He proposed a registration for salesmen who might take on new, small lines as one way to deal with competition from low-cost imports.[41]

By the end of the decade it was obvious that the local glove industry was shrinking. Even with relatively calm contract negotiations, the association decided to shorten its spring 1959 convention and eliminate the traditional dance and golf tournament.[42] This was no time for fun.

The NAGM spent the decade of the fifties fighting for tariffs and outwardly ignoring the way its members were moving overseas. Despite the fact that the association kept up the fight against free trade, a survey of its activities in the next 24 years shows that its members did little else of substance, beside engage in free trade. The notes summarizing the association's public image, the actions reported in the local papers, their press releases, the way people in the county came to know the manufacturers. There was another side, not publicized and difficult to discover, that shows local glovemen in a completely different light: the move overseas by county manufacturers.

While glove manufacturers cry out to state and federal officials for higher tariffs to block imports and protect local industry, one noted businessman disclosed that some manufacturers have plants in Hong Kong, the Philippines, and Japan, the same areas which are giving the glove industry a rough import problem.

The movement out of the country was led partly by conglomerates and larger companies, partly by a few of the county's traditional glove manufacturers, both large and small. In the forties and fifties, those concerns saw that labor shortages and increasing wages would inexorably depress local manufacturing.

Puerto Rico, which did not tax mainland companies that expanded there, had a growing cottage industry of women doing hand sewing and embroidery. Fulton County companies headed there first to take advantage of the tax breaks and low wages. With "Operation Bootstrap" the island grew increasingly attractive to numerous glove manufacturers.

When Ireland, Hilts-Willard, Gates-Mills, and later Grandoe established footholds in Puerto Rico, they sent cut gloves to the island to be sewn by hand. In the late 1940s, Gloria Dominech had a firm in Puerto Rico that employed thousands of hand sewers. She was an elegant lady, the wife of the mayor of Mayaguez. Grandoe in particular contracted with this firm, and the venture matured into a virtual partnership with Grandoe, with Dominech serving as local manager for Grandoe's contract work after 1952. Dominech's daughter, Celia, continued working with Grandoe. Celia and Joseph Morsheimer—who had married one of Schrecker's daughters (Schrecker was founder of the firm that became Grandoe)—established Grandoe's operation in Puerto Rico.[43]

Fownes was at one time the largest of the international companies with operations in Fulton County. This English firm, established in 1777, had expanded to America in 1887 in order to circumvent American tariffs. The company built a factory on South Main Street in Gloversville in 1908, and before World War I, the company had 60 to 75 cutters and 500 workers in all at that plant. The company's earnings began to shrink in 1947 and in 1960 it closed the Gloversville plant, putting 120 people out of work. Fownes moved its operations to Amsterdam, where it had a factory producing knit gloves.[44] In 1953, seven years before the closing of the Gloversville plant, the president of Fownes, Abe Sheer, traveled to Puerto Rico and bought Cayey Manufacturing Co., an existing glove company. The move halved the company's expenses for wages and overhead. Cayey was housed at first in an old tobacco warehouse, but Fownes quickly realized it needed a new factory. The Puerto Rico Industrial Development Co. built a factory for Fownes. The enterprise was named Rico Glove Co. and the factory produced fabric gloves that had been cut in the states. Around 1961, Fownes built a second Puerto Rican factory, Plata Gloves, which cut fabric gloves for both factories.

Also among the early pioneers in Puerto Rico was Roscoe R. Stanyon, Sr., who was born in England and came to Gloversville to train as a cutter at Jacob Adler Glove Co. He formed Imperial Glove Co. in 1919, and it became the largest manufacturer of pigskin gloves in the world. Around 1950, he started the RJD Corporation in Puerto Rico to manufacture leather gloves.

Hilts-Willard set up operations on the island in the 1940s and also employed Gloria Dominech's firm. The company later established a separate business there, Mohawk Products International.

By the end of the 1940s, all of the county's larger glove companies were importing gloves from the protectorate. Industry grew so fast that by 1956, Puerto Rico had attracted 350 businesses from the mainland and almost every Fulton County manufacturer of any size was sending work there. However, well before 1956 it became obvious that rising wages in Puerto Rico would soon change the economics of doing business on the island.

In only twelve years Puerto Rico's glove industry had grown so fast that it had as many employees as there were gloveworkers in Fulton County. The industry shifted from a cottage industry of handworkers to a "machine-sewn, highly modern and thoroughly integrated factory operation."[45] The industry's expansion owed much to the lower wage scales, but also to the absence of income taxes. "Some of the companies granted tax exemptions are wholly-owned subsidiaries of Johnstown and Gloversville factories."[46] While most factories received gloves cut in Fulton County, cutters were being trained on the island. Hilts-Willard sent Harwood Rowles to Puerto Rico in the early 1960s to teach islanders to cut gloves.

In 1957 the island's lower wages inspired the United Glove Workers to ask for a dollar an hour minimum wage for all machine operators on the island. Mrs. Florence Roberts, head of Fulton County's Operators Union, claimed that there were 10,000 factory and homeworkers in Puerto Rico and that its work force not only exceeded that of Fulton County but approached the level the county reached at its peak. The union believed that Puerto Rico's sewers were not only taking work from the county, but were actually destroying local industry.

In contrast, there is some uncertainty in determining who was first, who was bravest, in challenging the international scene to manufacture gloves in the Far East. Puerto Rico was a U. S. commonwealth; it was fairly close to the mainland; and it had close ties to America. Distance, unfamiliar cultures, and fear of the unknown discouraged many county manufacturers who had done business in Puerto Rico from going to Asia.[47] In any event, it was probably not a gloveman from Fulton County, but a Midwesterner who made the first move. Carl Ross, a manufacturer of dress gloves from Sheboygan, Wisconsin, went to the Philippines right after World War II.

Philippine production rose through the fifties; in 1958 it was almost five times that of 1956. Although the 12,371 dozen pairs of gloves exported was less than ten percent of domestic production, that country was poised for continued expansion.

Roscoe Stanyon

Roscoe Stanyon, Sr. was possibly the first county manufacturer to move to the Philippines. He established Crown Quality Glove Manufacturing Co. in Santa Rosa, a suburb of Manila, around 1953, only three years after he established a glove-manufacturing company in Puerto Rico. Later he built Batangas Manufacturing Co. in a more distant suburb where he and his wife lived for many years. The factory in Santa Rosa was a walled fortress with glass shards topping the thick masonry walls and towers at the four corners. There, Stanyon employed 500 to 600 workers.

In 1963 he formed the Sociedad Espagnold de Curtidos leather firm in Spain, one of the first fully-owned U. S. companies in that country. For all his expansion overseas, though, his company continued to produce gloves in the states. He acquired Crossley Glove Co. in Broadalbin, Serfis Glove Co. in Northville, and a small company in Lake Luzerne.

In the early 1980s, John Widdemer and his partner at the time, Jerry Wentworth, bought Stanyon's Batangas factory, naming it Berkshire Leather. After about eight years Widdemer sold his interests to Wentworth. Widdemer explained that the sale resulted from an inability to control inventory in the Philippines; in a one-year period $700,000 worth of inventory disappeared.

Aris Glove Company was also among the early firms to move to the Philippines. The company was originally a German firm. Adolph Steinberger started as an importer in New York City; in the early 1920s he bought a factory in Germany and took in his three sons, who had adopted the family name Stanton. The sons established Aris Gloves (Aris is an acronym of the first names of the three brothers, Arthur, Robert, and Irwin). To escape the problems faced by Jewish families in Germany in the 1930s, Aris bought Adam W. Klopot's glove factory on Phair Street in Gloversville and moved the firm there. The company also had a subsidiary, Buscarlet, which closed years ago. In the late 1950s, Aris sold its Gloversville plant and moved to the Philippines, and developed a larger operation than it ever had in Fulton County.

Elmer Little & Son moved to the Philippines shortly after Roscoe Stanyon. In 1954 William Dzierson was managing the company. (His wife was Elmer Little's daughter.) That year, Italian imports were putting so much pressure on Elmer Little's sales that Dzierson began shipping gloves cut in Fulton County to the Philippines where at first they were sewn by hand. This separation of tasks greatly reduced import duties since the value of the leather was exempt when gloves were cut in the United States.

Elmer Little

Such contract work enabled the Elmer Little Co. to experiment with production without a big investment. Then, in 1958, it acquired a factory, and Dzierson began to train cutters. He brought Tony Vincenzio, a Filipino, to Johnstown to learn cutting so he could teach his fellow countrymen. Dzierson spent about six months a year in the Philippines. He had sewing machines sent from Johnstown to the factory. In the 1960s, the company began using Japanese leather from Osaka tanneries for dress gloves. From these inexpensive leather splits, Dzierson worked with the Japanese to produce a cowhide leather that was as soft as sheepskin, and the company promoted the cowhide for gloves. By the early 1960s, most of Elmer Little's machine sewing was being done in the Philippines. Around 1965, the company acquired a larger factory and sent some clicker-cutter machines there, though power supplies continued to be a problem. Through the early 1970s the company was able to out-compete Gates-Mills and Fownes in their operations in the Philippines because Elmer Little used the lower-priced cowhides.

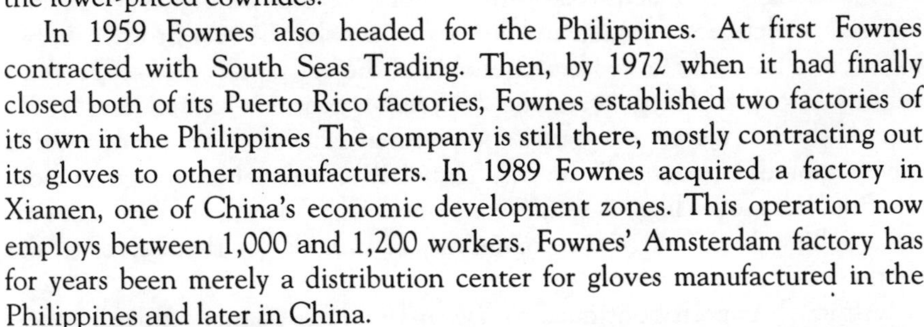

In 1959 Fownes also headed for the Philippines. At first Fownes contracted with South Seas Trading. Then, by 1972 when it had finally closed both of its Puerto Rico factories, Fownes established two factories of its own in the Philippines The company is still there, mostly contracting out its gloves to other manufacturers. In 1989 Fownes acquired a factory in Xiamen, one of China's economic development zones. This operation now employs between 1,000 and 1,200 workers. Fownes' Amsterdam factory has for years been merely a distribution center for gloves manufactured in the Philippines and later in China.

Jules Higier of Superb-Crescendoe did import Italian leather gloves and had knit gloves made in Hong Kong in the 1950s. However, his companies never expanded into to the Far East, mostly because neither he nor his son wanted to spend the necessary time there.

Manufacturing overseas was never easy. One local businessman said that when you form a partnership with a foreign enterprise to establish an overseas venture, "you really become a partner with the IRS." The IRS monitors the business very closely, determining how much profit is made overseas in order to establish whether profits are being sent overseas to keep them from being taxed in this country.

Not everyone went to the Philippines. Joe Perrella, with roots in Naples, sought out a partner there as did many European manufacturers. In 1958 Perrella contracted gloves from Antonio Gianella and later from Antonio's son Rocco. Perrella started small in Italy, then expanded there through the 1960s.

Perrella's business was divided equally between Italy and Fulton County; he had two factory sites in Gloversville and one in Northville, with a total of about 100 workers and many part-timers. Perrella appreciated the Neapolitans' fine soft leather and quality work, but by 1972 wages and costs in Naples were approaching the county's. Perrella gradually ceased contracting work in Italy and this led to his reducing his glove-making locally. Like many glovemen, Joe Perrella did cut gloves almost until his death.

Simultaneous with the transition from Puerto Rico to the Philippines or Italy, Fulton County glove manufacturers continued to protest the low tariffs on gloves. Casey and Moss objected to the 1957 proposal for a five-year extension of the tariff law. They joined the American Tariff League in requesting a study and a complete revision of tariff policies to one that would help other countries raise their standards of living, and their wages, thereby benefitting the county and its industry.[48]

Throughout the fifties, pressures from foreign imports continued to take their toll of county manufacturers. In late summer 1958, just at the time the glove business picked up as it did every year, Johnstown's premier and most fashionable leather-glove business closed its doors. Ireland Brothers had been making gloves for 84 years. The company reportedly had a peak business before World War II of $2.5 million a year. When it closed, its work force had shrunk from between 300 and 400 workers to one-tenth that number.[49]

The closing had much to do with the company's unwillingness to expand overseas, which seems strange in light of the fact that Ireland Brothers began to promote and sell gloves from Grenoble in the early years of the twentieth century. Douglas Hays, president of Ireland Brothers in its later years, apparently did not want to make the personal sacrifice such a move would have required. Undoubtedly he was financially comfortable enough to close the firm, but moves like his reinforced rumors that Johnstown manufacturers were pulling funds out of the community to provide for themselves to the detriment of their workers.

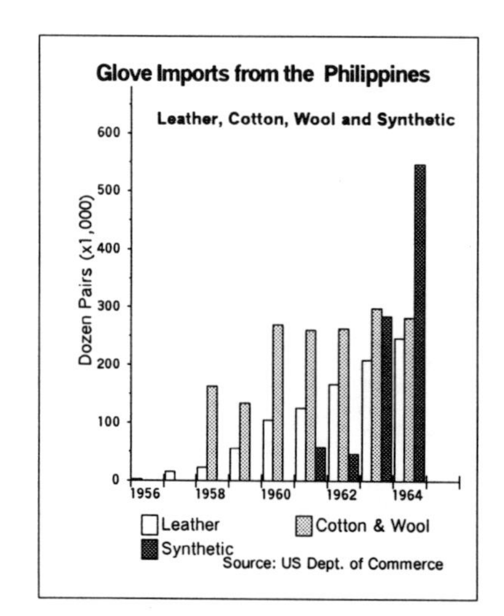

Although imports continued to rise in 1958, the county's glove business seemed to improve, though how much offshore production contributed to manufacturers' profits is not known. The county, too, seemed to be prospering economically in 1958, and unemployment was falling although it still remained very high. The tanning industry appeared to be looking up and a cold snap increased year-end glove sales. Despite all these positive signs, the future remained bleak. In his annual prediction (for 1959), Casey foresaw threats from increased imports and the devaluation of the franc.

For the first time, the manufacturers' duplicity was reported in the local newspaper. "While glove manufacturers cry out to state and federal officials for higher tariffs to block imports and protect local industry, one noted businessman disclosed that some manufacturers have plants in Hong Kong, the Philippines, and Japan, the same areas which are giving the glove industry a rough import problem."[50]

On top of an already bleak picture, the leather glove industry had to contend with the 1959 rise in the cost of skins worldwide. Russia joined the competition for skins and prices rose in every market from Ethiopia and the Sudan to Nigeria and Iran. Leather prices continued to increase through 1960.

In 1958 the manufacturers used the NALGM's spring convention as a forum for asking for a restoration of import duties through the application of "escape clause" relief. They formulated a request for the Federal Trade Commission to "promulgate rules and regulations to foster and promote the maintenance of fair, competitive conditions" in the industry.[51] Manufacturers based the request to apply the escape clause on the fact that Japan was producing 50 percent of all combined leather and fabric gloves, and they asked that the import of leather gloves be limited to 30 percent of the domestic market.[52] The request was accepted by the Tariff Commission, which scheduled a hearing. Again the entire community—glove manufacturers, tanners, union leaders, and local officials—filed briefs with the Special Senate Committee on Unemployment.[53] Casey and Clarence Hallenbeck, business agent for the joint board of the glove unions in the Amalgamated Clothing Workers of America (ACWA), AFL-CIO, took their case to the Tariff Commission, but were challenged by commissioner Schreiber, who took a dim view of "complaints against foreign dress glove competition by manufacturers who were themselves importing the same gloves."[54] Casey admitted that 75 percent of the county's manufacturers engaged in such importing. Commission chairman Joseph E. Talbot suggested that if these manufacturers just stopped importing, there would be more jobs. Hallenbeck replied that he thought it likely more glove shops would close if their owners could not send work overseas. Hallenbeck conceded that the manufacturers imported gloves to make money or to make ends meet, and he replied, "Yes," when the chairman asked, "Then part of the unemployment trouble is caused by plant owners?" Hallenbeck qualified his answer by protesting that the manufacturers had to do it to "maintain the work force they have now."[55]

(This statement proved prescient: It is ironic that in 1998, Joseph Conroy, the county's last substantial glove manufacturer, has to do exactly the same thing to maintain what is left of his work force.)

A French manufacturer told the Federal Trade Commission that if there were no imports and all the domestic leather cutters worked full time, they could produce only a small percentage more than they were at present, nowhere near enough to compensate for the loss of imports. The chamber of commerce added to the testimony statistics about the county in 1959: it was a terrible year in which county unemployment benefits amounted to five percent of the state's total and 800 workers ran out of benefits. In addition, local retail sales were dropping, numerous downtown stores were vacant, and an "atmosphere of doom emanated from the county."[56]

The Tariff Commission's rejection of the county's plea came in March 1960, with a report that noted domestic production of table-cut gloves had not declined much since 1954 (it had essentially disappeared by that time) and that manufacturers continued to make a profit. Senator Charles Keating and Congressman Sam Stratton blamed the rejection on the inadequacy of the escape clause and promised to introduce legislation to correct it.[57] Keating introduced such a bill and Senator Jacob Javits joined the opposition to the country's trade policies. Stratton entered a complaint in the *Congressional Record* stating that the Tariff Commission had failed to consider the unemployment situation in Fulton County.[58]

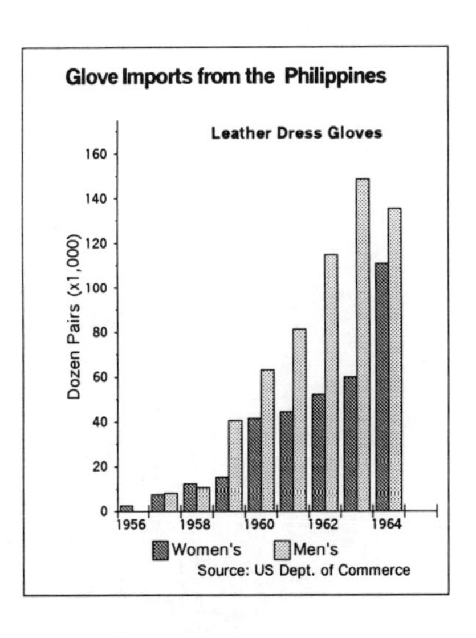

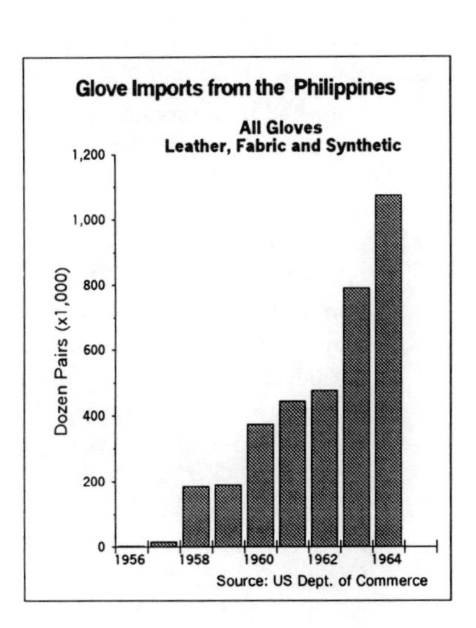

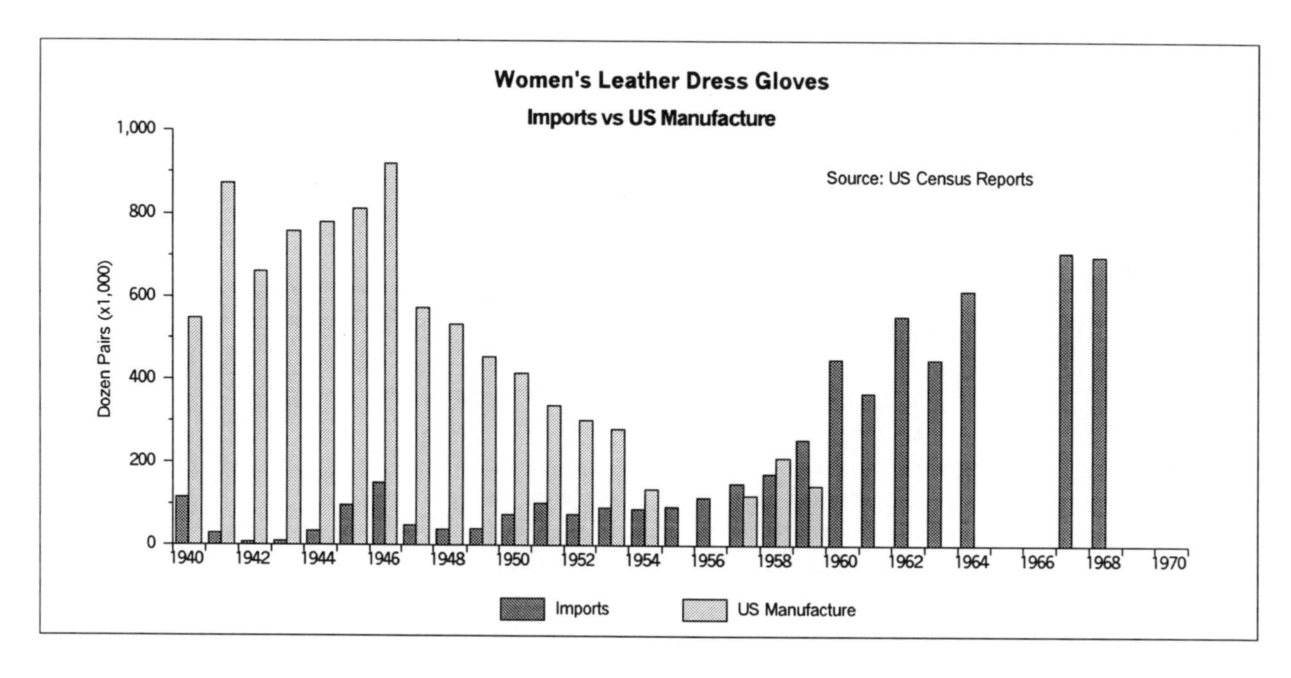

1960

Francis Sutton, owner with his brother, Milton, of Sutton Glove Co., died at age 61.

Bert S. Zimmer, owner of former W. N. Zimmer & Sons Glove Co., died at age 76. Bert S. took over the business in 1924 when his father died. Bert S. suffered a severe stroke in 1953 and the business was closed around 1957.

Joseph P. Conroy & Co. bought the former Superb Glove Co. building in Johnstown, May 1960. Conroy employed about 60 workers.

Joseph Perrone, who had liquidated his business in 1958, sold his factory to Alma Leather Co.

Illinois Glove Co. purchased the 107-year old Daniel Hays Co. of Gloversville, which for several years had been producing slippers, not gloves.

1961

Bela Albert Loose, owner of Triangle Glove Co., died at age 71. He was born in Hungary and worked as a glove cutter there until 1913 and in Gloversville. In 1929, with two partners, Herman Wille and P. Schnebel, he organized the Triangle Glove Co., which employed 16 workers in the forties. Wille had come to Gloversville in 1909 from Saxony where he had learned glovemaking.

The Sixties

Glove manufacturing in Fulton County in the sixties was little different from the 1950s. The decade saw county manufacturers continue to expand glove production in the Far East at the same time they continued to protest the country's move toward free trade. Unemployment was high, but the shortage of skilled workers became more acute. The biggest change from the previous decade was the growing shortage of skins, which, by the next decade, would completely change the county's tanning industry. Since the end of World War II, the style of gloves worn by women in America had changed from soft, tight-fitting, stylish gloves to utilitarian gloves or worse, no gloves at all. Jackie Kennedy made gloves fashionable again in the mid-sixties, but only for a short time.

An upward spiral in the cost of living in 1961 was accompanied by further increases in the price of leather and skins. Glove imports from Europe were rising again, this on top of a 34 percent increase in 1960.

Gloveman Joseph Perrella, speaking to the NALGM, gave an upbeat talk on the county's ability to compete with European gloves in quality and fashion. As 1961 ended, however, it became obvious that imports during the year might reach a 24-year peak.[59] Casey's year-end summary talked about the county's role in an international industry, but ventured little optimism and no solutions.[60]

Half the glove shops in business in 1960 would close or sell out to other manufacturers before the end of the decade. The demise between 1948 and 1950 of the huge number of postwar start-ups was an exceptional situation. The decline in the sixties was not—many of the shops that closed had been in business for a long time; 16 of them were major, well-established firms. Many closed because their owners simply did not want to do business overseas.

Those who did go overseas saw their business growth accelerate. Underscoring the incredible rate at which glove production had escalated in the Far East in the 1950s is a trip made by the association's executive director Jim Casey in spring 1961. Casey visited glove factories in Hong

Kong, China, the Philippines, and Japan on the way to a Rotary International convention in Tokyo. He returned in time to report his findings to the 44th annual association convention. He noted that both Hong Kong and Japan opposed U. S. import restrictions and that Japan was afraid of Hong Kong's growing glove industry, because Hong Kong's wage structure was even lower than Japan's.

Casey reported that graft and corruption appeared to be prevalent in the Philippines, and he described how manufacturers had barbed-wire fences around their factories and searched workers as they left the premises.[61] Parenthetically, it was at the convention where Casey described his trip that the association changed its name back to the National Association of Glove Manufacturers, recombining its concern with the two types of gloves, both of which were experiencing declines in domestic manufacturing.

1962

Edward F. Vonderahe succeeded Ralph O. Collins as president of Gloversville-Continental Mills. One of the founders of Gloversville Knitting in 1896 was Edward C. Collins, father of Ralph O. That company merged with Continental Mills of Philadelphia in 1960. Ralph O. Collins had been with the Gloversville firm since 1919 and became president on the death of Lucius N. Littauer in 1944.

In August 1963 more glove-making problems emerged in the Philippines: the U. S. put a quota on imports of cotton gloves and a dock strike tied up shipment of leather gloves. Faced with a loss of future orders, Philippine manufacturers resorted to chartering cargo planes to deliver gloves.[62] Expansion to the Philippines had many downsides, but county firms continued to set up businesses there through the sixties and into the seventies.

Forrest P. Gates

Gates-Mills had expanded in the county through the fifties, becoming the manufacturer and distributor of Mark Cross gloves in 1950 and purchasing the Artcraft Glove Co. of Johnson City, Tennessee, in 1955. A decade later the company bought the Daniel Hays Co., which had been owned by the Illinois Glove Co. between 1960 and 1965. In 1961 Gates-Mills added an annex and in 1966 a new shipping facility. All this expansion, while other county manufacturers were shrinking, was not enough to keep the company profitable, even as it became the specialist in men's gloves. According to William B. Gates, the company was losing out to European manufacturers who, because of their lower wages, could afford to pay more for finished skins and thus obtain the best grades. To remain competitive, Gates-Mills was faced with using cheap Iranian cape.

It was in this period of expansion that Gates-Mills went to the Philippines. The company started manufacturing there around 1967 and is still there. At first the company sorted leather in Fulton County and shipped it to a contractor in the Philippines. Starting in 1968, Chester Nessel traveled to the Far East many times to organize production for Gates-Mills' overseas operations. Nessel was the son of an immigrant from Austria who established a factory in Gloversville and became quite successful before the 1929 crash. Chester worked first for Gates-Mills as a salesman, later as a coordinator of the company's operations in the Philippines, then in Taiwan, and finally in Japan. For their Philippine operation in later years, Gates-Mills obtained Australian and New Zealand cowhides tanned in Japan.

Harold V. Pitman died at age 70. He operated the glove shop with his name from 1936 to 1960, when it was sold to Leon F. Swears, Inc.

The assets of the bankrupt Sheraton Glove Co. of Mayfield were sold at auction.

1963

Elmer E. Little, president of Elmer Little & Son Glove Co., died at age 68. The firm had been founded in 1893 by his father. The son began work at the factory in 1919 and became president in 1948 after his father's death.[5]

In 1961 Japan began exporting low-cost vinyl gloves that felt like leather. These inexpensive gloves sold out in 1962 and Japan planned to ship upwards of a million dozen pairs in 1963.[63] Casey used the word "optimism" in his 1962 year-end statement but noted the degree to which Japanese lined vinyl ladies' gloves had replaced the county's staple, lined leather gloves. These vinyl gloves were still creating problems for Casey at the end of 1963,

1963 continued

Louis Meyers & Son, Inc., approaching its hundredth year in business (founded in 1864), closed. Equipment, inventories, and gloves were sold at auction in June for $500,000. The firm had employed 200 workers.[6] Within a month of its closing, the company filed for bankruptcy, listing $2.8 million in liabilities, $1.4 million in assets. James F. Fox, president of the firm, was charged with a 302-count indictment for grand larceny, failure to pay full wages to employees, and conspiracy to commit both these crimes. The larceny involved theft of funds paid by employees to Blue Cross and Blue Shield. (In 1966, after Fox made restitution to the employees, charges were dismissed.)

Vincent Sanges died at age 75. He was born in Naples, Italy, and founded the firm with his name in 1935.

The Fabry Glove and Mitten Co. moved into a building formerly occupied by the Bohemian Bakery to increase the company's glovemaking capacity.

1964

Boyce-Lazarus bought the "Lucky 711" sporting goods division of Sanville Glove Co. to add golf gloves to its line.

Grandoe Corp. constructed a new 1-story addition to house automated shipping. County glovemen were surprised by the move because most firms, including Grandoe, were building factories overseas or switching to contract operations.

1965

Gelmart Knitting Mills, Inc. purchased Gloversville Knitting Co. of Schenectady and two related knitting mills.

Joseph Bove closed his glove shop, which had employed as many as 52 workers. Bove, a native of Naples, Italy, had been running the business for 24 years.

Crocetta Glove Co. ceased operations. Founded in 1919, the company employed 350 workers at its peak, less than 20 at the time it closed.

when it was estimated that Japan would ship 2.2 million dozen pairs in 1964. Japan's exports, when combined with Hong Kong's three million dozen pairs, would be more than stores could handle and would diminish sales of fabric gloves and leather-palmed wool gloves as well as domestically produced lined leather gloves.[64]

Foreign competition was hurting glove manufacturers in the Midwest as well as in the county. Eisendrath Glove Co. of Marinette, Wisconsin, closed in 1966, throwing over 300 out of work.[65] Four years later, Hansen Glove Co. of Milwaukee discontinued production of fabric and leather gloves.

Women's Wear Daily noted that by 1964 three factories had been built in Taiwan to produce knit gloves. Production costs were estimated to be 15 percent less than in Japan, 10 percent less than in Hong Kong.

Even though a few manufacturers had established operations or contracts in the Pacific rim, a considerable amount of gloves was still produced in Puerto Rico through the 1960s. Harry Pozefsky, attorney for the United Glove Workers, testified at a U. S. Department of Labor hearing in Puerto Rico that the minimum wage there should be raised to $1.25, a move opposed by county glove manufacturers. The union had tried many times to equalize wages between the island and the states, and it appears as if this latest attempt, in May 1965, might spur the glove industry's move away from the island to the Far East.[66]

Work in Puerto Rico was not seasonal as in the county. Gloveman John Widdemer speculates that this was because the cheaper manufacturing costs on the island encouraged county manufacturers to keep those factories running full time, while employing county workers only in peak times. In 1998, union leader Bill Towne told the author that he believed that the county always had more workers than it needed and that manufacturers encouraged the surplus to keep payroll costs low and be in a position to respond to the industry's seasonality. What happened in Puerto Rico seems to corroborate his conjecture.[67] However it is difficult to comprehend what caused the situation in which there were more workers than the county's manufacturers chose to employ full time at the same time they were claiming there was a shortage of workers. Was it because the shortage of skilled glove workers grew more pronounced in the sixties? What caused this strange dichotomy of declining jobs and a shortage of skilled workers? One has to conclude this was another result of inadequate pay and an aging work force.

The shortage of skilled glove workers grew more conspicuous after 1962 on top of an estimated 20 percent drop in available skilled workers in the five years before 1962.[68] The greatest need was for pique sewers, which required the highest level of skill. Instruction in pique sewing was added to the local school's glove-making curriculum, which was already attracting fewer students.[69] The expiration of the redevelopment act that provided federal funds to support glovemaking classes brought that program to an end in the spring of 1965. There would be fewer and fewer skilled glove workers in succeeding years. A surge of orders in the fall of 1963 was typical of the seasonality of the glove business, however, manufacturers actually failed to produce enough gloves to fill orders because of the shortage of skilled workers.[70]

The end of 1966 saw a rise in the county's jobless rate with nearly 2,700 out of work. Between 1958 and 1971 the county lost 2,000 jobs. The minimum wage was raised to $1.50 an hour at the beginning of 1967 at the same time leather prices were escalating. The few remaining manufacturers were being squeezed as never before. This combined with the rise in the rate of inflation at the end of the sixties accounted for the demise of a number of the glove firms.[71]

Throughout all this the National Association of Leather Glove Manufacturers did not change its point of view. At the spring 1960 NALGM convention, manufacturers did have one thing to cheer about: the glove industry was omitted from the list of commodities for which the government would consider making concessions at the upcoming GATT conference. But by the end of 1961 and into 1962, imports and quotas continued to focus the efforts of workers, glovemen, and local officials. Realizing that 1961 glove imports had hit an all-time high, Casey's year-end message had no words of hope.[72]

William H. Evans, head of the local chamber of commerce, took the county's plight to the U. S. Chamber's annual meeting and nearly succeeded in keeping that organization from supporting President Kennedy's free trade proposals.[73] Evans, who was also the new managing editor of the *Leader-Herald*, waged an exciting battle, and his attempts produced good copy, but no results. The import battle lasted all the way to the association's spring convention, which was attended by about half the number of glove firms of earlier decades.

In a 1962 debate entitled "Free Trade vs. Protectionism," Casey faced an economist who supported a world market and the total elimination of tariffs. Casey called his stance "utopian dreams" and said his support of a world common market was "so much bunk."[74] His year-end report was "apprehensive" about 1963.[75]

The Kennedy round of tariff negotiations (1967) considered giving most-favored nation status to Russia and Czechoslovakia, a step Casey thought might even drive France, Italy, and Germany—countries that already had that status[76]—out of the American market. Casey claimed the 1967 Geneva reductions would bring a sharp increase in the foreign share of the men's glove market. He also said that the foreign share of women's gloves had risen to "80 percent in the past three years."[77] His protests ignored the fact that the county's share of that market had always been about 20 percent.

In 1961 gloves accounted for almost a third of the $67 million worth of products the country imported annually. When the tariff cuts were announced, the tariffs on gloves were not reduced. Casey credited the fact that the glovemaking suffered the least of any industry to the constant fight waged by the county, the manufacturers, and unions. But, within a few months Casey was back in Washington asking the Tariff Commission to establish quotas for gloves.[78]

Through the 1960s, association meetings were remarkable for what they did not do. No discussions of the moves overseas were reported to the local papers.

Highlights of Association Activities

In 1962, for the first time there was talk of launching a membership drive. The association was still concerned with tariffs and the shortsightedness of retailers who place their orders so late in the season. The following year the convention focused on the emergence of mass retailing and the growth of large chain stores that would further complicate marketing gloves.

In 1966 a representative from IBM talked about the way computers could assist local manufacturers and how they would shortly be essential for data processing. With a few exceptions, most notably Jules Higier, local manufacturers entered the computer age rather late and very slowly.

1967

Adam W. Klopot died at age 97. He established the glove company that bears his name in 1901. That company employed 25 people in the forties. Later he was associated with Aris Glove Co. from which he had retired at the age of 86. A native of Vienna, Austria, he came to Gloversville in 1884.

The Alvord Glove Co. of Mayfield celebrated its 50th anniversary. The company, which had made gloves of many different skins, had switched to using only deerskins in 1953, a move that other county firms would follow.

1968

Consolidated Foods, Corp. a conglomerate from Chicago, acquired Aris Gloves, Inc., which reported sales of $7.6 million with a profit for the year ending April 1967 of $450,000,

Forrest P. Gates died at age 79. He had been associated with his father in the firm of Gates-Mills.

1969

Major independent manufacturers were Daniel C. Miller, Fred C. Miller, Vincent Sanges, R. J. Evans, Clair, Peter Rubin, West Brook, and Moderne glove companies, and G. Balzano & Sons, C. J. Bachner & Sons. (Daniel C. Miller—son of G. E. Miller a glove manufacturer for many years—established the glove company that bears his name in 1928. Frederick C. Miller, also a son of G. E. Miller, started the glove company under his name in 1921. It employed 75 workers in the forties.)

Wells-Lamont, Inc. of Chicago moved into a new building in Mayfield to begin manufacturing "Promark" gloves there. The modern factory was built with the help of the Fulton County Economic Development Corp.

Jacob Zuckerwar died at age 79. He was chairman of the board of Grandoe, president of J'Mar Glove Co. and of Bacmo Glove Corp.

The Seventies and Eighties

Highlights in the seventies

1970

John D. Widdemer, president of Hilts-Willard Glove Co. announced the company's headquarters were taking over the old Montgomery Ward building in Gloversville. He said the company's sales had grown from $200,000 to $3 million in the past eight years.[7] By the end of 1970, the company announced that it would stop making gloves locally.[8]

Grandoe, "the country's largest producer of men's and women's gloves," became a licensee of the Super Bowl.[9]

The Glove Fashion Council, funded by NAGM members, closed after only a year and a half of public relations on behalf of glove manufacturers.

Louis Reitzes died at age 79. He was born in Russia and came to Fulton County about 1900. He owned Mary's Glove Embroidery and the Supreme Glove Co.

1971

Henry Veghte, former Johnstown resident, sold the Killington Glove Co., a Rutland, Vermont firm that had been a subsidiary of Daniel Hays Co. until Veghte acquired it in 1953.

Wells Lamont Glove Co. in Mayfield closed and 70 workers lost their jobs. The company had moved to the new factory building with the help of the FCED Corp. only a year and a half earlier.

Snow caved in the roof of the LaRowe Co. factory in Northville.

Vincent Martorelli, who had operated Martorelli Brothers Co. with his brothers from 1916 to 1955, died at age 77. He was born in Naples, Italy, and came to America in 1913.

Fownes Bros. & Co., Inc. reported a sharp profit drop in 1971 with lower sales. Sales volume in 1970 was $10.3 million; in 1971 it was $8.48 million.

Inflation gripped the country in the early seventies. Local unemployment remained high as glove manufacturing continued its inexorable decline. The country's economic growth did nothing for glove workers.

Hilts-Willard's announcement in December of 1970 that it was no longer going to make gloves in Fulton County is a seminal event. At this time, Hilts-Willard had factories in Puerto Rico and controlling interests in firms in Europe and Japan. When it closed, the average age of the company's Gloversville employees was 65 years and their ages ranged up to 81 years. The actual closing was timed to the implementation date of the ACWU pension, April 1, 1971 (see pages 249-250).[79]

John Widdemer, president of the firm, said that the move was one of survival and that all the firms that did not expand overseas were doomed to fold. "We tried to train younger workers but couldn't get a quality product,"[80] he told the author in 1997.

Grandoe was among the last to start manufacturing in the Philippines. The company stayed as long as it could in Fulton County and Puerto Rico, but in 1977 built a factory in the Philippines that is now closed. Grandoe had one factory in Manila and another in Batangas, the same location as the Stanyon and the Willard factories. It hired about 75 cutters, of whom 25 were clicker cutters and the rest table cutters, "every bit as skilled as those in Fulton County."[81]

When wages of workers in the Philippines rose to $12 a day, many manufacturers began moving on to different countries in the Far East. The Philippines had been attractive because most people spoke English and glovemen were reluctant to leave, but the islands were becoming too expensive, not only because of wages but also because of government practices. Interviewees mention "grease" and "less than honest government officials."

In the early 1970s competition from Europe continued strong, but changed as eastern European countries entered the global market. Hungary, which had been third in the production of gloves behind France and Italy, became the leader.

In 1975 changes in the General System of Preferences, made it possible for certain developing countries to export ski and golf gloves and almost all sporting goods to America with no duties added. Manufacturers were planning moves to take advantage of countries that did not generate duties.

European countries, Czechoslovakia and Poland, and Korea and Taiwan had doubled their purchases of cattle hides and were beginning to look to the United States for these hides.[82] The shortage of raw skins and hides became so severe in 1979 that the jobs of 400,000 American leather workers were threatened, among them Fulton County's tanners. Senator Jacob Javits and Representative Donald J. Mitchell tried to help, but a Congressional bill to limit exports of American hides and skins was defeated.[83]

Imports in the work-glove market more than doubled between 1976 and 1980, rising to 36 percent of the total, but the change in the county's dress-glove industry was much greater—foreign firms supplied 77 percent of the total. Imports rose 93 percent between 1976 and 1979 to a total of 23.7 million dozen pairs of gloves.

Of the county's remaining manufacturers, 70 percent were importing or making gloves overseas. Production overseas spread from the Philippines, Hong Kong, and Korea to China in this interval. Curiously, exports of gloves increased, but two-thirds of the increase consisted of cut-up glove parts shipped to countries with low labor costs to be sewn and shipped back to America. The rise in this period occurred despite a 1977 dock strike that tied up the East and Gulf coasts and affected that 70 percent of the county's glove manufacturers because their shipments from overseas were delayed.

The last years of the National Association of Glove Manufacturers

Throughout the seventies, it is amazing to see how the association presented a picture of optimism in the midst of the organization's slow death. When outgoing president of the association Eric Dzierson spoke of a rebirth in the industry in 1978, he really was talking about the tremendous growth of the glove industry overseas and acknowledged that if the largest five local glove companies made all their gloves in Fulton County, they would require upwards of 30,000 workers. He noted how few trained workers were available and that workers overseas appeared to be more productive than those in the county.[84] What his statement implies is that those same manufacturers must have been making considerable profits because 30,000 workers can make a lot of gloves! Casey's year-end pronouncements again mentioned optimism, but it was apparent that it was no longer the county's industry. The larger manufacturers had become virtual importers, mere distribution centers, operating with the same seasonality as the old glove shops.

The 1983 year-end projections still talked of an upswing, but the following spring, the NAGM announced plans to discontinue operations.[85] Poor economic conditions and shrinking membership (only 38 remained out of a high of 200) were the reasons. The funds to pay an executive director were just not there.

A luncheon marking the end of the association occurred on the date that would have been the group's 66th annual convention. It was also a retirement party for Casey, who was praised by Richard C. Zuckerwar and Joseph P. Conroy. All along Casey had believed that no tariff could compensate for the disproportionately low hourly pay in foreign countries. But to the very end, he never publicly discussed the industry's move overseas. He preached what the local glovemen wanted to hear and kept their secrets. His business outlook was always optimistic, and he reassured the members that things would get better.

By 1983 the glove industry's payroll had shrunk to $20 million, while the tanneries' combined county payroll exceeded $50 million. This difference owes as much to radical changes in the leather industry as to the disappearing glove industry.[86]

1972

Walker LaRowe died at age 77, owner of LaRowe Glove Co. for 50 years.

Joseph Leibl, owner of Marguerite Glove Co. died at age 60. He had been born in Prague and moved with his parents to Milwaukee, where his father worked as a glove cutter. The son moved to Gloversville in 1928 and worked for various glove firms until he established the glove company with his own name in 1942. That company employed 25 workers in the forties and was renamed Marguerite after his principal trade name.

John E. Castiglione, retired owner of Castiglione Glove Co., died at age 89. He was born in Naples, Italy in 1882 and came to Gloversville around 1900.

C. E. Alvord, who founded the Alvord Glove Company of Mayfield with his late father, died at age 80

Harry Rubin died at age 70. He was one of four brothers who formed J. M. Rubin & Sons Glove Co. with their father.

James H. Casey, Jr, photo from the fifties

Highlights in the seventies, continued, and the eighties

1973

Fred Tatar, founder with his two sons of the Daytona Glove Co., died at age 80.

Gaetano Martorelli, founder and president of Martorelli Brothers Glove Co. for 40 years, died at age 80. He was born in Naples, Italy, and came to Gloversville in 1914.

Homer C. Van Vleet, formerly with the Van Vleet Glove Co. died at age 81.

Samuel Millstein died at age 73. He had owned the Crossley Glove Co. of Broadalbin.

Edmund J. DeLaney, owner of Dixon Glove Co. in Mayfield from 1937 to 1967, died at age 83.

1974

Henry Balzano, founder with his brothers of the Balzano Glove Co., died at age 60.

Joseph Bachner, II, died at age 57, vice-president of C. J. Bachner & Sons.

1975

James Rogers, for 56 years associated with Gloversville Silk Mills, died at age 90.

Patrick Crocetta, retired president of the Crocetta Brothers Glove Co., died at age 74.

1976

The Wilkins Glove factory in Mayfield, erected in 1879, was torn down. The frame structure was 50 by 130 feet.[10]

Joseph Lazarus died at age 66. He was president of Boyce-Lazarus Co.

The landmark Littauer Glove Co. building at the rear of 118 South Main Street in Gloversville was destroyed by fire. In recent years it had housed the Mosetti Glove Co.

Leon F. Swears, retired president of the knit glove firm bearing his name, died at age 80. He established the firm in 1921 and it ceased operations in 1970.

Carl M. Balzano, partner in the former G. Balzano & Sons Glove Co., died at age 60.

Louis Pisano died at age 81. He was born in Italy and was former owner of Pisano & Rossi Glove Co. In 1966-67 he operated a branch of that company in Puerto Rico.

1977

Harold W. Hutchens, former owner of Hutchens & Potter, died at age 88.

D. Douglas Hays, partner in Ireland Brothers Glove Co., died at age 75.

Park Hallenbeck, retired head of the former Mayfield Glove Co., died at age 60.

1978

Louis Vander Essen, operator with his wife of the Jayne LeVan Glove Co., died at age 70.

Anthony Crocetta, co-founder of Crocetta Bros. Glove Co., died at age 86. In the late 40s, he founded Artcraft Glove Co. in Johnson City, Tenn.

A. Theodore Goosen, president of the Arthur B. Goosen Glove Co. for 21 years, died at age 61.

Gates-Mills, Inc. moved some of its shipping operations into the former Johnstown Price Chopper building. With its other sites, the company now had the capacity to pack and ship up to 20,000 gloves a week. The company continued to make men's gloves, but most of its sales were of imported gloves. Gates-Mills, which billed itself as the largest manufacturers of fine men's gloves in America, continued to expand, acquiring the Superb Division of Superb-Crescendoe, Inc.

1979

William E. Dovey died at age 83. He was born in England and ran a glove company under his name from 1930 to 1965.

Joseph Stefic died at age 92. He had come from Austria and ran the Belle Glove Co. from his house until 1959.

Roscoe R. Stanyon, Sr. died at age 87. Born in England, he came to Gloversville and trained as a cutter at Jacob Adler Glove Co. He formed Imperial Glove Co. in 1919 and it became the largest manufacturer of pigskin gloves in the world. He was a pioneer glove manufacturer in the Philippines.

1980

The J. M. Rubin Glove Co. closed for a reorganization. The company had a plant in the Philippines.

Herman J. Serfis died at age 83, founder of the Northville glove company that carried his name.

The Van Buren Glove Co. of Mayfield, chartered in 1930, went out of business.

Artcraft Glove Corp., Allen H. Pulsifer president, incorporated.

Milton C. Sutton died at age 78. With his father and brother he founded Sutton's Gloves.

1981

Fred C. Miller, a partner in the glove company established in 1921 that bears his name, died at age 80. He was with the company for more than 50 years before his retirement in 1970.

Norman Blum, formerly of Buscarlet Glove Co., died at age 90.

1982

A. M. Papa, president of Mario Papa & Sons, Inc., died at age 66.

A California firm bought the Perrella Glove Co., with expectation that all 60 employees would remain on the job. The sale was assisted by the Fulton and Montgomery County Development Agency and a loan of $400,000 from Bankers Trust.

Highlights from the last years of the Association

1971
The NAGM Bulletin opined there would be an improvement in domestic production, especially of leather gloves. That prediction coincided with the announcement that Crescendoe was laying off help, but not folding. The company blamed the cutback on women rejecting gloves as a fashion note.[12]

The NAGM convention that year featured a seminar on international banking. Outgoing president Joseph Conroy spoke of shortages of trained labor and the need to engage in collective consultation between management and workers as a way to improve productivity.[13]

1972
Those attending the annual convention worried about tight leather markets and the high cost of credit.

Casey's year-end report used the word optimism again, as the number of glove firms kept dropping. He predicted prices of gloves would rise by 15 percent.

A spokesman for the Tanners Association had a dim view of what 1973 might bring glovemen because of the rising costs of hides and skins. European tanning capacity was increasing and competition for raw materials was great.[14]

1973
The 55th annual convention of the NAGM had to consider the association's sinking financial condition. Members learned about the Trade Reform Act of 1973 and how both Russia and China would receive favored nation status.

1974
NAGM president Dominic Papa was optimistic that gloves for special uses would provide opportunites for the county's glovemen. The 1975 convention encouraged members to innovate, create new markets, and sell gloves for other than warmth.

1976
Optimism heralded headlines describing the NAGM's 58th annual convention. The president urged members to forget about the past and focus on the future in order to be successful.[15] Casey even foresaw a brisk expansion coming.

1977
The NAGM moved its 1977 convention to the Gideon Putnam Hotel in Saratoga Springs. Speeches dished out the usual words of optimism. The association moved to new and smaller quarters on South Main Street in Gloversville. The group had been holding quarterly meetings of its board members for several years and they continued active in tariff concerns.

Association programs that featured gloves for fashion gave way to advertising campaigns for winter sports gloves. One manufacturer, Premier Glove Co., sold gloves at the Super Bowl.

1978
Dominic Papa talked of trade problems and concerns with letting foreign manufacturers bid on government contracts. He cited the decline in the leather glove industry and said, "there is not much room for making any further concessions unless you want to annihilate the industry completely."

1979
The shortage of leather and the increase in prices even convinced Casey that the situation in the glove industry was "terrible."[16]

The 1979 association dinner drew 110 participants and nostalgic comments on previous times when the event drew a thousand people. Casey's year-end report said prospects for 1980 were confusing.

1980
Tariff cuts on imported leather gloves were announced for the beginning of 1980. The spring 1980 convention of the NAGM heard president Chester Nessel say, "I never dreamed we could go through such a terrible year. . . . I wonder what could happen next."[17]

1981
Some things never change: attorney Herbert T. Posner, speaking at the 1981 convention, talked about the predatory ways of large department stores and the immense problem of consignment sales. These "allow the customer to place orders, but pay only for the gloves it can sell—at a mark-up no less."[18] He urged the manufacturers to change the practice, which had been going on for as long as the county had made gloves. True to form, some of the manufacturers present countered that if these sales "were curtailed, customers would be lost, production cut, and competitors would benefit."[19] An editorial in the local paper observed that the convention "had expressed degrees of optimism not heard for some time."

1983
The association curtailed its spring 1983 convention to a one-day affair, and although it went through the motions of electing a new president and board, the end was in sight. James H. Casey, Jr. was serving his 46th year as executive secretary with the organization. The outgoing president, Herman J. Steinberg of Amsterdam Glove Corp. said "things look much better, especially in the womens' line. We'll soon be back making ladies' gloves."[20] The headline in the local paper describing the convention once again used the word "optimism."

1984
Casey retired at the spring luncheon, which marked the end of the association.

The Leather Industry after 1950

Milestones in the tanning industry

1951
Martin-Deischel Leather Co. closed its doors. Formerly the Star Tannery, Martin-Deischel was incorporated in 1927. It had been one of three local companies tanning mochas and it closed because it could no longer obtain the needed Egyptian sheepskins. Only Geisler & Lehr continued to tan mochas.

1952
Melvin W. Cox and William Avery, Sr. acquired interests in Karg Brothers, the county's largest tannery.

1953
At the beginning of 1953, the mill and all the machinery of Geisler & Lehr, Inc. were sold to Triangle Finishing Corp. The 40-year old firm was the last of the mocha tanneries and it succumbed to the poor business climate and the high cost of raw skins.[11]

1954
L. James Risedorph, president of Filmer Leather, purchased the Reliable Tannery, one of the county's largest, The 60,000 square foot building, constructed by John Stockamore, was taken over by Martin & Littel in 1923 and by Reliable Tanners in 1936. Reliable was organized by Abraham S. Fink, son of an immigrant from East Prussia. The Filmer Tannery, formerly the Charles King tannery, burned in April 1954 and the county feared that the business would move away. Risedorph also established the tannery that bears his name. Risedorph was the son of an Otsego farmer.

As the leather glove industry declined, so did the county's tanning of leather for gloves. The county saw an initial decline in all forms of tanning in the late fifties and through the 1960s, fueled by the changes in the international markets for skins. Third-world countries, like Nigeria, that had exported raw skins destined for gloves, began to tan them as a way of creating jobs and greater revenues. This combined with increased worldwide competition for the limited supplies of skins and leather brought tanning of skins, such as hair sheep, almost to a halt in Fulton County. Since the mid-1980s, Europeans claimed the market for sheepskins tanned in Africa. (Domestic sheep have been bred for meat, not leather. Hence less desirable North American sheepskins cannot replace those from countries near the equator.)

Also in the late sixties, county tanners were already complaining that they had been shut out of the goatskin market and that a large percentage of raw American calfskins were being sent abroad. At the same time, worldwide shortages of skins were growing, partly as a result of the closing of the Suez Canal. New sources were found: skins exported from Iran and Iraq were joining those from Lebanon and Turkey in the global market, but these supplies were inadequate. Not only did the decline of available leather further the decline in leather glove manufacturing but it worked both ways: the declining glove business decreased the need for glove leather.

A shift to tanning for garment and shoe leather briefly reinvigorated the local tanning industry and created a boom that would burst in the eighties. This shift was completed in the 1960s, so that a very small proportion of local work went into the glove industry. Tanners thrived and expanded in the county through the sixties, but toward the end of that decade, even that portion of the local economy began to shrink. The rapid growth in the import of shoes curtailed domestic calfskin tanning. Tanners renewed their call for changes in the country's foreign trade policies and rejoined glovemen in protesting the country's move toward free trade.[87]

Leather dealers and contractors prominent in the second half of the twentieth century included men with origins in Africa and the Near East. Abe Seroussi, elected mayor of Gloversville in 1998, has been a leather middleman in Gloversville for years. He was born in Khartoum and his parents were Sudanese Jews. His family was connected with the Gloversville leather merchant firm of Horowitz & Arbib through his grandmother who was an Iraqi Jew. His father descended from a Jewish family from Tripoli. The father became a leather trader in Libya and northern Nigeria, and spoke Arabic, French, Italian, and English. He opened a pickling plant in Khartoum. When Rommel swept across northern Africa in 1940 and 1941, Jews had to leave Africa, and the family moved to New York. Abe Seroussi's uncles still have plants in Nigeria and Tanzania.

Another local leather dealer, Muhammed Legesse came from Ethiopia to settle in Gloversville. He still trades in skins from Ethiopia and the Near East.

Around 1970 there was a marked shift to cowhide tanning in Fulton County, illustrated by the design of the new sewage treatment plant. County planning for the project was based on the local industry's tanning of small animal skins. The plant opened in 1972, and by 1975 the tanneries were loading it with the much greater volumes of waste created by cowhide processing. The county's swift changeover to cowhide tanning quickly made the facility obsolete.[88] Tanner Rod Correll believes this resulted from a failure in planning, that evidence of the shift to cowhide was there before ground was broken for the plant. The system was enlarged to handle the tanner's needs, but the demise of cowhide tanning in the late 1980s meant that the county now possesses a system that probably would serve the normal needs of a population ten times greater.[89]

Wood & Hyde's history is typical of the enormous changes in the local tanning industry in the past four decades. From the twenties through the end of World War II, the company, under Donald Hyde, Sr. used its monopoly of South African skins to produce only glove leather. It lost that source after the war and shifted in the early fifties to tanning wool sheep from Iran and Morocco for garment leather, while continuing to produce glove leather from hair sheep obtained in Brazil, Sudan, and Nigeria. The company also had a large custom tanning operation, preparing skins for Grandoe, Perrella, and Superb as well as others.

In 1953 Benjamin Dennie bought Wood & Hyde, which had three plants, the company's large tannery and a small one originally owned by Levor, both in Gloversville, and another facility in Hagaman, near Amsterdam, NY. After he took over, the company gradually shifted away from glove leather to garment leather. In the seventies, when the company could no longer obtain skins from Iran, it began to import them from Afghanistan. By the early eighties, the company shifted to tanning cowhides, importing them from Argentina in the "wet blue," that is, partially tanned. The company no longer tanned glove leather. The firm, now owned by Genesco, a national corporation, continues to tan cowhides.

The experience of a second tannery further illustrates this transition period. Hermann Loewenstein, a tanner trained in Stuttgart, came to New York City in 1893 and set up an export-import firm there, exporting many kinds of American leather to Europe and importing leathers from South America and Europe for sale to American shoe and handbag manufacturers. Among them was Scotch grain, a pebbly-textured cowhide that excelled for Army boots in World War I. Loewenstein's company did well through the Depression and through World War II. His son, Rudolph, who adopted his mother's name, Correll, took over in 1945 on Hermann's death. Rudolph realized that he needed an upstate tannery and bought the Ellithorp Tannery in Gloversville. (That tannery was originally the Cane Tanning Co., producing glove leather. Under George Ellithorp, who continued running the tannery after its sale to the Loewenstein Company, the Ellithorp Tannery did contract tanning for Loewenstein, which principally produced shoe leather.)

That tannery continued to produce calf suede and white buck through the fifties. Rod Correll joined his father, Rudolph, in the business in 1957. Within a few years, Rod became convinced that a fundamental change was necessary because of the dwindling supply and high price of U. S. calfskins. The tannery began to tan cowhides in Gloversville in the early 1970s. (That tannery was probably not the county's first to tan cowhides, however. Dexter Risedorph told the author that he thought his father's tannery was the first to tan cowhides in the county.)

Rene Perrone, who had purchased Liberty Tanning from the Smicklers, owners of Illinois Glove Co., also tanned cowhides. By the late seventies most shoe manufacturing had moved offshore and the local shoe leather

1955

Peerless Tanning Co., Gloversville, whose building was destroyed by fire, acquired the facilities of Alma Leather Co. Peerless was founded in 1919 by J. Edward Lotze, who had worked for Littauers, Booth & Co., and Surpass Leather Co.

Karg Brothers took over the building and machinery of Teetz-McKay in order to increase its tanning capacity.

1956

Karg Brothers acquired the Cleary Tanning Co. mill, giving them three locations for their custom tanning operations.

1958

J. C. Bleyl's tanning and coloring operations moved to the New Hampshire plant of Bleyl's owner, Winslow Brothers & Smith, a subsidiary of Armour Meat Packing Co. Some finishing work remained in Gloversville.

1962

Samuel Rothschild, chairman of the board of G. Levor Co. and president of the F.J.& G. Railroad and the Littauer Hospital, died at age 81.

1964

The J. C. Bleyl Co. tannery was closed in November because of declining markets for the plant's sheepskins. The buildings were purchased by the Riss Tanning Corp., which planned to produce garment and shoe leather. Simon Riss was formerly vice president and general manager at Johnstown Tanning Corp.

1966

Rene Perrone and Jerome Ritter, owners of R & M Leather Corp. purchased Liberty Dressing Co.

The National Suede and Leather Refinishers of America held a convention in Fulton County, the first in the organization's eleven years to be held outside Chicago.

G. Alan Rothschild, president of G. Levor & Co., announced that that firm would close its shoe-leather operations at the end of 1966, displacing about 250 workers.

Cayadutta Tanning Co. purchased the former E. S. Parkhurst plant from Framglo and announced plans to tan cattle hides and buffalo, whale, and sealskins.

Menkes Feuer of Feuer Hide & Skin Co. announced the purchase of the former Crocetta glove building.

1968

Genesco Co. of Nashville, Tenn., a conglomerate made up of many shoe and leather companies and with sales over a billion dollars a year, purchased Wood & Hyde Leather Co. Joseph E. Wood established the latter company in 1891 and was joined by W. Donald Hyde in 1905. The president at the time of the sale was Benjamin Dennie, who had started working for the firm in 1919.

1970

Menkes Feuer, chairman of the board of Feuer Hide & Skin Corp. died at age 73. He had come to America in 1922 from Kalusz, Austria.

tanneries began to shrink. Liberty closed in the late seventies. Both the Ellithorp and Hermann Loewenstein tanneries closed in 1986.[90]

Several small cowhide tanners remained along with the Feuer-owned tanneries, which included the former Teetz-McKay Tannery, purchased in 1955 and the Cleary Tanning Co. purchased in 1956. Karg Brothers Tannery, the largest of the local tanneries owned by the Feuer group, was probably the biggest producer of cowhide leather in Fulton County from the late sixties to the mid eighties. The Feuer group also acquired the former Risedorph, Crown, and Pan American tanneries and Gloversville Leather, Elton Leather, and Star Leather. Karg's closing in 1994, described below, marked the demise of cowhide tanning in Fulton County.

About 1980 the situation in the local tanning industry had become acute because the United States was the only country that allowed unrestricted export of cowhides and American exports were climbing steeply. In summer 1979, county tanners, led by Frank Perrella of J. B. F. Industries, began a campaign to limit exports of cowhides. The U.S. was becoming a third-world, exporting country with respect to those natural resources. Statistics indicated that 83 percent of the country's cattle hides were exported, and that the U.S. produced 15 percent of the world's cattle hides, leaving the country's tanneries with half the raw hides they needed to keep going. Major producers like Argentina, Brazil, and Uruguay had some restrictions on exports. The price of raw cattle hides rose 154 percent in a year and a half.[91]

The situation, which had been developing for years as third world nations developed their economies, reached such proportions that the United States' imports of leather products created a trade deficit of $2.5 billion, ten percent of the total U.S. trade deficit in 1980. Japan and Korea were buying 50 percent of the country's hide exports, outbidding American manufacturers because of favorable exchange rates.

In 1981 there were 151 firms in Fulton County engaged in production of leather or leather products. These firms accounted for 51 percent of the county's manufacturing jobs, but only about 25 percent of the total work force.[92]

Although cowhide tanning revived the industry, it created numerous problems. In the seventies, as the county moved to tanning cowhide, it became obvious that pollution from processing these hides threatened local communities. A few owners did make the huge investments necessary to bring the old tanneries up to standards that met new Environmental Protection Agency (EPA) regulations. Frank Perrella at J. B. F. Industries and Harry Brace at Ellithorp were among them. However, many of the older facilities were just not worth fixing.[93]

In a move that would threaten the future of tanning locally, the city councils in both cities passed ordinances in 1978 requiring that waste water from the tanneries be pretreated before it was discharged into the local sewer systems.[94] Tanners protested that the compliance date, March 1, 1980, could not be met and estimated that the cost would be $20 million. The problems of tannery wastes had been escalating since the tanneries began using heavy metals like chrome in their operations.

In early 1979 Crescent Leather Finishing Co. claimed that it had found a way of reducing sulfides in the tanning process and virtually eliminating solids from industrial waste water.[95] The company's technical director, Eugene Spritzer, developed the process, which took longer than sulfide tanning, but saved the company the expense of installing new equipment.

New EPA regulations issued in 1980 placed further restraints on tanning operations. Even shavings and dust were labeled hazardous because they contained chrome.

In 1980 glove manufacturers feared that the EPA regulations concerning hazardous materials would apply to them in the disposal of trimmings and cuttings. The local chamber of commerce heard reports that the new regulations would mean that smaller businesses could no longer manufacture gloves.[96] The EPA put in place regulations that traced the disposal of all tannery wastes, and then, in October 1980, the EPA declassified those tannery wastes, that is took them off the regulated list.

But no problems were as threatening to the community as the array of chemicals used in cowhide tanning. Concern was growing over the use of such heavy metals as chrome, and tannery workers were developing real health problems. William Towne, deputy administrator of the Glove Cities Joint Board of the ACTWU took the lead in questioning chemical use, particularly dimethylformamide (DMF) used in dyeing leathers. He and other union officials believed the abnormally high occurrence of testicular cancer in leather shops (ten cases between 1974 and 1987) could be traced to DMF.[97] Doctors from Mt. Sinai Hospital in New York City conducted a program of health screening that was funded by the New York State Department of Labor. They found fifteen percent of the 160 workers tested had lung damage. Benzidine, also used in dyeing, had already been identified as a cause of bladder damage, and 20 out of the 160 screened had blood in their urine, a warning of bladder cancer. The union took credit for the fact that local tanneries stopped using dyes containing DMF and benzidine.[98]

In the early 1980s county tanners were fighting to maintain the business. The Tanners Association increased its activities in relation to the problems of tariffs, restrictions on sales of skins by producer countries, and regulations. They heard from a representative of the Tanners Council of America in the spring of 1982 which outlined that group's efforts on their behalf. But, in general, the Tanners Association was mostly a social club whose members never really pulled together on enviromental issues.[99]

Cowhide tanning became so competitive that the local industry again began to shrink. The resulting paradigm shift away from cowhide tanning in Fulton County meant that by the 1990s most local work in the leather industry was finishing and coloring. Argentine cowhides are brought here in the wet blue for leather to be finished for garments, shoes, handbags, and cheaper gloves. One firm in Fulton County, Pearl Leather, owned by the Ruggerio family, had the capabilities to finish 350,000 square feet a day in 1998. Other large finishing companies include Carville-National Leather in Johnstown; Fashion Tanning, owned by the Zambella family; and Townsend (formerly Crescent) Leather, owned by the Kucel family.

The trend away from cowhide tanning was so marked that by 1990 the county tanned primarily deerskins and a very few sheepskins and cowhides. A few tanners, mostly descendents of the Slovaks who came to work in the tanneries in the early part of this century, run the tanneries that do produce glove leather from deerskins. While this resurgence in the tanning of deerskins sustains an important component of the local tanning industry, it does very little for local glove manufacturing, because almost 80 percent of tanned deerskins are exported. Deerskin tanning had come full circle but no longer in partnership with the glove industry.

1971

McFeely and Cohn purchased Bert Kennedy's interests in Gloversville Leather Co.

Walter S. Mahoney, former president of a leather firm, died at age 79.

Ellithorp Tanning Corp. was acquired by Harry Brace of Gloversville and Shrut and Asch Leather Co. of Boston. The latter also bought an interest in Hermann Loewenstein, Inc., the tannery's former owner.

1972

Fire caused considerable damage to Liberty Tanning Co.

John F. Mahoney died at age 83. He was president of P. J. Mahoney & Sons Leather Co. and of Alma Leather.

1973

Fred L. Rulison, head of Fred L. Rulison & Sons, Inc., leather tanners in Johnstown, died at age 77. With his father and brother, he had started a tannery in Northville in 1919 and moved it to the old Herman Martin tannery site in 1930.

1974

David S. Van Santen, retired president of Karg Brothers Tannery, died at age 85.

Bert Kennedy, former president of Gloversville Leather, Inc. died at age 80.

1975

Robert J. McFeeley, 56, and Robert S. Evans, 38, president and technical consultant to Pan American Tanning Corp, formerly Gloversville Leather, died in a car crash. Around 1936, Evans and George E. Lewis had established the Lewis & Evans Glove Co., then was associated with the Main Glove Co.

1977

Everett E. Karg, partner with his father in Karg Brothers, Inc. tannery for 15 years, died at age 81.

1979

Arthur H. Cane died at age 82. He was born in England and was a partner in the Mills Bros. Tanning Co. which became the Cane Tanning Co. in 1930 with Cane as sole owner. The company manufactured glove leather, employed between 75 and 100 people, and was sold to Hermann Loewenstein in 1946.

James C. MacIntyre, for 45 years superintendent and treasurer of Karg Brothers tannery, died at age 70.

Hermann Loewenstein, Inc. sold to Katy Industries, a Chicago-based conglomerate.

1981

Lauren Berner, Sr., retired president and co-owner of Leavitt-Berner Tanning Co. died at age 60.

Dexter Risedorph purchased the Sheepskin Lining Co. and Corgay Leather, Inc.

1982

Harold A. Bernard, retired tannery superintendent at G. Levor, died at age 89.

Bill Studenic is one of the deerskin tanners and his family history typifies the county's experience in tanning. His grandfather, Andrew, came from Czechoslovakia in the early 1900s to work in the Topp shearling tannery. Andrew's two sons Alfred and Anthony were able to open their own tannery and did contract work until World War II, when they had enough funds to acquire half of a larger tannery, thus establishing Independent Leather. They tanned mostly garment leather from skins imported from Iran, Turkey, Syria, New Zealand, and Africa. Business was good, but in 1954 the brothers began fighting. Bill believes that Fred Simek, another tanner of Slovak descent, wanted to become a partner in the business and drove a wedge between the brothers. Bill's father was crowded out and with a settlement and financial help from gloveman Bert Kennedy he was able to buy and rejuvenate Gloversville Leather, a fine hair-sheep tannery.

Bill was not much interested in college, and even a tanning course he took at a technical school did not interest him. He put on rubber boots, gloves, and apron and became a tanner, learning the business from the bottom up. He was fascinated by "taking a skin in the pickle and turning it into leather." Bill's father had put a small laboratory in the tannery and hired "Dutch" Wilcox, Johnstown High School's chemistry teacher to run the lab. Bill learned to analyze steps in the process and later learned coloring leather from an expert. (Independent had a lab, but the only other tannery with a lab was G. Levor's tannery, at that time run by the Rothschilds.)

Bill became tannery room foreman at the age of 23. His father died in 1968, and Kennedy kept the business going, but the business of contract leather tanning was slowing down. Bill's pay was cut and he felt vulnerable. Kennedy sold stock in the business to some of the workers, but Bill decided he wanted to buy another tannery. In 1970, when the Wilson tannery was offered for sale, Bill and Joe Anadio were able to buy it. The tannery's strengths had been deerskin tanning, which was new to Bill. He saw the future of deerskins though his partner disagreed, so he bought Anadio out in 1974. Bill's company, Colonial Leather, now tans 1,500 deerskins a day, in addition to some custom tanning of glove leather. His tannery has two principal competitors, Twin City and Johnstown Leather, both owned by Slovaks.[100]

The deerskins tanned in the county come from deer killed in the wild. Butchers around the country get deerskins from hunters who bring their deer to be cut up. Collectors visit the butchers, paying upwards of $9 for each deerskin. Of the one million-plus deerskins tanned each year, about 80 percent are exported, most to Italy, where it is sent "in the stain," that is tanned but not finished or colored. The Italians' ability to do delicate work to finish and color deerskins places them ahead of the county. Some deerskins go to Japan and Korea.[101]

Mike Subik, whose grandparents came from Kuty, Czechoslovakia, and married here, is another tanner of Slovak descent. He is related to the Hladiks, who also worked in leather mills and his uncle, Marty Hladik, built tannery machinery for Travis & Oczko. Subik's father became a supervisor in a tannery. Mike Subik is the oldest son and started in the glove business in 1946 but did not like it. Without ever having worked in a tannery, he bought Key Finishing on State Street and named it Johnstown Leather. (The Cleary Tannery across the street is now owned by Fred Simek. In 1960 Subik needed a bigger facility and moved to the old Teetz-McKay Tannery. With 80 workers, the company colors leather and tans deerskins.

Subik believes that the union, and in particular Bill Towne, hurt the tanneries more than any other local industry by making them non-competitive with tanneries in other areas. Among the tanneries, Colonial, Johnstown Leather, Twin City Leather, Simco, Wood & Hyde, and Carville are union shops.[102] Owners believe that union tannery workers are well paid, averaging close to $15 an hour, with piecework bringing men who work the fleshing machines upwards of $1,000 a week, when there is work. Owners also believe that tannery workers' benefits—health insurance and pensions—are good.

Local tanning received its greatest setback in 1994 with the bankruptcy of the Feuer Leather Group. Feuer-owned Karg Brothers Tannery had the capacity to tan upwards of a million deerskins, at a time when the county could handle well over two million in a year. The loss of that capacity decreased county production, even though other tanners were able to pick up some of the slack. (Deerskins, another two million at least, are also tanned in Wisconsin, Colorado, Texas, and Oregon.)

Feuer closed Karg Brothers owing back sewer taxes and landfill fees and this brought about increased fees and financial hardship for the remaining tanners. The Karg site is a "looming environmental nightmare,"[103] on which back taxes totalling $830,000 are owed the city of Johnstown. Feuer's three plants (Karg, Pan American, and Allied Split) employed more than a thousand workers, yet now there are hardly a thousand tannery workers left in the county.

According to Mike Subik, Feuer Leather Group bled $68 million from the industry, most of it in Fulton County, the rest from tanneries in Mercersburg, Pennsylvania, and Pennicock, New Hampshire. The company's unpaid bills contributed to the bankruptcies affecting the Kilmer, Schaffel, and Gulick (Commonwealth Leather) tanneries.

Tanning in Fulton County circa 1998

Twin City Leather, Langdon Marvin, has the capacity to tan 200,000 deerskins, some shearlings, lamb, and goatskins.

Gloversville Tannery, formerly Napatan Tannery, has the capacity to tan 100,000 deerskins.

Colonial Tannery, Bill Studenic, with the capacity to tan 400,000 deerskins, also does some custom tanning of sheepskins, cowhides, and farm-raised alligator.

Johnstown Leather, Mike Subik, has the capacity to tan 700,000 deerksins, and tans some lamb and sheepskins, and cowhides.

Simco, David Simek (recent successor to his father, Fred) with the capacity to tan 200,000 deerskins, also tans some sheepskins and cowhides.

Wood & Hyde continues to tan cowhides.

Di Mis Tanneries has two locations and a small capacity to tan cowhides.

Alliance Tannery, formerly part of Karg Tannery, bought by Karg employees, now tans cow splits.

All of the county's other leather companies, which number approxixmately 30, only finish and color leather.

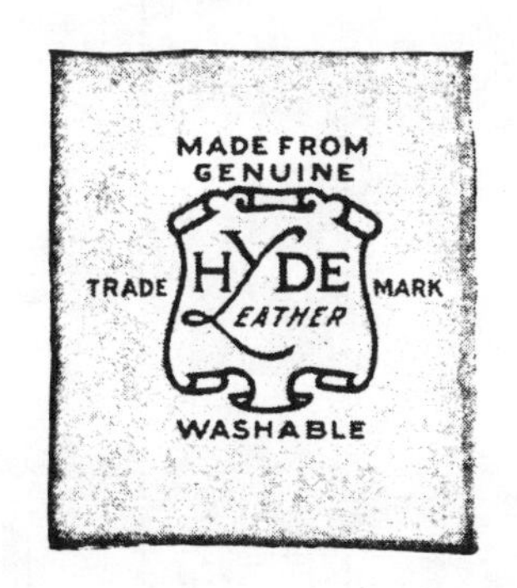

Wood & Hyde Company
GLOVERSVILLE, N. Y.

Unions

Other than joining community leaders in calling for more work and higher tariffs, the unions really did not help the declining job situation. On the other hand, union actions in the second half of this century were not as detrimental to the county's welfare as some have charged. In recent years, if you asked anyone in the industry and in much of the community what happened to the county's glove business, the one common explanation cited for its demise was union activity.

Contract negotiations, minor labor disputes, strikes, and struggles among and within the unions occupied an enormous amount of space in local newspapers, often the bulk of local news. Labor issues were thrust at the public and although the reporting seems fair, the sheer weight of union activity created the public impression that the unions were an overpowering force.

Through World War II and into the following decade, glove workers were well paid, undoubtedly as a result of union activity. However through succeeding decades, glove workers' wages began to decline in relation to manufacturing jobs elsewhere. The unions were no more fragmented than they had been earlier, but they became less effective until they finally joined together. Even then the union was unable to win wage settlements comparable with the rest of the country. The glove unions only began to win important benefits for workers in the late sixties, just as union membership began to plunge.

The decade of the fifties was one of struggle and strife; it got off to a poor start in 1950 with difficult labor negotiations that dragged on for six months beyond the time the old contract expired. Prolonging the negotiations were disputes among the three glove-worker unions over alleged pay differences between the unions. A compromise pleased no one and the Operators Union threatened again to strike. The settlement, which was only partially retroactive, provided no more than the 5 percent increase the manufacturers had initially offered.

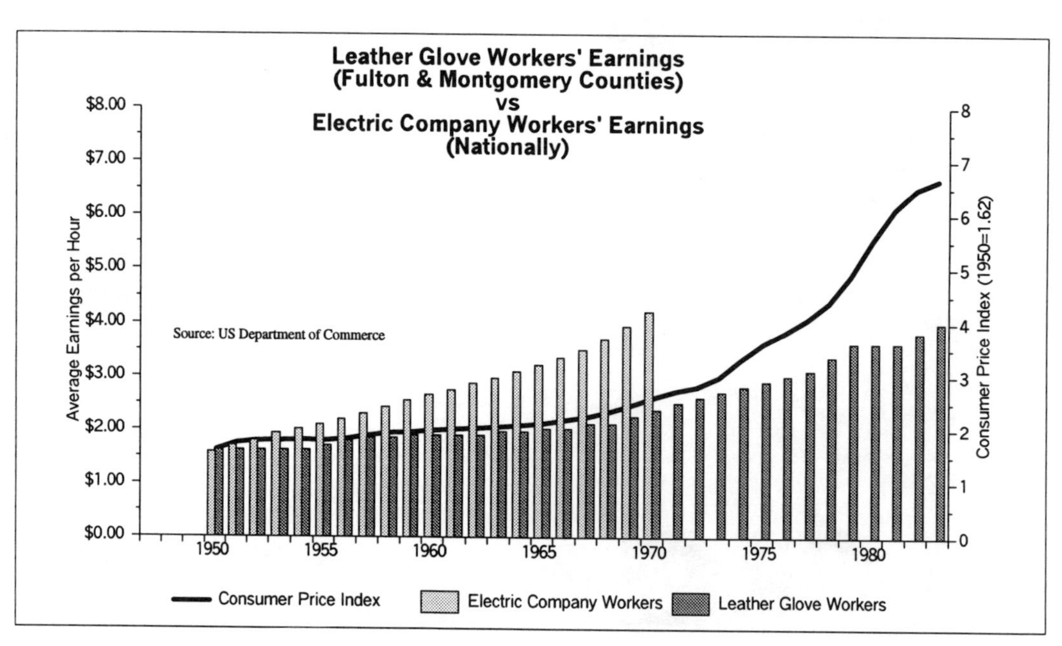

Leadership of the three unions had remained almost static. The manufacturers had divided into two groups for negotiation purposes: the Block Cut Manufacturers group chose Milton C. Sutton as president. The Table and Pattern Cut Manufacturers group chose Douglas Hays of Ireland Brothers as president, and attorney H. Andrew Schlusberg was appointed to head up its labor negotiations. Each union negotiated separately with the two groups, so there were three sets of talks with both groups of manufacturers.

Finally, in 1952, the three glove unions (Cutters and Shavers with 1,100 members; Operators and Day Hands with 3,000; and Layers-off with 300 members) began to negotiate together.[104] The three unions temporarily took on the title "Branch of the Glove Workers Union."

At the urging of the Layers-off union, the Amalgamated Clothing Workers Union, CIO began organizing the county's cutters in late 1952. The cutters had been represented by the Independent Cutters and Shavers Union since 1936, when the local group withdrew from the AFL Cutters Union. In 1940 the Independent Union, which had comprised table and pull-down cutters, expanded to include pattern and block cutters, shavers, and splitters, thus becoming the Consolidated Cutters Union. Dwindling membership (a decline of 1,500 to 1,100), insufficient funds to run the local union, and the prospect of a retirement plan within the national union made affiliation appear desirable.

Cutters' president Gordon Blake argued against affiliation, claiming that the national union could not provide union pensions. He said manufacturers had absolutely rejected a pension plan in the past and would not contribute more than two percent of wages to a union plan. He also argued that the current insurance plan was better than one the Amalgamated would offer, that 85 percent of Midwestern glove workers were affiliated with AFL unions, not the CIO, and that anyway, a national union was not the answer to local problems.[105] In early 1953, Blake won by a 373 to 240 margin and the union remained independent.

Contract negotiations took on a tediousness that mirrored the slowing business, but there was no strike. The contract with the glove workers' unions had expired on April 1, 1952, and talks dragged on into the summer of 1953. Vacation time, additional holidays, a change in the welfare plan, and other benefits held up settlement. The unions were unhappy also with the wording of cost-of-living raises or, as the manufacturers wanted, decreases, should the cost of living decline.[106]

Affiliation became an issue for county unions again later in 1953. The Layers-off Local 292 started a campaign directed at the Cutters-Shavers and Operators-Day Hands to encourage those unions to join the Amalgamated Clothing Workers, CIO. Frank McMaster, business agent of Local 292, stated that the county's glove industry would continue to decline without all the local unions joining together and affiliating with a national union.

Members of the United Tannery Workers, Local 1712, CIO, said they would welcome the two independent unions, with the expectation that this would create a joint board of glove and leather workers.[107] This failed, and Local 1712, membership still declining, decided in October 1953 to affiliate with the Amalgamated Clothing Workers. The newly renamed UTLWUFM (United Tannery and Leather Workers Union of Fulton and Montgomery Counties) asked for a 20-cent an hour raise. Local 1712's members voted to strike because of the impasse in negotiations with the tanners, but by the end of January 1954, the union reached an agreement for a three-cent-an-hour

Details of Union Activity

1950

- Manufacturers offered 5 percent wage increase.
- 3,100 operators and day hands and 300 layers-off rejected the offer, Cutters agreed.
- Settlement after 6 months.
- Some operators objected to settlement.
- Walkout threatened.
- Settlement with 5 percent raise as initially offered.

1951

- Cutters elected Gordon Blake to 16th term as president.
- Layers-off elected Nat M. Keene to 11th term as president.
- Operators elected Bertha Beach, replacing Leonard J. Hannig.

1952

- CIO tried to get Layers-off to become an affiliate.
- Tannery union, Local 1712, CIO, won a cost-of-living wage increase that meant the local minimum wage for tannery workers rose to $1.33 an hour.
- Membership in Local 1712 declined to 750 tannery workers.
- The Adirondack Leather Workers Union obtained a five percent raise and increased benefits for workers at the Hermann Loewenstein Tannery after a short strike.
- Local 1712 asked for a 15 percent overall raise that included added benefits but settled for a nine percent package.

1953

- Layers-off rejected CIO affiliation.
- Operators and Day Hands refused to join Amalgamated.
- United Tannery Workers Union, Local 1712, (CIO) affiliated with Amalgamated Clothing Workers Union (CIO) and became United Tannery and Leather Workers Union of Fulton and Montgomery Counties (CIO).
- Cutters and Shavers and Layers-off voted to join Amalgamated (CIO) as Local 1714.

1954

Group within Layers-off left Amalgamated and joined Independent Operators Union.

1955

Strike by Cutters involved 60 shops and 750 cutters.

Operators Union and Layers-off Union crossed picket lines.

Strike settled with no wage increase, but a package of benefits including a second week of vacations with pay and provisions for a union shop.

Amalgamated tried and failed to organize Operators and Day Hands Union.

Gordon G. Blake retired as president of Local 1714.

William Brooks succeeded Blake as president of Local 1714.

End of table cutting as a separate skill within union.

1956

Layers-off threatened strike.

Five-cent-an-hour average increase granted layers-off, making their average pay $1.80 an hour.

overall raise and other benefits. Their contract also called for a study of a way to provide pensions for workers.

At the end of 1953, in a surprise move, the Consolidated Cutters and Shavers Union voted to join Local 1712, UTLWUFM, establishing a joint board to cover all leather and glove workers under the Amalgamated Clothing Workers Union (ACWU).[108] The Consolidated Cutters and Shavers had been an independent union for nearly eighteen years. The ACWU claimed it could promote glove sales through a union label campaign. The Cutters and Shavers Union became Local 1714, still under Gordon Blake.

The Operators and Day Hands lost no time in rejecting an invitation to join the Amalgamated.[109] As the Amalgamated locals planned to move into new quarters, the Joint Board held elections, choosing John L. Noone as president, with minimal changes in the leadership of the branches.[110] Consolidation was anything but smooth with problems exacerbated by the fact the glove unions had had no signed contract for two years.[111] In April 1954, a dissident group within the Layers-off union Local 292, ACWU, followed the union's business agent, Frank McMaster, out of Local 292, which it had joined in 1941, and into the Independent Operators and Day Hands. At the NLRB election held in April, the layers-off voted three to one to withdraw from the Amalgamated.

April 1955 marked three years that the Cutters and Shavers in Local 1714 had worked without a contract. Workers at ten area firms walked out in what the manufacturers called an illegal action.[112] Issues included a three-cent-an-hour wage increase and increased benefits, but no pensions. This, the first official strike since the three-week walkout of 1939, spread to more than 60 shops and involved 750 cutters and shavers. That would have put all 4,000 county glove workers out of work, except for the fact that the Operators and Layers-off voted three to one to cross picket lines. They adamantly refused to support the striking CIO union.[113] This cutters' strike occurred in a slack time when work was already staggered. An editorial reflected the community's concern, which was not so much for the workers as for the cities' need to present the image of a place with a stable labor record.[114]

Members of Local 1714 picketed the George Johns nonunion glove shop. After the pickets left for the night, someone fired shots and threw rocks at the shop's door and tacked up a large derogatory sign. The strike was becoming ugly. Many operators would not cross the picket lines, and with shortages of cut leather developing, more than 1,500 sewers were not at work. As that number surged to over 2,000, it was estimated that production was cut by half.[115] The tannery workers in Local 1712 supported the strike but only with "voluntary contributions," not by contributing union funds or staging a sympathy strike. A mediator was able to bring about an agreement to end the strike after two weeks, without granting the workers an increase in pay.

Glove manufacturers felt they could not raise local wages significantly and survive, but union workers, whose wages had been above the national average, were beginning to lose ground. Their wages were declining in relation to the cost of living and wage scales in other industries. The inability of the unions to work together and their small achievements in the early fifties were disproportionately devastating because all this occurred as the local industry was shrinking and as the surviving manufacturers were moving their operations overseas.

Shortly after the strike, Gordon G. Blake retired as president of Local 1714, a position he had held for eighteen years. Blake started as a table cutter at the age of 14 in 1900 at the George Mandrill Co., where he earned between $15 and $18 a week (Table cutters' wages averaged $70 a week in 1954, so their wages rose between four and four and a half times over the 1900 rate. At the same time, the cost of living nationally, based on the consumer price index, rose to three times the 1900 level.) Blake became head of the cutters' union in 1935. He had witnessed the cutters' four major strikes, 1904, 1914, 1934, and 1955, which was a remarkably small number given the turmoil that surrounded contract negotiations. The first two strikes were for six months, the 1934 strike lasted six weeks. Blake had seen the number of cutters fall from 1,500 to less than half that number. Under his leadership, cutters had won their first benefit—a week's paid vacation—in 1944. They obtained hospitalization insurance in 1946 and paid holidays in 1950.

Blake waged as many battles in Washington on tariffs as did the executive director of the manufacturers' group. Blake fought there for higher minimum wages. He led the local when it became part of a national union, overseeing real gains in wages, though, like most other union leaders of the time, secured almost no gains in worker benefits.

What emerges from this record is the contrast between the number of skirmishes and struggles, constant union pressure, and real successes before 1950 on the one hand and the difficulty of achieving any gains for workers in this postwar climate. Blake must have found it much more difficult than it had been to lead the independent cutters out of the Depression and through the war.[116] How frustrating it must have been for him that in the few years prior to his retirement he was not able to continue the successes of earlier years. Even without having access to manufacturers' profit records and supporting financial information, one has to speculate that the manufacturers really could offer no more. This is one more sign that in the fifties the industry could not sustain itself without going offshore.

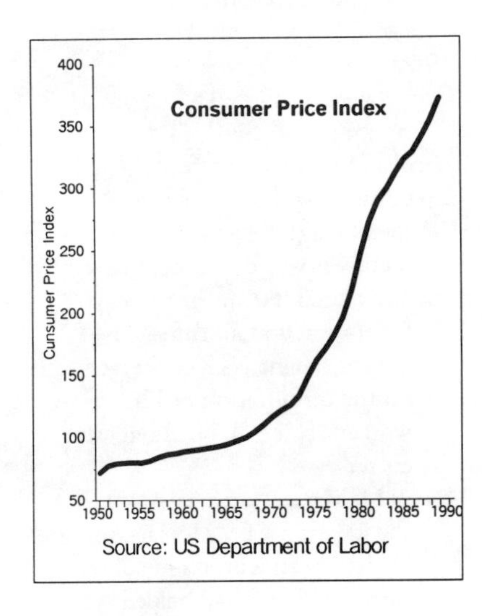

Source: US Department of Labor

With the dwindling number of cutters and changing times, the Cutters union agreed in 1955 to let any member work interchangeably at table, block, or clicker cutting.[117] The elite cadre of table cutters had lost their vigor. They were becoming obsolete as the newer clicker-cutting technology became more pervasive. Their decline also reflected changing styles: consumers no longer wanted tight-fitting gloves, just something warm and easy to put on. Table cutting was no longer needed and no longer justified, given its expense.

The drift toward national unions quickened in May 1955, when the 15-year old independent Adirondack Leather Workers voted to affiliate with the Leather Workers Organizing Committee, CIO. This was the union that had represented 400 workers at G. Levor's since the 1949 struggle, as well as workers at Framglo and Milligan & Higgins, the glue factory.

Because the Operators and Day Hands Union had also been without a contract for three years, the ACWA began organizing those workers, trying to draw them away from their independent union. The ballot for the July 1955 election offered three choices: the current independent union, the ACWA, or neither. The Amalgamated claimed it had been organizing in Puerto Rico to bring wages there to county levels and that it would work toward a pension plan. The independent, now under Mrs. Florence Roberts, joined a fight for survival armed with broadsides and ads to match the ACWA's. Both sides charged the other with financial irregularities. Out of

1957

Operators and Day Hands Union under Mrs. Roberts became United Glove Workers Union of America.

Casey warned manufacturers to "tread lightly" in negotiations because of increase of glove imports.

Manufacturers offered 5-cent-an-hour increase to glove workers.

Increase accepted by Local 1714 after initial rejection by Operators and Layers-off unions.Tannery workers won a small pay raise, about 3 cents an hour.

1959

Workers in all three glove unions won a 5-cent-an-hour raise.

No progress on ACWU's efforts toward a pension plan.

1960

Glove workers offered a 6-cent-an-hour raise.

Local 1714 accepted offer.

Executive Board of UGW urged members to reject offer, but members voted to accept raise.

Fownes closed its Gloversville Operation and all three glove unions sought NLRB intervention on the termination of 120 workers, some 30 of whom were cutters.

Frank McMaster, business agent for the Layers-off for 21 years, retired. He had been a union member since 1918 and had helped separate the Layers-off Union from the Cutters in 1932.

nearly 2,000 eligible voters, 1,379 cast votes and the independent won again 973 to 406.

By 1956 workers in all three unions were paid an average $1.80 an hour. Operators voted down an increase in union dues from $.50 to $1.00 a week. It is difficult to imagine running a union with these limited funds. None of the independent glove unions in the county were able to provide insurance or pensions; they could only negotiate these pensions as part of contracts. However, there was no guarantee that the manufacturers would renew the contracts or stay in business long enough to continue paying insurance policies. The fragmentation of the manufacturers and their precarious financial conditions were probably a greater threat to workers' benefits than the weakness of the unions.

The ACWA continued to try to expand its influence in the county's independent unions and this prompted Mrs. Roberts of the Operators Union to reach out to independent glove unions throughout the country. In early 1957 the independent styled itself the United Glove Workers Union of America, a reflection of Mrs. Roberts personal expansionist dreams.

The decade of the fifties ended as it has started, with union dissension and small gains in wages. The cost of living was rising nationally and union wage gains locally were failing to keep pace. Manufacturers chose not to or could not pay more, and many had already adopted a mode of survival by chasing cheaper labor overseas.

In the decade of the sixties, the glove workers' unions finally consolidated and achieved pensions for their workers. Union activity in the county picked up at the end of 1960 as both glove- and tannery-worker contracts were up for negotiation. Wage negotiations for tannery workers again dragged into the next year.

By 1963 the industry's decline was obvious. In the search for solutions to the industry's decline, Clarence Hallenbeck of the Local 1714, the cutters' union, offered to work with manufacturers when they proposed to set up an experimental plant to explore ways of improving production techniques, but nothing came of it.[118] Makers had sewn a complete glove as late as World War II. Specialization, or sectional work as it is referred to by makers, was slow to be adopted by glovemakers, although silking, hemming, and buttonhole-making had been separate tasks done by different workers since the late nineteenth century. Manufacturers claimed that the unions slowed changes that would have resulted in greater productivity. More likely the slow pace at which specialization was adopted had more to do with setting piecework schedules and the jealousies between different types of workers. Manufacturers could increase production by rearranging and streamlining glove shop operations. Specialization in sewing was gradually adopted. By the early sixties, when the union made the offer, the tasks of attaching thumbs, stitching fourchettes, and closing gloves were already being done by different workers. However, there was little else that manufacturers could do to improve the end result; greater productivity was illusory.

Nationally, the impetus for pension plans had escalated during the 1940s, when contributions to pension plans had been exempted from wage controls. The Taft-Hartley Act had required that pension plans be jointly managed by union and management appointed trustees. Through the fifties, workers in many industries obtained pensions, but they were still not available to glove workers.

When Local 1714 voted to strike in 1963, a principal issue was the union's demand for a monthly pension of $47 to $50 a month funded by the manufacturers, but that year's contract brought no pension settlement. The 1965 glove industry negotiations focused on obtaining a pension plan for glove workers similar to the one Local 1712 had obtained for tannery workers 15 years earlier. The unions sought additional benefits, vacations, and a rate-schedule increase. Local 1714 voted to go on strike on April 1, and with the cutters on strike and the other unions observing the picket lines, the manufacturers closed their shops. The Layers-off did not agree with the settlement to the 32-day strike and issued a 30-day strike notice. The conflict between the unions was growing. The Operators had been urged by Mrs. Florence Roberts Putnam, representing the UGW, to reject the settlement. Her objections were based on proposals for a pension plan. She wrote, "We do not want the Amalgamated Clothing Workers to tell us what pension plan to have. . . . your husbands have led you down the river." She told the operators that the ACWU would try to get them to join that union.[119]

When the Layers-off Union voted to accept a contract identical to the one gained by Local 1714, ACWU, Paul Hladick, head of the Layers-off union resigned, stating his dissatisfaction with the way his branch was forced to accept the same distribution of benefits as the other unions.[120] That fall, the Layers-off voted to pull out of the United Glove Workers and return to the Amalagamated as Local 292, putting the local back in the national union it had left more than a decade earlier.

In 1965 Mrs. Margaret Pedrick was elected president of the Operators and Day Hands branch of the United Glove Workers. (Mrs. Putnam chose not to run again.) This move portended a change in that union's policy that would finally bring about union cooperation.

In early 1966 the ACWU reached an agreement for a pension plan for Cutters and Layers-offs. Pension proposals were the stimulus that brought the Operators Branch of the UGW to a vote on joining the national union. Just days after the ACWU announced an agreement for the pension in August, 1966 the Operators again voted against joining the ACWU. The two other unions formally adopted the plan in early 1967. It is ironic that this occurred at a time when the industry had so declined that only 2,800 workers remained in all three uions.

The pension plan achieved by the ACWU unions as part of the new two-year contract would give workers $55 a month at age 65 and would go into effect on April 1, 1971. The national union required union workers to be employed in a union shop for 20 years in order to qualify for a pension. In the 1966 agreement, the union gave local workers a credit of 15 years, whether they had been members of the ACWU or not. This was a one-time offer, which only required that the worker be employed for an additional five years in a union shop, until April 1, 1971, in order to qualify for the pension. This extraordinary gift achieved the pensions local unions had been unable to negotiate previously. Pensioners would also receive Social Security benefits and could earn up to $1,500 a year without reducing union retirement benefits.

Although the union pension agreement that went into effect in 1971 granted workers credit for work in previous years even if the work was not done in a union shop, many thought the plan was less than generous. Further, the plan and subsequent changes in federal regulations have been confusing for union workers. More than a few workers had to work beyond

1963

Glove union talks stalled.

Local 1714 asked for a 25-cent-an-hour wage increase.

Local 1714 struck.

The other two unions joined in the strike.

Strike lasted ten days.

Glove workers won 7-cent-an-hour increase.

Tannery workers obtained a three-year contract, giving them a total raise of $.11 an hour, benefits, and increased manufacturer contributions to the pension fund.

1965

Cutters struck over wages, benefits, and vacations.

Cutters struck for 32 days.

Five-cent-an-hour raise offered all glove workers.

Cutters (Amalgamated) and Operators (United) accepted.

Layers-off (United) rejected offer, then accepted it.

Layers-off voted to leave United and return to Amalgamated.

Tannery workers accepted a 3- to 4-cent-an-hour raise to the average $2.25 hourly pay, after negotiating over piece rates.

1966

The ACWU reached an agreement for a pension plan for Cutters and Layers-off to take effect in 1971.

The Operators of UGW again voted against joining the ACWU.

1967

ACWU got a two-year contract with 10-cent an hour increase, plus a pension plan.

UGW got a similar contract.

Contract applied to 2,800 glove workers.

Local 1712 rejected a three-year contract giving a $.25-an-hour raise over the three years. The lowest minimum would have risen from $1.92 an hour to $2.17 and pieceworkers would have received just over $3 an hour in the third year.

1969

Operators (UGW) voted to join ACWU.

All three unions granted a $.43-an-hour increase over a period of three years.

normal retirement age to qualify for the pension. Bill Towne, the current local head of Amalgamated, said that retirees complained because they forgot that the initial plan was not even funded by local employers, but was essentially a gift from other union workers from both inside and outside Fulton and Montgomery counties. Towne also believes that it is ironic that many retirees began a decade-long complaint that it was the ACWU's fault that the pensions were so small, without acknowledging that 15 years of the pension plan was an outright gift and that they had turned down affiliation with the Amalgamated many times previously.[121]

On the other hand, when the plan was put into effect, union members who had worked all their lives in a union shop felt they had been deprived of adequate pensions. In part they felt cheated because the pensions had to cover so many workers, even those who had not worked in union shops all their careers. Union workers were also upset because the plan allowed credit for nonunion work. The one-time granting of credit for nonunion work also confused workers who later could not claim such nonunion work toward their pensions and were compelled to work in a union shop until their retirement.[122]

In 1974 the Employee Retirement Income Security Act (ERISA), a federal program regulating all pensions, was adopted. It was designed to eradicate employer and trustee abuses of the private pension systems. Among its provisions was the requirement that a worker had to work for an employer who was contributing to the pension plan for a minimum of ten years. These ten years would vest the worker in the pension plan; in other words, the plan would stay in effect as the worker moved among union shops. However, many glove workers moved from shops covered by the union plan to those not covered, and when they retired they received only what had been vested. And, they could lose that if the time worked for a non-covered employer was more than that for a covered employer. ERISA did not change the union pension plan, but only added to it. However, the complexity of the pension arrangements were an added source of confusion and discontent among workers.

The prospect of a pension plan had not been sufficient to induce the Operators Branch of the United Glove Workers to join the ACWU in 1967. So, in January 1969, for the second time in 14 years, the ACWU asked the NLRB to hold an election to determine whether that union should represent the Operators Branch. At first the Operators would not agree to the consent election, but it was finally held in June 1969; and 1,200 workers voted three to one to join the ACWU. This ended the Independent Operators Union, which had been founded in 1933 as an outgrowth of several smaller unions that primarily functioned as negotiating units for different types of sewers. At one time the independent Operators Union had 5,000 members. When it joined the ACWU, the demise of the independent glove and leather unions in Fulton County was complete. The new branch, Local 1715, immediately began negotiations on a new contract, which was quickly settled. It gave workers an average 43-cent an hour increase in a three-year contract signed by all three amalgamated unions. When the unions affiliated with the ACWU it meant that all workers were able to obtain pensions they had sought for decades.

Union membership continued to decline through the seventies. The labor scene was relatively quiet at the beginning of the decade, even during the 1972 contract talks, because the major pension struggle was over and the unions were no longer fighting among themselves. The ACWU brought demands for increased wages but union members voted quite peaceably, and with a margin of nine to one to accept the ten cents an hour offered by the manufacturers. The new contract stipulated that those who were drawing pensions and wished to continue working were not to be given work until there was full employment.

The 1974 negotiations brought a two-year contract with a $.20-an-hour package, but the number of workers in all three unions who were eligible to vote on the contract had dropped to 964. While the steepest decline in the number of glove concerns appears to have been in the 1960s, the decrease in the number of glove workers accelerated through the late sixties and into the seventies.

The 1976 union contract brought pieceworkers an average ten-cent-an-hour gain in each of the contract's two years and a mechanism for establishing a joint worker-management committee to air complaints and improve the industry.[123] That year, the Amalgamated Clothing and Textile Workers Union (ACTWU) was formed by a merger of the Amalgamated Clothing Workers of America and the Textile Workers Union of America.

For the first time in its history, the glove workers' contract was settled three months before the old one was to expire. The contract, agreed to at the end of 1977, called for a dollar an hour salary increase and 30 percent increase for pieceworkers over a 45-month span. Only 40 percent of the union's members bothered to vote on accepting the pact.[124]

Tannery workers, however, rejected a pact that called for $.25-an-hour increase for workers earning between $4.00 and $6.00 an hour and $.15-an-hour for workers earning over $6.00 an hour. They rejected a second contract before finally agreeing at the beginning of 1978 to a plan that called for much-improved medical benefits and a raise of $.25 an hour for the first year, $.35 an hour for the second year of the two-year contract. The county had approximately 1,050 union tannery workers. The increased membership reflected the changes in the tanning industry and its slow turnaround.

In mid-1980 the Amalgamated filed petitions requesting trade adjustment assistance for workers in five firms that had reduced employment because of foreign competition. Workers in those firms would receive up to 70 percent of their average weekly pay, plus help toward qualifying for and obtaining new employment. The firms were C. J. Bachner & Sons, producer of ladies' dress gloves; and Mario Papa & Sons; Gates-Mills; Joseph P. Conroy; and Pagano Gloves, makers of men's, ladies', and sport gloves. Similar petitions were filed for employees of sixteen tanning firms. Petitions had already been accepted for Pan American Tanning and Clair Glove.

The parent union ACTWU attempted to reopen the four-year contract that was to end in March 1982. A proposed contract was initially rejected by a large majority, although only half of the union's remaining 800 members voted on the contract proposal. When accepted in April 1982, the plan called for a two-year contract, but few other details about it were made public at the time.[125] That year, June was a remarkably placid month—all three unions agreed to the five percent increase offered by the manufacturers as a cost-of-living settlement. Leather workers received a five-cent-an-hour raise.

The tannery workers union, Local 1712, remained strong until the closing of the Feuer group of tanneries. Union membership declined by nearly 700; so by 1998 only 300 tannery workers remained in the local.

1971
ACWU Pension Plan went into effect.

1972
New two-year contract called for ten-cent-an-hour increase.

1974
New two-year contract called for $.20-an-hour increase.
Total glove union membership declineed to 964 workers.

1976
New two-year contract called for 10-cent-an-hour increase.
Amalgamated Clothing Workers and Textile Workers Union of America merged to form Amalgamated Clothing and Textile Workers Union

1978
New 45-month contract called for $1.00-an-hour salary increase, 30-percent increase for piecework.
Glove union membership declined to 850.

1980
Amalgamated requested trade adjustments assistance for five firms affected by foreign competition.

1982 New two-year contract called for 5-percent increase
Glove union membership declines to 800

1995 Amalgamated membership declined to 160 members, with approximately 12 working on gloves, the rest in glove distribution jobs.
Amalgamated merged with International Ladies Garment Workers Union to form Union of Needletrades, Industrial & Textile Employees (UNITE).

The ACTWU, which merged in 1995 with the International Ladies Garment Workers Union to form a new union, the Union of Needletrades, Industrial & Textile Employees (UNITE), now has about 160 members in its glove local 2486 in Fulton County and 60 members in another local at Fownes Brothers in Amsterdam. However, only about a dozen union members actually work on gloves, and all of these are at Joseph P. Conroy's glove company in Johnstown. Samco, Sam Greco's company, and Peter Kiernan's Pique (PK) gloves both produce gloves with nonunion workers. The rest of the union members sort, pack, and ship gloves made overseas, and the majority of them work for Grandoe.

As one more indication of the way the industry began to shrink many years ago, only 427 former glove workers received union pensions in 1998.

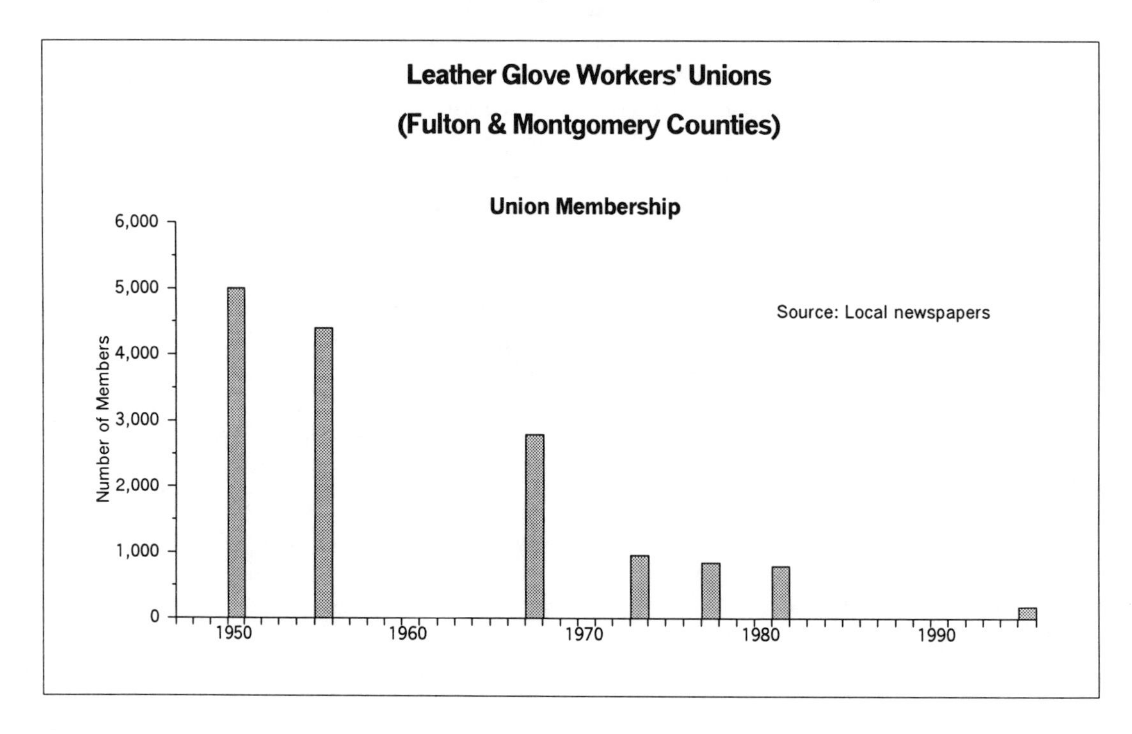

The Last Chapter

By the end of the 1990s a very short list of glove companies remained in the county and only a handful of them still manufactured gloves. Another handful are multinational that have no manufacturing facilities here. Bali Leather, Gates-Mills, Swany America Corp., and Grandoe, Inc. have only design and distribution facilities in the county as well as corporate offices.

The list of these survivors would be longer, except for the fate of New York City–based Aris Corp., whose experience shows just how uncertain it is to work overseas and organize production globally. In 1969 the Stanton brothers sold Aris to Sara Lee Corp.

Aris had developed the Isotoner ® glove, a one-size-fits-all glove made of a patented two-way stretch fabric with leather inserts and decorations. It could be produced cheaply and sold at a high price and great profit. Stores loved Isotoners because they did not have to maintain the complex inventory of gloves in many different sizes.

Aris's operation in the Philippines outstripped all others. By the early 1980s, its huge factory employed seven thousand workers. Between 1985 and 1990, the company was making 20,000 dozen gloves a week, equal to two-thirds of Fulton County's all-time peak production. Aris's production was greater than that of Fownes and Grandoe combined.

Under Sara Lee, Aris-Isotoner became one of the conglomerate's most profitable brands. Sales grew from $6 million in 1969 to $220 million in the early 1990s, when the company reported a profit of $35 million or 15 percent of sales. In the process, Aris won 75 percent of the department store market. The company's Manila factory, managed by Lari Stanton, son of one of Aris's founding brothers, was able to turn out 27 million pairs of gloves more profitably than factories in China.

In 1990, Sara Lee closed the Manila plant, which had a highly skilled work force. The parent company opened a plant in India and dispensed with Stanton. Sara Lee tried to extract even greater profits from its subsidiary, and new management turned to independent contractors to increase profitability. Aris discovered that the contractors were producing lower-quality gloves at a higher cost. Within four years the company's sales had decreased by half. Operating losses piled up even with an infusion of capital from Sara Lee. New executives failed to save the company and it was sold—"virtually given away"[126]—becoming Totes-Isotoner, which remains unprofitable. As of 1998, its production continues to decline.

Grandoe Corporation contracted glove manufacturing in Taiwan briefly, an operation that overlapped its work in the Philippines. In 1986 the company moved from the Philippines to China, where wages were about $3.00 a day. Zuckerwar's operation was the first American firm to make gloves in China. The company is now headed by Richard C.'s son Richard J. (locals also distinguish them by Sr. and Jr). Under Richard Jr. Grandoe added a factory in India in 1994, which employs close to 500 people.

In 1995 Grandoe moved to a new, larger factory in China. Richard J. Zuckerwar sent his nephew, a fourth-generation descendent of S. Schrecker, to China to locate a suitable site for the complex. The huge building, built by the Chinese in Fuzhou, houses one of the more modern glove factories in the world. It is wholly owned by a corporation set up by Zuckerwar.

The huge making room and one of the old clicker-cutting machines at Grandoe's Fuzhou glove factory. Photographs by the author

The factory is in an economic development zone planned to attract investments from Taiwan. Superhighways lined with trees and bicycle lanes, along with new bridges and a very modern airport, serve the zone. Skyscrapers rise in downtown Fuzhou, which a decade earlier was a small village set among rice paddies. Apartment buildings and factories face the new city's roads, but in late 1998 as many as half of the Chinese-built factories stand empty.

In 1998, the author visited the Fuzhou factory, and she made the following observations about the factory which employs about 840 workers: The cutting floor is filled with clicker-cutters, machines first shipped from Gloversville to the Philippines, then on to China. (Most of these old machines, some made by Curtin & Hebert of Gloversville, are controlled with one hand, something that OSHA would not permit. In the U.S., such machines must be equipped with two control levers so that it takes two hands to operate these fiercely stamping machines, thus protecting fingers.) Many sewing machines were also shipped from Fulton County, but are gradually being replaced by new Japanese machines, and more recently by those built by the Chinese. In the Fuzhou plant, the cutting room is on the ground floor because the factory could not support the clicker machines on a higher floor, so the work-flow design is not ideal.

The making room at Grandoe's Fuzhou glove factory. Photograph by the author.

The huge making rooms dwarf even Fulton County's largest. Initially fifteen managers from Grandoe's Philippine company began training Chinese counterparts, and in 1998 only nine remained. General manager Aniceto Delos Reyes also oversaw the India plant and contract work in Indonesia. He had had many years experience in the garment business and worked for Carl Ross Glove Co. of Wisconsin in the Philippines. Cesar A. Co was assistant manager in charge of the Fuzhou workers, who are mostly young women recruited from all over China. Co says the company is very strict about not hiring women under eighteen, unlike some shoe companies such as Nike, which also have factories in Fuzhou.

The Filipino managers do not speak Chinese, so English is the common language; this creates difficulties in communication because the Chinese workers understand little English. Initially, Chinese workers were very inexperienced and lacked a consciousness of quality and cleanliness. Constant attention by management and supervisors has dramatically improved quality and the factory is spotless.

Women workers live in barracks and rented rooms, taking only one week off a year to return to their homes for vacation. The ten-hour work days, six days a week, have shrunk to eight hours, five days a week.

The Filipinos all live together in a nearby hotel, work long hours, and feel this is no place to bring their families. The controller, who recently returned to the Philippines, was a woman whose young children were cared for by her parents in her native land. She could only return to the Philippines twice a year for nine-day leaves; Co has the same two vacations; and Ani Reyes has three week-long vacation periods.

There are no unions in China, but wages and production rates are negotiated with labor committees. Workers receive housing subsidies, and the minimum wage is 500 yuan ($65) per month. The work is still somewhat seasonal. The Chinese New Year coincides with the end of most contract work, so this vacation does not interrupt work schedules. In rush seasons, many workers put in overtime, which is well compensated, but limited to 36 hours of overtime a week. Factory conditions are better than in the shoe factories that make up the majority of Fuzhou manufacturing, so Grandoe experiences a low worker turnover rate.

Some things that happen in the factory sound just like Fulton County in its heyday—beauty contests, parties, dances, events to recognize longevity with the company. Other things are quite different—morning exercises and monthly meetings to reinforce China's birth-control policies.

Leather gloves are produced from pigskins from Taiwan, sheepskins from India, deerskins from the United States, cowhides from Japan, and goatskins from Pakistan. Ski gloves make up the bulk of production and these require about twice the work of a leather dress glove.

The company is experimenting with production teams, groups of approximately 20 women who work interchangeably at tasks to speed work. As a further incentive, the members of the group receive pay based on the output of the entire team. Workers do pitch in to increase the team's output, although there was initially resistance to group work and pay. This team approach has proved to be efficient and has meant that leather moving into the factory comes out as gloves in minimal time—about a week, versus four weeks previously. However, except for savings related to inventory costs, there have been no real savings in manufacturing. Further, inspections at four different steps are required to ensure quality.

Although most of the gloves are shipped out directly to large retailers, a significant amount is shipped in large containers by boat to New Jersey, then trucked directly to Gloversville for repacking and distribution. All Grandoe has left in Fulton County are three buildings, neatly painted, with spotless interiors. These structures house no manufacturing operations, only the warehouse for transhipping gloves, a design workshop and sample-making operation, and, of course, corporate headquarters, which will shortly be linked by one computer system directly to the Far Eastern factories. At Grandoe's distribution center, the shipping operation gives the appearance of the same friendly atmosphere, with camaraderie between managers and workers, that used to be the hallmark of many of the county's smaller glove shops. It is also plagued by seasonality, which limits full-time employment.

In the early 1990s the company produced 250,000 dozen gloves a year, a number that has been more than cut in half in recent years as production has shifted to ski and snowboard gloves. Employment levels have remained relatively constant.

ADIRONDACK

Gates-Mills also began to pull back from the Philippines in the 1970s, though it never left completely. The company went to Taiwan and Korea and contracted work in both places from the mid-1970s to the mid-1980s. It was still expanding in Fulton County, buying the leather-glove manufacturing Superb Division of Crescendoe-Superb Gloves in 1979.

Gates-Mills continued to focus on the manufacture of men's fine leather gloves. Sewing at the Johnstown factory declined gradually in the early 1980s, and by mid-decade all of Gates-Mills work was done overseas. The company even sent some deerskins to Taiwan from Fulton County to be sewn into gloves. Gates-Mills tried to operate in Indonesia, but transportation problems there made it impossible to stay. Then, in 1988, the company began to contract with a Chinese firm that now does work exclusively for Gates-Mills.

The company moved in 1987 to its present site adjacent to Gloversville's industrial park. Gates-Mills built its facility before the opportunity zone and the industrial park had been established there. In 1998 Gates-Mills did no manufacturing in Fulton County, but its manufacturing capacity overseas was greater than at any time it did operate locally.[127]

Joseph P. Conroy was among the last surviving county manufacturer to move overseas. Conroy became a gloveman by working at every aspect of glovemaking except sewing. He believes he was and remains successful because he "worked too much—days, nights, Saturdays, Sundays sometimes."

By 1998, only about 15 percent of the company's gloves were produced locally in two plants: one on Market Street in Johnstown, which originally housed Jules Higier's Superb Glove Co., and Norwell Gloves, Inc. in Northville. In 1998 the former was a union shop with about 15 workers, the latter a nonunion shop with 15 women sewing gloves.

Conroy began to contract gloves from the Philippines in the early 1970s and is still contracting gloves there and also in Sri Lanka. One of Conroy's trusted workers recalled that the first several batches of imported gloves were terrible, with different colored linings in a pair of gloves, poor stitching that left gaps in seams, and mismatched leathers. Gradually, however, the quality improved so that overseas production became every bit as good as American work.

Conroy, 87 years old in 1998, has found it difficult to operate overseas, planning a year ahead and tying up capital and inventory for long periods. However it is the overseas work that enables him to continue manufacturing in Fulton County. Most of his county employees have been with the company for 25 years or more and he worries that he will not have enough work here to keep them employed. "I always want to keep some business here."[128]

Bali Leather John Widdemer, who became associated with Hilts-Willard in 1957, pioneered in producing gloves in Japan in 1962, and produced gloves in the Phillipines in the seventies. In the eighties he formed Bali Leather, which by 1998 produced primarily golf gloves. His company participated in the global market in a smaller way than Grandoe or Gates-Mills, but the practices were similar. Sometimes his firm bought skins in Nigeria that had already been tanned using a process for washable leather developed for Bali. After he examined a sample of the skins in Nigeria, the skins were sent directly to a glove factory in Madras, India, which is jointly owned by Widdemer and an Indian partner. In 1990 this factory replaced a similar venture that Widdemer had in Korea. In this case, Widdemer had a Japanese partner who controlled the Korean factories. At other times, Widdemer has bought skins in Africa and has them tanned in Fulton County before shipping them to his factories overseas to be sewn.

Elmer Little - Swany Corporation Internationalization has not all been the movement of American companies abroad. Swany, said to be the largest glove-manufacturing firm in Japan, gained a foothold in America in 1987 by buying out Elmer Little & Son. Elmer Little had been able to expand through the 1970s, producing "The Warmer," a sandwich glove with a knit glove base, pile lining, and cowhide split leather on the back and palm.

Using the cowhide to cover 50 percent of the glove reduced the duties on their Philippine-made gloves by 10 percent, therefore giving the company an edge on the market and dominance over competing cheap PVC (polyvinyl chloride) gloves from Taiwan. This two-year crest was fueled by million-dollar-a-year sales on this glove alone. The company developed many new technologies, using fabric when the price of cowhide went through the roof in the late seventies. The business tripled between 1975 and 1980.

Then problems hit on many fronts: Aris, a principal competitor, advertised that it would accept all returns and allowed end-of-season payment after returns were made. (This had been tacit county policy, but it had never been so advertised.) This reduced cash flow, and combined with inflation, William Dzierson's illness, Elmer Little's leveraged position, and problems within its New York City bank, ultimately defeated the company. The bank cancelled its line of credit, and Eric Dzierson, who succeeded his father as CEO, decided in 1987 that selling the company was the only way out.

In 1986 the county's unemployment was rising, the population was shrinking, five leather manufacturers had recently closed, and Gloversville High School was experiencing a high drop-out rate. The glove industry was in its death throes. That year Gloversville was selected by the administration of New York Governor Mario Cuomo as one of the first areas to receive the designation "Opportunity Zone" or "Economic Development Zone (EDZ)." Given the county's problems it is easy to see why the local EDZ was approved.

The announcement that the Elmer Little & Son glove firm was to relocate from Johnstown to Gloversville was the opening act of one of the more bizarre and unfortunate last scenes in the closing years of the glove industry. The story of Swany's purchase of the company also exposes one of the sorriest chapters in the county's glove-making history. The way Swany manipulated benefits provided by the county, state, and federal government to attract business and jobs is a moral tale of the problems generated by economic development agencies.[129] Those details of Swany's history are beyond the scope of this book, but it is instructive to look at them briefly to understand the improbability of creating new glove manfacturing jobs in the county and, as a sidebar, how county residents continue to distrust unions.

In the process of acquiring Elmer Little & Son, Swany applied for certification as an EDZ business enterprise and in the process swore that the company had not shifted its operation from any other area of the state that was not designated an EDZ. Further, Swany maintained it would retain local manufacturing, keep existing employees, continue existing labor contracts, and enlarge its work force.

Within a few months, Swany asked for two million dollars in financing to fund a relocation and expansion project through the county Industrial Development Authority to erect a 57,000-foot warehouse and distribution center. The arrangement would give the company property tax abatements and wage tax credits. To take advantage of the EDZ opportunity, Swany moved Elmer Little's operation from Johnstown to Gloversville, a step contrary to EDZ requirements. Swany also applied for an Urban Development Agency grant to supplement funding raised through revenue bonds.

The issue of job creation became a contentious one. The company gave out various figures for the number of employees and jobs created and jobs terminated. This aspect brought local union leader Bill Towne into the fray and undoubtedly his efforts were primarily responsible for Swany losing its certification. But, the story is a very complex one, and the problems of a local group running a venture as complicated as the EDZ are so great, it is easy to understand how Swany was able to take advantage of the situation.

Swany already had a distribution center in nearby Fonda. The company proposed to move that operation to the new facility and this moving of jobs within the state was also contrary to the rules designating the Economic Development Zone.

Newspapers in Schenectady and Amsterdam joined the local press in trying to discover how the Fulton County Economic Development Council (FCEDC) was operating. Their editorials were as effective as the unions in calling attention to the Swany problem and the alleged misapplication of state Economic Development Corporation (EDC) funds. The union formally requested that Swany be decertified and stripped of the business incentives it obtained by moving into the local EDZ. The charges brought before the Department of Economic Development hearing were that Swany had failed to create new employment in the Gloversville EDZ; it failed to prevent loss of employment in the EDZ; and it falsified information on its application for certification.

The decertification hearing discovered the fact that Swany was merely shuffling jobs around. It never addressed the union's other contention that the company was just establishing low-paid jobs, not true manufacturing jobs. The union's charges of union busting were deferred to a later NLRB hearing. As a result of the hearing, Swany was decertified on the grounds that its application had contained inaccurate data, that the company transferred existing employment in the state to the zone, and that it failed to operate its facility in accordance with its application and thereby failed to create jobs.

The union's efforts to bring these charges to a hearing brought criticism to the union and polarized the community. People involved in the EDC, local government, and the chamber of commerce accused the union of being concerned only for union jobs, not with the larger picture of creating jobs under the FCEDC. Some felt that the union's actions seriously jeopardized the communities' efforts to attract new business.

It is also true that if the union had not acted, the problems of the local EDC with respect to Swany and the falsification of Swany's initial application for certification might never have been examined. The union saw primarily union busting, overwhelming the larger issues of Swany's failure to live up to conditions established by EDC. No one ever addressed the union leader's question, "Why did it have to be the union that exposed the Swany situation?" Details of this fray underscored the community's distrust of unions.

Parenthetically, Swany had made a stab at manufacturing machine-knitted gloves in the county, thanks to a Wal-Mart contract. This huge chain favored domestic products, but within a year, Wal-Mart began buying these gloves overseas, and Swany discontinued even this small-scale manufacturing in the county.

Although, contrary to opinion at the time, the local EDZ did manage to attract other new businesses to the depressed county, but there would be no more manufacturing of gloves. The EDZ concept's biggest shortcoming, according to Joseph P. Conroy, was the fact that it offered no help to existing companies.

Swany's example is probably more important for what it may tell of the future. Not only has the industry become globalized, but ownership of local firms by foreign companies, as in the Swany case, may expand in the future.

Government Contracts

Government contracts continued to sustain a small number of the county's glove manufacturers. These contracts totalled one million dollars in 1965, double that amount in 1966. The Vincent Sanges glove firm shared some of the larger orders with the Mario Papa & Sons firm; Grandoe and J. M. Rubin & Sons also won large contracts. In 1967, the Sanges firm won a governmental unit-quality award for its production.

The government had a policy of awarding only a portion of large contracts to the lowest bidder, and of apportioning as much as half the order among average bidders. This made bidding on government contracts quite profitable and served to spread the work around.[130]

The government requires that military gloves be manufactured in the United States. A few glovemakers were able to stay in business by doing government contract work to the exclusion of other work. One of those businesses had a precipitous and ultimately very sad ending.

Mario Papa & Sons was one of the county manufacturers that never went overseas; it tried to survive doing government work. Mario Papa, the firm's founder, was born in Naples, Italy. His family had a confectionery business, which his uncles took over on his father's death. He came to Gloversville in 1907 when he was only fifteen and was apprenticed to another uncle as a glove cutter.

Mario went to night school to learn English and in 1917 he became a laying-off contractor. His shop had a half-dozen employees. Dominic Papa, one of Mario's sons, remembers[131] how much help his father's firm was given to enable it to start and stay in business. He also remembers the cutthroat competition. George Curtin helped Mario acquire the needed steam tables, giving him used tools and machines. Curtin is remembered as a man who knew how to invest in people. Mario layed-off gloves for 25 firms, including Grandoe. On one occasion, when he needed a loan and Richard Zuckerwar, Sr., had no spare cash, Zuckerwar gave Mario his diamond ring to pawn.

In 1934 Mario began making gloves in a shop he established as Mario Papa & Sons. At first he sold gloves to Elite and C. J. Bachner, firms that had salespeople. Then he branched out, making men's pigskin gloves, 100 dozen a week. Dominic remembers that at one time Bachner failed to pay for gloves Mario had made and Mario was unable to meet a payday for his help. He went to Ellery Willard, who was a manufacturers' representative, and Willard loaned him the $1,800 payroll and quickly recouped his loan by selling the gloves Bachner had returned. Willard helped the Papas get into the retail business.

During the Korean War, the Papa firm produced many more pigskin gloves than it could sell. Mario "almost cried as he told Menkes Feuer that he could not pay the money he owed for the pigskins." Feuer picked up the phone and called Johnstown Tannery and told him to turn over to Mario Papa and Sons $30,000 worth of pigskins that Feuer had placed in the tannery to be tanned. He did not worry about credit, and told Mario that with four sons, he would succeed." John Naudin of Jones & Naudin also helped the Papas obtain credit in order to buy skins. Dominic remembers the firm also bought pigskins from Victor Arbib of Spanish-American Leather.[132] Arbib was Jewish, but spoke Italian fluently, and he too helped the Papas. The Papas had many ups and downs, especially in the fifties, but someone always helped them.

Throughout the fifties, Mario Papa & Sons kept winning government contracts, and Dominic Papa served on many advisory committees relating to government contracts. In 1952 Mario Papa & Sons received a Navy commendation for the quality of its government contract work.[133] In 1958 Dominic Papa was offered a position on the industrial advisory committee of the Army's quartermaster research and engineering command.[134] The company secured a $60,000 government contract in 1959, typical of the contracts it had won over the years. In 1960 the firm obtained a government commendation for responsible bidding, adherence to specifications and prompt delivery.[135] The company received another commendation in 1961.

The Papa company opened a subsidiary in Richmondville, Schoharie County, in 1961. At its peak, the company employed about 300 workers, 200 in Gloversville and others in Richmondville and Rutland, Vermont.

In the spring of 1962, Dominic Papa addressed the NAGM on how to obtain government contracts.[136] The firm was awarded more contracts in 1962 and 63. The Papa firm continued doing government work through the early 1980s, receiving commendations several times, among them a Defense Department award in 1981 for quality work.

In 1973 Dominic Papa was elected president of the NAGM. The next year he was named to the federal Leather and Leather Products Advisory Group of the U. S. Department of Commerce.

In an attempt to improve business, the Papa glove firm branched into knit hosiery in 1975. All along, bidding on government contracts was attractive because foreign firms, with their lower prices, were not permitted to make these bids. When the Trade Policy Staff Committee considered permitting foreign firms to bid on government contracts, the committee decided the prohibition was not a trade barrier. It was Mario Papa as a member of the advisory board who made the motion that permitted the prohibition to be taken to the Geneva Conference for final decision, where it was upheld.[137]

What happened to Mario Papa & Sons and Grandoe is a moral tale that sums up the problems local industry had in trying to survive with government contracts.

In December 1988 the antitrust division of the U. S. Department of Justice filed charges against Mario Papa & Sons and Dominic S. Papa, as president of the company, in the District Court for the Eastern District of Pennsylvania. The papers charged that:

> *Beginning as early as 1958 and continuing into 1988, the exact dates being unknown to the United States, the defendants and co-conspirators entered into and engaged in a combination and conspiracy to suppress and eliminate competition by rigging bids and allocating contracts for dress gloves for military personnel purchased by the United States Department of Defense. The combination and conspiracy unreasonably restrained interstate trade and commerce in violation of Section 1 of the Sherman Act.*[138]

Similar charges were filed against Grandoe Corporation and its chairman of the board Richard C. Zuckerwar, except the start date was "as early as 1979."[139] The individuals involved in both cases were charged with participating in meetings and telephone conversations to discuss and agree on prospective bids to be submitted; of allocating such contracts among the defendants and co-conspirators; and submitting collusive and rigged bids on such contracts.

Dominic Papa pled guilty to two counts. In March 1989 he was sentenced to 90 days on the first count, with probation to follow, and fined $100,000 for each count. His company was fined $300,000 on each count and assessed $150,000 in civil fines. At sentencing he told the judge, "I have been living in shame. I am sorry for the sorrow I have brought to my family, friends, and workers who are everything. I did something against the government I love."[140]

The Papa company, several of its officers, and three subsidiaries (Little Falls Glove Company, Ace Glove Company of Richmondville, and Elpam, Inc. of Rutland) were prohibited from bidding on government contracts for seven years. Government contracts had been such a major part of the company's business that within the year the company closed, leaving close to a hundred workers without jobs.

The bid-rigging scheme actually extended into the Midwest. The first company to be charged in this bid-rigging scheme was Illinois Glove Co. of Chicago. Gilbert Smickler, president of Illinois Glove Company, had "implicated Mario Papa & Sons in the bid-rigging conspiracy"[141] and received a lighter sentence and smaller fine (60 days in jail and a $300,000 fine). Charges were also filed against the Damascus Corporation of Rutland, Vermont, and its president Bernard Montant was fined $50,000. The last firm to be charged was the Steinberg Brothers Glove Company of Amsterdam (also known as Amsterdam Glove Co.) The two brothers each received $250,000 fines in addition to their company's million-dollar fine.[142]

Grandoe's business never depended that heavily on government contracts, so except for the fine the company was not severely affected by the federal case. Richard Zuckerwar, Sr., however, was devastated by his 60-day jail sentence and $390,000 fine.[143] He retired from the business, leaving Richard Jr. as head of the firm. The father—who many remember as one of the most refined, knowledgeable, and handsome of glovemen, one who was kind and generous and exuded an aura that made men proud to work for him—took personal responsibility for the company's problems.

It was quite a leap from the time local industry was encouraged to work together in the early days of the NRA to the Nixon era clamp-down on such collusion. In the interim the government permitted firms to bid jointly to aid the war effort in the forties and encouraged negotiated bidding during the Korean War to facilitate glove production. The many times that the government relaxed antitrust provisions may have blurred local manufacturers' perceptions of what was expected of them. On the other hand, the 1954 settlement of federal charges made it clear that manufacturers would never again engage in such practices.

Many of the manufacturers whom the author interviewed say that of course manufacturers discussed prices over the years. Often at the end of association meetings a small group would stay behind to discuss contracts. Dominic Papa said he felt "they had been encouraged by the government to do it [work together] all along."[144]

The county's most recent and probably most egregious criminal act with respect to government contracts occurred in the late 1990s. Everett D. Weber, president of the defunct Rubin Glove Company, pleaded guilty in 1997 in federal court to overstating the value of inventory in order to obtain an asset-based line of credit and to submitting false invoices to the Department of Defense in the completion of a $7.6 million contract with the government.

And, lest it be perceived that these manipulations of contracts and actions to defraud the government occurred only in recent years as the industry was declining, it should be noted that a similar cloud hung over Gloversville's biggest hero among glove manufacturers. During his tenure in Congress (1898-1907), it was alleged that Lucius Littauer interceded with the Quartermaster General's Department to secure a contract for his company for the production of gauntlet gloves for the Army. Littauer's company "had been prominently connected with glove contracts with the War Department"[145] and had such a contract during the Spanish-American War. Littauer's role was concealed in the activities of a middleman, the E. R. Lyon Co., and Littauer's involvement was revealed in 1903 when the Lyon company became bankrupt. This "gauntlet scandal," which Littauer claimed was politically motivated, brought an end to his aspirations for a position in Teddy Roosevelt's cabinet. (Such an appointment was not outside the realm of possibility in light of the fact Roosevelt was Littauer's friend and Harvard roommate.) The matter was allowed to drag on and never went to trial because of the statute of limitations. Littauer was never convicted, although his career in Congress ended as a result of the charges.[146]

Littauer was, however, convicted in 1914 of a charge unrelated to the glove business—he smuggled jewelry into the country to help his brother avoid paying customs. Both men were given suspended sentences and *The New York Times* made much of Lucius Littauer's two-faced actions—fighting for higher tariffs and protected markets to help his business but not paying duties when it suited him personally.[147]

Wrongdoing has permeated the local industry. There are numerous rumors of theft, and several cases involving stolen skins. One particularly large theft was settled in a 1977 court action that penalized many glovemen who had purchased stolen skins. All along, competition and just plain greed drove many to devious means.

The only large company still making gloves for the government in 1998 was the Smickler firm in Illinois, the same firm that blew the whistle in the case against Papa and Grandoe. No other large firms wanted to deal with the government: only a few small manufacturers, like Greco, continued to do so. The small firms engaged in such contract work mostly because the government had waived some specifications in order to entice them to bid. For a time the government even waived the requirement that gloves had to be produced in the country. All this limited manufacturing capacity and brought about higher prices for gloves bought for the military.

Who was left in 1998?

Joseph P. Conroy was the largest of the county's remaining manufacturers. Humbert Salluzzo had a small glove shop and retail business and the Vertucci glove shop on Mill Street had sold gloves seasonally; both were in Gloversville. Joseph Pagano had a small shop in Johnstown. Two new glove factories rounded out the very short list of those who still made gloves in the county.

Pagano Gloves, an archetype of Fulton County glove firms in the twentieth century, survived through 1998. Carmelo Pagano came from Sicily to Johnstown in 1930 with his family, which included four boys, Anthony, Salvatore, Carmen, and Joseph, who was seven years old. The father learned to cut gloves; the mother, who had family in the area and was the reason they moved to Johnstown, sewed. The father dreamed of setting up a glove shop, but there never was enough money. He became a glove-shop foreman and died just before World War II.

The sons took advantage of the upsurge in glove-making anticipated because of the coming war and in 1940 started a glove shop with, as Joe Pagano says, "nothing." They began in a room at the back of their home, expanded to the second floor of the building that later became the Rainbow Grill, and finally in 1953, bought the building between the post office and the YMCA, tucked beneath the imposing St. John's Episcopal Church.

The family all worked. They had so much work they had a permit to run on three shifts, six days a week, and at the company's peak around 1970, they employed 60 workers and still had to contract out most of their sewing. They had ten cutters, mostly Italians and French, "whoever was good." Virtually all of their gloves were fine table-cut dress gloves.

Their workers were well paid. Pagano says he never had labor problems. Despite the fact the business was a union shop, he gave raises or bonuses to those who earned them, telling workers not to let on. He was good to his help. He paid top money for leather, and at first specialized in pigskins. When asked how he built a reputation for making quality gloves, he says he sent samples to retailers large and small and produced exactly the quality and cost they desired. It took a while to build a reputation, but Pagano did, serving as salesman as well as managing the business, which grew so that it was competing with Superb. Pagano opened a satellite shop in Amsterdam with 30 employees. He counted Saks, Arnold Constable, and other prominent department stores among his customers. Pagano always ran a tight ship and he says he never "gave under the table" as others did; he did not have enough money to bribe buyers. He depended on the quality of his gloves.

Joe Pagano learned accounting when he was eighteen and always managed the company's business. His wife was always the firm's bookkeeper, despite the fact she had six children. Joe taught her how to become a bookkeeper. The oldest daughter looked after the younger children. In 1973 Pagano took a course to become a tax preparer and worked at that part-time as the glove business shrank.

From 1953 on, the firm was a member of NAGM, but Joe Pagano never felt that organization did much to help his business. Pagano's business began to decline along with everyone else's due to imports, cheaper overseas labor, the inability to pay what local labor should get. He was opposed to going overseas; he rejected all offers to train work forces overseas for other manufacturers. He was unhappy when others went offshore and clung to the idea that gloves could be made locally.

In 1998 Pagano was still making fine gloves and said, "If I retire, what am I going to do at home?" His gloves retailed at $50 to $70 a pair, $30 wholesale. He spent about $10 on the leather and paid a maker a bit more than $3 to sew a pair. He also paid for silking, but he did all the cutting, laying-off, and many other operations needed to produce a fine glove. He had reduced the business so that he could work three months of the year as a tax preparer, producing income that was essential to keeping his glove business going. None of his children are in the glove business; he encouraged them to find other professions. He had trouble finding good makers and mused about the demise of homework, "Who was it hurting?"

How did he succeed and how was he able to keep his business going as most others closed? He always ran his shop as a family business. He paid the best prices for the best leather and never had trouble buying skins. He said he was "just going to do a better job, not like other manufacturers." It was a family enterprise, and family members did not take much money out of it, keeping money in the business. Others, he said, paid less and wanted to make more, showing that successful glovemaking in Fulton County was always a frugal business.

In 1998 Joe Pagano (age 75) was virtually the last table cutter in Fulton County. At one time there were nearly 2,000 such skilled workers. And, of the 1,900 glove shops, large and small, counted over the years, Pagano's was one of the last four still manufacturing gloves in the county.

PK or Pique Gloves Peter Kiernan's paternal grandfather was a plant manager for Louis Meyers & Son and his maternal grandfather had a tannery. With glovemaking in his blood, Kiernan worked first for Grandoe, and then in 1987 established his own business in the old Joe Perrella shop on Gloversville's Union Street. Realistic enough to understand the limitations of manufacturing locally, Kiernan carved out a niche for himself in designing gloves for others and producing specialty gloves. By 1998 his small retail shop produced fancy work gloves for western ranchers and pique-stitched dress gloves, as well as specialties such as elegant driving gloves for Mercedes Benz and white dress gloves for Marine Corps bands. His shop emphasized quality over volume, and he experimented with a direct mail catalog.

When his shop was working full time he had a staff of eleven that included one cutter and six women sewing. His was one of the rare shops anywhere that still produced full pique gloves.[148] Kiernan has promoted his wares on television, on AP wire features, through regional magazines, and in a newsletter. He did not have the financial stature to bid on larger government contracts and he had no desire to expand overseas. With all his passion for the industry and ability to publicize his business, he admited that he will just be able to "carve out a living."

Samco Gloves Sam Greco's third-floor making room in Gloversville had the feel of an old-time glove shop, as well it should. The machines were antiques, the workers generally older women, the clutter typical. It was also a shop that could be picked up and relocated in a weekend. Greco was prospering, despite the financial commitment he had to make to establish a line of credit that would permit him to bid on government contracts. And, because his work was for the government, it could all disappear in a flash with a telegram from the government cancelling a contract. It was a risky business, dependent on his presence and that of his manager, but probably more than he admits on himself. The only time in the interview that the ebullient Sam Greco looked worried about his business was when he considered the difficulty of making government bids and the fact that should he fail to continue obtaining contracts his business would have to close.

Greco had many of the attributes that make a gloveman: He had long experience working for others like Steinberg and Fownes in Amsterdam. But he inherited his strongest attribute from his father, Joe Greco, who came to America as a young boy from Sicily. Joe was a born tinkerer and became one of the county's most proficient free-lance machinists, someone who could keep all the old machines working. Sam began to learn how to fix machines when he was twelve, and when he was sixteen went to work for Jules Higier. Joe Greco worked for Jules Higier at his Superb plant, Sam Greco at Higier's Crescendoe plant. Sam left a year before Higier died, bitter that he had not been given a raise he thought he deserved. Even when he was employed at other shops, he worked late afternoons to repair machines for the Perrella, Rubin, and Papa glove factories.

After a long career in politics and gloves, and in 1987 at an age when almost everyone else was thinking of retiring, Sam established his government contract business. His knowledge of machines and collection of old machines plus the credit to acquire skins were all he needed. (His attic and garage are stuffed with ancient machines, among them over 100 machines his father acquired for a dollar each when Boyce-Lazarus closed.)

Of his 45 employees in 1998, 35 were women who sew, six were cutters who worked out of a shop near Greco's house in Johnstown, and two and a part-time worker were layers-off. He hired the best makers he could find—mostly older women—and he trained a few younger sewers, some with grants for training workers. His wife helped with the books. He found enough leather from hair sheep tanned locally to make 300 dozen gloves a week. (Leather alone costs $30,000 a week.) He had enough machines to grow if he could, but he admitted that it was impossible to predict how long he could remain competitive with government contracts. In 1998 he said all he could do was hope for longer-term contracts that would provide a stable environment in which to increase production.[149] Only a few of his workers earned piece rate wages totalling $12 to $15 an hour, a rate that was barely competitive with other skilled work.

Samco employees highlight a work ethic that is still alive in Fulton County. In the last two years, Eleanor Cirillo has helped train some of Sam's sewers. Her father, Aniello Costa, was a table cutter trained in Naples, and her parents were among the first five families who came from Naples to Johnstown. They had twelve children, eleven of whom lived to marry. The older brother became a table cutter, but only three of the children went into the glove business.

Eleanor started work as a layer-off when she was 17 and two years later started sewing. A fast learner, she felt accomplished after only six weeks of her six months' apprenticeship. She sewed for Northrup and Aborn glove companies.

Eleanor, who left school at 16, married and had three children, "none in gloves." Her husband, a tannery worker, was employed at G. Levor for 35 years, later by Mike Subik. Eleanor worked for a number of shops. "Every place I worked closed up—Principes, Alexette, Vincent Sanges, Fownes, Suttons, Crescendoe, Papas, and Rubins—every place closed except Joe

Conroy's, where I worked ten years, and Gates-Mills." She never worked full-time, and was often laid off when work was slow. She was an in-seam maker, putting in fourchettes. When she first started, the whole glove was sewn by one person, then "sectional" work came in just before World War II. She joined the operators' union in 1934 when all three glove unions were separate. She had a union pension, but felt that "unions never did that much for me." Her retirement was reduced because she worked sporadically during the time her husband was ill so she could care for him. She lost her medical insurance when her last employer, Rubin Glove Co., closed. She worked 40 hours a week when she was 17 and 64 years later she was still working that many hours.

A year after our first interview with Eleanor Cirillo, when we visited Samco, there she sat, near the beginning of the production run, at age 81, still sewing fourchettes.

Glove work was always a hard business to leave. The Fugazzotto family's story of their father, John, tells it best. John, a cutter for Joseph P. Conroy, tried to retire every year from age 65 on. Every year, Conroy encouraged Fugazzotto, one of his best cutters, to continue. Finally, at age 83, John picked up a stack of skins, carefully cut them and tied the tranks, thumbs, and fourchettes into bundles. Then he untied the worn leather apron that he had used for years and cut it into glove parts. When he saw this, Conroy understood that Fugazzotto had really retired.

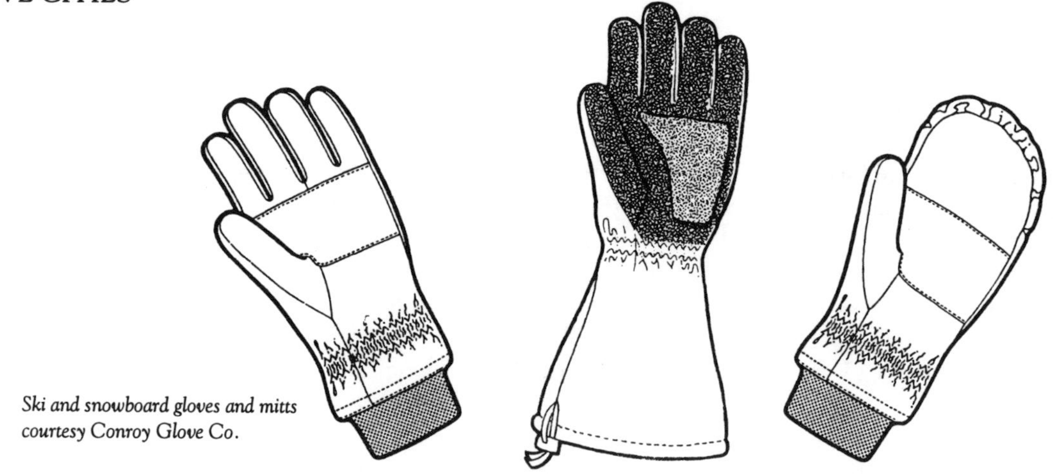

Ski and snowboard gloves and mitts courtesy Conroy Glove Co.

Concluding Thoughts

Few of the county's glove firms were ever really secure.
B. McMartin

Gloves are as important today as they were a hundred years ago, but for different reasons. We do not wear them just for fashion or to protect us when we are working. We wear them for comfort, for sports, for many different occupations. Johnstown and Gloversville made a lot of gloves, but never had a corner on the glove business, only on the manufacturing of fine leather dress gloves for men. But the pride the industry gave the cities as well as the comfortable living standards enjoyed by most residents are remembered and mourned as if these were the most special communities.

Despite the number of manufacturers, it is remarkable how so many aspects of the Fulton County experience had parallels in the rest of the country—the growth and expansion of unions, the effects of the National Recovery Act and the National Labor Relations Act, the loss of manufacturing capacity, upheavals caused by the trend toward free trade and overseas manufacturing, business expansions as a result of wars, and the outlawing of homework. The county never seems to have been the leader in any of these events, just a stolid and rather reluctant follower.

If this had been a book on Ford Motor Company or Endicott Johnson or another similar large company, it would have had the focus of one man or one family. Studies of cities with single industries have often been centered on a few large manufacturers. In Fulton County, one industry dominated two small communities and the satellite villages that ringed them, but with two facets that differentiate the county's experience from most other places: The single industry lasted over a very long time—almost 200 years—and it had an extraordinary number of manufacturers—1,900 or more.

As a first step in our research, and my husband played a big role in this phase, we tried to count how many glove shops there had been at different times, how many there were altogether, and how long individuals survived. We arrived at the astronomical number of 1,900 in 190 years based on actual named firms found in many sources: directories, census records, R. G. Dun manuscripts, and so on. Of course, this number reflects a huge proportion of small shops, but there were several hundred midsize (30 to 100 employees) to large (from 300 to 500 employees) shops. There were less than a dozen really large shops, some of which were very successful for a time, some of which had great problems.

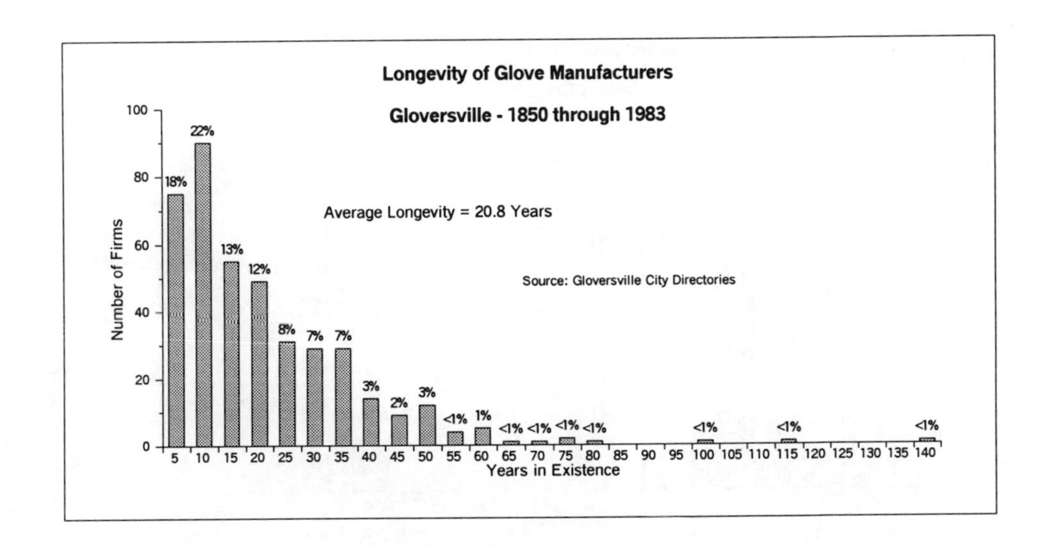
Longevity of Glove Manufacturers
Gloversville - 1850 through 1983
Average Longevity = 20.8 Years
Source: Gloversville City Directories
Number of Firms
Years in Existence

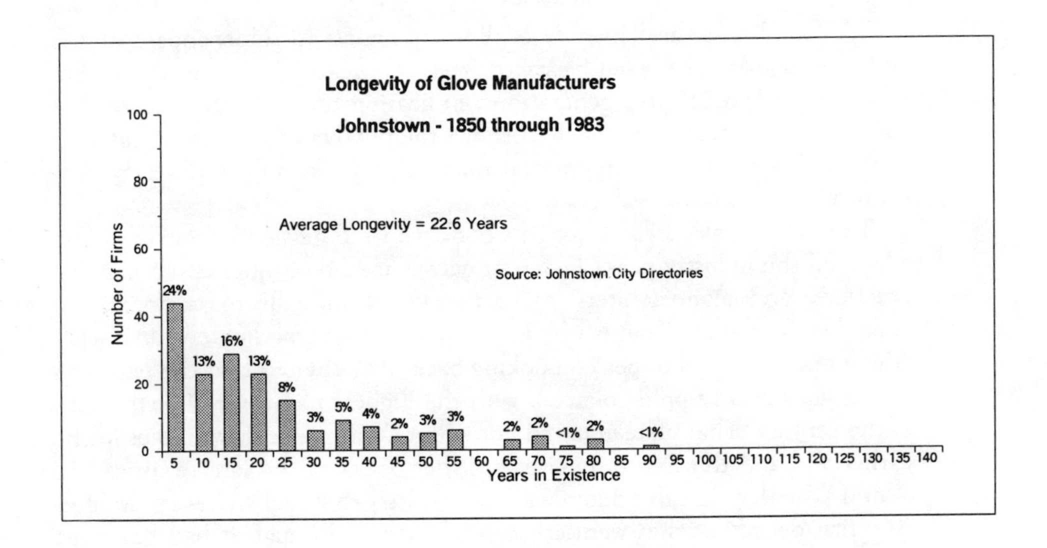
Longevity of Glove Manufacturers
Johnstown - 1850 through 1983
Average Longevity = 22.6 Years
Source: Johnstown City Directories
Number of Firms
Years in Existence

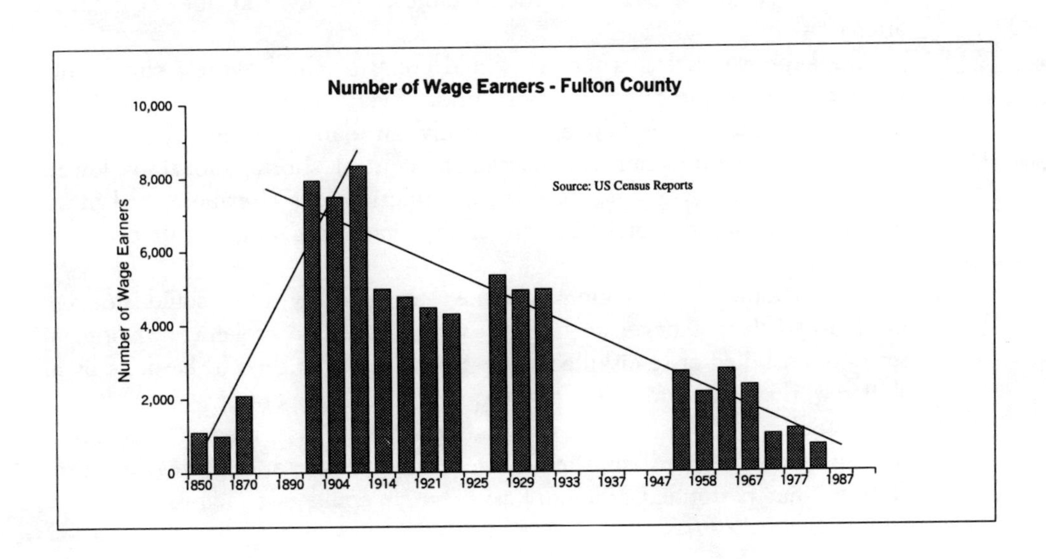
Number of Wage Earners - Fulton County
Source: US Census Reports
Number of Wage Earners

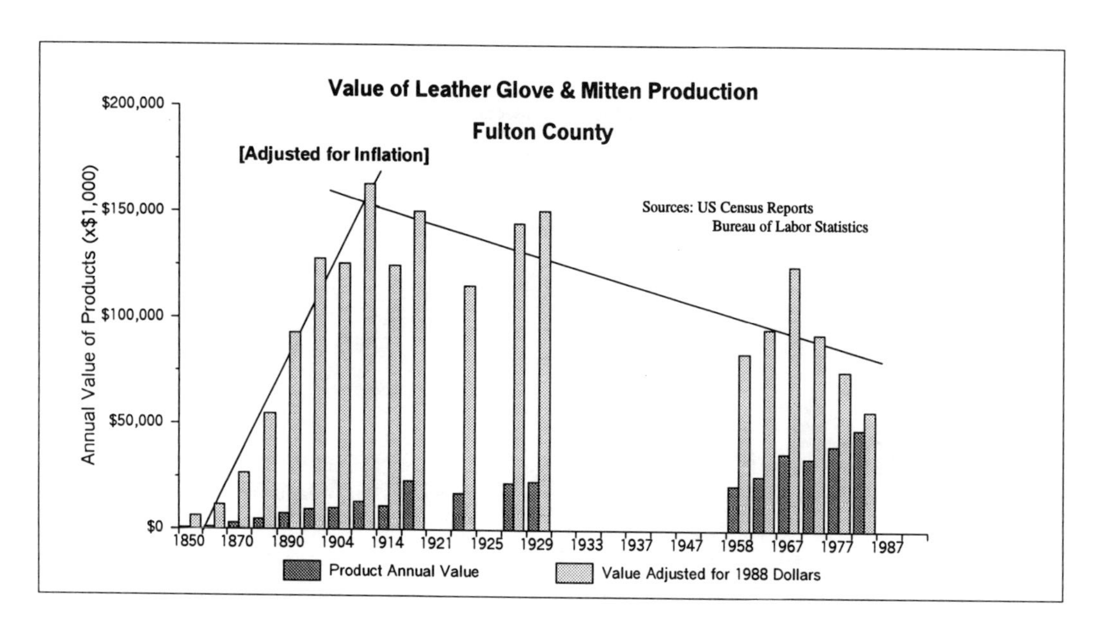

We found that the longevity of different shops was independent of size and ranged from just a few years to over 180 years. A surprising number survived for two or three generations, indicating the industry's remarkable stability. (The accompanying chart shows the number of workers at different census periods but achieving a total number of workers for the nearly two-century period is not possible.)

Throughout our research for this book we were nagged by one question: when did the industry peak? Different census methods, different accounting practices, and manufacturers' secrecy made it difficult to compare and compile information. That is why I have noted at several different times that "the industry seemed to peak." Looking back, it is obvious that the peak was a long, downward-tipping plateau, with the highest point just after the turn of the century. That plateau lasted until after World War II, with dips in the earlier war and the Depression years, lower peaks in the late twenties and World War II. What this describes is an industry that really never grew after that first decade of the twentieth century. And, although it had begun its inexorable decline about 1905, the precipitous decline did not occur until after 1950.

The memory of that [prosperity] is engraved in the minds of the people who lived in those years.
Letter to the Editor, *Leader Herald*,[4]

We kept wondering when we would come to the brightest times, the times county people remember with pride. Every time business looked up, something unfortunate happened, usually an outside event over which neither manufacturers nor workers had any control: shortages of skins, lower tariffs, losing homeworkers, wars, more attractive jobs elsewhere, and most important of all, the globalization of manufacturing and cheap overseas labor.

Throughout, glove-making remained an industry that could not be mechanized. It was never an industry which could be broken down into a series of unskilled or semiskilled tasks. Every operation had to be done by a skilled worker or by a machine that required a skilled operator.

In addition, it was an industry that resisted sophisticated management. Managers could speed up the transfer of materials and gloves between stations that performed different tasks, but it could not change the basic processes.

Even though there is no archetypical glove worker or manufacturer, there are a few common threads among both groups. Paramount, of course, was their independence, which has been noted in so many ways. Members of the community certainly did exhibit a strange and tenacious independence. John Lear, author of the *Saturday Evening Post* article, called them "the temperamental wizards."[1] However, the cutters were not just independent people, their work gave them a sense of prestige. They were never a cog in an industrial wheel, never just a part of a mechanized operation.

The owners were similarly independent, fighting and competing in "the last stronghold of untrammeled competition."[2] Without question, competition was the singular trait of manufacturers that made the glove business so difficult. Independence is part of the explanation of the reasons manufacturers never worked together, but it does not clarify certain of their attitudes, decisions, or actions: What made them so conservative? For instance, over many decades, manufacturers held to established ways in the face of indications that business would continue to decline and of prospects that tariffs would never be raised to levels that favored local employment. Almost all of the manufacturers left the industry because of retirement, death, bankruptcy, buyouts, or because they just gave up. Only a very few had the foresight, daring, or courage to expand in foreign markets. There were few mergers over the years because resistance to change was endemic; most manufacturers were afraid to try something new.

It has been impossible to profile and make human only a handful of the entrepreneurs who expanded the industry and the town. Their diversity and independence negates choosing one whose biographical record would typify the industry. So it has been frustrating to bring to this work the human element that inspires history.

Several county businessmen have read this book in draft and helped me shape my understanding of glovemen. We have speculated together on the limiting attributes of the glovemen's character. Some have suggested that it might be very rewarding to analyze glovemen from a psychological perspective. Even if that were within the scope of this book, the sheer number of glovemen makes this impossible.

Rod Correll, who was a second generation manager of a local tanning business, believes that the family nature of glove-making was one of its limiting features. After the success of a patriarchal entrepreneur, it has often been the case that sons and sons-in-law were afraid to take risks. That seems to be true of many, but not all, county glove-manufacturing families. Further, in the county, family businesses rarely hired the business specialists that aided success (Gates-Mills's survival may stem from hiring outsiders.) Correll believes that public ownership and business consultants could have helped glovemen survive and expand. He portrays local glovemen as proud and capable, but afraid to reach out, afraid they would be swallowed up by larger forces they could not understand.

As small manufacturers, most glove-shop owners were not business trained. Many of them acquired a liberal arts education at institutions such as Hamilton College. Like the cutters who served apprenticeships or learned from their fathers, the vast majority of manufacturers learned the business from relatives. It is significant that among the survivors the Widdemers, the Gates, and the Zuckerwars have carried on that tradition.

Would more consolidations have been a solution? There is something to be said for a small glove shop: the owner could keep his eye on things; there was no chain of command to manage; there were sales representatives who could assist him; and the owner could touch or sample all the leather that came through his shop. But could he respond to fashion? Certainly he was at the mercy of competitors that left him fearful of raising prices. Did the small entrepreneur actually make less money than the owners of the larger shops? Consolidation might have been a temporary solution, but even that would not have added many years to the local industry. Only the general move overseas and the demise of nearly all the firms that did not move overseas seems to have enabled the few multi-national firms to grow into really large companies.

Furthermore, not all of those who manufactured gloves overseas were large; a few small companies have been quite successful. What is surprising is how few manufacturers chose to move their businesses overseas when those opportunities arose, how few dared to confront the challenges of international business.

One has to recognize the astuteness of the remaining handful of manufacturers who continue to thrive with overseas operations. But one has to question the glovemen who made those initial steps offshore in the 1950s. It appears as if they left the county surreptitiously and without regard to the viability of the community. Certainly industry's flight from the county is no worse than the textile industry's move to southern states from New England. Many other places have been abandoned and their industrial structure left to decay. What makes it seem so bad today is that the community remembers just how well off were the majority of people at a time when most other workers were pawns in the industrial revolution. And, as workers nationally began to enter the middle class after World War II, the county experienced a reverse movement.

There was no real sense of manufacturers working together; even the National Association of Glove Manufacturers did not promote real cooperation. And, the role played by its executive director remains an enigma. Did Casey's perennial optimism hurt the industry? Did he encourage the individuality and independence of the manufacturers while failing to provide real leadership? Could he or anyone else have provided leadership to this group of independent individuals? Many in the county still blame the union leaders, especially Carr. Shouldn't Casey share some of the censure? How could he have challenged the statistics that showed the beginnings of the decline in the fifties and the accelerated decline of the sixties? Why did he never publicly address the industry's move overseas? James Casey and Harold Moss both had fine educations. They were men who felt comfortable appearing at hearings in Washington. They could see beyond the Mohawk Valley. What was it about them or the members of the associations they headed that limited their influence? Was Casey duplicitous in fighting tariffs while ignoring the fact that the members of the Glove Manufacturers Association who were succeeding were doing it only because they were abandoning the county?

Casey's perennial optimism was also a characteristic of both workers and manufacturers and created their feeling that they were almost at the center of the world even though they occupied an isolated backwater. With the exception of Clarence Carr and Lucius Littauer, most union leaders and manufacturers either lacked the desire or the will to reach outside the area. No single union leader represented the whole industry. Only Clarence Carr stands out above the others, and his story within the community is far from typical.

Glovemen sought their own niches, even before specialization became essential to survival. Every one sought his own way. A few were very successful, but only the Littauers appear to have pulled out of the business with a considerable fortune and they did so long before the industry experienced difficult times.

Another common thread among glove workers and manufacturers was the fact that glove-making was a very satisfying craft. For most of the history of the industry there seems to have been a contentment among workers who created a fine product with their hands. But, underlying that contentment, workers appear to have realized that there were better jobs, better industries in which to work, better professions. Workers—more than manufacturers—seem to have encouraged their children to seek other opportunities, to move away from the community.

Much has been written about workers who became unhappy with mechanized jobs in an industrial society. Perhaps the converse of this principle is true: that people were so happy with their jobs, fueling their sense of creativity, craft, and control, that the jobs were seen to be better in retrospect than they actually were. This aspect of the glove business kept both workers and employers happy even as jobs disappeared and children went on to other jobs.

For the vast majority of shops where the owner kept his hands in the business, it is obvious that the manufacturers enjoyed the same sense of pride from the craft as did their workers. The few owners of larger shops who did not maintain a hands-on involvement were never as much a part of the community. For all the satisfaction that the smaller manufacturers enjoyed, there was never any guarantee of success. Still, love of their craft enhanced their sense of independence and kept them satisfied, probably long beyond the time their Fulton County businesses were truly viable.

Workers, for all their independence, were as conservative as manufacturers. Most union members were content with their local representatives and resisted change. Perhaps individualism and independence were at the bottom of this resistance—no worker wanted an outsider to speak for him.

Despite the fragmentation of the unions, the unions did bring workers important and necessary achievements. The unions were certainly weak in obtaining worker benefits for members. In many interviews I heard the comment "the unions ruined the glove business." Nothing could be further from the truth. Glove workers were fairly well paid from 1915 to 1945, but after World War II, wages constantly fell behind other manufacturing industries.

The union leaders were all local people who came up through the ranks. Carr was a tannery worker; even today's head of the former Amalgamated Union, Bill Towne, started as a staker in a tannery. A few local union heads, however, did see the need for affiliation with national organizations and were able to bring in deeply committed leaders to advise them, and some of these principals were highly educated.

The glove workers in Fulton County felt comfortable as members of middle-class America, and the majority of the manufacturers were of the same class. The small size of most shops meant workers, managers, and owners had close personal relationships. The small percentage of unskilled craftsmen created a bond among the craft or skilled workers. There may have been a social stratification between tannery and glove workers, but the community as a whole displayed a strange kind of homogeneity, born of the smallness of the communities. As Bill Towne wrote, "There was no place to hide. Workers lived next door to owners, they went to the same churches and schools. Workers became owners. These conflicting and changing relationships strained the typical labor/management relationship. The community was less marked by homogeneity than by an uneasy peace."

There were distinct differences between Gloversville and Johnstown and between the various immigrant groups. The glove industry brought a degree of leveling to the social fiber of the communities. The different family structures displayed by groups of immigrants shaped the glove industry's development: The conservative Scots and English thrived in Johnstown. Strong family ties and frugal ways—with every member contributing to the business—typified Italian glove shops. The greater entrepreneurial leaps of Gloversville's Jewish glovemen explained the growth of many large factories. But, there are exceptions to all these stereotypes, which at best only hint at the different levels of success among individual firms.

Immigrant workers undoubtedly made it possible for the industry to continue operating in the county far longer than would be expected from such a craft industry. Around World War II, new workers stopped arriving. Few other places experienced such a decline in immigration in the last half of the twentieth century.

Many other places experienced the same vitality that immigration brought to the county. Waves of immigration and the encouragement of manufacturers in general created an oversupply of workers. Fluctuations in production and the scourge of seasonality meant that manufacturers needed more workers for the peak periods. In the end, manufacturers could not control the market's seasonality.

All this still does not constitute a satisfying explanation of what happened to the Glove Cities, mostly because it does not address the enigma of the manufacturers' roles. "Why," as Tom Willard observed, "did such smart and hard-working men continually 'milk the cash cow,' and position their business for liquidation rather than growth?" Bill Towne said, after reading a draft of this book, that he agreed that "the industry's demise was predetermined. The historical record makes this clear: The impossibility of turning a craft industry into a mass-producing work culture, ethnic diversity, geographic isolation, lack of formal education, fierce independence, the extraordinary number of manufacturers and organizations, complex personal relationships all added to problems created by the outside world." He also observed that what had developed over time "was not a deliberate and conscious resistance to change, but rather a passive acceptance of fate." That strikes me as a very important part of the explanation, but I have one more theory, also unprovable, of why the glovemen acted so conservatively and rigidly.

I believe that the experience of the majority of glovemen was so fraught with problems out of their control, so terrifying in the way they had to finance raw materials in a global market and constantly gamble that they could repay loans, that fear ultimately dominated their decisions. The constant risk-taking must have made them afraid to hope and robbed them of ambition and flexibility. They were unable to relinquish their role in a small firm, to merge with others who ultimately had no better ability in the business. It seems to me that fear must have played as great a role as fate in the demise of county glove-making.

Sad ending

The end of American innocence was part of a great tragedy, but it was not, in itself, an unmitigated disaster. Those who look at it with dismay, or those who deny that it happened, do so because they expect true stories to have a completely happy ending. This is a kind of innocence American history must get over.
Henry May in *The End of American Innocence*[5]

Still, hindsight offers nothing that would have changed the outcome. Large-scale local industry was doomed and its doom was sealed over a century ago. Now all that remains is to fathom the destiny of the Glove Cities. The failure of the area to attract new industries for so many decades is not as simple as many claimed—that local manufacturers tried to keep them out. The failure had more to do with the fact the area did not have the elements that could attract new endeavors: transportation; a young, trained work force; factories in good enough condition to be used for other purposes. Some attempts at economic development have failed, but in the last decade there have been some successes, although not enough to bring about an increase in population.

Local political leadership supported the manufacturers from the start. It helped manufacturers during the long strikes. It joined with the manufacturers to keep tariffs high and talked of ways to keep jobs in the county. Organized labor believes that this support of "business interests, to the detriment of labor and the community at large, has contributed to the present economic condition."[3] This view fails to recognize the fact that without the enterprising manufacturers, there would have been no industry. Further, as this work shows, most—a vast majority—of manufacturers rose from the ranks of workers. In few other industries are the roles of manufacturer and worker so blurred.

Today, the glove cities themselves appear almost frozen in time. One of the most interesting aspects of our research for this book was to drive around Johnstown and Gloversville with copies of the 1868 and 1905 maps and some old directories and see where all the glove factories and tanneries were and where their owners and workers lived. Every street revealed a piece of glove or leather history.

Several remaining huge frame tanneries are quite rundown. Some frame tannery buildings have been given new life for finishing or coloring skins. The deerskin tanneries look very little different from their original state.

We were surprised to discover just how many buildings that once housed glove shops remained, how many still stood among residential areas. There are quire a few of the small buildings that housed 19th century glove shops, tucked behind their former owner's homes. A few of the old shops have been replaced by parking lots, grocery stores, and even a high-rise senior-citizen complex. Some are forlorn structures with gaping holes for missing windows; the most decrepit are the frame glove shops and they are resolutely irretrievable, destined to be torn down. A few brick and stone or cement-block glove shops house other businesses. A very few are beautifully maintained: Conroy's shop in Johnstown is in mint condition; Grandoe's buildings in Gloversville are too, but they serve primarily as offices and warehouses.

The old shops and tanneries are ubiquitous, monuments to a long ago time. Along with the ornate brick buildings that line the main streets, the glove shops are reminders of another time. The inner cities still retain a beauty that could be reinvigorated. Outside both cities are sprawling industrial areas filled with soulless structures, boxy warehouses and modular factories. If only life and work could be reinvented, reintegrated, to restore these once beautiful cities.

I began to write this book with a sense of pride in the area and the industry. I finished it with deep sadness, mourning the fact that its success was limited and the industry's demise was so predetermined. Many studies have been written about workers, and quite a few have analyzed single companies. Few have had the challenge of trying to understand an industry with so many manufacturers. My methods evolved as my research progressed. I realized that it was necessary to see the industry's achievements from the perspective of the community and the people who experienced it. I found far too few first-hand accounts, but I have incorporated all that I could discover.

There is no question but that I have a totally different understanding of the industry than I had when I started. My approach was necessarily subjective, but I trust it begins to answer the many question about the industry's rise, problems, and demise.

The slow but inevitable attrition from the 1950s through the 1980s was almost the mirror image of the growth in the 1820s through the 1850s. The ebullience of the expanding years contrasts starkly with the depressing aura of the declining years. From the research for this book emerges the fact that even the best times were burdened with problems; the good times were ephemeral. It is human nature to recall pleasure more than pain; county residents have a wonderfully positive collective memory of times gone by. I did not realize when I started this book that my research would show such a dark side to the cherished past.

Appendix - Creation of the Data Base

This is basically the story of how the production of leather gloves emerged, evolved, and then disappeared in Fulton County. Initially, leather production was inseparable from glove manufacturing. Later, leather production became separate, but it was an integral part of the county's economic base. Leather was initially produced primarily for gloves, but shoe and garment leather gradually dominated the production of glove leather. For all these reasons, this book focuses on glove leather and treats the production of other types of leather peripherally.

The production of silk for glove linings expanded in the county and spawned the growth of knitting mills. After World War I, fabric gloves become an important part of the local economy, but they were produced in great quantities elsewhere. They are of interest to the county's story because the tariff problems of the fabric glove industry parallel those of the leather glove industry. Again, even though this book discusses fabric gloves, it does not analyze the production levels of fabric gloves in the same way it does leather gloves.

Given these constraits we determined the existence of 1900 separate glove and glove-leather firms. Nineteenth century statistics rely heavily on the **U. S. Census of Manufactures for the years 1850, 60, 70, and 80.** Much has been written about the errors, omissions, and incompleteness of these census records. The Fulton County records are in general quite complete. All the data from the census was entered into a spread sheet. All the steps described below were completed and then once we had become familiar with the names, the quirks of spelling, and the bad handwriting, we went through these steps second time - after correcting the initial data taken from the census. The results are not perfect, but, after determining such things as the fact that one business had been spelled four different ways, the results are quite good.

Frothingham's *History of Fulton County* is a superb source for the industry before 1890. He gives dates for the creation of many firms, identifies the founders and officers of many, and lists some firms that are just getting under way. This data was put on a spread sheet in an attempt to extend the census records one more decade.

Notes were compiled from **R. G. Dun** records from the beginning, circa 1865, to the end of the 1880s. Many short-lived firms emerged from this information.

Listings from the **Directories for Johnstown and Gloversville** for all glove and leather manufacturers were added to the data base. Spread sheets show addresses, officers where known, as well as type of work done by each firm. The years in the data bank are 1876, 1880, 1890, 1900, 1910, 1920, 1924, 1933, 1943, 1953, 1963, 1972, and 1983. When it was determined that key information would be available from some interim years, information was added to the final charts from the years 1885, 1895, 1905, 1915, 1928, 1938, 1948, 1958, and 1968, although spread sheets were not created for these years. Unfortunately the directories do not contain information on the outlying communities in the county.

Through about 1930 to 1940, it was relatively easy to trace the family businesses as they passed from father to son, rarely to wife, and to third and fourth generations because most business were given their owners' names. In the 1930s and after, many firms were incorporated and given modern names - Superb, Pearl, Crescendoe, etc. Sometimes the Directories listed the officers. Other times, local businessmen in the glove industry were consulted to determine chains of ownership.

All these data were combined and cross checked to eliminate redundant records. All those references which appeared only once were given numbers and tallied. The rest, those businesses which existed for at least one decade, were graphed on a large chart showing beginning and ending dates.

This chart, created at first by hand, then completed by computer, was devised to show all the substantial firms, through their various changes of style (name), owners, and partnerships. We used this as a working tool; it is much too cumbersome to be reproduced with this book.

From the data so obtained we determined the total number of firms existing between the beginning, circa 1825, and today. That number is **1,900**. Of that, **700** glove firms and **300** leather frims existed for at least a decade, and **900** existed for shorter periods (**650** glove firms and **250** leather firms). Summarizing the number of short and long term businesses at different times presents a picture of when the local economy expanded (in particular the relation to the three postwar periods) and when it contracted,.

Also the charts we created show the family businesses with greatest longevity, the strength of family relationships, and the businesses which lend themselves to more detailed analysis. Fortunately, a number of these substantial firms have descendents still in the business or continuing to live in Fulton County.

These charts are too complicated to reproduce easily, but a copy has been given to the Gloversville Free Library.

Guide to the Endnotes

All secondary sources are cited in the corresponding endnotes. Most of the research for this book involved first sources, which are described below, along with the word or acronym used to identify them in the endnotes.

Clipping refers to items in a set of scrap books prepared by Miriam Sesonske, secretary in later years to the National Association of Glove Manufacturers. The entries are not always identified as to source, *The Leader Republican* (**LR**), *The Morning Herald* (**MH**), *Women's Wear Daily*, *The New York Times*, or the *Schenectady Gazette*. In 1955, the two local papers combined and from then on all clippings, not otherwised identified, are from the one local paper, *The Leader-Herald* (**LH**). In the case of the local sources, the papers usually ran parallel stories so the general term clipping has been used for items from all papers not otherwise identified in the scrapbooks. The notebooks are remarkably complete for the years 1938 through 1984, with the exception of the three months at the end of the tannery strike in 1949-1950. All the notes from this period came from microfilms at the *Leader Herald* office.

Hearing refers to the 700-page transcript of the State Board of Mediation and Arbitration, New York State Department of Labor hearing into the cutters strike of 1914. A microfilm of the manuscript is at SUNY Albany and the full text is available on "The Glovers of Fulton County," a web site linked to SUNY Albany and prepared by the history department under Prof. Gerald Zahavi.

Report refers to *Homework in the Glove Industry in New York State*, Volumes I and II, a report prepared by the Division of Women in Industry and Minimum Wage of the New York State Department of Labor, 1941. Attorney A. Schlusberg's copy was given to Eleanor Reppenhagen and she allowed the author to copy it.

TGR refers to *The Glovers Review*, bound copies of which are in the Gloversville Library.

R. G. Dun reports refers to material in the Baker Library at Harvard University, the volumes for Fulton County covering the years 1865 to the mid-1880s.

Correspondence refers to letters I have received and kept. Many but not all of the **Interviews** were taped and I have kept the tapes. All taped interviews were made in 1996 through 1998.

An undated and unpaged notebook in the Gloversville Library with no author identified contains a number of biographies of prominent Gloversville businessmen and details of their families. These sketches, alphabetically arranged, were probably written around 1947 and most of the individuals had glove or leather businesses that were active in the late 1930s and in the World War II years. Endnote reference to these biographies are listed as **Biog. Gl.** It was used as a source for the short notes on pages 181 through 184.

The vertical files of the Gloversville Library provided information on churches and are the source for the Carr writings, the Lear article, and the Redmond monograph.

John Widdemer loaned the copy of *Charles Booth, A Memoir*, London, Macmillan and Co., Ltd. 1918.

Endnotes

Notes from pages 1 - 58

---

1 Utica, New York: North Country Books, 1992

2 There are no records in the Johnson papers to indicate that any of the people brought by Sir William actually set up glove shops. That they did seems to have been a myth to explain the origins of the industry. There are records of tanning deer to make breeches, of woolen factories, and grist mills, but none of actual glove shops. Many local historians have tried to document these origins. Bethune M. Grant, Jr. wrote of a visit to Perth by the grandfather of glove manufacturer M. S. Northrup. Around 1875, the grandfather encountered an elderly woman whose family had come with the first Johnson immigrants and who had been members of the Glovers Guild in Perthshire, Scotland. According to her family tradition, these first settlers did make gloves. It must be understood that the 1760s were rough frontier times, with communities dominated by subsistence farmers. Only gradually did individuals start mills and manufactures. It is not surprising that there is no evidence extant that can trace glovework from the early days in Perth to the earliest recorded glovers at the end of the first decade of the nineteenth century.

3 Johnstown paper

4 Ibid.

5 F. W. Beers, *History of Montgomery and Fulton Counties*, NY: F. W. Beers & Co., 1878, reprint 1979, p 201. Beers says that a Jonathan Sedgwick proposed the name Stump City in 1816.

6 Washington Frothingham, *History of Fulton County*. Syracuse, NY: D. Mason & Co., 1892. Frothingham gives a later date for the beginning of the Heacock family business, but a license to make leather issued to Lemuel Heacock in 1815 disproves the historian.

7 Frothingham, p 154

8 While most of the notes from these early days come from Frothingham, they are generally confirmed by a treatise written by Horace Sprague in 1859 called Gloversville

or the Model Village. Sprague's start dates differ slightly from Frothingham's, but Sprague mentions that Mills and Burr only manufactured leather from deerskins before 1810. Their mitten-making came after that date. A transcription of this treatise is in the papers of Robert Bedford.

[9] Note - Even if the Census numbers are correct, it is generally only possible to compare production values through averages of firms in a region because there were so many different types of mittens and gloves produced with different qualities and values.

[10] Sprague, no page numbers.

[11] Diary of E. P. Parmalee, of Broadalbin and Gloversville, 1857-1864, Manuscripts and Special Collections, New York State Library.

[12] *Leader Republican Anniversary Issue*, 1937

[13] The article is in a scrapbook in the Gloversville Library. It is undated and there is no indication which paper it came from. However, it appears to have been printed around the turn of the century.

[14] In the hemlock-bark industry where the cost of imported hides was so great - one raw hide being worth as much as or more than an acre of frontier land - the year 1857 had numerous bankruptcies.

[15] The Census figures relating the production of dozens of pairs of gloves to different amounts of skins is given to show the size of the industry only. Different production levels relate to the different types of skins used and gloves produced, the various amounts of skins on hand, and so on.

[16] The 1860 Census for the Town of Johnstown gives no reports on sewing machines, even though they are tallied for outlying villages. This is probably just an aberration of the census taker.

[17] Such handwork remained a part of glovework up to the time - the 1950s - when manufacturers sought foreign workers for handwork

[18] J. Jay Stranahan & Beach Nichols, *Atlas of Montgomery and Fulton Counties, NY*, 1868.

[19] Tamara K. Hareven, *Family Time and Industrial Time: The relationship between the family and work in a New England industrial community*. Cambridge and New York: Cambridge University Press, 1982.

[20] *Ibid.*

[21] These books are in the Fulton County Museum, Gloversville.

[22] From a family history and collection of letters written by William D. Foote, compiled by my great-aunt Lulu, Mary Louisa Foote

[23] *The Glovers Review*, (TGR), June 1937, p 33.

[24] Hareven, notes that seeking this balance was very important for workers in Amoskeag's textile mill.

[25] R. G. Dunn

[26] Jonathan Garlock, *Guide to Local Assemblies of the Knights of Labor*, Greenwood Press, 1952, pp 308-9.

[27] Caroline F. Ware. *The Early New England Cotton Manufacturer*. Boston and New York: Houghton Mifflin & Co., 1931.

[28] Tamara K. Hareven, *Ibid.*

[29] *Ibid.*, pp 112, 113

[30] Judith A. McGaw, *Most Wonderful Machine*. Princeton: Princeton University Press, 1987.

[31] Carole Turbin, *Working Women of Collar City*. Chicago: University of Illinois Press, 1992.

[32] *Ibid.*

[33] Alan Dawley, *Class and Community - The Industrial Revolution in Lynn*. Cambridge, Mass.: Harvard University Press, 1976.

[34] Dawley, p 8.

[35] John T. Combler, *Working-Class Community in Industrial America, 1880-1930*. Westport, Conn.: Greenwood Press, 1979.

[36] Peter Lawson-Clarke. *The Glovers of Yeovil*. Privately printed, 1996.

[37] *Ibid.* p 31.

[38] *Ibid.* p 33.

[39] *Ibid.* p 37.

[40] Eileen Boris, *Home to Work: Motherhood and the Politics of Industrial Homework in the United States*. New York: Cambridge University Press, 1994, p 11.

[41] Frothingham

[42] Bethune M. Grant, Jr., *Gloves Magazine*, April 1935, p 26

[43] Letter to the author from editor of the Stanton-Anthony Papers.

[44] Boris, p 13

Short-note references, pages 1 - 58

[1] Washington Frothingham, *History of Fulton County*, Syracuse, New York: D. Mason & Co., 1892, p 155.

[2] Frothingham

[3] TGR, July 1918, p 31

[4] Frothingham, p 154

Notes from pages 59 - 118

[1] In 1890, there were 212 establishments with 6,208 workers, producing $7,369,730 worth of gloves. In 1900, 244 establishments with 9,889 workers produced $10,835,898. If the figures are correct, this implies a 59% increase in the number of workers. Since the 33% population increase could not produce all of it, it seems that there must have been a huge increase in part-time, homeworkers.

[2] It did this with 43.6% of the total number of U. S. factories, 61.3% of the total capitalization, 55.9% of the wage earners and 60.6% of the value of raw materials.

[3] Hearing, p 421

[4] As quoted in TGR, Dec. 1908, p 35

[5] Daniel W. Redmond, *The Leather Glove Industry in the United States*. Columbia University, Ph. D. Thesis, 1913.

[6] A series of hearings dealt with the stitching on the back of foreign gloves. The use of one thread did not invoke additional duties, but using more than one thread did. The arcane arguments surrounding this issue went on for nearly two years.

[7] TGR, July 1909, p 8

[8] *Ibid.*, p 9

[9] Hearing, p 185

[10] Hearing, p 212

[11] Clippings from a scrapbook in the possession of William Hutchens, grandson of the co-owner.

[12] *Morning Herald*, series end of March and early April, 1913.
[13] Although many manufacturers voted Republican, and not solely because of the tariff issue, not all were Republicans in this county—which to this day remains strongly Republican. At least one son of James I. McMartin was a Democrat.
[14] TGR, May 1913, p 7
[15] Hearing, p 286
[16] TGR, Nov. 1913, p 31
[17] TGR, Sept. 1909, p 11
[18] Hearing, p 128
[19] After the closing of the James I. McMartin's Sons glove shop, my grandfather, Daniel McMartin (1854-1936) became an importer of mocha skins. I was too young when he died to have learned about the business from him, but several of the glove men, notably Joe Perella, who bought mocha from him described his sales to me. He apparently was very successful. Joe Conroy knew my grandfather and recalled that he "really knew leather, he was a very clever businessman."
[20] TGR, Oct. 1909, pp 9-11
[21] Hearing, p 336
[22] *The Gloversville Daily Leader* for February 27, 1902 describes the floral decorations in the family's home for the wedding of Mr. and Mrs. Gustav Levor's daughter to Sidney New of New York City. To an impressive list of guests (all Jewish) from out of town were added a few local glovemen. The local paper described Levor as "a successful businessman ... and all who have met him in Gloversville have found him to be a very agreeable gentlemen in every respect."
[23] Irving Howe. *World of Our Fathers*, New York: Harcourt Brace Jovanovich, 1976.
[24] Howe, p 139.
[25] Statistics derived from the directories of Gloversville and Johnstown
[26] Statement on company letterhead, copy given to the author, dated Dec. 29, 1914
[27] Account book in the possession of Bert S. Zimmer's granddaughter, Ann Lee Clough.
[28] Martin Fishbein, "The Gloversville Strike," *The Leather Workers of Fulton County*, pamphlet, p 3
[29] Hearing, p 205
[30] Hearing, p 220
[31] For details of the glove manufacturers' association and their schedule of wages, see pages 81, 82.
[32] Hearing, p 166
[33] TGR, Jan. 1903, p 10
[34] Clipping, Hutchens scrapbook
[35] Hearing, p 423
[36] Susan E. Hirsh, *Roots of the American Working Class*, University of Pennsylvania Press, 1978, p 22.
[37] TGR, Feb. 1902, Aug. 1902, Jan. 1903
[38] See page 53 for definition of pull-down cutting
[39] TGR Apr. 1903 p 13
[40] TGR Apr. 1903 p 16
[41] TGR May 1903, p 13
[42] TGR June 1903, p 10
[43] TGR July 1903, p 11
[44] TGR Apr. 1904, p 10
[45] TGR Sept. 1903 p 10
[46] TGR Oct.1903 p 11
[47] TGR Oct. 1903, p 4
[48] TGR Jan. 1904 p 11
[49] TGR Jan. 1904 *Ibid.*
[50] TGR June 1904 p 10
[51] TGR July 1904 P 10
[52] TGR, Aug. 1904, pp 6-7
[53] *Ibid.*
[54] Hearing, p 184
[55] Ehrlich, Hearing, p 639
[56] TGR, Aug. 1906, p 16
[57] TGR, Jan .1903
[58] TGR, Aug. 1909
[59] TGR, Aug. 1904
[60] Hearing, p 425
[61] TGR, Dec. 1905
[62] *Leader Republican*, Dec. 18, 1913 and Dec. 31, 1917.
[63] TGR, May 1912, p 33
[64] There is no evidence that this mill made glove linings throughout its long tenure until today. At present it does make linings for Samco, one of the few glove manufacturers left.
[65] 1890 U S Census
[66] Hearing, *passim*
[67] Confirmed by John Widdemer, William Gates, and Joseph Conroy.
[68] Redmond, *Ibid.*
[69] Hearing, p 76
[70] Hearing, p 136
[71] Hearing, p 223
[72] Schulenbergs in the late 30s
[73] Hearing, p 657
[74] Hearing, p 242
[75] Hearing, p 166, this referred to the practices of taxing and chasing scraps described on pages 110, 112
[76] Interview with William Gates
[77] Hearing, p 577
[78] Hearing, p 586
[79] Hearing, p 346
[80] Hearing, p 386
[81] Hearing, p 570
[82] Hearing
[83] Hearing, p 318, p 393
[84] U. S. Department of Labor, Bureau of Labor Statistics
[85] Howe, p 145
[86] Hearing, p 241
[87] Hearing, p 571
[88] Hearing, p 609
[89] Hearing, p 643
[90] TGR, Feb. 1903, p. 8
[91] TGR, Oct. 1904, p. 11
[92] TGR, Aug. 1909, p. 39
[93] Hearing, p 274
[94] Hearing, p 75
[95] Hearing, p 54
[96] TGR, May 1910, p. 46
[97] Hilts-Willard, as reported by John Widdemer
[98] Hearing, p 403
[99] TGR, Aug. 1914, p 37
[100] TGR, Sept. 1914
[101] Hearing, p 281-6
[102] Hearing, p 669
[103] Hearing, p 167

[104] Clipping from the scrapbook of William Hutchens, grandson of the owner.
[105] Hearing, pp 639-40
[106] Hearing, pp 648-9
[107] Morning Herald, Mar. 21, 22, 1913
[108] *Ibid.*
[109] Hearing, p 66
[110] TGR
[111] In modern usage the term jobber has taken on the meaning of one who supplies materials. It was used at this time in Fulton County to mean a manufacturer whose shop made gloves for another.
[112] Hearing, pp 415-6
[113] Hearing, p 405
[114] Hearing
[115] Hearing, p 609
[116] Hearing
[117] Hearing, p 363
[118] Hearing, p 406
[119] Hearing, p 372-3
[120] Hearing
[121] Hearing
[122] Hearing, pp 374-5
[123] Hearing, p 372
[124] Hearing, pp 414-5
[125] Hearing, p 514
[126] Conversation with John Widdemer
[127] Hearing, p 238
[128] Hearing, p 205
[129] Hearing, p 455
[130] Conclusion of Hearing, p 3
[131] *Ibid.*
[132] *Ibid.*
[133] A third brother, Joseph, was a principal in the Bachner-Moses-Louis Company, later called Bacmo.
[134] Herbert M. Engel, *Ibid.*, p 106
[135] TGR
[136] Hearing, p 492

Short-note references, pages 59-118

---

[1] *Leader Republican*, Dec. 18, 1913 and Dec. 31, 1917
[2] TGR, May 1912, p 23

Notes from pages 119 - 178

---

[1] Kessler-Harris, *Out to Work—A History of Wage-Earning Women in the United States*. New York: Oxford University Press, 1982, p 152 for numbers in other cities, author's graphs page for county immigrant levels.
[2] Kessler-Harris, p 124
[3] TGR, Feb. 1915, p 18
[4] TGR, June 1916, p 15
[5] TGR, May 1918, p 17
[6] TGR, Nov. 1917, p 25
[7] TGR, Nov. 1918, p 20
[8] TGR, Feb. 1916, p 16
[9] TGR, May 1918, p 17
[10] Robert H. Zieger, *American Workers, American Unions, 1920-1985*. Baltimore: The Johns Hopkins University Press, 1986, p 8.
[11] TGR, Jan. 1918, p 25
[12] Leader Republican, 1937 Anniversary Issue
[13] TGR, Jan. 1919
[14] The United States Tariff Commission, Second Annual Report, 1917-1918.
[15] TGR, May 1919, p 20
[16] TGR June 1922, p 21
[17] TGR, Jan. 1922, p 22
[18] TGR, June 1934, p 4
[19] Variously referred to also as the Associated Glove Manufacturers of the State of New York
[20] TGR, July 1928, p 20
[21] TGR, July 1929, p 18
[22] *Ibid.*
[23] Figures quoted from government sources by Donald R. Vosburgh, Gloversville, New York: *A Community Study of Industrial Transition and Social Change*, Ph. D. Thesis, Syracuse University, 1953. p 60
[24] TGR, Dec. 1922, p 18
[25] TGR, June 1927, pp 28-29
[26] TGR, Feb. 1929, p 49
[27] TGR Feb. 1920, p 29
[28] Zieger, pp 5-6
[29] Gerald Zahavi, *Workers, Managers, and Welfare Capitalism*. Chicago: The University of Illinois, 1988, p 40.
[30] TGR, Oct. 1920, p 51
[31] TGR, Mar. 1923, p 24
[32] TGR, July 1926, p 25
[33] TGR, Jan. 1924, p 19
[34] TGR, Aug. 1921, p 23
[35] *Morning Herald*, Mar. 2, 1944
[36] *Business Week*, June 7, 1933, "Gloversville—Technocrat's Utopia," pp 20-21
[37] Twenty-first Congress, Session II, Ch. 497, 1930, p 667, par. 1532
[38] *Leader Republican*, April 23, 1935
[39] TGR, Apr. 1937, p 35
[40] Clipping, Feb. 6, 1935
[41] Clipping, Mar. 11, 1938
[42] TGR, Nov. 1937, p 18
[43] Inventory book in the possession of Bert S. Zimmer's granddaughter, Ann Lee Clough.
[44] *Morning Herald*, Aug 8, 1935
[45] Announcement, Marshall Field & Company, April 1, 1938
[46] *Morning Herald*, Jan. 15, 1937
[47] Conversations with Morris Evans
[48] Contradictory information permeates sources used in research for this book.
[49] Clipping, June 13, 1938
[50] *Ibid.*
[51] Clipping, June 23, 1938
[52] Clipping, Apr. 2, 1940
[53] For background on the NRA, I relied on Arthur M. Schlesinger, Jr.'s trilogy, *The Age of Roosevelt*. Boston, Houghton Mifflin Co., 1959. Specifically, *The Coming of the New Deal*, pp 97-102, 121-150, 385-408.

[54] TGR, Aug. 1919
[55] TGR, 1934
[56] TGR, July 1933, p 13
[57] *Ibid.* p 14
[58] *Ibid.* p 26
[59] TGR, Apr. 1934, p 25.
[60] *Ibid.*
[61] TGR, Apr. 1934, p 23
[62] *Leader Republican*, March 12, 1935
[63] *Ibid.*, dispatch from Washington.
[64] *Morning Herald*, Jan. 24, 1935
[65] *Morning Herald*, Jan. 23, 1935
[66] Schlesinger, *Ibid. The Politics of Upheaval*, 263-290.
[67] Zieger, p 40
[68] GM August 1935, p 11
[69] Clipping from *The New York Times*, April 16, 1935
[70] Clipping, June 1935
[71] Zieger, p 22
[72] *Ibid.*, p 26
[73] *Ibid.*, p 34
[74] *Ibid.*, p 28
[75] Zahavi, p 4
[76] Gerald Zahavi teaches at SUNY Albany and his special interest has been Communist and left-led CIO unions.
[77] *Morning Herald*, Oct. 11, 1933
[78] MH, Oct. 16, 1933, p 5
[79] Interview with Lydon Maider
[80] MH, Oct. 23, 1933, p 3
[81] MH. Oct. 26, 1933, p 3
[82] MH, Oct. 31, 1933, p 3
[83] MH, Nov. 7, 1933, p 3
[84] Zahavi, p 7
[85] Bill Towne is among them, notes to the author.
[86] MH, Oct. 25, 1933, p 3
[87] Zahavi, p 12
[88] Clipping, July 24, 1935; *Gloves Magazine*, Aug. 1935, p 31
[89] Clipping, June 1935
[90] LR, June 17, 19, 1935
[91] Zahavi, p 14
[92] Clipping, Nov. 16, 1939
[93] Clippings, Mar. 3, 1938 and Apr. 2 and 6, 1938
[94] Clipping, Aug. 9, 1938
[95] Clipping, Aug. 15, 1938
[96] Clipping, Apr. 27, 1938
[97] Clipping, Apr. 6, 1938
[98] Clipping, July 1, 1938
[99] Clipping, Aug. 6, 1938
[100] Zieger, p 54
[101] Philip S. Foner, *The Fur and Leather Workers Union*, Newark, NJ: Nordan Press, p 561 ff
[102] Leo Cyril Brown, *Union Policies in the Leather Industry*. Harvard University Press, 1947, p 141
[103] Carr, p 2
[104] *Ibid.*
[105] MH Oct 6, 1938, p 3
[106] Clipping, Mar. 1939
[107] Clipping, Mar. 20, 1939
[108] Clipping, May 14, 1940
[109] Zieger, p 72
[110] *Ibid.*, p 73
[111] Clipping, Sept. 6, 1940
[112] Clipping, Dec. 12, 1940
[113] Clipping, June 30, 1941
[114] Clipping, Jan. 9, 1940
[115] Clipping, June 31, 1944
[116] Clipping, July 30, 1940
[117] Conversations with Joe Conroy.
[118] Clipping, Oct. 29, 1940
[119] *Ibid.*
[120] Edw. I Saickman, letter to the editor, *Leader Herald*, March 30, 1940.
[121] This undoubtedly refers to Mrs. Bunn
[122] Clipping, June 5, 1940
[123] *Ibid.*
[124] Lester Pross, written for a freshman class in composition at Oberlin College in October 1941.
[125] Notes from Leon Jacobsen
[126] Clipping, Apr. 17, 1935
[127] Clipping, June 14, 1938
[128] Clipping, Nov. 9, 1938
[129] Clipping, Dec. 30, 1938
[130] AP, Jan. 5, 1939
[131] *Homework in the Glove Industry in New York State, Vol. I and II*, prepared by Division of Women in Industry and Minimum Wage, May 1941 (hereafter *Report*), p 155
[132] *Ibid.*, p 157
[133] *Ibid.*, Appendix Table XLVI
[134] *Ibid.*, p 45
[135] *Ibid.*, pp 67, 75
[136] *Ibid.*, p 73
[137] *Ibid.*, Appendix, Table XLI
[138] *Ibid.*, p 145
[139] Clipping Apr. 8, 1941
[140] Letter, May 1, 1941
[141] *Ibid.*
[142] Clipping, May 29, 1941
[143] Clipping, May 26, 1941
[144] Clipping, May 23, 1941
[145] *Report*, p 87
[146] *Ibid.*, Appendix, Table XLVII
[147] *Ibid.*, p 166
[148] *Ibid.* p 180
[149] Notes from Leon Jacobsen, whose father had a glove shop on Main Street in Gloversville that closed in 1938.
[150] Clipping, June 4, 1941
[151] LR, June 6, 1941
[152] Among those to speak on the possibilities of increased public welfare expenses if homework were to be curtailed was the Johnstown City Health Officer, my father, Dr. Malcom McMartin.
[153] MH, June 7, 1941
[154] Clipping, June 18, 1941
[155] LR, June 17, 1941, p 5
[156] One speaker mentioned homeworkers as having to purchase and keep their sewing machines in repair. This was a common, but not universal practice. Some companies loaned machines to homeworkers.
[157] *Report*

[158] Clipping, Nov. 1939
[159] Clipping, Nov. 18, 1938
[160] Clipping, Mar. 29, 1941
[161] Clipping, Feb. 11, 1941
[162] Clipping, Sept. 9, 1943
[163] MH., June 23, 1941
[164] Clipping, Jan. 5, 1941

Short-note references, pages 119 - 178

[1] TGR, June 1918, p 15
[2] Schleshinger, vol II, page 401
[3] *Ibid.*
[4] *Ibid.*, p 23

Notes from pages 179 - 212

[1] Zieger, p 73
[2] Zieger, p 85
[3] *Ibid.*, p 86
[4] Clipping, June 12, 1943
[5] Zieger, p 93
[6] Clipping, Aug. 22, 1942
[7] Clipping, Jan. 6, 1942
[8] *Morning Herald*, editorial, Feb. 3, 1942
[9] The committee consisted of Patrick Crocetta, George Hackney, Homer Van Vleet, Andrew Belman, Frank Kiernan, Richard Zuckerwar, Leo Lewis, James Green, Max Rubin, Samuel Starr. Clipping, Jan 10, 1942
[10] *Ibid.*
[11] Conversation with Sam Greco
[12] *Ibid.*
[13] *Ibid.*
[14] Clipping, June 11, 1942
[15] Clipping, Aug. 4, 1944
[16] Van Vleet, Crocetta Brothers, Daniel Hays, Gates-Mills. Clipping, July 12, 1945
[17] Clipping, Jan. 30, 1945
[18] Clipping, July 8, 1943
[19] Clipping, June 12, 1944, $4,000 worth of skins taken from Speare Co.
[20] Clipping, Sept. 29, 1943
[21] Clipping, Oct. 25, 1943
[22] Clipping, Nov. 16, 1939
[23] Clipping, Feb. 27, 1942
[24] Clipping, Aug. 26, 1942
[25] Clipping, May 5, 1943
[26] Clipping, Sept. 5, 1945
[27] Clipping, Mar. 13, 1946
[28] Clipping, Mar. 27, 1943
[29] Clipping, May 18, 1943
[30] Clipping, July 20, 1943
[31] Clipping, Mar. 13, 1945
[32] *Ibid.*
[33] Clipping, June 12, 1945
[34] Clipping, Aug. 1, 1946
[35] Clipping, June 6, 1947
[36] Clipping, June 20, 1944
[37] Clipping, Nov. 2, 1945
[38] Clipping, Apr. 9, 1946
[39] *Ibid.*
[40] Clipping, Sept. 9, 1943
[41] Clipping, July 17, 1943
[42] Clipping, May 15, 1944
[43] Clipping, Nov. 13, 1945
[44] Clipping, Sept. 18, 1946
[45] Clipping, May 31, 1946
[46] Zieger, p 108
[47] Clipping, Feb. 28, 1947
[48] Clipping, Mar. 30, 1948
[49] This story was told to the author by George Agar, officer of State Bank of Albany involved in the case.
[50] Clipping, Mar. 27, 1947
[51] Clipping, Apr. 30, 1947
[52] Clippings, Mar. 28, 1948
[53] Clipping, June 19, 1943
[54] Clipping, June 19, 1948
[55] *Women's Wear Daily*, Sept. 3, 1948
[56] Clipping, Oct. 23, 1948
[57] Clipping, Dec. 1948, quoting James Casey.
[58] Clipping, Sept. 1945
[59] Clipping, Apr. 4 1947
[60] Clipping, May, 1947
[61] Clipping, Nov. 20, 1947
[62] Clipping, Jan. 21, 1948
[63] Clipping, Jan. 28, 1949
[64] *Women's Wear Daily*, Nov. 25, 1949
[65] Clipping, May 11, 1950
[66] *NYT*, May 28, 1950
[67] Clipping, June 13, 1950
[68] Clipping, May 9, 1951
[69] Clipping, June 2, 1951
[70] Clipping, Feb. 1, 1949
[71] Clipping, July 3, 1949
[72] Clipping, July 16, 1949
[73] Clipping, Sept. 14, 1949
[74] Clipping, Sept. 19, 1949
[75] Clipping, Sept. 16, 1949
[76] *New York Herald Tribune*, Sept. 11, 1949
[77] Clipping, Oct. 13, 1949
[78] Clipping, Oct. 14, 1949
[79] Clipping, Oct. 15, 1949
[80] Clipping, Nov. 22, 1949
[81] Clipping, Nov. 29, 1949
[82] Clipping, Nov. 25, 1949
[83] *Ibid.*
[84] Clipping, Dec. 1, 1949
[85] LR, Dec. 12, p 3
[86] Interview with Lydon Maider
[87] *Ibid.*, Dec 15, p 20
[88] *Ibid.*, Dec 17, p 3
[89] MH, Dec 27, p 1
[90] LR, Jan. 4, 1950, p 3
[91] *LR*, Jan. 23, 1950 p 3
[92] Records of the City of Gloversville, January 31, 1950
[93] LR, Feb. 3, 1950, p 3
[94] MH, Feb. 4 and 6, 1950.
[95] MH, Feb. 6, 1950, p 3
[96] LR, Feb. 7, 1950, p 1
[97] LR, Feb, 21, 1950, p 7
[98] LR, Mar. 1, 1950, p 3; Clipping, March 20, 1950
[99] As quoted by Fishbein in *The Leather Workers of Fulton County*, p 9

[100] The privately printed booklet has no publishing identification. A copy can be found in the Gloversville Free Library.
[101] *Ibid.*, p 9
[102] Foner, p 673
[103] Bill Towne, modern union leader, believes that Carr's downfall can be attributed to his lack of understanding of the national political scene.
[104] *Ibid.*, p 11
[105] Clipping, May 9, 1950
[106] Clipping, Apr. 1, 1950
[107] This number may be low, because of the number of new firms around 1948. A net loss of 76 firms is still substantial.
[108] Clipping, July 7, 1950
[109] Clipping, Nov. 24, 1953
[110] Clipping, Aug. 11, 1954. Charges against county firms were dropped when they agreed not to engage in such practices, but a Milwaukee firm decided to fight those charges, and in 1954, the Federal government issued an injunction against that firm to stop the alleged practices.
[111] Clipping, Apr. 4, 1951
[112] Historian Gerald Zahavi has attempted to learn more of Carr's later years, with little success.

Short-note references, pages 179 - 212

[1] As remembered by his granddaughter's husband, John Widdemer.

Notes from pages 213 - 267

[1] The sharp increase in glovemaking at the end of the war encouraged manufacturers in related industries like box making. In 1953 there were six box makers in the county including J. W. Sisson & Co., which had been in business since 1860.
[2] Clipping, June 3, 1952
[3] Zieger, p 138
[4] Zieger, p 148
[5] Conversations with Joe Conroy, Paul Pollak, and Bill Towne.
[6] *New York State Industrial Bulletin*, Apr. 1951.
[7] Census data are often conflicting or not comparable, and figures as low as 77 percent and as high as 95 percent appear in different contexts.
[8] Clipping, Feb. 14, 1951
[9] Clipping, Mar. 13, 1951
[10] Clipping, Mar. 26, 1952
[11] Clipping, May 1, 1952
[12] Clipping, May 7, 1952
[13] Clipping, Nov. 14, 1953
[14] Clipping, *Schenectady Union Star*, Dec. 9, 1955
[15] Clipping, Feb. 4, 1956
[16] Clipping, Feb. 20, 1959
[17] Clipping, July 1959
[18] Clipping, Jan. 2, 1952
[19] Clipping, Mar. 26, 1952
[20] Enrollment figures quoted by the Fulton County Board of Elections in Vosburgh, *Ibid.* p 126.
[21] "The Fight over GATT," *Time*, June 6, 1955, p 94.
[22] File in Gloversville Library containing clippings from January and February 1955 from *Women's Wear Daily*, *New York Herald Tribune*, et al.
[23] Letter, clipping, May 21, 1958
[24] *Ibid.*
[25] Clipping, June 20, 1953
[26] Clipping, Feb. 2, 1954
[27] Advertisement in *Women's Wear Daily*, Oct. 31, 1952, p 27
[28] *NYT*, Feb. 7, 1955
[29] *Ibid.*
[30] Conversation with his son, Tom Willard
[31] Clipping, Mar. 25, 1955
[32] Clipping, Aug. 27, 1955
[33] Clipping, July 3, 1953
[34] Clipping, Mar. 28, 1964
[35] Clipping, Mar. 28, 1952
[36] Clipping, Aug. 2, 1952
[37] *Boston Globe*, Jan. 2, 1954
[38] Out of 239 listed in the U. S. Census of Manufactures as leather glove manufacturers.
[39] Clippings, June, 1957
[40] Clipping, Aug. 27, 1957
[41] Clipping, Sept. 26, 1957
[42] Clipping, May 20, 1959
[43] Conversation with George Madnick
[44] Clipping, Jan. 14, 1960
[45] Clipping, May 25, 1965
[46] *Ibid.*
[47] Many manufacturers and executives interviewed by the author spoke of not wanting to go abroad or live there. Many were offered the chance and declined. Among those who did not want to go were Joe Morsheimer, Douglas Hays, and Joe Pagano.
[48] Clipping, Feb. 3, 1958
[49] Clipping, July 28, 1958
[50] Clipping, July 28, 1958
[51] Clipping, July 27, 1959
[52] *WWD*, Aug. 4, 1959
[53] Clippings, Jan. 8, 1960
[54] *Schenectady Gazette*, Jan. 21, 1960
[55] *Ibid.*
[56] Clipping, Feb. 10, 1960
[57] Clippings and telegram, Mar. 21, 22, 1960, *WWD*, Mar. 25, 1960
[58] *Congressional Record*, House, 1960, pp 5949-50
[59] *WWD*, Dec. 9, 1960
[60] Clipping, Dec. 31, 1960
[61] Clipping, June 22, 1951
[62] Clipping, WWD, Aug. 16, 1963
[63] Clipping, WWD, Mar. 1, 1963
[64] Clipping, Jan 17, 1964
[65] Clipping, *Green Bay Press Gazette*, Oct. 9, 1966

[66] Clipping, May 25, 1965
[67] In conversations with the author, Towne has asserted that there always was an oversupply of labor. He finds it hard to believe that there ever was a labor shortage. The shortage seemed to keep pace with the move of work away from the county.
[68] *LH*, Mar. 3, 1962, p 14
[69] Clipping, Sept. 14, 1962
[70] Clipping, Oct. 25, 1963
[71] Clipping, *Albany Times Union*, Jan. 1972
[72] *WWD*, Jan. 5, 1962
[73] Clippings, May 3, 1962
[74] *Albany Times Union*, Nov. 2, 1962
[75] Clipping, Dec. 31, 1962
[76] Clipping, Apr. 19, 1967
[77] Clipping, May 16, 1967
[78] Clipping, Nov. 16, 1967
[79] Clipping, Dec. 11, 1970
[80] Interview with John Widdemer
[81] Conversation with Joe Morsheimer
[82] Clipping, Jan. 6, 1976
[83] Clipping, Sept. 21, 1979
[84] Clipping, *LH*, Nov. 29, 1978
[85] Clipping, May 21, 1984
[86] Clipping, Editorial: "Opinion", Jan. 4, 1983, p 4
[87] Clipping, Jan. 20, 1967
[88] Lillian Pierson Cohen, "Fulton County: Tanning Center," *The J. C. C. Journal*, Aug. 20, 1982
[89] Conversations with Roderick Correll and Dudley Ferguson
[90] Interview with Roderick Correll
[91] Clippings July 7, Aug. 27, Sept. 10, 1979
[92] Clipping, Dec. 31, 1981
[93] Interview with Dexter Risedorph
[94] Clipping, Nov. 21, 1978
[95] Clipping, Mar. 6, 1979
[96] Clipping, Aug. 13, 1980
[97] *LH*, Sept. 18, 1987
[98] Bill Towne, "Union Screening Scores for Tannery Workers," *New Solutions*, *A Journal of Environmental and Occupational Health Policy*, pp 40-42
[99] Interview with Bill Studenic
[100] *Ibid.*
[101] Conversations with Warren Dennie
[102] Interview with Mike Subik
[103] *LH*, July 19, 1998, p 1
[104] Clipping, Feb. 19, 1952
[105] Clipping, Mar. 9, 1953
[106] Clipping, Sept. 30, 1953
[107] Clippings, Oct. 29, Jan. 11, Sept. 2, and Dec. 19, 1953
[108] Clipping, Dec. 16, 1953
[109] Clipping, Jan. 9, 1954
[110] Clippings, Mar. 18, 1954, Apr. 26, 1954
[111] Clipping, Apr. 20, 1954
[112] Clipping, Apr. 11, 1955
[113] Clipping, Apr. 14, 1955
[114] Editorial, Apr. 26, 1956
[115] Clippings, Apr. 15, 18, 19, 21, 22, 1955
[116] Clippings, Apr. 29, 30, 1955
[117] Clipping, May 11, 1955
[118] Clipping, *WWD*, June 7, 1963
[119] Clipping, *LH*, May 3, 1965
[120] Clipping, June 11, 1965
[121] Letter to the author, November 1998
[122] Union leader Bill Towne told the author that this is the root of the dissatisfaction with union pensions that persisted into the 1990s.
[123] Clipping, Apr. 5, 1976
[124] Clipping, Dec. 19, 1977
[125] Clipping, Apr. 15, 1982
[126] *Forbes*, Oct. 20, 1997, p 61
[127] Interview with William B. Gates
[128] Interview with Joseph Conroy
[129] William E. Towne, *The Decertification of the Swany USA Corporation*, 1996, unpublished manuscript. The discussion of Swany is based on this thesis written for a master's degree in Labor and Policy Studies at SUNY, Empire State College in 1996. The author is assistant manager of the Amalgamated Northeast Regional Joint Board AFL-CIO, which represents the county's unionized glove and leather workers' locals. Towne believes that the Swany debacle was an effort to destroy labor, and in this author's opinion, while he fails to place the problem in the larger perspective of global competition, his analysis is factual and complete.
[130] Clipping, June 4, 1966
[131] Interview with Dominic Papa, taped
[132] This firm was later owned by Henry Tauber
[133] Clipping, June 18, 1952
[134] Clipping, Aug. 1958
[135] Clipping, Feb. 4, 1960
[136] Clipping, June 23, 1961
[137] Clipping, Dec. 10, 1977
[138] Documents No. 88-524-1 & 2, 15 U. S. C.
[139] Document No. 89-00135, 15 U. S. C.
[140] *LH*, Mar. 6, 1989
[141] *LH*, July 6, 1989
[142] *Schenectady Gazette*, Nov. 1, 1990
[143] *Ibid.*
[144] Interview with Dominic Papa
[145] TGR, Nov. 1903, p 13
[146] Engel, *Ibid.* pp 24-25
[147] *Ibid.* pp 26-28
[148] Lisa C. Rabon, "Glovers Grip New Markets," *Bobbin Magazine*, Jan. 1998, p 29.
[149] Rabon, *Ibid.*, p 25

Short-note references, pages 213 - 267

[1] *Time* magazine, May 9, 1977
[2] Advertisement in *Women's Wear Daily*, Oct 31, 1952, p 27
[3] Clipping, May 13, 1953
[4] Clipping, July 9, 1956
[5] Clipping, Feb. 14, 1963
[6] LH and WWD, June 20 and 21, 1963
[7] Clipping, Feb. 20, 1970
[8] Clipping, Dec. 11, 1970
[9] Clipping March 6, 1970
[10] Clipping, LH, Jan 27, 1976
[11] Clipping, Jan. 2, 1953
[12] Clipping, Dec. 9, 1970
[13] Clippings, June 11, 1971
[14] Clippings, Dec. 30, 1972, Jan. 5, 1973
[15] Clipping, June 10, 1976
[16] Clipping, Feb. 17, 1979
[17] Clippings, June 13, 16, 1980
[18] Clipping, June 20, 1981
[19] *Ibid.*
[20] Clipping, June 17, 1983

Notes from pages 268 - 276

[1] *Saturday Evening Post*, May 17, 1947
[2] *Ibid*, p 150
[3] Towne, p 13
[4] Leslie Massad, in letter to the editor, LH, June 4, 1997
[5] Henry F. May: *The End of American Innocence* (New York: Columbia University Press, 1959, 1992). May directed these sentences at the intellectual history of a short period before World War I. I feel his words apply equally to the end of this era.

Index

Note: When a company is named for the owner it is usually indexed by the owner's last name, i.e. J. M. Rubin & Sons is listed as Rubin, J. M., & Sons.

Barbara McMartin is the author of sixteen guidebooks, all but one on the Adirondacks. This is her sixth history. She has written: *The Great Forest of the Adirondacks; Hides, Hemlocks, and Adirondack History; Caroga - An Adirondack Town Recalls Its Past; To the Lake of the Skies;* and *The Adirondacks - A Wildlands Quilt.*

She grew up in Johnstown and has always wanted to write about the glove industry. She has had several different careers: as a mathematician, an outdoorsperson and guidebook writer, an environmentalist, and an historian. She is very much enjoying her latest endeavors as an economic and industrial historian.